EFFECTIVE SUPERVISION:
A PRACTICAL APPROACH

McGRAW-HILL SERIES IN MANAGEMENT

FRED LUTHANS AND KEITH DAVIS, CONSULTING EDITORS

Allen: The Management Profession

Arnold and Feldman: Organizational Behavior

Benton: Supervision and Management

Buchele: The Management of Business and Public Organizations

Cascio: Managing Human Resources: Productivity, Quality of Work Life, Profits

Cleland and King: Management: A Systems Approach

Cleland and King: Systems Analysis and Project Management

Dale: Management: Theory and Practice

Davis and Frederick: Business and Society: Management, Public Policy, Ethics

Davis and Newstrom: Human Behavior at Work: Organizational Behavior

Davis and Newstrom: Organizational Behavior: Readings and Exercises

Del Mar: Operations and Industrial Management: Designing and Managing for Productivity

Dobler, Lee, and Burt: Purchasing and Materials Management: Text and Cases

Dunn and Rachel: Wage and Salary Administration: Total Compensation Systems

Feldman and Arnold: Managing Individual and Group Behavior in Organizations

Finch, Jones, and Litterer: Managing for Organizational Effectiveness: An Experiential Approach

Flippo: Personnel Management

Gerloff: Organizational Theory and Design: A Strategic Approach for Management

Glueck and Jauch: Business Policy and Strategic Management

Glueck and Jauch: Strategic Management and Business Policy

Glueck and Snyder: Readings in Business Policy and Strategy from Business Week

Hampton: Management

Hampton: Inside Management: Readings from Business Week

Hicks and Gullett: Management

Hicks and Gullett: Modern Business Management: A Systems and Environmental Approach

Hicks and Gullett: Organizations: Theory and Behavior

Hodgetts: Effective Supervision: A Practical Approach

Jauch and Townsend: Cases in Strategic Management and Business Policy

Johnson, Kast, and Rosenzweig: The Theory and Management of Systems

Karlins: The Human Use of Human Resources

Kast and Rosenzweig: Experiential Exercises and Cases in Management

Kast and Rosenzweig: Organization and Management: A Systems and Contingency Approach

Knudson, Woodworth, and Bell: Management: An Experiential Approach

Koontz, O'Donnell, and Weihrich: Essentials of Management

Koontz, O'Donnell, and Weihrich: Management

Kopelman: Managing Productivity in Organizations: A Practical, People-Oriented Perspective

Levin, McLaughlin, Lamone, and Kottas: Production/Operations Management: Contemporary Policy for Managing Operating Systems

Luthans: Organizational Behavior

Luthans and Thompson: Contemporary Readings in Organizational Behavior

McNichols: Executive Policy and Strategic Planning

McNichols: Policymaking and Executive Action

Maier: Problem-Solving Discussions and Conferences: Leadership Methods and Skills

Margulies and Raia: Conceptual Foundations of Organizational Development

Mayer: Production and Operations Management

Miles: Theories of Management: Implications for Organizational Behavior and Development

Miles and Snow: Organizational Strategy, Structure, and Process

Mills: Labor-Management Relations

Mitchell and Larson: People in Organizations: An Introduction to Organizational Behavior

Molander: Responsive Capitalism: Case Studies in Corporate Social Conduct

Monks: Operations Management: Theory and Problems

Newstrom, Reif, and Monczka: A Contingency Approach to Management: Readings

Parker: The Dynamics of Supervision

Pearce and Robinson: Corporate Strategies: Readings from Business Week

Porter, Lawler, and Hackman: Behavior in Organizations

Prasow and Peters: Arbitration and Collective Bargaining: Conflict Resolution in Labor Relations

Quick and Quick: Organizational Stress and Preventive Management

Reddin: Managerial Effectiveness

Rue and Holland: Strategic Management: Concepts and Experiences

Rugman, Lecraw, and Booth: International Business: Firm and Environment

Sartain and Baker: The Supervisor and the Job

Sayles: Leadership: What Effective Managers Really Do . . . and How They Do It

Schlesinger, Eccles, and Gabarro: Managing Behavior in Organizations: Text, Cases, Readings

Schroeder: Operations Management: Decision Making in the Operations Function

Sharplin: Strategic Management

Shore: Operations Management

Steers and Porter: Motivation and Work Behavior

Steinhoff and Burgess: Small Business Management Fundamentals

Sutermeister: People and Productivity

Vance: Corporate Leadership: Boards, Directors, and Strategy

Walker: Human Resource Planning

Weihrich: Management Excellence: Productivity through MBO

Werther and Davis: Personnel Management and Human Resources

Wofford, Gerloff, and Cummins: Organizational Communications: The Keystone to Managerial Effectiveness

EFFECTIVE SUPERVISION: A PRACTICAL APPROACH

RICHARD M. HODGETTS

PROFESSOR OF MANAGEMENT

FLORIDA INTERNATIONAL UNIVERSITY

McGRAW-HILL BOOK COMPANY

NEW YORK   ST. LOUIS   SAN FRANCISCO   AUCKLAND   BOGOTÁ

HAMBURG   JOHANNESBURG   LONDON   MADRID   MEXICO

MILAN   MONTREAL   NEW DELHI   PANAMA   PARIS

SÃO PAULO   SINGAPORE   SIDNEY   TOKYO   TORONTO

This book was set in Zapf Book Light by Better Graphics (ECU).
The editor was Kathleen L. Loy; the designer was Hermann Strohbach;
the production supervisors were Joe Campanella and Friederich W. Schulte.
R. R. Donnelley & Sons Company was printer and binder.

EFFECTIVE SUPERVISION: A PRACTICAL APPROACH

1 2 3 4 5 6 7 8 9 0 D O C D O C 8 9 4 3 2 1 0 9 8 7 6

ISBN 0-07-029155-1

Library of Congress Cataloging-in-Publication Data

Hodgetts, Richard M.
    Effective supervision.

    Includes bibliographies.
    1. Supervision of employees.   2. Personnel
management. I. Title.
HF5549.H5185   1987   658.3′02   86-20037
ISBN 0-07-029155-1

ABOUT THE AUTHOR

Richard M. Hodgetts is currently a Professor of Management at the College of Business at Florida International University (FIU) in Miami. He received his bachelor's degree in business from New York University, his master's degree in business from Indiana University, and his doctorate in business from the University of Oklahoma. Dr. Hodgetts was a Professor of Management at the University of Nebraska, Lincoln, for 10 years, one of which he spent as a Visiting Professor at Texas Tech University. He joined FIU in 1976 and currently teaches in the general management area.

Dr. Hodgetts has written numerous articles, some of which have appeared in such journals as the *Academy of Management Journal, Personnel Journal, Personnel Management*, and *Training and Development Journal.* He is also the author or coauthor of 14 hardcover books, including *Modern Human Relations at Work* (Dryden Press), *The American Free Enterprise System* (Addison-Wesley), *Effective Health Care Administration* (Academic Press), and *Effective Small Business Management* (Academic Press).

Dr. Hodgetts is president of Hodgetts & Associates, Inc., and is active in training and consulting in industry in both the United States and South America. Much of his work is in the area of effective supervision, where his clients come from such diverse areas as banking, police enforcement, energy, health care, real estate, insurance, transportation, and the hotel and restaurant industry. At the present time Dr. Hodgetts is engaged in a South American project for a large international oil firm and a national government that are seeking assistance in more effectively employing their human resources.

In his spare time Dr. Hodgetts coauthors a weekly business newspaper column entitled "Minding Your Business." He is also the consulting editor of the management series for a large national book publisher.

To John Beishline

Who helped point me in the right direction.

CONTENTS

xi

PREFACE

There are many supervision books on the market today. Unfortunately, after using a fair number of them in the classroom and in supervisory training programs, I was forced to admit that none presented supervision the way I saw it being practiced in the real world. I found that most books fell into one of two categories: theoretical or "hands on." The theoretical books are very similar to basic management texts except that the writer replaces the word *manager* with the word *supervisor*. The texts are much too general and nonapplied. The hands-on texts are limited in scope and spend most of their time telling the reader "how to do it." The biggest shortcoming here is that these books do not tell the supervisor enough, and in some cases the advice is limited to a specific industry or type of company. I have written *Effective Supervision* to overcome these deficiencies and to offer teachers and practitioners a useful alternative.

OBJECTIVES

Effective Supervision is designed to span the gap between the theory on which effective supervision is based and the practice that is so crucial to the subject. Theory helps explain *why* supervisors act as they do; practice describes *how* they act. Each needs the other. The supervisor who is too theoretical is out of touch with the workplace. The supervisor who knows only the practical side of the job is unable to adapt quickly to changing conditions because there is no fundamental understanding of basics. Theory and practice, as a composite, form the basis for practical supervision and that is my objective in this book: to blend the foundations of effective supervision with a how-to emphasis.

ORGANIZATION

This book follows a natural progression, beginning with foundations of supervision and moving on to supervising people, supervising the work environment, and supervising oneself. Each part of the book addresses one of these major areas.

   Part One examines the fundamentals of effective supervision. These include planning, organizing, decision making, controlling, and managing conflict and change. Attention is focused on the success factors that help differentiate effective supervisors from their less effective counterparts.

Part Two addresses the behavioral side of supervision. Some of the major areas of consideration here include recruiting, training, communicating, motivating, leading, appraising and rewarding performance, and supervising protected groups.

Part Three is devoted to supervising the work environment. At this point attention is directed to: ensuring worker safety and health; dealing with unions, grievances, and discipline; and improving productivity and cost control.

Part Four focuses on supervising oneself. The three primary topics of discussion here are time management, stress management, and the development of a career plan.

SPECIAL FEATURES

Many supervisory texts discuss their practical focus. In this book I have attempted to go one step further and provide the reader with an opportunity to put these ideas into action. Every chapter begins with a case that calls for a solution. After reading the case, the reader can write down his or her answer and then compare it to the one provided at the end of the chapter. I believe that this approach gets the individual into the chapter by focusing his or her thinking on key issues that are about to be discussed.

A second special feature is the two "You Be the Supervisor" cases found at the end of each chapter. These cases permit the application of chapter ideas to real-life problems.

A third special feature is the "Supervision in Action" stories provided in each chapter. These stories present actual case situations and/or practical guidelines that have been found to be used by effective supervisors. They help form the basis for a practical approach to supervision.

A fourth special feature is the self-assessment quiz in every chapter. This quiz is designed to provide the reader with some insights into his or her own knowledge, understanding, perceptions, or behaviors as they relate to a supervisory topic or issue.

Effective Supervision is also accompanied by a complete resource for instructors and students. The *Instructor's Manual* contains, for each chapter: chapter objectives, lecture outline, answers to chapter questions, case solutions, and examination questions (with answers provided). A set of transparency masters completes the contents of this guide.

The *Study Guide* contains, for each chapter: a chapter review/outline that can be completed as the student studies the chapter; true/false, multiple-choice, and short answer questions; and a Definitions and Concepts section, containing the key words used in each chapter.

TARGET MARKET

Many individuals can profit from this book. In particular, I have written it for four specific groups:

Students. Individuals who have never supervised anyone will find this book to be a helpful, practical introduction to the management of workers. Its blend of supervisory theory and practice make it ideal for supervisory management courses at the junior college or 4-year level.

Supervisors. Practicing supervisors will find material in this book that is not presented in the typical supervision text or training seminar. Even for those with a wealth of experience, this book is designed to be a handy reference for dealing with typical supervisory problems and challenges of the 1990s.

Superiors. Managers who are directly responsible for handling supervisors will find that this book contains a great deal of useful information both for managing and for coaching and counseling. The book can serve as a primer for those who provide on-the-job guidance and mentoring to supervisors.

Training directors. Training directors who are responsible for supervisory training will find this book to be an excellent supplement to their lectures and a handy reference in answering questions and formulating practical, hands-on assignments.

A NOTE TO THE READER

In order to maximize the value of this book, you should approach each chapter as a self-contained unit. The objectives, or goals, stated at the beginning of the chapter relate directly to the "Review Your Understanding" questions at the end. When you have finished reading a chapter, go back and reread the objectives and then work on answering the review questions. This before-and-after approach helps, from a learning standpoint, to knit the material together into a cohesive unit.

Second, after you read the starting case, write down your answers and put them aside. Then read the chapter. When you have finished, review your answers and modify them as needed. Then compare your case answers to those given at the end of the chapter. This approach helps you see your own progress; your initial answer provides insight into your knowledge of the subject matter before you studied it formally, and your revised answer provides feedback on what you have learned in the chapter. Your comparison of your answer to the one presented at the end of the chapter allows you to see how realistic your solution was.

Third, when you have finished reading the chapter, review the key terms in "Build Your Supervisory Word Power" and be sure you understand each of them. If you do not, go back into the chapter and reread the section where each was presented and explained.

Fourth, carefully read the "Summary of Key Points" at the end of the chapter. If any of the major points is unclear, go back into the chapter and reread that material. Use this review to ensure that you have mastered the basic material in the chapter.

Fifth, remember that in the final analysis this book is written with you in mind. I have attempted to present my ideas in an interesting, insightful, comprehensive, and useful way. If you find the material to be enjoyable as well, so much the better. The important thing is that you derive value from the book. When you have finished the text, plan on putting it on your bookshelf for handy reference or passing it on to someone else who can profit from its use.

ACKNOWL-EDGMENTS

Every book contains errors of omission or commission. I accept all responsibility for these and welcome any advice or corrections that readers may wish to send to me.

On the other hand, there are many things in this book that warrant praise and attention. Regrettably, I cannot take total credit for any of them and, in some cases, openly admit that they were the result of advice and suggestions provided by those who read and reviewed the manuscript. In particular, I would like to thank my friend Fred Luthans. Over the last 20 years he and I have collaborated on many books and articles, but this is the first time I have had the pleasure of writing for the management series on which he serves as coconsulting editor. He provided me with, among other things, a suggested revised outline for the book that greatly clarified my ideas and allowed me to present them in a more coherent, interesting, and practical way. Other reviewers who read and commented on parts of the text included: David Bateman, Southern Illinois University; Marie Dalton, San Jacinto College; Herbert Engelhardt, New York University; Cliff Goodwin, Purdue University at Indianapolis; Larry Heldreth, Danville Community College; Dewey E. Johnson, California State University at Fresno; Fred Luthans, University of Nebraska; Charles Yauger, Arkansas State University; and Richard Whiting, California State University at Los Angeles. I also would like to thank my colleagues at Florida International University and other academic institutions who provided me personal suggestions and guidelines that helped fashion the final product. In particular, these people are: Dean Charles Nickerson, College of Business, Florida International University; Provost Steven Altman and professors Enzo Valenzi, John Morse, and Karl Magnusen, all of Florida International University; Professor Jane Gibson of Nova University; and Professor Ronald Greenwood of General Motors Institute.

Richard M. Hodgetts

EFFECTIVE SUPERVISION:
A PRACTICAL APPROACH

PART ONE

FUNDAMENTALS OF EFFECTIVE SUPERVISORY MANAGEMENT

The purpose of this part of the book is to examine the fundamentals on which effective supervision is based. These can be categorized into two groups: technical and managerial. On the technical side, the supervisor must know what he or she is supposed to do in the role of first-line manager. Chapter 1 addresses the overall nature of the supervisor's job, giving attention both to why some supervisors succeed and why others fail. Attention also is focused on the nature of supervision and how the supervisor's job has changed over the last couple of decades.

On the managerial side, the supervisor must know how to use the basic principles of supervisory management. In the main, this involves such management functions as planning, controlling, decision making, organizing, and the management of conflict and change. Chapter 2 addresses the way in which supervisors plan and control work. In the first part of the chapter, attention is focused on the planning process, the advantages of planning, and the reasons why planning sometimes fails. Then consideration is given to the controlling process, characteristics of effective control, and common control techniques. The last part of the chapter integrates planning and control considerations via a detailed discussion of how management by objectives can be used in organizing both of these functions.

Chapter 3 presents the ways in which supervisors make effective decisions. After the decision-making process is described, an explanation of cost-benefit analysis is presented. This is followed by a discussion of group decision making and the ways in which creativity can be used to improve decisions. The latter part of the chapter examines realism in decision making and gives tips for improving decision making.

Chapter 4 focuses on how supervisors organize for results. The nature of the organizing process is described, and common organizational designs are presented. Key factors in effective structural design are then discussed. The chapter closes by offering a series of useful tips for effective organizing.

Chapter 5 deals with the management of conflict and change. Conflict can be disruptive, and it is important that the supervisor know how to manage it effectively. Change is any alteration of the status quo. Regardless of whether change is good or bad, it is an inevitable occurrence in modern organizations. As a result, the supervisor must understand how people respond to change, their reasons for resisting it, and how it can be managed effectively.

When you have finished reading all the material in this section, you will understand the nature of the supervisor's job and the managerial challenges that face the individual. You also will know the basic principles of effective supervisory management.

CHAPTER 1

THE SUPERVISOR'S JOB

**GOALS OF
THE CHAPTER**

Modern supervisors have demanding, challenging, rewarding jobs. As management's link with the workers, supervisors must assume two major responsibilities: carry management's message to the employees and represent these workers to management. The supervisor is the "individual in the middle," and over the last decade this person's job has taken on added dimensions. The overriding purpose of this chapter is to examine what the supervisor's job is all about. When you have finished reading all the material in this chapter, you will be able to:

1. Explain who supervisors are, where they come from, and what functions they perform.
2. Compare and contrast the scientific management, human relations management, and human resource management approaches to supervision.
3. Identify and describe some of the factors that help account for supervisory success.
4. Explain why supervisors sometimes fail in their jobs.
5. Describe the format and approach that will be taken in this book in studying effective supervision.

Before beginning your examination of effective supervision, however, take a couple of minutes to examine a real-life case and see what you can make of it. Each of the chapters will begin with one of these starting cases. They are designed to help you focus on the major issues in the chapter.

A STARTING CASE: JEANNE'S DECISION

Seldom is there a sales supervisory opening at the Carter Company. However, last year one of the supervisors announced that he was taking early retirement. Following its policy of promoting from within, the firm offered the position to its number one salesperson, Jeanne Shirling. After thinking about it for 2 weeks, she accepted the job.

Jeanne was located in the southeast region of the United States. Her new

3

territory was in southern California and it took her a month to settle all her business in the east and get relocated. She took over a sales force of 27 people. A review of their sales records showed that 10 of them were excellent, 12 were average, and 5 were poor performers. Jeanne decided to focus her attention on the latter.

For the first 3 weeks she was in the office only 1 day. The rest of her time was spent on the road with the salespeople who were not doing well. Jeanne believed that if she stayed with them and taught them the fundamentals of selling, she could increase their sales revenue 40 percent by the end of the fiscal year.

At the end of her first 3-week stint, Jeanne had helped raise the average of the five salespeople by a weekly gross of 12 percent. She had plans to go out on another 3-week swing through areas that she and these salespeople had not yet worked. However, she first had to take care of all the work that had piled up on her desk. This took 4 full days, and she was glad to be done with it.

Her second 3-week stint was better than her first. By its conclusion the average gross weekly increase per salesperson was now up to 27 percent. Jeanne would have liked to go on the road again; however, the paperwork was so great that she felt compelled to stay in the office for the 10 days it took to clear up everything. Jeanne was beginning to feel that the paperwork side of her job was taking a lot of time, and she looked forward to getting on the road again. Unfortunately, the next week was taken up with semiannual perform-ance evaluation reviews, followed by a 5-day supervisory management retreat. During this week-long getaway, Jeanne's boss had some time to sit down and talk with her. Part of his conversation went as follows:

> Usually I spend a week or two working with new supervisors. However, you've been on the road so much that I just haven't been able to touch base with you on a good time for the two of us to get together. Over the next couple of days, I'd like to talk to you about next year's plan.

When the two did talk, Jeanne learned that her boss wanted her to spend more time in the office taking care of reports and studying market surveys. "I want you to develop your people into effective salespeople," he said, "but I don't want you to spend so much time on the road. It takes away from your managerial responsibilities." Jeanne tried this approach for 3 months. It was the most excruciating work experience she had ever had.

Last month the firm announced that it was opening an office in Alaska. Basically, the job was to call on new accounts and try to gain a foothold in the area. The company was asking for one person to do this initial work and, if things worked out, more would be added later on. Jeanne called her boss and said that she would like the job. He was bewildered by her request, but since no one else from inside had asked for the assignment, he submitted her name to headquarters and she was given the territory. She left for Anchorage yesterday. When the president of the firm heard about the move, he called up her boss and asked why she had left her job for a remote assignment. "I just don't know," the boss said. "I thought she liked her supervisory job, but apparently she didn't. It's a mystery to me why she wants to go back to selling."

What happened? Why did Jeanne leave her job? What was she looking for that she did not find in her role as a supervisor? Will she be happy in her new job? Sketch out your answers to these questions. We will return to them at the end of the chapter.

THE NATURE OF SUPERVISION

Supervisors are first-line managers who are directly responsible for overseeing the workers. Figure 1-1 provides an illustration of a typical organization chart. Notice that the supervisors are located just above the workers. This is why they are often referred to as first-line managers.

Who is a supervisor?

The most accurate way to answer this question is by focusing on what supervisors do. Supervisors are managers who directly interact with, give orders to, and evaluate the performance of workers. These managers have many different titles, depending on where they work. The following are all

Figure 1-1. Place of the supervisor in a typical organization (partial chart).

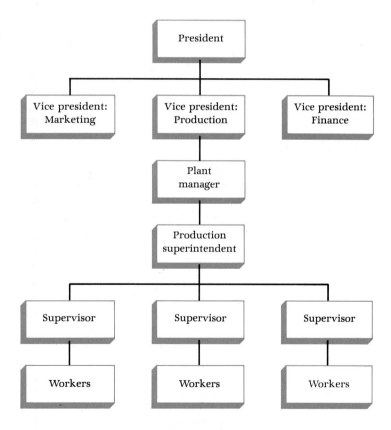

examples of supervisory job titles, although one would not automatically know this because the word *supervisor* is not always in the title:

Office manager

Senior training specialist

Cost control chief

Section head

Assistant supervisor for
   secretarial services

Materials foreman

Shift supervisor

Lead person

Documents chief

Safety director

Where do supervisors come from?

Most supervisors are promoted from the worker ranks. Often the best workers are recommended for these promotions. Management's reasoning is quite simple: Those individuals who know how to do the work are in the best position to train and guide others in how to do it. Of course, this reasoning can be wrong. Many workers are effective at their jobs but are ineffective in managing others. They can take care of themselves, but they cannot oversee and direct the work of anyone else. One of their biggest failings is that they view the technical aspects of their job as more important than the human relations aspects. The result is that they are overly concerned with the work and in the process fail to communicate with, motivate, or lead their people.[1]

Some supervisors are brought in from the outside. Many of these people have had first-line management experience with other firms but have changed jobs because they either disliked their work or felt that their efforts at further promotion were limited. Others have done very well at the worker level but been unable to move up because there were no openings for first-line managers; as a result, they have moved to other firms where supervisory openings were available. Still others have had no work experience at all; they are hired right out of college and put into a first-line position. Many firms like to recruit college graduates and start them at the lower ranks. This provides the company with a pool of well-educated managers that learn the business from the ground up.

What do supervisors do?

The supervisor has often been called "the man in the middle." This cliché refers to the fact that the individual is the link between the management ranks and the workers. In this capacity, the supervisor has a responsibility to carry out management directives and to look after the people in the unit; these two functions are spelled out in Supervision in Action: Two of the Supervisor's Most Important Responsibilities. The supervisor is also responsible for communicating and coordinating with other supervisors to ensure that all units are working in the same direction. The manager also has a responsibility to comply with requests from staff departments (personnel, legal, engineering, quality control, etc.) and to consult with them when their expertise is needed in problem solving. Finally, the supervisor has a responsibility to the union in terms of being knowledgeable about the labor agreement and how it affects supervisor-worker relations and attempting to maintain a relationship that is helpful to long-run union-management accord.

SUPERVISION IN ACTION: TWO OF THE SUPERVISOR'S MOST IMPORTANT RESPONSIBILITIES

Supervisor's responsibilities to employees. Some people might argue that a supervisor's main responsibilities are to the employees in his department. Certainly, responsibility to management and to employees are the two most important. What is interesting about the downward responsibilities of the supervisor is that most of them, though directed toward the employees, are also in the best interests of higher management. This is another way of saying that a generally satisfied work group is in management's long-term best interests.

Employees place leadership expectations on the supervisor. They expect him to provide them with direction and support. They expect him to be their representative to higher management. They expect him to look after their needs—social needs and personal needs as well as work-related needs. Perhaps employees should not expect all of this from their leaders— but nevertheless many of them do—and the supervisor must deal with these expectations.

Many of the topics in the management/supervisory literature deal more comprehensively with the supervisor's responsibilities to employees, so for best results, what is presented here must be combined with other writings dealing with communication, human behavior, leadership, and so on. For the present, let us sketch out what are a number of the supervisor's responsibilities to his employees. The supervisor should:

- Establish a warm and trusting *working climate* within the department.
- *Handle employee problems promptly.*
- *Be fair* in all departmental matters.
- Explain to employees all matters connected with their jobs.
- *Train* employees when needed.
- Assume the role of *counselor* on occasions.
- *Discuss proposed changes* before change takes place.
- Maintain a *safe* and *clean* work area.
- Provide sound policies for employee personal problems (when not provided by higher management).
- *Explain* fringe benefit plans and pay systems.
- Orient new workers.
- Coordinate and plan work so that workloads are as stable and predictable as possible.
- Develop good morale.
- Stand up for employee when being treated arbitrarily from above.

Supervisor's responsibilities to coworkers. The supervisor's responsibilities to his coworkers (other supervisors) are not quite as pressing as the above-mentioned two categories. Nevertheless, he does have responsibilities relative to these other supervisors. In summary form they may be stated as follows. The supervisor should:

- *Coordinate* whatever *work flows* or *paperwork* that needs to be exchanged among supervisors.
- *Communicate* with other departments about mutual needs and problems.
- Give them support as members of the same management team.
- *Coordinate policy interpretations* with other departments to assure consistency and uniformity.

It can be seen here that the supervisor's role is somewhat less demanding with respect to his coworkers.

Source: Archie B. Carroll and Ted F. Anthony, "An Overview of the Supervisor's Job," *Personnel Journal*, May 1976, pp. 230–231. Reprinted by permission of *Personnel Journal*, Costa Mesa, Calif.; all rights reserved.

Management functions. In carrying out these responsibilities, supervisors perform four functions: planning, organizing, directing, and controlling.

PLANNING. The specific plans and objectives to be pursued are provided by higher-level management. It is the supervisor's job to see that these are attained. Most of the objectives are measurable since they relate to specific things that have to be done: e.g., produce 35,000 assembled units per week; maintain scrap costs within 5 percent of total production costs; limit overtime to 300 hours per month; keep rejects below 1 percent of all manufactured units; hold machine downtime to an average of 1 hour per machine per month. Notice that these objectives are spelled out in terms of what is desired and the time frame within which the objective is to be attained. Objectives that are not specifically stated are still quantified to the highest degree possible. For example, if the supervisor is told to minimize machine downtime, the individual will coordinate with the maintenance department to find out how often each machine requires preventive maintenance. Then maintenance will be scheduled so as to ensure that needed repairs are made before the machine goes down.

ORGANIZING. In the organizing process the supervisor assigns the work to the individuals in the unit. This involves a clear delegation of authority and responsibility. It is a natural follow-on to the planning process because the work assignments are all in accord with the objectives. Many firms have their own procedures for work assignments; for example, it is common to find the supervisor sitting down with each subordinate, discussing what the individual is to do over the next 6 months, talking about problems that are likely to arise and how they can be dealt with, and concluding by urging the individual to ask questions or seek assistance if something comes up that cannot be handled personally. There are many other activities in the organizing process, including redefining of job descriptions and reorganizing the work units; however, these do not take up much of the individual's time because the supervisor is too involved with day-to-day operating matters.

DIRECTING. In the directing process the supervisor is concerned with human relations. Specifically, the manager uses communication, motivation, and leadership to get things done. *Communication* is the process of conveying meanings from one party to another. In this process the supervisor works to get the subordinates to understand what they are to do, when, and how. If they have questions, they are then free to ask them, and through this feedback process the supervisor attempts to clear up any misunderstandings or gaps in the communication and to win their support for the job. *Motivation* is effort directed toward the accomplishment of an objective; the greater this effort, the higher the likelihood that the subordinates will get things done right and on time. In this process the supervisor attempts to increase their efforts by providing them rewards. *Leadership* is the process of influencing people to direct their efforts toward the accomplishment of specific objectives. In this process the supervisor uses that style of direction (authoritarian leader, participative leader, etc.) which is most likely to influence the subordinates to get their assignments done within time, cost, and quality parameters.

Of all four functions, directing is usually the most difficult because to a large degree it is outside the control of the supervisor. For example, the effectiveness of a communication often rests on how the other party interprets what is being said. The supervisor cannot make people "hear" things the way he or she would like them to be heard; the supervisor can only encourage feedback for the purpose of determining what the other party did hear properly.

Similarly, motivation is an internal process, and while the supervisor can offer rewards to those who do the best work, this does not always motivate them to work even harder in the future. What is a motivator or reward for one person may not be so for another person. Motivation is determined by the worker, not by the supervisor. The latter tries to establish a climate conducive to motivation, but in the final analysis it is the worker who determines how successful these efforts have been.

The leadership style is chosen by the supervisor, but the workers determine whether or not it is the right style. Moreover, the style that is effective with one person may be totally inappropriate with another. So the supervisor must use a contingency approach to leadership, varying the style to match the worker and the situation.

CONTROLLING. In the controlling process the supervisor checks to see how well things have been going and then uses the results to determine what must be done in the future. Controlling is an ongoing process. The supervisor will be confronted daily with problems such as machine breakdowns, late delivery of materials, and tardiness and absenteeism by the employees. These must be controlled at that time. Maintenance must be provided for the machine; an immediate follow-up on the status of the materials must be undertaken to determine when they will be received and a new source found if the delivery time is too late to be acceptable; workers must be reminded about (and, if necessary, have their pay docked for) unexcused lateness and absenteeism. Periodically, the supervisor must also evaluate the personnel in the unit; quite often this is done on a 6- or 12-month basis. At this time the manager sits down with each person, reviews how well he or she has done, and then makes assignments for the next period. This evaluation review helps point out where the individual is doing a good job and where additional assistance, training, or greater effort is needed.

Management skills. In carrying out these four functions, the supervisor makes use of three management skills: technical, human, and administrative.

Technical skills are those related to how things work. Individuals with technical skills have a fundamental grasp of machines, processes, and production methods. When they are given a piece of machinery and a user's manual, they are able to read the booklet quickly and understand what the writer is talking about. They can then set up the machine and have it operating in far less time than can the average individual. These people have an engineering-type understanding of how things work. Supervisors need technical skills because they directly manage individuals who are responsible for getting work done. Supervisors who understand "how to do it" are in an excellent position to manage those who are actually carrying out the work.

Human skills are those related to interacting with the individuals who are doing the work. They were discussed above in terms of communication, motivation, and leadership. Most supervisors have technical skills; they know how the work ought to be done. However, they lack human skills and so they never manage to get the most out of their people. Two industry experts stated it this way: "Many supervisors rise on their technical competency without any training in the area of supervisory skills, e.g., being able to recognize what motivates people. When there are numerous supervisors that do not know how to supervise, there is bound to be trouble such as: high turnover, low morale, sloppy work habits, and inefficiency."[2]

Administrative skills are those related to how all parts of the department or organization fit together. They cover many activities, from formulating organizational objectives, policies, and procedures to developing techniques for handling office work flow and to coordinating a host of seem-

Figure 1-2. Management skills needed at different hierarchical levels.

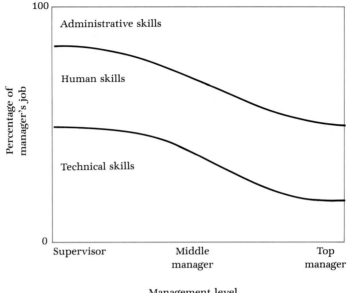

ingly unrelated functions that enable the enterprise to operate as an integrated unit. These skills are of more importance at the upper levels of the hierarchy than they are at the supervisory level. Nevertheless, the supervisor does require some of these skills because coordination of overall unit effort is important. As seen in Figure 1-2, administrative skills gain in importance as one moves up the hierarchy, while technical skills decline in importance. For the supervisor, the order of importance is: technical, human, administrative.[3]

MODERN SUPERVISION IN PERSPECTIVE

The job of the modern supervisor has changed dramatically since the turn of the century. Part of the reason can be found in technology; machinery and equipment have been greatly improved, and the way that work is done has changed to accommodate these factors. More important, however, the values of the workers have changed and supervisors have come to realize that the old ways of managing the personnel are no longer effective. This transition from the turn of the century to the present time can be divided into three distinct phases: scientific management, human relations management, and human resource management.

Scientific management

At the beginning of the twentieth century the United States was in the scientific management era. The factory system was in full swing and management's primary concern was how to increase worker productivity. Scientific managers, many of whom were mechanical engineers by training, had entered industry and were helping management run the workplace through the use of better materials flow, improved machine operation, sophisticated time and motion studies, and other efficiency-oriented procedures. In this process, the scientific managers sought to bring together the workers and the work in the most efficient way possible. The worker was viewed as an adjunct of the machine. The most important concept of scientific management was the *task concept*, which spelled out exactly what the worker was to do, how it was to be done, and the amount of time allotted for its completion.[4] As a result of their efforts, the scientific managers were able to achieve dramatic increases in productivity. Workers who used to load 10 tons of coal per day or produce 5 units per hour now found themselves able to do 2 and 3 times as much work without any increased effort.

The large gains in productivity resulted in dramatic bottom-line increases in profit. Business firms began to realize that with scientific management, previously marginally profitable operations could now be turned into highly profitable ventures. In the process, management began to accept certain basic ideas about the workers. One was that the average individual needed to be carefully trained and directed in carrying out the work; people basically were not very smart, but with the effective use of the task concept, these shortcomings could be overcome.

A second assumption of management was that people were most motivated by money. If the company gave them a chance to increase their pay, they would work as long and as hard as they had to for this economic reward. Many scientific managers developed wage incentive systems in which workers were paid on the basis of how much work they did. The most famous of these systems offered two rates of pay: one for those who did less than what was expected and one for those who attained or surpassed this minimum. For example, on a job with a minimum of 25 assembled units per day, the pay rate would be something like 4 cents per unit up to 24 units and 7 cents per unit for all units if the worker attained 25 units or more. Consider the difference in pay between a person who assembled 22 units and one who turned out 26 units. For 22 units the individual would receive 88 cents (22 $\times$ 0.04), while for 26 the person would make $1.82 (26 $\times$ 0.07). Under this incentive pay arrangement, individual workers had to reach the minimum number of units assigned for the job if they hoped to make a good wage; otherwise, they were confined to the lower piece rate.

Supervisors during these times were expected to keep their personnel working at all times, and anyone who did not attain the minimum output requirements of the job was put on notice. If the individual was still unable to reach this output level, he or she was dismissed. The supervisor's role was one of closely monitoring and controlling worker output. If any workers had a problem getting their work done, the supervisor would check to see if perhaps the tasks could be broken down into simpler operations, ensure that the machine was properly maintained, make certain that materials for processing were being received promptly, etc. Supervisors concerned themselves with the work environment; the closest they came to worrying about the worker was to ensure that the latter understood the company's payment plan and was aware of the risk associated with falling behind in output. Basically, the supervisor and management at large believed that if the tasks were simple enough and the personnel were controlled, the workers would produce the established minimum for the job.

Human relations management

As industrialism took hold in the United States, a major union movement started to emerge. Workers began to realize that a strong union could be an important asset in negotiating with management and getting increased salary and benefits. At the same time, personnel values were changing.

By the early 1920s, many of the scientific managers and early factory owners were gone. They had been replaced by people born in the late 1800s. These latter individuals had grown up under conditions quite different from the earlier generation. They were not convinced that people worked for just money alone. They realized that there were other ends that people pursued in the workplace. Additionally, they understood that life at work is sometimes more important than the pay that people receive for putting up with these conditions. A human relations orientation was beginning to gain a foothold in the management ranks.

From the early 1920s to the early 1960s, human relations played a major role in the way that first-line supervisors managed their people. In one sense, this approach was different from that of the earlier managers because it was based on a philosophy of "money alone does not motivate." It was also supplemented with the belief that people wanted to be treated well and to feel that they were members of a team. In short, workers wanted to satisfy more than economic needs; they wanted to fulfill social needs as well.

In this environment, the supervisor's role was expanded. Rather than just focusing on job assignments (the task concept) and control, the supervisor now tried to make the workers feel useful and important. The supervisor kept them informed about what was going on and listened to their objections and complaints about work-related matters. In addition, the personnel were treated with some degree of trust and confidence; the supervisor allowed them to exercise self-direction and self-control on routine matters. Rather than managing them as little children, which is what earlier supervisors had done, first-line managers now treated their people the way that parents would handle adolescent children.

Supervisors believed that if they shared routine decisions with their people, the latter would be able to satisfy their needs to belong and to feel important. In turn, this would lead to an improvement in morale, a reduction in resistance to formal authority, and an inducement to the subordinates to cooperate in getting things done.

On the one hand, the human relations approach was a major adjustment in supervisory thinking. Anyone who stood off to the side and watched supervision during the scientific management and the human relations eras could easily see the difference in the approaches.

On the other hand, there were many similarities, especially during the early years of the human relations era. The most significant similarity was that human relations thinking did *not* displace scientific management with its hard-nosed view of the workers; it merely complemented it by adding a human dimension. The supervisor during the scientific management era would be likely to tell a worker who had just made a mistake on an important job, "You'd better do this right or else!" This threatening tone was replaced by the candy-coated one of the human relationists. Now the supervisor would tell the worker: "You really shouldn't have done the job that way. You should have been more careful." The threat was veiled in more humanistic terms, but it was still there. Supervisors still believed that workers were motivated by money and the fear of losing their job. However, they also began to realize that if opportunities for socializing with the other personnel and interacting with one's boss were made available, the workers would do an even better job. Early human relations was nothing more than an attempt to manipulate the workers by substituting kind words and good intentions for threats and close control. If these did not work, of course, the supervisor would resort to the earlier tactics.

As management moved through the 1930s and 1940s and into the 1950s, the economy changed dramatically. The great depression gave way to the post-World War II economic boom. A new generation of managers began arriving on the scene, bringing with them a new set of values regarding what motivates people and how they should be managed. This was the beginning of the human resource management movement.

Human resource management

The era of human resources began to emerge during the 1960s. In contrast to the scientific management and human relations movements that preceded it, this latest era represents a different perception of the workers and is a major break with the past. The assumptions, policies, and expectations that modern supervisors have of their people are dramatically different from those of earlier generations of first-line managers.

Today's supervisors believe that most workers are capable of exercising a great deal of self-direction and self-control. It is basically a waste of time to hover over them, looking at everything they do, prepared to swoop down the minute a mistake is made; this approach is not only time-consuming but results in poor worker performance. A better approach is the use of general control in which the supervisor keeps abreast of what is going on and has time to focus on any major problem areas that develop. Modern supervisors also realize that most workers are much more creative than their jobs require. Are you very creative? Take Self-Assessment Quiz 1-1 and gain some insights to the answer.

SELF-ASSESSMENT QUIZ 1-1: HOW CREATIVE ARE YOU?

Carefully read each of the following statements and place an X next to the response that most accurately describes you.

	Mostly true	Mostly false
1. You are not just bright, you are brilliant.		X
2. You can often quickly generate many different ideas for solving a problem.	X	
3. You have a positive self-image.	X	
4. In problem solving, you are most concerned with the small details.		X
5. You are sensitive to the world around you.	X	
6. You are frequently a nonconformist.	X	
7. You tend to be more impulsive than reflective in problem solving.		X
8. You lead a rich, almost bizarre, fantasy life.	X	
9. You think in black-and-white terms; right is right and wrong is wrong.		X
10. You are motivated by challenging problems.	X	
11. You do not take rules and regulations too seriously.	X	
12. You like to dress well; you never dress shabbily.	O	X
13. You believe in business before pleasure.	O	X
14. Vague instructions or directions make you nervous.		X
15. You prefer fiction books to nonfiction.	X	
16. You like detective or investigative types of problems.	X	
17. You rarely read more than 10 hours per week.	O	X
18. You are more interested in why people are nice to you than in the fact that they are nice.		X
19. It is more important to you to please others than to please yourself.	O	X
20. If you work long and hard enough, you can find answers to most problems.	X	

Of course, not every supervisor uses a human resource management approach and not every organization would profit from one. In assembly-line work the personnel are tied to the line. There is little opportunity for creative thinking or self-direction; they have been told what to do and how to do it. The situation is very similar to that of the old scientific management era. However, many organizations can profit from human resource manage-ment supervision. This is particularly true of white-collar businesses. Any time that individual creativity or initiative will result in increased efficiency, a human resource approach has merit. This is particularly true in organiza-tions in which the personnel are well educated and/or well trained. In this book we are going to study the ways in which supervisors can implement a human resource approach to management. The focus is going to be heavily practical.

SUCCESS IN SUPERVISION

Over the last decade a great deal of attention has been directed toward identifying those factors which lead to supervisory success. The following seven factors have been found to be important to supervisors. Managers who have these competencies tend to do better than those who do not.[5]

Efficiency orientation

Efficiency is measured by the equation: output/input. If a supervisor can increase the amount of work the personnel are doing while leaving the inputs the same, efficiency rises. Likewise, if the individual can increase output at a faster rate than input or cut back input faster than output, efficiency increases will result.

Supervisors with an efficiency orientation are good at writing or describ-ing plans for accomplishing tasks or achieving goals. These plans take into account such things as identifying actions to be taken, resources needed in accomplishing goals, and obstacles that may prevent goal attainment. These supervisors also organize their resources in such a way as to reach the goal(s) more efficiently than before, and they tend to think in efficiency terms. Manufacturing supervisors think in terms of specific increases in production units and decreases in waste allowance. Sales supervisors think in terms of specific sales targets. Cost control supervisors think in terms of cost per unit.

Research shows that the most effective supervisors place greater empha-sis on efficiency than do other supervisors. Additionally, when contrasted with middle- and top-level executives, these supervisors have a greater efficiency orientation.

Self-control

Effective supervisors have high self-control. Research reveals that people with this trait tend to weigh the costs and benefits to themselves, their work group, and the organization at large before expressing or acting on personal needs or desires. In contrast, supervisors with low self-control tend to think of immediate, self-centered gratification or satisfaction.

When verbally attacked or aggressively confronted by someone, effective supervisors tend to remain calm. Their first attempt is to determine why the other party is angry. This is then followed by an attempt at a logical, rational explanation to the situation, such as "I made that decision because I feel that overtime work should be rotated among everyone who wants it rather than just given to the first person who asks." This approach is quite different from that used by supervisors who lack self-control. The latter are likely to respond, "I made the decision and that's it!" Research has found that self-control is more important at the supervisory level than at the middle or upper levels of the hierarchy.

Open expression

Open expression, or *spontaneity* as it is sometimes called, is the ability of individuals to express themselves freely or easily. Effective supervisors have high spontaneity. Additionally, they are often able to verbalize what others are merely thinking. Individuals with high spontaneity are also quite secure in their expression of feelings and opinions. The following is an example reported from a research interview related to spontaneity:

> We had been working on a problem in the furnaces. Some of the engineers had figured out that a chemical reaction was taking place and producing a gas that we didn't want in the furnace. We were working on it flat out. One afternoon we were taking stock. One engineer had presented a theoretical idea as to what was happening. Another guy came up with an alternative way of setting up the furnace. Another engineer had an idea about a different alloy that wouldn't cause the same reaction. We were bouncing these ideas around. We were confused but pretty worked up about the problem. Finally, I said, "Enough talk. By God, let's just go out and squeeze some of that stuff and try it out." This eventually led to the solution to this problem that the plant had had on and off for four or five years.[6]

Spontaneity is more common among superior performing supervisors than it is among their counterparts at the middle and upper levels of the hierarchy.

Objectivity

Objectivity is the ability of a person to be relatively unbiased and not limited by excessive personal prejudices or perspectives. Individuals who possess this objectivity are able to see the other person's point of view. For example, supervisors who have this competence are able to discuss a conflict that exists between two subordinates in such a way as to reflect each side's point of view accurately. In fact, even when personally involved in a conflict, these supervisors are able to understand the other party's side of the argument. The following is an example:

> Dave Pauling is a newly hired supervisor in his company. Dave has heard from some of the other supervisors that his boss, Jim King, is a difficult person to get along with. However, Dave believes in finding out things for himself. During the first meeting they had, Dave went out of his way to tell Jim about his previous supervisory experience. He also made it a point to have all of his reports in 2 days early. Jim and he now get along extremely well. In the process, Dave has learned that Jim is not tough to get along with unless you fail to do your job properly. He is only rough on ineffective supervisors, believing that they must either shape up or ship out. Dave is glad that he waited until he got to know Jim better before making a decision regarding the type of manager he is.

Research reveals that effective supervisors have greater personal objectivity than do average or poor supervisors.

<table>
<tr><td>

Use of individual power

</td></tr>
</table>

Use of individual power is the use of influence to obtain compliance. People who use this type of power give orders, directions, or commands that are based either on their formal authority in the organization or on the policies of the enterprise. They do not necessarily solicit the opinion or input of others. They give orders and expect them to be obeyed. The following is an example:

> José Rodriguez is a supervisor in an industrial products company that has established specific procedures and methods of operation for its newly established production line. These procedures are designed to ensure the safety of personnel by protecting them from the hazards of chemicals with which they work. José had instructed his people on the specific safety activities and procedures that were to be followed. However, one of the production workers, Greg Williams, stopped wearing protective gloves during the second week of operation of the production line. José told him to put them back on, but later that day he again found Greg not wearing the gloves. When he approached Greg to restate his directive, Greg insisted that there was no danger from the chemicals and that he could operate his machine better without the gloves. José wasted no time with him. "This isn't a point of discussion. Wear the gloves or get the hell out of the plant!" he told him. Since then, José has had no problem with people breaking this safety rule.

Research reveals that among supervisors, the best performers tend to have much higher use of unilateral power than do average or poor performers. When it is required, they exercise unilateral control.

Use of group power

Use of group power is the use of influence forms like alliances, networks, coalitions, and teams in getting things done. People who use socialized power tend to see themselves as members of a team or group. They view their relationship with their boss as an important coalition. They also try to get their own subordinates to accept certain standards of behavior, and they work to ensure that their people continue to perform at this level. If conflict ensues, they attempt to resolve the situation through building coalitions or using existing ones. The following is an example of one reported use of socialized power:

> I was asked to sit in on a review project, to represent the marketing perspective. The manufacturing committee was set up to assess the status of our suppliers. I did some analysis on my own and felt that by focusing on one supplier for a commodity that was critical to our production we were foolish. What if [that supplier] should fail? What if [it] could not grow fast enough to keep pace with our demand? I presented my argument to the manufacturing committee. They thought it was reasonable but started raising objections. They claimed that we had already spent a lot of money with two previous companies and had problems. They said that the current supplier was doing fine and working with them on delivery issues and quality concerns. I backed down

at that point. I knew that several manufacturing engineers were on the committee. So I went to the design engineers and explained some of the dilemmas I saw in the situations. I explained to them the potential problems from a tooling standpoint, and they agreed. They also agreed to come to the next manufacturing committee meeting with me. It was a ploy in my negotiating with the committee. Having one engineer talk to another engineer can lead to an understanding sooner; it's a peer thing. It worked. The manufacturing engineers saw the point and pushed the rest of the committee to address my concern from several perspectives. Soon after, we started purchasing from several suppliers, which I think was the right decision.[7]

Concern for impact

Effective supervisors are concerned with the impact that power symbols have on others. Prestige and status are important to them and they understand the importance of acting "appropriately." For example, they dress in a manner that indicates that they are supervisors who manage others. Their office is set up in such a way that those who enter it are given clues regarding who they are and what they do. The following is an example:

Bill White, a new supervisor, replaced a retiring first-line manager last year. The previous supervisor had a great deal of difficulty dealing with his people; quite often they argued with him and there always seemed to be ongoing fighting. Bill is a much different person. In contrast to his predecessor, he wears neatly pressed slacks, a shirt and tie, and a jacket. Bill's office wall has a number of awards he has been given for outstanding work performance as well as his undergraduate degree from State University. He keeps his desk clear of any papers except those he is working on, and whenever anyone enters his office, the door is closed behind them so that the two can talk in private. Over the last 6 months, productivity in Bill's work group has risen by 18 percent.

What makes Bill effective? One answer is the impact he has on his people. He acts like a supervisor. He dresses the part and lets everyone around him know that he is a manager. In contrast to his predecessor, Bill is aware of his image among the workers. Successful supervisors have very high concern for the symbols of power and know how to use them. Research shows that of all three managerial groups in the hierarchy, effective supervisors have greater concern for this area than do the others.

WHY SUPERVISORS FAIL

The above section described some of the major competencies of successful supervisors. Unfortunately, not all first-line managers are successful. There are various reasons for this. One is that they lack the competencies identified above. A second is the lack of a desire to do the job. A third is a lack of proper training. A fourth is the inability to adapt to changing conditions. The following discussions examine these last three.

Lack of desire

Perhaps the biggest reason why supervisors fail is that they do not want to be first-line managers. They enjoy being their own boss and not having to worry about others. As workers they are excellent because their job allows them to focus on one major area and not be concerned with what goes on around them. Additionally, they only have to make one person happy: themselves. If they produce the desired amount of quantity and/or quality work, their boss leaves them alone. Unfortunately, in many firms there is the belief that the best workers want to be promoted and move up the line. It is assumed that no one, especially at the lowest levels of the hierarchy, really wants to stay where he or she is. So when there are job openings at the supervisory level, the people at the lowest levels are offered the position. Management fails to realize that these people may not want the job or, worse yet, do not have the skills for carrying it out. See Supervision in Action: Learning the Ropes.

SUPERVISION IN ACTION: LEARNING THE ROPES

When you are promoted to the job of supervisor, many more things change for you besides your title. Immediately, a whole new set of relationships is created with other people—with your supervisor, your employees, and your colleagues in other departments. Your supervisor starts to let you in on management concerns and to look to you to achieve results through your work team. You move from being a member of a group of friendly coworkers to being the group's supervisor. Your former coworkers treat you differently even though you may think that you are the same as before. No matter what you do to prevent it, they may be apprehensive, waiting to see how you are going to behave as their leader. At the same time as they are finding fault with you, they are looking to you for leadership, direction, help, and answers.

Further, colleagues in other departments look to you for assistance in matters that affect them. Your new desk is a collecting place for many kinds of projects and problems. Usually, not everything goes well. Many things new to you have to be decided, planned, and carried out in the midst of pressures, opportunities, and constraints.

As you race from one new experience to another, you begin to reflect on your situation. A common first reaction is "What hit me? I like the idea of being supervisor, but I am not so sure that I like all this tension." Later, you may think, "This supervisory work is harder than it looked. If I'm to master this job, I'd better understand a little better what a supervisor is."

What is a supervisor?

How does a supervisor differ from an employee? Do supervisors frown more? Sprout horns? Hunt less and eat more yogurt? Maybe, but not necessarily. As you may have observed, supervisors have different responsibilities and authority. As an employee your responsibility was to do the job that had been assigned to you. Now your job is to set and accomplish objectives through your work team, plan and organize the work, implement those plans, and solve problems of many kinds—employee's mistakes, their complaints, substandard performance, broken equipment, and the like. You will be expected to interview and select job candidates, train employees, and give them performance feedback. If they fail and you have done all you could do to salvage them, you may have to fire some. When the group falls behind schedule, or output drops, you are expected to create a motivational climate. When there is a discipline problem and all else has failed, you may have to be the heavy. You will see problems from a different perspective than you did as an employee.

Becoming a supervisor

How should you go about learning to become an effective supervisor?

As a starter, new supervisors need to know how to supervise themselves, motivate employees, listen, plan, delegate work, correct mistakes, solve problems and make decisions, give performance feedback, coach, and discipline. These skills are part of one continuous interrelated process—the supervisory process. Seeing them as such can expedite your learning to do them. . . .

Completing your education

If you're typical of most new supervisors, you have a good technical background in your specialized field. This was probably one of the prerequisites to your being chosen leader of your group. Nevertheless, there are probably still things about accounting, programming, manufacturing, engineering, or whatever your specialty that you may need to master. Completing your technical education or keeping up to date on technical matters should be a personal goal of high priority.

Equally important to succeeding in your new role is understanding company operations and how things are done within your organization. Thus of immediate concern to you as a new supervisor is to learn how your division, section, or department operates; what it is supposed to accomplish; how it is related to other departments; and how you are to work together with these other groups. You are expected to understand the company's objectives, customers, and products. You should be able to explain and interpret your employees' work in the light of these overall objectives. It is also important to learn procedural matters thoroughly. This includes personnel policies and practices, budgets, department schedules, and any data processing systems related to your work. Set objectives to do this and do it.

Lack of training   Before workers are allowed to run machinery, they are taught how to do it. The same is true in the case of supervisors. They must be trained. Few individuals can supervise effectively by simply doing what comes naturally.

Additionally, the type of training they need is usually nontechnical in nature. For example, many supervisors have technical tasks, such as filling out budget requests, reporting work output, and keeping track of employee tardiness and absenteeism. These are usually not very demanding and can be picked up on the job.

On the other hand, human relations skills often require training in order to be improved. How does one go about motivating the personnel? What steps should a supervisor take in developing employees? Why do communications break down and what can the manager do to prevent this? These questions all get into areas that the average supervisor does not know much about. Table 1-1 provides a summary of responses from 190 first-level supervisors. The individuals were asked to indicate the type of training they needed. If they said they needed a little training in the area, their response received a score of 1; if they reported a need for some training, the response was given a score of 2; if they said they had a great need for this type of training, the response was given a score of 3. Notice from the table that, on average, 11 of the areas received a score of 2 or higher. Additionally, when comparing the areas that were ranked highest with those that were ranked lowest, behavioral training proved to be more important than technical training.

Table 1-1. Supervisory training needs ($n = 190$)

Ranking		Weighted score	Mean score
1	Motivating	459	2.42
2	Developing employees	457	2.41
3	Communications	442	2.33
4	Leadership	420	2.21
5	Planning/Organizing	409	2.15
6	Human relations	407	2.14
7	Performance appraisal	398	2.09
8	Disciplining	390	2.05
9	Decision making	385	2.03
10	Handling complaints/grievances	381	2.01
11	Management methods (e.g., MBO)	380	2.00
12	Reporting systems (written information)	366	1.93
13	Counseling	359	1.89
14	Functioning in the organization	356	1.87
15	Time management	349	1.84
16	Delegation	338	1.78
17	Affirmative action/EEO	334	1.76
18	Safety (e.g., OSHA, FIRST AID)	332	1.75
19	Conducting meetings	318	1.67
20	Termination procedures	309	1.63
21	Interviewing	307	1.62
22	Hiring procedures	279	1.47
23	Budgeting	255	1.34

Source: Katherine Culbertson and Mark Thompson, "An Analysis of Supervisory Training Needs," *Training and Development Journal*, February 1980, p. 59.

Lack of adaptability

The environment in which the supervisor works is a changing one. Many supervisors are unable to adapt to these conditions. Three of the major changes that confront supervisors are in the areas of technology, personnel, and industry conditions.

Technology has changed dramatically over the last decade, and greater changes can be expected in the future. Computers have invaded the workplace and, along with improvements in machinery and equipment, have changed the old ways of doing things. Today's employees have to work smarter, not harder. Supervisors are continually having to learn new ways of getting things done as they hurry to keep up with new work procedures and developments. Those who are unwilling to learn will fail as supervisors.

At the same time, the personnel are changing. People born and raised during the 1930s are leaving the work force while those from the 1970s are entering. The latter have different values and interests and they bring them to the workplace. Today's young workers are less willing to put up with regimentation and authoritarian leadership. They want a say in what goes on and expect to be involved in decisions that affect them. They are far more vocal than their predecessors, and supervisors are finding that if they cannot adjust to the needs of these workers, they are unable to keep them.

Coupled with the above developments, the environment of most businesses is changing. Deregulation and merger are having a major impact on the way that firms do business. This impact is being felt all the way down the line. Supervisors are finding that their units must be more productive than ever as their firm hurries to remain competitive. Artificial price controls and government regulations that protected inefficiency are now being swept away. Those firms which cannot meet the challenge are finding themselves being pushed aside by major competitors who can adjust and survive in this environment. At the same time, many large firms are buying up the smaller, more efficient ones in their industry in an effort to strengthen their foothold.

These developments are placing great demands on supervisors. It is no longer business as usual. The knowledge, information, and training of the 1970s is not enough to see the first-line manager through. The individual needs to know more. This book is designed to provide that information.

DESIGN OF THE BOOK

This book has four major sections. The first, of which this is the initial chapter, examines the fundamentals of supervisory management. These are the basics that every first-line manager must know. They include planning and controlling work, making effective decisions, organizing for results, and managing conflict and change. The principles and guidelines set forth in these chapters form the foundation of modern supervision.

The second part of this book addresses the subject of supervising people. This involves the nuts and bolts of what supervisors do on a daily basis.

Consideration is given to recruiting, communicating for results, motivating the employee, leading effectively, and training the personnel, appraising and rewarding performance, and supervising protected groups, such as minorities, women, and older workers.

The third part of the book focuses on supervising the work environment. This involves consideration of employee safety and health, dealing with unions, grievances, and discipline problems, and improving productivity and cost control.

The last part of the book addresses the ways in which the supervisor can manage himself or herself. The two major areas of attention here are time and stress management and developing a career plan.

Throughout the chapters, the focus of attention is on how effective supervision can be achieved through a practical approach. Where needed, consideration is given to the theoretical aspects of supervision. However, in every case an attempt has been made to translate this theory into practical, how-to-do-it terms that produce bottom-line results. This is the world of supervision: efficiency, shortcuts, street smarts, and a leadership style that is a result of more than just common sense. So come with us now as we begin our journey into the exciting world of effective supervision. We start with what many management experts believe is the heart of effective supervision: communicating for results.

JEANNE'S DECISION: STARTING CASE REVISITED

Having read the chapter, you should now realize that Jeanne's biggest problem is that she lacks the desire to be a supervisor. She is more interested in selling than in supervising those who are selling. Notice that when she was out on the road with the personnel, she loved the work. When she was in the office doing paperwork or handling administrative chores, she did not like the work. Basically, Jeanne is an action-oriented person who likes to roll up her sleeves and go out and sell. She is a classic example of the person who can sell well but does not have the desire to direct others who are selling. Her decision to go to Alaska is a good one because it puts her back in the work environment she knows and loves best.

One other point that is made indirectly in the case is that the firm promotes from within and gives first shot at supervisory openings to its best sales people. This is a mistake because there is no proof that those who sell best can manage best. If the firm goes on doing this, it is looking for more trouble. The firm needs to focus on the factors that result in succesful supervisory management. Although a supervisor who is also an effective salesperson may thus be better able to evaluate and direct subordinates, sales skills alone are not enough to ensure successful supervision.

INTERPRETATION OF SELF-ASSESSMENT QUIZ 1-1:
HOW CREATIVE ARE YOU?

1. Mostly false. Highly creative people tend to be bright but not brilliant.
2. Mostly true. Creative people are able to come up with a great many solutions (regardless of how useful the solutions actually are) in a short period of time.
3. Mostly true. Creative people feel good about themselves.
4. Mostly false. Creative people tend to be more concerned with the overall picture than with the small details. They are macro rather than micro people.
5. Mostly true. These people tend to be very aware of what is going on around them.
6. Mostly true. Creative people tend to like to do things differently from the crowd.
7. Mostly false. Creative people are more reflective than impulsive; they think about things before taking action.
8. Mostly true. Creative people tend to live in their own world without losing touch with the world around them.
9. Mostly false. Creative people are flexible in their thinking. They perceive many shades of gray.
10. Mostly true. Creative people like challenging problems.
11. Mostly true. Creative people look on rules and regulations as general guidelines, not as absolutes.
12. Mostly false. Creative people do not worry too much about how they dress. They are not out to impress people.
13. Mostly false. Creative people believe in the maxim "Make yourself happy first." They are most creative when they are in the best frame of mind; they believe in pleasure before business.
14. Mostly false. Creative people do not let unclear directions get them down. They improvise and figure out how to do things on their own.
15. Mostly true. Creative people like fiction more than nonfiction. It stirs their creative thought processes and helps them develop new ways of looking at things.
16. Mostly true. Creative people like detective or investigative types of problems; they enjoy solving "think" problems.
17. Mostly false. Creative people read a lot, often in the range of 15 to 25 hours per week.
18. Mostly false. Creative people like to be treated nicely; it makes them happy and helps create the right environment for creative thinking.
19. Mostly false. Creative people are more interested in why people treat them well than in the fact that people do treat them well.

20. Mostly true. Creative people believe that most problems can be solved, given sufficient time and energy. They also believe that they can solve most problems regardless of how difficult it may appear at the outset.

How well did you do? Most creative people get at least 14 of these correct. If you did not, take heart, for this does not mean that you are not creative. There are many ways of gaining insights into creativity, including having people work on various types of creative problems. This quiz is designed only to give you insights into your own behaviors and to provide you with general information regarding how creative people, in general, behave.

SUMMARY OF KEY POINTS

1. Supervisors are first-line managers who are directly responsible for overseeing the workers. While they have various titles, supervisors are the first link between management and the workers. In many cases supervisors are promoted from within, although some are hired from the outside.

2. Supervisors perform four functions: planning, organizing, directing, and controlling. The specific nature of each was described in the chapter. In carrying out these functions, supervisors use three management skills: technical, human, and conceptual.

3. Modern supervision has been the result of an evolutionary process that began at the turn of this century. At that time, scientific management held sway, with its emphasis on the task concept, time and motion, and efficiency. This approach was gradually complemented by human relations management in which the workers were allowed to exercise a minimum of self-direction and self-control and were kept informed about much of what directly affected their work. The human resources era began to emerge in the 1960s. Today's supervisors believe that most workers are capable of exercising a great deal of self-direction and self-control. Additionally, they focus attention on providing an environment in which the workers can exercise their creativity and talents to the best of their abilities.

4. Many factors help account for supervisory success. Seven of the most important are: an efficiency orientation, self-control, open expression, objectivity, use of individual power, use of group power, and concern for impact.

5. Supervisors fail at their jobs for many reasons. One is the lack of factors such as those noted above. Others include lack of desire, lack of training, and lack of adaptability.

BUILD YOUR SUPERVISORY WORD POWER

These key terms are presented in their order of appearance in the chapter. Practicing supervisors have a working knowledge of these terms.

Supervisor. A first-line manager who is directly responsible for overseeing the workers.

Technical skills. Skills related to how things work.

Human skills. Skills related to interacting with subordinates. The skills encompass communicating, motivating, and leading.

Administrative skills. Skills related to how all parts of a department or organization fit together.

Task concept. The spelling out of what a worker is to do, how, and by when.

Efficiency. A measure of how well people are doing. Efficiency is determined by dividing output by input.

REVIEW YOUR UNDERSTANDING

1. In your own words, what is a supervisor? What title does the individual commonly carry? How do people become supervisors? Explain.
2. What do supervisors do during the planning process? How do they go about organizing? What types of activities do they carry out? In each case, give an example.
3. How do supervisors go about directing their people. What is involved in this process? How do they carry out the controlling function? Explain.
4. Supervisors make use of three management skills: technical, human, and conceptual. What does this statement mean? In your answer be sure to describe each of the skills.
5. How did supervisors view the workers during the era of scientific management? How did this approach to management change during the era of human relations? In your answer be sure to compare and contrast the two approaches.
6. How do supervisors in the human resource era differ from those in the scientific management and human relations eras? Cite at least three examples in your answer.
7. Explain how each of the following factors helps supervisors do a better job: efficiency orientation, self-control, open expression, objectivity, use of individual power, use of group power, and concern for impact. In each case, give an example of how the effective supervisor would use the factor.
8. Why do supervisors fail? Identify and describe three reasons.

SUPPLEMENT YOUR KNOWLEDGE

In addition to the references listed at the end of this chapter, the following provide important, practical information that is of use to supervisors in managing their people:

Begosh, Donald G.: "So You Want to Be a Supervisor . . .," *Supervisory Management,* February 1978, pp. 2–10.

Bittell, Lester R., and Jackson E. Ramsey: "The Limited, Traditional World of Supervisors," *Harvard Business Review,* July–August 1982, pp. 29–33.

Coleman, Daniel: "Style of Thinking, Not I.Q., Tied to Success," *New York Times,* July 1984, pp. 1–18.

De Long, Thomas: "What Do Middle Managers Really Want from First-Line Supervisors?" *Supervisory Management,* September 1977, pp. 8–12.

Johnston, Robert: "What You Need to Know to Be a Supervisor," *Supervisory Management,* March 1983, pp. 35–42.

Mangrum, Claude T.: "Making the Transition to Supervisor," *Supervisory Management,* September 1978, pp. 7–13.

Margerison, Charles: "Where'd You Learn to Be a Manager?" *Supervisory Management,* February 1981, pp. 40–43.

McClelland, David C.: "Testing for Competence Rather than for 'Intelligence,' " *American Psychologist,* January 1973, pp. 1–14.

Sasser, W. Earl, Jr., and Frank S. Leonard: "Let First-Level Supervisors Do Their Job," *Harvard Business Review,* March–April 1980, pp. 113–121.

YOU BE THE SUPERVISOR: FINDING OUT ABOUT THE JOB

Jill Bowlen is scheduled to be graduated from college next month. She has been interviewing with a number of different firms, and the one she has been most interested in has an opening at the supervisory level.

The recruiter, Tom Yost, had explained to Jill that his firm likes to hire new, young college graduates as supervisors. The company had found these people to be fast learners and much more motivated than those recruited from other sources. The job that Tom was talking about is in the receiving department of a large warehouse. The warehouse takes in over $8 million of materials per month and the supervisor is responsible for overseeing the acceptance, storage, and eventual disbursement of these materials.

Tom had explained to Jill that the company has a policy of promotion from within. All middle managers are chosen from the current group of supervisors; all top managers are drawn from the middle-management ranks. This policy was one of the reasons why Jill was attracted to the firm. However, she was concerned that the job would be more than she could handle. "I've never had a full-time job before," she told Tom. "This is my first step into the real world and I'm afraid that I'll end up getting in over my head. I don't know much about supervising people. What exactly will I be doing? What responsibilities will I have? How will I be evaluated?"

Tom had tried to put her mind at ease. He explained that each year the company hired approximately one hundred new supervisors right out of college. "We've had plenty of experience teaching young supervisors what they need to know," he said. "No one right out of college has the foggiest idea of what a supervisor's job entails. That's not important. We're looking for people with intelligence, achievement drive, a good education, and a willingness to learn. We'll do all of the rest. Think it over. If you're interested, call me and I'll take care of the rest."

Jill thought about the job for over a week. "If a hundred people a year take a job with the firm," she reasoned, "it can't be that difficult to master. Perhaps I'm making a mountain out of a molehill." Picking up the phone, she called Tom and told him she would take the job on one condition: "I'd like to talk to one of the supervisors who was hired right out of college. If possible, I'd like it to be someone who has not been on the job more than a year."

Tom agreed and called her back an hour later. "OK," he said, "I've got it all set up. You're to go over to 100 Billard Avenue in an hour. We have a plant there. Six of the supervisors we hired last year work at this plant. I've asked the plant manager to get one of them loose for a couple of hours to talk to you. He'll choose someone who'll give you the straight story. At the same time, this person will probably show you around the plant and give you an idea of what they do there. We've got two supervisory openings at Billard, and you just might end up there yourself. So be sure to ask the individual all of the questions you can think of. Then call me tomorrow and let me know how it went. If you want to see anyone else, just let me know and I'll schedule another visit for you. Otherwise, you can spend a couple of days relaxing before reporting to work next Monday."

Jill was extremely pleased with the arrangements. As soon as she hung up, she jumped in her car and drove over to the plant. When she entered the building she noticed that the supervisor was already waiting for her. As she approached, the supervisor said, "I thought I was the only person who ever asked for a prejob conference with a supervisor. I'm delighted to know that there are others who feel the same way. C'mon, let me show you around and answer your questions."

1. If you were the Billard supervisor whom Jill just met, what types of questions would you expect her to ask? List five.
2. If Jill asked you what a supervisor does, what would you tell her without getting too technical in your answer? Provide a general overall picture of the first-line manager's job.
3. If you were giving Jill recommendations on the types of training she should have in order to do a good job, what would you recommend? Be complete in your answers.

YOU BE THE SUPERVISOR: GETTING THE RIGHT PEOPLE

The Cappaole Company was founded 3 years ago. The firm specializes in sub-contract work for electronics and computer firms. Since its founding, the work force has grown from 37 to 254 people. The supervisory staff has increased from 3 to 28. Unfortunately, while business has boomed (sales are up 87 percent over the last year), the company has been having trouble finding and keeping qualified supervisors.

In the past 6 months there has been a 39 percent turnover in supervisors. Most of this has resulted from management actions. The president of the firm explained the situation to one of the major stockholders by noting: "We seem to be having trouble finding the right people. We hire lots of supervisors, but they don't work out. Oh sure, a couple of them are fine, but most of them simply can't manage. I don't understand what the problem is. We go out of our way to get the best. We have a recruiting firm that looks over all applications and screens out those who do not have the right qualifications. The rest are sent over to us and we choose the ones who we think will do the best job. However, something seems to be wrong. Either we're not being sent the best people or we're failing to pick them out. In any event, I intend to bring in a consultant next week to look over the problem and give me some recommendations."

The consultant who was brought in had a great deal of experience in the business. The first thing he did was interview some of the newly hired supervisors. He then talked to some of those who had been around since the beginning. From this, he was able to piece together the following facts:

1. The recruiting firm uses a number of different methods in deciding whether or not someone will make a good supervisor. One of these is an intelligence test that measures general knowledge. A second is a manual dexterity test that measures how fast the individual can assemble a semisophisticated piece of equipment following a blueprint and written instructions.
2. A high school diploma is considered mandatory for the job. Non-high school people are rejected outright. On the other hand, so are college graduates. The recruiting firm will not send anyone over to the plant who has more than 3 years of college experience.
3. Past supervisory experience is given very little attention. Most of the people who have been hired as supervisors have had less than 1 year of experience, and the majority of them have had none.
4. Age seems to be very important to the screening firm. All of the supervisors they have sent over to Cappaole are between 24 and 29 years of age.

While the consultant found out other things about the supervisory work force, the above four were the most important. Based on this information, the consultant went back to the president and told him that he felt the biggest problem was that the selection firm was not doing a good job in screening supervisory candidates: "You ought to have them send over anyone who meets minimal requirements and have your own supervisors talk to them. After all, who knows more about the characteristics for supervisory success at this company than those who are doing this work?" The president agreed and said that he would take care of everything.

1. What types of people are being recommended for the supervisory jobs at the company? What do they have in common?
2. If you were a supervisor at this plant, what types of characteristics would you expect supervisors to have? Identify and describe five.
3. How would your approach to choosing supervisors differ from that of the recruiting firm? Compare and contrast the two. Why would yours be better? Explain.

NOTES

1. Katherine Culbertson and Mark Thompson, "An Analysis of Supervisory Training Needs," *Training and Development Journal*, February 1980, p. 58.
2. Culbertson and Thompson, p. 58.
3. Robert L. Katz, "Skills of an Effective Administrator," *Harvard Business Review*, January–February 1955, pp. 33–42.
4. Frederick W. Taylor, *Principles of Scientific Management*, New York: Harper & Brothers, 1911, p. 39.
5. The material in this section can be found in Richard E. Boyatzis, *The Competent Manager*, New York: Wiley, 1982.
6. Boyatzis, p. 153.
7. Boyatzis, p. 124.

CHAPTER 2

PLANNING AND CONTROLLING THE WORK

GOALS OF THE CHAPTER

In managing day-to-day operations, the supervisor wears many hats. Sometimes the manager must convey new work orders, sometimes must train and direct new employees, and other times must check work progress to see that everything is on schedule. All of these activities are tied to an overall plan that guides the unit's operations. Sometimes this plan is formally written down; other times it is informal and conveyed by word of mouth. In any event, planning is an important part of the supervisor's job. Controlling, the process of seeing that everything is being done according to plan, is directly linked to these efforts because it helps the supervisor keep track of work progress and make any changes that are necessary to ensure the success of the plan. The overriding goal of this chapter is to examine how supervisors go about planning and controlling the work in their units. When you have finished reading all the material in this chapter, you will be able to:

1. Define the term *planning* and discuss the steps in this process.
2. Explain how rules, procedures, and policies help supervisors carry out plans.
3. Identify major advantages of planning and discuss why planning sometimes fails.
4. Define the term *controlling* and discuss the steps in this process.
5. Relate some of the major characteristics of effective control.
6. Describe some of the most common control techniques used by supervisors, including: budgeting, work distribution charts, the Gantt chart, and PERT.
7. Explain how management by objectives works and discuss some of the benefits it offers.

A STARTING CASE: THE NEED FOR A NEW APPROACH

When Sam Levy first started with his company, there were only six employees. That was 25 years ago. Since then the firm has grown dramatically. Sam and the four other workers all reported directly to the owner-manager, Paul

Adams. "Paul was the owner and supervisor, all rolled into one," Sam reminisced. "Now I've got more people reporting to me than we had in the entire company back then." Sam's remark referred to his current status as head supervisor of group 2.

Sam became a supervisor almost 20 years ago. Paul assigned two people to report to him and told Sam, "I want you to coordinate their efforts, help them with their work, and see that they're kept busy at all times." Over the years the number of subordinates increased to five. Last year, however, the company had a major reorganization and decided to increase the number of workers in each supervisory group. Sam was assigned nine more people. Since then things have not gone well for him.

Sam has been having three major problems. First, the work output per person has dropped by 8 percent. Second, some of the people report that they spend as much as 30 minutes per day waiting for Sam to assign them additional work. Third, Sam is finding it impossible to check everyone's work and spend as much time as he feels is necessary in providing guidance and assistance.

Earlier this week Paul called Sam in for a talk. "You seem to be having trouble managing 14 people," Paul said. "What exactly is the problem?"

Sam explained it this way: "In the old days I used to have no trouble handling things. However, with 14 people, I have too many things to do. I used to be able to tell the workers what I wanted done and they would do it. Now it seems that I have to write things down in order to be sure that both of us remember what was said. Also, I like to check to see that things are done right. This probably takes more of my time than actually delegating and explaining what's to be done. The upshot of all of this is that I'm overworked."

Paul pondered Sam's comments. "I don't know if you're as much overworked as you are in need of a better planning and control system," Paul said. "You need to work smarter, not harder. Rather than giving people something to do for the next day or so, you have to assign them more long-range jobs that will keep them busy for a week or two. This is the only way to free yourself up for handling problems and for getting your own work done." Sam has promised to look into developing a better approach, but he is confused as to what form that system should take. However, he does realize that he has to do something different.

Why is Sam having problems? What does he need to do differently? How should he go about it? Write down your suggestions and then put them off to the side. We will return to them later.

THE PLANNING PROCESS

Planning is the process of setting objectives and determining the steps that will be taken in attaining these ends. There are four steps in this process. The following examines each.[1] Before reading on, however, take Self-Assessment Quiz 2-1 and determine how much you know currently about the two main areas of focus in this chapter: planning and controlling.

SELF-ASSESSMENT QUIZ 2-1:
WHAT DO YOU KNOW ABOUT PLANNING AND CONTROLLING?

Carefully read each of the following statements and place an *X* in the appropriate column. When you have finished, check your answers at the end of the chapter to see how well you did. This quiz should provide you useful input regarding your current knowledge of these two important supervisory functions.

	True	*False*
1. When workers have participated in the establishment of goals, they tend to be motivated toward attaining them.	X	
2. Effective supervisors find that it is more efficient to assign workers 8 to 10 objectives than it is to assign them three or four objectives.		X
3. Believe it or not, most supervisors do no planning at all.		X
4. Workers tend to meet and exceed expectations when they have participated in the establishment of these objectives.	X	
5. When possible, supervisors should assign objectives that are measurable.	X	
6. Planning helps supervisors overcome their need to live with ambiguity.		X
7. Good supervisors try to develop contingency plans.	X	
8. It is sometimes difficult to determine where planning ends and controlling begins.	X	
9. Most effective supervisors are able to control all aspects of their unit's performance.		X
10. Close control tends to be much more effective than loose control.		X
11. Control is most effective when established at strategic locations at the lowest level of the operating process.	X	
12. Effective supervisors often directly control only a small percentage of their employees' work.	X	
13. Computerized control printouts have more reliability with supervisors than do typewritten or handwritten control reports. *They do but shouldn't*	0	X ✓
14. All deviations from plan should be investigated.		X
15. Budgeting is a common supervisory control tool. *not good one*	X	

Ⓛ
Setting objectives   Planning begins with the formulation of objectives. At the supervisory level, the objectives are usually specific and measurable. Examples include: produce 600 units per day; keep quality rejects to 1 percent of all produced units; hold the scrap rate to 2 percent of all material costs; reduce overtime by 25 percent by the end of December. These types of objectives have two

characteristics: they are short-run in orientation and they are measurable. Of course, sometimes the supervisor will have to pursue objectives or assign goals that do not have these characteristics, but this is more the exception than the rule.

The objectives of the unit are determined by the supervisor's boss. The first-line manager, in turn, first decides how to break these objectives into subobjectives and then communicates them to the personnel. In large organizations this step is often carried out as part of the formal planning process and the objectives are committed to writing. In small organizations the approach is often informal, with the supervisor simply discussing with the subordinates what needs to be done and then assigning work to them.

Getting employee understanding and cooperation ②

Having told the individual what is to be done, the supervisor must now step back and let the worker talk. Perhaps the individual is unsure of what the supervisor meant by saying, "The reason I want you to operate this new machine is that you're the best worker we've got, and with you I know that 500 units a day is a realistic objective." The worker may want to know whether that is 500 units every day or an average of 2500 units per week. The individual may also be concerned that while 500 a day is not asking too much, this goal may be unrealistic until the individual becomes familiar with the new machine. Additionally, many employees are concerned that they will be overworked while others will be given easier jobs that require far less effort. The supervisor may need to point out that everyone else will be operating old machines and, as usual, will be turning out an average of 450 units per day.

The other thing the supervisor must do is gain the workers' support. Telling people what to do is not enough; the manager must win them over. This often means explaining to them how the unit will be operating for the next 3 to 6 months, what types of work changes can be expected, and what their roles in the entire process will be. At this stage of gaining the workers' cooperation, the supervisor employs the ideas of human resource management (discussed in Chapter 1) in terms of showing how the work objectives can help the individual use his or her abilities and talents.

Developing a contingency plan ③

Not everything will go according to plan. The supervisor may delegate work to all of the subordinates and then find that one of them is quitting and that it is impossible to get a replacement in less than 10 days. Or a machine may go down and the maintenance people may report that it will be 4 days before the factory can send another part. Or a key worker may be ill, causing overall output to suffer. Many times there is nothing the supervisor can do about these things. However, when there are alternative steps that can be taken, a contingency plan is helpful.

Most supervisors do not draw up formal contingency plans. They simply think through what they will do if certain things go wrong. These plans are usually based on technical and human considerations. For example, a supervisor who is familiar with all of the equipment in her work area will already have figured out in her head that if the photocopying machine breaks down and blueprint copies cannot be made, she can place a call to a nearby copying service that offers a 2-hour turnaround. It will cost more money than doing it in-house, but the work will get done on time. Likewise, if a word processing machine breaks down, the supervisor may simply have all of the important work that was assigned to that machine divided up among the other typists. In this way, only minor typing work will fall behind schedule.

Sometimes contingency plans cannot be implemented without assistance from other departments. For example, if a machine goes down, the supervisor may find that she is fourth in line for servicing. It will be 3 days before the maintenance people can get to her machine. However, if she knows a supervisor in another department who does not have pressing work and she can talk him into helping out, he may trade places with her on the maintenance schedule list. This is the human consideration side of contingency plans. To a large degree, these considerations are a result of the supervisor's power base (a topic discussed in Chapter 1 under Success in Supervision).

Converting the plan into action

The final phase of the planning process is to implement the plan by converting it into action. This phase is multifaceted. It involves checking on schedules to ensure that everyone who has been assigned a job will have the needed materials and equipment, that work progress has been tied to objectives, and that budgets have been developed for everything. This is the phase in which planning formulation (what the supervisor has decided to do) gives way to planning implementation (actually getting it done). The talking stage is over; the doing stage is here.

In making things happen, the supervisor often has a lot of leeway. However, there are still organizational guidelines that must be followed. For example, many firms have rules, procedures, and policies, and plans must be formulated and implemented within these guidelines. In fact, these three are often referred to as *types* of plans because they regulate organizational activity and keep it heading toward overall enterprise goals. While often used interchangeably by supervisors, there are some very important differences between rules, procedures, and policies.

A *rule* is an inflexible regulation that must be followed at all times. The following are rules:

- No smoking in this area.
- Safety glasses must be worn by everyone entering this room.
- Only employees may enter this area.

The purpose of a rule is to direct action along a specific line. By following the above three rules, the supervisor ensures that safety regulations are carried out and that only company personnel are allowed into the area.

These rules are designed to help the manager reduce accidents and keep nonauthorized personnel away. Remember that if a rule is given any leeway, it stops being a rule. If the supervisor allows some people to smoke in the area or permits some workers to enter the room without first putting on safety glasses, we no longer have a rule. At best it has become a general guideline that is offered as a piece of friendly advice: i.e., you really should not smoke in this area; it is advisable to wear safety glasses in this room; nonemployees should not be invited into this area.

Procedures are guidelines to action. They set forth chronological steps that are to be followed in achieving an objective. For example, in a business office when materials are received, it is common to have the person signing for them follow these procedures: (1) Check the list of items against the materials that have been delivered to ensure that the list and the delivered materials are in accord, (2) sign the receipt and get a copy of the list, and (3) give the list and the materials to the lead secretary who will make a detailed physical count to ensure that everything is in order. In a retail store when someone returns merchandise because it is defective or otherwise un-acceptable, the departmental personnel are instructed to do the following: (1) Check the buyer's receipt against the merchandise that is being re-turned; (2) if the receipt and the merchandise are in accord, give the buyer a receipt for the purchase price of the merchandise; (3) direct the individual to the customer service area where the receipt can be exchanged for cash; (4) enter the name and address of the buyer, as well as a brief description of the merchandise, into the merchandise returns book; and (5) send the buyer's receipt to the customer service department and the merchandise to the central purchasing department. Notice in both cases that procedures call for following a host of steps. Both examples are incomplete in that they do not cover every eventuality; for example, in the retail store case it was never made clear how the worker should handle the situation if the person returning the merchandise did not have a receipt. Detailed procedures would cover such eventualities. Additionally, if there were a problem, the worker would call for the supervisor.

Policies are guidelines to thinking and action. On the one hand, they set forth some action that must be taken. On the other hand, they allow for some interpretation or flexibility in implementation. For example, consider the following policy regarding the hiring of supervisors: We hire only college graduates as supervisors. Does this mean that a new supervisor must provide evidence of having attained a formal degree from a college? Not if the company regards this statement as a policy, for there may be an equivalency line: 3 years of college and 5 years of work experience may be regarded as the equivalent of a college degree. Or consider another com-mon policy: We promote from within. This means that if the company can find a qualified in-house person to fill a job opening, the individual is offered the position; on the other hand, the company has the flexibility to go outside if it determines that there are no qualified in-house personnel. Finally, consider this fairly common policy: Satisfaction or your money back. What is meant by the word *satisfaction*? This is determined by the company; otherwise, the firm would be at the mercy of the customer. For example, the supervisor may agree to take back a suit that has a torn sleeve and give the customer a cash refund; however, the manager may refuse to have the coat fixed free of charge because it was bought 6 months ago and it is evident that the suit has undergone considerable wear.[2]

One thing to remember about rules and policies is that the former are inflexible while the latter are not. Quite often supervisors confuse the two, as in the case of the manager who tells a customer, "It's our policy not to take back merchandise after 30 days." This is not a policy. It is a rule. A policy would be much more flexible, such as "It's our policy not to take back merchandise that has been subjected to excessive wear." A second important thing to remember is that rules, procedures, and policies help the supervisor implement the plan. They provide the individual with additional inputs that help direct, limit, and focus the plan.

The above steps are the most critical ones in planning. However, there are many other things that practicing supervisors need to know about planning. Supervision in Action: Some Useful Tips presents other points that are of value.

SUPERVISION IN ACTION: SOME USEFUL TIPS

The planning process

Effective planning is simply a process of reasoning and thinking. To focus thinking, the following steps should be followed:

- Have an overall goal for the plan (quality improvement, plant maintenance, or the like).
- Collect information on what the current situation is and describe it in simple statements.
- Collect information about what the future may hold for your work group and describe it realistically.
- Identify the important threats that may prevent your group (or company) from achieving its goal.
- Identify the big opportunities.
- Try to identify *several* choices in dealing with threats and opportunities.
- Evaluate the advantages and disadvantages of each choice, including the resources required to make each one work.
- Identify the roadblocks to successful implementation of each.
- Develop an overall action plan that has the best chance of succeeding.
- Develop a contingency plan for dealing with the unexpected.
- Set specific objectives along the way as a means of determining whether the plan is on schedule.

Sounds simple, doesn't it? Yet the process requires a lot of attention. It can run aground for a variety of reasons.

One has to do with the system itself. Organizations often develop complicated systems for planning around these 11 points. The idea is to force managers who might otherwise not plan to follow the process. But too often managers instead become buried under layers of paperwork that end up collecting dust.

When those who plan don't involve those who will execute the plan, problems also arise. The manager who involves people, instead of simply data, in the planning process will likely have a more effective plan. There are two reasons why—quality and acceptance.

First, groups always produce higher-quality planning outcomes than a manager working alone, for groups can identify threats and opportunities that the manager on his or her own might miss.

Second, and more important, participation in the planning process increases acceptance of the plan by those who must make it work.

Another reason that plans fail is that the planner tries to look too far into the future. This can be just as bad as not planning at all. Although different levels within an organization require different planning timeframes, for the most part it's best not to look beyond a year as the basis for a realistic plan.

The most important factor in the success of the planning process is the plan itself. The quality of the plan can be evaluated by asking the following questions:

- Is it clear? Do people understand it?
- Does it agree with the values and purpose of the organization?
- Does the plan deal effectively with both the threats and opportunities identified?
- Does it identify the items of importance to the work group?
- To what extent are there specific, measurable goals and objectives?
- Is the plan a real basis for action?
- Does the overall plan contain contingencies in case of a serious internal or outside event?
- Does the plan include a way of obtaining feedback on its success?
- Is the plan flexible enough in case it needs to be changed?

Planning begins "at home"

Many managers blame their company for their inability to plan. Although you may work for an organization that lacks direction and doesn't reward or support planning, that shouldn't stop you from planning. Someone must deal with the uncertainty created for your work group.

Make no mistake about it; good planning pays off. It creates shared values; it creates direction; it creates work excitement; it increases one's ability to manage. And that's what you are paid for.

Source: Donald O. Jewell, George E. Manners Jr., and Sandra F. Jewell, "For the First-Time Planner," *Supervisory Management*, July 1984, pp. 41–42.

ADVANTAGES OF PLANNING

Planning has many advantages for the supervisor. One of the most important is that it forces the individual to focus on the future. Rather than taking a wait-and-see attitude toward things, the manager begins thinking about what has to be done and how these objectives should be pursued. The individual adopts an active rather than a passive approach.

Second, planning forces the supervisor to think in terms of specific objectives. It gives the supervisor goals to pursue and provides a basis for answering the question How well are things going?

Third, planning provides a basis for teamwork. When goals are clearly defined, the supervisor is able to determine work assignments for all of the people in the unit and to coordinate their activities. This, in turn, can lead to useful interaction and communication among the personnel and can thus result in higher morale and espirit de corps.

Fourth, planning helps the supervisor develop the talents of the personnel. By determining who is able to do what, the supervisor begins to realize what everyone's abilities are and can use work assignments to sharpen skills and/or build competencies.

Fifth, planning helps the supervisor learn to live with ambiguity. Quite often things will not go according to plan. There will be unexpected roadblocks or problems. By learning to face these, the supervisor gains experience that will be profitable later on at the middle and upper levels of the hierarchy. Planning helps develop the first-line manager for future responsibilities.

WHY PLANNING SOMETIMES FAILS

Plans fail for a number of reasons. At the supervisory level, most of these can be explained in terms of four causes.

First, sometimes the objectives are unclear. When this happens, the personnel do not know precisely what they are supposed to be doing. For example, the supervisor who tells a worker, "Get this done as soon as you can," may not realize that the individual will put aside the rush job he was working on and devote his efforts to this new assignment. The worker substitutes one objective for another and in the process overall progress suffers.

Second, sometimes the workload is not properly distributed. When this happens, the supervisor ends up overloading some of the workers while others have very little to do. This is common when a great deal of work has to be done and the manager wants to make sure that all workers are given enough to keep them busy. Quite often the supervisor will give too much to the best workers because in the past they have proven most reliable. In the process, these people end up being weighted under with their volume of work, and project completion is late.

Third, some plans are based on erroneous information. For example, the supervisor is given a major project and told, "All of the material you need will be provided, and maintenance has been told to give you first priority." The project plan is drawn up under the assumption that all the necessary support help will be forthcoming. Halfway through the project, however, materials start arriving late and the maintenance people are unable to free up the necessary people to ensure that the supervisor's machine downtime is minimized. As a result, everything starts to back up and the project completion date has to be pushed weeks into the future.

Fourth, some plans fail because there is not proper coordination of effort and work between the unit personnel. For example, the assembly people are scheduled to turn out 500 units per day, but the test and quality control people are scheduled to handle only 400 units per day. Quite obviously there is a problem. When the overall plan for the project was worked out, someone overlooked the gap of 100 units per day. If the project must stay on a 500-units-per-day schedule, more assistance must be provided to the test and quality control people. If 400 units per day are required, the number of people doing the assembling is too great. One or more should be rescheduled to other jobs that warrant additional personnel.

THE CONTROLLING PROCESS

Controlling is the process of seeing that everything is done in accordance with the plan. In practice, it is often difficult to determine where planning ends and controlling begins because the two are so closely intertwined. The controlling process has four basic phases. The following examines each.

Setting standards

Controlling begins when standards are set. This phase is at least partially completed in the planning process, for standards are objectives, or goals. However, they are often refined in the controlling process. For example, an objective set in the planning process may be the production of 100 units per day. In order to ensure that this objective is met, the supervisor may set minimum control standards of 12 units per hour. In this way the supervisor can easily determine progress toward the objective. In other cases an objective may be much more broadly based, such as to provide immediate servicing of customer accounts. What does the word *immediate* mean? The supervisor may determine that it means responding to a customer query or complaint within 3 hours of the time it is received. In this case the standard is set in terms of response time. Now when the supervisor checks on work progress, he or she will look at the pile of customer service requests in ascertaining whether each is being handled within a 3-hour time span.

Gathering information

Controlling requires the supervisor to compare desired progress against actual progress. The supervisor needs feedback information in order to do this. In the above paragraph this feedback was easily available to the supervisor. When it is not, the individual must take steps to obtain it. For example, if one of the supervisor's objectives is to keep the cost per unit at $12.54 or less, the individual needs feedback from the accounting department or from whomever is charged with gathering cost and production information. Additionally, the supervisor needs to have this data on a timely basis. It does no good to find out today that the cost per unit last month rose from $12.43 to $12.98 and appears to be still climbing.

In carrying out this step, the supervisor must develop sources of information that provide the necessary information. At the time the objective was first formulated, the manager should have asked, "How will I be able to monitor progress toward this objective?" In the case of cost per unit, the individual should already have placed a telephone call to the person who would have this information and have arranged for it to be provided on a timely basis.

Comparing results against expectations

In the examples thus far, it was quite easy to compare results against expectations. The objectives were all quantified. The supervisor merely had to look at the desired and achieved results to determine how well things were going. However, sometimes results are qualitative or call for a judgment call. For example, a supervisor in the public relations department may have an objective of improving the firm's public image. How can this objective be measured? What types of results should be examined? Would the number of positive stories in the local newspaper be a gauge? What about the number of luncheon talks given by the supervisor and the staff at community functions? How about participation in the United Fund and the company's summer jobs program for high school students? Where does one draw the line regarding the types of results to use in this comparison stage? How does one quantify these results? Finally, if the results are not quantifiable, how should they be used? These types of questions are not easy to answer, but they do point out that supervisors sometimes have a difficult time comparing results against expectations because the former cannot be easily measured or used for comparison purposes.

Taking appropriate action

The last phase of the control process is that of taking appropriate action. In light of the results, what should be done? The first thing the supervisor must realize is that appropriate action sometimes means doing nothing. For example, one of the supervisor's best people has gone to the west coast to make a comprehensive health and safety insurance presentation to an old client. The latter has done business with the firm for years. However, this time the salesperson fails to get the account. Why? Because the president's brother-in-law has just opened an insurance brokerage of his own and is specializing in health and safety coverage. The president wants to keep the business in the family and so he switches the account to the new firm. Who is to blame? No one; this is one of the risks of doing business.

A second important thing the supervisor must keep in mind is that sometimes the difference between expected and actual results does not warrant action. For example, a health care clinic supervisor has set an objective of filing all insurance forms within 24 hours of the time that a person receives medical care. Over the last 6 months the reputation of the clinic has grown so widely that the office is jammed with patients from 8 A.M. until well after 5 P.M. The paperwork is piling up and it now takes an average of 1½ days for a form to be filed. Is a half-day difference significant enough to worry about? The answer is no. The delay is a result of the increased workload, not of employee incompetence.

In deciding whether any action is required on his or her part, the supervisor should follow the *exception principle of control.* This principle holds that corrective action should be taken only in those cases in which the results are outside of acceptable limits. If things are about as expected, no action is necessary.

CHARACTERISTICS OF EFFECTIVE CONTROL

Effective control systems have a number of important characteristics. The following are four of the most important.

Provide useful information

The supervisor's control system must be designed in such a way that it provides useful information. If the manager needs to know about daily productivity, these figures should be provided in an understandable fashion.

The biggest problem that supervisors run into is being given more information than they need. For example, in addition to productivity information, it is not uncommon for managers to be provided with weekly data related to the number of personnel who were at work, the number of machines that were fully functioning, and the amount of electric power that was consumed. Unless the supervisor is expected to control these other areas, the information is superfluous and should be deleted.

A second major problem that supervisors face is having to analyze control reports in order to find what they are looking for. Within a massive array of data are the two or three statistics they need.

In both of these above cases, the problem can be overcome by getting the manager involved in fashioning the reporting system. If the individual is allowed to relate what is needed and in what form, the firm should be able to follow on from there and see that it is provided.

Be timely

Information must be timely. It does the supervisor no good to receive control information after the problem has become a major one. Managers need to know what is going on soon after it happens. For example, if a supervisor is asked to expand her northeastern U.S. sales force into Canada in an effort to gain a foothold in that market, a control system should be set up for providing sales feedback, such as weekly sales figures. In this way, if after a predetermined time the firm has been unable to penetrate the market, sales activity can be curtailed and losses held to a minimum. Timely information is vital to effective control.

Be economical

Control systems have to be worth the expense. There is no sense having supervisors fill out a weekly employee tardiness and absenteeism report if these supervisors are the only ones who are going to use this information. They can gather this data on an informal basis and forgo the time spent in filling out the formal report. Likewise, if the computer department prepares monthly cost control reports for every unit but most supervisors find these to be of no value in monitoring operations, the report is worthless and should be scrapped. The rule to be followed in developing and using control techniques is: The benefits should sufficiently outrun the costs. Some things can be controlled informally; others can be controlled with a small number of key data, and all supplemental information can be omitted because the expense of collecting it is too great.

Lead to corrective action

An effective control system must lead to corrective action. It is not enough merely to uncover deviations from the plan; the supervisor also has to be provided some insights regarding what to do about them. For example, if the supervisor is given a weekly printout showing how many units are being manufactured by the work group, this allows the supervisor to compare total output against expected output. However, the supervisor does not know if everyone is doing the amount of work he or she should be doing; some people may be doing more than their share and others may be doing less. If the weekly printout provides a production breakdown by individual worker, this problem will not arise. If the printout does not provide it, the only way for the supervisor to determine how much work everyone is doing is through personal observation. This is often called management by walking around (MBWA) and can be an effective supplement to the regular methods of controlling operations. However, it is only one of many. The following section examines other popular techniques.

COMMON CONTROL TECHNIQUES

Budgeting

Supervisors use many different types of control techniques. The following examines four of the most common.

The budget is one of the supervisor's most commonly used financial control techniques. A *budget* is a plan that specifies anticipated results in numerical terms and serves as a control device for feedback, evaluation, and follow-up. Typically, the supervisor submits a budget proposal, which is modified by higher-level management and then approved. The first-line manager is then responsible for operating within these financial limits.

In white-collar organizations, the proposed budget typically entails employee salaries, travel and entertainment, maintenance of office equipment, supplies, and other direct out-of-pocket expenses. Sometimes organizations also make an allocation of other expenses, such as floor space and office security. In these cases, a supervisor with a large work area will have a monthly expense tied to the amount of room the unit occupies. If the firm is paying $25,000 annually to rent one floor of an office building and the work unit occupies 20 percent of this space, the annual rent charge will be $5000. Likewise, 20 percent of all indirect expenses, such as office security and utilities, will be allocated to the group. This approach is common in sales-oriented organizations, in which the total cost of maintaining a sales unit can be compared to the total revenues brought in from its operation.

In blue-collar organizations, budgets usually incorporate such expenses as direct labor, indirect labor (clerical, supervision), overtime, materials, supplies, maintenance, and utilities. At scheduled intervals (biweekly, monthly) the supervisor is provided information regarding how well actual expenditures are adhering to the budget. If they are running ahead of projections, the manager will attempt to get them in line by reducing or eliminating overtime, opting for minimum maintenance, and/or urging everyone to turn off lights or machines that are not being used. At the end of the fiscal year, the actual and budgeted expenses are then compared for the purpose of overall control and, based on forecasts, new budgets are drawn up.

Work distribution charts

Another approach that has proven useful in controlling operations is the *work distribution chart*, which helps supervisors assign work to employees in the unit. This chart can be used for blue-collar operations but more commonly is employed with white-collar employees because of its value in scheduling and controlling office work. Table 2-1 provides an illustration.

Notice that the chart brings together both the work and the people. From here the supervisor need merely keep track of work progress, ensuring that all workers are doing their jobs. The biggest problem with the work distribution approach is that it does not lend itself to specific control. For example, as seen in the table, both Chell and Davis are responsible for photocopying. However, how much work should they be doing each hour? Perhaps they should each be given a specific amount of work, such as 12 copies per minute or 600 copies per hour. Despite this shortcoming, however, work

Table 2-1. Work distribution chart for scheduling and controlling office work

Work to be done	Hours per task	Weekly work distribution in hours per employee					
		Able	Baker	Chell	Davis	Early	Fitts
Transcription	30	15	15				
Typing	30	15	15				
Dictation	10	5	5				
Photocopying	20			10	10		
Filing	30			25	5		
Mail in	10				10		
Mail out	10				10		
Word processing	70					35	35
Total hours	210	35	35	35	35	35	35

distribution remains a very popular control technique because it is both simple and comprehensive in nature.

Gantt chart

The *Gantt chart* is a planning and controlling technique that graphically illustrates work progress over a period of time. Figure 2-1 provides an illustration. The figure shows five jobs. The dark line running across the chart indicates that each job is scheduled to take 5 days. The *V* after Wednesday means that progress is being plotted as of the end of business on this day. The dotted lines running across the chart indicate progress. Notice that job 1 is a day ahead of schedule; job 2 is on time; job 3 is a half day behind; job 4 is on time; and job 5 is a full day behind. Based on this information, the supervisor will want to schedule the worker(s) on job 1 for an additional assignment on Friday. The manager will also want to check with the workers on jobs 3 and 5 to find out why they are behind and to see what can be done to get them back on schedule.

The Gantt chart is very useful in planning and controlling work projects. It is widely used in manufacturing work in which many projects must be controlled simultaneously. By simply looking at the chart, the supervisor is able to identify those jobs which are being completed on time and those which warrant attention.

Program evaluation and review technique

Program evaluation and review technique (PERT) is particularly useful for new or sophisticated projects as well as for scheduling and controlling jobs that are interrelated. In the majority of important projects, only 10 to 20 percent of the jobs are critical and need to be closely monitored. The rest

Figure 2-1. Illustration of a Gantt chart.

Order number	Monday	Tuesday	Wednesday	Thursday	Friday
1	Manufacturing		Assembling	Testing	
2	Manufacturing		Assembling		Testing
3	Manufacturing			Assembling	
4		Manufacturing		Assembling	
5		Manufacturing		Assembling	

are of minor importance because they are either simple or can be done as time allows. PERT helps the supervisor focus on the most critical jobs.

The first step in designing a PERT network is to identify all of the tasks, or events (as they are called in PERT jargon), that have to be completed and to determine in what order they must be done. For example, in building an aircraft, the engines will not be attached before the wings are put on, and the seats cannot be put in before the carpeting is laid.

Secor d, the activities needed to complete each event must be deter- mined. These activities are expressed in terms of time, such as 2, 4, or 6 days.

Third, a network diagram of the project must be constructed. In this process, each event is given a number and each activity is represented by an arrow and the time associated with it. For example, if it takes 3 days to complete event 4, that part of the diagram would be drawn this way:

Figure 2-2 illustrates a PERT diagram for a project with eight events. Notice from the diagram that each event has an activity except for the first one, which is simply the beginning of the project and calls for the undertaking to start. As a result, event 1 takes no time.

Fourth, the paths through the network must be computed. In Figure 2-2, along with their respective times, they are:

Path	Time	Total
1–2–5–7–8	2–9–4–1	16
1–3–5–7–8	8–6–4–1	19
1–4–6–7–8	7–5–3–1	16

The longest path through the maze is known as the *critical path*. It should take 19 days to complete this projet. If it becomes necessary to reduce the project time, the most effective way of doing this is to cut down the number of days in the critical path. For example, by reducing the time associated with event 3 from 8 days to 6 days, the total time can be cut by 2 days.

Figure 2-2. Illustration of a PERT network.

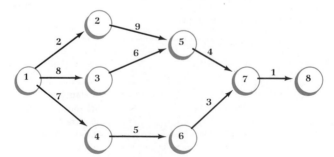

PERT helps supervisors control operations by breaking projects into events, assigning times to these targets, and allowing the supervisors to monitor each event. If there is slippage in any part of the network, this can be identified. For example, if event 2 takes more than 2 days, the supervisor will know about it by the third day. Problems can be identified quickly and corrective action begun.

MANAGEMENT BY OBJECTIVES

In many organizations, management by objectives is used to coordinate both the planning and the controlling responsibilities. *Management by objectives* is a process by which the supervisor and the subordinate jointly identify goals for the latter, define expected results, and use these measures as a basis for control and future planning.

The MBO cycle

Management by objectives (MBO) is a six-step process. Figure 2-3 illustrates the steps involved.

The supervisor begins by identifying the goals that the department or unit will be pursuing. The supervisor typically does this for a 12-month period

Figure 2-3. The basic MBO cycle.

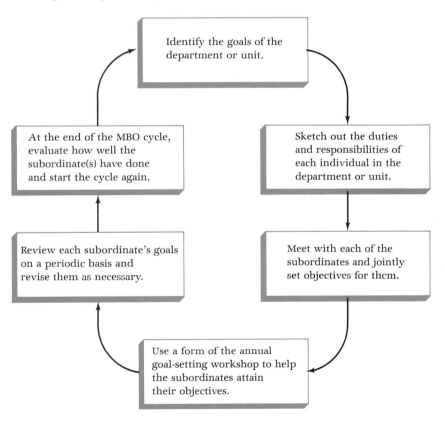

Identify the goals of the department or unit.

Sketch out the duties and responsibilities of each individual in the department or unit.

Meet with each of the subordinates and jointly set objectives for them.

Use a form of the annual goal-setting workshop to help the subordinates attain their objectives.

Review each subordinate's goals on a periodic basis and revise them as necessary.

At the end of the MBO cycle, evaluate how well the subordinate(s) have done and start the cycle again.

since most organizations plan and evaluate operations on an annual basis. The specific goals that the supervisor identifies are often expressed in terms of sales, profits, revenues, costs, time, and other measurable objectives.

Second, the supervisor clarifies the organization chart for the department or unit. The actual organization of the group is sketched out, including the titles and duties of each person. In doing so, the supervisor answers questions such as: Who is in this department? What does each person do? How does each interact or coordinate with the others?

Third, the supervisor sits down with each subordinate, and together they set goals for the latter.[3] This process usually has five steps:

1. The supervisor asks each subordinate to make notes on those objectives which he or she would like to pursue during the next year.
2. The supervisor then works up a list of objectives that he or she would like to see each subordinate pursue.
3. During each meeting, both lists of objectives are reviewed. First, the subordinate identifies those goals which he or she would like to attain. Then the supervisor presents those objectives which he or she would like to see the subordinate pursue. Using two-way communication, the two discuss these objectives and work out a final list.
4. Two copies of the final draft of the objectives are typed. One is given to the worker, and the other is kept by the supervisor.
5. Before the meeting ends, the supervisor asks the subordinate if there is any assistance the subordinate will need. These requests are written down and used by the supervisor in preparing his or her own list of objectives. At this point the meeting is formally ended.

This meeting is extremely important because everything in the MBO process revolves around objectives. In working out these goals, effective supervisors follow a number of important guidelines. These are set forth in Supervision in Action: Setting MBO Objectives.

SUPERVISION IN ACTION: SETTING MBO OBJECTIVES

In setting objectives in the MBO process, supervisors typically start off by doing three things. First, they determine those objectives which they would like each subordinate to pursue. Second, they examine the objectives the subordinate is proposing. Third, they mesh the two lists. This is done by working up a series of questions and answering each as it relates to every worker in the unit. Some of the most common questions that supervisors use in this process are the following:

1. In order to attain the overall objectives of my department or unit, what contributions do I need from this individual?
2. What specific objectives should this person pursue in order to make the above contribution?

3. Do the objectives that this person has recommended mesh with those identified above? If not, how can they be brought into line? What changes are needed in his or her list and in my own in order to arrive at a final set of subordinate objectives.
4. Does the individual have a sound plan for accomplishing these objectives? If not, how can I help? What can I do to assist this subordinate in working out a game plan for achieving these goals?
5. How will progress toward these objectives be measured? How frequently should the individual provide me feedback on this progress? How else can I go about evaluating the individual's progress?

During the meeting, the supervisor focuses on identifying specific and measurable goals. Objectives are expressed in terms of dollars, ratios, percentages, costs per unit, delivery time, quality, etc. The supervisor avoids using vague words, such as *approximately* (the worker will produce approximately 10 units per hour), *as soon as possible* (this objective will be accomplished as soon as possible), *maximum* (the individual will work at maximum speed at all times), and other terms that make objectives difficult to measure. Additionally, the supervisor is guided by the following principles of workable goals: (1) Limit the number of goals per person to five or six, since any more than this often proves unwieldy or overly time-consuming; (2) make sure that the individual's goals support those of the overall unit; (3) make the goals as explicit and measurable as possible; (4) set goals that are ambitious enough to offer the individual a challenge and a feeling of accomplishment when they are achieved; and (5) review the goals periodically to be sure that everything is going along well and that if the individual needs any help, it can be provided as expeditiously as possible.

By following these steps, practicing supervisors admit that they are better able to use the MBO process. As one of them put it, "It's an invaluable approach to managing people and work."

Fourth, in pursuing objectives, it is common for each subordinate to use a goal-setting worksheet. Quite often the format of this sheet is drawn up by measurement and used by everyone involved in the program. Most worksheets have a layout similar to the one in Figure 2-4, which illustrates what a supervisor's worksheet might look like. Subordinates would be pursuing more limited objectives and their worksheets would not be as comprehensive. The objectives on the sheet are those which come out of the joint manager-subordinate meeting. The way in which progress is evaluated is also a result of this meeting. The supervisor will already have explained how progress toward the objectives will be measured. Quite often these are spelled out in such a way that progress can easily be determined. For example, if one of the objectives is to decrease the cost per unit from $1.22 to $1.18, this can be done by dividing the total costs allocated to the units by the number produced. The cost accounting department or whatever unit is

Figure 2-4. An annual goal-setting worksheet.

NAME George Mathis   DATE January 1, 1986

POSITION   Supervisor: Engine Manufacturing Work Group #3

Objectives	Major Steps for Achieving Objectives	Method(s) of Measuring Progress
Increase weekly production from 150 to 175 machines by June 30, 1986.	Install three new machines by March 31, 1986. Have personnel fully trained and prepared to operate these new machines by April 15, 1986.	Weekly production master control report.
Reduce worker overtime 25 percent by December 31, 1986.	Provide additional training to all machine personnel. Hire one new expediter to assist in ensuring speedy delivery of all needed materials.	Weekly time cards and monthly cost control reports.
Cut rework costs from 2 percent of overall production costs to 1.5 percent.	Conduct a quality assurance study to determine specific causes of rework costs. Identify the amount of reworking required by each person. Report reworking costs to each individual on a weekly basis. Determine the feasibility of rewarding the individual with the lowest reworking cost and discipline all whose reworking costs are above 2.5% of overall production.	Monthly cost control report.

responsible for providing direct cost figures will be called upon to get this information to the worker and supervisor on a periodic (weekly, biweekly) basis. In this way, the worker will be able to monitor his or her own progress and know how well things are going. The major steps for achieving the planned objectives are determined by the worker. After all, who better knows how to pursue these objectives than the individual who is responsible for them?

Fifth, during the year each worker's goals are checked to see how well things are going and to determine if any changes in these objectives are needed. The supervisor may find that some individuals are having trouble meeting their goals because there is a shortage of materials or the machines are requiring more maintenance than before. In these cases the manager will want to revise the production objectives downward. In other cases the supervisor may find that the individual is learning the job faster than expected and can be assigned greater responsibility at an earlier date. The most important thing the supervisor does at this stage is to assist those who are having trouble meeting their objectives. This is particularly important when the failure is no fault of their own.

Sixth, when the period covered by the MBO cycle is over, the supervisor evaluates the overall results and begins the process again.

Notice that in this cycle the manager performed a number of important functions, including the two examined in this chapter: planning and controlling. MBO helps the supervisor manage more effectively.

Benefits of MBO

MBO is widely used for a number of reasons. One is that it is both comprehensive and easy to understand. When each manager coordinates with the people in his or her unit in determining what the latter are to do, there is a coordination of effort. Everything the workers do supports the supervisor's objectives. Everything the supervisor does supports the objectives of the person at the next level in the management hierarchy. MBO brings about organizational teamwork because everyone is moving in unison toward the same basic objectives.

Second, MBO encourages both supervisors and subordinates to think and talk in terms of specific, measurable, quantifiable objectives. Of course, it is not always possible to express goals in this way. A new supervisor who is told to improve the morale of the work group will be unable to measure this objective directly. However, the individual will be able to measure factors that help identify morale and provide insights regarding whether it is going up or down: i.e., absenteeism, tardiness, turnover, scrap cost, productivity, etc. To the extent that these are used in the MBO process, objectives can be approached in terms of dollars, cents, time, and other measurable quantities.

Third, MBO helps keep the focus on the organization's key objectives. If every manager up and down the line follows the cycle set forth in Figure 2-3, each will be pursuing the major objectives of the respective unit or department. This will help ensure that the focus on overall objectives does not get lost in day-to-day operations.

Fourth, MBO helps the supervisor delegate minor tasks, thereby freeing time for more important planning and controlling activities. It helps the supervisor manage, reducing the likelihood of the individual being tied up in time-consuming, trivial matters.

Finally, MBO helps the supervisor train and develop the subordinates by setting objectives that "stretch" these individuals in the pursuit of difficult, but attainable, goals. In this way, the supervisor is able to help subordinates meet their desire for interesting, challenging work while at the same time creating a group of highly skilled, motivated people.

THE NEED FOR A NEW APPROACH: STARTING CASE REVISITED

Having read the chapter, you should now realize that Sam's problem is that he has been managing his group of 14 the way he handled his group of five. He has not adjusted his approach to meet the additional challenges.

What he needs to do is opt for some form of management by objectives. Remember from the case that his basic problems are planning and controlling. MBO lends itself to handling these functions. Also, Sam has to make greater use of the exception principle. He cannot afford to control all aspects of the work of his people.

Of course, these ideas are going to be new to Sam. He is used to doing things as best he can. Much of what he has learned about supervising people has been acquired on the job. The introduction of more formal techniques is likely to come as a shock to him. Nevertheless, if he does not opt for some of the ideas set forth in this chapter, he is not going to resolve his current problems.

INTERPRETATION OF SELF-ASSESSMENT QUIZ 2-1:
WHAT DO YOU KNOW ABOUT PLANNING AND CONTROLLING?
---

1. True. Participation tends to increase goal-directed motivation.
2. False. It is better to focus on just a handful. Too many objectives are confusing to the subordinate and difficult to control by the supervisor.
3. False. Effective supervisors do more planning than do their ineffective counterparts.
4. True. Participation often results in a greater-than-expected work output.
5. True. This approach is helpful to both the supervisor and the workers.
6. False. Planning helps them live with ambiguity but not overcome it.
7. True. These managers realize that they need a game plan in the event that something goes awry.
8. True. The two functions tend to overlap.
9. False. They do not even try to control all aspects of the unit's performance; instead, they focus their attention on the most important areas and let the rest go.
10. False. Loose control tends to be more effective than tight control.
11. True. In fact, this is one of the most effective ways of controlling operations.
12. True. Effective supervisors are selective regarding what they control.
13. True. Although not covered in the chapter, this question points out the importance of putting control information in the right form. Computerized printouts tend to be overrated and this sometimes leads to serious mistakes.

14. False. It is not worth the manager's time to investigate all deviations from plan; just the important ones warrant consideration.
15. True. In fact, for many managers it is the most commonly used control tool.

SUMMARY OF KEY POINTS

1. Planning is the process of setting objectives and determining the steps that will be taken in attaining these ends. There are four steps in the planning process: setting objectives, achieving employee understanding and cooperation, developing a contingency plan, and converting the plan into action.
2. Rules, procedures, and policies are useful when implementing plans. A rule is an inflexible regulation that must be followed at all times. A procedure is a guide to action. A policy is a guide to thinking and action.
3. Planning has a number of important advantages. Some of these include: It encourages the supervisor to take an active rather than a wait-and-see approach to things, it helps the manager think in terms of specific objectives, it provides a basis for teamwork, it helps in the development of subordinates, and it assists the supervisor in learning to live with ambiguity.
4. Sometimes plans do not work out as expected. There are various reasons for this, including: unclear objectives, an improper distribution of the workload, reliance on erroneous information, and improper coordination of effort and work between the unit personnel.
5. Controlling is the process of seeing that everything is done in accordance with the plan. There are four steps in this process: setting standards, gathering information, comparing results against standards, and taking appropriate action in light of the results.
6. Every effective control system has a number of similar characteristics. Four of the most important are: Provide useful information, be timely, be economical, and lead to corrective action.
7. Supervisors use many different types of control techniques. Four of the most common are: budgets, work distribution charts, the Gantt chart, and PERT. Each was described in the chapter.
8. Management by objectives (MBO) is a process whereby a supervisor and subordinate jointly identify goals for the latter, define expected results, and use these measures for control and future planning. MBO is a six-step process (see Figure 2-3). The specifics of the process were described in the chapter.
9. Many supervisors like MBO, and it has proved to be a very effective planning and control tool. Some of its specific benefits include: comprehensiveness; ease of understanding; a focus on specific, measurable, quantifiable objectives; a focus on key objectives; the help it offers in delegating minor tasks; and the opportunity it provides the supervisor for training and developing the subordinates.

BUILD YOUR SUPERVISORY WORD POWER

These key planning and controlling terms are presented in their order of appearance in the chapter. Practicing supervisors have a working knowledge of them.

Planning. The process of setting objectives and determining the steps that will be taken in attaining these ends.

Rule. An inflexible regulation that must be followed at all times.

Procedure. A guideline to action.

Policy. A guideline to thinking and action.

Controlling. The process of seeing that everything is done in accordance with the plan.

Exception principle of control. Corrective action should be taken only in those cases in which the results are outside of acceptable limits.

Budget. A plan that specifies anticipated results in numerical terms and serves as a control device for feedback, evaluation, and follow-up.

Work distribution chart. A control tool that helps the supervisor assign work to the employees in the unit.

Gantt chart. A planning and controlling technique that graphically illustrates work progress over a period of time.

PERT. An acronym that stands for program evaluation and review technique. PERT is a planning and control tool that helps supervisors identify the various tasks that have to be accomplished in a sophisticated or one-of-a-kind project and then monitor progress toward these particular goals.

Events. All of the tasks in a PERT network.

Activities. The times associated with each event in a PERT network.

Critical path. The longest path through a PERT network.

Management by objectives. A process by which the supervisor and subordinate jointly identify goals for the latter, define expected results, and use these measures as a basis for control and future planning.

REVIEW YOUR UNDERSTANDING

1. What is meant by the term *planning?* What are the four basic steps in this process? Describe each.
2. How does a rule differ from a procedure? How does a procedure differ from a policy? In your answers be sure to define your terms and to provide an example of each.
3. What are the advantages of planning? Identify and describe four of them.
4. Why do plans sometimes fail? Identify and describe four basic reasons.
5. What is meant by the term *controlling?* How does the process work? Identify and describe it.
6. Effective control systems have a number of important characteristics. What are four of the most important? Identify and describe them.
7. What does a supervisor need to know about the budgeting process? Be as helpful as possible in your answer.
8. How do work distribution charts help the supervisor both plan and control? Be complete in your answer.
9. How does a Gantt chart work? When would a supervisor use it? Of what value would it be to the individual? Explain.
10. Of what value is PERT to the supervisor? When would it be used? How would the manager construct a PERT chart? Be sure to include a discussion of events, activities, and the critical path in your answer.
11. What is meant by *management by objectives?* What are the steps in the process? Identify and describe each.
12. Why do many supervisors like MBO? What benefits does it offer? Identify and describe four.

**SUPPLEMENT
YOUR KNOWLEDGE**

In addition to the references listed at the end of this chapter, the following provide important, practical information that is of use to supervisors in planning and controlling their units:

Beam, Henry H.: "Bringing MBO Back to the Basics," *Supervisory Management*, July 1979, pp. 25–30.

Fannin, William R.: "Making MBO Work: Matching Management Style to MBO Program," *Supervisory Management*, September 1981, pp. 20–27.

Horgan, Neil J.: "Will Your MBO Program Fly or Fizzle?" *Supervisory Management*, December 1981, pp. 21–24.

Jewell, Donald O., George E. Manners, Jr., and Sandra F. Jewell: "For the First-Time Planner," *Supervisory Management*, July 1984, pp. 40–42.

Kress, Thomas G.: "What Every Supervisor Should Know About Financial Control," *Supervisory Management*, January 1977, pp. 30–34.

Martin, Robert A., and James C. Quick: "The Effect of Job Consensus on MBO Goal Attainment," *MSU Business Topics*, Winter 1981, pp. 43–48.

Mittra, Sitansu S.: "PERT, LOB, and MOST: United for More Efficient Project Scheduling," *Supervisory Management*, November 1976, pp. 30–35.

Young, A. E.: "Capital Budgeting: Plan Your Work and Work Your Plan," *Supervisory Management*, January 1979, pp. 31–38.

**YOU BE THE
SUPERVISOR:
TODD'S
APPROACH**

It took a year for Bill Barnes to make up his mind. Finally, last month he informed Todd Knapp, his subordinate, that Todd was being demoted and moved to another department. Todd seemed genuinely surprised by the news.

"I thought things were going along fairly well," Todd said. "Oh sure, work output has been down for the last year, but when you and I talked 3 months ago, you admitted to me that things were beginning to improve."

Bill agreed that he had made this statement and that things had been slightly better over the past 90 days. However, as far as Bill was concerned, this degree of improvement was just not good enough. "When you took over the unit a year ago, Todd, things were in good shape. Work output was on target and there were no tardiness or absenteeism problems. After you took over, output went down and tardiness and absenteeism began going up. For the last 9 months you and I have been talking about ways of reversing the situation, but very little change has occurred. I think it's time for a new supervisor." Todd disagreed, but Bill was adamant.

Before bringing in a new first-line manager, Bill felt that it would be important to find out what had been going wrong with the unit. For the past 2 weeks he has had the temporary supervisor of the unit talking to the personnel to find out how things could be improved. The temporary supervisor has uncovered three worker complaints:

1. Todd had confused many of the workers by drastically altering the number of objectives they were pursuing. Under the previous supervisor, each worker was given four or five objectives that were to be attained every 6 months. Todd changed all of this and gave them between 12 and 15 objectives each.

2. The workers received two performance appraisals from Todd during the last year. In each case most of the workers admitted that they did not understand how Todd had arrived at his appraisal. The majority of the personnel said that they thought they were doing a good job but that Todd gave them only

satisfactory ratings. On the other hand, some workers did less than the average but received very good ratings.

3. Todd was seldom available to help out when the workers had problems. Usually he gave his people things to do and then had little more to do with them until performance appraisal time.

The temporary supervisor capped these comments by noting: "Todd really didn't have a management system for getting things done. He simply told his people what he wanted done, and that was that. I don't know what his idea of a supervisor's job was, but it certainly didn't involve managing people."

1. Assume that you have been appointed in Todd's place. How would you go about using management by objectives to straighten things out? Explain.
2. Why is it a good idea to assign only four or five objectives per worker rather than 12 to 15? Defend your answer.
3. How could MBO help you do a better job of planning and controlling the unit? Explain.

**YOU BE THE
SUPERVISOR:
A PERT PROJECT**

Frances Aherne manages a group of high-tech supervisors. Her firm, a medium-size contractor, has been very successful in designing and building computer disk drives. They have also taken on subcontract work, building and delivering computer systems and microcomputers for some of the nation's largest computer manufacturers.

Frances has recently been placed in charge of a new project to design and build a prototype for a new generation of microcomputers. The basic technology is being supplied by the major computer firm. Frances's job is to see that the prototype is built within time, cost, and quality parameters.

Her firm has never built a prototype before. This is why they chose Frances to head the project. She has worked for the company for 10 years and is one of their best head supervisors. In previous years she has been assigned projects that have fallen behind schedule or have been having cost overruns. In every case Frances was able to turn around the situation and bring the project in on time and within the contract price. Since this latest project is so important to the future business of the firm, the head of manufacturing decided that Frances was to manage the undertaking.

Upon learning the news, Frances balked. She felt that the project would be too difficult. "We've never done anything like this," she told her boss. However, after meeting with some of the people in production planning and control and learning how PERT works, Frances changed her mind. "This PERT concept is a really good one," she told her boss. "I think we can successfully complete the project, thanks to the benefits PERT offers in terms of both planning and control."

After carefully studying the prototype and how the project would have to be approached, Frances designed the PERT network presented below. The production planning and control people have looked it over and agree that the network has been properly designed. Frances has exactly 6 months in which to finish the project. The head of manufacturing has told her that he will provide all of the assistance needed to get the project done on time. Frances is convinced that with this type of support, she can do it.

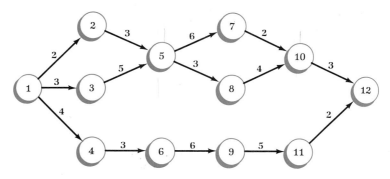

1. Assume that you are a supervisor reporting directly to Frances and charged with helping her manage the project. How long will it take to finish the project, given the data in the PERT network above? Calculate the critical path.
2. Based on your answer to the above question, what does Frances have to do? Explain.
3. In what way can you and Frances use PERT to help control the project? Cite two examples in your answer.

NOTES

1. For more on this subject, see: George Miller, "Management Guidelines: The Art of Planning," *Supervisory Management*, May 1981, pp. 24–31; and H. Kent Baker and Stevan R. Holmberg, "Stepping Up to Supervision: Planning for Success," *Supervisory Management*, November 1981, pp. 12–18.
2. For more on this subject, see: Stuart P. Bloom, "Policy and Procedure Statements that Communicate," *Personnel Journal*, September 1983, pp. 711–718.
3. C. R. Dillon, "MBO: Part I: Setting Objectives," *Supervisory Management*, April 1978, pp. 18–22.

CHAPTER 3

MAKING EFFECTIVE DECISIONS

GOALS OF
THE CHAPTER Decision making is a critical part of the supervisor's job. This is particularly true because the individual has to make a great number of decisions on a daily basis. The overall objective of this chapter is to examine how decision making is carried out and note some of the ways in which supervisors can do this more effectively. When you have finished reading all the material in this chapter, you will be able to:

1. Describe the steps in the decision-making process.
2. Relate what cost-benefit analysis is all about and how it can be of value to the supervisor.
3. Discuss the benefits and limitations of group decision making.
4. Explain how creativity can be used in decision making.
5. Describe some of the realism factors that influence the decision-making process.
6. Discuss some of the most useful tips for improving supervisory decision making

A STARTING CASE: DECIDING WHAT TO DO

When Julia Jackson accepted the promotion to nursing supervisor of floor 3, she looked forward to the new job. Julia had been in health care for 6 years, but this was her first managerial job. Floor 3 is devoted to critical care and Julia felt that her previous technical training and experience made her a good choice for the promotion. However, soon after she took the job she began to realize that staffing was a major problem. Because of the nature of the health care being provided, it is necessary to have a greater nurse/patient ratio on the third floor than on any other in the hospital. The schedule calls for each nurse to show up 15 minutes before her shift begins in order to review the status of the patient charts and to ensure an orderly transfer between the incoming and outgoing nurses. It is also important for all paperwork related to patient care to be finished before the shift is over.

It took Julia almost a week to realize that there was a problem in the coordination of the two shifts. Some nurses were showing up at the last minute and, while the staff on duty was always adequate to handle the situation, this was against hospital policy. Julia mentioned this to two of the nurses and was told: "Oh, it's no real problem. No one leaves before her replacement gets here. There is no threat to the patients, and this is all that's important."

Julia also noticed that the paperwork was beginning to pile up. Some nurses left their shifts without finishing their reports, and the nurses on the next shift did not always complete them. Julia also brought this to the attention of some of her people and was again told that since the paperwork that was not finished on time was minor and in no way affected the health care being provided, it was no problem.

After mulling over both of these problems, Julia called on the previous supervisor and discussed the situation with her. The previous supervisor admitted that these two developments had never occurred when she was in charge but urged Julia to proceed slowly in dealing with the problem. "The union contract will expire in 10 more days and the union has been pushing for an increase in the nurse/patient ratio on your floor. This may be nothing more than a ruse to show that the nurses are overworked and need more help." This idea sounded realistic to Julia, but when she mentioned it to one of the people on her shift, the individual acted surprised. "I don't think it's a matter of overwork. I think we're just a little busier this year than we are usually. It'll all straighten out in a couple of weeks."

Julia is not sure what to make of the situation. She does not want to take any action if the problem will rectify itself. On the other hand, she does not want to let things get worse if they can be straightened out now. Yesterday she told her husband, "I'm going to have to find out what the problem really is and then decide how to deal with it. Right now I'm getting conflicting signals. I don't know what to do, but I do know that some form of investigation is needed."

What is the problem confronting Julia? Put it in your own words. How should she go about investigating the problem and deciding what to do? Outline a course of action. Then put your paper aside. We will return to it later.

THE DECISION-MAKING PROCESS

Decision making is the process of choosing from among alternatives. Supervisors use decision making in dealing with problems and in exploiting opportunities.

In the case of problems, there are two types. One type is problems that have already occurred; in these cases the supervisor needs to straighten out the situation. The other is problems that are in the future. In these instances the supervisor either (1) is aware of their impending nature and must decide how to minimize or eliminate them or (2) believes that they may occur and wants to take action to prevent them. Much of the supervisor's decision-making time is used for dealing with problems.

Sometimes the first-line manager has a chance to take advantage of a situation or exploit an opportunity. For example, a supervisor has just learned that management is about to hire ten new people. If this supervisor can talk his boss into giving him two additional people, the current work project can be brought in 1 week early. The supervisor must decide how to exploit this chance. Should he approach the boss directly and ask for the new people? Or should he point out that with additional people he can bring the project in early and then let the boss raise the issue of giving him additional personnel?

Whether the supervisor is solving (or preventing) problems or taking advantage of opportunities, the decision-making process is the same.[1] The following examines the eight steps involved.

Define the problem or opportunity

The first thing the supervisor must do is clearly define the problem or opportunity. For example, if tardiness has increased over the last month and the supervisor feels that this is a problem, it should be stated in specific terms. "I am having a problem with tardiness" is not a specific statement of the problem. On the other hand, "Tardiness is up 23 percent over the last 4 weeks" is a specific statement of the problem. Or consider the work-project opportunity mentioned above. "I need more people in order to get the project completed ahead of schedule" is too general a description of the opportunity. "I need two more people in order to bring in the project 5 days ahead of schedule" is a specific statement of the opportunity. Remember that the more clearly and specifically the supervisor can state the problem or opportunity, the easier it is going to be to carry out the rest of the decision-making process. A well-defined statement helps point the way for action.

Gather information relevant to the issue

In the case of problem solving, the supervisor now needs to gather information related to what is going wrong. Who has been guilty of tardiness? When is tardiness the highest? When is it the lowest? Information of this type will give the supervisor additional insights to the problem. In the case of the work-project opportunity, the supervisor will gather information related to how much more has to be done on the project, how much work the average person is doing currently, the amount of money each person is being paid, and what other approaches (more machinery, for example) can help reduce the project completion time.

Identify ways of dealing with the situation

In the case of problem solving, this step involves listing possible causes of the dilemma. There may be many reasons why tardiness has increased in recent weeks. By looking at who is late and when, the supervisor may be able to identify possible reasons. For example, if most people are late on Monday morning but no other day and fishing season began 4 weeks ago, these workers may be spending the entire weekend out on a lake and be returning home very late on Sunday evening, resulting in their tardiness the next morning. If most of the people who are late are tardy almost every day and they all belong to one work group, it may indicate that the supervisor has done something to anger them. Sometimes an analysis of the information related to the problem helps pinpoint possible causes.

In the case of opportunities, the supervisor will want to list the possible ways of taking advantage of the situation. In the above example, what are four or five of the most reasonable ways of reducing the work-project time?

Choose the most likely cause

Of all the alternatives listed in the above step, the supervisor must now choose the one that offers the best chance to solve the problem or take advantage of the opportunity. The supervisor may feel that since most of the tardiness occurs on Monday morning, the fishing season explanation is the most likely one. Something must be done to get people to return home earlier so that they can get to work on time on Monday morning. Meanwhile, the easiest way to deal with the work-project opportunity is to have two additional people assigned to the undertaking.

Formulate a plan of action

At this stage the supervisor has to decide what should be done. This calls for a plan of action. In the case of the tardy workers, the supervisor may decide that everyone who is late for work on Monday morning will be docked an hour's pay. In the case of the work project, the supervisor may decide to spell out the advantages associated with putting more people on the project and let the boss volunteer to provide two additional people.

Evaluate the plan of action

How likely is it that each of the approaches will work? The supervisor may believe that each will indeed provide the desired results; however, before implementing them the supervisor needs to step back and look them over with a critical eye. Is the approach as realistic as initially assumed? Will it work? Or is there some flaw in the approach? One of the easiest ways of answering this question is to discuss the approach with someone else, usually a fellow supervisor. Quite often this person will have faced a similar problem and be able to offer useful advice. The boss is another valuable asset, especially if some disciplinary action is being considered. Often this person has had experience in these matters and can provide important guidance and direction.

Implement the plan of action

Having decided what to do and having modified it in light of the above step, the supervisor must now implement the plan. To the extent that the decision-making process has been carefully carried out to this point, implementation often proves to be one of the easiest steps. Most problems will have been anticipated and sidestepped.

Control the process

Sometimes things do not go according to plan. The implementation may not solve the problem or capture the opportunity. In this case the supervisor must go back and review the steps in the process to see where things went wrong. Quite often a different approach is needed. In this case the supervisor must review information that has been gathered (in the second step above) and formulate a new approach. If, however, none of the information lends itself to formulating what the supervisor feels is a feasible approach, additional information must be collected and the supervisor must plunge back into the middle of the decision-making process. Fortunately, this is not often necessary, particularly if the supervisor has carefully conducted cost-benefit analysis.

COST-BENEFIT ANALYSIS

The supervisor often uses cost-benefit analysis in the decision-making process even though perhaps not calling it by this name. *Cost-benefit analysis* involves a comparison of the costs and benefits associated with a particular decision.

Understanding the basics

The basics of cost-benefit analysis are fairly simple, although there are some parts of it that require the careful attention of the supervisor. Let us use a version of one of the examples discussed in the previous section. A supervisor has found that by adding two more people to a project it will be possible to cut 5 days off the completion time. Should the supervisor add the two people? This will depend on how much these additional personnel will cost and how much the firm stands to gain from early completion time.

The first thing the supervisor must do is to gather data related to both the costs and the benefits. If the personnel will cost $9/hour, the labor cost is $720 ($9 $\times$ 8 hours $\times$ 5 days $\times$ 2 people). Additionally, there will be benefit costs, such as medical insurance, social security, and disability coverage. When the supervisor hires the people, all their expenses must be included. Assume that these expenses are $30, bringing the total to $750.

Now the supervisor has to calculate the benefits associated with bringing the project in early. Quite often projects that are being completed for other firms under subcontracting agreements have bonuses associated with early completion. If this is not true in this case, the supervisor need go no further. It is a waste of money to bring the project in early. If there is a bonus, the supervisor must find out how much. If it is $100/day, the costs outrun the benefits, and unless the firm feels that this loss is justifiable because it will ensure future business from the major contractor, the supervisor should not hire the two people. The benefits must outrun the costs before it pays to bring on the two people. If the benefits turn out to be $770, should the supervisor add the personnel? Not necessarily. At this point, cost-benefit analysis will be subjected to "adequate" return on investment. The firm may have a standing rule of charging "2 times direct cost," which means that if it takes on a $1 million project, its labor, materials, and other expenses directly associated with the undertaking must be kept to $500,000. What happens to the other $500,000? This goes to cover administrative expenses (managerial salaries), indirect expenses (lighting, plant security, insurance, etc.), and profit. Unless the total benefit is $1440 or more, the supervisor will not add the two people.

This approach to cost-benefit analysis assumed that the supervisor needed to gather data on the expenses and payoffs associated with the project. Many times the supervisor will mentally make these calculations.

The individual will often be knowledgeable regarding early delivery bonus money and will have a working knowledge of the cost of adding a person to the project. Quickly comparing these numbers, the supervisor will know whether it is worth pursuing the matter or simply dropping it. On the other hand, there are times when the supervisor cannot get by with just mental calculations because the problem is too complex. A good example is a project that has multiple parts. In this case, marginal analysis is often required.

Marginal analysis

Marginal analysis is an economic concept that is concerned with the extra output that can be attained by adding an extra unit of input. Quite often the concept focuses on *marginal revenue,* which is the amount of money the firm stands to earn for doing additional work, and *marginal cost,* which is the expense associated with doing the additional work. For example, if the company will agree to manufacture one more component, the major contractor will pay $1000 for it. This is the marginal revenue. The total cost of building the component, say $700, is the marginal cost. The additional profit, of course, is $300. The idea is fairly simple if per-unit costs remain the same. However, if they change, then marginal analysis must be carried out.

Consider the following example: A small manufacturing firm has been offered a contract to build up to 10 major subsystem components for the National Aeronautics and Space Administration (NASA). NASA would like to know if the firm would be willing to accept this contract. The purchase price per component is $20,000 and NASA will allow it to build any number up to 10. The project is turned over to a supervisor who gathers cost figures on building each of the 10. These data are provided in Table 3-1. Notice from the table that the setup costs are high and that the firm will have to produce at least three units before it will make any money on the project. More important, after the sixth unit the overall profit will decline. The marginal costs associated with building any more than this are greater than the marginal revenues obtained. For example, the sixth unit will cost $18,000 to build and will generate $20,000 of revenue. On this unit the firm will make $2000. The seventh unit, however, will cost $26,000 to build and the firm will

Table 3-1. Costs and revenues associated with a subcontracting agreement

Number manufactured	Total revenue	Total cost	Total profit	Marginal revenue	Marginal cost
1	$ 20,000	$ 40,000	($20,000)	$20,000	$40,000
2	40,000	50,000	(10,000)	20,000	10,000
3	60,000	58,000	2,000	20,000	8,000
4	80,000	72,000	8,000	20,000	14,000
5	100,000	88,000	12,000	20,000	16,000
6	120,000	106,000	14,000	20,000	18,000
7	140,000	132,000	8,000	20,000	26,000
8	160,000	160,000	0	20,000	28,000
9	180,000	194,000	(14,000)	20,000	34,000
10	200,000	234,000	(34,000)	20,000	40,000

lose $6000 on this one. The same is true for all remaining units; the costs are greater than the revenues.

What should the supervisor recommend be done? Using marginal analysis, the decision is clear-cut. The firm should agree to build six units for NASA. At this point the profit is maximized. If the company builds any less or any more, project profits will decline. In employing marginal analysis, the supervisor needs to remember the *profit maximization rule:* Produce to the point where marginal revenue and marginal cost are equal; if they are never equal, produce to the last point where marginal revenue is greater than marginal cost.

Expected value

Sometimes the supervisor does not know with certainty what the future holds. In the two earlier examples in this section the supervisor had no trouble determining costs and benefits or revenues. However, what if the supervisor has four alternative approaches to getting a job done? How should the supervisor decide which one to use? The answer is fairly simple. The supervisor should determine, if only mentally, which of the approaches has the greatest likely payoff for the firm. In doing this, the supervisor ends up assigning probabilities to each of the alternatives. Keep in mind that these probabilities are highly subjective, based on past experience and knowledge of the work. The supervisor does not know if the probability assignments are precise, but given the situation, this is the best that he or she can do.

Let us be a little more precise regarding how probability assignments are used by supervisors. A first-line manager has been given four contract projects by the boss and asked to choose the one the firm should accept. Whichever it is, this supervisor will then head up the project team. Each of the projects requires skilled personnel, and the penalties for late completion are very severe. The supervisor examines the profit the firm stands to make from each project and then computes the probability of successfully completing each project. Here are the supervisor's results:

Project	Overall profit	Success probability
1	$1,000,000	.05
2	800,000	.10
3	750,000	.20
4	400,000	.65

Which project should the supervisor choose? In answering this question it is necessary to multiply the overall profit by the probability of success. Remember that even if the profit is very great, the company will be unwise to opt for this alternative if the chance of completing the project is very small. When profit and probability are multiplied, the result is known as the *expected value.* In the above case, the four expected values are computed:

Project	Overall profit	Success probability	Expected value
1	$1,000,000	.05	$ 50,000
2	800,000	.10	80,000
3	750,000	.20	150,000
4	400,000	.65	260,000

The supervisor should opt for project 4. While it offers the smallest profit, its success probability is so high that it has the greatest expected value. Keep in mind that supervisors often make these calculations mentally. They do not compute an exact success probability, nor do they refer to the results of their calculation as expected values. However, they are doing the same thing as presented here. In their own way, they are using cost-benefit analysis.

GROUP DECISION MAKING

While the supervisor often makes decisions alone, there are times when the individual can profit from having a group make the decision. The key question for the supervisor is: When is individual decision making superior to group decision making and vice versa? In answering this question, the supervisor needs to compare the benefits of a group approach against the liabilities.[2]

Benefits of group decision making

Group decision making has a number of benefits. One is greater knowledge and information. Quite often a group will be able to provide more information about a problem than will an individual alone, regardless of how well trained or educated the person is. If the group members have some knowledge of the problem, they are usually able to make contributions to its solution.

A second benefit is the variety of approaches. An individual usually brings one perspective to a problem. A group offers many. Each member has a personal approach that is somewhat different from the others. As a result, the number and types of alternatives are superior to those of the individual working alone.

A third benefit is acceptance of the final decision. When a group has played a role in formulating a decision, the members are more likely to accept the outcome even if their decision was not the final choice of the group.

A fourth common advantage is reduced communication problems. Since the group participated in the decision, the members are all aware of the situation, and the implementation of a solution can usually proceed smoothly. Questions, objections, and roadblocks that typically confront decision implementation are often nonexistent as a result of group decision making.

**Drawbacks
of group
decision making**

Group decision making also has drawbacks. One of the major ones is social pressure to conform. While everyone in the group is supposed to feel free to offer suggestions and recommendations, sometimes there is pressure for everyone to get together and go along with the general consensus. Often referred to as *groupthink,* this pressure can result in the group overlooking good advice from some of the members. The latter are pressured into getting in line and going along with the majority.

A second drawback is dominance by one individual over the others. This person may have greater status or position in the organization or simply have a more dominating personality. In any event, the individual perseveres and gets everyone else to go along.

A third drawback is *hidden agendas,* a term which means that people in the group are working on achieving their own ends rather than those for which the group has been convened formally. A member who is opposed to solution A to the problem works to turn the other members away from this alternative without revealing why the solution is unacceptable. There are many reasons for hidden agendas, including protection of one's position, personal pride, desire for acceptance, and personality conflict. Whatever the reason, hidden agendas keep the focus on personal interests instead of on problem solving.

A fourth drawback is compromise. Sometimes a group will get bogged down, unable to agree on which of the solutions to recommend. Determined to make a decision, members are encouraged to compromise or to give in by accepting a version of their solution. This drawback is common when the group breaks into smaller groups, with each small group supporting a different solution.

Conservative shift

**Making group
decision making
work**

Group decision making can be used effectively if the supervisor manages the situation properly. One of the most important things is to win the support of the group members by pointing out the value of their contribution to the problem. A second useful approach is to give everyone in the group specific things to think about or do. In this way, each person can recognize his or her own contribution. A third useful approach is to create an environment in which people can express themselves openly and freely, thereby encouraging both creative inputs and discussion regarding shortcomings or pitfalls that might lie ahead. The latter is particularly important in overcoming groupthink. Additional suggestions regarding group decision making are provided in Supervision in Action: Making Group Decision Making Work.

Sometimes the problem or opportunity under analysis requires a creative approach. In meeting this challenge, the supervisor will sometimes rely on his or her own ability and experience. However, it is more likely that the individual will turn to the work group for help. The following section examines how this is often done.

SUPERVISION IN ACTION:
MAKING GROUP DECISION MAKING WORK

To be truly effective as a means of reaching organizational objectives, work-group communication development needs to include a goal orientation. After all, the purpose of a work group is to combine the energies of several people so that output is more than what would be produced if the same individuals worked separately.

As a supervisor, you want to forge a communication system that encourages input for group goal attainment from all group members. Such an approach is a far cry from calls to simply get people talking; we want to focus their energies through Goal-Directed Group Support (GDGS). This approach was developed for use in improving communications within work groups in organizations of all types. In essence the approach has five steps.

Step no. 1: weekly or biweekly group meetings. An essential step in the process is the establishment of formal meetings to discuss progress and problems in the work environment. It is extremely important that there be constant communications and feedback within the work group and between the supervisor. These meetings can be brief, and they should be scheduled at sufficient intervals so that problems and frustrations are not allowed to build within the work group and prevent the manager and work team from accomplishing their mutual goals.

Step no. 2: at the meeting—a diagnostic problem-solving approach (DPS). Instead of the usual approach of finding fault when things are going wrong, the GDGS approach fosters a diagnostic approach to communications. The manager's role at the meeting is directed toward finding solutions to problems rather than attempting to assess blame. The supervisor must maintain a very low profile and encourage subordinate input into the resolution of problems. He or she should say, for example, "There has been an increase in the scrap rate in the past week. What do you think we can do to lower the rate?"

Step no. 3: solution development. It is important for the manager to assume the role of a resource person rather than that of an active participant. The manager should try to limit himself or herself to pointing out how upper-level management may react to potential solutions. The supervisor should not monopolize the conversation or actively direct the discussion. If the work group gets the feeling that the decision has already been made, then the whole effort will have been in vain. In fact, in most cases, a feigned attempt at group inclusion in decision making is a greater disaster than no attempt. In the former, the manager is dishonest with his or her group; in the latter, at least the supervisor is forthright and not pretending to be democratic.

It is very useful to write down each proposal and develop a list of solutions before any one idea is discussed at length. In this manner all possible ideas are presented by the group for its consideration. Encourage a wide range of ideas. Look for that new, unexpected idea that might mean a breakthrough in problem solution.

Once the list is of sufficient length, the next step is group discussion of the solutions. In this part of the process the supervisor should attempt to indicate his or her initial feelings on the subject, then open the discussion for comments with an open mind. A true discussion is desired—one in which the supervisor provides the managerial framework within which the merits of each proposed solution may be evaluated by the work group.

Step no. 4: discussion of the final solution. After the various proposals have been examined by the group, the supervisor must select the best solution. Hopefully, it will be one upon which the group has reached a consensus. The selection may or may not take place at the same meeting, depending upon the amount of additional information that may be needed. It is beneficial if the supervisor discusses the various proposals and indicates why they were or were not chosen. Thus the group may be able to understand the decision-making process; even if its solution was not chosen, it may understand why not.

Step no. 5: feedback. Once a solution is decided upon and implemented, the supervisor should provide feedback as to the success of the solution and what sorts of problems were encountered in its implementation. While current management literature would indicate that allowing participation in decision making is one of the most effective ways of increasing performance and satisfaction, we would add that providing feedback is equally essential to maintaining a high level of interest in what is going on in the organization. Feedback not only on group performance, but also on other aspects of the internal and external environment that may affect the work group in the future, is important to the satisfaction of the work group with its job—and with your job of managing.

In summary, the GDGS system attempts to bring into focus the important contribution that the group can make in decision making. It is a systematic approach to foster group participation in problem solving. GDGS is more than just a communication tool; it is a carefully managed work-group activity that is directed toward problem solving. As such, it is an important supervisory skill for the supervisor with a work group that can no longer be expected to follow blindly and that wants to make important contributions in many areas formerly reserved exclusively for management.

Source: Ken Thompson and Robert E. Pitts, "The Supervisor's Survival Guide: Involving Your Staff in the Decision-Making Process," *Supervisory Management*, April 1979, pp. 34–36.

CREATIVITY AND DECISION MAKING

Cost-benefit analysis and group decision making are useful in decision making, but sometimes the supervisor needs to be less analytical and more creative. This is often more difficult than it first appears because many supervisors have not been trained to use their creative talents. If anything, they have been taught to examine information and to make decisions based on these data. Intuition, imagination, gut feelings, hunches and other less-than-scientific approaches have been discouraged. Today there is a strong move toward encouraging creativity, although many supervisors find it hard to adjust to these new conditions.

How supervisors think

The brain has two sides: left and right. Individuals tend to prefer one side to the other and this affects the way they make decisions. Of course, depending on the situation, people can move from one side to the other. However, they do tend to have one dominant side.[3] Before reading on, take Self-Assessment Quiz 3-1 and find out which side of the brain is your dominant one.

SELF-ASSESSMENT QUIZ 3-1: LEFT-BRAIN, RIGHT-BRAIN THINKING

Everyone has a dominant side of the brain that influences the way he or she thinks and makes decisions. Read each of the following statements and circle the alternative that best describes you. Remember that this is a forced-choice quiz, so even if you do not like either alternative, choose the one that comes closest to describing you.

1. In handling day-to-day activities, which approach is most typical of you?
   a. You plan your day, blocking out time for each activity.
   b. You just let things happen.
2. How do you feel about daydreaming?
   a. It's an important tool for future planning.
   b. It's a waste of time.
3. How well organized are you when it comes to managing information, materials, etc.?
   a. Not very well organized.
   b. Extremely well organized.
4. How do you go about solving problems?
   a. Wait and see if things will straighten themselves out.
   b. Ponder the situation, write down alternatives, arrange them by priority, and pick the best one.
5. How well do you verbally express yourself?
   a. Very well.
   b. Rather poorly.
6. When you want to remember something, which of these two approaches is most representative of you?
   a. Write it down.
   b. Mentally visualize the information.
7. Do you have frequent mood changes?
   a. Yes.
   b. No.

8. Do you enjoy taking risks?
   a. Yes.
   b. No.

9. When you are asked to speak extemporaneously, how do you proceed?
   a. First make a quick outline to guide you.
   b. Simply stand up and say as little as possible.

10. What type of social situation do you prefer?
    a. Spontaneous.
    b. Planned in advance.

11. Are you goal-oriented?
    a. Yes.
    b. No.

12. How do you feel about hunches?
    a. Never rely on them.
    b. Often follow them.

13. How good are you at remembering faces?
    a. Very good.
    b. Not good at all.

14. In a communication situation, which do you like to be?
    a. The speaker.
    b. The listener.

15. Which school subject did you like better?
    a. Geometry.
    b. Algebra.

16. Can you usually tell how much time has passed without looking at your watch?
    a. Yes.
    b. No.

17. Do you tend to decide issues on the basis of information or on the basis of gut feeling and intuition?
    a. Information.
    b. Gut feeling.

18. When you take notes, do you print them out?
    a. Often print them.
    b. Never print them.

19. After you have attended a musical, which do you remember best?
    a. The lyrics.
    b. The music.

20. How good are you at interpreting body language?
    a. Very good.
    b. Not good at all.

An interpretation of your answers can be found at the end of the chapter.

Left-brain thinkers are very common in the business world. They are analytical, verbal, active, and goal-oriented. When they approach a problem, they get the facts, analyze them carefully, and then decide what should be done. They also tend to be rational, explicit, and concrete in their approach. They do not spend much time daydreaming or thinking about what could have been. They deal with the here and now and spell out a specific course of action. In the extreme, they are a no-nonsense group.

Right-brain thinkers are not as common in the business world. They are intuitive, nonverbal, emctional, and visual in their approach. They approach a problem by going outside the facts and adding in information that is not totally justified by the facts. They often visualize in their heads a solution to a problem. They are not as precise in explaining things as are their left-brain counterparts, but they tend to use colorful, emotional, sweeping terms. They also tend to take things in stride, feeling that if the problem is not resolved today, it can be solved tomorrow.

From the above description, right-brain people are obviously more creative in orientation than are left-brain people. However, this does not mean that the supervisor cannot use creative approaches to decision making or that the individual cannot learn to be more creative. There are tools and techniques that can enhance the individual's ability to generate creative solutions to problems. Before examining what these are, however, let us take a look at the creative thinking process.

Creative thinking process

There are four steps in the creative thinking process. Typically they are carried out in the order presented below. However, the amount of time spent on any one will vary depending on the situation.

Preparation. Preparation is that stage at which the supervisor gets mentally prepared. If the result is to be a creative decision, this stage is characterized by a definition and analysis of the problem. During this period the individual becomes saturated with data. In fact, the more information the supervisor can obtain about the problem, the more likely it is that the individual can be innovative or creative.

Incubation. During this phase the individual thinks about how the data can be used to generate a unique approach to the problem. However, the supervisor does not hurry the solution. In fact, if the supervisor is unable to think of a solution, it is not uncommon for the individual to sit back and let the subconscious mind work on an answer. If no answer is forthcoming within a predetermined time, say 10 days, then the individual will go back to the preparation stage and review the data again.

Illumination. Illumination occurs when the supervisor suddenly realizes the answer to the problem. This phase is often characterized by the cliché "a bolt out of the blue." The individual now knows how to proceed. In the decision-making process, this step occurs when the supervisor selects a course of action.

Verification. The last step in the creative thinking process is verification of the solution. The supervisor has to check to ensure that the answer will work. Quite often there is a need to refine or rethink part of the solution. The answer that comes as a result of illumination is often not in final form. There are some modifications or adjustments that are needed. Trial-and-error work must be done to eliminate minor bugs. Once this is done, the solution should provide the desired results.

Creative thinking approaches

There are many creative thinking approaches. Quite often these are group participation approaches. The best known is that of brainstorming, although the Gordon technique is also fairly popular.

Brainstorming is used when the supervisor needs to generate a large number of ideas for solving a problem or taking advantage of an opportunity. The focus is on quantity as well as quality. After presenting the situation to the members of the group, the supervisor encourages them to be as imaginative and creative as possible. Criticism is not permitted, so people can say whatever comes into their minds. Additionally, if someone can piggyback on an earlier idea by expanding or refining it, so much the better. Brainstorming sessions can result in many useless ideas. However, they can also generate solutions and suggestions that could not have been obtained any other way.

The *Gordon technique* is similar to brainstorming, although it tends to be used more for handling technical problems than any other type. Free association is used, and the participants are encouraged to build on ideas that have been suggested by others. However, in contrast to brainstorming, in this technique the group members are usually not told the problem; they are simply given a hint or stimulus. For example, the supervisor might tell them, "Reduce tardiness," and it is up to them to determine how to proceed. (Some of the rules and suggestions for using brainstorming and the Gordon technique are presented in Table 3-2.)

The *nominal grouping technique (NGT)* involves a formal meeting of the group members. During the meeting each member silently writes down his or her ideas about the problem and its solutions. There is no discussion or consultation with other members. Then each person, in turn, shares one of his or her ideas with the group. This continues in round-robin fashion until all of the members' ideas have been expressed. During this process one person writes down the ideas on a flip chart or board. All of the ideas on the board are then discussed in regard to their merits and feasibility. The group then silently votes on the ideas. This is usually done in terms of a rank order

Table 3-2. Brainstorming and the Gordon technique: rules and suggestions for use

Osborn brainstorming	General suggestions that apply to both techniques
Rules: 1. Judicial thinking or evaluation is ruled out. 2. Free wheeling is welcomed. 3. Quantity is wanted. 4. Combinations and improvements are sought. *Suggestions for the Osborn technique:* 1. Length: 40 minutes to one hour, sessions of ten to fifteen minutes can be effective if time is short. 2. Do not reveal the problem before the session. An information sheet or suggested reference material on a related subject should be used if prior knowledge of the general field is needed. 3. Problem should be clearly stated and not too broad. 4. Use a small conference table which allows people to communicate with each other easily. 5. If a product is being discussed, samples may be useful as a point of reference. **Gordon technique** *Rules:* 1. Only the group leader knows the problem. 2. Free association is used. 3. Subject for discussion must be carefully chosen. *Suggestions for the Gordon technique:* 1. Length of session: two to three hours are necessary. 2. Group leader must be exceptionally gifted and thoroughly trained in the use of the technique.	1. Selection of personnel: a group from diverse backgrounds helps. Try to get a balance of highly active and quiet members. 2. Mixed groups of men and women are often more effective, especially for consumer problems. 3. Although physical atmosphere is not too important, a relaxed pleasant atmosphere is desirable. 4. Group size: groups of from four to twelve can be effective. We recommend six to nine. 5. Newcomers may be introduced without disturbing the group, but they must be properly briefed in the theory of creative thinking and the use of the particular technique. 6. A secretary or recording machine should be used to record the ideas produced. Otherwise they may not be remembered later. Gordon always uses a blackboard so that ideas can be visualized. 7. Hold sessions in the morning if people are going to continue to work on the same problem after the session has ended; otherwise, hold them late in the afternoon. (The excitement of a session continues for several hours after it is completed and can affect an employee's routine tasks.) 8. Usually it is advisable not to have people from widely differing ranks within the organization in the same session.

Source: Charles S. Whiting, "Operational Techniques of Creative Thinking," *Advanced Management*, October 1955, p. 28. Reprinted by permission.

of preference. The lists are then tallied and the overall rankings of the group are revealed.

The *Delphi technique* is similar to NGT except that the group members are usually physically dispersed. Each receives a questionnaire asking for answers to questions or for solutions to problems. The results are then compiled and fed back to the entire group. Using the information provided about everyone else's responses, the participant is asked to fill out the questionnaire again. As this continues through four or five rounds, a general consensus begins to emerge as more and more participants agree on answers or solutions to the problems under discussion.

There are many other types of creative thinking approaches that can be used. The important thing to remember is that creativity is often stimulated in a group situation. If the supervisor can maintain this creative attitude in the workplace, creativity can become a daily occurrence.[4] For more on this, see Supervision in Action: How to Nourish the Creative Employee.

SUPERVISION IN ACTION: HOW TO NOURISH THE CREATIVE EMPLOYEE

The best supervisor is not necessarily the one who tries singlehandedly to come up with solutions to organizational problems. A more important quality is the ability to channel employee ideas into the mainstream of the organization. To do that requires an understanding of the care and feeding of the creative employee.

The following quiz is a test of your capacity as a supervisor for managing creativity. . . . Be honest with yourself in answering the questions, and try not to look at the answers before giving your opinion. Answer each question as true or false. The correct answers are explained beneath each question.

The human aspects of creativity

1. Creativity and personal growth are interrelated.
   TRUE. When employess are treated as adults who can creatively contribute to the success of the organization, they mature as human beings. An environment conducive to creativity is a prerequisite for self-fulfillment since creativity is in the main a personal expression of one's self. The individual releases creative energies that provide personal fulfillment and satisfaction, which according to Abraham Maslow is an indication of a "healthy personality."

2. Employee creativity is the result of planned management action.
   FALSE. Creativity will exist independent of management's actions. Management's role is to direct the creative behavior. As an example, one researcher found that where work methods were strictly prescribed, employees engaged in a variety of creative activities, including different types of games, purposeless antics, and singing. In this case, the creative behavior that was used to counter job monotony was harmless. Creativity can, however, have more harmful manifestations, including clever methods to restrict output—even sabotage. It is the nature of the frustrated employee either to withdraw by engaging in daydreaming and absenteeism or to exhibit aggressive behavior in overt violations of organizational rules.

3. There is no proven correlation between creativity and employee performance.
   FALSE. Many managers feel that creativity has a detrimental effect upon productivity. They believe that employees who are thinking about ideas are wasting time that should be spent producing. But research conducted by myself and others shows a statistically significant correlation between employee creativity and job performance. Creative employees seem to have a zealous regard for long hours and hard work.

4. Creative problem solving is a function of the left hemisphere of the brain.
   FALSE. The right half of the brain controls the creative thought process used in solving problems. It is also the source of thought in initiating

new programs and analyzing contingencies. The left half of the brain controls logic and decision making based on the routine and familiar. While right hemispheric thought leads to new hypotheses, it is the left side that verifies and rationally analyzes those hypotheses. Studies have shown that in the proper environment people can be induced to utilize the right half of their brains and thus develop their creative abilities.
5. Supervisors could be aided considerably if only there were some means of measuring creativity.
FALSE. There is already a considerable body of research regarding the measurement of creativity. The problem is putting those findings to work.

Source: Donald W. Myers, "How to Nourish the Creative Employee," *Supervisory Management,* February 1981, pp. 31–32. Reprinted by permission.

REALISM IN DECISION MAKING

While the decision-making process described at the beginning of this chapter accurately described how supervisors choose from among alternatives, it did not directly address some of the factors that influence the process. Four of the most important of these factors are discussed below.

The time factor

Decisions are commonly made within time constraints. For example, the average supervisor must set objectives, complete budget proposals, and submit performance evaluations on unit personnel. All of these must be done within time limitations. The supervisor often finds that there is a specific time period, i.e., 2 weeks, during which subordinate objectives must be formulated and submitted to higher management. Analogously, performance evaluations must often be completed within a predetermined time after the end of the performance cycle.

How long will it take the supervisor to carry out all of these decisions? This will depend on the situation. If the supervisor has a light workload, there will be adequate time to get everything done. However, if the supervisor has a heavy workload, these decisions will be squeezed into whatever time is left. Quite often the latter is more common than the former. Additionally, supervisors are sometimes given assignments for which important decisions must be made as soon as possible. In such cases, time is a crucial factor. To the extent that it is limited, supervisors will not have all of the necessary time to analyze and evaluate problem-solving alternatives fully. They simply will do the best they can.

Satisfactory solutions

When the supervisor investigates and analyzes a problem, there may be a great deal of information that needs to be processed. For example, a nursing supervisor has been asked by her superior to provide input regarding what management should include in its new wage-and-benefit package. How many people should she talk to in gathering this data? How much time should she spend formulating a list of inputs? How detailed should this list be? As the supervisor ponders these questions, she will arrive at a cutoff point. For example, she will talk to five subordinates and come up with three to five factors that should be included in the new wage-and-benefit package. Notice that in these cases the supervisor neither talked to everyone in her work unit nor considered every possible wage and benefit that could be included. Once the supervisor had talked to a sufficient number of personnel to generate the desired number of inputs, she ceased her data-gathering and -analysis activities. She had attained a satisfactory solution to her problem.

This idea of satisfactory solutions is very common in decision making. Few supervisors need to come up with the best possible answers to problems; they merely need to be in the ballpark. The costs of determining the best solution are sometimes so high that it does not pay to pursue this avenue of investigation. More easily identifiable and acceptable alternatives are preferred.

Willingness to take risk

The willingness of a supervisor to assume risk will influence decision making. Many first-line managers, for example, will judge how much risk they should assume in order to get acceptable results and/or increase their chances of promotion. If a supervisor finds that by playing it safe he can get ahead, this is the strategy he will use. If another first-line manager realizes that she must take risks in order to succeed, she will do it. Consider the following payoff table:

Decision	Probability of success	Payoff
A	.1	$250,000
B	.2	150,000
C	.3	50,000
D	.4	20,000

A low-risk-taking supervisor would opt for strategy D because it has the greatest probability of success (or least probability of failure). A high-risk-taking supervisor would opt for strategy A because it offers the highest payoff. Notice that the decision choice is dictated by risk propensity rather than by expected value. Which decision is best? It is decision B that offers the highest expected value, as shown by the calculations in the following table:

Decision	Probability of success	Payoff	Expected value
A	.1	$250,000	$25,000
B	.2	150,000	30,000
C	.3	50,000	15,000
D	.4	20,000	8,000

Based on the risk propensities of the two supervisors, decision B would be the third choice of the low-risk-taking supervisor and the second choice of the high-risk-taking supervisor. Realistically speaking, risk propensity sometimes influences decision choice regardless of the expected values of the alternatives.

Rationalization

In some cases the best decision is the one the supervisor can defend or live with. For example, a supervisor has submitted a request for a personal computer to be used in controlling warehouse inventory. Higher management approves the request but leaves the specific choice of machine to the supervisor. While the supervisor personally thinks that Digital Equipment offers the best computer for this purpose, he is concerned about what will happen if the machine needs servicing at a crucial time. In order to protect himself from criticism, he opts for an IBM PC. If the machine does break down at a key point in time, the supervisor feels that no one will fault him for having bought an IBM because of its reputation for quality and service. So in making the final decision, he does not ask which alternative is best but which alternative is defensible.

Another common example of rationalization occurs when the supervisor decides what to do before examining all of the data. For example, she must decide which of five candidates to hire. The first person does not impress her, but the second does. The individual has had experience in the field and is highly articulate, two traits the supervisor feels are important to the job. Before the interview with this candidate is over, the supervisor has made up her mind to hire the individual. However, she does not stop the interviewing process at this point. The three remaining candidates are all given a chance to meet with her, but each falls short of the second candidate in terms of experience and/or articulateness. The supervisor has established criteria that are used to rationalize her choice, i.e., this person does not have as much experience as candidate 2; the next individual is not as articulate as candidate 2, etc. Far from giving each an equal chance, the supervisor develops screening criteria and allows these to rationalize the final choice.

TIPS FOR IMPROVING DECISION MAKING

Use cost-benefit analysis

There are many things that supervisors should know in improving their decision-making ability. The following presents five of the most useful tips.

While cost-benefit analysis is important, the supervisor must determine how much analysis to use. In doing so, the individual must be careful not to fall prey to the *law of triviality*, which holds that there is an inverse relationship between the cost or value of a decision and the amount of time spent analyzing it. Low-cost decisions receive a great deal of attention, while high-cost decisions are taken care of in a matter of minutes. Supervisors must realize that time is money and the amount of analysis must be commensurate with the expected payoff.

Avoid crisis decisions

Some supervisors do not see major problems on the horizon; they become aware of them only when a crisis has developed. Other supervisors do see major problems developing but wait until the last minute to make decisions. In both cases the supervisors have allowed crises to develop. There are two ways of avoiding these problems. First, supervisors must develop what is called a proactive stance toward problem-solving. This means that they must continually ask themselves, "What major problems are likely to develop over the next 60 to 90 days and what can I do to head them off now?" Second, they develop a bias for action.[5] This cliché means that the supervisors prefer to solve problems rather than to allow the problems to solve themselves. Sometimes, of course, problems will go away without any action by the supervisor. However, this is more the exception than the rule. A willingness to solve problems before they become crises is a better operating philosophy.

Rely on established procedures

Some problems are going to be difficult and/or critical. These will require careful analysis and decision making. Most, however, can be handled by using established procedures. They are routine, day-to-day issues. In dealing with them the supervisor should use the simplest, most direct approach possible. Many of the rules, procedures, and policies that have been developed by the organization can be used. Additionally, the supervisor does not need to deal personally with many of these matters. They can be delegated to subordinates while the manager focuses on more important decisions.

Consult with others

When decisions are going to affect others, the supervisor should talk to these people and get their input. Often these individuals are willing to go along with the decision if they can be shown how it can be of value to them. Additionally, if the decision is a major one, the supervisor would be wise to consult with other supervisors, as well as with the boss, in discussing how to handle the matter. Quite often outside input will provide important information that can be used to improve decision implementation.

Remember: No one is right all the time

No matter how hard the supervisor tries, the individual is going to make mistakes. Some management experts argue that if a supervisor is right just over 50 percent of the time, the individual will be successful. The important thing is that regardless of how poorly the decision turns out, tomorrow is another day. The supervisor has to learn to live with mistakes. That is part of the cost of being a supervisor. If the individual uses the decision-making process spelled out in the beginning of this chapter to help identify what went wrong and why, he or she can learn from these mistakes. In the future, the individual's decision-making ability will improve, and this is of immense value to both the manager and the organization. Supervisors who are afraid to make a decision because they do not want to be wrong will not do very much for the organization. Those who are willing to learn from their mistakes will eventually develop into top-management timber.

Managerial Decision Making (Hubert)

DECIDING WHAT TO DO: STARTING CASE REVISITED

The case points up a problem that is confronting Julia. However, there is not sufficient information regarding the cause of the problem. Julia needs to investigate what is causing the problem. One cause alluded to in the case is the impending contract negotiations. Another may well be poor morale on the part of the nurses, although the previous supervisor gave no indication of this. A third may be Julia's leadership style. From the case, we know that she talks to her people about the problem. Is this considered appropriate? If not, the nurses may be deliberately misleading her because they feel it is not their business to help her manage the floor. Remember that this is Julia's first managerial position.

What should she do? She should use the decision-making process to investigate the problem, gather information, formulate possible causes, and begin working to alleviate these causes. She should use the decision-making process just as it has been spelled out in the chapter.

INTERPRETATION OF SELF-ASSESSMENT QUIZ 3-1:
LEFT-BRAIN, RIGHT-BRAIN THINKING

This quiz is not designed to give you a definitive answer to whether you are a left-brain or right-brain person. However, it does provide some insights regarding whether you tend toward one of these sides or are in the middle somewhere: a whole-brain thinker. Take your answers to the 20 questions and enter them below by putting a check mark next to the answer you gave for each respective question.

Question	Answer		Question	Answer	
1.	a. ✗	b. ✔	11.	a. ✔	b.
2.	b.	a. ✔	12.	a.	b. ✔
3.	b. ✗	a. ✔	13.	b.	a. ✔
4.	b. ✔	a. ✗	14.	a.	b. ✔
5.	a. ✔	b.	15.	b.	a. ✔
6.	a.	b. ✔	16.	b.	a. ✔
7.	b. ✗	a. ✔	17.	a.	b. ✔
8.	a. ✔	b.	18.	b.	a. ✔
9.	a. ✔	b.	19.	a.	b. ✔
10.	b.	a. ✔	20.	b.	a. ✔
				Total __5__	__15__

Your total on the left indicates the number of times you opted for a left-brain choice; your total on the right reveals the number of times you made a right-brain choice. If your score is lopsided, you now know whether you are basically left- or right-brain-oriented. However, if you have an about even score (no more than 12 on either side), then you are a whole-brain thinker. If you want further insights, examine the questions you were asked and note how left- and right-brain types differ in their approach to things.

Remember that this quiz is only a general indication. All of the alternatives were weighted equally, but experts in the area know that some of these answers are more important than others in helping determine your thinking preferences. Finally, you might find it interesting to know that most people who take this quiz are left-brain-oriented. Were you?

SUMMARY OF KEY POINTS

1. *Decision making* is the process of choosing from among alternatives. This process has eight basic steps: (a) Define the problem or opportunity; (b) gather information relevant to the issue; (c) identify ways of dealing with the situation; (d) choose the most likely cause; (e) formulate a plan of action; (f) evaluate the plan of action; (g) implement the plan of action, and (h) control the process.

2. One of the most useful approaches in analyzing decision-making alternatives is cost-benefit analysis. In decisions with multiple or interrelated parts, it is common to make use of marginal analysis. Another popular approach is the computation of expected value.

3. Group decision making is sometimes a very useful approach in choosing from among alternatives. The benefits and drawbacks of this approach were discussed in the chapter, as were suggestions regarding how to make group decision making work.

4. Sometimes supervisors need to make creative decisions. This is a right-brain function, and many first-line managers have been taught to be left-brain thinkers. They are unaccustomed to using the four steps in the creative thinking process: preparation, incubation, illumination, and verification. For this reason, it is common to find them using group approaches to creative thinking. Two of the most popular are brainstorming and the Gordon technique. Both were described in the chapter.

5. While decision making follows the steps described above, some factors influence the way in which the process is carried out. These include: time; a willingness to accept a satisfactory (as opposed to the best) alternative; the varying risk-taking propensities of supervisors; and rationalization.

6. The last part of the chapter set forth five useful tips for improving decision making. These tips draw together much of what was said in the chapter but present it in more action-oriented terms.

BUILD YOUR SUPERVISORY WORD POWER

These key terms are presented in their order of appearance in the chapter. They are terms for which supervisors have at least a working knowledge.

Decision making. The process of choosing from among alternatives.

Cost-benefit analysis. A comparison of the costs and benefits associated with a particular undertaking.

Marginal analysis. An economic concept that is concerned with the extra output that can be attained by adding an extra unit of input.

Marginal revenue. The amount of money that a firm stands to earn for doing one unit of additional work.

Marginal cost. The expense that is associated with producing one unit of additional work.

Decisions

1. Involve others?
① Quality?
② Acceptance or Understanding
③ Improve or develop?
*   personnel?*
④ would waste time.
⑤ damage subordinate
*   relationship w/peers.*
form a group?

Increase motivate
Involve yourself

Profit maximization rule. A rule which holds that a firm should produce to the point where marginal cost and marginal revenue are equal; if they are never equal, the firm should produce to the last unit where marginal revenue is greater than marginal cost.

Expected value. The result of multiplying the profit or gain associated with a decision by the probability of the success of that particular alternative.

Groupthink. Social pressure used to get group participants to conform with the overall thinking of the group.

Hidden agenda. A term that refers to those objectives or goals which are being pursued by individual group members rather than to those for which the group has been formally convened.

Preparation. The first stage in the creative thinking process, it is characterized by the supervisor getting mentally prepared to deal with the problem under consideration.

Incubation. The second stage in the creative thinking process, it is characterized by the supervisor sitting back and letting the subconscious mind work on an answer.

Illumination. The third stage of the creative thinking process, it is characterized by the supervisor realizing the answer to the problem.

Verification. The last stage of the creative thinking process, it is characterized by an implementation, and sometimes modification, of the solution to the problem.

Brainstorming. A group creative thinking technique, it is characterized by a focus on as many different approaches to the problem as the group can generate, by freewheeling, by piggybacking on other people's ideas, and by a lack of criticism of anything people say.

Gordon technique. A group creative thinking technique, it is most commonly used in generating novel approaches to solving technical problems.

Nominal grouping technique. A group creative thinking technique, it is characterized by the participants silently writing down their solutions, communicating them to the group, discussing the various recommendations, and then silently voting on the merits of the recommended solutions.

Delphi technique. A group creative thinking technique that requires the participants to fill out a questionnaire and then, upon receiving feedback regarding how everyone responded to the questions, to fill out the questionnaire again; this continues for four or five rounds, by which time a general consensus is usually achieved.

REVIEW YOUR UNDERSTANDING

1. In your own words, what is meant by the term *decision making?* What are the steps in this process? Describe each step, using a common example throughout.
2. What is meant by the term *cost-benefit analysis?* Why do many supervisors do cost-benefit calculations in their heads? Explain.
3. A supervisor has determined that the cost of a particular decision will be $800 and the benefit will be $900. Based on this information, the manager decides against implementing the decision. What is the logic behind this decision? Explain.
4. How do marginal cost and marginal revenue enter into cost-benefit analysis? Use an example in your answer.
5. What is the profit maximization rule? How does it help the supervisor in choosing from among alternatives? Explain.

6. What are some of the most common benefits of group decision making? What are some of the most common drawbacks? Identify and describe three of each.
7. Most supervisors are left-brain thinkers. What does this statement mean? How do these supervisors differ from right-brain thinkers? Compare and contrast the two.
8. How does the creative thinking process work? Choose a problem that might be solved using this process and then discuss the creative thinking steps as they would be applied to this problem.
9. How do brainstorming and the Gordon technique work? What types of problems might each be used to help solve? Give an example in each case.
10. A number of factors influence the way that decision making is carried out. What are four of these factors? Identify and describe each.
11. A supervisory friend of yours has come to you for some tips on improving his decision making. Drawing on the material in the chapter, what are four things you would tell the individual? Describe each tip in some detail.

SUPPLEMENT YOUR KNOWLEDGE

In addition to the references listed at the end of this chapter, the following provide important, practical information that is of use to supervisors in making decisions:

Ford, Charles H.: "Manage by Decision, Not by Objectives," *Business Horizons*, February 1980, pp. 7–18.
Hoh, Andrew K.: "Styles of Decision Making," *Supervisory Management*, May 1981, pp. 19–23.
Kirby, Peter G.: "How to Make Different Kinds of Decisions," *Supervisory Management*, February 1977, pp. 2–8.
McAlindon, Harold: "Toward a More Creative You: Developing the Whole Person," *Supervisory Management*, March 1980, pp. 31–35.

YOU BE THE SUPERVISOR: TO PRODUCE OR NOT TO PRODUCE

Wyatt Inc. is a small manufacturing firm that has done quite well in the subcontracting business. The firm accepts many types of subcontracts but tends to specialize in small production runs that are too expensive or low-profit for prime contractors to handle themselves.

Last week Wyatt received a proposal for a bid on inexpensive gears that are used in hand-held power machinery. The markup in the industry is 200 percent, so the contractor cannot afford to expend a great deal of money building the machinery and still remain price-competitive. The proposal is for production runs in batches of 10,000. The price per bolt is $1 and the company can bid on as many batches as it wants up to a total of 10, the total number being requested.

Wyatt has done a cost breakdown on the batches and determined that with initial setup expenses, it will cost more to produce the first couple of batches of 10,000 than the contractor is willing to pay. By the third batch of 10,000, however, the cost of the batch will be equal to the incoming revenue. More specifically, the table on the next page shows how the company has priced out the cost per batch.

Batch	Cost
1	$15,000
2	12,000
3	10,000
4	8,000
5	6,000
6	7,000
7	9,000
8	11,000
9	13,000
10	16,000

In addition to the above information, which represents direct costs of production, the company would like to make a profit margin of 12 percent. This margin will cover all indirect costs associated with the manufacturing and still leave an adequate return on investment.

A company representative has contacted the contractor to see if the $1/unit price is flexible. It is not. The contractor is unwilling to pay any more than $1, although it is willing to give the company an added bonus of $25,000 if it agrees to manufacture all 10 batches. The reason for the bonus is that the contractor prefers to deal exclusively with one subcontractor rather than spread the job out among two or more.

1. Assume that you are the supervisor who is responsible for deciding how many batches to manufacture. Overlooking the return-on-investment consideration and the bonus, how many batches would you recommend that the firm manufacture? Show your work.
2. Would your answer to the above question change in light of the return-on-investment consideration? Explain.
3. Would the bonus influence you to produce all 10 batches? Explain, and if your answer is no, relate how large the bonus would have to be before you would recommend that the firm agree to produce all 10 batches.

YOU BE THE SUPERVISOR: A CREATIVE APPROACH

For the past 75 years a private university located in the northeast part of the United States has offered only daytime programs. The university began as a liberal arts college and gradually added engineering, business, and law schools. During the last two decades a graduate college has been established, offering course work toward master's and doctor's degrees in the arts, sciences, and business.

Earlier this year the president of the university and the board of trustees decided to expand the scope of the institution by offering night school classes as well as weekend courses. They also approved extension courses in the form of correspondence study. The president is convinced that unless the university begins reaching out to the community and making an effort to capture the adult and working person market, overall enrollment will eventually decline and the institution will lose money. Projections by the planning committee of the university show that enrollments have just about peaked and that over the next 10 years the enrollment of full-time students will decline by approximately 12 percent.

The university has hired a staff of ten people to head the continuing education department, which will be responsible for coordinating and managing the activities associated with the adult and working person market. Chairpeople throughout the university have already been contacted, and they have all added night sections and weekend courses to their class schedules for next semester. They have also designated courses that they feel can be taken through independent study, and faculty members have been assigned to write these courses. The continuing eduation department, which is headed by a supervisor, is charged with coordinating this overall effort and keeping in close contact with the professors to ensure that the courses are completed on time. In addition to the above, the department is charged with seeing that all correspondence study materials are printed, bound, and stored in the university warehouse. The department also has the responsibility of advertising these new courses and handling all of the accompanying enrollments.

The major problem facing the supervisor is how to advertise these courses. The supervisor knows that the market for the courses is quite different from that of full-time day students. After giving the matter a great deal of thought, the supervisor has decided to call together the work group and discuss the nature and form of the advertising program. In particular the supervisor is interested in developing a creative approach that will catch the attention of the adult market and influence these people to write for more information and/or sign up for courses. Four other major universities in the local area offer courses for this market niche, and the supervisor realizes that the ad campaign will have to distinguish between its courses and those of the competition. The group is scheduled to have its first meeting tomorrow.

1. Assuming that you are the supervisor of this group, what approach would you use in generating creative ideas from the group? Be as specific as possible in describing the approach.
2. What form will the creative thinking process take? What phases will the group members go through?
3. After the ad campaign is formulated, how will cost-benefit analysis enter into the decision-making process? Explain.

NOTES

1. Don Caruth and Bill Middlebrook, "How to Make a Better Decision," *Supervisory Management*, July 1981, pp. 12–17.
2. John J. Sherwood and Florence M. Hoylman, "Individual Versus Group Approaches to Decision Making," *Supervisory Management*, April 1978, pp. 2–9.
3. Jacquelyn Wonder and Priscilla Donovan, *Whole-Brain Thinking*, New York: William Morrow, 1984.
4. Harold R. McAlindon, "Toward a More Creative You: The Actualizing Climate," *Supervisory Management*, April 1980, pp. 35–40.
5. Thomas J. Peters and Robert H. Waterman, Jr., *In Search of Excellence*, New York: Harper & Row, 1982.

CHAPTER 4

ORGANIZING FOR RESULTS

**GOALS OF
THE CHAPTER**

Every supervisor relies on the work-unit personnel in getting things done. The process by which work assignments are made and activities are coordinated is known as organizing. The purpose of this chapter is to examine the ways in which the supervisor organizes for results. When you have finished reading all the material in this chapter, you will be able to:

1. Define the term *organizing*.
2. Compare and contrast a bureaucratic design with a contingency organizational design.
3. Identify nine principles of organizing that can be of benefit to supervisors.
4. Describe the most common organizational designs used by supervisors.
5. Relate the importance of job definitions to effective organizing.
6. Explain how span of control affects organizational design and how the supervisor should go about choosing an ideal span.
7. Discuss how delegation works and why many managers are reluctant to delegate.
8. Identify seven useful tips for effective organizing.

A STARTING CASE: TRYING TO KEEP UP

Richard Folkes is a supervisor in the claims department of a local insurance firm. Richard has worked here for 2 months, and he greatly enjoys the job. His work group's responsibilities are to investigate auto claims from clients. Richard often gets calls from his firm's clients reporting that they have been involved in auto accidents. "What do I do?" is usually the person's first question. Richard takes down the information and sends out one of his people to look at the car and find out what happened.

Richard's department is responsible for appraising the company's liability and getting the customer a check to cover the repair work or the value of the car (in the case of a total wreck). Since insurance is paying the bill, the company has the right to choose where the car will be repaired. Richard knows some of the best repair shops in town, and in the case of major damage he often personally calls one of them to negotiate the final price. "I can usually save the firm $50 to $75 with just one call," he explained to his boss last month.

"And if I can do this 5 times a week, it just about pays the annual salary of one of our people in the field."

Richard's firm also insures personal residences against the usual calamities: fire, flood, theft, personal accident and injury, etc. The procedures are similar to those described above, except that there is usually much more negotiation between either the insurance firm and the homeowner or the firm and the injured person, as in the case of a guest who falls on the property and is injured. Last week Richard personally handled one of these cases. A car had missed a curve, driven onto the grass, and crashed into a 6-foot wall surrounding a large house. The damage to the wall was $5100, and to the shrubbery on the inside of the wall it was $3800. Richard agreed to pay the $5100 but allowed only $1300 for the plants. It took over an hour to explain to the owner that in the case of plants the insurance company does not pay the full replacement value.

Earlier this week Richard received a call from his boss: "Your paperwork is 9 days behind schedule. What's going on? I want you caught up within a week." The phone call left Richard confused. He currently supervises 15 field people and finds that he has little time to handle paperwork. The amount of time taken up with day-to-day matters in the field leaves him with only about one hour in the office. On the other hand, there are five other supervisors who hold positions similar to Richard's, and none of them has any trouble keeping up with his or her paperwork.

What is Richard's problem? What is he doing wrong? How can he tackle the paperwork problem and still handle day-to-day field concerns? Write down your suggestions. We will come back to this case at the end of the chapter.

THE NATURE OF ORGANIZING

Organizing is the process of assigning duties and coordinating the efforts of the personnel for the purpose of efficiently attaining predetermined objectives. The supervisor does not have to carry out this process from the ground up. The basic organizational design, procedures, policies, and rules are typically already in place. Working within this framework, the supervisor delegates tasks to the subordinates and sees that everything is done in accord with these instructions.

If the first-line manager has been using MBO or some similar approach, many of the above ideas have already been implemented. Now the individual need merely keep things moving along by ensuring that everyone is making satisfactory progress and, as people finish assigned tasks, by giving them new ones.

Bureaucracy

To the extent that the supervisor functions in a highly structured organization in which operating procedures are spelled out in detail, the individual manages in a *bureaucracy*. Some of the specific characteristics of an ideal bureaucracy are:

1. Everyone is given a specific, detailed work assignment.
2. There is a strict hierarchy of command, with each person closely controlled by his or her boss.
3. There are rules and standards that ensure uniformity of performance and coordination of activity.
4. All personnel carry out their jobs in an impersonal way, showing no real concern for other people in the organization.
5. Employment is based on technical qualifications, so that those who do their job well get to keep it and the others are dismissed.

On the positive side, a bureaucracy is designed for efficiency. And while little personal concern is shown for the worker, if the individual does adequate work, he or she is protected from arbitrary dismissal. On the negative side, bureaucracy encourages mediocrity. People do whatever is necessary to get by, but no more. No one wants to be creative and find out that he or she has broken a rule or procedure in the process and is now about to be dismissed. Nor does anyone want to do too much work, because there are clear-cut work assignments that relate how much to do. The ultimate result is that everyone stays within the rules, working in a uniform and even-paced manner. Those who are creative, hard working, and/or daring soon quit and move to organizations in which they can exercise their individual initiative.

How common is the bureaucracy? An organization having all the bureaucratic characteristics described above is not very common. However, there are many organizations that have some of the characteristics of the bureaucratic form. In enterprises in which things have to be done by the book and the individual can easily be replaced if he or she does not measure up, bureaucratic rules are in evidence. Blue-collar work, especially on assembly lines, is a good example. On the line, things are done "by the numbers." No one improvises or breaks with the daily pattern of work routine.

Today's supervisor is finding that the bureaucratic approach is becoming less common. More and more organizations are changing their organizational designs to incorporate the needs and desires of the situation and the personnel. The result has been the emergence of contingency design structures.

Contingency organizational design

Contingency organizational design is based on the principle that the structure must accommodate the specific needs of the situation. A bureaucracy may be designed so that every supervisor has exactly seven subordinates. In an organization constructed along contingency lines, however, the number of subordinates is determined by a host of factors, including the difficulty of the tasks the people are performing, the importance of the jobs to the overall success of the unit and the enterprise, and the style of leadership that is most effective for the supervisor. Following these guidelines, some supervisors have very few subordinates reporting to them, while others have many subordinates.

In many white-collar organizations and enterprises that operate in a dynamic and changing environment, contingency organizational designs are common. The supervisor will adjust them to meet the situation. For example, if there is a special assignment that must be completed within 2 days, the supervisor often will assign people to it and tell them to do whatever is necessary to complete the task on time. "Get back with me if you need some assistance," the supervisor will say, "otherwise, do whatever is necessary to finish by tomorrow at 5 P.M." Rather than following rules and procedures, the supervisor will give the subordinates the authority to do whatever is required to ensure on-time completion.

In another case the supervisor may find that two salespeople have to be halfway across the country by the next morning in order to make a presentation of the company's latest product line. There is no time to fill out the usual requisition for travel and send it up the line for approval. The supervisor will explain the situation to his boss and together they will decide how to get the air tickets and room reservations handled. By the time the two salespeople return from the trip, the paperwork will be complete and simply backdated. In a bureaucracy where everything is done according to the rules, these types of crises involve a lot of red tape and employee time. With a contingency approach, faster and more effective decisions can be made.

Every organization operates somewhere along the line between pure bureaucracy and pure contingency-based design. However, to the extent possible, each follows some common organizing principles.

Common organizing principles

Most enterprises use a number of basic organizing principles. The supervisor often employs them without knowing them by their title or name. The following are nine of the most common.

Unity of command. This principle holds that everyone should have one and only one boss. In some cases this principle is violated, but in the main it is one of the pillars of organizational design. Most supervisors would find their authority undermined if their people were reporting to at least one other manager.

Scalar chain. This principle holds that there should be a clear line of authority running from the top to the bottom of the organization. When this is done, all people know to whom they report and who reports to them. The scalar chain forms an organizational ladder with each level of the hierarchy serving as one of the rungs.

Span of control. This principle holds that there is a limited number of subordinates that a supervisor can manage effectively. The principle does not state what this number is but encourages the manager to identify those factors which will influence the number and to use them in deciding how many subordinates to have. If the supervisor finds that he or she cannot directly manage all the people in the work unit, it may be necessary to form two or more groups and have the supervisor work with an informal leader in each group. In this way the direct span of control can be reduced.

Authority-level principle. This principle states that the supervisor should delegate authority for operating decisions to the individual responsible for making them. In short, authority for a decision should rest at that level at which the operating decision is made. In implementing this principle, the manager gives subordinates control over their day-to-day work activities.

Parity of authority and responsibility. This principle holds that authority and responsibility should be equal. If the supervisor delegates a task to someone, that subordinate also should have the necessary authority to get the job done. This principle seeks to overcome the all-too-common management practice of delegating responsibility while holding on to authority.

Unity of management. This principle holds that there should be one manager and one plan for all operations having the same objective. If the supervisor is given six goals to attain, the supervisor should use these objectives to develop an overall plan for pulling everyone together into a cohesive unit.

Stability of tenure. This principle holds that to the extent that a supervisor can maintain the services of the personnel, unit efficiency will be enhanced. The logic behind the principle is that if there is a great deal of turnover in the unit, the supervisor will continually have unskilled or untrained personnel learning their jobs. A group of good workers who remain with the unit is preferable to a group of excellent workers who stay but a short time before moving on to jobs elsewhere.

Principle of subordinate involvement. To the extent that the supervisor can get the subordinates involved in planning and controlling their own work, motivation will increase. This principle is based on the *rule of ownership*, which holds that when people have control or ownership of their work, they are more likely to exercise initiative, creativity, and effort.

Principle of brevity. This principle holds that in delegating work to people, the supervisor should be brief and to the point. There is an inverse relationship between the length of a message and the likelihood that the subordinate will listen, understand, and react in the desired manner.

Figure 4-1. Functional departmentalization.

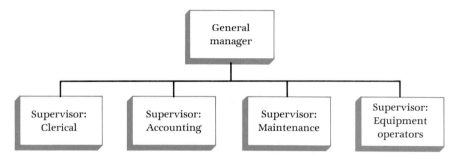

COMMON ORGANIZATIONAL DESIGNS
Functional departmentalization

Many different types of organizational designs are used in industry today. In the main, however, they fall into the following five basic categories.

Functional departmentalization is an organizational design in which the personnel are assigned to work groups based on their jobs. Clerical people are put in one group, accounting people in a second, maintenance people in a third, equipment operators in a fourth, etc. Figure 4-1 provides an illustration.

Under a functional departmentalization arrangement, the supervisor manages a homogeneous work group. This allows the supervisor to become an expert in how the work is done. In fact, because of the focus on work specialization, it is common to find supervisory vacancies being filled by promotion from the ranks. Quite often the most proficient worker, or the one with the greatest seniority, is offered the job. Because of its simplicity and emphasis on job specialization, functional departmentalization is the most popular form of organizational design.

Product departmentalization

Product departmentalization is an organizational arrangement in which work groups are constituted on the basis of a product or service. This arrangement is quite common in department stores in which there are supervisors for the various departments: i.e., toys, shoes, appliances, men's wear, etc. It is also used by manufacturing firms which build complete units in a single department or which have multiple product lines, each of which functions as an entity unto itself. Figure 4-2 illustrates the way a bank would organize in order to provide services to its customers.

Figure 4-2. Product departmentalization in a bank (partial form).

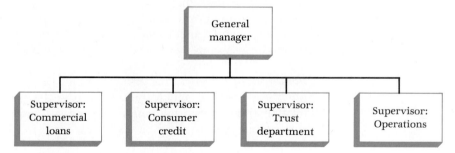

Under this organizational arrangement the supervisor learns to develop general management skills. Rather than being an expert in one particular area, the supervisor has to become proficient in many. The supervisor must also learn to think in broad terms, i.e., a product line rather than just an activity involved with selling that line. Where possible, many firms look at product lines as profit centers and they evaluate the supervisor on the basis of how well he or she has done in terms of product-line profit and return on investment. These supervisors operate their units like little businesses that function under the umbrella of the overall enterprise.

Geographic depart- mentalization

Geographic departmentalization is an organizational arrangement in which work groups are constituted on a territorial basis. This type of arrangement is quite common among enterprises that are situated in many different locales. For example, an insurance firm that is headquartered in Chicago with regional offices in Omaha, Kansas City, and Dallas would likely be organized territorially. The regional offices would be similar in organization to the main office so that each could offer the same product lines and services in the regions that are offered to customers in the Chicago area. Another common example is department stores that are part of a retail chain. There will be stores all over the region, but within each the structure is the same. As a result, while the organization chart will show regionally based stores, within each the goods and services will be similar and for all practical purposes the supervisor will not be directly affected. The situation will be the same as that in product departmentalization.

Geographic departmentalization affects the supervisor when the specific approach made by the firm differs from region to region. In one section of the country the firm may focus more heavily on one type of good or service than in another. For example, retail stores in Florida will usually not have the same marketing approach as those in Maine. If nothing else, weather conditions dictate the need for some different product-line offerings. Also, with a territorial approach the supervisor is able to get training in many different locales and become familiar with the many market niches the firm is pursuing.

Matrix depart- mentalization

Matrix departmentalization is a hybrid form of organizational design that draws upon both the functional and the product departmentalization arrangements. Figure 4-3 provides an illustration. Notice that the supervisor of project A reports directly to the general manager. The same is true of the other two supervisors. Each supervisor is responsible for the completion of a project, and in getting this done, the individual must rely on the expertise and assistance of the functional managers. The project supervisor has authority that cuts across the organization. It is authority related only to the project and is used in getting the functional managers to provide the necessary assistance for completing the project and to coordinate the work of the project personnel. The supervisor who is in charge of the project acts

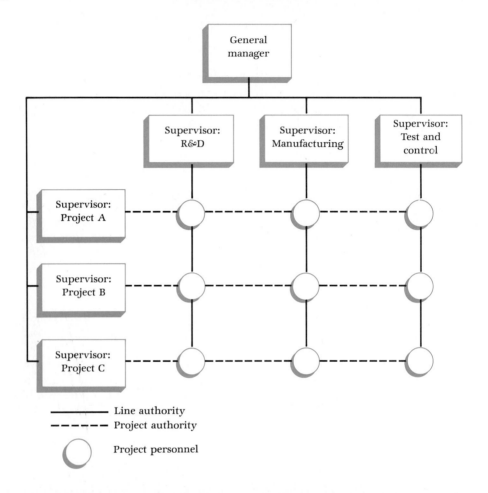

Figure 4-3. Matrix departmentalization.

———— Line authority

– – – – – Project authority

◯   Project personnel

like a business manager, concerned with seeing that the undertaking is completed on time and within cost and quality parameters. The functional managers provide the resources necessary for getting the project accomplished within the predetermined guidelines by assigning people and equipment to the undertaking. The functional manager has *line authority*, which is direct authority. This allows the supervisor to give orders to his or her subordinates and to control their work. Supervisors have line authority over their regular personnel. The project supervisor has *project authority*, which is the authority to give orders to personnel in project-related activities only.[1]

The matrix structure is popular in industries such as aerospace and construction as well as among firms engaged in new product development. This is true despite the fact that some of the principles spelled out in the previous section are violated in matrix designs. The best example is unity of command, in that the personnel who help the project manager report to the latter on project-related matters but still remain members of the functional department. Supervisors who head projects have the opportunity to use all of the managerial functions that were discussed in Chapter 1. They also learn that formal rules and regulations are not enough to ensure project completion. The use of persuasion, negotiation skills, and trading of favors is also important in getting the functional managers to provide them the assistance they need. Project supervisors often find this experience to be very useful later on when they become department and division managers.

Committees

The committee form of organization does not stand alone. It usually supplements one of the above-mentioned designs. For example, it is common to find committees used in functional, product, or geographic structures. Sometimes these committees are formed to help resolve a particular problem and are then disbanded. In this case they are known as *ad hoc committees.* In other cases there are permanent committees, such as the finance committee, the personnel committee and, in the case of corporations, the board of directors. These are known as *standing committees.*

When supervisors serve on committees, these are usually ad hoc committees. There are many reasons for such a committee. Sometimes the manager will want to get feedback from the personnel on various matters, such as how to handle the introduction of new technology. A small unit work group will be appointed to study the most effective means of implementation. More commonly, the supervisor will be appointed to serve as a member of a committee that involves people from a number of different units. For example, the general manager may decide that a computer must be introduced into the workplace. Rather than making this a unilateral decision, the individual decides to form a committee consisting of supervisors and workers from all of the units that will be affected. The committee will review the advantages and disadvantages associated with computerization and then present its recommendations to the general manager.

Regardless of the reason for the committee, it is important that the advantages and disadvantages be weighed against each other. Some of the important advantages of committees include: (1) They can often produce a better decision than can one person working alone, (2) they are extremely useful in coordinating plans and transmitting information throughout the organization, and (3) the motivational value they create among the members can result in both enthusiasm and support for their decisions. Some of the important disadvantages include: (1) They can be a big waste of time and money, (2) sometimes they are used for making decisions that are best handled by the individual manager, and (3) when a deadlock is reached, the decision of the committee is sometimes a compromise that produces a truly inferior result. Nevertheless, if the supervisor runs the committee meetings properly, the advantages can be obtained while the drawbacks are minimized or avoided. Some of the most useful techniques for conducting successful group meetings are presented in Supervision in Action: Holding Successful Meetings.[2]

SUPERVISION IN ACTION: HOLDING SUCCESSFUL MEETINGS

Committees spend a great deal of time in meetings. It is common to find the members attending regular weekly or biweekly meetings, at which time progress is evaluated, problems are discussed, issues are resolved, and the members are given things to do prior to the next meeting. Unfortunately, sometimes these meetings get very little accomplished and the members begin wondering why the supervisor has called them together. Effective supervisors realize the need to make each meeting count. As a result, it is common to find them following these eight guidelines:

1. *Make certain a meeting is necessary* to achieve the desired objective. Don't call a meeting if the same result can be achieved by personal visit, memo, phone call, etc.
2. *Develop an agenda* and send it out in advance. The agenda should clearly indicate the item(s) to be covered, appropriate supporting materials, time and place of the meeting, approximate time the meeting will require, and some indication of what is expected in the way of participation from the members, e.g., to give advice or make a decision.
3. *Give careful consideration to those being invited to the meeting.* Invite only those people who need to attend. Inviting individuals who have no reason for attending can actually be disruptive or counterproductive, especially if they are vocal.
4. *Give the meeting your undivided attention.* Hold the meeting where distractions and interruptions can be held to a minimum.
5. *Be prepared.* There is no substitute for adequate preparation. Know what it is you want to accomplish and do your homework in such a way that all necessary information is available. Anticipate questions and issues which may arise.
6. *If participation by the members is important,* be prepared to ask the right questions to stimulate discussion. Encourage everyone to get involved. Avoid questions which stifle discussion. Reserve personal opinions or judgments until later in the discussion; otherwise, the members might be unduly biased by your comments and fail to provide the type of input really desired. Don't allow one or a few members to monopolize the conversation.
7. *Keep to the agenda.* Encourage members to express themselves, but don't permit them to wander off the subject or waste time with long-winded dissertations.
8. *Conclude the meeting by summarizing the highlights,* including action to be taken as a result of the discussion. Follow up the meeting with a set of accurate and detailed minutes, distributing them to all present.

Source: Larry G. McGougle, "Conducting a Successful Meeting," © January 1981. Reprinted by permission of *Personnel Journal,* Costa Mesa, Calif.; all rights reserved.

**OTHER
KEY FACTORS
IN ORGANIZING**

Departmentalization is one of the four basic factors in organizing. The other three that are of importance to effective supervision are: job descriptions, span of control, and delegation of authority. The following examines these three.

Job descriptions

Job descriptions are statements of the duties and functions to be performed by a person holding that job. The general purpose of a job description is to explain the duties, responsibilities, requirements, and qualifications of anyone who has to recruit, screen, interview, or orient an employee for that job. Figure 4-4 provides an example of a job description for a service and safety supervisor. Notice how detailed the information is. Job descriptions serve as the basis for all organizing activities. The supervisor typically does not write these descriptions; however, the supervisor does use them both in recruiting and in work delegation. They provide the manager with information regarding what the unit personnel should be doing. The descriptions also serve for organizing people on the basis of experience and expertise.[3]

Span of control

Span of control refers to the number of subordinates who report directly to a supervisor. A narrow span (two or three subordinates per supervisor) results in a tall structure (many levels in the hierarchy), while a wide span (7 to 10 subordinates) produces a flat one. There is no agreement as to the ideal span of control; it depends on the situation.

From the supervisor's standpoint, the main question is, What span is most effective? The answer depends on a number of factors. One is the activities that the subordinates are carrying out. If everyone is doing fairly simple work, the supervisor can manage more people because each will require very little time; on the other hand, if the subordinates are carrying out complex tasks, the supervisor will have to provide constant, close supervision. A second, and related, factor is training. The greater the amount of training, the less assistance and guidance the subordinates will require. A third factor is geographic distance between subordinates. If they are all located in one place, it will be easier to supervise a large number than if they are in field offices and the supervisor has to travel out to them. A fourth factor is the supervisor. If the individual has a great deal of energy and enjoys working with a large number of subordinates, the manager will do better with a wide span of control; if the individual has less-than-average energy and prefers to work with only a handful of subordinates, the supervisor is more likely to have a narrow span of control. A fifth factor is the subordinates. If they enjoy close control, the supervisor will tend to use a narrow span of control; if they prefer loose control, the manager will employ a wide span of control.

In determining the ideal span, the supervisor must look at variables such as those discussed above. The ideal span for one manager will not be the best for another. The most important thing to remember, however, is that many supervisors tend to exercise too much control. If they were to widen

JOB TITLE: SERVICE AND SAFETY SUPERVISOR

DIVISION: Plastics	D.O.T. CODE: 889.133-010
DEPARTMENT: Manufacturing	EEO-1/AAP CATEGORIES: 1/2
SOURCE(S): John Doe	WAGE CATEGORY: Exempt
JOB ANALYST: John Smith	VERIFIED BY: Bill Johnson
DATE ANALYZED: 5/26/83	DATE VERIFIED: 6/5/83

JOB SUMMARY

The SERVICE AND SAFETY SUPERVISOR works under the direction of the IMPREGNATING & LAMINATING MANAGER: **schedules** labor pool employees; **supervises** the work of gardeners, cleaners, waste disposal and plant security personnel; **coordinates** plan safety programs; **maintains** daily records on personnel, equipment, and scrap.

JOB DUTIES AND RESPONSIBILITIES

1. **Schedules** labor pool employees to provide relief personnel for all manufacturing departments: **prepares** assignment schedules and **assigns** individuals to departments based on routine as well as special needs in order to maintain adequate labor levels throughout the plant; **notifies** Industrial Relations Department weekly about vacation and layoff status of labor pool employees, contractual disputes, and other employment-related developments.

2. **Supervises** the work of gardeners, cleaners, waste disposal and plant security personnel: **plans** yard, clean-up, and security activities based on weekly determination of needs; **assigns** tasks and responsibilities to employees on a daily basis; **monitors** progress or status of assigned tasks; **disciplines** employees as necessary in accordance with labor contracts.

3. **Coordinates** plant safety programs: **teaches** basic first-aid procedures to security, supervisory, and lead personnel in order to maintain adequate coverage of medical emergencies; **trains** employees in fire fighting and hazardous materials handling procedures; **verifies** plant compliance with new or changing OSHA regulations; **represents** division during company-wide safety programs and meetings.

4. **Maintains** daily records on personnel, equipment, and scrap: **reports** amount of waste and scrap to cost accounting department; **updates** personnel records as necessary; **reviews** maintenance checklists for towmotors.

5. **Performs** other miscellaneous duties as assigned.

JOB REQUIREMENTS

1. Ability to apply basic principles and techniques of supervision.
   a) Knowledge of principles and techniques of supervision.
   b) Ability to plan and organize the activities of others.
   c) Ability to get ideas accepted and to guide a group or individual to accomplish a task.
   d) Ability to modify leadership style and management approach to reach a goal.
2. Ability to express ideas clearly both in written and oral communications.
3. Knowledge of current Red Cross first-aid procedures.
4. Knowledge of OSHA regulations as they affect plant operations.
5. Knowledge of labor pool jobs, company policies, and labor contracts.

MINIMUM QUALIFICATIONS

Twelve years of general education or equivalent; and one year supervisory experience; and first-aid instructor's certification.

or

Substitute 45 hours classroom supervisory training for supervisory experience.

JOB SPECIFICATIONS

1. Knowledge: Knowledge of supervisory principles/techniques; knowledge of first-aid procedures sufficient to teach others; familiarity with federal safety regulations.
2. Mental application: Applies effective principles of supervision to direct and motivate employees.
3. Accountability: Directly supervises the work of up to 25 laborers and security personnel; responsible for ensuring proper towmotor maintenance.

Figure 4-4. Example of a job description. (From Mark A. Jones, "Job Descriptions Made Easy," © May 1984. Reprinted by permission of *Personnel Journal*, Costa Mesa, Calif.; all rights reserved.)

their span of control and spend less time looking over their subordinates' shoulders, they would be more effective.

Delegation of authority

Delegation is the process by which the supervisor distributes work to the subordinates. This process involves three steps: (1) communicating the work to the subordinate, (2) giving the latter the authority to get the work done, and (3) creating an obligation whereby the subordinate assumes the responsibility to complete the task satisfactorily.

For supervisory purposes, the major problems facing the manager are: (1) knowing what to delegate, (2) being willing to delegate, and (3) overcoming subordinate resistance to delegation. Before continuing on, take Self-Assessment Quiz 4-1 and see how you score as a delegator.

SELF-ASSESSMENT QUIZ 4-1: HOW WELL DO YOU DELEGATE?

In answering this quiz, think of how you supervise other people, whether it be on the job, as a member of a social organization, when working for a charitable organization, etc. Mentally picture the job and stay within this framework in answering all of the questions. An interpretation of your responses is provided at the end of the chapter.

1. How well organized are you?
   a. Not well at all.
   b. Average.
   c. Better than average.
   d. Extremely well.
2. Do you establish procedures for what must happen when you are absent?
   a. Yes.
   b. Usually.
   c. Sometimes.
   d. Never.
3. How clear and straightforward are the orders and instructions you give to subordinates?
   a. Not very clear.
   b. Fairly clear.
   c. Usually quite clear.
   d. Very clear.
4. How much confidence do you have in your subordinates?
   a. Total.
   b. A great deal.
   c. A fair amount.
   d. Very little.
5. How do you divide your working time between handling details and working on planning and supervision?

a. Most time is spent working on details.

b. Working on details takes more time than planning and supervision.

c. Relatively little time is spent on details; most of the time is spent on planning and supervision.

d. Almost all the time is spent planning and supervising.

6. In projects that you delegate, do you overrule or reverse decisions made by your subordinates?

a. Almost never.

b. Occasionally.

c. Quite a bit.

d. Almost always.

7. Do you ever desert your subordinates or revoke their authority before they complete their project?

a. Almost never.

b. Occasionally.

c. Quite a bit.

d. Almost always.

8. Are you interrupted by subordinates who come to you for advice, for decisions, or with questions?

a. Almost never.

b. Occasionally.

c. Quite a bit.

d. Almost always.

9. Do you specify the results you expect from delegated work, or do you specify the tasks to be done?

a. Almost always the focus is on the results.

b. Usually the focus is on the results.

c. Usually the focus is on the tasks to be done.

d. Almost always the focus is on the tasks to be done.

10. Do you ever have unfinished jobs accumulating and find it difficult to meet deadlines?

a. Almost never.

b. Occasionally.

c. Quite a bit.

d. Almost always.

11. Do your subordinates take the initiative in expanding their authority with delegated work, or do they wait for you to initiate all assignments?

a. They almost always take the initiative.

b. They occasionally take the initiative.

c. Once in a while they take the initiative, but usually they wait for me to determine the assignment.

d. They almost always wait for me to initiate the assignment.

12. How cluttered is your desk?

a. Very cluttered with all sorts of material.

b. Somewhat cluttered, mostly with things that need to be filed.

c. Somewhat cluttered with things I'm working on and other things that need to be filed.

d. Almost clean; only things that I'm working on are on the desk.

13. When problems arise in regard to matters that you have delegated, how often do you ask for your subordinates' ideas and opinions in straightening things out?

a. Almost always.

b. Usually.

c. Occasionally.

d. Never.

14. Are you irritable, tired, or worried because of job pressure?

a. Almost always.

b. Usually.

c. Occasionally.

d. Never.

15. Do you have to take work home with you or work late at the office?

a. Almost every night.

b. More often than not.

c. Occasionally.

d. Almost never.

To see how well you did, turn to the back of the chapter.

What to delegate—and not to delegate. Most supervisors do not delegate enough work to their subordinates, and when they do they often delegate the wrong things. Some activities have a high potential for delegation.[3] These include such things as paperwork, routine matters, and technical matters. Paperwork jobs are often more busywork than anything else. Cutting and pasting materials for a rough draft of a report can often be delegated to subordinates. So can routine tasks like checking inventory levels, verifying time cards, or ordering weekly supplies. Others can do these things as well as the supervisor can. The same is true for technical matters, such as adjusting machine settings or designing weekly cost control reports. There are workers who can do these things. The supervisor should not personally have to get involved in these kinds of activities.

On the other hand, some tasks should not be delegated. Personnel matters such as hiring and dismissing members of the work unit, resolving work-group conflicts, employee coaching and counseling, performance evaluations, and salary recommendations are jobs for the supervisor alone. So, too, are confidential activities such as policy changes or meetings involving how to deal with union demands. The supervisor must assume the responsibility for these tasks. The same is true for those jobs which the superior has directly assigned to the supervisor.

Basics of delegation. In delegating authority, the supervisor must keep a number of things in mind. Supervision in Action: Guidelines for Effectiveness describes some of these. In addition, there are other basic facts the supervisor must remember. First, the right person must be selected for each task. All employees do not have the same ability, and the supervisor should try to match the work to the skills of the subordinate. Second, the worker must be given the necessary authority to complete the task, and the supervisor must allow the worker to exercise it. Third, after the task has been completed, the supervisor should couch all criticism in constructive terms.

SUPERVISION IN ACTION:
GUIDELINES FOR EFFECTIVE DELEGATION

Many important guidelines can be useful to the supervisor in his or her efforts to delegate effectively. The following are nine of the most useful:

1. Be certain you clearly establish the required standards of performance. This may be in the form of a written job description supported by periodic meetings with individual staff members. These sessions serve to reinforce the required job standards, in addition to permitting the employees an opportunity to express any concerns, feelings, or interests in taking on additional responsibilities, and so forth. Reiterating the standards of performance leaves little room for misinterpreting instructions.

2. Be sure you clearly define tasks being delegated as well as those not being delegated. When employees are given an assignment, they should know exactly what they have the authority to do and what is expected of them. Moreover, you should provide information regarding how their assignment fits into the overall scheme of things; elaborate on just who is handling what aspects of the assignment, yourself included. This way employees will know if they are on target and functioning as required.

3. Make clear the extent of support and direction those delegated to do the job may expect. Let them know where they can go for additional information, when they should come to you with problems, and whom they should not approach for advice. Imparting this information makes your task as coordinator of activities that much more manageable.

4. Once the limits have been set, encourage as much creativity and independence as the nature of the task permits. Express to your employees your confidence that they can handle the tasks assigned by allowing them the option of determining how the task can best be accomplished. By doing this you are telling them you are assured of their skills, and this, in turn, will encourage them to do the best job possible.

5. Make certain that you clearly communicate the nature of each task. Be conscious of using terminology with which the employee may not be familiar. Be sure you do not make unfounded assumptions regarding the employee's prior knowledge of the task. Allow sufficient time to

explain the assignment and do not conclude the session until you are satisfied that the employee understands what is being expected of him or her.

6. Throughout the process of any assignment, one of your responsibilities as a supervisor is to assure that all is proceeding according to schedule. This means requesting progress reports and communication concerning any difficulties encountered by your delegates. Checking progress, however, does not mean asking daily how the assignment is progressing. Your intentions may be sincere enough, but the effect may well be that your employees will feel you do not have confidence in their abilities.

7. Depending on the length and relative importance of the project, periodically assess results. Correct errors where appropriate and straighten out any misunderstandings that may have occurred. It is helpful always to begin by pointing out those aspects of the task that have been completed satisfactorily and then pointing out those areas requiring improvement. When pointing out areas needing correction, be particularly conscious of your tone so that the sermon does not become disciplinary in nature. Employees should leave your office feeling challenged by the task set before them and anxious to correct any errors that may have been made.

8. Communication is not only a verbal or written skill. Your facial expressions and physical mannerisms have as great an impact on an employee's incentive to proceed with a task as your other messages. Failure to communicate in a positive, nonverbal way can be as detrimental as overt negative statements.

9. Once a task has been accomplished, those employees involved should be apprised of your general assessment of their performance. This includes not just their ability to meet the deadline, but all the aspects involved, such as gathering information, working with peers and management, following through, and handling other work in addition to this assignment. Even if employees know that they have done a good job, reinforcement from you can provide the impetus necessary to motivate them the next time. This aspect of delegation, the conclusion, is critical. To recognize employee's achievements—whether verbally, in the form of a memo in the file, or by way of a celebration for the staff that worked together on a project—is essential for the continuity of the rapport that must be maintained between yourself and your staff.

By understanding the importance of allowing employees to do their own job as their abilities dictate, carefully assessing each person's demonstrated skills, potential, and interest, and adhering to the basic guidelines for providing direction, you will develop a stronger staff support system, increase rapport, and thereby enhance your effectiveness as a supervisor.

Source: Diane Arthur, "Guidelines for Effective Delegation," *Supervisory Management,* October 1979, pp. 12–13. © 1979 by AMACOM, a division of the American Management Associations, New York. Reprinted by permission of the publisher; all rights reserved.

Rather than telling the individual what he or she did wrong, the supervisor should explain things in terms of how these mistakes can be avoided in the future and/or used as important lessons in better understanding what to do next time.

Failures to delegate. Some supervisors do not delegate enough work. While there are many reasons for this situation, usually they relate to the supervisor and/or the subordinate.[4] Some supervisors fail to delegate because they feel that they can personally do the job better than anyone else. Other common reasons include: (1) a lack of confidence in subordinates, (2) an inability to communicate ideas effectively to subordinates, and (3) an unwillingness to take a chance on things going wrong. Quite obviously these reasons are interrelated. For example, many supervisors who have a lack of confidence in their people are also unwilling to take a chance on them.

Subordinates are also a cause of the failure to delegate. Some of the main reasons include: (1) They lack self-confidence, (2) they take up a lot of the manager's time with questions and other delegation-related issues, (3) they are afraid of doing the work poorly, and (4) there is not sufficient incentive for them to take on the tasks. These events all result in the subordinate being reluctant to accept delegated work. When taken in conjunction with the reasons in the above paragraph, it becomes obvious why many supervisors do not delegate as much work as they should.

A third reason for the failure to delegate is that the supervisor does not think there is any reason for it. He or she will argue: "Heck, I don't really have that much work to do. Why bother someone else with it? I have plenty of time to do it myself." While this may be true, quite often supervisors are doing more than they realize. Slowly, often over a period of 1 or 2 years, their workload builds up and they are unaware of how much more they are doing now in contrast to 24 months ago. There are a number of telltale signs that the supervisor is doing too much and should start delegating. Some of these include:

1. The supervisor is working longer hours than any of the subordinates, arriving 30 to 60 minutes before anyone else and not leaving until well after the last person has gone.
2. The supervisor takes work home every night, including weekends, when the pile of material is larger than ever.
3. The manager's in basket is continually full, no matter how much work the individual gets done each day.
4. The first-line manager is beginning to rush to meet deadlines, something that he or she never used to do before.
5. The individual is doing a lot of routine or technical tasks, in contrast to think work or administrative chores that are more managerial in nature.

6. The supervisor is beginning to experience more and more pressure and stress, and there are fewer time periods when the individual feels relaxed.

7. The manager is making most of the decisions in the unit, not allowing the subordinates to participate as much as they have in the past.

8. Subordinates are beginning to realize that they do not have authority to do anything unless it has been cleared in advance with the supervisor.

When these signs are present, delegation is in order.

TIPS FOR EFFECTIVE ORGANIZING

Much of the material in this chapter has offered useful suggestions regarding how supervisors can more effectively organize their work units and delegate tasks to their personnel. The following complements these ideas by presenting seven specific tips that make organizing in general, and delegation in particular, easier to carry out.

Make use of job descriptions

Many supervisors fail to tell their people what they want done or how they want it to be done. This is a result of poor communication. Much of this problem can be overcome if the organization has well-written job descriptions.[5]

In large organizations, it is common to find the personnel department working with the unit managers in seeing that these descriptions are properly written. However, in small firms there are usually no descriptions or the supervisor, personally, is expected to write them and/or see that they are kept up to date. In the beginning, this is going to take time. The supervisor will not know what to put in and what to leave out of the description, what format to use, or how detailed to be. Once the first-line manager begins to learn how to write these descriptions, however, he or she is going to save a great deal of organizing time. Rather than verbally having to explain the job to new employees, the latter can be given the job description and a short orientation period and then left alone. If nothing else, the job description saves the supervisor time that can be allocated to more important duties.

Use job matching

Some jobs can readily be assigned to people on the basis of their expertise. The supervisor can give accounting-related tasks to the accountant, letters and memos to the secretary, and requests for quality control data to the engineer. However, sometimes there are tasks that do not fit neatly into any one job category, or there is more than one person who can do them. In these cases the supervisor must decide to whom to assign the work. In doing so, job matching is an excellent approach.[6]

Job matching is the process of bringing together the work and the people in such a way that the requirements of the former and the skills and abilities of the latter complement each other. Some workers are extremely good at detailed work; some can produce a great quantity of work in a very short period of time; some are extremely well organized and can arrange and coordinate activities and reports in a logical way; some are very creative and can generate new ideas and solutions for solving recurring problems; others are very good promoter types and can quickly win people over to their way of thinking. No one is good at everything, but most people have one or two skills or abilities that are higher than average. By finding out what each does well, the supervisor can match tasks and people. This approach is not only efficient but gives the personnel an opportunity to excel at those things which they do best.

Delegate in small bites

When new tasks are delegated, many subordinates try to avoid them because the supervisor frightens them. They are given a great deal of work or an extremely important assignment and told: "I need this finished in 2 days. The instructions are on the first page. Just follow them to the letter and get back to me with the finished material the day after tomorrow." In a matter of 1 or 2 minutes the subordinate is swamped with a major work assignment.

What the supervisor needs to do is delegate in small bites, breaking major projects into three or four phases. One way to begin is by telling the subordinate: "Here is a project that must be finished by tomorrow afternoon. I want you to read the instructions on the first page of this report, look over the accompanying data, and then come back to see me in an hour. At that point we'll talk about how the report is to be written." After the two talk, the supervisor should then have the individual start working on the project and say something like, "Come to see me at 4 P.M. this afternoon and let's review where you are and what else needs to be done." By following this piecemeal approach, the worker realizes that he or she will have continual access to the supervisor and can ask questions and discuss progress. This bit-by-bit approach reduces tension and anxiety and lets the subordinate know that as far as the supervisor is concerned, "We're both in this together."

Be firm

Sometimes the supervisor will attempt to delegate work to a subordinate and be told, "I can't get to that for at least a week," or "That's not really my cup of tea. Why not ask George?" Some supervisors accept this rebuff and look for someone else. However, effective supervisors stand firm. If the supervisor has already determined that this person is the right one to do the job, then no is an unacceptable answer. Surprising as it may seem, effective supervisors turn the tables on the subordinate and say: "You can put that stuff you're working on to the side. I need this finished by late this afternoon," or "You've done this kind of work before. That's why I'm giving it to you again. George is going to be working on something else." New supervisors often believe that they will be more effective if they go along with the workers. Experienced supervisors know that if they have carefully thought the situation over and made the right decision, they should push it through. Once it becomes clear to the workers that the supervisor knows what he or she is talking about and will not be sidetracked, subordinates become more willing to undertake the assignment.

Don't dump, delegate

Delegation calls for the assignment of both authority and responsibility.[7] *Dumping* occurs when the supervisor gives the subordinate something to do but undermines the individual's authority in carrying out the assignment. One of the most common forms of dumping is when the supervisor goes around the subordinate and countermands some of the latter's decisions. Another is when those who are given orders by the subordinate bypass this individual and go back to the supervisor either to ask for clarification or to indicate in some way that they will respond to the supervisor but not to the person who has been put in charge of handling the assignment. Unless the supervisor makes it clear that they are to do as the subordinate wants, the supervisor is undermining the subordinate. When these things happen, it becomes obvious that the supervisor has dumped the work on the subordinate but has not given the individual the requisite authority for seeing things through.

Reward good performance

One of the surest ways of getting people to do what needs doing is to reward them for their performance. When the personnel begin to realize that those who do the most and/or the best work are given higher salaries or bonuses or recommended for promotion, enthusiasm and morale increase. On the other hand, if the subordinates realize that there is no payoff for getting involved, they will do the least amount of work possible. Additionally, if the supervisor is a stern taskmaster and berates, ridicules, or punishes those who make mistakes, no one will want to accept work assignments. The subordinates will reason that the best they can do is avoid punishment, for there are no rewards if they do things well. This situation, all too common in some firms, eventually results in serious productivity problems.

Examine your personal behavior

The best way for the supervisor to overcome such organizing problems as dumping and the failure to reward performance is to become aware of them and then to develop a concerted strategy for overcoming them. This is easier said than done. Many supervisors believe that they are extremely effective in organizing; they see themselves as using loose control, giving people interesting and challenging assignments, and always being available to discuss job-related problems. Employee attitude surveys reveal a quite different picture, however. Many supervisors are seen as exercising close control, being delegators of boring and routine work, and seldom available to help out with job-related problems. How can supervisors overcome these perception problems? The most effective way is by opening up two-way communication channels with the personnel and getting feedback. Tapping into the informal network is another useful method. Then, based on the feedback, the supervisor can adjust his or her behavior. Remember, sometimes the supervisor must give people assignments they do not want or like. However, by explaining why it must be done, the supervisor often can reduce or eliminate negativism on the workers' part. Most subordinates want to pitch in and help out. What they resent is not being told why they have to do things or feeling that they are being used by the supervisor. To the extent that the supervisor can put his or her ego on the shelf and focus on developing a meaningful work relationship with the subordinates, the supervisor's effectiveness will increase.

TRYING TO KEEP UP: STARTING CASE REVISITED

Richard's problem is one of work delegation. He has 15 people in the field and spends most of his time there. Additionally, while in the office he handles calls from clients who need information. In both of these cases, the main question is, Why?

Richard needs to delegate more authority to his people and let them handle things. In the office, he should have someone taking those calls from clients. Richard is too directly involved in the day-to-day contacts with customers. Instead of functioning as a supervisor, he is acting like one of the field staff.

Finally, remember from the last part of the case that no other supervisor is having the same problems. So the source of Richard's problem cannot be just the number of his subordinates or the nature of his work; it must have to do with his organizing approach. Perhaps he is afraid to delegate. Maybe he believes that he can do things better than his field personnel can. In any event, he needs to change his style of delegation and begin relying more on the personnel to handle day-to-day matters while he focuses on handling managerial responsibilities.

INTERPRETATION OF SELF-ASSESSMENT QUIZ 4-1: HOW WELL DO YOU DELEGATE?

Below, circle your answer to each of the questions and then add up the number of circles in each column. Give yourself 1 point for each circle in column I, 2 points for each circle in column II, 3 points for each circle in column III, and 4 points for each circle in column IV.

Question	I	II	III	IV
1.	a	b	c	d
2.	d	c	b	a
3.	a	b	c	d
4.	d	c	b	a
5.	a	b	c	d
6.	d	c	b	a
7.	d	b	c	a

Question	I	II	III	IV
8.	a	b	c	d
9.	d	c	b	a
10.	a	b	c	d
11.	d	c	b	a
12.	a	b	c	d
13.	d	c	b	a
14.	d	c	b	a
15.	a	b	c	d
	_ × 1 +	_ × 2 +	_ × 3 +	_ × 4 = _____

Here is a scoring key in evaluating your effectiveness as a delegator:

Points   *Interpretation*

15–25   Poor. You do very little delegating. You need to examine your practices closely to find ways of improving.

26–35   Average. You delegate some of the work but could do better.

36–45   Good. You delegate quite a bit to your subordinates. You are above average.

46–60   Excellent. You delegate as much as possible. You are in the top 10 percent of all people who take this quiz.

SUMMARY OF KEY POINTS

1. Organizing is the process of assigning duties and coordinating the efforts of the personnel for the purpose of efficiently attaining predetermined objectives. To the extent that the supervisor functions in a highly structured organization in which operating procedures are spelled out in detail, the individual operates in a bureaucracy. On the other hand, if the organizational design is flexible and modified to meet environmental conditions, the supervisor operates in an organization designed along contingency lines.

2. A number of common organizing principles are of value to the supervisor. These include: unity of command, the scalar chain, span of control, the authority-level principle, parity of authority and responsibility, unity of command, stability of tenure, the principle of subordinate involvement, and the principle of brevity. Each was described in the chapter.

3. Many different types of organizational design are used in industry today. Some of the most common include: functional departmentalization, product departmentalization, geographic departmentalization, matrix departmentalization, and committees. Each of these was discussed in the chapter.

4. Job descriptions are statements of the duties and functions to be performed by the person holding that job. These descriptions are particularly useful to the supervisor in managing the unit.

5. Span of control refers to the number of subordinates who report directly to a supervisor. A small number results in a tall structure, while a large number brings about a flat structure. The main question for the supervisor is, What span is most efficient? Key factors influencing the answer were presented in the chapter.

6. Delegation is the process by which the supervisor distributes work to the subordi-

nates. There are a number of reasons why supervisors do not delegate and subordinates are reluctant to accept assignments. These were discussed in the chapter. So, too, were tips designed to help the supervisor overcome these problems and more effectively carry out the organizing process.

BUILD YOUR SUPERVISORY WORD POWER

These key organizing terms are presented in their order of appearance in the chapter. Effective supervisors have a working knowledge of them.

Organizing. The process of assigning duties and coordinating the efforts of the personnel for the purpose of efficiently attaining predetermined objectives.

Bureaucracy. An organizational structure in which everyone has specific work assignments, there is a strict hierarchy of command, there are uniform rules and procedures, all personnel do their jobs in an impersonal way, and employment is based on technical qualifications.

Contingency organizational design. An organizational design based on the principle that the structure must accommodate the specific needs of the situation.

Unity of command. The principle that everyone should have one and only one boss.

Scalar chain. The line of authority that runs from the top to the bottom of the organization.

Span-of-control principle. The principle that there is only a limited number of people that a supervisor can manage effectively.

Authority-level principle. A principle of organizing which states that the supervisor should delegate authority for operating decisions to the individual responsible for making them.

Parity of authority and responsibility. An organizing principle which holds that authority and responsibility should be equal.

Unity of management. The principle that there should be one manager and one plan for all operations having the same objective.

Stability of tenure. A principle of management which holds that to the extent that a supervisor can maintain the services of the personnel, unit efficiency will be enhanced.

Principle of subordinate involvement. To the extent that the supervisor can get the subordinates involved in planning and controlling their work, motivation will increase.

Principle of brevity. In delegating work to people, the supervisor should be brief and to the point.

Functional departmentalization. An organizational design in which the personnel are assigned to work groups based on their jobs.

Product departmentalization. An organizational design in which work groups are constituted on the basis of a product or service.

Geographic departmentalization. An organizational design in which work groups are constituted on a territorial basis.

Matrix departmentalization. A hybrid form of organizational design that draws upon both functional and product departmentalization arrangements.

Line authority. Direct authority.

Project authority. Authority to give orders to personnel regarding project-related activities only.

Ad hoc committee. A committee formed to solve a particular problem and then disbanded.

Standing committee. A permanent committee.

Job description. A statement of the duties and functions to be performed by the person holding that job.

Span of control. The number of subordinates who report directly to a supervisor.

Job matching. The process of bringing together the work and the people in such a way that the requirements of the former and the skills and abilities of the latter complement each other.

Delegation. The process by which the supervisor distributes work to the subordinates.

Dumping. Giving a subordinate something to do and then undermining the individual's authority to carry out the assignment.

REVIEW YOUR UNDERSTANDING

1. In your own words, what is meant by the term *organizing?* What activities does it require the supervisor to perform? Explain.
2. How does a bureaucratic design differ from a contingency organizational design? Compare and contrast the two.
3. There are many useful organizing principles. Four of these are: unity of command, the scalar chain, span of control, and the authority-level principle. How is each of these of value to the supervisor? Explain.
4. Describe the ways in which the following principles help supervisors manage more effectively: parity of authority and responsibility, stability of tenure, the principle of subordinate involvement, and the principle of brevity. Be specific in each of your descriptions.
5. How are personnel organized under each of the three arrangements—functional, product, and geographic—and when would each be preferable to the others? Explain.
6. How does matrix departmentalization work? Describe it, being sure to explain the type of authority the project supervisor has. What challenges does this organizational arrangement present to the supervisor? Explain.
7. In what way is a committee an organizational form? When do supervisors use committees? Why do they use them?
8. How are job descriptions of value to the supervisor in organizing the work unit? Explain.
9. What is meant by the term *span of control?* How is this organizing concept used by the supervisor in effectively managing the work unit?
10. What is meant by the term *delegation?* What are some things a supervisor should delegate? What are some things a supervisor should not delegate? Explain.
11. Why are some supervisors reluctant to delegate? Why are some subordinates reluctant to accept delegated tasks? How can the supervisor become a more effective delegator? Offer five specific tips. Describe each.

SUPPLEMENT YOUR KNOWLEDGE

In addition to the references listed at the end of this chapter, the following provide important, practical information that is of use to supervisors in organizing the work and the people:

Bernstein, Ellen Joy: "Employee Attitude Surveys: Perception Vs. Reality," *Personnel Journal*, April 1981, pp. 300–305.

Bourdon, Roger D.: "A Basic Model for Employee Participation," *Training and Development Journal*, April 1980, pp. 24–29.

Brown, John L., and Neil McK. Agnew: "The Balance of Power in a Matrix Structure," *Business Horizons*, November–December 1982, pp. 51–54.

Caruth, Don, and Bill Middlebrook: "How to Delegate Successfully," *Supervisory Management*, February 1983, pp. 36–43.

Day, Dave: "Effective Delegation," *Personnel Journal*, November 1983, pp. 916–919.

Henderson, Richard I.: "Job Descriptions—Critical Documents, Versatile Tools, Part 4: Getting It on Paper," *Supervisory Management*, February 1976, pp. 12–21.

Malinowski, Frank A.: "Job Selection Using Task Analysis," *Personnel Journal*, April 1981, pp. 288–291.

Miller, George: "Management Guidelines: Building an Effective Organization," *Supervisory Management*, July 1981, pp. 35–41.

Montana, Patrick J., and Deborah F. Nash: "Delegation: The Art of Managing," *Personnel Journal*, October 1981, pp. 784–787.

Potter, Beverly A.: "Speaking With Authority: How to Give Directions," *Supervisory Management*, March 1980, pp. 2–11.

Scanlan, Burt K., and Roger M. Atherton, Jr.: "Participation and the Effective Use of Authority," *Personnel Journal*, September 1981, pp. 697–703.

YOU BE THE SUPERVISOR: THE NEW PROJECT

The Wittkins Corporation has decided to expand its focus of operations. The firm currently designs, manufactures, tests, and ships computer hardware. These parts are purchased by both large and small computer firms that find it cheaper to subcontract this work than to perform it personally. After receiving the material from Wittkins, the companies then do their own assembling and marketing of the finished products. Wittkins's basic organization chart is the following:

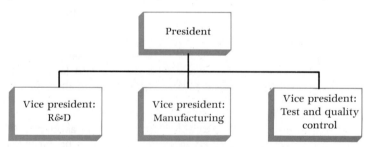

The research and development people are responsible for seeing that the hardware is state of the art. The manufacturing people are responsible for building the hardware according to design specifications. The testing and quality control people are responsible for performing both of these functions as well as for shipping the units to the respective customers.

Wittkins recently signed a contract to design, manufacture, test, and ship completely assembled computers that the customer need only market. The firm that gave Wittkins the contract also provided it with the blueprints for building the machine. It is to be a lightweight, inexpensive model that will retail for $1500. The company believes that there is a demand for at least 25,000 of these machines. However, since there is likely to be strong competition within 9 months, the firm intends to get in and out quickly. Wittkins's contract calls for 5000 of these computers to be built and delivered within 90 days.

The contract is a lucrative one for Wittkins, assuming that the machines can be built and delivered within the agreed-upon time. For this reason the president has decided to appoint a supervisor to act as the project manager in coordinating and expediting the work. This individual will report directly to the president and will have the authority to organize the project as he or she sees fit. "I don't care about organizational design," the president has said; "what I want is organizational performance."

1. Assuming that you are the supervisor in charge of the project, what would the organizational structure look like? Use the chart in the case as your point of departure.
2. What type of authority would you have? What problems might confront you in getting the project in on time? Explain.
3. Which tips from the chapter would be of most value to you in running the project? Identify and describe the most useful three.

YOU BE THE SUPERVISOR: A BACKLOG PROBLEM

Supervisors at Temp Inc. are given 3 weeks' vacation each year. The company staggers these vacations so that there are never more than two first-line managers gone at the same time. Some supervisors prefer summer vacations so that they can travel around the country, some like to get away during the winter for an extended skiing trip, and others tie theirs to school schedules so that they can be with their children just before the school year starts or during semester break.

By staggering the vacation schedules, the firm is able to cover these vacancies with two floating supervisors. These first-line managers move from one unit to another as needed.

Last week one of them was assigned to a work group of 12 people. These individuals are all members of a design department and are responsible for taking contract proposals and working up finished designs to accompany them. Most of their workday is taken up with two tasks: (1) studying contract proposals and putting together preliminary designs, and (2) meeting with those making these proposals in order to discuss modification and refinement of the designs.

When the floating supervisor arrived in the department, she found a 2-week backlog of work. She also discovered that the regular manager viewed herself as a member of the work group and took on as many design chores as the average worker. In an effort to get work progress back on track, the floating supervisor decided to check everyone's work status, expedite the jobs, and assign more work. However, this proved more difficult than she had thought that it would be.

Most of the personnel were reluctant to take on new tasks without first sitting down and discussing the current one with the supervisor. Each wanted to be sure that what he or she was doing was correct. Additionally, those who had questions or concerns did not hesitate to come by and ask for assistance. Most would stop what they were working on until they had been assured that they were doing the work right. During the first week with the group, the supervisor found that the backlog of work rose by 2 days. When she checked past work-progress reports, it turned out that ever since the regular supervisor had taken over, the work output in the unit had been the lowest in the organization. The reason it had never become a major problem was that every couple of months the backlog had been cleared simply by dividing it up among other units.

1. If you were the floating supervisor in this department, to what would you attribute the slow work progress? Defend your answer.
2. Of the organizing principles identified in this chapter, which would be of most use in correcting the backlog problem? Identify and describe how four of these principles could be used.
3. Specifically, what needs to be done to correct this situation? Is there anything that you could do immediately? What does the regular supervisor have to do now? Offer at least three recommendations for action.

NOTES

1. C. Edward Kur, "Making Matrix Management Work," *Supervisory Management*, March 1982, pp. 37–43.
2. For more on this subject, see: Henry A. Tombari, "Making Your Meetings Count," *Supervisory Management*, July 1979, pp. 35–39.
3. Don Caruth and Trezzie A. Pressley, "Key Factors in Positive Delegation," *Supervisory Management*, July 1984, pp. 6–11.
4. A. T. Hollingsworth and Abdul Rahman A. Al-Jafray, "Why Supervisors Don't Delegate and Employees Won't Accept Responsibility," *Supervisory Management*, April 1983, pp. 12–17.
5. James Evered, "How to Write a Good Job Description," *Supervisory Management*, April 1981, pp. 14–19.
6. Ann Coil, "Job Matching Brings Out the Best in Employees," *Personnel Journal*, January 1984, pp. 54–60.
7. Marion E. Haynes, "Delegation: There's More To It Than Letting Someone Else Do It," *Supervisory Management*, January 1980, pp. 9–15.

CHAPTER 5

MANAGING CONFLICT AND CHANGE

**GOALS OF
THE CHAPTER**

Conflict in modern organizations is inevitable. So is change. The supervisor cannot prevent these occurrences—but can learn to manage them constructively. The overriding goal of this chapter is to examine what conflict and change are all about and to discuss ways of dealing with them to the benefit of the organization and the personnel. When you have finished reading all the material in this chapter, you will be able to:

1. Define the term *conflict* and discuss how the management of organizational climate can help the supervisor uncover brewing conflict.
2. Describe how organizational climate can be measured.
3. Compare and contrast work-unit-level conflict with organizational-level conflict.
4. Explain how the supervisor can constructively manage conflict.
5. Define the term *change* and describe how the change process works.
6. Discuss some of the most common responses to change and the reasons for resistance.
7. Explain how the supervisor should go about managing change.

A STARTING CASE: BUSINESS AS USUAL?

The secretarial pool at Beller & Company consists of 50 typists and other support people. Up until a few months ago, the company had relied heavily on electronic typewriters, dictating machines, photocopying equipment, and other noncomputer-based technology. Management then decided to switch over to microcomputers and word processing equipment. "We can get 30 percent more work done with the same number of people," the head of administrative services told Jane Geblen, senior supervisor of the secretarial pool. "We'd be foolish not to do it."

The two managers talked about the change for over an hour. They agreed to bring in salespeople from three of the largest office computer firms both to examine their operations and to submit proposals for computerizing operations.

Over the next month, representatives from the computer firms came by to look at the equipment in the secretarial pool, study the flow of work, and make recommendations regarding how to improve efficiency through computerization. In the process, the representatives interviewed a number of secretaries regarding their work assignments and how they handled day-to-day operations. The workers' interests were aroused by the visitors and they began to ask Jane what was going on. However, she remained tight-lipped, saying only that "We're looking into ways of making your work easier to perform." This explanation was not well accepted by the secretaries, and the informal network began to hum with information. The most accepted rumor was that management intended to computerize operations and cut the secretarial pool by half. The monies for the new equipment would be saved through the personnel cutback.

Jane heard these rumors, especially the one about the cutbacks. She told the person who shared the latter rumor with her that it was not true. "There is going to be no reduction in personnel in this department," she said. However, she refused to elaborate or to explain why the computer company representatives had been coming to the firm.

Two weeks ago the computer firms submitted their proposals, and one of them was chosen to implement its plan. The new machinery will be installed next week. In the interim, Jane thought it would be a good idea to call together her people and tell them what was going to happen. The meeting was held earlier today and it did not go well.

After Jane told her workers about the decision to bring in microcomputers and other state-of-the-art word processing technology, she was inundated with questions regarding work changes, layoffs, and firings. No one seemed willing to believe that it was going to be business as usual. When the meeting ended, Jane went to talk to her boss. He told her, "I think you'd better schedule another meeting with your people. This computerization decision may require more selling on your part than we initially thought."

What went wrong? Why are Jane's people upset? How could she have prevented this? What should she do now? Write down your answers. We will return to them at the end of the chapter.

THE NATURE OF CONFLICT

Conflict is a condition that occurs whenever the goals, methods, or objectives of two or more parties are in opposition. The more serious the opposition, the greater the conflict. Many years ago, supervisors believed that all conflict was bad and should be eliminated. Today this view has changed. It is now realized that if managed properly and kept within bounds, conflict can be helpful to the organization. One of the biggest problems for the supervisor is learning to recognize the symptoms of conflict. Quite often the manager does not know there is a conflict brewing until it breaks out. Some organizations try to get a reading of this psychological state of the organization by monitoring its organizational climate.

Organizational climate

There are many types of organizational climate, depending on one's place in the hierarchy. Climate tends to be affected by what goes on at the top of the structure. If things are run smoothly, if there is a general concern for the people, if trust and communication are high, and if the personnel feel that the enterprise is a good place to work, the climate at the upper and middle levels will be good. In turn, this will affect the way the people farther down the line are treated and how they feel about the organization.

In specific terms, *organizational climate* refers to a set of work-environment properties which are perceived by individuals who work there and which serve as a major force in influencing job behavior. These properties include leadership style, organizational structure, job descriptions, performance standards, rewards, work values, and supportiveness.[1] These properties, in turn, affect worker production, efficiency, and satisfaction. For example, consider a company into which a new supervisor has been brought to replace a retiring one. The new supervisor is a hard-nosed individual, which is in sharp contrast to the previous supervisor, who was a flexible leader. The new supervisor is changing the organizational climate, and the result will soon be felt on the bottom line. The personnel are unaccustomed to this type of leadership, and their trust, willingness to work hard, and generally positive attitudes are going to decline. This will eventually result in a drop in work output.

The organizational iceberg. A change in organizational climate is not easily seen. Even those who are directly affected may not notice it at first. In the above example, the personnel may feel a little uneasy with the new manager. They may even bristle when treated as lazy or unwilling to assume responsibility. Yet they may not feel their attitudes changing or their hostility toward the new supervisor beginning to grow. This may take a month or two. So even the new supervisor's boss may be unaware of brewing conflict, for although some aspects of organizational life are easily seen, others are not readily observable.

The aspects easily seen include such things as financial resources, the goals of the enterprise, the skills and abilities of the personnel, performance standards, and overall output. The financial resources are evident to anyone who examines the company's books; the goals are written out in black and white; the skills and abilities of the personnel can be observed by watching them carry out their jobs; performance standards have been written out for each job; output is measured and, in all likelihood, recorded on a daily basis.

The aspects not readily observable include such things as the attitudes, feelings, values, norms, supportiveness, and satisfaction of the workers. These things can be measured only indirectly. The supervisor cannot see a worker's attitude change but can infer that the attitude has changed based on the individual's behavior. If the worker used to be happy and cheerful and is now sullen and angry, the manager can conclude that attitude has changed. Likewise, if the person used to be the highest producer in the department and now turns out only an average amount of work, his or her work values have undoubtedly changed.

Figure 5-1. The organizational iceberg.

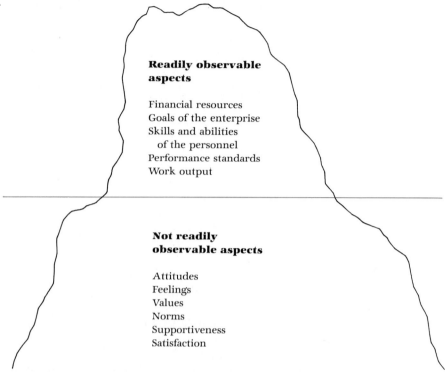

Readily observable aspects

Financial resources
Goals of the enterprise
Skills and abilities
   of the personnel
Performance standards
Work output

Not readily observable aspects

Attitudes
Feelings
Values
Norms
Supportiveness
Satisfaction

The difference between the seen and unseen aspects can be likened to an iceberg (see Figure 5-1). That part of the iceberg which is above water can be seen; that part below the water cannot be seen. The latter often provides insights regarding conflicts that exist either between the workers and the supervisor or between the workers themselves.

Measuring organizational climate. One way of identifying brewing conflict is by measuring the organizational climate periodically and comparing the results. This can be done in a number of ways. One is through the use of structured survey instruments in which the workers are asked to evaluate climate-related factors. Figure 5-2 provides an example. The figure represents only a small number of questions that might be asked (given the wide scope of its inquiry, note that no subheadings divide the questions into categories); in many surveys the workers are given a series of questions in areas such as leadership motivation, communication, decision making, goal setting, and control.[2] The responses are tabulated for each work group. The supervisor can learn how things are going in the work unit simply by comparing past profiles with the current one. For example, if in the previous three surveys all of the responses fell in category III and this time most responses are in category II, it indicates that things are changing for the worse. Notice how such a response would indicate that the workers were

	I	II	III	IV
How often does your supervisor communicate with you?	Never	Seldom	Often	All the time
How often is your supervisor available to answer questions and provide needed direction?	Never	Seldom	Often	All the time
How much trust does your boss have in you?	None	A little bit	Some	A lot
How often does your boss involve you in decisions that directly affect your work?	Never	Once in a while	Usually	Always
Does your supervisor tell you in advance about work-related changes?	Never	Occasionally	Usually	Always
How much confidence does your boss have in you?	None	A little bit	Some	A lot
How much authority do you have to carry out your job-related tasks?	Very little	Some	A lot	Total
How does your supervisor attempt to motivate you?	Fear and threats	Fear, threats, and sometimes rewards	Rewards and sometimes involvement in decision making	Rewards and involvement in decision making
What is the usual flow of job-related information in your work unit?	Down only	Down and sometimes up	Up and down	Every which way
How much close control does your boss exercise over you?	A great deal	Quite a bit	Some	Not very much

Figure 5-2. Measuring organization climate: an evaluation instrument (partial form).

feeling less confidence, trust, and supportiveness in the supervisor. Conversely, if the latest findings were all, on average, in category IV, this would indicate that things were being perceived as better than ever.

Attitude surveys are very useful in helping management get beneath the surface of organizational activity and find out what is really going on. If this can be done, conflict can be minimized or properly managed.

Types of conflict   Conflict can emerge in many different areas. The two that are of most importance to the supervisor are conflict in the individual work unit and conflict in the organization at large.

Work-unit-level conflict. The most common types of conflict with which the supervisor must deal occur at the work-unit level. The following examines three of the most likely.

FRUSTRATION. *Frustration* is the unpleasant feeling that occurs whenever someone is prevented from reaching a desired goal.[3] A typical example occurs when a supervisor can give the highest evaluation in the work unit to only one person because the performance evaluation system requires that the workers be ranked from first to last in terms of overall contribution. There can be no ties. In this case, if more than one person wants to get the highest evaluation in the unit, there is likely to be frustration.

Individuals deal with frustration in a number of ways. Some people use *withdrawal,* as in the case of a worker who goes off in the corner and sulks. Some use *aggression,* as in the case of the person who calls the decision stupid or confronts the supervisor with the decision and voices displeasure in a loud, angry tone. Others use *compromise,* in which case they try to find intrinsic satisfaction in the job and not let the evaluation ranking get them down. Whenever there is a situation in which one person can succeed only at the expense of others, frustration is probable.

GOAL CONFLICT. *Goal conflict* occurs whenever an individual has to choose between two goals. Sometimes these goals are both attractive, sometimes they are both unattractive, and other times their attractiveness changes.[4]

One form of goal conflict is known as *approach-approach conflict.* This takes place when a worker has to choose between two mutually exclusive, equally desirable goals. For example, because of new territory assignments, Bill can have either the northeast or southwest territories of the country. Both promise to be lucrative and he is hard-pressed to choose between them.

A second form of goal conflict is *avoidance-avoidance conflict.* This occurs whenever a worker is forced to choose between two mutually exclusive, equally unattractive goals. For example, Mary must decide whether to do her tour of field duty in the Atlanta or the Dallas office. Either choice means that she will be away from her family for 3 weeks. This type of conflict often requires the individual to choose the lesser of two evils.

A third form of goal conflict is *approach-avoidance conflict.* This is the most common type of goal conflict. In this type of conflict a worker begins to have second thoughts as he or she nears the attainment of the objective. For example, for a long time Carla has been working to obtain a promotion to the home office. When she learns that her promotion has gone through, she is elated. However, as the day for her to move to the home office draws closer, she begins wondering whether she made the right decision. Perhaps she should have stayed in the branch office, where she knows everyone and things are much less hectic. Perhaps she will not work out well in the home office and her career will be sidetracked. Perhaps she has made a mistake in pursuing the promotion. These types of doubt are common whenever one is moving into a new job or assuming different responsibilities.

ROLE CONFLICT. Role conflict is another major type of work-related conflict. *Role conflict* occurs whenever a person tries to undertake two or more mutually exclusive roles. For example, a supervisor has learned that in order to be effective in the organization, two things must be done: (1) Get higher output from the work unit than any other supervisor and (2) get along well with upper-level management. The supervisor has learned that his particular work group responds best to participative management; he always gets his workers involved in decision making and tries to make each feel that each is an integral part of the team. Earlier this week the supervisor received a memo from his boss saying that from now on anyone who breaks safety rule violations is to be reported and a formal letter of reprimand is to be placed in the individual's personnel file. Most of the safety rules are unnecessary, and the supervisor has found that his people work faster if these rules are not enforced. In fact, one of the things they like best about him is his willingness to overlook these types of violations. They feel that it differentiates him from all of the other supervisors, who are always doing things by the book. In this case, the supervisor has a role conflict. He cannot enforce the safety rules and continue to maintain his image with the workers.

This type of conflict helps explain why the supervisor is sometimes known as "the man in the middle." He or she must keep both the workers and the management content; and each wants to think of the individual as a member of his or her team. Workers who are expected to adhere to group norms while simultaneously receiving pressure from management to increase their output also have role conflict problems. It is a common phenomenon at the supervisor-worker level.

Organization-level conflict. Supervisors also face conflict at the organizational level. This takes two forms: institutionalized and emergent.

INSTITUTIONALIZED CONFLICT. *Institutionalized conflict* is built into the organization. There are various ways in which this typically occurs. One of the most common is through departmentalization, in which the enterprise groups its personnel into major departments, such as production, marketing, and finance. When people are assigned to a particular department, it is common for them to become more concerned with the overall good of this group than that of the organization at large. At budget time, for example, the production people request more machinery, the marketing people ask for more money for advertising and salespeople, and the finance people urge fiscal conservativeness. Each group or department seeks its own ends over those of the other groups. Since these conflicts result in winners and losers, one or more groups always end up feeling hurt.

Another type of institutionalized conflict emerges because of the organization's hierarchy. Those at the top of the structure are most concerned with strategic planning; they have long-range interests and are most concerned with what is going to happen over the next 1 to 3 years. Those in the middle are concerned with intermediate- range planning; they are most concerned with what is going to happen over the next 6 to 12 months. Those at the supervisory level are most concerned with short-range objectives; they are most concerned with what is going to happen over the next 6 months. When top managers talk about the future, many supervisors could care less. When supervisors talk about problems on the production floor, top managers feel that they are failing to see the forest for the trees. Each group—top, middle, and lower—is looking at things from its own point of view. As a result, there is often conflict between them because each feels that the others fail to appreciate its particular point of view.

A third type of institutionalized conflict is the all too common one between the line and staff people. The line people, who are in direct control of operations, have an approach that is often quite different from that of the staff people, who provide advice and assistance. For example, line people are often action-oriented; they want to get things done right away. Staff people want to study the problem in depth before making any recommendations. Line people tend to be highly intuitive; they do what they feel is best. Staff people are highly analytical; they examine things very carefully before deciding on a course of action. Line people tend to be shortsighted; staff people tend to be too long-range in orientation. Line people want simple, easy-to-use solutions; staff people like complicated solutions that take every facet of the problem into consideration. Line people are accustomed to examining some of the available alternatives and choosing one of them to solve the problem; staff people are interested in examining many available alternatives and choosing the best one without regard to time and/ or cost restraints. Line people are highly protective of the organization; staff people tend to be very critical of the organization. These are only generalized statements, but there is a good deal of truth in them. Most supervisors are line people and it is common for them to have running conflicts with staff personnel. They do not trust the latter; they feel that the latter make unrealistic recommendations; they resent the fact that staff people can give suggestions but not have to assume the responsibility if these suggestions prove to be wrong.

EMERGENT CONFLICT. *Emergent conflict* arises from personal and social causes. The supervisor must deal with a number of types of emergent conflict. One of the most common is the conflict between the formal and informal organizations. This arises any time the goals of these two groups are incompatible. A typical example is when the work output levels of the formal organization are higher than those of the informal organization.

A second form of emergent conflict is a result of *status incongruency,* which occurs whenever people have greater or lesser status than their formal position dictates. For example, the supervisor who has a smaller office and less support help than all of the other supervisors suffers from a lack of status. There is an incongruency between the amount of status the individual should have and the amount the person does have. Conversely, the machinist who is continually called to the plant superintendent's office to advise the latter on new machinery purchases has more status than the supervisor. This, too, is incongruent because if one were to follow hierarchical lines, the person who advises the plant superintendent should be the supervisor, not the machinist. Any time that one's status is out of line with his or her formal position, status incongruency exists.

Emergent conflict situations are personal and social in nature. They typically involve individual and group norms. Whether or not there is a conflict depends on how the people, themselves, view the situation. An informal organization which feels that management's work quotas are too low may have no trouble accepting them. A supervisor who is oblivious to status symbols may not feel any inconsistency problem if the organization fails to provide a large office and support help.

MANAGING CONFLICT

Some of the types of conflict examined in the previous section cannot be prevented by the supervisor. Nor can the individual always resolve them. They simply must be tolerated. An example is institutionalized conflict; a conflict between line and staff people will exist regardless of how hard the supervisor tries to overcome it. On the other hand, there are some things the supervisor can do to manage conflict regardless of how institutionalized it is. The following discussions examine six of the most effective ways of doing so.

Before reading on, however, take a moment to examine your own conflict management leadership style. How would you go about resolving conflict if you were the supervisor? Self-Assessment Quiz 5-1 provides you some initial insights.

SELF-ASSESSMENT QUIZ 5-1:
YOUR CONFLICT MANAGEMENT LEADERSHIP STYLE

Of the many strategies that can be used in managing conflict, the choice of the best one to use in any situation is obviously going to depend on the situation. However, without going into specifics, think of the basic leadership style that you would normally use in any conflict situation. Then read the strategies below and place a 1 next to the one that best describes your leadership approach to managing conflict; place a 2 next to the strategy that is second most representative of you, and continue on down to a 5 next to the style that is least descriptive of you. Interpretations of this quiz can be found at the end of the chapter.

___2___ I would be most concerned with the people who were being affected by the conflict. I would go out of my way to make sure that they were not hurt. I wouldn't worry much about myself for I'll always get through. It's the others who would have me concerned.

___4___ Conflicts should be avoided, and I would go out of my way to see that they are. I would try to find out what the groups to the conflict want and to see if a compromise could be worked out that would keep everyone at least somewhat happy.

___5___ Conflict is caused by troublemakers, and as the supervisor I would have to put my foot down. I would remind them that I was in charge and would not stand for these types of problems. They would either have to shape up or ship out.

___1___ I would call together those involved in the conflict and, working as a team, try to solve the situation. I would confront the problem directly and work with the personnel until the conflict was satisfactorily resolved.

___3___ I would not do anything about the problem because there is always going to be conflict in the organization. The best approach is to avoid direct contact; let the participants work it out for themselves.

Use direct constructive confrontation

Sometimes direct constructive confrontation is best. This is particularly true when there are opposing parties with which the supervisor must deal. The issue cannot be ducked. It must be met head on. There are a number of important things that the supervisor must remember about direct confrontations. Some of these are spelled out in Supervision in Action: Constructive Confrontation.

SUPERVISION IN ACTION: CONSTRUCTIVE CONFRONTATION

Conflicts over performance and other job-related issues are inevitable, even natural, between manager and employee, but far too many supervisors and foremen lack the ability to deal with such disagreements constructively.

If a dog doesn't like you, it looks at you and growls. Not so with people.

When we become irritated with another's actions, we are not always willing to express our discontent. Instead, we tend to keep our feelings inside and avoid the person with whom there is a problem. In doing so, the severity of the problem is compounded.

Some people have an actual phobia about confrontation—a fear of turning friendships into hardships or rapport into rancor.

Rather than waste energy eluding an unpleasant situation (and it takes a tremendous amount of energy to do so), today's managers must be able directly to confront the individual who is the source of a problem. They must learn a much-neglected skill that we call constructive confrontation.

What are the causes of this fear of confrontation, how can we overcome these fears, and what traps should we avoid in the process?

The monster: fear

Fear of confrontation stems primarily from ineptitude; that is, the lack of knowledge or skills in dealing with the confrontation. We worry that any misdirected or poorly focused actions we take in confronting an individual will only serve to worsen the undesirable situation. Lacking confrontation skills, we fear that our ignorance might result in the loss of a good employee or friend. In addition, we foresee the advent of possible retaliation or revenge.

Here are some practical strategies that will curtail our fears and help us take a constructive approach to confrontation. These guidelines will be especially useful to supervisors or foremen in dealing with performance and discipline problems.

- Be well prepared. Use specifics when discussing the situation. Know exactly what the problem involves, and be able to state it clearly.
- Get to the point immediately. Voice your intentions directly without making the confrontee play guessing games.
- Don't be subjective. Remain as objective as possible in evaluating the situation. Try to understand why the person behaves a certain way. Don't say, "You're irresponsible." The person will feel personally attacked. Give a sound reason for your objection to his or her behavior. Show how the behavior affects you. "I get angry with you when you're late because I feel you've let me down." The person will empathize with your feelings even though he or she may not fully comprehend the cause.
- Don't be vague about encouraging alternative conduct. Cite the specific changes you want to see and communicate them clearly. For example: "I would rather you devote your time to completing this project than devoting energies to that one."
- Give sufficient warning. Inform the person of the consequences that may result from the unsuitable behavior. If the annoyance continues, you at least know you have given a word of caution before any drastic action takes place.
- Encourage two-way, open communication. Each party must be able to voice opinions and comprehend what is being said.
- Remember the valuable aspects of your relationship. When two people successfully confront their problems, they can also strengthen their commitment to one another.
- Don't overlook good intentions. At a large manufacturing company, a manager became annoyed over one of the clerk's tardiness in submitting reports. The manager needed the reports to meet his own deadline for a more extensive report to his boss.

    The problem continued for several weeks until a confrontation was unavoidable. Fortunately, the manager had been trained in confrontation skills. He was able to discover that a computer malfunction was causing inaccurate information to be produced as input for the initial report. The clerk was consuming extra time by painstakingly correcting errors.

As a result of the confrontation, the problem was quickly resolved.

What to avoid

Steer clear of the following two pitfalls in confrontation:

- Don't argue. If the other party becomes defensive upon confrontation, don't let yourself get involved in an argument. It only muddles up the major problem and decreases the chances of a positive solution.
- Stick to the issue. Don't let the other person go off on tangential subjects. The problem at hand should be solved before any other matters are introduced.

People don't find it easy to confront others, especially those who are close to them. However, in the long run, a well-planned approach with direct communication will result in a sense of relief and accomplishment.

Source: Roy Trueblood, "The Constructive Approach to Confrontation," *Supervisory Management,* September 1980 © 1980 by AMACOM, a division of American Management Associations, New York. Reprinted by permission of the publisher; all rights reserved.

Identify hidden agendas

Quite often, as seen in Figure 5-1, conflict has both an identifiable and a hidden side. The hidden side sometimes contains agendas that must be brought out into the open. For example, work groups A and B may be in conflict with each other because, in the words of group A, group B is sending it too many units that need reworking. "We have so much reworking to do that we are falling behind in forwarding these units to the packing group," the spokesperson for group A explains. In truth, group B may be angry that group A averaged 3 percent more in raises than group B did. Group B feels that it is not being rewarded fairly and is striking out as best it can. These hidden agendas tell the real story behind the conflict, and to the extent possible, the supervisor must be prepared to discuss the problems of the two groups to the point of identifying these agendas and getting them out on the table.

Minimize status differences

Differences between people or groups can be worked out more effectively if both are placed on the same footing. This means minimizing differences in *status,* which is the relative rank that one person has in relation to another. For example, if the supervisor has a problem with one of the workers and wants to talk it out, the supervisor's office is not a good choice of location. In this setting the supervisor has more status than the worker. By choosing a neutral area where both can talk as equals, these status differences are minimized.

In the case of subordinates who have problems, the supervisor often faces the same type of situation. If one of the workers is the shop steward and the other is a regular line worker, the latter may feel that the steward will use his or her union affiliation to gain power or status. The supervisor can minimize this by forcing both people to stick to the problem at hand and refusing to acknowledge any differences between the two.

Focus on issues, not blame

In most conflict situations each party attempts to blame the other for what has happened. "He is supposed to provide us with new materials twice a day," argues one of the workers, "but he only brings them around in the midmorning. Half the time we have to stop working to wait on him." The other counters by saying: "My job is to make sure that everyone has materials. But if people run out of materials, they're supposed to page me and let me know, not sit down and wait for me to make the rounds back to their work station. Anyone who calls me gets additional materials within 15 minutes. They enjoy finishing their work and then sitting down and waiting for me to come by. It gives them a break and a chance to put the blame on me." Quite obviously each side feels that the other is wrong. However, the issue is not who is wrong but what to do about it. The supervisor should focus on the problem and how to resolve it. If someone has deliberately done something wrong, that can be taken care of later on. Additionally, it does the supervisor no good to comment on who is right or wrong because this ends up with the individual choosing sides and alienating one of the parties.

Focus on mutual agreement and benefits

Once the problem has been identified, the supervisor should work to get both parties to agree on how it can be prevented in the future. This is called *co-opting*, which involves making the participants to the conflict parties to its solution. For example, after listening to both sides the supervisor may try to co-opt them by saying: "Well, it seems that the problem is more a matter of work procedures than anything else. I think we need to change these procedures to ensure that no group ever runs out of inventory again. Jack, I'd like your group to place a call to Neil when you're down to your last 15 minutes of inventory. This will give him time to get more materials to you. And Neil, I'd like you to agree that from the time you get a call from Jack's group, you'll be at their work station within 15 minutes with more materials. What do you say, fellas? Can I rely on you to help work on this problem?" Notice how the supervisor worked to get both parties to the conflict to agree on how they could mutually help out.

After both agree to do their part, the supervisor can then close by noting how much their cooperation is appreciated and noting that this will be remembered when their next performance evaluations are filled out. In this way the supervisor focuses on the benefits available to those who pitch in and help out.

Sometimes time delays are important

The above tips were all directed toward helping the supervisor quickly resolve conflict problems. However, sometimes the issue is much more serious than just one or two work groups that cannot get along. If the matter is extremely critical, the supervisor may need to have two or three meetings with the groups and may also need to check with his or her boss in deciding what to do. Additionally, even if one solution does seem to be the best, the supervisor is wise to give it some thought before setting it forth. This is particularly true when one of the parties offers the solution. "Boss," someone may say, "if we get Harry to take over the lathe machine and Jean becomes responsible for the quality control part of the job, this would solve all of our problems." At first blush this may indeed appear to be the answer to the problem. However, if there is a great deal at stake, the supervisor should delay giving an OK. There may be something wrong with the solution, and the supervisor may thus have to back off from the implementation later on. Sometimes quick action is not the best means of resolving the conflict.

THE NATURE OF CHANGE

Change is any modification or alteration of the status quo.[5] Sometimes change is a good idea; other times it turns out to be a mistake. In either event, the process itself always remains the same.

The change process

In the change process three things happen: (1) There is change in the status quo, or the way things exist currently; (2) some force(s) cause(s) the change to come about; and (3) as a result of these forces, a new status quo results. This change process can be best illustrated through *force-field analysis*, a technique used to analyze a change situation. Figure 5-3 provides an illustration.

Figure 5-3*a* depicts the current status quo and the forces pushing for and against changing this current status. The forces on each side are equal in strength and so there will be no change for the time being. In order for change to occur, (1) the forces in favor of the change have to be strengthened over what they are in Figure 5-3*a*, (2) the forces in favor of maintaining the status quo have to be weakened over what they are in Figure 5-3*a*, or (3) some combination of these first two events must take place. Figure 5-3*b* illustrates what happens when the forces favoring the change gain strength; Figure 5-3*c* illustrates what happens when the forces opposing the change lose strength. In practice, some combination of both of these latter figures usually occurs.

Any change the supervisor attempts to bring about can be illustrated using the above figures. For example, consider the case of a firm that is installing new computer equipment in order to increase efficiency. The forces pushing for the change could be that (1) the change will make our work easier, (2) the change will ensure our ability to keep up with the

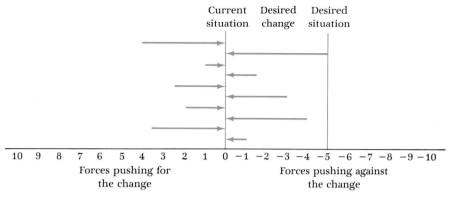

(a) Current versus desired situations

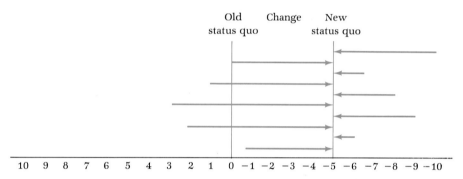

(b) Change brought about by an increase in factors pushing for change

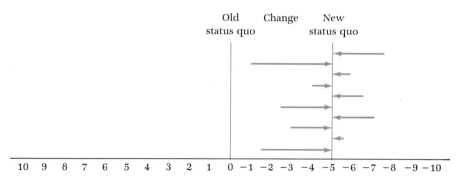

(c) Change brought about by a decrease in factors pushing against the change

Figure 5-3. Force-field change analyses. (a) Current versus desired situations; (b) change brought about by an increase in factors pushing for change; (c) change brought about by a decrease in factors pushing against the change (partial form).

competition, and (3) computers will result in increased profits and we will all stand to benefit as a result. The forces pushing against change could be that (1) the machines will replace some of us, (2) management will change the work rules and make us all do more work, and (3) it will take a lot of effort to master computerized operations. Each force will have a particular strength, and depending on which set of forces is stronger, either the change will be accepted or there will be strong resistance.

RESPONSE TO CHANGE

Workers have many different responses to change. Before examining these, however, test your knowledge about the change process by taking Self-Assessment Quiz 5-2.

SELF-ASSESSMENT QUIZ 5-2:
WHAT DO YOU KNOW ABOUT THE CHANGE PROCESS?

Carefully read each of the following statements and then check whether each is basically true or basically false. Answers are provided at the end of the chapter.

	Basically true	*Basically false*
1. Most employees do not like change; it tends to scare them.	✕	
2. Most work changes bring about immediate increases in productivity.		✕
3. Most supervisors are delighted with newly announced organizational changes.		✕
4. Unions tend to resist new work changes.	✕	
5. Most organizational changes are designed to increase efficiency.	✕	
6. A manager with a get-tough approach usually attains faster results than does a manager with a participative approach.	✕	
7. Most workers enjoy resisting change and giving the organization a hard time.		✕
8. People like advance notice about change; they do not want it sprung on them.	✕	
9. Over the long run, get-tough managers have better results than do participative managers.		✕

10. The computer has been responsible for massive unemployment in industry.   _____   ___✓___

11. If their coworkers oppose a change, most workers will also oppose it.   ___✗___   _____

12. Most workers either outrightly reject or accept change.   _____   ___✗___

13. One major reason for resistance to change is the fear of losing one's job.   ___✗___   _____

14. Worker participation in the change process often reduces employee opposition to change.   ___✗___   _____

15. Most supervisors overrate the amount of time needed to implement change effectively.   _____   ___✗___

Rejection

Rejection takes place when a change is seen as potentially destructive and the workers refuse to go along with it. This is one of the most serious responses to change and is usually confined to those matters which the workers see as job-threatening. For example, if a company decides to computerize operations and knock out 20 percent of the work force, the remainder might well use rejection in the form of absenteeism or turnover. Unions often use rejection in the form of a strike or walkout to oppose such things as threats to seniority rights or the failure of management to meet their bargaining demands for what are considered minimum wage-and-benefit concessions.

Resistance

Resistance is used when workers feel threatened by a change or are extremely anxious regarding its impact on them. In contrast to rejection, with resistance the workers do not leave the job; they stay and fight it in the workplace. In the extreme, it can manifest itself in outright sabotage of equipment. More commonly, however, it takes the form of lower work output. Sometimes it even takes the form of feigned acceptance of the change. For example, under the guise of helping management implement the change, the workers go out of their way to make the implementation as difficult as possible. Data are misfiled, materials are misplaced, machines are run at improper speeds, etc. The workers do not reject management's efforts to implement the change; they simply resist by making it difficult for the change to come about.

Tolerance

When workers are neutral about a change or have equal positive and negative feelings, they tend to *tolerate* the change. This is the most likely response to change in a healthy organizational environment. The workers do not particularly like the change, but they are not prepared to resist either. They feel that the management basically looks after their interests and treats them well, and they are willing to go along with the change.

Tolerance is particularly evident when the change does not threaten the workers in any way. For example, if management insists that in the future all workers wear safety equipment while in a particular area of the factory and that they refrain from smoking during this time, it is unlikely that anyone is going to oppose management's directive.

Acceptance

When the forces favoring a change are much stronger than those opposing it, the workers tend to *accept* the change. For example, when management installs new safety equipment that makes jobs easier and safer to carry out, workers tend to accept these changes with no trouble at all. Anytime the workers can see that they stand to benefit from the change, acceptance becomes a common form of response.

REASONS FOR RESISTANCE TO CHANGE

There are many reasons for resistance to change. In most cases it is a result of conscious thought. Workers examine the value of the change for them and then make a decision. In most cases they either resist or tolerate the change. Outright rejection or acceptance are uncommon. The following examines some of the most typical reasons for resistance.

Fear of economic loss

Sometimes change results in the worker's job skills becoming obsolete. For example, if a company decides to introduce computers, those individuals who were performing these tasks by hand or with semiautomatic equipment may now be replaced. Of course, this may not be true at all. The firm may intend to use them in conjunction with the computer. However, the workers are likely to believe the worst and fight the implementation in an effort to keep their jobs.

Changes in the status quo

Even if changes do not result in any loss of income, they often require workers to do things a different way. The individuals have to adjust to the new technology. This means learning new work procedures, rules, techniques, etc. For the first couple of months, the work may be unpleasant as the personnel seek to master their jobs. Even when change is helpful, it is not uncommon to find people fighting it because the changes mean having to give up old routines and comfortable ways of doing things.

Lack of information

Many times people fight change because they do not fully understand how it will affect them. They are not provided with sufficient information regarding how, when, where, and why the change is being implemented. There is an important rule in the introduction of change: The greater the impact of the change on personnel, the more advance notice and information the supervisor should provide about the change. When workers are kept in the dark, they tend to resist the change if for no other reason than: "If the change were good for us, management would already have told us about it. The reason they are delaying doing so is because some of us are going to be let go or shipped off to other departments." When there is a lack of information, the informal network carries rumors that fill in the gaps and explain what management is up to. Many times these rumors are false. However, the workers believe them because there is no information to the contrary.

Group pressure

If a group is highly cohesive, the members will act in unison. When changes are introduced, if the group feels threatened it has a reason for sticking together. Cohesion now increases, and even those who believe the change may be helpful feel the pressure to conform, and they do. Peer pressure serves to keep everyone in line, united against the change.

Shortsightedness

Many people look at change from a short-run view. They ask themselves, what impact will this change have on me over the next 1 or 2 months? They do not consider the effect over the next 6 to 12 months. The supervisor may try to explain to them that things will be hectic for a while but will then straighten out and the work will be a lot easier to perform given the new work changes. However, the personnel do not hear the last part of this statement. They only listen to the part that says things will be hectic.

MANAGING CHANGE

Change does not have to result in chaos or friction among the employees. If managed properly, workers will not only tolerate change but will sometimes accept it. In managing this process, the supervisor must realize that change involves four steps. These should be carried out sequentially as each builds on the previous one.

Define the change

The first step in managing change is to define it: What is the change going to involve? There are two important groups to be considered in this process: the supervisor and the workers. The supervisor needs to understand the change thoroughly before attempting to introduce it. If the change involves new technology, the supervisor must be aware of such things as how the equipment will be used, what type of worker retraining will be involved, who will have to be transferred to other work units, and what impact the change is likely to have on the current work group. In defining the change this way, the supervisor begins piecing together any domino effect that may occur. For example, if the transfer of workers to other units will break up a highly efficient work group, will the new technology offset this loss of morale and teamwork?

Identify the situational factors

The next step is to translate the answers to the above questions into situational factors: Will there be resistance to the change? Who is likely to be most resistant? What types of approaches should be used in meeting this resistance? How much advance notice should be given about the change?

Answers to these questions help the supervisor identify those areas that must be incorporated into the general change strategy. They force the supervisor to confront the major stumbling blocks that will have to be surmounted in successfully implementing the change.

Develop a change strategy

This is the most difficult and comprehensive step of all. The supervisor must now determine how to handle the change. There are many ways of doing this, depending on how much worker involvement is best. Supervision in Action: Formulating the Most Effective Change Strategy explains some of the major steps that are often taken at this point.

SUPERVISION IN ACTION: FORMULATING THE MOST EFFECTIVE CHANGE STRATEGY

Develop a change strategy. Once the supports and blockages to change are identified, a change strategy can be developed. Understanding the overall process of change can help here.

Three distinct stages are involved in any change program—unfreezing, thawing, and refreezing. Before a change is introduced, a specific status quo exists; people have preconditioned attitudes and behavior patterns. The unfreezing stage requires that the old patterns be "thawed out" and replaced by a desire for new behaviors. The introduction of the change attempts to shift the status quo by actually teaching employees new behaviors. To avoid returning to the old status quo, the refreezing stage "firms up" the new attitudes and behaviors so that the change is firmly in place.

A change strategy attempts to exploit positive factors and neutralize negative ones. In other words, the change process is facilitated more by removing or neutralizing the forces that resist change than by increasing the pressures to bring about the change. . . .

A supervisor has many strategies for change implementation at his or her disposal, each with advantages and drawbacks. Depending on the strategy chosen, a supervisor exerts different degrees of pressure to get his employees to accept change.

- *Give explanations.* A supervisor explains the change—what it is, why it is worthwhile, and how it will affect subordinates. Employees often resist change because they fear the unknown. They lack information or have inaccurate information. Supplying the facts enables them to evaluate how the proposed change will affect their own situation. This approach takes time and effort but reduces misunderstanding. With in-depth knowledge about the change, subordinates are less likely to exhibit blind resistance.

- *Allow participation.* Another strategy for bringing about change is to permit those affected by it to participate in the decisions involved in the change. This strategy is especially appropriate when subordinates possess relevant information or have considerable power to resist the change. When subordinates are involved in the change process, they tend to be more committed to the outcome. This approach does have its drawbacks because involvement is time-consuming and may not lead to the best solution.

- *Provide support.* Sometimes all that subordinates need to accept a change is their supervisor's support. Support may be in the form of training assistance, an open ear, or reassurance. Facilitative strategies are particularly appropriate when fear and anxiety are at the heart of the resistance. Training subordinates to perform jobs required by a change reduces anxiety and increases confidence in their ability to implement the change. These strategies are also useful when subordinates recognize that they have a problem and are willing to accept help in adjusting to the change. Supportive strategies are not very effective when the resistance to change is great. Subordinates must be open to change and be willing to accept help to achieve it. This support may be costly from the viewpoint of a supervisor's time.

- *Use persuasion.* Persuasive strategies attempt to create change by reasoning, urging, and inducements. The message may be presented in a biased manner in order to sway opinion. Such strategies are desirable when subordinates lack commitment or are highly resistant to change, when the magnitude of change is great, and when the use of power is inappropriate. Providing rewards or inducements to subordinates to accept the change may also reduce their resistance. Persuasive strategies have the additional benefit of being relatively quick.

- *Apply power.* Unlike persuasion, power strategies involve some type of coercion, manipulation, or threat to gain compliance. Power strategies are used when speed is essential and when employees show a low need for change. To use power, a supervisor must first possess it. The costs to the user may be high if subordinates retaliate through such means as a work slowdown.

Supervisors should remember that different situations require different change strategies. A common mistake is to use only one or a few strategies regardless of the situation. Managing change requires flexibility. No strategy is best all the time.

Source: H. Kent Baker and Stevan Holmberg, "Stepping Up to Supervision: Coping with Change," *Supervisory Management*, March 1982, pp. 24–26. ©1982 by AMACOM, a division of American Management Associations, New York. Reprinted by permission of the publisher; all rights reserved.

Implement and monitor the change

The last step in the change process is to implement the strategy and then follow up to be sure that everything is going according to plan. No matter how well thought out a change strategy is, something usually goes wrong. For example, subordinates who appeared very positive about the change suddenly begin having second thoughts; machinery that was supposed to be easy to use turns out to be extremely complex to master, and work output begins to fall off precipitously; people who were supposed to be transferred to another department find that they are temporarily laid off because the other department cannot hire them until the beginning of the new fiscal year in 3 weeks. The supervisor has to expect these types of problems. The important thing is that they not be allowed to upset the implementation of the change. While working to straighten them out and get everything back on an even keel, the supervisor must keep his or her eye on the changes that have been introduced and ensure that they are kept in place. If the supervisor fails to manage the change, all previous efforts will prove to be fruitless.

BUSINESS AS USUAL?: STARTING CASE REVISITED

Having read the chapter, you are now aware of some of the important steps that should be followed in implementing change. One is the need for advance notice regarding what is to happen. Remember the rule mentioned in the chapter: The greater the change, the more the advance notice that should be given.

Why did Jane not tell the workers what was going on? The case never provides an answer. Perhaps she thought the personnel would like it better if they were surprised. Maybe she was unsure of how or when to tell them. Perhaps she was waiting for her boss to tell her that it was OK to pass on the news.

In any event, the workers are now upset and Jane has to do something about it. She should begin by fully explaining the types of machines that will be brought in and how they will help the personnel work smarter, not harder. Second, Jane must explain how any work assignments will change and what effect this will have on current work procedures. Finally, she must emphasize that there will be no layoffs or firings and even go to the extent of putting this in writing. The two main reasons for resistance to change in this case are: dislike of the changing status quo and fear of economic loss. Jane must work to counter both of these.

INTERPRETATION OF SELF-ASSESSMENT QUIZ 5-1: YOUR CONFLICT MANAGEMENT LEADERSHIP STYLE

The five choices in this quiz correspond roughly to the five basic leadership styles that most supervisors have. The first conflict style is used by managers who attempt to oblige their people. They are very personnel-oriented. The second style is used by managers who attempt to use compromise to deal with conflict. They try to balance a concern for the personnel with a concern for the work to be done. The third conflict style is used by supervisors who attempt to dominate the problem. They are very work-oriented and want everyone to quit fooling around and get back to work. The fourth conflict style is used by supervisors who attempt to integrate their personnel into the solution of the problem. These managers have a high concern for both the people and the work. The last conflict style is used by supervisors who attempt to avoid the problem altogether. Of course, five sample statements are not enough for you to identify your conflict management style totally. However, this short quiz should give you some insights regarding how you tend to approach conflict management.

INTERPRETATION OF SELF-ASSESSMENT QUIZ 5-2:
WHAT DO YOU KNOW ABOUT THE CHANGE PROCESS?

---

1. Basically true. Most employees like the status quo.
2. Basically false. It requires some time before the impact of most work changes becomes evident.
3. Basically false. Most supervisors, like workers, enjoy the status quo.
4. Basically true. Most unions tend to fight new work changes because they feel that this is an attempt by management to undermine the workers in some way.
5. Basically true. The purpose of most organizational changes is to make things easier and faster to do.
6. Basically true. In the short run most get-tough managers are able to produce better bottom-line results than are their participative management counterparts.
7. Basically false. Most workers have better things to do than to resist change. However, when they feel that they are threatened in some way, they will resist.
8. Basically true. In fact, the greater the change, the more the advance notice that people would like.
9. Basically false. Get-tough managers have good short-run results, but over the long run they tend to have poorer results than do participative managers.
10. Basically false. While computers have accounted for a small amount of unemployment, they have been responsible for the creation of many jobs.
11. Basically true. Most workers will go along with the rest of their work group. Group norms are a powerful force in dictating individual behavior.
12. Basically false. Most workers wait and see what impact the change is going to have on them before deciding what to do. Acceptance or rejection is then a matter of degree.
13. Basically true. This is not the only reason for resistance to change, but it certainly is one of the major ones.
14. Basically true. Getting the personnel involved in the change process is one of the best ways of winning their support for the change.
15. Basically false. Most supervisors underrate the amount of time needed to implement change effectively. It takes longer than they originally thought it would.

**SUMMARY OF
KEY POINTS**

1. Conflict is a condition that occurs whenever the goals, methods, or objectives of two or more parties are in opposition. One way of determining the current state of conflict is by measuring the organizational climate. This can be done with instruments similar to that presented in Figure 5-2.

2. Many types of conflict can emerge in organizations. One is work- unit-level conflict. This can take a number of different forms, including frustration, goal conflict, and role conflict. Another is organization-level conflict. Two of the most common forms of this are institutionalized conflict and emergent conflict.

3. Supervisors need to know a number of things about managing conflict. Six of the most useful are: Use direct constructive confrontation; identify hidden agendas; minimize status differences; focus on issues, not blame; focus on mutual agreement and benefits; and remember that sometimes time delays are important.

4. Change is any modification or alteration of the status quo. When change takes place, the forces pushing for change are greater than those pushing against change, resulting in a new status quo.

5. Workers can have many different responses to change. One is rejection, which takes place when a change is seen as potentially destructive. A second is resistance, which is used when workers feel threatened and/or are extremely anxious regarding the impact of the change on them. A third is tolerance, which occurs when workers are neutral about the change or have equal positive and negative feelings. A fourth is acceptance, which occurs when the forces favoring a change are stronger than those opposing it.

6. There are many reasons for resistance to change. Some of the most common are: fear of economic loss; changes in the status quo; a lack of information; group pressure; and shortsightedness.

7. In managing change, there are four steps the supervisor needs to take. First, the change must be defined. Second, the situational factors must be identified. Third, a change strategy must be developed. Fourth, the change must be implemented and monitored.

**BUILD YOUR
SUPERVISORY
WORD POWER**

These key conflict and change-management terms are presented in their order of appearance in the chapter. Effective supervisors have a working knowledge of them.

Conflict. A condition that occurs whenever the goals, methods, or objectives of two or more parties are in opposition.

Organizational climate. A set of work-environment properties which are perceived by individuals who work there and which serve as a major force in influencing job behavior.

Frustration. The unpleasant feeling that occurs when someone is prevented from reaching a desired goal.

Withdrawal. A frustration reaction in which the person draws away from the source of frustration.

Aggression. A frustration reaction in which the person confronts the source of frustration and often vents his or her anger on it.

Compromise. A frustration reaction in which a person works to find satisfaction in other ways so that the frustration is minimized.

Goal conflict. Conflict that occurs whenever a person has to choose between two goals.

Approach-approach conflict. Conflict that occurs whenever a person has to choose between two mutually exclusive, equally desirable goals.

Avoidance-avoidance conflict. Conflict that occurs whenever a person has to choose between two mutually exclusive, equally unattractive goals.

Approach-avoidance conflict. Conflict that occurs whenever a person begins to have second thoughts as he or she nears the attainment of a particular objective.

Role conflict. Conflict that occurs whenever a person tries to undertake two or more mutually exclusive roles.

Institutionalized conflict. Conflict that is built into the organization; a classic example is that between line and staff people.

Emergent conflict. Conflict that arises from personal and social causes, such as the conflict between the formal and informal organizations and status incongruency.

Status incongruency. Conflict that occurs whenever people have greater or lesser status than their position dictates.

Co-opting. A process of making participants to a conflict parties to its solution.

Change. Any modification or alteration of the status quo.

Force-field analysis. A technique used to analyze a change condition.

Rejection. A response to change, it occurs when workers see the change as potentially destructive and refuse to go along with it.

Resistance. A response to change, it occurs when workers feel threatened and/or extremely anxious regarding its impact on them.

Tolerance. A response to change, it occurs when workers are neutral about a change.

Acceptance. A response to change, it occurs when the workers are in favor of the change.

REVIEW YOUR UNDERSTANDING

1. In your own words, what is meant by the term *conflict?* Is all conflict bad? Explain.
2. What is organizational climate? What are some of the factors that help determine whether a climate is good or bad?
3. An organizational iceberg is made up of two parts: readily observable aspects and not readily observable aspects. What does this statement mean? Be complete in your answer.
4. How can organizational climate be measured? Give an example in your answer.
5. The most common types of conflicts are those which occur at the work-unit level. What are three of these types of conflicts? Identify and describe each.
6. How does organization-level conflict occur? In your answer, give an example of both institutionalized and emergent conflict.
7. How can a supervisor constructively manage conflict? Offer at least four guidelines, being sure to describe how to use each one.
8. What is meant by the term *change?* Describe the process by using a force-field analysis approach.
9. There are four common responses to change. What are they? Identify and describe each.
10. Why do workers resist change? Cite and describe at least four reasons.
11. How can a supervisor effectively manage change? Identify and describe the four steps in the process, being sure to provide sufficient detail in the third step.

SUPPLEMENT YOUR KNOWLEDGE

In addition to the references listed at the end of this chapter, the following provide practical information useful to supervisors in managing conflict and change:

Baetz, Stephen: "I Win—You Win: Negotiating for Commitment," *Personnel Journal,* March 1980, pp. 237–239.

Baker, H. Kent, and Stevan R. Holmberg: "Stepping Up to Supervision: Coping with Change," *Supervisory Management,* March 1982, pp. 21–27.

Berry, Waldron: "Overcoming Resistance to Change," *Supervisory Management,* February 1983, pp. 26–30.

Ford, Jeffrey D.: "The Management of Organizational Crises," *Business Horizons,* May–June 1981, pp. 10–16.

Grove, Andrew S.: "How to Make Confrontation Work for You," *Fortune,* July 23, 1984, pp. 73–75.

Kleiner, Brian H.: "How to Make Conflict Work for You," *Supervisory Management,* September 1978, pp. 2–6.

Labovitz, George H.: "Managing Conflict," *Business Horizons,* June 1980, pp. 30–37.

YOU BE THE SUPERVISOR: FINDING THE RAINCOAT

Things usually run quite smoothly in Terry Anderson's department. However, a problem arose last month between two of his people. One, Sara Gutierrez, is in charge of processing all expense vouchers and seeing that everything is in order before submitting them to central payroll for reimbursement. In accord with company guidelines, Sara has developed a two-page set of procedures that spell out exactly how bills are to be submitted, what types of receipts are required, etc. The other party to the conflict, Randy Dowler, is a salesperson. Randy was sent to London to close a major sale with a new customer there. During the trip it was unseasonably rainy and Randy bought a raincoat. When he submitted his vouchers, there was a bill for $125 for the raincoat.

Sara looked the expenses over and called Randy to tell him that the raincoat was not a reimbursable item. Randy explained that he had bought the raincoat strictly for business reasons and would be happy to turn it over to the company. All he wanted was to be reimbursed. When Sara stood her ground, the conversation grew heated and within a few minutes the two were screaming at each other. Terry came out of his office to ask what the problem was. Five minutes later both Sara and Randy were in the supervisor's office. Terry did not mince words with them. Without letting either of them say a thing, he began to talk: "I don't know what the problem is and I don't want to know. We run a business office around here and I'm not going to be having people yelling and screaming. Now I don't care how you solve the problem, just solve it, and don't let me hear another word about it."

With this, the meeting ended and both left the office. Randy walked over to Sara's desk, removed the receipt for the raincoat from the expense voucher packet, and walked off with it.

Last week Randy returned from a 2-week sales trip to Japan. He had over $13,000 of expenses. Everything was itemized in longhand on three legal-size pages. Sara looked it all over carefully and could find nothing wrong. However, just as she was about to have the voucher typed, she noticed a penciled-in asterisk next to the overall total. She looked farther down the page to see what this asterisk meant. At the bottom of the sheet was another asterisk with a question in Randy's handwriting. It asked, "Can you find the raincoat?"

Sara was extremely angry. She took the vouchers to Terry's office along with Randy's note. "I think something has to be done," she told her boss. "I'm not going to be treated like this." Terry suggested that she knock out $125 of reimbursable expenses, but Sara pointed out that Terry had itemized receipts for the entire amount. "I think we're going to have to have another meeting on this matter," she said. Terry just looked out the window and made no reply. He was unsure of what to do.

1. If you were the supervisor, how would you have handled the initial meeting? What would you have done differently?
2. What type of conflict exists here? Put it in your own words.
3. If you were the supervisor, what would you do now? How would you resolve the conflict? Be complete in your answer.

YOU BE THE SUPERVISOR: PLANNING FOR CHANGE

Hopkins Manufacturing, founded in 1905, is an old-line production firm in the northeast. The current factory was built in 1908. Over the years a number of changes have been made to modernize the building and equipment. However, by the late 1970s management realized that a whole new facility would be needed.

Three years ago the company signed contracts to build the most modern plant in the industry. Now built, the plant has carefully laid-out work stations, computerized material-flow control, equipment designed to make the work easier and faster to complete, more spacious work quarters for getting the work done, a large employee cafeteria, and spacious recreational grounds just outside the plant.

The formal move to the new facilities is scheduled to take place in 1 month. For all practical purposes, the plant could be moved into today, but there are still some minor things that have to be completed.

The company's biggest concern right now is how well the workers will accept the new conditions. According to the 3-year contract hammered out by management and the union last year, the firm has the right to move to the new facilities and require that the employees undertake whatever work changes are necessary to adjust to the line. On paper, management has the right to demand that the workers accept the new conditions and do all that is called for in the contract. In reality, the firm is concerned that there will be a great deal of resistance to these new changes. For this reason it called a meeting of the supervisory staff yesterday. The company would like to have suggestions regarding how the smoothest transition can be made in moving the workers from the old to the new plant. The head of manufacturing put it this way:

> We've operated out of the same facility for over a half century. A lot of our people have been with us for 20 or more years. This new move may be well accepted by a small percentage of the people, but I think we're going to find that most of them are unsure of what we now expect of them. They are going to be confronting new machinery, new work procedures, computerized operations, etc. This is a whole new ball game for most of them. When we talked over the proposed new plant with the union, we were able to sell them on it because we showed how both of us would gain from a modern facility. However, that was only the talking part. Now we have to implement that decision by moving the workers into the new plant and getting them to accept these new conditions.

This may be a lot harder to do than any of you think. While the new plant makes sense from a dollar and cents standpoint, this doesn't mean that it will be quickly accepted by the workers. We need to think of ways of reducing any resistance to this new change and getting the new conditions accepted as soon as possible. Over the next 3 days I want all of you to think of ways that we can do this. We're going to have a meeting again next week, and at that time I'd like to have your ideas.

1. What types of resistance would you expect to the new conditions? Why would there be this resistance? Explain.
2. What types of things could management do to make the transition from the old to the new factory easier? Offer at least three suggestions.
3. If you were a supervisor in this plant, what type of change strategy would you try to implement? Be as complete as possible in your answer.

NOTES

1. For more on this, see: Rensis Likert and Jane Gibson Likert, *New Ways of Managing Conflict*, New York: McGraw-Hill, 1976, p. 76.
2. Likert and Likert, chap. 5.
3. John P. Houston, Helen Bee, and David C. Rimm, *Invitation to Psychology*, 2d ed., New York: Academic Press, 1983, p. 358.
4. For more on this, see: Fred Luthans, *Organizational Behavior*, 3d ed., New York: McGraw-Hill, 1981, pp. 371–374.
5. Richard M. Hodgetts, *Modern Human Relations At Work*, 2d ed., Hinsdale, Ill.: Dryden Press, 1984, p. 392.

PART TWO

SUPERVISING THE PEOPLE

The purpose of this section of the book is to examine the ways in which supervisors directly manage their subordinates. In the main, this involves a study of how supervisors staff their units, train their personnel, and interact with and lead their people. All of this requires a solid understanding of behavior at work.

Chapter 6 addresses the ways in which the staffing and training functions are carried out. The first part of the chapter looks at the ways in which personnel recruitment and selection are handled. Attention also is focused on the legal aspects of these two functions. Then consideration is given to orienting and training people. The last part of the chapter discusses the importance of evaluating the training effort.

Chapter 7 examines how supervisors communicate for results by identifying communication barriers, understanding nonverbal communications, working with the informal organization, getting feedback, and developing effective listening habits.

Chapter 8 extends this behavioral emphasis by examining the subject of employee motivation. In addition to explaining why people work, it focuses attention on individual differences that help explain why employee motivation must often be approached on a person-by-person basis. At the end of the chapter, guidelines for effective motivation are offered.

Chapter 9 focuses on the topic of effective leadership. In addition to examining the nature of the subject, it presents supervisory styles and contingency approaches to leadership. The last part of the chapter offers practical tips for increasing leadership effectiveness.

Chapter 10 examines how employee performance is appraised and rewarded. After reviewing how the performance appraisal process works, it presents common appraisal forms and discusses appraisal problems. The latter part of the chapter focuses on validity, reliability , the appraisal interview, and the importance of rewarding performance.

Chapter 11 addresses the supervision of protected groups. Included within this discussion are women, handicapped workers, and older workers. The nature of the challenge is presented and recommendations for action are offered. Attention also is given to the area of reverse discrimination.

When you have finished studying all the material in this part of the book, you will know how supervisors carry out the management functions. You also will be aware of many dos and don'ts that help the individual increase his or her supervisory effectiveness.

CHAPTER 6

RECRUITING AND TRAINING THE PERSONNEL

Often it is necessary to recruit, select, orient and/or train personnel. In small firms these functions are typically carried out by the supervisor. In large firms the personnel department handles many of them, with the supervisor getting involved only in the final selection of the new personnel and the training of the people in his or her work unit. The objectives of this chapter are to examine how effective staffing and training of the personnel are carried out. In the latter area, consideration will be given to training both the workers and the supervisors. When you have finished reading all the material in this chapter, you will be able to:

1. Relate the role of human resource forecasting to the recruitment process.
2. Identify and describe the internal and external sources used in recruiting personnel.
3. Describe the seven stages in the personnel selection process.
4. Explain how the orientation process works and what its value is to the organization.
5. Discuss some of those laws affecting the recruitment process with which the supervisor should be familiar.
6. Describe some of the most common methods for training workers.
7. Describe some of the most common methods used for training supervisors.
8. Explain how training programs can be evaluated.

A STARTING CASE: THE TRAINING RESULTS

Every week Josh Robinson receives material in the mail announcing a training program being sponsored by a university or professional training group. Josh has been on a number of these mailing lists ever since he attended a seminar entitled "The Role of the Supervisor."

Two months ago Josh received an announcement for a program entitled "More Effective Employee Communication." The brochure did not tell a great deal about the conference, but from what Josh could glean, the seminar was designed for people who needed to improve their in-house communication. One of the examples provided in the brochure pointed out the importance of communication for those people who have to coordinate their efforts with members of other departments. This example caught Josh's eye because as supervisor of the quality control and delivery (QCD) department, he has people who need just such training.

QCD has two major functions. First, it is responsible for checking the output of all manufacturing units to ensure that quality standards are met. Second, it is charged with seeing that the goods are shipped to the customer. In handling the first of these functions, the departmental personnel interact with pre-assigned people in each of the manufacturing units. In taking care of the second, production output schedules are used to coordinate in-house manufacturing with the shipping schedules of the outside transportation firm.

Josh believed that the scheduled seminar would be a good one for some of his key people. As a result, he wrote a request and got an OK for six of them to attend. That was a month ago. Last week Josh received a memo from the vice president of personnel asking him to relate the specific value that the seminar had had in terms of his work unit's performance. Josh spent the next 3 days checking quality control reports and shipping schedules. He found that there had been no change in quality control; the reject rate had held steady at 11 percent for the last 18 months. He also found that there had been no noticeable change in the service being provided by the transportation company. Prior to the training the company was late with 3.5 percent of its deliveries. Since the training the firm had been late with 3.48 percent of deliveries.

In an effort to gain more insights into the seminar, Josh called in all six of the people who attended and asked them about the 1-day meeting. They told him that the speaker was interesting, entertaining, and informative. However, they were unable to give Josh one idea that they picked up at the seminar that they were able to bring back to the job and use.

Josh has 3 more days in which to write to the vice president of personnel. He is concerned that if he does not tell the individual something positive, he will not be given an approval to send any of his people to future programs. On the other hand, he is not sure what they learned from the program, and so he is uncertain of what to put into the memo.

In your own words, what is Josh's problem? How did he get into it? Could it have been avoided? What should he do now? Write down your answers and put them aside. We will return to them later.

RECRUITING PERSONNEL

The supervisor's work unit will sometimes undergo personnel changes. Some workers will resign, retire, be promoted, or be transferred. If economic conditions are poor, some will be laid off. If the economy turns up and business orders increase, more will have to be hired.

In the short run, many supervisors operate with reduced work forces while the firm goes about recruiting job applicants. At some point, however, these shortages must be made up. If the organization has a personnel department, the supervisor will usually not get involved in much of the recruiting and screening. The individual will wait until the personnel department has recruited and made an initial screening of the candidates. Then the supervisor will interview the remaining applicants and make the hiring decision. Much of the following discussion on recruiting and selecting covers duties handled by the personnel department; in small firms, however, the supervisor will personally do these things. The first step in the process is human resource forecasting.

Human resource forecasting

Human resource forecasting is the process of adjusting personnel inflows and outflows so that the number of people in the organization is equal to the number required to get the work done. This forecasting is usually done by the personnel department or by higher-level management. The supervisor gets involved to the extent that it affects his or her work unit.

One of the most direct ways of forecasting the need for additional people is through the demand for goods and services provided by the unit. As this demand increases, the supervisor will have to ask for more personnel. In the production of goods, increased machine efficiency will temporarily resolve the problem; however, this solution is short-run in nature, for if more personnel and machines are not allocated to the unit, production will level off. In the case of services, the situation is more critical. For instance, an insurance supervisor cannot expect the claims personnel to handle more work just because there are more claims; if it takes an average of 2 hours to process a claim, the typical worker will handle no more than 20 claims a week, and if more personnel are not provided to the unit, the work will begin to pile up. Services often require the personal attention of people; increased workloads cannot be handled through the mere addition of machinery. Restaurants, banks, stock brokerages, and other institutions in which face-to-face contact between the personnel and the customer-client is vital, all require accurate human resource forecasting.

This forecasting is typically done by asking the supervisor how many new people will be needed in the unit over the next 3 to 6 months. In addition to examining the amount of work that must be done each week, the supervisor will consider the likely number of personnel who will quit or ask for a transfer. The supervisor will also take career-planning changes into account; these are a result of unit personnel being promoted into supervisory positions. In some organizations this is done on a seniority basis; those with the greatest job tenure are offered the next supervisory opening. In many firms, however, experience is only one of the important factors. Others include performance rating and promotion potential. The latter is determined by the supervisor and his or her boss. The result is a supervisory replacement chart such as that presented in Figure 6-1.

Firms that fill supervisory openings with the use of replacement charts do not have to worry about recruiting and selecting first-line managers. However, for worker-level positions they do, and the first step is job analysis.

Figure 6-1. Supervisor replacement chart.

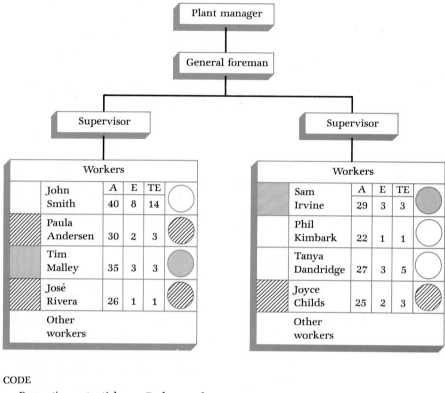

Job analysis

Job analysis is an evaluation of a job, including the work activities, machines, tools, equipment, job-related knowledge, and work experience required to perform adequately the tasks associated with the job. From this analysis, job descriptions and job specifications are determined. Job analysis also serves as a basis for determining how to recruit, select, orient, train, and evaluate the person(s) who will be assigned this job. If the firm is small, the supervisor may have to conduct the analysis. If the enterprise is large, the personnel department will usually handle this function.

Internal personnel sources

When possible, many organizations prefer to fill job vacancies with in-house personnel. They know who these people are and have some record regarding their previous performance. They are not buying a pig in a poke.

When supervisors have to fill positions, it is common to find job posting or bidding being used. Employees are notified of job vacancies through notices on bulletin boards or through in-house publications, such as a weekly company newsletter. They are then free to bid for the job.

If these approaches are successful, the supervisor will fill the vacancy. If they are not, other internal sources will typically be tapped. One of the most common is applicant files, consisting of résumés of people who previously applied for jobs but were not hired. Quite often these are individuals who came by and filed applications even though there was no job opening at the time.

External personnel sources

If internal sources do not produce the necessary personnel, external sources will be used. For workers at the lower ranks, newspaper ads are one of the most popular recruiting methds. People looking for work often scan the help-wanted sections. Sunday papers are a particularly good choice because they often carry a special help-wanted section.

Another source is employment agencies. There are state employment agencies in every state, and private employment agencies can be found in most cities. For a fee paid by the employer and/or employee, the agencies will do some of the preliminary screening and put the organization in touch with the applicants.

A third source is the competition. From time to time a competitor will lay off people or have dissatisfied employees who quit. While these people often are contacted through newspaper ads or employment agencies, sometimes they are told about the job by current employees who know them socially.

SELECTING PERSONNEL

The supervisor is usually not very involved in the recruiting process. After relating the number and type of personnel needed, the supervisor steps out of the picture. Once the recruitment efforts bear fruit, however, the supervisor again enters the scene. If the company is small, the first-line managers may do virtually all of the personnel screening. If the firm has a personnel department, the supervisor usually gets involved only after the candidate has successfully completed the preliminary phases of the screening process. This process, as seen in Figure 6-2, has seven stages.

Preliminary screening

The first step in the selection process is to have job applicants fill out an application blank. Small firms often use one that asks for basic information, such as name, address, previous work experience, and references. Larger firms have more detailed applications that quickly allow them to determine those who have the necessary job requirements and those who do not (see Figure 6-3 for an illustration of an employment application blank). For example, if the job requires someone who has had special training in operating computer-related equipment, more detailed application blanks are likely to pick this up.

Application blanks are particularly useful when a large number of people

Figure 6-2. Steps in the selection process.

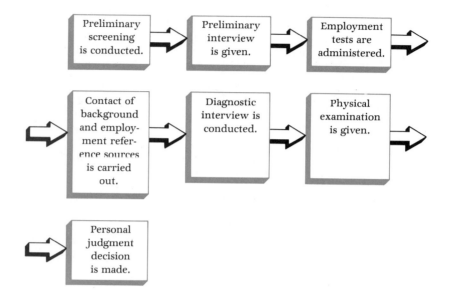

apply for the same job. Those lacking the necessary experience or training can quickly be screened out, thereby reducing the list to a more manageable number. What the firm must keep in mind is that none of the questions on the form should illegally discriminate against job applicants; this includes the use of non-job-related questions about sex, age, race, religion, education, marital status, arrest records, and credit rating. The best way to avoid this problem is to ensure that all questions are related to the job itself. [1]

Preliminary interview

The objective of this step is to screen out any unsuitable or uninterested applicants who have passed the preliminary screening phase. At this time the interviewer will gather more information from the applicant regarding work experience, job-related strengths and weaknesses, and purposes in seeking the job. In a one-on-one interview, it is often possible to eliminate those who slipped by the preliminary screening.

Employment tests

The purpose of employment tests is to find out how well the applicant can do the job. There are many types of tests tha can be administered, depending on the job. However, all should have both validity and reliability.

Validity is present when a test measures what it is supposed to measure. If a test is designed to determine if someone is a good typist, it should measure outcomes such as typing speed and accuracy. Typically the job applicant is given a couple of letters or a short report and then timed to see how long it takes to type the material. Errors are usually incorporated into the results by adding a predetermined number of seconds per mistake to the overall typing time. Based on past scores and work performance, the organization knows that those individuals with the lowest times are judged

MR.
MS.
MRS.

DATE

FIRST NAME   MIDDLE   MAIDEN (if any)   LAST NAME

PERSONNEL USE ONLY

INSTRUCTIONS: The careful and thoughtful completion of this application is an important step in our consideration of individuals for career opportunities. This application provides information which enables us to determine whether an applicant has the interests, background, and experience to be given additional consideration. In most cases, circumstances may prevent a preliminary interview. The conscientious completion of this form will supply much of the information normally covered in such a session. Please use separate sheets to complete answers wherever necessary. Please print in ink and use your own handwriting.

CURRENT STREET ADDRESS

1. POSITION(S) APPLIED FOR

CITY   STATE   ZIP CODE

2. SALARY EXPECTED   /Mo.

3.   SOCIAL SECURITY NO.

LOCATION PREFERENCE   LOCATION RESTRICTION   PHONE NO.

NEAREST AIRPORT TO YOUR CURRENT ADDRESS SERVED BY EASTERN AIRLINES

ARE YOU WILLING TO RELOCATE?
☐ YES ☐ NO

HOW SOON AFTER NOTICE CAN YOU REPORT TO WORK?

LAST PREVIOUS ADDRESS

AVAILABLE FOR EMPLOYMENT AS CHECKED:
☐ PERMANENT or ☐ TEMPORARY
☐ FULL TIME or ☐ PART TIME

ARE YOU WILLING TO WORK NIGHTS/ WEEKENDS/HOLIDAYS/SHIFTS?
☐ YES ☐ NO

CITY   STATE   ZIP CODE

HAVE YOU APPLIED PREVIOUSLY TO EASTERN? IF YES, WHERE?
☐ YES ☐ NO

HAVE YOU EVER BEEN EMPLOYED BY EASTERN? IF YES, WHERE?

MONTH/YEAR   WHAT POSITION?   MONTH/YEAR   WHAT POSITION?

WHAT LANGUAGES DO YOU SPEAK FLUENTLY, OTHER THAN ENGLISH?

IF UNDER 21 YEARS OF AGE, PLEASE GIVE BIRTH DATE   (MO/DAY/YEAR)   HEIGHT   WEIGHT

ARE YOU A U.S. CITIZEN? IF NOT, DO YOU HAVE AN ALIEN REGISTRATION CARD?
☐ YES ☐ NO

DO YOU HAVE ANY IMPAIRMENTS, PHYSICAL, MENTAL, OR MEDICAL, WHICH WOULD INTERFERE WITH YOUR ABILITY TO PERFORM THE JOB FOR WHICH YOU HAVE APPLIED?
☐ YES ☐ NO

IS YOUR SPOUSE EMPLOYED? IF YES, WHERE?
☐ YES ☐ NO

IF YES, EXPLAIN

EDUCATION RECORD   NAME AND ADDRESS OF COLLEGES OR UNIVERSITIES ATTENDED

DATE ATTENDED
FROM   TO   MAJOR SUBJECT   CREDIT HOURS COMPLETED   DEGREE & DATE RECEIVED   GRADE AVERAGE

CIRCLE THE HIGHEST LEVELS OF EDUCATION YOU HAVE COMPLETED

HIGH SCHOOL   10 11 12
COLLEGE   13 14 15 16 17 18
BUSINESS/ TECHNICAL   1 2 3 4

NAME AND ADDRESS OF BUSINESS/TECHNICAL AND/OR MILITARY SCHOOL ATTENDED

DATE ATTENDED
FROM   TO   TYPE TRAINING STUDIED   CREDIT HOURS COMPLETED   DID YOU GRADUATE?   LICENSE/ DIPLOMA RECEIVED   GRADE AVERAGE

IF YOU DO NOT HAVE A HIGH SCHOOL DEGREE, DO YOU HAVE AN EQUIVALENCY DIPLOMA (G.E.D.)? ☐ YES ☐ NO

ISSUING AGENCY OR NAME OF HIGH SCHOOL ATTENDED

Figure 6-3. Example of an employment application blank (partial form). (Reprinted by permission of Eastern Airlines.)

to be the most qualified typists. Notice that the test is valid because it measures typing ability. If the applicants were asked to fix photocopying machinery, the test would not be valid because this is not a measure of typing skills.

Reliability is present when a test is consistent. If qualified typists get high scores every time they take the test and nontypists get low scores, the test is reliable. The important thing to remember is that a test can be reliable without being valid. If all typists are given three similar screening tests, all designed to measure general knowledge of world events, and those who do well on the first also score well on the next two, the test is reliable. However, since the instrument did not measure typing ability, it is not valid.

In overcoming validity problems, effective organizations do three things. First, they design tests that are job-related. Second, they give the tests to people currently doing the job to ensure that they are measuring job-related behavior. Third, they rely on more than one test in determining how well the person has done. Multiple testing helps ensure that an accurate appraisal is being made of the person's ability.

Contact of background and employment reference sources

Contact of background and employment reference sources is used to obtain a more objective evaluation of the applicant. It is particularly important if previous work experience is crucial. For example, if the firm is hiring salespeople with a minimum of 2 years' selling experience because it finds that these people are most effective in selling the company's office equipment, work experience should be proven. The easiest way of doing this is to call and talk to the previous employer. At the same time, it is possible to ask about the individual's performance, reliability, and salary. Many firms are unwilling to answer these latter types of questions because they are afraid of saying something they should not. However, they are usually willing to confirm whether the individual has worked there, in what position, and for how long. Some are also willing to answer the question; Would you be willing to rehire this person? The answer to this often provides a great deal of information.

Diagnostic interview

The supervisor often meets the applicant for the first time at the diagnostic interview. Having had the pool of job seekers reduced from perhaps 10 to a more workable number of 3, the supervisor is now called on to make the final decision.

This interview can take one of three forms: structured, unstructured, or semistructured. A *structured interview* is one in which all of the people being interviewed are asked the same questions. This ensures that the supervisor covers all of the areas critical to employee selection. An *unstructured interview* is one in which the supervisor knows the basic direction the interview is to take, but the questions are not written down and followed in sequential order; instead, the interview is allowed to develop spontaneously. A *semistructured interview* combines features of both the structured and unstructured versions, usually by employing a handful of specific questions coupled with general discussion.

The supervisor often begins by asking the individual some job-related questions and then allowing the applicant to take it from there. Occasionally, the manager even uses open-ended questions, such as "How do you think your previous work experience has prepared you for this job? What do you think are your biggest assets? Why would you like to work for us?" In order to prevent the interview from getting too far afield, however, there are a number of things the supervisor should do, including: (1) Plan the interview in advance, (2) establish and maintain rapport with the applicant, (3) keep in mind that the primary goal is to gather information that will help in making the employment decision, and (4) take notes during the meeting so that all pertinent facts can be reviewed later on when applicants are being compared.

At the same time, the supervisor wants to be careful not to ask any questions that violate the individual's right of privacy. Are you aware of what is and is not an acceptable question? Check your knowledge by taking Self-Assessment Quiz 6-1.

SELF-ASSESSMENT QUIZ 6-1: WHAT CAN YOU ASK A RECRUITEE?

Interviewers are not allowed to ask some questions because they are a violation of the individual's right to privacy. On the other hand, there are many questions that can be asked. Assume that you are the supervisor who is interviewing a job applicant. Read the following questions and then indicate with an X whether it is all right to ask the question (mark in Yes column) or it is not (mark in No column).

	Yes	No
1. Are you aware of the amount of manual labor required by this job?	X	
2. Are you planning on getting married in the near future?		X
3. I have decided to hire you but need to fill out this insurance form for medical benefits; what is your marital status?	X	
4. Do you and your spouse intend to start a family soon?		X
5. I'll get back to you on my decision within a week. Do you have a phone number where I can reach you?	X	
6. Do you own your own home or rent?		X
7. How much do you weigh?		X
8. We require a physical exam before hiring anyone. When could you come in to be examined by our doctor?	X	
9. We do not allow smoking during working hours. Would you be able to comply with this rule?	X	
10. You look like you're in terrific shape. How old are you?		X

Physical examination

After the applicant has completed the previouly described steps, he or she often is required to take a physical exam. There are a number of reasons for this, including: (1) to ensure that the person is physically able to do the job and (2) to determine the individual's eligibility for life, health, and disability insurance. The first of these is most important to the firm because it does not want to assign people activities that they are physically incapable of performing. Additionally, if there is something physically wrong with a person, the company wants to know about it from the start. An individual who has had a heart attack and wants a job as a maintenance worker responsible for moving heavy equipment may fail to indicate this information on the application form; however, the physical exam will pick this up and the individual will be screened out.

Personal judgment decision

Having completed all the screening steps, the supervisor must now decide whom to hire for the job. If there is only one applicant left, the supervisor's task is simple. If two or more are left, a final cut must be made. Some organizations try to make the decision as logical and straightforward as possible by designing and using an evaluation instrument. Working with the supervisor, a higher-level manager or a member of the personnel department will identify those factors which are most important for the job. Table 6-1 provides an illustration.

Notice in the table that there are three important factors on which candidates are rated: work experience, job knowledge, and personal characteristics. The first and last each carry weights of 20 percent, while job knowledge carries a weight of 60 percent. The way these percentages are allocated is illustrated by the weight factor in the table. Each individual can receive up to .10 point for familiarity with noncomputerized inventory system, up to .15 for knowledge of different inventory control system, up to .10 for interpersonal skills, etc. The most important factor is knowledge of computerized production systems, which carries a value of .30. By evaluating each person on the subcategories of the three job factors, the supervisor gets a total score for each person. In Table 6-1 the job would be offered to applicant B. This individual has a total score of .90 out of 1.00, which is higher than anyone else's. If there were a tie, it would be broken by choosing the most important subfactor and determining who had the highest score here. For example, if applicant B turns down the job and so does applicant C, there are two people tied for third place: applicants A and E. Who should be chosen? The most important subfactor is knowledge of computerize production systems, which carries a weight of .30. Applicant E has a higher score on this factor than does applicant A, and so the former would be offered the job.

RECRUITING AND SELECTING: THE LEGAL ASPECTS

Supervisors are not experts in understanding the legal side of recruiting and selecting. However, there are some laws with which they should have a basic familiarity. The following examines these.

Table 6-1. A job applicant comparison form

	Work experience (20%)		Job knowledge (60%)			Personal characteristics (20%)			Total
	Familiarity with non-computerized information systems	Familiarity with computerized information systems	Knowledge of computerized production systems	Knowledge of different inventory control systems	Knowledge of program control systems	Effective oral communication	Effective written communication	Interpersonal relations	
Weighted factor	.10	.10	.30	.15	.15	.05	.05	.10	1.00
Applicant A	.05	.08	.25	.17	.15	.04	.05	.06	.85
Applicant B	.07	.10	.30	.12	.12	.05	.05	.09	.90
Applicant C	.10	.06	.24	.14	.15	.04	.04	.10	.87
Applicant D	.10	.05	.22	.15	.13	.04	.04	.07	.80
Applicant E	.03	.10	.30	.14	.15	.03	.05	.05	.85

Race and sex discrimination

Title VII of the *Civil Rights Act of 1964,* along with its amendments, outlaws discrimination based on race, color, religion, national origin, or sex. Specifically, the act applies to firms with 15 or more employees, labor unions with 15 or more members, employment agencies, and state and local governments. Some of the ways that Title VII affects recruitment and selection were presented in Self-Assessment Quiz 6-1. There are others.

One is that government contractors must not only have a plan for ensuring equal opportunity of the personnel but must also hire minorities. It is required by the contract, and they must be prepared to document their efforts.

Another major piece of legislation is the *Equal Pay Act of 1963,* which requires equal pay for individuals doing jobs that require substantially equal skills, responsibility, and effort while working under similar working conditions. In recent years women have won a number of equal pay lawsuits in which they have received settlements for back wages and have also had their current pay levels raised.

Age discrimination

The *Age Discrimination in Employment Act* protects people between the ages of 40 and 70 from discrimination in hiring, retention, compensation, and other conditions of employment. This means that firms cannot discriminate against people because of their age. In fact, when evaluating an applicant, a supervisor should not write any notes on the official evaluation that relate to age. Comments such as "Very qualified, but let's try for a younger person" or "This person is 58. We ought to get someone who will be able to stay with us for at least 20 years" are discriminatory under the law. If people are qualified to do the job, they must be considered regardless of the fact that they are middle-aged.

Handicapped

Handicapped people are also protected by law. The *Rehabilitation Act of 1978* requires organizations to take affirmative action for the employment of individuals with physical or mental handicaps. Specific regulations have been developed and issued by the federal government that set forth the kinds of organizations that must comply with this law and the actions that must be taken. Those firms affected by this law are required to develop specific programs aimed at increasing employment opportunities for the handicapped. Included in this group are all organizations doing more than $2500 worth of business with the federal government.

Meeting the challenge

The above represent only a handful of the laws that affect the recruiting and selecting of personnel. There are many others, such as the *Fair Credit Reporting Act,* which requires an organization to tell an applicant who was refused employment on the basis of information received from a credit-reporting service the name and address of that reporting service. Additionally, if the applicant was refused a job because of a reference, the individual must be informed of this fact and can request a summary of the information contained in the reference letter.

The supervisor will not be an expert on the legal aspects of recruiting and selecting. However, the individual can meet the challenge by remembering that the most important thing in choosing job candidates is to focus on work-related issues. Experience, job knowledge, job training, etc., are all important areas of consideration; sex, age, physical characteristics, and religion are not. To the extent that the organization makes the supervisor familiar with what is legal and with the proper way to interview and screen candidates, discrimination will be minimized. It is a challenge that must be faced by both the supervisor and the organization.

ORIENTATION

Orientation is the process of introducing a new employee to the job by telling the individual how things are done and creating the basis for inter-personal relations between the new individual and the regular work force. Supervision in Action: Effective Orientation details some of the most common steps taken by supervisors in orienting new employees.

SUPERVISION IN ACTION: EFFECTIVE ORIENTATION

There are many ways of orienting a new worker. The approach will vary from department to department and from job to job. However, there are five elements common to most orientation programs. In checklist form, they are the following:

1. ***Department functions***
   - ☐ Goals and current priorities
   - ☐ Organization and structure
   - ☐ Operational activities
   - ☐ Relationship of functions to other departments
   - ☐ Relationships of jobs within the department
2. ***Job duties and responsibilities***
   - ☐ Detailed explanation of job based on current job description and expected results
   - ☐ Explanation of why the job is important, how the specific job relates to others in the department and company
   - ☐ Discussion of common problems and how to avoid and overcome them
   - ☐ Performance standards and basis of performance evaluation
   - ☐ Number of daily work hours and times
   - ☐ Overtime needs and requirements
   - ☐ Extra duty assignments (e.g., changing duties to cover for an absent worker)
   - ☐ Required records and reports
   - ☐ Check-out on equipment to be used

☐ Explanation of where and how to get tools, have equipment maintained and repaired
☐ Types of assistance available: when and how to ask for help
☐ Organization and structure
☐ Relations with state and federal inspectors

3. Policies, procedures, rules, and regulations
☐ Rules unique to the job and/or department
☐ Handling emergencies
☐ Safety precautions and accident prevention
☐ Reporting of hazards and accidents
☐ Cleanliness standards and sanitation (e.g., cleanup)
☐ Security: theft problems and costs
☐ Relations with outside people (e.g., drivers)
☐ Eating, smoking, and chewing gum, etc., in department area
☐ Removal of things from department
☐ Damage control (e.g., smoking restrictions)
☐ Time clock and time sheets
☐ Breaks/rest periods
☐ Lunch duration and time
☐ Making and receiving personal telephone calls
☐ Requisitioning supplies and equipment
☐ Monitoring and evaluating of employee performance
☐ Job bidding and requesting reassignment
☐ Going to cars during work hours

4. Tour of department
☐ Rest rooms and showers
☐ Fire-alarm box and fire extinguisher stations
☐ Time clocks
☐ Lockers
☐ Approved entrances and exits
☐ Water fountains and eyewash systems
☐ Supervisors' quarters
☐ Supply room and maintenance department
☐ Sanitation and security offices
☐ Smoking areas
☐ Locations of services to employees related to department
☐ First aid kit

5. Introduction to department employees

Source: Walter D. St. John, "The Complete Employee Orientation Program," © May 1980. Reprinted by permission of *Personnel Journal*, Costa Mesa, Calif.; all rights reserved.

Common approaches

Small firms tend to be informal in their approach to orientation, while larger enterprises follow a carefully laid-out series of procedures. In either case, it is common to take the new worker on a tour of the facilities, introduce him or her to the people in the work unit, make the individual familiar with the history of the firm and what it is doing currently, provide a brief description of the company's goods and services, explain what the organization chart looks like, provide a brief rundown of personnel policies, benefits, and services, and let the individual know the rules and regulations that everyone is required to follow.

Small firms often do these things verbally. The supervisor will discuss them with the individual as they walk about the facilities and, if the worker has any questions (such as specific types of health coverage or the particulars of the retirement program), refer the person to someone in the organization who is charged with handling that specific area. Large firms often provide their new people with a booklet or brochure that spells out much of this information. In fact, it is common to find many people being given a series of handouts: one for insurance, one for work-related rules, one for the history of the firm, etc. The individual is encouraged to read these at his or her leisure. If there are any questions, the supervisor will answer them or send the individual to the personnel department, where there is someone who can provide the information.

Advantages of orientation

In recent years, there has been an increase in the number of firms offering orientation to their people. The major reason is that they are finding that oriented workers do a better job and stay with the firm longer than do those who are not given orientation. For example, research reveals that better-oriented personnel reach standard performance faster than do their counterparts who are not so oriented.[2]

A second major advantage is the reduction in anxiety associated with job failure. By making new people familiar with what is expected on the job and how long it will take to become proficient at the work, the initial nervousness that often accompanies new assignments is greatly reduced. Proper orientation also makes the individual aware of some of the hazing techniques often employed by older workers and allows the new person to "catch on" earlier.

A third benefit is a reduction in employee turnover. Orientation has proven to be an effective way of showing new people the importance of their job and the role they play in the scheme of things. This helps bring about a feeling of self-esteem and leads to longer employee tenure with the firm.

A fourth benefit is the time saved by supervisors and coworkers. The better the individual's orientation, the less time the individual will take from others for answering questions, showing how the work is to be done, etc.

A fifth benefit is that a well-designed orientation program helps the worker develop a positive attitude toward the employer. The individual begins identifying with the enterprise and the work. The result is higher job satisfaction and better work performance than from those who have not had orientation.

TRAINING OF PERSONNEL

Training is the process of systematically changing the behavior and/or attitudes of employees in order to increase their organizational effectiveness. There are many types of training from which personnel can benefit. All

NAME _____

BUREAU _____

PLEASE INDICATE YOUR LEVEL OF SUPERVISORY RESPONSIBILITY BY CHECKING ONE OF THE FOLLOWING:

☐ first-line supervisor (the employees you supervise do not supervise others)

☐ second-line supervisor (you supervise employees who also have supervisory responsibilities)

☐ management level

    I. PLEASE INDICATE BY CHECKING THE APPROPRIATE COLUMN THE DEGREE OF NEED YOU THINK EXISTS FOR TRAINING FIRST-LINE SUPERVISORS ONLY.

	Great need	Some need	Little need
1. Communications			
2. Interviewing			
3. Counseling			
4. Disciplining			
5. Hiring procedures			
6. Termination procedures			
7. Developing employees			
8. Motivating			
9. Human relations			
10. Handling complaints/grievances			
11. Planning/organizing			
12. Performance appraisal			
13. Decision making			
14. Leadership			
15. Functioning in the organization			
16. Delegation			
17. Management methods (e.g., MBO)			
18. Budgeting			
19. Time management			
20. Conducting meetings			
21. Reporting systems (written information)			
22. Safety (e.g., OSHA, first aid)			
23. Affirmative action/EEO			

II. PLEASE INDICATE ANY OTHER SUPERVISORY SKILLS FOR WHICH YOU FEEL THERE MAY BE A NEED. LIST THEM BELOW AND CHECK THE APPROPRIATE BOX INDICATING THE DEGREE OF NEED.

	Great need	Some need	Little need
1.			
2.			
3.			
4.			
5.			

Figure 6-4. Survey of supervisory training needs. (From Katherine Culbertson and Mark Thompson, "An Analysis of Supervisory Training Needs," *Training and Development Journal,* February 1980, p. 60).

of these programs, however, should begin with a determination of training needs.

**Determining
training needs**

There are many ways in which the supervisor can determine that workers in the unit require training. Common examples include: excessive scrap, an increase in the number of accidents, a rise in the turnover rate, a failure to meet the work standards of the unit, excessive employee fatigue, or too many bottlenecks in the operation. Other reasons for training include: new job assignments, introduction of new machinery and equipment, and/or establishment of new work procedures. In all of these cases, training is needed. Many organizations attempt to identify the specific type of training by having the personnel fill out training forms. (Figure 6-4 illustrates such a form used to determine training needs at the supervisory level.)

   If the firm is small, training is usually done by the immediate superior or by experienced personnel at the same level of the hierarchy. For example, the supervisor or a worker with 2 or 3 years of experience will train a new person in how to run a piece of machinery or fill out the monthly cost control report. However, in handling less technical areas, such as how to manage one's time more effectively or how to communicate with people, it is common to find outside trainers being brought in or, if the firm is large, the personnel department running the program. This requires a well-thought-out approach, beginning with an overall design of the program.

**Designing
the program**

Regardless of who does the training, there should be an identification of training objectives and a determination of the criteria that will be used in evaluating the results. Figure 6-5 illustrates this training cycle.

Figure 6-5. The training cycle.

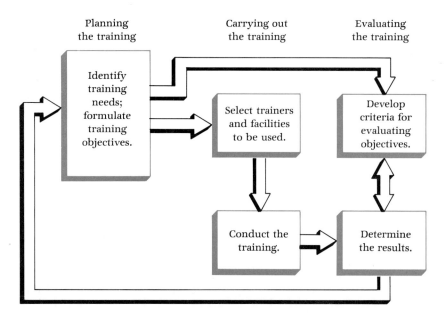

Notice from the figure that program design has three basic phases. In the first phase training needs and training objectives are identified. In the second phase the trainers and facilities to be used are determined and the training is carried out. In the final phase a comparison of the evaluation criteria and the actual outcomes of the training are made. In carrying out the overall design, there are three important things the supervisor should keep in mind:

1. **Make the material meaningful.** The trainees should be given an overview of the program so that they know what to expect. The material should then be presented in a logical sequence with familiar examples so that the participants can follow what is being communicated. Where possible, visual aids and handouts should be used to supplement verbal presentations. Finally, the trainer should be careful not to move too quickly. Feeding people new information in small bites is infinitely preferable to giving them a great deal of information to digest all at once.

2. **Make the training realistic.** The participants should be given as much hands-on training as possible. If there is some theory involved, this should be woven in with actual practice. If the individuals are being taught how to operate a piece of equipment or fill out a report, the trainer should give them the opportunity to do so. At some point the individual has to stop talking, step back, and let the participants take a turn. Additionally, if the training can be done out on the line or in the actual workplace without disturbing others, this should be done. For example, learning to run a machine in a quiet classroom is not the same as operating it in a loud factory area. When possible, the training environment should simulate the actual workplace.

3. **Allow for feedback.** The trainees should be given the chance to obtain feedback on how well they are doing. If they make a mistake, this should be pointed out to them along with some discussion regarding how they can avoid making this error in the future. Sometimes participants can tell how well they are doing and the need for feedback is minimized. However, in those cases in which this information is not readily evident, feedback from the trainer is extremely important in reinforcing correct behaviors and eliminating incorrect ones.

Types of training

There are two types of training that supervisors need to know about. One is the training of subordinates; the other is supervisory training. The following examines both.

Subordinate training. Whether the supervisor provides the training or it is done through the personnel department or an outside trainer, most employee training is designed to be practical, hands-on, and immediately useful. The four most common methods are: (1) on-the-job training, (2) vestibule training, (3) off-the-job training, and (4) coaching and counseling.

ON-THE-JOB TRAINING. *On-the-job training* (OJT) is the most widely used method of training employees. With this training the employee is placed in the work situation and showed how to do the job either by the supervisor or by an experienced worker. Table 6-2 illustrates the steps used in OJT when teaching someone to handle equipment, materials, tools, or other lower-level mechanical jobs. This type of training is typically carried out in the supervisor's own department.

VESTIBULE TRAINING. *Vestibule training* takes place in an environment that simulates the workplace. Quite often this is a nearby area of the plant or building that is set up for training purposes. A common example is a large area where individuals are taught to run different pieces of equipment under the watchful eye of a trainer. Once the individual knows how to use

Table 6-2. The four-step method of on-the-job training

Step 1: Preparation of the learner

1. Put the learner at ease—relieve the tension.
2. Explain why he is being taught.
3. Create interest, encourage questions, and find out what the learner already knows about his job or other jobs.
4. Explain the why of the whole job, and relate it to some job the worker already knows.
5. Place the learner as close to his normal working position as possible.
6. Familiarize him with the equipment, materials, tools, and trade terms.

Step 2: Presentation of the operation

1. Explain quantity and quality requirements.
2. Go through the job at the normal work pace.
3. Go through the job at a slow pace several times, explaining each step. Between operations, explain the difficult parts, or those in which errors are likely to be made.
4. Go through the job at a slow pace several times, explaining the key points.
5. Have the learner explain the steps as you go through the job at a slow pace.
6. Have the learner explain the key points as you go through the job at a slow pace.

Step 3: Performance tryout

1. Have the learner go through the job several times, slowly, explaining to you each step. Correct his mistakes, and, if necessary, do some of the complicated steps for him the first few times.
2. You, the trainer, run the job at the normal pace.
3. Have the learner do the job, gradually building up skill and speed.
4. As soon as he demonstrates that he can do the job, put him on his own, but don't abandon him.

Step 4: Follow-up

1. Designate to whom the learner should go for help if he needs it, or if he needs to ask questions.
2. Gradually decrease supervision, checking his work from time to time against quality and quantity standards.
3. Correct faulty work patterns that begin to creep into his work, and do it before they become a habit. Show him why the learned method is superior.
4. Compliment good work; encourage him and keep him encouraged until he is able to meet the quality/quantity standards.

Source: William Berliner and William McLarney, *Management Practice and Training*, 6th ed., Homewood, Ill.: Richard D. Irwin, 1974, pp. 442–443. © 1974 by Richard D. Irwin, Inc. Reproduced by permission of the publisher.

the equipment properly, he or she is sent back to the department. In a vestibule training situation the primary responsibility for training rests with the person who supervises the simulated work area. Quite often this individual is a professional trainer who knows how to explain things, to pick up mistakes when they occur, and to show the trainee how to avoid them in the future. When organizations have a large number of people who need vestibule training, it pays to invest in these facilities and take the supervisor out of the role of primary trainer.

OFF-THE-JOB TRAINING. Sometimes workers need technical training but the organization cannot afford the time or facilities to provide it. *Off-the-job training* is a good substitute. Under this arrangement, workers are sent to institutes or vocational schools where they learn the necessary job-related skills. This form of training is often used in teaching people how to run machinery, operate equipment, and handle other types of technical jobs.

COACHING AND COUNSELING. Sometimes workers need more than just technical training. They need the supervisor to coach them by answering their questions and explaining how to do things. They also need counseling in the form of guidance and assistance in how to get along with others and make decisions regarding issues such as their career with the firm. In this form of training, the supervisor provides the individual with information regarding what he or she is doing well and how the employee can improve in the future. This feedback is often behavioral in nature: i.e., "Here is how you should do that"; "You need to write this report in more direct terms; it is too general"; "Don't bring that matter up until you have discussed these three because the group won't be receptive to your idea until these others have been handled." In each of these cases the supervisor is offering personal guidance and assistance. Coaching and counseling are particularly important in helping workers refine their approach to things and improve the nontechnical side of their performance. It is also important in getting the worker prepared to move up to the supervisory ranks. (See Supervision in Action: Developing a Coaching Style.)

Supervisory training. When supervisors need training, this is commonly provided by the immediate superior, the personnel department, or an outside trainer. The four most common methods are: role playing, the in-basket technique, the case method, and coaching and counseling.

ROLE PLAYING. *Role playing* consists of the spontaneous acting out of a situation involving two or more people. The purpose of the training is to acquaint the participants with the proper way to handle a given situation. For example, one supervisor may be given the role of a person who is being fired because of excessive tardiness, and another is assigned the role of the individual who is doing the firing. Each plays the scene as realistically as possible while the rest of the supervisors in the session look on. When it is

---

SUPERVISION IN ACTION: DEVELOPING A COACHING STYLE

The first step for anyone who wants to become a better "coach" is to make time available to spend some with his people as individuals. If a supervisor thinks that he can't spare the time or take the time, he needs to rethink his priorities. Supervisors on the move are those who give time to the right functions. Others have found time by working through their coffee breaks, coming to work early, or, best of all, utilizing their time more effectively. Whatever one's technique is, additional time simply must be gained to spend with the company's most important resource: people.

When I work with supervisors on becoming better coaches, I give them these words of advice: Go gentle into the first coaching session you have with each individual. Think back to your first job and how you felt. You were uneasy and uncertain, weren't you? You need a plan to make your employee feel more at ease, and probably the best plan is to make clear at your first session that your purpose is to help him achieve some of his goals. It is even better if you tell the employee the specific purpose of the meeting before the session begins, so his stomach won't be churning while he's waiting for the unknown.

At the first meeting, the supervisor should start off by discussing some recent event that has happened in his section, department, or company about which the employee is bound to have an opinion or comment. Unless the two know each other fairly well already, it's best to stay away from talk about the employee's spouse, family, or hobbies. Most of those questions he'll answer with, "Oh, they're fine," and then the conversation is back at a standstill. After spending some time with "shop talk," the supervisor can more easily move to such questions as:

- What procedures and techniques of your job do you feel that you have thoroughly mastered?
- What procedures seem difficult? What suggestions do you have to improve them?
- What unit rules or company policies do you have questions about? (The supervisor might ask the employee to give his feelings about a specific policy, such as how sick leave is accumulated.)
- What would you like to be doing 1 year from now? What about 3 years from now?
- What do you thing would be the best way to get where you want to be in the future?

The supervisor shouldn't be thrown off if the worker hasn't thought much about what he wants to do in the future. After all, one of the purposes of the coaching session is to get him to start thinking *about* himself, *for* himself.

Source: Will Lorey, "Coaching: A New Look at an Old Responsibility," *Supervisory Management,* May 1977, pp. 27–28. © 1977 by AMACOM, a division of American Management Associations, New York. Reprinted by permission of the publisher; all rights reserved.

over, the trainer discusses what went well during the scenario and what was not handled correctly. In this way, both the supervisors directly involved in the role playing and those in the audience learn ways to deal with this type of situation. By running everyone through a series of problems likely to be faced on the job, role-playing sessions allow supervisors to confront important issues and learn the proper responses before they face them on the job.

IN-BASKET TECHNIQUE. The *in-basket technique* involves giving a supervisory trainee a box of materials (which contains typical items found in the supervisor's in-box) and a telephone and asking the individual to make decisions regarding what should be done. All of this has to be accomplished in a limited time period, after which the person is evaluated and critiqued on the number of decisions made in the allotted time. Some of the items in the box are very important and should be handled as soon as possible. Some are minor and can wait or simply be delegated to others. For example, there may be a memo saying that inventory must be reordered today in order to avoid a stockout. There may be another saying that next week there will be a meeting of all supervisors for the purpose of discussing the budget and everyone is to call a particular phone number, confirm that he or she will be there, and take down the specifics regarding the meeting room and time. There may be a third asking the manager to look over a two-page cost control report and by next month to send the superior a brief evaluation of the value of this report to unit operating efficiency. Note that all three of these memos will take some time but that they do not all need to be handled right now. The first should get highest priority, and the last can be left for a later date. The purpose of the in-basket technique is to help train supervisors to allocate their time and effort effectively.

THE CASE METHOD. The *case method* involves group discussion using a written case in which a situation is presented to the reader and a course of action is required. The supervisor must carefully read the case, analyze it, and then offer recommendations for action. In supervisory training, these cases are usually quite short, often running no more than two or three pages.

A typical example would be a case about a worker who has been caught stealing company property. The individual is the firm's leading salesperson. What should now be done? The objective of the case is to get the supervisor to weigh (1) the importance of enforcing rules with (2) the consequences that can result from such action. In this case, most firms insist that the person either be fired or penalized in some way (2 weeks off without pay) regardless of his or her sales performance. The objective of the case is to help supervisors understand the company's position on enforcement of the rules.

Another case might relate the story of the firm's best production worker, who, after 6 months on the job, is found to have lied on the application blank. The worker claimed to have had 5 years of previous work-related experience. What should be done? Most firms insist that the worker be fired for lying. Their argument is that honesty is too important a characteristic to compromise.

The case method approach to training is extremely useful in dealing with issues that cannot be adequately covered through lectures or written material alone. Interaction and discussion are needed.

COACHING AND COUNSELING. Just like their subordinates, supervisors need coaching and counseling. This can take numerous forms. One of the most useful is the example set by the boss. Supervisors tend to emulate their superiors, and to the degree that the latter are effective, first-line supervisors also tend to be effective. The boss has a tremendous effect on how the subordinate will perform. Another coaching and counseling technique is to call in the subordinates, discuss their progress, and offer them helpful advice regarding the overall management of their unit. A third, and related, approach is to be available to answer questions and provide answers to job-related problems. A fourth is to serve as a mentor or advisor regarding career problems and choices. While there are many ways of coaching and counseling supervisors, the important thing is that the boss provide the right climate for learning and growing. If this environment can be created, supervisors will be both creative and efficient in their work-related duties.

**EVALUATION
OF TRAINING**

The last phase of training is an evaluation of the results. Did the subordinates and supervisors learn what was taught to them? Are they applying it on the job? Was the time and/or money well spent? As seen in Figure 6-5, evaluation is the stage that ties together the planning (what was supposed to be done) with the outcome (what actually was accomplished).

Evaluation targets

What can be evaluated? This will depend on the specific type of training that was given. However, some of the major categories that often serve as evaluation targets include the following:

1. Quantity of work output
2. Quality of work output
3. Application of the subject matter to organizational problems
4. Improved attitudes among the participants
5. Development of strong esprit de corps within the work group

Notice that some of these are directly measurable and that others can be determined only indirectly. For example, both the quantity and quality of work output can be directly measured. If the firm keeps output records, it should be quite easy to determine if the amount of work has gone up and if the overall quality of the output has increased. On the other hand, improved attitudes and esprit de corps can be measured only indirectly. For example, if the supervisor notices that the workers tend to be more friendly toward each other and there seems to be more teamwork in tackling difficult problems, the manager may conclude that there is higher esprit de corps than before. However, the individual will usually base the judgment on work quantity or quality. If these start to increase, the manager may conclude that it is a result of improved attitudes. The supervisor infers a relationship between the two. Since attitude, morale, and other psychological variables are not directly seen, their presence is assumed based on directly observable results like work quantity and work quality. What this means in terms of evaluation is that the supervisor should focus on measurable changes in work performance.

Most important, the end points that are being measured should have been determined in advance. The supervisor should not say: "Let's see now. The training is over and I have to find out if it was useful. How should I do this?" Instead, the supervisor should have determined what can be measured, how it can be measured, and when this evaluation should be done. Asking participants in a training session to give their evaluation of the session is a good way to find out if the speaker was well-organized and maintained interest. However, in finding out if the training paid off, it is often necessary to wait a few weeks and then ask the participants if they are using any of the ideas or techniques they learned and how valuable these are proving to be.

Carrying out evaluations

Two primary groups are qualified to make an evaluation of the training: the trainees and their bosses. The trainees can relate how clear the training was, whether it was relevant to their needs, and what additional types of training are still required. The supervisors can evaluate the training based on how well the personnel are now performing their jobs.

If the training is done by the supervisor, there is usually no formal evaluation of the training. If the supervisor feels that additional assistance is needed, it will be provided. If the first-line manager feels that based on the individual's performance there is no need for additional training, no more will be given. This decision is based on the worker's job performance.

On the other hand, if the training has been conducted by the personnel department or an outside trainer, it is common to find a formal evaluation being used. Table 6-3 provides an illustration. Quite often the evaluation provides for both positive and negative feedback. In particular, the individual will be asked to rate the value of the training and discuss how it could be improved. Some organizations use two evaluation efforts. The first, given after the training is complete, is used to measure trainee response and initial impressions. The second, given a couple of weeks later, is used to determine if any of the ideas or techniques from the training are being used on the job. The reason why many firms like a second evaluation is that it gives the participant a chance to look at the training after the initial impres-

Table 6-3. Evaluation form for a training program

Date _____   Title of the program _____

Instructor's name _____

Please evaluate the instructor and the training. Do not leave out any questions. *Do not sign your name*.

Inadequate	1
Well below average	2
Average	3
Well above average	4
Excellent	5

Using the above 5-point rating scale, please give your evaluation of the following:

Course

Objectives were made clear at the beginning of the training.   _____
The lecture material was relevant to the objectives.   _____
The discussions were relevant both to the objectives and to the course content.   _____
Assignments were made clear and their relevance to the objective was explained.   _____
The training provided new ideas, techniques, insights, etc., and a chance to
    apply these to job-related situations.   _____

Instructor

Was well prepared.   _____
Presented the material in an organized and systematic way.   _____
Used examples and materials that were relevant and job-related.   _____
Was able to maintain interest and direction during the meeting.   _____
Was able to relate to the participants.   _____

What did you learn during this training that was most beneficial to you?

What were the major shortcomings or problems with this training?

Overall, how useful was the training? Be as detailed as possible in your answer.

---

sion has worn off. Quite often companies find that the first evaluation is very positive but that the follow-up is not. The trainer was interesting, entertaining, and motivational, but the ideas were of very little value.

THE TRAINING RESULTS: STARTING CASE REVISITED

Having read the chapter, you should now realize that Josh sent his people to a training program without fully understanding what its benefits would be. Josh read the announcement of the program and some of the things it promised to do, but apparently these goals were not attained. How could Josh have avoided making this mistake?

There were only two steps he could have taken. The first is to have called and talked to the person conducting the seminar to find out exactly what the individual hoped to accomplish and to obtain the names of some satisfied past participants with whom he could have talked. However, keep in mind that this suggestion is really pie in the sky. It would be time-consuming and the trainer might well give Josh the names of those who were going to give the program a good review. The second thing Josh could have done was to send just one person and find out how valuable the program was. This is the best he really could have done.

In terms of handling the memo to the vice president of personnel, Josh should come right out and tell the individual that the response was not very good and that in the future this program will not be attended. If the vice president asks all supervisors who send their people to seminars to write memos regarding the value of the training, the executive either has a lot of memos admitting that things did not go well or a lot of managers who hedge the truth. The objective of this introductory case is to point out the need to evaluate training programs. Many of them are not worth the time and effort that companies spend on them because they are neither well-designed nor well-implemented. When they are, however, they are an important source of training for both workers and managerial personnel.

INTERPRETATION OF SELF-ASSESSMENT QUIZ 6-1: WHAT CAN YOU ASK A RECRUITEE?

1. Yes. You can ask job-related questions.
2. No. This is none of the recruiter's business even if the individual would prefer to hire someone who is unmarried because the individual will have to spend a lot of time on the road. Of course, if the other party volunteers this information, that is another story.
3. Yes. After hiring, such information can be requested for insurance purposes.
4. No. this is no concern of the recruiter.
5. Yes. The recruiter is within proper limits since the telephone number is job-related.
6. No. This has no bearing on the applicant's qualifications.
7. No. If weight is a job-related issue, it can be determined during the physical exam.
8. Yes. It is a job-related question.

9. Yes. The individual is providing job-related information and a company is within its rights to prohibit smoking.

10. No. Age is usually not a hiring requirement, and if it is (e.g., the firm is bonded by an insurance company but the coverage extends only to people 18 years of age or older or there is mandatory retirement at 70 years of age), this information can be obtained from the employment application.

How well did you do? Most people get only six right. The thing to remember is that many supervisors unintentionally ask questions that are not supposed to be asked. This is why many firms provide training regarding what can and cannot be said to applicants.

SUMMARY OF KEY POINTS

1. From time to time, every organization must recruit personnel. In balancing the demand for workers with the number on hand, many firms are turning to human resource forecasting. They also make use of job analysis.

2. There are two sources that firms can use in recruiting: internal and external. Quite often supervisors are able to fill available positions through job posting and bidding. Externally, advertisements, employment agencies, and hiring from the competition are very popular approaches.

3. In selecting personnel from among a group of applicants, seven steps are commonly employed: preliminary screening, a preliminary interview, employment tests, contact of background and employment reference sources, a diagnostic interview, a physical exam, and a personal judgment decision by the supervisor in whose department the individual will work.

4. Supervisors are not experts in understanding the legal side of recruiting and selecting. However, there are some laws with which they should have a basic familiarity. Some of these include: the Civil Rights Act of 1964, the Equal Pay Act of 1963, the Age Discrimination in Employment Act, the Rehabilitation Act of 1978, and the Fair Credit Reporting Act.

5. Orientation is the process of introducing a new employee to the job by telling the individual how things are done and creating the basis for interpersonal relations between the new person and the regular work force. Oriented employees, it has been found, tend to do a better job and to stay with the firm longer than do those who are not given orientation.

6. Training is the process of systematically changing behavior and/or attitudes of employees in order to increase their organizational effectiveness. Every effective program should be carefully designed, make use of meaningful training materials, make the training as realistic as possible, allow for feedback from the participants, and have criteria for evaluating the program. At the worker level some of the most common types of training include: on-the-job training, vestibule training, off-the-job training, and coaching and counseling. At the supervisory level some of the most common types of training include: role playing, the in-basket technique, the case method, and coaching and counseling.

7. The last phase of training is an evaluation of the results. The criteria used in this evaluation should be as clear and measurable as possible. Many training programs fail because they either do not measure up to expectations or it is impossible to say exactly what impact they had on the performance of those who attended.

BUILD YOUR SUPERVISORY WORD POWER

These key recruiting, selecting, orienting, and training terms are presented in their order of appearance in the chapter. Effective supervisors have a working knowledge of them.

Human resource forecasting. The process of adjusting personnel inflows and outflows so that the number of people in the organization is equal to the number required to get the work done.

Job analysis. An evaluation of a job, including the work activities, machines, tools, equipment, job-related knowledge, and work experience required to perform adequately the tasks associated with the job.

Validity. As applied to test measures, it is present when a test measures what it is supposed to measure.

Reliability. As applied to test measures, it is present when the test provides consistent results.

Structured interview. An interview in which all of the people being interviewed are asked the exact same questions.

Unstructured interview. An interview in which the interviewer knows the basic direction the interview is to take, but the questions are not written down and followed in sequential order.

Semistructured interview. An interview that combines features of both the structured and unstructured version, usually by employing a handful of specific questions coupled with general discussion.

Civil Rights Act of 1964. Federal legislation that outlaws discrimination based on race, color, religion, national origin, or sex.

Equal Pay Act of 1963. Federal legislation that requires equal pay for individuals doing jobs that require substantially equal skills, responsibility, and effort while working under similar working conditions.

Age Discrimination in Employment Act. Legislation designed to protect people between the ages of 40 and 70 from discrimination in hiring, retention, compensation, and other conditions of employment.

Rehabilitation Act of 1978. Legislation that requires organizations to take affirmative action for the employment of individuals with physical or mental handicaps.

Fair Credit Reporting Act. Legislation that requires an organization to tell an applicant who was refused employment on the basis of information received from a credit reporting service the name and address of that reporting service.

Orientation. The process of introducing a new employee to the job by telling the individual how things are done and creating the basis for interpersonal relations between the new individual and the regular work force.

Training. The process of systematically changing behavior and/or attitudes of employees in order to increase their organizational effectiveness.

On-the-job training. Training that is provided to people in their place of work. It is usually given by the supervisor or an experienced worker.

Vestibule training. Training that takes place in a simulated work environment.

Off-the-job training. Training that is provided away from the firm, often at institutes or vocational schools.

Role playing. The spontaneous acting out of a situation involving two or more people.

In-basket technique. A supervisory training approach designed to evaluate and teach managers how to allocate their decision-making tme.

Case method. A supervisory training approach consisting of having the manager read a short case, analyze it, and then offer recommendations for action.

REVIEW YOUR UNDERSTANDING

1. How does human resource forecasting help an organization plan its recruiting efforts? What role does job analysis play in this overall process? Explain.
2. How will an organization attempt to fill in-house vacancies with internal personnel? If it does go outside, what sources is it likely to use? Give examples of both in your answers.
3. There are seven steps in the personnel selection process. What takes place in each? Explain.
4. Identify what a supervisor needs to know about the following laws: Civil Rights Act of 1964, Equal Pay Act of 1963, Age Discrimination in Employment Act, Rehabilitation Act of 1978, and Fair Credit Reporting Act. Offer at least one thing the supervisor should know about each.
5. How does the orientation process work? Describe it. Of what value is it to organizations? Explain.
6. How can a supervisor determine that workers in the unit need training? Explain. And what things can the supervisor look for? Cite at least three.
7. In carrying out the design of a training program, there are three things the supervisor should keep in mind. What are they? Explain each.
8. Describe how the following types of training help employees do a better job: on-the-job training, vestibule training, off-the-job training, and coaching and counseling. In your answer be sure to describe when each of these types of training would be used.
9. Describe how the following types of training help supervisors do a better job: role playing, the in-basket technique, the case method, and coaching and counseling. In your answer be sure to describe when each of these types of training would be used.
10. What do supervisors need to know about the evaluation of training programs? Be complete in your answer.

SUPPLEMENT YOUR KNOWLEDGE

In addition to the references listed at the end of this chapter, the following provide important, practical information that is of use to supervisors in selecting, orienting, and training their people:

Alpander, Guvenc G.: "Training First-Line Supervisors to Criticize Constructively," *Personnel Journal*, March 1980, pp. 216–221.

Langford, Harry: "Needs Analysis in the Training Department," *Supervisory Management*, August 1978, pp. 1–25.

Mealiea, Laird W.: "The TA Approach to Employee Development," *Supervisory Management*, August 977, pp. 11–19.

Sharinger, Dale H.: "Avoidance of Pitfalls in Supervisory Development," *Personnel Journal*, October 1981, pp. 92–96.

Shaw, Malcolm E.: "The Model Manager: Management Development Through Behavior Modeling," *Supervisory Management*, Janary 1979, pp. 14–21.

Smith, Terry L.: "Coaching the Troubled Employee," *Supervisory Management*, December 1981, pp. 33–36.

YOU BE THE SUPERVISOR: SUSAN'S JOB INTERVIEW

The Shardin Corporation has been expanding operations for 6 months. The initial recruiting was for line personnel and then for administrative people. The firm is now in the process of hiring support help, most noticeably typists and other office staff. One of the typing applicants, Susan Berdine, was in last week for her interview with the office supervisor. Part of the interview went as follows:

Susan, we're looking for people who are going to stay with us for at least 5 years. Do you have any plans for marrying and then quitting work?

None at all. I'm not even engaged, and my boyfriend has just started as a management trainee with a company across town. If I do marry, I'll be staying here.

Fine. Oh, by the way, we're looking for people in the 21 to 25 age range for our more advanced office personnel positions. How old are you?

I'm 22.

Great, well I guess that about wraps it up. By the way, where do you live? I haven't written it on my interview sheet as I should have.

I live at 2506 East Elm with my parents.

Is that an apartment or a house?

A house.

OK. We'll be in touch.

On the way out, Susan met one of the other candidates, Julie Phillips. Julie was not very optimistic about her chances. "Besides the interview," she told Susan, dates are being selected on the basis of past work experience and I don't have any. Oh, I'm sure that personal appearance and the ability to speak well all help. But it's job performance they're looking for. I did fine on the typing test, but that's still not as important as past experience."

Four days later Susan bumped into Julie again. The two had been sent letters indicating that they were hired and were to report for orientation. Yesterday they found that they will both be working in the same unit. "I guess that work experience isn't everything," Susan told her new friend. "Your typing test must have impressed them also." Julie agreed.

1. What types of screening procedures did the firm use? Were they job-related? Explain.
2. If you were the interviewer, which questions would you not have asked? What other questions would you have asked? Explain.
3. How would you handle the orientation process for Susan and Julie? What would you do? Describe it in your own words.

YOU BE THE SUPERVISOR: PLANNING THE TRAINING

The people in Jan Stevenson's department all have one common goal: to provide support help to the other departments in the organization. The largest group (10 people) in the department consists of typists who handle general typing from the administrative offices. The second largest group (7) consists of computer specialists who are responsible for processing information and seeing that each department has a weekly computer printout of all its financial and sales activities from the previous week. The rest of Jan's department consists of two assistant supervisors (one for the typists and one for the computer specialists) and the supervisor's administrative assistant, who serves as a typist and receptionist for her.

Every December the personnel department sends around a memo asking all management personnel to identify the types of training they feel that their people need. Since this is Jan's first year as a supervisor, she is not sure exactly what type of training to recommend for anyone in the department. However, one of her friends who has been a supervisor for some time explained to her that she should call together the people in the department, ask them the type of training they feel would be of most benefit to them, supplement it with her own judgment, and send it in. "For example," her friend told her, "last year one of my typists told me that she would like to take a course in word processing because she had learned that we were going to be putting personal computers in the departments and she could use one of these machines to handle letters, memos, reports, etc. It was an excellent idea and I sent her name in for the program. However, 3 months later she came by to see me to tell me that she heard there was a new word processing program that had just hit the market and she wanted to learn it because it would speed up her typing. I checked and found out that once you learn one word processing program, it usually doesn't pay to learn another. The time involved in learning is not offset by the time saved in typing. So I turned her down. The lesson is simple: Give people the basics, but don't recommend programs that are going to be of marginal value."

Jan feels that this is good advice, and she intends to talk to the people in her department to see what types of training they would like. She also intends to talk to her boss to see if he can give her some suggestions that will guide her in deciding what type of training each person should get. However, there is one thing that has her slightly upset. The memo from the personnel department also said that each program would be evaluated later on to see if it was worth the cost. "Please do not send people to programs that have marginal value for them," read part of the memo. "Evaluations of all programs will be conducted within 2 weeks of the time they are held." Jan does not know exactly what this means. "Perhaps," she has told herself, "I should talk to the boss about this also."

1. Put yourself in Jan's shoes. What types of training would you recommend for typists? Computer personnel? Supervisory personnel? Be specific in your answer.
2. What type of training would be most helpful to a person like Jan? Explain your answer.
3. How should Jan go about evaluating the training? Be complete in your answer.

NOTES

1. U.S. Equal Employment Opportunity Commission, *Affirmative Action and Equal Opportunity—A Guidebook for Employers*, vol. 2, Washington, D.C.: U.S. Government Printing Office, 1973, pp. 40–44.
2. William F. Glueck, *Personnel: A Diagnostic Approach*, 3d ed., Dallas, Texas: Business Publications, 1982, chap. 11.

CHAPTER 7

COMMUNICATING FOR RESULTS

GOALS OF THE CHAPTER

Supervisors are more concerned with day-to-day operations than is any other management group. For this reason, it is vital that they be able to communicate effectively with their people. If there is a failure or breakdown of communication at this level, it is very likely that the results will show up on the bottom line in the form of reduced profit, output, or efficiency. The primary goals of this chapter are to examine the ways in which communication takes place and to note some of the major steps that supervisors can take to improve their communication ability. When you have finished reading all the material in this chapter, you will be able to:

1. Describe how the communication process works.
2. Relate the two most common forms of communication media and note some practical guidelines that should be followed in using each.
3. Identify and describe two common barriers to communication and ways that supervisors can effectively deal with each.
4. Explain how an understanding of nonverbal communication can help supervisors better manage their people.
5. Discuss the nature of the informal organization and some things that supervisors should know about it.
6. Define the term *feedback* and identify some useful tips for developing and maintaining feedback from the employees.
7. Compare and contrast the listening habits of poor and effective listeners.
8. Explain what active listening is all about and the value it has for effective supervisory communication.

A STARTING CASE: PAUL'S TARDINESS DECISION

As he arrived for work, Paul Donnelly saw two of his people just entering the building. Usually Paul is in the office by 9 A.M., but because he had been out at the airport dropping off a top manager, he was 30 minutes late getting in.

There is no set policy regarding tardiness, although it is expected that everyone will be on time for work. If someone does start coming in late, most supervisors will call in the individual and discuss the situation. This usually straightens out the problem. If it does not, the annual performance appraisal will pick it up and the individual is likely to get a smaller-than-average raise.

Paul recognized the two people who came in late. However, he was reluctant to confront them directly. Besides, he thought, they may not be the only ones guilty of tardiness. He concluded that the best way to handle the situation was to write a detailed memo setting forth his policy on tardiness and indicating what the penalties would be.

The memo was three pages long. It detailed the need for people to arrive to work on time and not to leave early. One entire page was devoted to the penalties for tardiness. Anyone coming late, regardless of the reason, would have his or her pay docked for the missed time. Anyone coming late more than once a week would be sent home and lose a day's pay.

Paul had the memo typed up and tacked on the bulletin board in the main work area. The workers always kept track of what was on the board. They could not help but see the new memo.

Yesterday Paul found two workers coming in late. He informed both that he would have their pay docked for the missed time. Both seemed surprised by his actions but said nothing. Earlier today one of the workers was late again and Paul sent him home. Before the worker left, however, he and Paul had quite a row. The worker said he had never heard of any policies related to tardiness. Paul countered by pointing to the memo on the bulletin board. The worker seemed genuinely surprised. "What memo?" he yelled. "I've never seen any memo about tardiness." With that, he stalked to the parking lot and drove off.

Why did the worker not read the memo? What did Paul do wrong in communicating his policy on tardiness? How should he have communicated with his people? What should he do now? Offer him some practical advice.

HOW COMMUNICATION WORKS

Communication is the process of conveying meanings from sender to receiver. Sometimes this is done verbally; other times it is done in writing. Quite often the supervisor uses the process to convey directives and orders to the workers. Other times the supervisor employs it to pass on information to the boss. The following examines how this process works.

The process

Supervisory communication has five main elements. First, there is the supervisor who is conveying information. This person is known as the *sender*. It is this individual's job to determine what is to be communicated and to figure out how this should be done so that the person getting the message will understand it.

Second, there is the means used to convey the message. The supervisor must use an appropriate form of the communication *media*. This can be a conversation, a picture, a diagram, a chart, or whatever the individual feels will be most effective in getting the worker to understand the message.

Third, there is the *receiver* who gets the message and must interpret what it means and what, if any, action should be taken as a result.

Figure 7-1. The communication process.

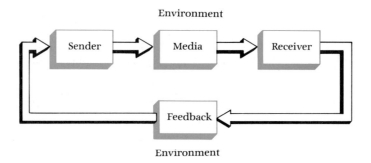

Fourth, there is *feedback,* with which the individual indicates that the message is clear and will be complied with or asks for further assistance or clarification.

Fifth, there is the *environment* in which the message is communicated. Sometimes, *where* the communication takes place is more important than anything else. For example, if the supervisor's boss calls the individual into the office to talk about something, this may indicate a serious problem. The supervisor does not have to wait to determine how important the matter is; he or she already knows this based on where the discussion is taking place. If it were a minor matter, the boss would talk to the supervisor in the hallway or over a cup of coffee in the cafeteria.

Figure 7-1 illustrates the communication process in action.

Communication media

There are many forms of communication media that supervisors use in conveying messages. In general terms, they fall into two categories: verbal and written.

Verbal communication. Verbal communication is fast and provides the opportunity for immediate feedback. The two most common forms of verbal communications are face-to-face communication and telephone conversations.

Face-to-face communication is regarded as the most effective medium because it provides for immediate feedback. If the worker misunderstands something or needs additional information, the supervisor can provide it then nd there. Even when messages should be committed in writing, it is beneficial to follow up and supplement them verbally.

Telephone messages are not as effective as face-to-face communications because the supervisor cannot see the other party. Nonverbal feedback (body language) is denied to the individual. He or she must rely on what the other person is saying (or not saying) in determining whether the message is clear. On the other hand, the telephone offers rapid transmission and the opportunity for immediate feedback. If the worker has any questions or needs more data, it can be requested at this time.

Written communication. Written communication can take many different forms. Examples include memos, personal letters, bulletins, official reports, directives, and newsletters. Most supervisors do not use all of these things. Aside from filling out performance evaluations, the most common form of written communication is the memo.

Memos are brief written messages usually of 250 words or less. Their purpose is to provide information to a group of people in a fast, inexpensive, and uniform manner. They also provide a permanent record for both parties. In writing them, the supervisor should make use of the following guidelines:

1. Review the purpose of the memo. What message is to be conveyed?
2. Consider the target group. Who is to receive the memo?
3. At the top of the page, note to whom the memo is directed, from whom it is coming, and what the purpose of the message is.
4. Organize the ideas in a logical and sequential order. Make it easy for the reader to move from one idea to the next.
5. Be concise. Short memos tend to be read and remembered by more people than do long memos.
6. Edit the first draft by eliminating unnecessary words and by expanding any areas where questions are likely to be asked. Write the second draft with the objective of minimizing the need for any verbal follow-up to complement or explain the memo.
7. Have someone else read the second draft and react to it. If the individual raises any questions or problems, address them before finalizing and sending the memo.[1]

Supervisors are seldom expert writers. Written communication is not one of their major job requirements. For this reason, it is important for them to supplement the above advice with a knowledge of what is called the *fog index*; this index measures the degree of difficulty in a written memo or report. The greater the fog index, the more difficult it is for workers to understand the message. (See Supervision in Action: Eliminating the Fog.)

SUPERVISION IN ACTION: ELIMINATING THE FOG

In reducing the fog index in writing, there are four basic rules that supervisors must follow:

1. Select one or more samples. Count out 100 consecutive words at random. If you are testing a lengthy report, two or more samples may be taken. Count each word, even "a's" and "I's." Do not count figures that are not spelled out. Count hyphenated words as one word.
2. Find the average number of words per sentence. This is done by dividing the total words in the sample by the number of sentences.
3. Find the percent of difficult words in the sample. Count the number of difficult words and divide by the total number of words.

- *Include* each word of three syllables or more as a difficult word.
- *Exclude* words of three syllables or more that are capitalized (except words that are capitalized because they start sentences).
- *Exclude* words of three syllables or more that are formed by two simple words, such as "chairperson" or "businessman."
- *Exclude verb forms of three syllables in which the third syllable is es* or *ed,* such as "processes" or "converted."

4. Add the average number of words per sentence and the percent of difficult words. Then, multiply this sum by 4 in order to determine the readability level (in terms of grade level).

Here is an example of how the index is computed using the following 113-word sample:

In order to maintain stability in the work force and help ease the situation connected with the dislocation of employees due to some major changes in our operations, the following procedures should be followed:

No full-time employee is to be hired in the company without first checking to see whether there is a qualified person elsewhere in the company available for the job. Ralph Johnson will act as a clearinghouse for all new hires or layoffs. He will attempt to match jobs and people, considering their qualifications. He will also instigate the necessary procedures in order to accomplish this objective. Supervisors will be asked to evaluate qualifications of all persons involved in these moves.

Step 1. The sample contains *113* words.

Step 2. The sample contains *six* sentences.

$$\frac{113}{6} = 18.83 \text{ words per sentence}$$

Step 3. The sample contains 23 difficult words. The verb form "connected" was excluded.

$$\frac{23}{113} = 0.2035$$

$$0.2035 \times 100 = 20.35 \text{ difficult words}$$

Step 4.

$$
\begin{array}{r}
18.83 \text{ words per sentence} \\
+ \ \underline{20.35 \text{ difficult words}} \\
39.18 \\
\times \ \underline{0.4} \\
\end{array}
$$

15.67 or 15.7 grade level in readability

Here is how to reduce the fog:

How would you rewrite the memo in order to cut the fog? Rewrite it, then compare your work with the following:

We have made some *operational* changes to upgrade our firm. These changes may result in some job changes and new *opportunities*. To help in this process, these steps will be taken:

1. Our employees will be informed and given first priority in consideration for new job opportunities within our firm.
2. Mr. Ralph Johnson will handle all new hires and layoffs.
3. Further, Mr. Johnson will attempt to match new jobs with our present employees where he can. He will set up the procedures to do this.
4. Supervisors will be asked to assess the qualifications of those involved in these moves.

Step 1. The sample contains *98* words.
Step 2. The sample contains *eight* sentences.

$$\frac{98}{8} = 12.25 \text{ words per sentence}$$

Step 3. The sample contains 10 difficult words.

$$\frac{10}{98} = 0.102 \times 100 = 10.2 \text{ difficult words}$$

Step 4.

$$
\begin{array}{r}
12.25 \text{ words per sentence} \\
+ \ 10.20 \text{ difficult words} \\
\hline
22.45 \\
\times \ \underline{0.4} \\
\hline
8.98 \text{ grade level in readability}
\end{array}
$$

Now this is more like it. The readability level of the memo is the 9th grade. The memo was rewritten to gain economy and clarity in expression. Unnecessary words, particularly difficult words, were eliminated. More sentences were used. Some sentences were numbered.

Source: Dan W. Swenson, "Write Clear Reports: A 'Readability' Index," *Supervisory Management,* September 1980, pp. 29, 31–32. © 1980 by AMACOM, a division of American Management Associations, New York. Reprinted by permission of the publisher; all rights reserved.

BARRIERS TO COMMUNICATION

Not all supervisory communications are successful. Sometimes barriers exist and cause communication breakdown. Two of the most common communication barriers are perception and inference.

Perception

Perception is a person's view of reality. Since no two people have ever had the exact same experiences, their perceptions of things will vary. Sometimes this will cause communication problems. These problems fall into two categories: sensory and normative.

Sensory perception is one's view of physical reality. When a supervisor says, "The lathe in work area A needs maintenance," the repair person knows which machine the manager is talking about. Unless there is more than one lathe in the area that needs maintenance, the repair person should have no trouble finding the machine. On the other hand, sensory perception can cause communication prolems because people do not always perceive what literally is presented to them. For example, look at the following statement:

MANY FOREMEN AND OTHER SUPERVISORS OF WORK FACTORY FIVE HAVE BEEN FOUND COMING TO WORK LATE. THIS PRACTICE OF TARDINESS MUST STOP EFFECTIVE IMMEDIATELY!

Now go back to the statement and this time, using just your eyes, quickly scan the material and count the number of times the letter F appears. Begin!

How many times does the letter F appear? Most people say six, found in the words *foremen, factory, five, found,* and *effective.* Actually there are eight; the other two F's are in the words *of.* Why do most people miss the last two? Because they are accustomed to glancing over short words, not really paying close attention to them. The same is true when written messages are sent to workers. Sometimes the personnel read them too quickly and do not pick up everything that is there. This is why it is useful to supplement written communiques with verbal follow-up related to the individual's understanding of the memo. In doing so, the supervisor must be sure not to ask *whether* the individual understands, because the worker is almost always going to say yes. The supervisor must ask *what* the individual understands by using questions such as: What is your understanding of the new work rules? How are these rules going to affect you? Do you agree with these new rules and if not, why not? Make the individual talk about his or her comprehension and perception of the rules.

Normative perception is a person'a view of interpretive reality. It comes into play when things are a matter of opinion. Normative perception can be illustrated best with diagrams. Look at Figure 7-2. What do you see? How about Figure 7-3? The first is called the Peter-Paul goblet. Some people see the profiles of two individuals facing each other. Other people see a goblet or drinking cup. The second has two common interpretations: a bird with a long beak or a rabbit (the bird's beak becomes the rabbit's ears).

Figure 7-2. What do you see?

Figure 7-3. What do you see?

This basic idea of interpretive reality carries over to supervisory communication whenever the manager conveys anything that can be interpreted in a manner other than that which was desired. For example, a supervisor tells her subordinate, "This work change will not only increase your output but will ensure you a good performance rating and a chance at promotion." However, the subordinate disagrees. The only thing he can see is that the work change will mean that he will have to do more work. There is something in it for the company; there is nothing in it for him. The most effective way of getting around normative perception problems is for the supervisor to encourage feedback. She should ask the worker, "How do you feel about the new work change?" The subordinate may indicate that he thinks it is going to be of no value for him. Whether he is right or wrong, that is his view of reality. It does no good for the supervisor to say, "Well you're totally wrong." This is not a question of right or wrong. It is a matter of perception. The supervisor must work on selling the individual on the change or encouraging the person to wait and see how things come out. "You're going to be pleasantly surprised with the eventual outcome," she can tell him. "This work change will be for your benefit. Just give me a chance to prove it to you."

What the supervisor must remember is that everyone has his own view of reality. Whether it be sensory or normative reality, what is real to people may differ from person to person. The only way to change this view is by providing additional feedback that will serve to clarify things and show how they are of value to the other person.

Inference

An *inference* is an assumption made by the receiver of a message. Inferences are common when messages contain gaps that must be filled in. For example, the supervisor tells the subordinate, "We're going to start giving out the biggest raises to the best workers." What does this mean? How large will the biggest raises be? When will this start? How will performance be measured in determining the "best" workers? All of this is unclear. The receiver will begin drawing inferences and filling in the gaps. This is how rumor and gossip get started. In overcoming inferences, the supervisor needs to promote and encourage feedback from the personnel. The manager also needs to phrase both verbal and written messages in such a way as to reduce the number of gaps by being as complete and detailed as possible. Can you spot inferences when they appear? Try Self-Assessment Quiz 7-1 and see how well you do.

SELF-ASSESSMENT QUIZ 7-1: CAN YOU SPOT INFERENCES?

Carefully read the following story. When you have finished, read the statements that follow and circle the correct answer in each case. Remember that some of the statements will be true (T) because the story reported the information just this way; some will be false (F) because the story said just the opposite; and some will be inferential (I) because the story does not make it clear whether they are true or false and to reach a conclusion about them you have to fill in the gaps.

The story

Chuck Preston is a supervisor at the Willowby Company. Last Tuesday Chuck was late for the second time that week. His car had broken down. Chuck's boss suggested that he get a new car, but with the price of cars so high, Chuck has been reluctant to do so. Earlier today his boss informed him that the company's business has been doing so well that there will be overtime for the next 6 months. If Chuck would like, he can have 4 hours of overtime every day and can also work on his days off. Overtime pays supervisors 1½ times their calculated hourly rate. Working on days off carries 1½ times the regular rate for the first day and double time for the second. With this new development, Chuck realizes that he can now afford to replace his clunker. Additionally, the overtime work should be fun because four of the people in his regular work group have indicated that they, too, would like to work overtime every day as well as on their days off. Chuck intends to work overtime 4 hours per day during the regular 5-day week and 8 hours per day on each of the other 2 days.

Questions

Without going back and looking at the story, answer the following questions by entering an X in the appropriate column.

	T	F	I
1. Chuck is a supervisor at the Willowby Company.	X		
2. Chuck supervises a production group.			X
3. Chuck was late for the first 2 days of his workweek.			X
4. Chuck wants to buy a brand new car.			X
5. The company's business is beginning to slow up.		X	
6. Chuck wants to work overtime.	X		X
7. There will be overtime for the next 6 months.	X		
8. Chuck intends to work 28 hours overtime per week.		X	
9. There are eight people in Chuck's regular work group.			X
10. Chuck intends to replace his old car with the money he earns with overtime pay.			X

The answers to these questions are provided at the end of the chapter.

UNDERSTANDING NONVERBAL COMMUNICATION

In addition to knowing how to avoid barriers to communication, the effective supervisor has to have an understanding of nonverbal communication. This can take many forms, including facial expressions, gestures, posture, and the way people use physical space. For supervisors, the two most important components of nonverbal communication are kinesics and proxemics.

Kinesics

Kinesics is the study of communication through body movements and facial expressions.[2] These movements and expressions transfer meaning to others. As a result, they can be just as important as verbal activity. By looking at the individual's body language, the supervisor can learn to pick up cues regarding how the person feels about what is being communicated.

The eyes have been found to be the best conveyors of information, and the face, in general, provides more accurate nonverbal feedback than any other part of the body. For example, studies and observations have found that eye contact is extremely important when the supervisor communicates with a worker because it is generally seen as a sign of honesty, interest, openness, and confidence.[3]

Posture is another important form of nonverbal communication. It provides clues regarding confidence, aggressiveness, anxiety, fear, rejection, etc. For example, workers who stand erect tend to be sure of themselves; those who slouch are usually not. Posture is also important when the supervisor wants to convey a message. For example, by standing, leaning over the desk, and peering down at the employee, the individual can create the right atmosphere for delivering a reprimand or making an important point.

Proxemics

Proxemics is the study of how people use physical space and what this use says about them. People are territorial animals who lay claim to areas and defend them against intruders.[4] The way space is used serves to communicate with others. This becomes clearer by examining the three types of feature space.

Fixed feature space consists of the permanent parts of a building or room: walls, ceilings, partitions, windows. A supervisor with a window office has more status than does a supervisor without one. When subordinates communicate with the former, they know (or soon learn) that this person has authority and power. He or she is not to be fooled with.

Semifixed feature space consists of those things in a room which can be moved: chairs, desks, tables, lamps, etc. These can be arranged in such a way as to communicate a message. For example, most supervisors sit behind their desk, with the worker on the opposite side. This formality communicates the message: "I am in charge; that's why I'm behind the desk. You are here to take orders; that's why you are in front of the desk." By arranging the office so that the visitor sits in a chair on the side of the desk, the supervisor can reduce this formality. "Let's talk openly and freely," the individual is saying. If the supervisor has two chairs on the other side of the desk and walks around and sits next to the subordinate, this is even more informal. The message now is, "Let's talk as equals." To the extent that supervisors have a need to increase or decrease formality, semifixed features in the room can be adjusted.

Informal feature space is the physical distance people maintain between themselves and others. There are four such distances or zones (see Figure 7-4). One is *public distance*, which extends from about 12 to 25 feet. It is the

Figure 7-4. Personal space categories.

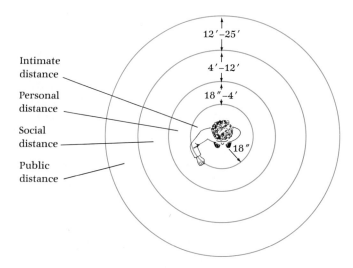

Intimate distance

Personal distance

Social distance

Public distance

12'–25'

4'–12'

18"–4'

18"

farthest distance at which people can communicate effectively on a face-to-face basis. This distance is ideal when talking to groups of people. The second zone is *social distance,* which extends from 4 to 12 feet. Most business is transacted at this distance. The third is *personal distance* and can range from 1½ to 4 feet. This zone is usually reserved for good friends. The fourth is the *intimate distance* and extends up to 1½ feet from the other person. This zone is reserved for only the closest of friends. As the supervisor allows workers to move from the public to the personal zone, informality, closeness, and trust are encouraged. Through the use of physical distance, the supervisor can add a nonverbal dimension to communication efforts.

WORKING WITH THE INFORMAL ORGANIZATION

Not all the supervisor's communications are through formal channels. Quite often the individual will need to tap into the informal network to find out information or to convey messages. In so doing, the supervisor needs to understand how the grapevine works.

The grapevine

The *grapevine* is a term used to describe the informal organizational communication system. It refers to any communication taking place outside of prescribed formal channels. Despite its often negative connotations, the grapevine flourishes in every organization and manages to serve some very important employee needs of both supervisors and employees. In general, the grapevine has six characteristics:

1. **It transmits information fast.** In contrast to the slow nature of formal communications, the grapevine can handle rapid exchanges of information. By cutting across organizational levels and avoiding red

tape, the grapevine is perhaps the fastest source of information retrieval.

2. ***It is predominantly oral in nature.*** The grapevine relies most heavily on word-of-mouth transmission. The formal system largely deals with written communication. Since many supervisors and employees do not want to go "on the record" with their concerns and questions, the grapevine is ideal for them.

3. ***It is geared toward handling out-of-the-ordinary events.*** The formal system, when functioning adequately, can effectively process routine messages. If something unusual happens, such as the unexpected departure of a powerful supervisor, the formal system has to pull back and decide how to deal with this information. On the other hand, the grapevine is literally pulsing with the news. Unlike the formal hierarchy, the grapevine takes nonroutine, unexpected news in stride.

4. ***It is people-oriented rather than things-oriented.*** Informal communications buzz with information about people: what they said, what they did, and how they behaved. Formal communications tend to steer away from these types of messages and focus instead on news about things: strategies, policies, procedures, rules, etc.

5. ***It is controlled and fed mainly by the workers.*** Unlike the formal system, which is largely controlled and monitored by management, the organizational grapevine by and large is the communication vehicle of the employees. Of course, supervisors use the grapevine; but even if they did not, it would flourish.

6. ***It is employee motivating.*** The grapevine keeps employees alert, interested, and motivated in their social surroundings. In particular, it provides them the opportunity for chatting with coworkers and satisfying social needs.

Advantages and disadvantages of the grapevine

An active grapevine is one indication of organizational health. A lively grapevine reflects the psychological need of people to talk about their jobs and their company as a central life interest.

Another advantage of the grapevine is its candidness. It provides a barometer of employee opinion in the organization. If the supervisor is sensitive to this, he or she can gather a great deal of information about the attitudes and interests of the workers.

A third advantage is that the grapevine acts as a sounding board, a place for employees to let off steam and air their anxieties and frustrations. This psychological safety valve can be very important to the long-term, smooth operation of the organization.

Fourth, the informal system greatly influences the environment and the quality of work life. A healthy grapevine promotes social compatibility and a cooperative, team-oriented work group. It is the informal system that really establishes the behavioral norms and quickly socializes newcomers as to what is, and what is not, acceptable behavior.

Finally, informal channels take up slack by processing information not handled by formal channels. The grapevine helps to get the work done. If only formal channels were used by supervisors and employees, work output would not be as great as it could be. In particular, decision making would take much more time. As an example, consider the following story. (Use Figure 7-5 to follow the flow of communication.) Roberta is appying for a job as assistant production supervisor with the XYZ Company. She knows that there are many other applicants but feels that she is very well qualified. Her cousin, Paul, is director of purchasing for the firm, and she calls and asks him for help in getting the job. In turn, he calls his friend Tom, who is the corporate comptroller, and asks for help in getting Roberta hired. Tom calls his friend Jean, who is the production manager, and relates a very positive picture of Roberta. Finally, Jean calls Jack in personnel and asks him to send down Roberta's file right away. The conversation goes something like this:

> I've heard really good things about one of the applicants for the job of assistant production supervisor. Her name is Roberta Smithfield.

> Yes, I've got her application right here. But to tell you the truth, we've got others who are as qualified as she.

Figure 7-5. An informal system in action.

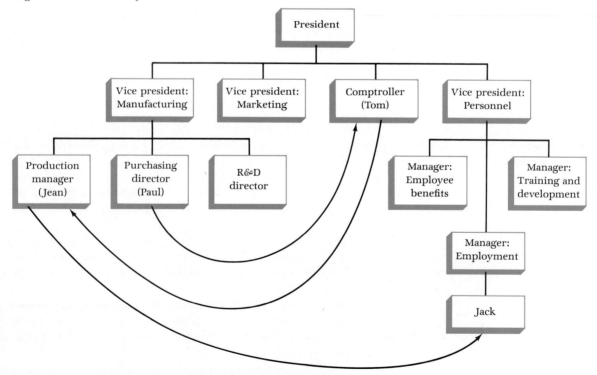

Well, written qualifications don't tell the whole story, Jack. It takes more than formal education to get along in our department. I've heard Roberta has what it takes. I'd like you to get her in to see me as quickly as possible.

I really wanted to set up appointments with you for four or five others as well.

Listen, Jack, my schedule is jammed. Get Roberta in here first. If I need to see anyone else, I'll let you know.

Roberta comes in for the appointment the next day and is formally on the job by Monday morning. Is this a realistic scenario? Very! Oftentimes the hiring of a new employee is a result both of the informal and the formal communication systems.

The informal organization also has disadvantages. One of the most important is that there is often some degree of error in the grapevine. However, it should be remembered that this error is not as great as many people think. One research study found that 75 to 95 percent of grapevine information was accurate.[5]

Second, employees sometimes feed the grapevine with self-serving information. They create "facts" rather than simply report them. They attempt to influence things through the use of selective inputs.

Third, information processed by the grapevine is not protected by limited responsibility. When someone puts a message into the formal system, he or she takes responsibility for it. If there are questions or comments about it, people know where to find the source. This is not true, however, with the informal communication system, and this lack of focused responsibility can cause confusion.

Fourth, the grapevine sometimes carries unfounded rumors. These rumors are based, at best, on inference rather than on fact and can cause a great deal of damage if not quickly set straight.

Grapevine chains

It is possible to depict graphically how grapevine messages travel. In the case of the XYZ Company mentioned earlier and presented in Figure 7-5, the situation was that a message was passed from one person to another. This is called a *single-strand chain* and is actually the least used informal channel. Figure 7-6 depicts the single strand as well as the other three common grapevine paths.

The *gossip chain* is characterized by one person telling all the others, usually in rapid succession. Speed is important because without it someone else will probably carry the news. Like the single srand, this chain is seldom used in organizations.

The *probability chain* is one in which information is passed in an unpredictable pattern. The first person randomly tells one or a few others and they in turn arbitrarily pass the message to still other people. This chain is more commonly used than are the single-strand or gossip chains.

The *cluster chain* is the most frequent grapevine mode and is charac-

Figure 7-6. Grapevine chains.

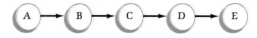

Single-strand chain

Gossip chain

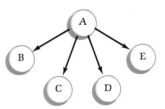

Probability chain

Cluster chain

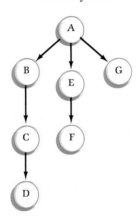

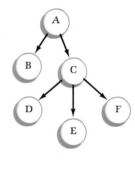

terized by *selective* patterns of communication. For example, A may regularly pass information to B and C because he knows he can trust them with the message. If it is confidential, they will keep it that way. If it can be communicated further, but not everyone should know, A is certain that B and C will be discreet with regard to whom they tell. Notice from Figure 7-6 that B has chosen to tell no one, while C has told D, E, and F. If anyone tells the message to someone he should not, he runs the risk of being excluded from future informal communiques.

Managing the grapevine

Supervisors must pay heed to the grapevine and actively get involved in using it to supplement their formal chain of communication. To ignore the grapevine is to cut oneself off from a valuable communication resource. Studies show, for example, that five out of every six messages processed by an organization are carried via informal channels.[6] As a result, supervisors need to learn to adapt to, to manage, and to control the grapevine. One approach is to open up all organizational communication channels, fight rumors with a positive presentation of facts, and develop a long-term credibility of managerial communications. This, of course, requires the creation of a trust relationship between the supervisors and the employees.

If this can be accomplished, it will go far toward eliminating the negative consequences of the grapevine while nurturing its benefits. Such a relationship also helps squelch rumors, which tend to flourish when employees feel insecure and have limited access to information.

The best way to control rumors is by providing substantial and accurate information. If rumors do occur, the effective supervisor can then pick up on them and short-circuit them by providing correct information. In turn, the rumor will have provided the manager with insights regarding where the workers lack information and/or have concerns. The supervisor's role in influencing the informal organization is to: (1) Accept and understand the informal organization; (2) consider possible effects on informal systems when taking any action; (3) integrate, as far as possible, the interests of informal groups with those of the formal organization; and (4) keep formal activities from unnecessarily threatening the informal organization in general.

FEEDBACK

Feedback is information that facilitates the understanding and/or control of communications, enabling the sender to adapt or adjust messages for greater clarity. Feedback turns communication into a two-way street, allowing the sender to become the receiver and vice versa. This process is particularly important to supervisors because workers greatly benefit from such feedback. This was clearly illustrated in a study conducted among clerical employees of a large eastern insurance company. The workers were asked the frequency and usefulness of different types of feedback. Figure 7-7 presents the findings. Most significantly, the workers reported that while they received only a moderate amount of feedback from their supervisors, they felt that this information was extremely useful to them.[7] Feedback helped them do a better job.

Supervisors need to remember a number of things about feedback. The following detail six of the most useful tips for improving effectiveness through feedback.

1. ***Immediate feedback is important.*** When people do something well or poorly, the supervisor should let them know this has not gone unnoticed. In the case of a worker who does an outstanding job, immediate feedback serves to reinforce the behavior and ensure that the individual will try to do it again. In the case of a person who does a very poor job, immediate feedback serves as a warning that things will have to improve. Rapid feedback is a learning reinforcement tool that can be used to shape employee behavior.

2. ***Supervisory feedback should complement work-related feedback.*** Some people have jobs that provide them work-related feedback, so they know how well they are doing. A salesperson does not need the sales supervisor to say, "Hey, you sold 10 percent more than

Figure 7-7. Frequency and usefulness ratings of various sources of feedback. (Reprinted by permission of the publisher from Phillip L. Quaglieri, "Feedback on Feedback." *Supervisory Management*, January 1980, p. 37. © 1980. Published by AMACOM, a division of American Management Associations, New York. All rights reserved.)

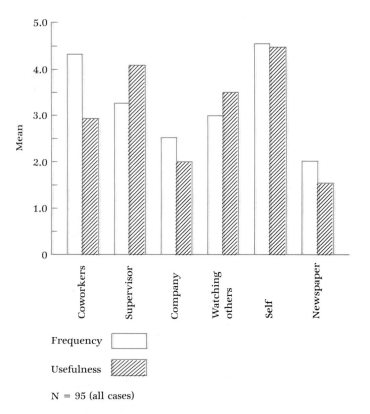

Frequency

Usefulness

N = 95 (all cases)

quota last month." The salesperson already knows this. Nor does a machine operator need to be told, "Your output last month was 15 percent greater than your assigned goal." The individual knows how much he or she is producing. On the other hand, these people still like to be praised by the supervisor. While they know they are doing a good job, verbal feedback from the boss lets them know that this person is also aware of their progress.

3. ***Positive feedback produces the best results, but negative feedback is better than none at all.*** Praising people for what they do well encourages them to do it again. Workers like positive feedback. They also welcome advice and assistance in areas where their performance is not up to par. Naturally, no one likes to be criticized or ridiculed. However, people would rather be told what they are doing wrong and how they can improve than not be given any feedback at all. In the latter case, the worker will never get any better. Without feedback, improvement is unlikely to occur.

4. ***Verbal feedback should accompany nonverbal feedback.*** Many supervisors smile at their people, nod at what the workers say, and pat them on the back before walking away. All of these nonverbal behaviors

indicate that the boss is pleased with their performance—and this may be the case. However, these behaviors should be accompanied by verbal feedback. The supervisor should literally tell them what the smile, the nod, and the pat on the back mean. This behavior not only reinforces the nonverbal feedback but helps the workers better understand what the boss wants done in the future.

5. ***Workers remember longest what they hear first and last in a message.*** When providing feedback, the initial comments set the stage for what is to follow. If the supervisor begins with a smile and a kind word, the listener is likely to be receptive. If the boss starts off with a scowl and a criticism, the worker is likely to be defensive. This will influence how well the person listens to what is communicated. Likewise, the last comments influence the receiver because he or she will use these as a means of determining what has been said. If the supervisor winds up a conversation by noting three things he wants the worker to do, the latter is likely to conclude that these are the major points with which to be concerned. If the individual wraps up the meeting by making flippant remarks, the worker may conclude that the boss was not serious about anything that was said.

6. ***Feedback is the only way of learning how people think and feel about things.*** Unless the supervisor provides feedback to the workers, they have no way of knowing how well the boss feels that they are doing. Unless the supervisor gets feedback from the workers, he or she has no way of determining what things they are satisfied, discontent, or indifferent about. One way of establishing feedback is to talk to the workers on a regular basis, asking questions and providing candid answers. A second way is to encourage them to ask questions and raise issues that are of personal concern. A third is to supplement face-to-face meetings with such techniques as employee suggestion plans. The latter are particularly effective in generating work-improvement ideas. (See Supervision in Action: Getting Feedback through Employee Suggestion Plans at Kodak.)

SUPERVISION IN ACTION: GETTING FEEDBACK THROUGH EMPLOYEE SUGGESTION PLANS AT KODAK

How the plan works

Rather than have one giant administrative and processing system, each of Kodak's major divisions in the United States and Canada has its own suggestion office. A full-time suggestion secretary administers the system for each division.

When an employee comes up with an idea that he or she feels would improve a company product or operation, suggestion blanks are readily available. The suggester is encouraged to seek the advice and help of a supervisor in completing the suggestion blank, which may be placed in the plant mail or in special collection boxes located in different areas of the plant.

Each suggestion is then delivered to the suggestion secretary and promptly acknowledged—if the suggester's name appears on the form. If desired, the suggester can elect to remain anonymous. The suggestion is then controlled by its preassigned number. Later the suggester can telephone to learn whether the numbered suggestion has been adopted. Lists of adopted suggestions submitted anonymously are also periodically published in the company newspaper and may be posted on bulletin boards.

The suggestion secretary submits each suggestion to those members of management and those staff groups best qualified to consider the suggestion. The proposal may be put to a trial test to determine its merit, if this appears necessary. But any investigation must be prompt and thorough.

In some large departments, the recommendations for both adopted and declined ideas are reviewed and approved by department suggestion committees before final results of the investigation are relayed back to the suggestion secretary. Following a thorough investigation by all interested parties, all reports and comments are reviewed by the plant suggestion office or committee acting in behalf of the plant manager.

Adoptions and awards

Where applicable, standard methods developed from years of experience determine the value of an adopted suggestion and the amount of the cash award to be given to the suggester. Most suggestions relating to production can be measured accurately. In such cases, the award is a percentage of the suggestion's value for the first 2 years in which it is utilized.

Those suggestions that do not readily lend themselves to standard methods of evaluation—for example, a suggestion that would improve the safety of an operation—are just as carefully considered by the suggestion committee. Estimates of the value of these suggestions are made on the basis of staff or the opinion of some other qualified authority. Award lists in each plant are made up periodically and checks distributed by the suggestion secretary to various department heads and superintendents for personal presentation to the recipients.

Source: Allan W. Bergerson, "Employee Suggestion Plan Still Going Strong at Kodak," *Supervisory Management,* May 1977, pp. 34–35. © 1977 by AMACOM, a division of American Management Associations, New York. Reprinted by permission of the publisher; all rights reserved.

EFFECTIVE LISTENING

Supervisors need to be good listeners because they spend more time listening than they do reading, writing, or speaking. One way of improving listening effectiveness is by developing good listening habits.

Good listeners have habits quite different from those of poor listeners. Nichols, a prominent researcher in the field, found 10 differences between the two.[8] Here are the habits found among effective listeners:

1. ***Listen with an open mind.*** Before the worker ever begins speaking, supervisors who are poor listeners have made up their minds that the subject will be uninteresting. This negative mind-set serves as an excuse for daydreaming or engaging in other non-listening-related activities. Supervisors who are effective listeners may find the subject boring, but they make the most of the situation. They focus on the worker's message, determined to derive something from the encounter.

2. ***Focus on what is being said.*** Supervisors who are poor listeners concentrate on the negative mannerisms of a mediocre speaker. The worker's clothes are not in style; he needs a haircut; her accent is difficult to understand; he repeats himself too often; she says, "OK," after every other sentence. Effective listeners also recognize the poor delivery of the speaker; however, they quickly put it in the back of their minds and focus on what is being said rather than on how it is being delivered.

3. ***Remain calm.*** Poor listeners hear just a brief part of what the speaker is trying to convey and interrupt at the first pause. When they are finished, the other person will often say, "Well, if you had waited, I was about to make that point," or even worse, "I *just* said that a minute ago." Ineffective supervisors rob their employees of the chance of making a point, even going so far as to refuse the speaker the psychological satisfaction of being heard out. When effective supervisors listen, they practice the cliché "Hear the worker out." They do not jump to conclusions about what the worker is saying. They wait for the person to finish before starting to develop their own ideas.

4. ***Focus on main ideas.*** Invariably, poor listeners try to remember specific facts. In so doing, they usually miss the main idea. Good listeners look for the main ideas. Once the gist of the talk is determined, the facts are remembered as logical supporting evidence.

5. ***Listen for the overall message.*** Supervisors who are poor listeners have a habit of taking copious notes and outlining the conversation. Their effective counterparts listen for the main points, realizing that in general conversations most people do not present their ideas in a totally logical fashion. So it is better to listen for important ideas than to try to outline the total message.

6. ***Pay attention.*** Poor listeners are often tired, lazy, bored, or preoccupied. They pay the speaker the courtesy of an attentive posture, such as leaning forward in the chair, chin resting on hand. From this position, however, they proceed to ponder their personal problems or

compose that memo that needs writing. The effective listener not only hears what is said but observes the nonverbal signals from the speaker—tone of voice, gestures, and facial expression—all of which add up to *real* understanding of what is being communicated.

7. ***Fight distractions.*** There are many distractions that can interfere with listening. The poor listener does nothing about these distractions, allowing them to sidetrack his or her attention. Effective supervisors try to control their environment by screening out distractions. They choose a quiet place to listen, refuse phone calls, and close their office doors to avoid intrusions.

8. ***Face up to difficult material.*** Many times supervisors find conversations difficult to follow. The degree of detail or technical depth is extensive. Poor listeners do not fight these feelings; they avoid anything that is challenging, quickly tuning out what they do not easily understand. Good listeners, on the other hand, occasionally seek out difficult subjects to challenge their listening skills. They are determined not to let a complicated presentation get the better of them. They typically spend time training their ear by listening to challenging material.

9. ***Avoid becoming emotional.*** There are certain terms, phrases, and words that affect people in an emotional way. For example, the supervisor who is pleading her case for a new employee may suddenly become irate when she hears her boss give a counterargument about "budget constraints." Or consider the supervisor who becomes angry when he hears someone say, "This is what the union wants," or the production employee who shouts, "Is management trying to replace us?" when she learns that some automated manufacturing processes are to be installed. The poor listener stops listening when confronted with emotion-packed words and starts flying off the handle. Effective listeners examine those words and phrases which tend to have an emotional effect on them. By doing so, they usually become more adept at controlling their emotions. In a one-on-one or small-group situation, they often discuss this problem frankly, even asking the other person to refrain from these terms. Above all, the awareness of this problem helps them conquer this listening barrier.

10. ***Do not daydream.*** Studies show that the average person speaks at about 125 words per minute while thinking at 400 to 500 words per minute. Poor listeners employ this slack for thinking about other things, such as where to go for lunch or when to call a staff meeting. At first, the poor listener tunes in and out, loosely keeping track of the speaker's conversation. All too often, however, he or she becomes too involved in an interesting daydream and forgets to tune back in, thereby missing most of the message. Effective listeners also find something to fill in the extra time, but they remain tuned in to the

speaker while doing so. They often make mental summaries of key points or try to read between the lines. They also reflect on the evidence while attempting to draw conclusions about the situation.

Active listening: The key to effectiveness

Effective listening involves more than just paying attention. It also includes active, empathetic, and supportive behaviors that tell the speaker, "I understand. Please go on." This mode of response is called *active listening.* Many people believe that they are active listeners. Are you? Find out by taking Self-Assessment Quiz 7-2. The analysis of your answers follows the quiz.

SELF-ASSESSMENT QUIZ 7-2:
IDENTIFY YOUR LISTENING RESPONSE STYLE

Carefully read each of the following comments and circle the response you would make in reply.

1. "I don't know what to do first. My boss has given me two special projects to do on top of everything else. There just aren't enough hours in the day."
   a. How about asking your boss what he wants done first?
   b. You always worry unnecessarily about things.
   c. What exactly do you have to do?
   d. We all get real busy sometimes; things will calm down.
   e. You seem frustrated by the workload.
2. "The word from the home office is that 10 percent of our sales force is going to be laid off because of the overall failure to make quota. This would be the worst possible time for me to lose my job."
   a. Why don't you ask the branch manager if you're likely to be one of the 10 percent?
   b. You're a good person and they know it. They'd never lay you off.
   c. Why do you think you might be one of the 10 percent laid off?
   d. Don't worry. Chances are, you won't be affected.
   e. You seem nervous about the possibility that you might be one of the 10 percent to go.
3. "That clerk we fired last week is threatening to bring a discrimination suit against us. She says she was fired solely because she was a woman. This could be a real messy situation. You know how the boss hates lawsuits."
   a. You'd better talk to the company lawyer right away.
   b. She couldn't be that foolish; it'll never happen.
   c. What could she base her suit on?
   d. If she does, nobody can say it's your fault.
   e. You appear concerned that this situation could become messy.
4. "If I take the promotion, I'll have to move to Pittsburgh. If I refuse it, the company probably won't offer me another one. I just don't know what to do."

a. Let's look at the pros and cons of living in Pittsburgh.

b. You'd better take this offer while you can.

c. What's so bad about Pittsburgh?

d. This seems a big problem now, but in the long run everything will work out.

e. You appear concerned about what to do.

5. "Jerry is the poorest worker in our group. He's a constant complainer. If he isn't griping to me about the rest of the group, he's complaining about his salary. He's really getting on my nerves."

a. Complaints often point to a larger general dissatisfaction.

b. That's because you always lend a shoulder for people to cry on.

c. Why do you think he's so unhappy?

d. Don't let that bother you. Every office has a Jerry.

e. You seem aggravated because Jerry complains to you so often.

6. "I'm delighted I got this new job, but I'm scared I won't be able to learn quickly enough to keep up with everyone else."

a. I'm sure the other workers will help you learn quickly.

b. You should be grateful you got promoted into this work unit.

c. What new things do you need to learn?

d. Everyone feels that way about a new job.

e. You sound both happy and nervous about this new job.

Answers

Count up how many checks you had for each *a, b, c, d,* and *e*. The one with the most is your dominant listening response mode. The title or word that describes each of these modes is the following:

a. Directive
b. Judgmental
c. Probing
d. Smoothing
e. Active

In the quiz, you were given the opportunity to choose a response statement. Answer *e* in every case is that of the active listening supervisor. This individual is called an active listener because he or she assumes a very definite responsibility. The person does not passively absorb the words spoken; instead, the individual actively tries to grasp the facts and feelings of the speaker and through active listening help the other person deal with the situation. Of course, not all supervisors are active listeners. Many fall into one of the other four response modes. The following is a brief description of all five, beginning with the directive orientation.

1. ***Directive.*** The directive listener leads the speaker by guiding the limits and direction of the conversation. Consider an employee telling the supervisor of his inability to get along with a coworker. The direc-

tive supervisor would make a reply such as, "If I were you, I'd just ignore him," or "Don't worry about it—everybody thinks he's a pain in the neck."

2. ***Judgmental.*** The judgmental listener introduces personal value judgments into the conversation. The listener tends to offer advice or make statements regarding right or wrong behavior. In responding to the employee's plight described above, the judgmental listener might say, "You'll just have to learn to get along with your coworkers," or "You're absolutely right; Tom is impossible to get along with."

3. ***Probing.*** The probing listener asks a lot of questions in an attempt to get to the heart of the matter. This individual tends to lead the conversation and satisfy his or her personal needs rather than those of the speaker. A probing listener might answer the above employee by saying, "Exactly what has this person done to you so that you can't get along?" or "What do you want me to do about it?"

4. ***Smoothing.*** The smoothing listener tends to pat the speaker on the head and make light of the problem. The underlying belief here is that conflict is bad and should be avoided at all costs. The smoothing listener would tell the employee in this example something like, "You and Tom just had a bad day. Don't worry, tomorrow it will all be forgotten."

5. ***Active.*** The active listener tries to create an encouraging atmosphere for the speaker to use in expressing and solving the problem. Active listeners tell the speaker what they hear the individual saying in order to (a) establish that understanding has occurred and (b) allow the speaker to continue. The active listener might respond to the employee in this example by saying, "It seems you are troubled by the fact that you and Tom can't seem to get along."

The active approach is not always the best one. Sometimes the supervisor needs to use a directive style; at other times a probing style is best. The manager must be flexible. At the same time, the individual has to remember that feedback comes from the other party; it is not self-generated. Of all five listening styles, however, the active one is the most effective at promoting feedback. For this reason it is, on average, the most useful one for supervisors.

PAUL'S TARDINESS DECISION: STARTING CASE REVISITED

The reason the workers did not read the memo is that it was too long and detailed. A second reason is that no one was ever told about the supervisor's decision. It was simply put into writing and placed on the bulletin board for the workers to read. Paul chose the wrong communication medium as the primary one. He should have used verbal communication to convey the message directly and then followed up by putting the written memo on the bulletin board. The verbal communique would have provided face-to-face interaction, with the chance for immediate feedback. The written communique would also have provided a permanent record for future reference.

What Paul needs to do now is call together the workers, review the memo with them. address any questions or concerns, and be sure that everyone knows what the penalties are for tardiness. He must not only communicate with his people but be sure that feedback channels are opened so that information flows both ways.

INTERPRETATION OF SELF-ASSESSMENT QUIZ 7-1: CAN YOU SPOT INFERENCES?

---

1. True. The story states this fact in the first sentence.
2. Inference. We do not know what type of group Chuck supervises. It might be a production group, but the story never states this.
3. Inference. Chuck was late on Tuesday for the second time that week. However, we do not know whether he works a Monday-Friday schedule. The story is unclear on this point. He may be working a Friday-Tuesday workweek.
4. Inference. The story says that he wants to get a new car, but does the word *new* mean brand new or just another car (which would be a new one for him)?
5. False. The story states just the opposite.
6. True. Chuck does want to work overtime.
7. True. The story says that there will be overtime for the next 6 months.
8. False. Chuck intends to work 4 hours overtime per day during the regular 5-day week (20 hours) and 8 hours per day during each of the other 2 days (16) for a total of 36 hours.
9. Inference. We do not know how many people are in Chuck's regular work group. We simply know from the story that there are more than four.
10. Inference. The story does not say that he intends to replace the car; it says that he can afford to replace the clunker. It is implied that he will get another car, but this is not directly stated.

How well did you do? Most people are able to identify only two inferences. They fill in the gaps and assume things to be in evidence that actually are not.

SUMMARY OF KEY POINTS

1. Communication is the process of conveying meanings from sender to receiver. This process has five main elements: sender, receiver, media, feedback, and the environment in which the message is communicated.
2. There are many forms of communication media. The two most common are verbal and written. Verbal communication usually takes the form of face-to-face communication or telephone conversations. Written communications commonly take the form of brief memos.

3. There are a number of important barriers to communication. One is perception, which is a person's view of reality. The two most common types of perception are sensory and normative. A second barrier to communication is inference, which is an assumption made by the receiver of a message and which is commonly employed when there is a need to fill in gaps.

4. Nonverbal communication can take many forms, including facial expressions, gestures, posture, and the ways that people use physical space. Supervisors need to be most concerned with two components of nonverbal communication: kinesics and proxemics. Kinesics is the study of communication through body movements and facial expressions. Proxemics is the study of how people use physical space and what this use says about them.

5. Supervisors need to be able to work with the informal organization. This means understanding both the nature and operation of the grapevine. The ways in which this can be done were explained in the chapter.

6. Feedback is information that facilitates the understanding and/or control of communications. Without feedback, supervisors really do not know how well their messages are being received or what types of questions their people would like answered. The chapter provided a numer of useful tips for creating and maintaining feedback.

7. Good listeners have quite different habits from poor listeners. The last part of the chapter compared and contrasted these two types of listeners and then explained the nature and value of active listening.

BUILD YOUR SUPERVISORY WORD POWER

These key communication terms are presented in their order of appearance in the chapter. Effective supervisors have a working knowledge of them.

Communication. The process of conveying meanings from sender to receiver.

Sender. The person who conveys information.

Media. The means used to convey a message.

Receiver. The individual who gets a message and must interpret its meaning.

Environment. The milieu in which a message is communicated.

Memo. A brief written message.

Fog index. A method of measuring the degree of difficulty in a written memo or report.

Perception. A person's view of reality.

Sensory perception. A person's view of physical reality.

Normative perception. A person's view of interpretive reality.

Inference. An assumption made by the receiver of a message.

Kinesics. The study of communication through body movements and facial expressions.

Proxemics. The study of how people use physical space and what this use says about them.

Fixed feature space. The permanent parts of a building or room.

Semifixed feature space. Those things in a room which can be moved, including desks, chairs, tables, and lamps.

Informal feature space. The physical distance people maintain between themselves and others.

Grapevine. A term used to describe the informal organizational communication system.

Single-strand chain. An informal communication chain in which information is passed from one person to the next in single-file fashion.

Gossip chain. An informal communication chain in which one person passes information to all the others.

Probability chain. An informal communication chain in which information is passed in an unpredictable fashion.

Cluster chain. An informal communication chain in which information is passed on a selective basis.

Feedback. Information that facilitates the understanding and/or control of communications, enabling the sender to adapt or adjust messages for greater clarity.

Directive listening. Listening in which the speaker is guided by the limits and direction of the listener.

Judgmental listening. Listening that is characterized by the listener introducing personal value judgments into the conversation.

Probing listening. Listening that is characterized by the listener asking a lot of questions in an effort to get to the heart of the matter.

Smoothing listening. Listening that is characterized by the listener tending to make light of the speaker's problem.

Active listening. Listening that is characterized by the listener trying to create an encouraging atmosphere for the speaker to use in expressing and solving the problem. The listener often uses neutral summaries to indicate that understnding has occurred and to allow the speaker to continue.

REVIEW YOUR UNDERSTANDING

1. How does the communication process work? In your answer be sure to incorporate all five main elements of the process.

2. What are the two most common forms of verbal communication? What is the most common form of written communication? What do supervisors need to know about using the latter form of communication? Explain.

3. In what way is perception a barrier to effective communication? Provide an illustration of sensory perception as a barrier. Then provide one of normative reality as a barrier.

4. How is inference a barrier to communication? Give an example.

5. In what way is an understanding of kinesics of value to the practicing manager? Explain.

6. How can an understanding of proxemics be of value to the practicing manager? In your answer be sure to include a discussion of all three types of feature space.

7. What are some of the characteristics of the grapevine? What are some of its primary advantages and disadvantages? Be as complete as possible in your answer.

8. Describe how the following grapevine chains work: single-strand, gossip, probability, and cluster. Which is of most importance to the supervisor? Why? Explain your answer.

9. What is meant by the term *feedback?* How can a supervisor improve his or her feedback? Offer the individual at least four tips for improving feedback effectiveness.

10. How do effective listeners differ from ineffective listeners? Identify and describe at least five different habits that effective listeners have.
11. What is active listening all about? Of what value is it to supervisors? Explain.

SUPPLEMENT YOUR KNOWLEDGE

In addition to the references listed at the end of this chapter, the following provide important, practical information that is of use to supervisors in communicating with their people:

Barnard, Janet C.: "The Principal Players in Your Organization's Information System." *Supervisory Management*, June 1983, pp. 20–25.

Diffie-Couch, Priscilla: "How to Give Feedback," *Supervisory Management*, August 1983, pp. 27–31.

Driver, Russell W.: "Opening the Channel of Upward Communication," *Supervisory Management*, March 1980, pp. 24–29.

Fielden, John S., and Ronald E. Dulek: "How to Use Bottom-line Writing in Corporate Communications," *Business Horizons*, July–August 1984, pp. 24–30.

Haynes, Marion E.: "Becoming an Effective Listener," *Supervisory Management*, August 1979, pp. 21–28.

Kikoski, John F.: "Communication: Understanding It, Improving It," *Personnel Journal*, February 1980, pp. 126–131

Levine, Edward L.: "Communicating with the New Worker," *Supervisory Management*, August 1980, pp. 12–23.

Powell, Jon T.: "Listen Attentively to Solve Employee Problems," *Personnel Journal*, July 1983, pp. 580–581.

Samaras, John T.: "Two-Way Communication Practices for Managers," *Personnel Journal*, August 1980, pp. 645–648.

Schachat, Robert, and Joel Anastasi: "Face-to-Face Communication: Breaking Down the Barriers," *Supervisory Management*, April 1979, pp. 8–14.

Treece, Maira: "Cut the Cost of Communicating," *Supervisory Management*, February 1976, pp. 6–11.

YOU BE THE SUPERVISOR: INSIDE INFORMATION

Judith Shapiro was hired 6 weeks ago as a production supervisor for a precision equipment manufacturer. Judy has had no business experience. She took this job a week after being graduated from college.

The firm has a supervisory training program for new people, and Judy spent a week learning the company's philosophy and approach to the supervision of the personnel. Most of this time was spent explaining production control procedures and how to use them. Very little attention was devoted to such supervisory ideas as motivation, leadership, or effective communication. One of the things Judy did learn was that upward communication is important to effective quality control. "The workers know a lot about how to improve product quality," the trainer told her group. "They know when something is wrong and will often call it to your attention. Listen to them and you'll find that they'll help you do your job."

Judy likes the job and the people. She has especially enjoyed the chance to have coffee and lunch with other supervisors in the quality control area. Her best friend at the firm, Tony Labiano, has been with the company for 5 years. Tony has one of the poorest performance records because the quality reject rate from his work group has been high. Over 5 percent of the group's output fails to pass inspection. Tony explained the reason to Judy in this way: "These workers are basically lazy. They deliberately do sloppy work. If it weren't for my keeping my eye on them all the time, the reject rate would be double what it is. Let me give you an example. Last month one of my people recommended that we have an hourly meeting every Wednesday to discuss ways to improve production quality. This idea is a waste of time. I don't listen to anything they tell me."

Last week Judy had a visit from two of her people. They recommended that she stop production on Friday morning and devote time to preventive maintenance. "We're scheduled for this maintenance on Wednesday, but it ought to be done earlier. The wear and tear on three of the machines has been so great that they probably won't last until Wednesday."

Judy thought the matter over and decided to go with the maintenance as scheduled. The following Monday the three machines went down. It took twice as long as usual to carry out the preventive maintenance and her department lost a half day's production. Judy's boss was not pleased with the results. He met with her yesterday and told her: "How could those machines have broken down? Didn't any of the workers tell you that early preventive maintenance was needed? You're new at this job and should be more receptive to your people's ideas. Whom are you listening to these days?"

1. Is Judy a member of an informal group? Explain.
2. Why did Judy overlook the advice of her workers? What communication barrier accounted for this? Be complete in your answer.
3. If you were a fellow supervisor advising Judy, what advice would you give her? Explain.

YOU BE THE SUPERVISOR: A HOME OFFICE ASSIGNMENT

Two months ago Jennifer O'Keefe answered a help-wanted ad for a supervisory trainee in the claims department of a large insurance company. She was hired and sent to the firm's 7-week management training program. The program is designed to acquaint the participants with all phases of supervision.

When the typical program is over, the participants are assigned to different offices throughout the city. In Jennifer's case, there were no openings for the first week and so she was assigned to work in the main office. One of the other trainees, Jason Heldug, also was sent here to work.

Within a few days, Jennifer learned that there was an opening in the home office for a new supervisor. Either she or Jason would get this position. The other would be assigned to a branch office. One of the female supervisors she had befriended, Paula Sharpe, told Jennifer to work hard to impress the boss because it was he who would make the assignment decision. Jennifer followed this advice to the letter. She showed up early for work every day and made it a point to stay busy at all times. On a number of occasions the boss needed someone to run special errands. Jennifer cheerfully carried them out.

At lunch hour she, Paula, and some of the other female supervisors in the office would get together. All of them would offer her advice regarding what to say and do back at the job. On the day before the decision was to be made, one of the women told Jennifer, "I hope you get assigned here. The other opening is at the Quincy branch uptown. That would be another 40 minutes of commuting for you." This information encouraged Jennifer to work even harder.

On Friday the boss called Jennifer in for a meeting. The conversation went as follows:

I've decided to assign you to an opening we have here at the main office. Paula will be in charge of helping you learn the ropes. Is that OK with you?

It sure is. I love working here. Besides, if I had to go to the Quincy office it would mean having to get up an hour earlier in the morning.

The boss said nothing about her remark. However, he did spend the next week trying to find out how Jennifer knew where the other assignment was. He asked Paula to learn who leaked the news, but she reported back that she was unable to locate the source.

1. If you were the supervisor, how would you go about learning who is in the informal organization? What steps would you take?
2. Would you have asked Jennifer how she learned about the Quincy office assignment? Why or why not?
3. How would you attempt to use the informal organization to help you get things done? Explain.

NOTES

1. Walter St. John, "In-House Communication Guidelines," *Personnel Journal,* November 1981, p. 873.
2. Julius Fast, *Body Language,* New York: Pocket Books, 1971.
3. Jane W. Gibson and Richard M. Hodgetts, *Organizational Communication,* Orlando, Fl.: Academic Press, 1986, chap. 5.
4. Edward T. Hall, *The Hidden Dimension,* Garden City, N.Y.: Doubleday, 1966.
5. Reported in Gibson and Hodgetts, chap. 5.
6. Gibson and Hodgetts, chap. 5.
7. Phillip L. Quaglieri, "Feedback on Feedback," *Supervisory Management,* January 1980, pp. 34–38.
8. These basic ideas can be found in Ralph Nichols, "Listening, What Price Inefficiency?" *Office Executive,* April 1959, pp. 15–22.

CHAPTER 8

MOTIVATING THE EMPLOYEE

**GOALS OF
THE CHAPTER**

Motivation is a major challenge for supervisors. The primary reason for this is that because workers have different needs, the motivational package for one does not have the same value for another. Additionally, many supervisors seem confused regarding the value of money as a motivator: How important is it and how should it be used? The same is true for psychological motivators like challenging work and increased responsibility. Many supervisors report that while they hear a great deal about the importance of such motivators, none of their workers say anything to them about wanting such things. The result is that many supervisors are not sure what motivation is all or how they can develop a meaningful motivational plan for achieving higher employee output and productivity.

The primary goal of this chapter is to examine the nature of motivation and discuss what supervisors can do to improve employee motivation. When you have finished all the material in this chapter, you will be able to:

1. Define the term *motivation* and describe the three links in the motivation chain.
2. Explain, in terms of the need hierarchy, why people work.
3. Discuss the value of the motivation-hygiene approach in developing an effective strategy for motivation.
4. Relate the value of money and other physical rewards to effective employee motivation.
5. Explain how supervisors can identify what motivates an individual employee and tailor-make an approach for that person.
6. Describe 10 useful guidelines that can help supervisors develop the right climate for motivation.

A STARTING CASE: BACK TO THE OLD JOB

Judy Travers is a new supervisor at the Davidson Company. Judy has been with the firm for over 18 months and, early on, was identified as supervisory material. She first came to the attention of her boss when she completed a 2-week work project in 4 days. Her superior was so surprised with her progress that he personally went through the report page by page. He could not find a single error.

During the months that followed, Judy was given a number of important assignments. Some of these required her to work overtime and on weekends. This did not phase her at all, although she was glad that Davidson paid time and a half for any work over 35 hours a week, double time on Saturday, and triple time on Sunday. During her first year Judy's overtime earnings equaled 25 percent of her regular income.

Judy's high performance rating qualified her for the supervisory list and she was promoted last month. Because of the company's policy of never reducing a person's annual income in a promotion, she received a salary 10 percent higher than that of the average new supervisor. Judy no longer qualifies for overtime pay but believes that she will more than make up for this lost income with supervisory raises.

During her first week as supervisor, Judy worked hard to learn about her work group. The most productive member is Judd Hertz. Judd reminds Judy a lot of herself. He turns out 15 percent more work than any other member of the unit and is always ready to work on Saturdays and Sundays.

Three weeks ago management decided that it would be less expensive to have a quality inspector in each department than to handle this function out of a central unit. All supervisors were asked to nominate one of their people for this job. The assignment carried a salary 5 percent greater than the base rate earned by Judd and his coworkers. However, there is no overtime associated with the work.

Judy called Judd in and told him about the opening. "I think you'd be ideal for this job, and when promotions come up next year you'd be able to show the committee that you already had some managerial experience. This is bound to get you the promotion. This would mean an additional 10 percent increase in salary. What do you say? Can I nominate you for the job?" Judd told Judy that he would prefer to stay where he was but that if she felt it was best for his career, he would go along.

Two weeks ago Judd started the new job. After 1 week he dropped by to see Judy to ask her to move him back to his old assignment. "I liked my old work better," he explained. "I don't get a chance to interact as much with the guys any more, and the money isn't really very good compared to what I was earning before." Judy agreed to his request and yesterday Judd got his old job back. The new person whom Judy appointed was delighted. "I wish you'd asked me in the first place," she told her boss. "I really like the work and the money is great."

Why did Judd give up his old job? What was he looking for that was not present in the work? What motivates Judd? What does the new quality inspector like about her job? What motivates her? Sketch out your answers to these questions. We will return to them at the end of the chapter.

WHAT IS MOTIVATION?

Motivation is effort directed toward the accomplishment of an objective. This effort sometimes takes the form of physical movement, such as a worker rapidly feeding material into a machine; other times it is mental in content, such as an employee quietly reading a monthly control report. What the supervisor must realize is that motivation is an internal, psychological process. It takes place within people. The manager cannot demand that people be motivated. Instead, he or she must work to create the right climate for motivation. This can be done by addressing the three main links in the *motivation chain:* ability, desire, and payoff.

When a person is motivated, it is because he or she is able to do the job, has a desire to do it well, and wants the payoff or reward that follows from doing the work. This chain of events, diagrammed in Figure 8-1, begins with ability.

Ability

The first link in the motivation chain is ability. The worker must have the capacity to do the job. Sometimes this takes the form of physical dexterity, such as fast reflexes or good hand-eye coordination. A person who lacks such dexterity will never do well as a typist no matter how much the person wants to succeed in this job. Likewise, an individual who is slight in build will not be able to carry extremely heavy loads of material for long periods of time. The person lacks the right physique. For some jobs, inborn ability is important.

Many times, however, people have the ability to do the job well. All they require is the proper education or training for developing that ability. For example, the average person can be taught to type quickly and accurately. Likewise, most people can be trained to use office machinery and equipment efficiently. To the degree that the supervisor spends time showing them how to do the work, they will be effective.

Another facet of ability is supervisory coaching. While many workers can be taught the basics of a job, they often need follow-up training and guidance to reinforce correct habits and help eliminate mistakes. By telling them what they are doing well and how they can improve their overall performance, the supervisor ensures that they will continue to improve and to work at peak ability.

Desire

While ability is important, the desire to do the best possible job is more important. Without this drive for excellence, ability is of limited value. There are two ways in which supervisors can build this desire. One is by making clear the rewards for performance. What will they get for doing a good job?

Figure 8-1. The motivation chain.

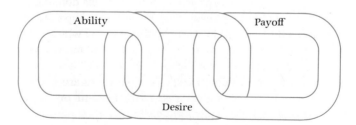

By answering this question, the supervisor establishes a link between performance and rewards.

The second is by letting workers know how performance will be measured. The supervisor who tells his people, "Those who do the best work will be recommended for the highest raises," is not relating what is meant by "the best work." If the individual is talking about work output, he or she should say, "Those who turn out the most widgets will be recommended for the highest raises." If work quality is as important as work quantity, the individual should modify this by noting, "Those who turn out the greatest number of properly assembled widgets will be recommended for the biggest pay increases."

Payoff

People work hard when they are rewarded for what they do. If this payoff is fair, the personnel will continue to perform well; if the rewards are not viewed as fair, work performance will decline. In incorporating this idea for a payoff into the motivation chain, the supervisor must remember two important facts.

First, people are motivated in different ways (see Supervision in Action: Superstars at Sheraton). Some people are more motivated by money than anything else, some are more motivated by interesting, challenging work, and others are looking for the opportunity to move up the hierarchical ranks. A highly motivational payoff for one employee may have little attraction for another. The best way for the supervisor to answer the question What motivates my people? is to get to know what each is looking for. So while the rewards the supervisor can give are usually limited in scope, the supervisor will still be able to do a better job if he or she has some reading of the payoffs the workers are seeking. In general, what do you think motivates workers? In answering this question, take Self-Assessment Quiz 8-1 and then read the interpretation at the end of the chapter before continuing on.

SUPERVISION IN ACTION: SUPERSTARS AT SHERATON

When Sheraton Corporation purchased what is now The Sheraton Centre at 7th Avenue and 52nd Street in New York, it had to do more than physical renovation. Employee morale was down and attitudes were poor, says Jean-Robert H. Cauvin, executive assistant to the vice president and area manager.

"In the service industry, employees do not perform when morale is low. If employees do not perform, then guests don't receive services." So Cauvin, the hotel's troubleshooter, started the "Superstar Program" to identify employees who do an outstanding job and who are, in a word, superstars.

"We wanted them to know that management cares about them and recognizes when they do a good job," says Cauvin. "We explained that attitudes on the job and with customers are important." The hotel stressed that survival of the hotel is dependent on long-term relationships and continued patronage of guests.

To reach employees with this message, The Sheraton Centre developed the Superstar Program, as outlined by Cauvin:

- *Monthly superstars.* Hotel guests are given a "starcard" at check-in, in the rooms, at food and beverage outlets, and at the front desk so they can vote for the hotel personnel who are particularly pleasant and efficient on their jobs. The starcard plays up the "star quality" of the employees and encourages guests to participate. The ballots are totaled monthly, and a total of 20 "superstars" are chosen based on the balloting, a review by the division supervisor and past employment record. The superstars and their achievements are announced at a monthly employee meeting and are awarded a certificate and $100.

  A "Super, Superstar" employee of the month is chosen from the 20 finalists, and is awarded a $100 check and a trophy. And finally there is a Super, Superstar employee of the year who receives a $1,000 check and a trophy.

- *Publicity.* In addition to the monthly employee meetings, superstars winners are announced in the "Superstar News" newsletter. In the beginning, the program was promoted through posters, decals, buttons, and a letter from the vice president and managing director announcing the program.

- *Superstar contest.* The contest, which is mailed to all employees, offers them a chance to test their knowledge about hotel courtesy and to win prizes for doing so. There is a series of multiple-choice questions on hotel procedures and a bonus question asking for the employee's definition of quality as it relates to his or her job. These questions are designed to make employees think about the kinds of qualities and actions needed on the job. The first-place winner of the contest wins an all-expense-paid trip to Hawaii, including spending money.

"At first there was some negative feedback to the program and some jealousy," says Cauvin, "because when someone is on top there is someone else on the bottom who is not going to like the program." But after almost two years of operation, "I would say that the program is well-accepted."

SELF-ASSESSMENT QUIZ 8-1: WHAT MOTIVATES THE WORKERS?

One of the most effective ways of learning about motivation is to examine it from a personal perspective: What motivates today's workers? In answering this question, put yourself in the shoes of the supervisor. In the list below, rank from 1 (most important) to 20 (least important) those factors which personnel look for in their work. Start by identifying the most important and least important factors and then work your way into the middle. This approach will save you time. When you have finished, turn to the end of the chapter, enter your answers, and then review the interpretation of your responses.

Rank *Factor*

Rank		Factor
7	1.	Pay
1	2.	Job autonomy
11	3.	A feeling of personal importance
19	4.	Extended sick leave benefits
20	5.	An impressive job title
10	6.	Job independence
9	7.	Good working conditions
8	8.	A feeling of self-worth
12	9.	The work itself
7	10.	Recognition for a job well done
15	11.	A stock option plan
13	12.	Improved insurance coverage
17	13.	A company car
3	14.	Interesting work
16	15.	Increased vacation time
5	16.	A chance to achieve
4	17.	Challenging work
14	18.	Cost-of-living increases
18	19.	Guaranteed severance pay
6	20.	Increased responsibility

Second, workers are motivated when they feel that they are being given proper rewards. This is known as the *equity* approach to motivation. How do workers know if their rewards are equitable or fair? In one sense, they do not know. They only have a *perception* of fairness. However, this perception is very important and it involves both themselves and the other workers in the unit. In making this mental determination, they first compare what they are getting from the organization with what they are giving to it. They then make a similar calculation for other people in the work unit. If an individual feels that she is doing 100 percent of what is asked of her and is getting no more rewards from the company than someone who does only 75 percent of what is required, she will feel that the payoffs are unfair. The company is not giving her an equitable reward.

The supervisor can deal with this equity problem in three ways. First, and most important, those workers who do the best work should be recommended for the biggest increases in salary and given the most rewards. Second, where possible, the supervisor should work to motivate everyone to give 100 percent. Third, the manager should deny, if possible, rewards to those who do not carry their own weight. Many workers admit that they are more motivated by a supervisor who gives them only a small increase in salary but refuses to give any increases to poor workers than they are by a supervisor who gives them excellent rewards and gives poor workers good rewards. The motivational rule is a tough one for most supervisors, but it is a realistic one: *Do not reward those who do not perform.* Even in organizations in which this rule can be implemented, many supervisors refuse to go along with this rule because of the pressure they get from those who are bypassed for salary raises, etc. They prefer to spread the rewards across the board even though it means a loss of motivation among their best people.

WHY PEOPLE WORK

Why do people work? The answer to this question strikes at the very heart of the motivational process. If the supervisor could identify exactly why someone worked, it would be a simple matter of constructing the best possible motivational package for the person. Unfortunately, individual motivation is too complex for this. However, there are some basic facts that supervisors can use in understanding why people work. Perhaps the most encompassing is the "needs" explanation.

Needs

A *need* is a desire for something. Everyone has needs. Some of these are physical; some are psychological. Abraham Maslow, the noted psychologist, identified five human needs.[1] These needs can be explained in terms of a hierarchy (see Figure 8-2). At the bottom of the hierarchy are the most basic needs. These are more important than the upper-level ones in that if they go unsatisfied, the individual will die. An example is food. While someone could refrain from eating for 30 days, this fast would most assuredly endanger the individual's life. On the other hand, the upper-level needs are often what make the job interesting. They provide workers with a feeling of accomplishment and self-satisfaction. The following examines each of these five levels in terms of both content and satisfaction.

Physiological needs. Physiological needs are physical needs. They include such things as food, clothing, shelter, and comfort. If workers were denied the satisfaction of all needs, these would be most important to them because they are the most basic. On the job, the supervisor works to help people satisfy these needs by providing good wages, labor-saving tools and devices, and efficient work methods.

Safety needs. Safety needs include such things as security, avoidance of physical harm, and avoidance of risk. People want to feel safe in their environment. On the job, the supervisor and the organization can offer a number of benefits that help meet this need. One is job seniority, in which those with the greatest time on the job are the last to be let go. Under many arrangements, if a department is cut by three workers, those with high seniority and previous experience in other departments around the firm are allowed to go into these departments and "bump" someone who is less

Self-actualization needs	Job-related satisfiers
Self-expression	The opportunity to perform creative work
Independence	The freedom to make decisions that directly affect one's work
Competence	Mastering and doing one's job well
Esteem needs	Job-related satisfiers
Recognition	Status symbols
Responsibility	Increased authority
Feeling of accomplishment	A chance to share in decision making
Social needs	Job-related satisfiers
Companionship	The opportunity for interaction with other group members
Acceptance	Become an accepted member of the work group
Belongingness	High team morale
Safety needs	Job-related satisfiers
Security	Job seniority
Avoidance of physical harm	Safe working conditions
Avoidance of risk	Insurance program and other fringe benefits
Physiological needs	Job-related satisfiers
Food, clothing, shelter	Wages or salaries
Comfort	Labor-saving tools and devices
Self-preservation	Efficient work methods

Figure 8-2. The human need hierarchy and job-related satisfiers.

senior. In this way, the company ensures that senior people are let go only as a last resort. Another need is that of avoiding physical harm. Supervisors can help meet this need by ensuring that there are safe working conditions. A third common safety need is the avoidance of risk, such as financial calamity caused by an extended stay in the hospital. This help is commonly addressed through the organization's insurance program.

Social needs. Social needs are desires for meaningful relationships with others. These needs can take many forms. One is a desire for companionship, which can be satisfied on the job through interaction with other group members. Another is the need for acceptance, which can be met by becoming a fully accepted member of the work group. A third is the desire to belong, which can be satisfied through the development of high team morale. Notice that social needs can partially be satisfied through supervisory efforts. The manager can allow, and even promote, the chance for interaction with other group members. However, the supervisor cannot demand that the work group accept all of the workers as full-fledged members. This is a decision that rests with the group itself. Likewise, the supervisor can work to develop high morale among the group members, but to a large extent the success of these efforts is determined by the members, not by the supervisors. Social needs are only partially under the control of the supervisor.

Esteem needs. Esteem needs are desires to feel important and to have self-respect. The need for recognition is one of these and is often satisfied through status symbols, such as job titles, an office with a window, or a special parking spot. Another is the need for responsibility, which is commonly satisfied by giving the individual increased authority. A third is the desire for a feeling of accomplishment, which can be addressed by allowing the worker to share in decision making. In overall terms, the personnel attempt to fill their esteem needs through the acquisition of prestige and power.

Self-actualization needs. Self-actualization needs are desires to maximize one's full potential, to become all that one is capable of becoming. This need is often satisfied through self-expression. One way this is done is by performing creative work. A second self-actualization need is that of independence, which can be satisfied by giving employees freedom to make decisions that directly affect their work. A third need is that of achievement, which can be addressed through meaningful goals. Self-actualization needs are psychological in content. They are satisfied to the degree that the worker feels that they have been met. If a worker is carrying out what she believes is boring, routine work, the supervisor's argument that "Your work is interesting and challenging" is not going to change her mind. Psychological needs are satisfied by people themselves. The logic of this statement helps explain why the motivation-hygiene approach to supervising people has proven so popular with many first-line managers.

Motivation-hygiene theory

Quite obviously, not everything a supervisor does for a subordinate will motivate the latter. For example, if everyone in the department is given a 5 percent raise, no one may be particularly motivated by the salary increase, especially if everyone in the industry received the same amount. If someone received less than 5 percent, he or she may be dissatisfied, but getting 5 percent does not ensure that the person will be satisfied. This idea of dissatisfaction-satisfaction has been of particular interest to those studying what motivates workers. It has even resulted in the formulation of a motivation-hygiene theory, popularized by Dr. Frederick Herzberg.[2]

In essence, the motivation-hygiene approach holds that there are two sets of factors that are important in the motivation picture. One consists of *hygiene, or maintenance, factors.* These do not bring about satisfaction; they merely prevent dissatisfaction. Hygiene factors ensure that employees will put forth an average commitment in time and effort and not feel that they are getting ripped off. These factors tend to be heavily physical in nature and include:

Economic factors—wages; salaries; fringe benefits

Working conditions—adequate light and heat; a safe physical environment

Security—seniority privileges; grievance procedures; fair work rules; company policies and rules

Social factors—opportunities to interact with other workers and socialize on the job

Status—job titles; corner offices with windows; a key to the managerial bathroom

Herzberg reports that when hygiene factors are missing, employees tend to be dissatisfied. Hygiene is necessary because it helps maintain a minimum amount of satisfaction. In providing these factors, Herzberg recommends, "Give them out and then shut up about them." This is because people expect hygiene factors. If they do not get them from one company, they can usually get them from the competition.

The other set of factors consists of *motivators.* These are the psychological factors that provide the extra something that so many people look for in their work. When they are present, satisfaction tends to increase. Some of the most important of these factors are the following:

Challenging work—the opportunity for self-expression and personal growth

Feelings of personal accomplishment—the belief that one is contributing something of value

Recognition for a job well done—the acknowledgment that one has done important work

Achievement—the chance to accomplish things

Increased responsibility—the acquisition of new duties and tasks that expand the job and give the individual greater control over it

Herzberg's theory is similar to Maslow's need-hierarchy approach in that it addresses both upper- and lower-level need satisfaction. However, it is a more applied approach because of the attention it gives job satisfaction and the need to provide, at a minimum, hygiene factors.

Money and other physical rewards

There is a great deal of confusion regarding the role of money and other physical rewards in the motivational process. The previous discussion pointed out that psychological need satisfaction is important because it focuses on internal factors, and since motivation is an internal process, it often spells the difference between motivated and unmotivated people. On the other hand, money should not be overlooked when we discuss psychological factors. It can help one satisfy physiological needs because food, clothing, shelter, and physical safety can all be ensured with money. Moreover, money can also help open social doors to people, serve as a basis for feeling good about one's self, and be a source of feedback regarding how well one is achieving personal goals. When viewed in this context, money helps satisfy needs at all levels of the hierarchy.

Perhaps the biggest problem that supervisors have in determining the value of money and other physical rewards in motivation is that they tend to overrate it. They believe that these factors are more important to the workers than they really are. For example, some supervisors feel that their people work for money alone. The adage "money motivates" summarizes their entire philosophy of worker motivation. Others believe that their employees are looking for jobs that do not require a great deal of hard physical work. Still others feel that their people have little desire to develop their skills and abilities. Actually, workers are motivated by *both* physical and psychological factors. And while money is at the top of many of their lists, other factors are also important.[3] Table 8-1 illustrates this. As seen from the table's data, both supervisors and workers were asked to rate 16 factors according to their importance to the workers. Some of the supervisory answers were exactly right. Many, however, were wrong.

Table 8-1. Factors that are of importance to employees

Factors	As ranked by	
	Supervisors	Employees
Pay	1	1
Chance to develop skills and abilities	14	2
Friendly coworkers	4	3
Good pension plan	10	4
Recognition for a job well done	6	5
Not being caught up in a big impersonal organization	7	6
Chance to make a lot of money later on	13	7
Interesting work	11	8
Chance to use one's mind	9	9
Job in growing field or industry	15	10
Participation in decisions regarding job	8	11
Not expected to do things not paid for	5	12
Not too demanding a job	3	13
Seeing the results of one's work	12	14
Having a job that does not involve hard physical work	2	15
Socially useful work	16	16

Source: Andrew K. Hoh, "Interpreting Employee Needs: Assuming vs. Understanding," *Supervisory Management*, April 1980, pp. 31, 33.

Of the many things that supervisors need to realize about the value of money and other physical rewards, two warrant specific discussion.

First, many supervisors are *high achievers.* They are goal-oriented and tend to measure progress toward these goals in quantitative terms. For them, money and other concrete measures are used as feedback in determining how well they are doing. For example, high achievers will compare this year's salary with last year's salary in evaluating their progress. They will also look at their benefit package, the size of their office, and the number of people they have reporting to them in evaluating their career progress. If something cannot be measured, high achievers tend to ignore it or assign it a low priority. Quite obviously, money is an important measure of how well they are doing. They pursue it if only for the feedback it provides regarding their progress. What supervisors fail to realize is that most people are not high achievers and that what motivates a first-line manager will not necessarily motivate a worker. As a result, they overrate the value of money as a motivator.

Second, and perhaps more important, money and other physical factors are under the control of the supervisor. If a person does a good job, the supervisor can recommend the individual for a higher-than-average raise. If the person does a poor job, the supervisor can write a poor evaluation and recommend the person for a less-than-average raise. If workers are totally motivated by physical rewards, then the manager has total control over them, for it is the supervisor who can give or withhold these payoffs. If the workers are most motivated by psychological rewards, however, the situation is reversed. Now it is the workers who decide what motivates them, and the supervisor is relegated to a secondary position. The latter condition is preent more often than first-line managers would like to believe. This is why it is important for supervisors to realize that in most cases they have spent too much time managing the work and not enough time managing the desire of the personnel to work. They need to focus more on the environment in which the work occurs and less on trying to manipulate and control the personnel. (See Supervision in Action: A Psychologist Looks at Motivation.)

SUPERVISION IN ACTION:
A PSYCHOLOGIST LOOKS AT MOTIVATION

"Motivation is something that comes from within," says clinical psychologist Dr. Peter Whitmer. "It's up to the manager and the company to set the stage to allow the employee's internal motivation to appear."

To do so, "you need to tailor rewards and recognition to individual motivation. Any kind of reinforcement should be geared to each individual's scheme of needs or psychological support," Whitmer explains. "Finding out what makes an individual tick is very complex, and individuals are not always reinforced by the same things all the time."

Whitmer, a consultant with Smith and Donahue, Inc. in Wellesley, Massachusetts, identifies three basic concepts of motivation: power, affiliation and achievement.

For those motivated by achievement, Whitmer says, you give them bigger and better jobs and a chance to show they can do these jobs. "Sometimes, achievement-oriented employees will take bigger and better jobs even with a pay cut," says Whitmer.

For those motivated by affiliation, recognition means acceptance by a peer group. And for those motivated by power, recognition is the ability to command more troops (authoritative types) or to work through more people (cooperative types).

What does this mean for personnel practices? "You have to compensate or recognize the individual differences which make people tick. For some, financial reward is what I call their 'hot' button; for others it's something different," says Whitmer. "If you don't, you risk giving the wrong kind of award."

According to Whitmer, this approach is particularly important for management- and vice-presidential-level employees. For more general programs aimed at larger groups of employees, Whitmer suggests offering, at the minimum, a "smorgasbord approach" to recognition awards because it allows individuals to choose the award that makes them tick.

Whitmer also points out that recognition programs should not remain static. "When we give a bonus or a trip to Hawaii, we call it an incentive," says Whitmer. "What it really is, is a reward for a particular behavior and an attempt to encourage similar behavior in the future."

"But once an award is given, it loses its potency to motivate, because it becomes expected." The result, says Whitmer, is that we continually have to create different ways to recognize and reward employees. And in recognition and reward, Whitmer suggests that we shouldn't overlook job enrichment and job development, along with performance appraisal, as part of our recognition program.

Source: "Employee Recognition: A Key to Motivation," © February 1981. Reprinted by permission of *Personnel Journal,* Costa Mesa, Calif.; all rights reserved.

ADDRESSING INDIVIDUAL DIFFERENCES

We have noted the importance of both physical and psychological motivators, pointing out that the latter are particularly important in getting people to do things. What combination of the two should the supervisor use? This will depend on the individual worker. Some firms have attempted to resolve this issue by offering cafeteria incentive plans.

Cafeteria incentive plans

A *cafeteria incentive plan* is one in which people are allowed to select their benefits. The organization tells them the options, and the workers decide what they want. For example, in many organizations it is common to allow workers to choose between (1 a health plan that is administered by Blue Cross/Blue Shield and (2) a health maintenance organization (HMO). The first allows the participant to choose his or her own doctor, and after a deductible (commonly $100 per person, $200 per family) is met, the individual pays 20 percent of all medical expenses while the health plan picks up the rest. The HMO arrangement requires the individual to choose one of the doctors in the plan and carries a much higher monthly premium to be paid by the worker. On the other hand, the cost of doctor visits and hospital stays is lower than that of the Blue Cross plan. Each person can examine the medical needs of his or her own family and decide which is best.

This same approach is used in choosing other forms of compensation. People are allowed to tailor-make their own plans. A number of criteria will affect these choices, including marital status, sex, and age. This was clearly indicated in a recent cafeteria incentive plan that was instituted in a retail store chain (Table 8-2).[4] Three types of incentives were offered to the workers. Those with the highest sales in a department over an 8-week period were allowed to choose one of four options in the first tier or two of the options from either the second or the third tier. Those who attained midrange sales were allowed to take one of the options from the second tier or two from the lowest tier. Those who attained minimum-range sales were allowed to choose one of the incentives from the third tier.

The choices that the workers made are presented in Table 8-3. Notice that single people chose gift certificates or portable TVs, while married people preferred days off or more freedom over their work environment. Males

Table 8-2. Three-tiered cafeteria incentive plan

Highest sales in a department
1. Selection of any merchandise
2. Dinner for two
3. Portable TV
4. $75 gift certificate

Midrange incentives
1. Day off with pay
2. Birthday off with pay
3. Ten gallons of gas or $15 worth of bus tokens
4. Two sets of movie tickets
5. Appointment as "Employee for a Day" (get picked up for work, taken out to lunch, and driven home)

Minimum-range incentives
1. Freedom to schedule own average weekly hours (for 1 week)
2. Coffee breaks free for 1 week (free coffee or tea)
3. Choice of day off
4. One-half-hour extended dinner/lunch hour (for 1 day)
5. Assistant manager for a day

Source: Linda L. Neider, "Cafeteria Incentive Plans: A New Way to Motivate," *Supervisory Management*, February 1983, p. 32 © 1983 by AMACOM Periodicals Division, American Management Associations, New York. Reprinted by permission of the publisher; all rights reserved.

Table 8-3. Ranking of top three incentives in a cafeteria incentive plan

	Marital status		Sex		Age			
Rank	**Single**	**Married**	**Males**	**Females**	**18–21**	**22–30**	**31–50**	**50–Up**
1	$75 gift certificate	Day off with pay	Portable TV	Merchandise at cost	Portable TV	Day off with pay	Day off with pay	Schedule own hours
2	Portable TV	Schedule own hours	Dinner for two	Schedule own hours	Day off with pay	Choice of day off	$75 gift certificate	Day off with pay
3	Dinner for two	Choice of day off	10 gallons of gas/bus tokens	$75 gift certificate	2 sets of movie tickets	Dinner for two	Merchandise at cost	"Employee for a day"

Source: Linda L. Neider, "Cafeteria Incentive Plans: A New Way to Motivate," *Supervisory Management*, February 1983, p. 33 © 1983 by AMACOM Periodicals Division, American Management Associations, New York. Reprinted by permission of the publisher; all rights reserved.

chose specific gifts, while females opted for more flexible rewards. Younger people (ages 18 to 21) were more likely to choose physical rewards, while older people opted for greater control over their jobs.

This study is not representative of all people. Some young workers want more freedom over their work. Some older workers desire greater pay and monetary benefits. The supervisor must try to identify the needs of the workers and then address them. This really is not as difficult as might appear at first blush.

Individual worker needs and supervisory effectiveness

Pulling together much of what has been discussed in this chapter, it is possible for the supervisor to develop a very practical approach to motivation. The first thing the individual must do is identify employee needs. What do the workers want? In answering this question, the manager must start by identifying how people behave. This is an important clue to what motivates them. Based on this, the supervisor can then formulate an effective plan of action. Since few workers give evidence of physiological-need deprivation, let us begin with the second level of Maslow's hierarchy and show what the supervisor can do.[5]

Safety needs. Workers who desire safety-need satisfaction have a number of behavioral patterns. They tend to be precise, orderly, and systematic in their approach to things.[6] Most are conscientious and determined to do a good job. Quite often they go out of their way to avoid antagonizing others. When discussing reward systems, these workers often talk about security programs and benefit packages. These behaviors are found among both new employees who are unsure of themselves and veteran workers for whom safety and security have always been important needs.

What do these people want from their jobs? Some of the most important things include job security, clear job descriptions, plenty of notice about job changes, support of the supervisor in getting things done, and reassurance from the latter that they are doing a good job.

How should the supervisor deal with these people? Some of the most important steps include:

1. Make sure the job is clear. Also provide careful, detailed instructions for doing things.
2. Encourage the worker to keep trying. This will build the person's confidence.
3. Give periodic praise for jobs well done. This reassurance will serve as an important psychological motivator.
4. Be available to provide support, especially when things get difficult and the worker has a lot of questions or needs more than the usual assistance.

Social needs. People who have a desire for social-need fulfillment tend to be very friendly and outgoing. They try hard to associate with other workers, are cooperative, and sometimes are overly anxious to please people. They make exceptionally good team members.

These workers seek to be accepted, both professionally and personally, by others. They particularly like to be praised for their accomplishments because this gives them a feeling of appreciation for their efforts. They welcome sincerity in interpersonal relations and are quickly demotivated by phony or manipulative behavior. These people also like to be told in advance about changes; failure to do so is often seen as a lack of concern for them as people. Some of the most useful steps to follow in motivating these workers to do the best possible job include:

1. Show a sincere interest in the worker as an individual.
2. Give periodic reassurance and praise for all accomplishments. This shows them that the supervisor really cares about them.
3. When appropriate, provide tangible rewards or awards. These can range from an employee-of-the-month certificate to a lunch at which the supervisor tells the worker what a great job he or she has been doing.
4. Show the individual ways that will make the job easier to accomplish. This serves to illustrate that the worker is an important person and has been accepted by the supervisor as a full-fledged member of the unit.
5. Give forewarnings and explanations of any changes to be introduced. If possible, solicit input from the workers regarding the change.

Esteem needs. Workers with strong esteem needs tend to be very sociable and outgoing. They not only take the initiative in meeting others but are often socially aggressive, sometimes to the point of making themselves the center of attraction. They are also poised, confident, and personable. There are few social settings in which they find themselves ill at ease.

These workers want recognition, status, and popularity. They also seek variety in their jobs and respect from others because of their ability, knowledge, and accomplishments. These people often form a close identity with their work unit. However, they do not like regimentation, close control, or petty detail. They want the opportunity to show what they can do. Some of the things that supervisors can do to increase the job motivation and effort of such people include the following:

1. Provide the individual with opportunities for group work. This interaction and chance to excel helps meet esteem and recognition needs.
2. Look for opportunities to provide variety in work assignments. Where possible, give the individual a special project to do.
3. Give the worker a chance to show off personal accomplishments. Then follow up and give the individual the deserved recognition.
4. Since the worker does not like close control, let the individual work under loose supervision. However, periodically meet with the worker, review how well the person is doing, discuss future assignments, and then let the individual continue on under loose reign.

Self-actualization needs. Workers with high self-actualization needs like to keep technically up to date in their occupation or profession. They particularly like to ask questions, analyze how and why things work as they do, solve problems, and improve things. They often display a minimum of emotion; their focus is on fact and objectivity.

One of the most important things these people want from their jobs is challenge. They like to feel stimulated by difficult but attainable tasks. New assignments and problems are welcomed. At the same time, they seek to learn, to grow, and to do things that are worthwhile.

In managing these people, the supervisor can do a number of things. Four of the most important are:

1. Periodically provide them with new work assignments or expose them to new knowledge. They like to solve problems and to take on special projects or creative tasks.
2. If work changes have to be introduced, consult with them before finalizing the implementation plan. They often can provide insights and analyses that will improve the plan and make its implementation simpler and easier.
3. Provide them with help toward self-improvement. Where possible, share relevant knowledge with them. They also welcome coaching that is designed to increase their job development.
4. Give them the opportunity to apply the results of their self-development efforts. This feedback reinforces their desire for more assignments and creative projects.

GUIDELINES FOR MOTIVATION

In addition to addressing the satisfaction of individuals' needs, supervisors can profit from guidelines that help develop the right climate for motivation. The following are 10 of the most useful:

1. ***Match the people and the work.*** Everyone has certain strengths. Some people are good at detailed work; others do a better job at more broadly based tasks. Some perform best when left alone; others like a lot of guidance. To the extent that the supervisor can match the personalities of the workers with the demands of the task, the people will be motivated to do a good job.

2. ***Make the task clear.*** As surprising as it is to the average supervisor, many personnel do not fully understand what they are supposed to be doing or how actually to get the job done. The workers give it their best shot, but they are not sure whether their efforts are being properly directed. To the extent that the job is clearly explained and its steps are spelled out, motivation can be enhanced.

3. ***Give positive feedback.*** Supervisors should let their people know when they have done a good job. Verbal acknowledgments usually take only a few minutes, and if the person did an exceptional job, a memo for that individual's personnel file is in order. This feedback serves as an incentive for repeat performances. Effective supervisors know the importance of catching a subordinate doing something *right.*

4. ***Tell people what they are doing wrong.*** When subordinates make mistakes, the supervisor should patiently explain to them what they have done wrong. This is the best way to ensure that they do it right the next time. Research shows that those supervisors who use mistakes as an opportunity to correct behaviors are more productive than those who use them as a basis for punishing their people. In correcting mistakes, the supervisor should explain what the person did wrong, why it was wrong, and how it ought to be done differently. For example, a worker who enters a hard-hat area without wearing a protective hat may feel that since he is only going to be there for a minute, the rule does not apply. By explaining that the insurance company has based its premiums on everyone in the area having a hard hat and is not responsible for any accidents to those not wearing them, the supervisor conveys both the reason for the rule and what the worker should do differently.

5. ***Let people know the rewards.*** Most subordinates try to do a good job, but they would work even harder if they were sure of the rewards they could attain. By making clear the relationship between performance and different types of payoffs, the manager can "hook" them on doing a good job.

6. ***Personalize the reward system.*** Not everyone is motivated by the same things. By individualizing the rewards so that people are better able to achieve what they want, the supervisor can ensure a higher-motivated work force. This is particularly true in the case of non-monetary rewards. Some people work better if they are given praise, some prefer to be left alone, and others like the manager to drop by

and talk to them on occasion. Supervisors should strive to accommodate all of the subordinates.

7. ***Never make promises that cannot be kept.*** To the extent that promises are kept, the supervisor establishes credibility with the workers. This is important in future dealings, especially when there is to be an introduction of change or a cutback in employment. If the trusted supervisor says, "I have gone over the plan for the installation of a computer in this department and can assure you that no one is going to be laid off because of it," the personnel will believe the individual, and resistance to the change will be negligible. On the other hand, if the supervisor has given promises before and these have not been kept, the workers are unlikely to believe these latest reassurances. The manager was wrong before, they will reason, and is wrong now.

8. ***Make the consequences equal to the behavior.*** If a worker does something extremely well, the individual should be given a greater reward than someone who does something fairly well. The same holds for punishments. If a worker breaks a major rule, he or she should receive a penalty that is much stronger than that given to someone who commits a minor infraction. The supervisor must also remember that rewarding people in front of their peers adds to the value of the reward. On the other hand, punishment should be carried out privately. If the supervisor discusses a worker's failure to complete a report on time in front of the other workers, the person being reprimanded is made to look foolish or ridiculous in front of peers. Unless there is some reason to make a public example of the worker, such situations are best handled within the confines of the supervisor's office.

9. ***Remove the roadblocks.*** Effective managers understand that their personnel will occasionally have trouble getting things done because of supervisory or organizational roadblocks. Sometimes the manager will have to change an order because it is resulting in too much red tape. Other times the supervisor will discover that there are not sufficient organizational resources to get a job done and find it necessary to fight for more funds. These efforts result in a removal of roadblocks, leading to both higher employee motivation and work output.

10. ***Be a good role model.*** Workers look at their supervisor as a role model. If the supervisor comes to work late and leaves early, the workers are likely to start doing the same. If the supervisor fails to follow safety procedures, the workers will also disobey these guidelines. Many of the group's norms grow up around the boss's behavior. By personally following company rules and setting an example for the work group, the supervisor ensures that they will do so too. Keep in

mind, however, that this does not mean following the adage "I wouldn't ask my people to do anything that I wouldn't do," for there are many times when the supervisor must ask people to do things that he or she cannot. Operators who are specially trained to run new equipment often know a great deal more about how to operate the machine than does the supervisor. The supervisor's job is to motivate people to do their jobs well, not to learn how to do it for them. Effective role modeling does not require the manager to operate the machine; it requires the manager to get the workers to do their job.

BACK TO THE OLD JOB: STARTING CASE REVISITED

Having read the chapter, you are now in a much better position to answer the questions that followed the introductory case. Review your answers and change them in any way you would like. When you have finished, read on.

The major reason why Judd gave up his job was that he was swayed by Judy's argument about getting managerial experience. However, two things are apparently missing from the new job: money and interaction with the other workers. Both are important to Judd. On the other hand, the new quality inspector loves her job. We are given little information about her. However, it seems at first blush that the salary raise and the nature of the work are both important motivators for her.

Finally, it is important to point out that the reason why Judy recommended Judd for the job was that he reminded her of herself. She thought that the same things that motivated her were those which motivated Judd. She was wrong. Judd is apparently much more interested in enjoyable work and in the amount of money he can make right now than he is in the future that awaits him in the management ranks. Judy misread the situation because she tried to motivate Judd by using her own values. Judy did not fashion a motivation plan designed to help Judd; she used one which she, herself, liked. She did not spend enough time learning about what motivated Judd, and her approach showed it.

INTERPRETATION OF SELF-ASSESSMENT QUIZ 8-1: WHAT MOTIVATES THE WORKERS?

There is no right answer to this quiz. The importance of motivational factors will vary based on the individual, the organization, the economy, and a host of other factors. However, your responses do reveal some things about you because they help indicate how you would try to motivate people if you were a supervisor. To clarify what your responses reveal, enter them in the form below; be sure to match the number (1 to 20) you gave to each question with the question number below. Then add up the numbers in each column.

	Group A		*Group B*
1.	2	2.	1
4.	19	3.	11
5.	20	6.	10
7.	9	8.	8
11.	15	9.	12
12.	13	10.	7
13.	17	14.	3
15.	16	16.	5
18.	24	17.	4
19.	18	20.	6
Total	143	Total	67

The 20 items that you ranked have been divided into two categories: physical and psychological. The physical payoffs are in group A and involve such things as pay, extended sick leave, good working conditions, and cost-of-living increases. The psychological payoffs are in group B and involve such things as job autonomy, a feeling of self-worth, recognition for a job well done, and a chance to achieve. The first group can be given by the supervisor and, if workers do not do a good job, can be withheld or denied. The second group is given to the workers by themselves; its payoffs are internally generated. The supervisor cannot stop someone from having a feeling of self-worth or believing that he or she is getting recognition for a job well done.

The lower your total in each column, the greater the degree of importance you assign to those factors. (Remember, you gave a 1 to the most important, on down to a 20 to the least important.) Which was most important for you, group A or group B? Whichever one it was, this says something about you, for managers tend to motivate people based on what they themselves believe the workers want. Most supervisors have a lower total in group A because they believe that physical rewards are more important to the workers than are psychological rewards. Without considering whether or not this is an accurate perception, use your totals above to gain an understanding of how *you* would try to motivate your supervisory personnel.

SUMMARY OF KEY POINTS

1. Motivation is effort directed toward the accomplishment of an objective. This is an internal, psychological process. It takes place within people. For this reason, the manager cannot demand that the workers be motivated. Instead, he or she must work to create the right climate for motivation. This is done by addressing the three links in the motivation chain: ability, desire, and payoff. Ability is the capacity to do something. Desire is the drive to do the best job possible. Payoff is the reward for doing the work.

2. People work for many different reasons. One of the most comprehensive ways of explaining a person's motivation to work is the needs approach. Everyone has five needs:

- Physiological—food; clothing; shelter; comfort
- Safety—security; avoidance of physical harm; avoidance of risk
- Social—meaningful relationships with others; companionship; acceptance
- Esteem—self-respect; responsibility; a feeling of accomplishment
- Self-actualization—creative work; self-expression; achievement

3. Both physical and psychological rewards are important to people. This has been made particularly clear with the motivation-hygiene approach, which holds that hygiene factors will not create satisfaction but will help prevent dissatisfaction; conversely, motivational factors will help create satisfaction. Examples of hygiene include economic factors, working conditions, security, social factors, and status. Examples of motivation factors include challenging work, feelings of personal accomplishment, recognition for a job well done, achievement, and increased responsibility.

4. Money is a major motivational factor. However, many supervisors tend to overrate it. One reason is that they are high achievers and tend to place a great deal of attention on quantifiable factors. Another is that money is at least partially controllable by the supervisor, who would like to think that money is a major motivator, for it gives the supervisor power over the subordinates.

5. Effective motivation requires the addressing of individual differences. One way in which some companies have attempted to do this is with cafeteria incentive plans, which allow workers to choose their benefits. A second useful approach to individualizing motivation is to examine the worker's behavior, determine what needs the individual wants satisfied, and develop a strategy to address them.

6. In addition to the above, supervisors need to develop practical approaches for managing their people. The last part of the chapter offered ten useful guidelines for motivation.

BUILD YOUR SUPERVISORY WORD POWER

These key motivational terms are presented in their order of appearance in the chapter. Effective supervisors have a working knowledge of them.

Motivation. Effort directed toward the accomplishment of an objective.

Ability. The capacity to do a job.

Payoff. A reward for doing work.

Equity. An approach to motivation, it involves comparing one's own work/reward ratio to that of others in the unit of determining the equity of personal payoffs or rewards.

Need. A desire for something.

Physiological needs. Physical needs like food, clothing, shelter, and comfort.

Safety needs. Needs for security, avoidance of physical harm, and avoidance of risk.

Social needs. Desires for meaningful relationships with others. These are often satisfied through social interaction and acceptance by group members.

Esteem needs. Desires to feel important and to have self-respect. These are often satisfied through the acquisition of prestige and power.

Self-actualization needs. Desires to maximize one's full potential and to become all that one is capable of becoming. These are often satisfied through self-expression, independence, and achievement.

Hygiene factors. Factors that help maintain a minimum level of satisfaction. Examples include wages, salaries, fringe benefits, a safe environment, and opportunities to interact with others.

Motivators. Factors that increase job satisfaction. Examples include challenging work, recognition for a job well done, achievement, and increased responsibility.

High achievers. Individuals who are goal-oriented and tend to measure progress toward these goals in quantitative terms.

Cafeteria incentive plan. An incentive plan that allows people to select their benefits from among a host of options. The purpose of the plan is to tailor incentives to individual needs.

REVIEW YOUR UNDERSTANDING

1. In your own words, what is meant by the term *motivation?* In what way is a knowledge of the motivation chain of practical value in motivating people?
2. Everyone has five basic needs. What does this statement mean? In your answer be sure to describe each of these needs.
3. How can organizations help people satisfy their needs? In your answer be sure to provide guidelines and suggestions for needs at each of the five hierarchy levels.
4. How does a hygiene factor differ from a motivator? Of what practical value is this information to supervisors? Explain your answer.
5. Why do many supervisors overrate the value of money as a motivator? Cite and explain two reasons.
6. One of the ways of motivating people is to offer them cafeteria incentive plans. How do these plans work? Of what value are they in addressing the individual motivational needs of people? Explain.
7. How can a supervisor determine what needs people want fulfilled on the job? How can the supervisor address each of these needs? In your answer be sure to address safety, social, esteem, and self-actualization needs.
8. In what way do the approaches identified in the above question change as one goes farther up the hierarchy? What does this say regarding the need of the supervisor to use physical versus psychological rewards?
9. What are some of the most useful guidelines that supervisors can use in motivating their people? Identify and describe five.

SUPPLEMENT YOUR KNOWLEDGE

In addition to the references listed at the end of this chapter, the following provide important, practical information that is of use to supervisors in motivating their people:

Collins, Samuel R.: "Incentive Programs: Pros and Cons," *Personnel Journal*, July 1981, pp. 571–575.

Cook, Curtis W.: "Guidelines for Managing Motivation," *Business Horizons*, April 1980, pp. 61–69.

Dwortzman, Bernard: "The ABCs of Incentive Programs," *Personnel Journal*, June 1982, pp. 436–442.

"Employee Recognition: A Key to Motivation," *Personnel Journal*, February 1981, pp. 103–107.

Franklin, William H., Jr.: "Why You Can't Motivate Everyone," *Supervisory Management*, April 1980, pp. 21–28.

Hanson, Charles A., and Donna K. Hanson: "Motivation: Are the Old Theories Still True?" *Supervisory Management*, June 1978, pp. 9–15.

Mode, V. Alan: "Making Money the Motivator," *Supervisory Management*, August 1979, pp. 16–20.

Nirenberg, John: "Motivate as if People Matter," *Supervisory Management*, October 1981, pp. 22–25.

Rosenbaum, Bernard L.: "Understanding and Using Motivation," *Supervisory Management*, January 1979, pp. 9–13.

YOU BE THE SUPERVISOR: WHAT MOTIVATES PEOPLE?

The Hudson Insurance Company is a large metropolitan-based firm located in southern California. The company has over 5000 office personnel nationwide. In an effort to remain as competitive as possible, the company spends a great of time and money recruiting and training supervisors. "If our supervisors can manage their people well," Harry Hudson told the board of directors last month, "we can keep our operating costs below that of the industry. Too much money is wasted at the lower levels of the hierarchy. At Hudson we aim for the highest managerial efficiency in the industry. Supervisory training plays a large role in this effort."

Part of the company's overall plan for excellence at the supervisory level is a 1-week seminar for new supervisors. It is conducted by a professional training and development group that works closely with Hudson. One day of the seminar is devoted to the subject of effective motivation. At the beginning of the day, all of the participants are given a list of motivational factors that workers at Hudson would like. They are asked individually to rank the list, answering the question: What do workers at Hudson Insurance want from their jobs? They are then put into groups of four and asked to come up with one overall list for the entire group. They are then provided with a list that shows what the workers themselves actually said. The results from both the most recent group of supervisors to take the training and the workers in the firm are shown in the accompanying table.

Factors	What the average new supervisor said	What the groups of four said	What the worker at Hudson said
Full appreciation for work done	8	7	1
Feeling "in" on things	10	10	2
Sympathetic understanding of personal problems	9	9	3
Job security	2	2	4
Good wages	1	1	5
Interesting work	5	6	6
Promotion and growth with the company	3	5	7
Management loyalty to the workers	6	4	8
Good working conditions	4	3	9
Tactful disciplining	7	8	10

1. In comparing the responses of the average new supervisor to those of the employee, what conclusions can be drawn regarding what the first-line managers believe motivates the workers? As a supervisor, would you agree or disagree with the accuracy of these rankings? Explain.

2. In what way do the responses of the individual supervisors and those of the groups differ? In what way are they the same? Are the group's responses closer to those of the individual supervisors or to those of the workers? Are the group's rankings accurate? As a practicing supervisor, how much faith would you place in them? Explain.

3. If you were a supervisor at Hudson, how would you attempt to motivate your people? In what way would your perception agree with that of the new supervisors? In what way would it differ from theirs? Explain.

YOU BE THE SUPERVISOR: TAILOR-MAKING AN INCENTIVE PLAN

The Intech Corporation is a high-tech firm in the computer field. The company produces many types of computer hardware under subcontracting agreements with major firms in the industry. There are two key factors for success in the business: on-time delivery and high quality. For this reason, Intech works hard to keep its output high and its quality rejection rate low. Production supervisors are continually urged to maintain high morale among their people, and those supervisors who are most successful in this effort receive large end-of-the-year bonuses.

Recently the corporation decided to extend this idea of bonuses to the workers in the form of an annual incentive award. The company plans to give these awards to the 10 production workers this year who turn out the greatest number of shipped units. (A shipped unit is one that has passed quality inspection.) The personnel department conducted a number of extensive interviews with the workers and then put together a questionnaire designed to identify the form of bonus they want. The company intends to make each award worth approximately $2500, although because of special arrangements with the company the actual retail value may be in excess of this amount. The results of the questionnaire were broken down by worker, age, marital status, and sex. They revealed the following:

Characteristics	Desired award
Age	
21–30	$2500 cash
31–50	$5000 savings bond
51+	Four extra weeks of vacation at full pay
Marital status	
Married	$3000 gift certificate redeemable at any of 10 major retail stores
Single	A giant color TV, stereo, TV camera, VCR unit and 100 blank tapes, and assorted movies (total retail value: $2525)
Sex	
Male	One-week prepaid vacation to London and Paris (total value: $2675)
Female	Twenty extra days off per year whenever the worker chooses to take them (3 days' advance notice is required)

1. On the basis of the preceding information, if you were the supervisor, how would you attempt to motivate unmarried males? Married females? Discuss your strategy, being sure to include in your answer the types of needs that each group would like to satisfy and how your strategy would be helpful in this regard.

2. Based on the information above, if you were the supervisor, how would you attempt to motivate unmarried females? Married males? What types of needs would your strategy address and what specifically would the strategy include? In your answer be sure to discuss specific things that you would do in motivating this group.

3. Again referring to the information above, if you were the supervisor, how would you attempt to motivate young workers? Middle-aged workers? Older workers? In what way would your strategy vary from one group to another? In your answer be as detailed and practical as you can.

NOTES

1. Abraham H. Maslow, "A Theory of Human Motivation," *Psychological Review*, July 1943, pp. 370–396.

2. Frederick Herzberg, Bernard Mausner, and Barbara Bloch Snyderman, *The Motivation to Work*, New York: Wiley, 1959.

3. Andrew K. Hoh, "Interpreting Employee Needs: Assuming vs. Understanding," *Supervisory Management*, April 1980, pp. 29–34.

4. Linda L. Neider, "Cafeteria Incentive Plans: A New Way to Motivate," *Supervisory Management*, February 1983, pp. 31–35.

5. Arthur Sondak, "The Importance of Knowing Your Employees," *Supervisory Management*, May 1980, pp. 13–18.

CHAPTER 9

LEADING EFFECTIVELY

GOALS OF THE CHAPTER

Supervisors must be able to lead their people. The overriding goal of this chapter is to examine the nature of the leadership process and explain how effective supervisors can go about carrying it out. In particular, attention is directed to practical guides and tips that can be of value to supervisors in leading effectively. When you have finished reading all the material in this chapter, you will be able to:

1. Define the term *leadership* and discuss some of the most common characteristics of successful leaders.
2. Compare and contrast Theory X views of the workers with Theory Y views.
3. Define the term *power,* identify five different types of power, and explain how supervisors can expand their power base.
4. Identify and describe how the following types of leaders go about supervising their people: authoritarian, paternalistic, participative, and laissez-faire.
5. Explain the value of the managerial grid and the path-goal approach in effective supervision.
6. Identify a handful of useful supervisory leadership tips.

A STARTING CASE: UP AND DOWN

When Susan Phelps became office supervisor at Downtown Hospital, things were not going well. Susan's department is responsible for the billing and collection of patients' accounts receivable. The previous supervisor had been a very easygoing, kind person who had been at Downtown for over 25 years. For most of this time, things went well. They only started to get out of hand when errors began to appear in the patients' bills.

This began about 18 months ago and within 4 months it had reached epidemic proportions. Over 25 percent of the patients were reporting that they had received someone else's bill or that some of the charges were for services that had not been provided. An investigation by a special hospital committee revealed that the patients were right. The administrator called in the head of the unit, who explained that half of the department consisted of newly hired people and that everything would soon straighten out. Unfortunately, just the opposite happened and the administrator felt compelled to replace the department head. This is when Susan Phelps became the supervisor.

Susan took over the department a year ago. Within 2 weeks it was evident that some of the people were poorly trained and that others simply had no facility for the work. No matter how many times Susan explained things to them, they still made billing mistakes. A month from the day she was appointed, Susan took action. She fired half of the personnel and allocated their work to the remaining six people. "We may fall behind in the billing," she told them, "but everything will get done right." The personnel agreed with her decision. They felt that something had to be done and that Susan had done it.

Over the next 2 months, three more people were hired. This was enough to take care of things, thanks to the increased efficiency. Susan got a full day's work out of everyone. Personnel coming late had the time docked from their pay. Anyone who sent out more than two erroneous bills in a week was dismissed.

Six months ago an audit of operations revealed that Susan's department was one of the best run in the hospital. She was given a 20 percent salary raise. The in-house newspaper ran her picture and a quote regarding how proud she was of her authoritarian, work-centered approach to getting things done.

The latest audit of operations presented a much different picture. Over the last 90 days, four of Susan's workers had quit and most of the remaining had asked for transfers to other departments. The replacement help has been unwilling to submit to Susan's leadership style, and patient billings are again becoming a major problem. The administrator has told Susan that if things do not straighten out, he will have to transfer her to another department.

What happened? Why was Susan successful in the beginning? Why is she having trouble now? Write down your answers. We will return to them at the end of the chapter.

THE NATURE OF LEADERSHIP

Leadership is the process of influencing people to direct their efforts toward the achievement of some particular goal(s). There are many ways in which supervisors can do this, depending on personal style and the demands of the situation. There is no ideal profile of the successful supervisor, but there are some general characteristics that the individual often possesses.

Characteristics for success

Until fairly recently, many people were interested in identifying universal traits or qualities that distinguished effective supervisors from their less effective counterparts. Were there some traits that were possessed only by effective supervisors? The answer turned out to be no, although there are personal characteristics that do help the supervisor influence subordinates.

Superior mental ability. Supervisors tend to be more intelligent than the average of their followers. Some researchers argue that an IQ in the 120 to 135 range is ideal.[1] The logic is that a supervisor who is average or a little higher in mental ability will be at a distinct disadvantage because some of the subordinates will always be one step ahead of the manager. On the other hand, a supervisor with an IQ in the superior range will be at a disadvantage because most subordinates will have a hard time following what the person wants done and why. What is obvious to the supervisor will not be obvious to the workers, who will find themselves continually confused by the boss's rapid way of handling things.

Emotional maturity. Supervisors are self-confident and sure of what they are doing. They know what they want their people to do and are prepared to deal with mistakes in a mature manner. If someone does make an error, they try to use the mistake as a learning experience rather than as an opportunity to punish. This approach builds confidence in the subordinates, who realize that if they do assume greater responsibility for work assignments, they can rely on the supervisor to help them out and provide them guidance should they run into difficulty.

Need-achievement drive. Successful supervisors have a need to achieve. They like to set difficult, yet attainable, objectives for themselves and then reach them. In terms of motivation, they are more interested in fulfilling their needs for esteem and self-actualization than they are in satisfying lower-level needs. They tend to have subordinates with like interests, for those workers who cannot get their jobs done on time and who lack high need-achievement drive tend to transfer to other departments where the supervisors are not as demanding. In large measure, high-achieving supervisors thus have high-achieving subordinates.[2]

Problem-solving skills. Effective supervisors have problem-solving skills. They know how to differentiate between cause and effect and then to focus on the former. They have also learned how to direct resources toward the solution of these problems. Quite often they run the most efficient operations, not because they are any better at handling day-to-day problems but because they know how to sidestep or minimize problems that cause bottlenecks and delays. Effective first-line managers are also moderate risk takers because they know that many problems cannot be solved with a low-risk approach. They are not afraid of failing once in a while if it means that over the long run they will succeed.

Empathy. Effective supervisors have *empathy*, the ability to identify with others emotionally. They are able to see things from the worker's point of view, although this does not mean that they necessarily agree with the worker. By being able to get into the other person's shoes, they have a vantage point from which to lead. The effective supervisor knows what management wants done and how the workers feel about things. He or she can then translate management's desires into objectives and assignments

Figure 9-1. The linking pin function.

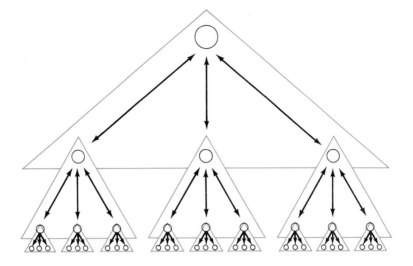

that will be of benefit to both groups: the organization and the workers. Empathy provides the basis for communicating things to people from their own points of view. By telling workers what is in it for them, the supervisor stands an excellent chance of winning their confidence and support.

Representation upward. The best supervisors know that they must represent their people up the line. The first-line manager is a link between the workers and the next level of management. Figure 9-1 illustrates this idea for the organization at large. To the degree that the supervisor represents the workers, ensures that they are treated fairly, and conveys an image of them as a hard-working, unified group, worker support will be strong and supervisory influence over the group will be great.

Supervisory assumptions

The above characteristics are not possessed by every supervisor. Some lack a sufficiently high mental ability, some do not yet have the experience for carrying out effective problem solving, and others are handicapped by their own biases or assumptions regarding worker behavior. In an effort to influence their people, all supervisors begin with a series of assumptions. Some people believe that their people are tough to work with, will goof off any chance they get, and work strictly for the money. Others believe that their people try hard, often assume more responsibility than they need to, and are motivated by many things, of which money is only one. These assumptions form a basis for the supervisor's leadership efforts. They are best illustrated in terms of Theory X and Theory Y.[3]

Theory X. Theory X is a set of assumptions that supervisors have about their people. These assumptions, in the main, hold that the workers are basically lazy and that in order to get them to do things, punishment and coercion are necessary. More specifically, as applied to supervisory workers, these assumptions include:

1. By their very nature, people dislike work and will avoid it when possible.
2. Workers have little ambition, like to be directed, and tend to shirk responsibility.
3. They want security above all else.
4. In order to get them to pursue work goals, it is necessary to use close control, threats of punishment, and coercion.[4]

These assumptions are used by supervisors who believe that their people are most motivated by lower-level-need satisfaction. These supervisors also believe that close control is in the best interests of both the organization and their personnel. Proceeding from these assumptions, the supervisors use what they feel is an appropriate leadership style. In most cases, over an extended period of time this thinking proves to be wrong. Especially in white-collar jobs and/or with well-trained and -educated workers, Theory X assumptions result in the use of an improper leadership style.

Theory Y. Theory Y is a set of assumptions that, in the main, hold that workers are self-motivated and have potential that often goes untapped in modern industrial life. As applied to supervisory workers, these assumptions include:

1. For most people, the expenditure of physical and mental effort is as natural as resting or playing.
2. Commitment to objectives is based on the rewards associated with reaching these objectives. When workers are committed to certain tasks, they typically exercise self-direction and self-control. Coercion and threats of punishment are not necessary.
3. If the conditions are right, the average worker will not only accept responsibility but seek it.
4. Many workers have a high degree of imagination, creativity, and ingenuity, but in modern industrial life only a small degree of this ability is ever tapped.[5]

Successful supervisors work to tap the natural abilities of their people through interesting and challenging work assignments. However, sometimes this is not possible because the human element is secondary to the physical surroundings. The assembly line is a good example. No matter how much creativity or ingenuity a worker has, the supervisor cannot help the individual use it. The worker must perform by rote whatever function has been assigned, such as installing air conditioners. In some jobs the people adjust to the work rather than vice versa. In many blue-collar jobs effective supervisors are more accurately described in Theory X than in Theory Y terms. Conversely, in many white-collar jobs effective supervisors are more Theory Y advocates than Theory X. Regardless of which theory the supervisor most subscribes to, there is a little of the other in the individual. No supervisor is totally Theory X or totally Theory Y. Successful first-line managers know what leadership style works best in their job and they adopt it.

Foundations of power

Power is the ability to influence, persuade, or move another to one's point of view. All supervisors need power, and depending on the situation, the specific type of power can vary. While there are many types of power, they can be condensed into five categories. These are: legitimate power, coercive power, referent power, reward power, and expert power.[6]

Legitimate power is vested in the supervisor's position. When a person is appointed a supervisor, he or she automatically receives some power as a result of the position. Quite often this power is spelled out in the job description. Formal authority is another name for legitimate power.

Coercive power is held by supervisors who can bring sanctions against those subordinates who do not comply with orders. Some of the most common forms of sanctions include docking a subordinate's pay because the individual was late for work, putting a formal reprimand into the worker's personnel file because the individual violated a major work-safety rule, or firing the person. Not all supervisors have the same amount of coercive power. In unionized organizations, the supervisor may be able to carry out the first two of these while the third may require an OK from the boss, who reviews the particulars of the situation to ensure that the action will stand up should the union appeal it to an arbitration committee. In many white-collar organizations the supervisor does not have the authority to dock pay, although the individual can dismiss someone for excessive tardiness.

Referent power is based on the subordinates' identification with the supervisor. If they like the supervisor, the individual's power increases; if they dislike the supervisor, the individual's power decreases. When supervisors have referent power, their people look up to them and believe that they are trustworthy and reliable. When supervisors have referent power, they are able to lead based on who they are rather than what they say. The subordinates have faith in them and will do as asked. The supervisor does not have to explain why; the fact that the individual gave the order is good enough for the workers.

Reward power is held by supervisors who can give monetary or physical rewards to those workers who do things well. Examples include good performance evaluations, higher-than-average pay raises, recommendations for promotion, first choice on job assignments, etc. Notice that reward power differs markedly from coercive power. Here the supervisor is rewarding people who perform well, while with coercive power the individual is punishing those who do things poorly. The logic behind the effective use of reward power is that those who are rewarded for doing a job well are likely to repeat this performance in the future. As the link between performance and rewards becomes clear to the workers, those who are motivated by these benefits will work hard to attain them. Most supervisors have some degree of reward power, although in organizations where higher-level managers exercise strong control, this power is limited. In turn, the ability of the supervisor to influence and persuade the workers is reduced. Why, they will argue, should we work hard when this person cannot do much for us?

Expert power is held by those supervisors who are seen by their people as having useful job-related knowledge and expertise. Managers who know how to cut through red tape, who can analyze, evaluate, and reach conclusions on difficult problems, and who have had experience handling a wide range of job-related problems are able to illustrate their expertise. Workers, in turn, are impressed with this ability and look up to these supervisors. The result is an increase in the individual's overall power.

Using power

While every supervisor has legitimate power, the individual must supplement this with other forms. Which is best? This depends on the situation. For example, in an organization in which efficiency is low and a get-tough manager is needed, a new supervisor who exercises coercive power in running out the dead wood may well be looked upon favorably by the other workers who have been carrying the load all along. As a result, referent power may increase. On the other hand, coercive power can be overused and in many cases should be a last resort. For example, on the basis of studies in five organizations (including a branch office, a college, an insurance company, a public utility, and some production work units), one group of researchers came up with the following conclusions regarding power:[7]

1. Expert power was most strongly and consistently related to satisfaction and performance.
2. Legitimate power, along with expert power, was the most important in attaining compliance with a leader's wishes.
3. Referent power was of intermediate value in getting workers to comply with directives.
4. Reward power was also of intermediate value in securing compliance.
5. Coercive power was the least valuable, and those supervisors who used it extensively had the lowest organizational effectiveness.

These findings indicate that informal power tends to be more important than formal power. Coercive and reward measures were least effective in getting things done. To the extent that this is true in many organizations, the supervisor must work to build power. Some of the ways in which this can be done are spelled out in Supervision in Action: Building a Power Base.

SUPERVISION IN ACTION: BUILDING A POWER BASE

Supervisors need to supplement their delegated power. There are many ways of doing so. The following are six of the most valuable:

1. ***Develop peripheral organizational vision.*** It is not enough to focus on one's own job. Supervisors must keep their eyes on what is going on around them. For example, when getting feedback from subordinates on proposed work changes, the manager needs to pay attention to the listeners as well as to the speaker. By watching the ways that members of the group react to statements by another worker, the supervisor can get an idea of who agrees with the changes and who disagrees. The manager can also get feedback regarding who the informal group leader is in this case and can begin to formulate a strategy for selling this person on the changes.

2. ***Keep people in your debt.*** Whether it is subordinates or other supervisors, strive to do them a favor or help them out on something. In this way they owe you one. Then go out of your way not to ask for the favor back. When people owe you, they will do little things for you even if you do not ask them to do so. You keep getting interest on the debt without ever touching the principal.

3. ***Be good at your job.*** Both subordinates and bosses regard this as one of the most important characteristics of an effective supervisor. Additionally, know what aspects of your work are regarded as most important and work to be best at these. For example, if the organization feels that quality is more important than quantity, have the lowest quality rejection rate. This will help you develop an image as a competent, proficient supervisor, and when you ask the boss for something, you are likely to get it. After all, the boss needs to keep good people satisfied.

4. ***Develop an image of yourself as a team player.*** Do not fight with people or take sides in all-out wars between groups. These supervisors are not regarded as team players, and the organization is reluctant to give them too much leeway for fear it will look like management is encouraging infighting among the personnel.

5. ***Volunteer for committees or other assignments that will give you visibility outside your work area.*** This increases your organizational contacts and lets people know who you are. If you need help from outside the department, you may already know those who can provide it.

6. ***Assume as much responsibility as you can handle.*** If there is a chance to increase the size of your budget or your work unit, take it. When promotions are given out, those supervisors with the largest departments are often considered first. Even if you are not promoted, if you have a large department you will have the power that goes with it. You can then work on building additional sources of influence.

SUPERVISORY LEADERSHIP STYLES

There are a number of basic supervisory leadership styles. On a continuum ranging from heavily work-centered to highly unconcerned, there are four: authoritarian, paternalistic, participative, and laissez-faire. Depending on the situation, any one of these can be effective.

Authoritarian leaders

Authoritarian leaders are heavily work-centered. They are most concerned with work output. The personnel are of secondary importance to them, often viewed more as factors of production than anything else.

The autocratic style was very common years ago. Today it is not as popular because of the nature of the work and the workers. Nevertheless, an autocratic approach is still useful in certain situations. One is during a crisis. Get-tough supervisors are more effective in handling these situations than are other managers because of their focus on the task. They do not let personal feelings get in the way of crisis resolution. Autocratic supervisors are also effective in dealing with highly inefficient operations where a lid must be put on costs and employee absenteeism and tardiness need to be sharply reduced.

Autocratic supervisors are found more commonly in blue-collar than white-collar occupations. They also tend to work better with manual than clerical types because the nature of the jobs often lends itself to a work-centered orientation. Figure 9-2 illustrates the typical interaction pattern of authoritarian (autocratic) leaders.

Figure 9-2. Leader-subordinate interactions.

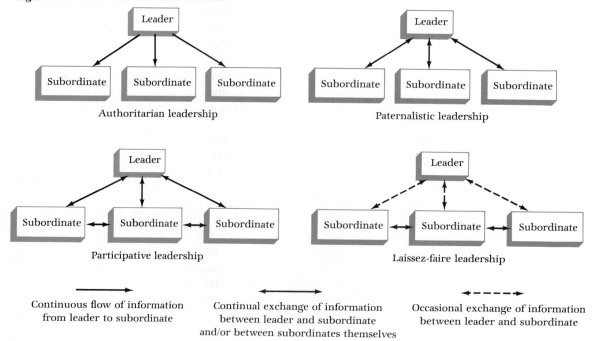

Authoritarian leadership

Paternalistic leadership

Participative leadership

Laissez-faire leadership

Continuous flow of information from leader to subordinate

Continual exchange of information between leader and subordinate and/or between subordinates themselves

Occasional exchange of information between leader and subordinate

Paternalistic leaders

Paternalistic leaders are heavily work-centered but, unlike their autocratic counterparts, also have a concern for the personnel. Their basic philosophy is, "Work hard and I'll take care of you." They deal with their workers the way a parent does with children. They are concerned with the worker's welfare and do not want anything to happen to the person; at the same time, they demand obedience and conformity to authority.

In Theory X and Theory Y terms, paternalistic leaders are known as soft Theory X types. They do not believe that their workers are totally lazy or interested only in job security. They feel that the subordinates enjoy social interaction and want to be active, contributing members of the work group. However, these supervisors like to maintain control over their people and operate the work group as one big happy family with themselves at the top.

If a worker does something the supervisor does not like, the subordinate is often chastised the way an errant child would be. "You really shouldn't have moved that material onto the loading dock until the pickup truck had actually arrived," the supervisor will say. "That's the rule everyone has been taught to follow. Your actions could have resulted in an industrial accident. For the next week you're to switch jobs with Andy. He'll do the unloading instead of you. The next time you do this work, I expect you to do it right or I'll reassign you again. The rules are there to protect everyone and you have to follow them." Notice that the supervisor did not yell or scream the way an autocratic manager might have. Yet the manager did remain in control while sticking to the basic philosophy of the paternalistic supervisor, i.e., I'm doing this for your own good. This same approach is used when workers make requests with which the supervisor does not want to comply. For example, if someone asks to be recommended for a promotion to another area of the organization and the manager does not want to do it, the individual will phrase the reply like this: "Gee, Mary, you just wouldn't be happy in that department. In a couple of weeks you'd be asking for a transfer back. I just couldn't let you make a mistake like that. I'd never forgive myself." Again the supervisor has prevailed by using the paternalistic approach.

The interaction between manager and subordinate is diagrammed in Figure 9-2. Notice that there is a two-way exchange of information under a paternalistic style. However, the control still rests with the supervisor.

Participative leaders

Participative leaders have high concerns for both the people and the work. In getting things done, these supervisors share authority with their people. They are best described in Theory Y terms, although not all of them subscribe fully to each of the basic tenets of this theory. Some managers are mildly participative; others are very strongly oriented in this direction.

Participative supervisors encourage their people to play an active role in operating the unit, although they reserve the right to make the final decision on important matters. These managers delegate; they do not abdicate. Some of the guidelines they follow include:

1. Delegation of work authority to those subordinates most able to assume these tasks
2. Clearly stated job descriptions and work assignments so that all subordinates understand their responsibilities
3. An encouragement of feedback from the subordinates so that there is a continual two-way flow of information
4. Trust in the ability and judgment of the subordinates
5. Creation of strong esprit de corps throughout the group

In recent years the trend toward participative management has increased. Part of the reason is found in the values of the work force; more and more people are demanding a say in what goes on. A second reason is the increase in job complexity brought about by competition and technology. In order to meet these demands, many supervisors are finding that they must delegate work so as to free themselves for additional assignments that require their exclusive attention. However, this does not mean that all effective supervisors use participative management. If the organization has been successful with a nonparticipative style, this may be the best one.

Laissez-faire leaders

Laissez-faire leaders have a lack of concern for the people and the work. They basically do not get involved. If there is any ongoing exchange of job-related information, it takes place between the workers. There are a few instances when a laissez-faire supervisory style is more effective than any other. When this is true, two conditions must be present: (1) The work group must be highly motivated and (2) the members must be extremely good at their jobs. Given these two conditions, the supervisor's laissez-faire approach cannot impede their work progress. In fact, the workers really do not rely on the supervisor for much of anything. The supervisor may handle routine paperwork or participate on a companywide efficiency committee, but the supervisor's interaction with the workers is minimal.

CONTINGENCY APPROACHES TO LEADERSHIP

A close analysis of the four supervisory styles described above reveals that there are two basic dimensions to leadership: concern for work and concern for people. Every supervisor uses some combination of these two and will vary them depending on the situation. This contingency approach results in the supervisor choosing different versions of these styles. In recent years this idea of contingency approaches to leadership has been brought down to an applied level through the use of tools such as the managerial grid and the path-goal approach.

Managerial grid

The *managerial grid* is a tool that can be used, among other things, for identifying one's basic leadership style. The grid itself, depicted in Figure 9-3, has two dimensions: concern for production and concern for people.[8] A

Figure 9-3. The managerial grid. (Reprinted by permission from the April 1978 issue of *Training, The Magazine of Human Resources Development.* © 1978 Lakewood, Minneapolis, Minn. All rights reserved.)

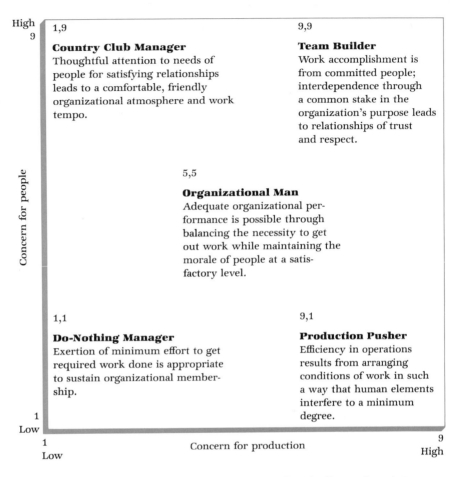

close look at the figure reveals nine degrees of each dimension. A 1 represents a low concern for that dimension; a 9 represents a high concern for it. For purposes of analysis, however, attention is focused only on the five critical ones in the figure. Before continuing, read the five styles in Figure 9-3 closely and decide which would be best for you as a supervisor. Then measure your own leadership style by taking Self-Assessment Quiz 9-1.

SELF-ASSESSMENT QUIZ 9-1:
WHAT IS YOUR SUPERVISORY LEADERSHIP STYLE?

Five supervisory leadership areas are identified below: planning, directing, managing subordinate friction, dealing with information required by subordinates, and controlling operations. These are not the only five things that supervisors do, but they will provide you insights regarding your own supervisory leadership style.

Read the five statements that follow each of these areas and then rank each statement in terms of your own behavior. Place a 1 next to that supervisory behavior which is (or would be) most typical of you, a 2 next to the second most typical behavior, etc., on down to a 5 next to that behavior which is least typical of you. Then transfer your responses to the answer sheet at the end of the self-assessment and total each column in the answer sheet. An interpretation of your supervisory leadership style can be found at the end of the chapter.

Planning

Rank   Behavior

_____ a. I jointly review the whole picture and get reactions, ideas, and commitment from subordinates who have relevant facts. In the process, goals, schedules, responsibilities, and checkpoints are jointly developed.

_____ b. I plan the work for each subordinate after discussing targets and schedules with that individual. I make individual assignments but ensure that each person knows that he or she can check back with me if further assistance is needed.

_____ c. I suggest what should be done next and offer my assistance to subordinates in arranging their activities.

_____ d. I give subordinates the responsibility for planning their own jobs.

_____ e. I do all the planning for my people, set quotas where they are needed, and assign the steps to be followed. I also establish checkpoints that can be used for measuring performance.

Directing

Rank   Behavior

_____ a. Once I have clearly explained the plans and assignments, I keep up with each person's performance and review the individual's progress. If the person is having difficulty getting the job done, I lend assistance.

_____ b. After giving my subordinates their assignments, I stand back and take very little on-the-spot action. I prefer to let my people solve their own problems.

_____ c. Once having discussed their next assignments with them, I stay in touch with my people in order to show them that I am interested in how well they are getting along.

_____ d. Once plans have been formulated, I keep up with the progress of my people. I also help out when needed by defining problems and removing roadblocks.

_____ e. After I have spelled out the plans and instructions, I monitor the work of the subordinates closely and make any changes that are necessary.

Friction between subordinates

Rank   Behavior

_____ a. I expect my people to work out differences between themselves.

_____ b. I emphasize the constructive aspects of the situation and encourage the subordinates to cooperate with each other.

_____ c. I conduct a joint examination of causes of conflict underlying subordinate friction and do not allow the discussion to terminate until I have found ways of eliminating the difficulty.

_____ d. I let my people know that friction between them is not acceptable and that corrective action will be taken if the friction does not stop.

_____ e. I talk to each of my people privately to explain that their friction is apparent to others. I then encourage each to do what he and she can to reduce the difficulty.

Information requested by subordinates

Rank   Behavior

_____ a. I get the information that is needed and keep my people fully posted.

_____ b. I determine whether an answer is needed, and if it is, I report back factually what is required.

_____ c. I pass the request up the line to my own boss.

_____ d. I find personal satisfaction in being helpful to my people in these matters.

_____ e. I get the necessary information, but for the overall good I edit it as I deem necessary.

Controlling

Rank   Behavior

_____ a. I make on-the-spot corrections as work goes along. When an activity is completed, I evaluate everyone's performance and based on overall results, give recognition or make recommendations for changes.

_____ b. I review the ongoing activity of the subordinates as well as the final results of their efforts. I examine both strong points and weaknesses in detail in order to provide points for improving subordinate performance. When merited, I give recognition for contributions on a joint basis.

_____ c. When reactions to their work are brought to my attention, I pass these on to my subordinates.

_____ d. I compliment my people who do well and invite their ideas for improvements. I find that criticism tends to arouse tension and make people defensive.

_____ e. I point out both personal strengths and weaknesses to my people and give each an opportunity to introduce suggestions for improvements.

	I	II	III	IV	V
Planning	b. _____	d. _____	e. _____	a. _____	c. _____
Directing	a. _____	b. _____	e. _____	d. _____	c. _____
Friction between subordinates	e. _____	a. _____	d. _____	c. _____	b. _____
Information requested by subordinates	e. _____	c. _____	b. _____	a. _____	d. _____
Controlling	e. _____	c. _____	a. _____	b. _____	d. _____
Total	_____	_____	_____	_____	_____

The self-assessment quiz provides insights regarding your preference for each of these styles. For purposes of effective supervision, it is important to remember that most first-line managers have both primary and secondary styles. For example, a supervisor might be a 9,9 manager who uses a 5,5 style when the 9,9 is inappropriate. This does not mean that he never uses the 1,9 style, 9,1 style, or 1,1 style; it merely means that these are seldom employed, for he can get by without relying much on them. Another supervisor might be a 1,9 manager who uses a 9,9 style as secondary; more than any other style, she uses a high concern for people and low concern for work. A high concern for both people and work is her second favorite style.

When given leadership preference tests like the one in the self-assessment quiz, most white-collar supervisors have the following order of leadership style preference: 9,9; 5,5; 1,9; 9,1; and 1,1. Most blue-collar supervisors have a somewhat different overall order of preference: 9,9; 9,1; 5,5; 1,9; and 1,1.[9]

Not all supervisors follow the above patterns. However, it is interesting to note that those in a given organization who are most successful tend to have similar leadership patterns. The same is true for their less successful counterparts. If the most productive supervisors have primary and secondary leadership styles of 9,9 and 5,5, respectively, there must be a reason for it. The nature of the business and the types of workers there call for these approaches. Supervisors who use a 9,1 and 1,9 style are not likely to be effective in this organization. Of course, in identifying the most productive style it is necessary to get feedback from the workers as well as from the supervisors. In this way, biased self-perception on the part of the first-line managers can be reduced. (See Supervision in Action: Measuring Supervisory Leadership Styles.)

SUPERVISION IN ACTION:
MEASURING SUPERVISORY LEADERSHIP STYLES

Many organizations are interested in helping supervisors identify their leadership styles. However, in order to prevent bias, there are usually three major steps involved.

First, supervisors are administered some type of leadership-style test. Quite often it is a pen-and-pencil test such as that presented in Self-Assessment Quiz 9-1. The supervisors are asked to fill it out in order to gain some insights regarding the type of leadership style(s) they prefer. This is known as the self-perception side of leadership. It represents the way the supervisor sees himself or herself.

Second, the supervised personnel are given the same leadership-style test and asked to fill it out in terms of describing the way that the supervisor actually goes about leading them. This is the subordinate-perception side of leadership.

Finally, someone appointed by the organization takes the results of both groups, the supervisors and their personnel, and compares them for purposes of determining how accurate the supervisor is in identifying personal leadership style. Quite often the supervisor turns out to be more work-oriented and less people-oriented than he or she believes. In any event, if there is any discrepancy between the way the individual supervisor sees himself or herself and the way the subordinates do, there is a basis for self-improvement. The supervisor is never shown the individual subordinate responses. However, the manager does get to see a composite. On the basis of subordinates' perceptions, the supervisor's boss then sits down and discusses how the first-line manager can develop a more effective style. Quite often this means becoming more interested in the people and less in the work. In particular, many of these self-descriptive leadership-style tests are designed to help people identify those areas in which they are not acting the way they should. For example, a supervisor may do many things well, but when it comes to decision making, the individual tends to make too many decisions without consulting the personnel. The individual needs to work on the more participative management techniques. Another supervisor may do a very fine job of counseling the people but be extremely poor in providing feedback on how well the workers perform. These problem areas can be identified and steps developed for improving performance.

Supervisors who have participated in these types of programs report that they like the feedback from subordinates because it helps open their eyes to what is going on around them. As one of them put it: "Until I saw the way my people evaluated my leadership style, I thought I was very good at promoting feedback but very poor in spelling out work assignments. As it turned out, they saw things in just the reverse order. Thanks to this information, I think I'm doing a much better job than before."

The path-goal approach

The managerial grid is a useful way of discussing leadership styles and deciding which most benefits the organization. However, most supervisors require even more hands-on assistance. The *path-goal approach* is a supervisory theory that helps managers balance the needed concern for work with the requisite concern for people.[10] (Figure 9-4 illustrates how the supervisor should do this.) The logic is that the supervisor should be concerned with clearing a path for the worker so that the latter can attain desired goals.

Jobs can be classified into two basic types: structured and unstructured. Structured tasks require very little guidance or direction from the supervisor. If the leader provides low directiveness, there will be high job satisfaction, as seen by points A and A' in Figure 9-4. On the other hand, if the supervisor provides a great deal of direction on unstructured tasks, job satisfaction will be low. This is illustrated by points D and D' in Figure 9-4. A high work-centered approach on structured tasks is seen as interference by the workers. If the supervisor wants to interface with them, he or she should focus on providing praise and encouragement. In managerial grid terms, a 1,9 style is appropriate.

In the case of unstructured tasks, the workers do look for assistance and guidance. When job assignments are unclear or there is a lack of knowledge regarding how to do the job, they welcome assistance. Face-to-face communication, coaching, training, and development are some of the common ways of providing this. If the manager does these things, employee satisfaction will be high and work output should improve. (See points C and C' in Figure 9-4.) If the supervisor fails to provide such assistance, employee satisfaction will suffer (see points B and B' in Figure 9-4). The supervisor in

Figure 9-4. The path-goal approach.

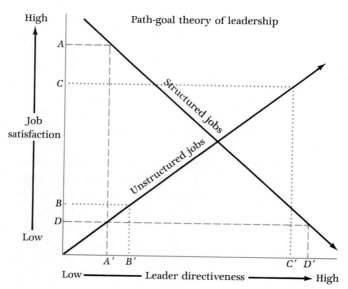

this case is choosing the wrong leadership style. In managerial grid terms, a 9,1 style is most appropriate.

The path-goal approach is a useful contingency concept because it helps the supervisor balance a concern for work with a concern for people. In particular, it focuses on the need for supervisors to help subordinates get their work done without doing it for them.

TIPS FOR EFFECTIVE LEADERSHIP

A number of useful tips can help supervisors lead their people more effectively. The following are six of the most beneficial.

Know your people

Supervisors have to learn what their people can and cannot do. They also have to understand what motivates each person. In this way they can tie together leadership and motivation. There is no sense clearing a path to a goal if the subordinate is not motivated to accomplish this objective. Additionally, a knowledge of the personnel provides the leader with insights regarding the amount of directedness or control that each person needs. Without a knowledge of the people, a supervisor cannot effectively use such ideas as the path-goal approach.

Match the people to the work

There are some tasks that everyone in the work group can do. There are other tasks at which some workers will excel. In ensuring the greatest efficiency, the supervisor must match the people to the work, starting with the most difficult or challenging jobs. Once these are taken care of, the manager can assign the less talented people to the easier tasks. Of course, it is unlikely that there will ever be a perfect match between the people and the work. In low-level jobs many individuals will be working beneath their level of ability. However, the best the supervisor can usually do is to make a "best fit" between the people and the work.

Change situations, not personalities

People basically remain the same. If a supervisor is a calm, easygoing person, the individual is unlikely to work well in an environment in which effective supervision requires a lot of running around, yelling, and screaming. In an office environment the individual might do quite well; in a frenzied blue-collar operation the person would be at a loss. The same analogy holds for the workers.

When people find themselves in environments in which they have trouble adjusting, one of two things must be changed: personality or situation. It is much too difficult for people to change their personalities. At best this is a time-consuming undertaking. It is easier to work on changing the situation. For example, if the supervisor finds that his or her job is too unstructured and this is frustrating and difficult to deal with, the individual should work on formalizing the requirements of the position. If the supervisor finds that he or she has little formal authority over the workers, efforts should be made to supplement this authority with informal means (see Supervision in Action: Building a Power Base).

Likewise, if subordinates have trouble working in their environment, the supervisor should help change these conditions. If the worker is encountering frustration because needed materials are not being delivered on time, efforts should be made to eliminate this bottleneck. If the worker finds it difficult to get cooperation from other people in the unit, the supervisor should step in and work to resolve the problem. If it turns out that one of these people is unable to offer the necessary cooperation, this individual should be reassigned to other work. Remember, it is more efficient to alter situations than to modify personalities. People are what they are and supervisors must work within these constraints.

Act appropriately

Some subordinates like a supervisor who is easygoing; others prefer an individual who goes by the book. These desires dictate what the individuals see as appropriate behavior. To the extent that the supervisor can live up to this image, effectiveness will be enhanced. However, this does not mean that the supervisor must focus squarely on the workers' needs and abandon his or her managerial role. In fact, if the supervisor must choose between supporting the workers or supporting the organization, the latter is the right choice. The workers may not like it, but they will understand that the supervisor is a member of the management team. If the manager opts for the workers' position, this will be seen as a sign of weakness and/or inappropriate behavior.

Be flexible

Every supervisor has a primary and secondary leadership style. However, this does not mean that the individual never uses any other styles. From time to time a manager who typically employs a 9,1 or 5,5 style will find a 1,9 style to be more effective than any other.

At the same time, a supervisor who usually employs a 9,9 or 9,1 style will need to use a 1,9 style. Most of the supervisor's personnel may respond best to a 9,9, but the most effective salesperson may require a 1,9 approach. Naturally, the supervisor is unlikely to be as good at using these styles as at employing primary and secondary ones. However, to the extent that the manager can be flexible, his or her effectiveness will increase.

It is important to remember that in most cases the supervisor should stay with these primary and secondary styles, because doing so helps subordinates interact more effectively with him or her. They are better able to read and respond to a supervisor whom they understand than one whose chameleonlike changes of leadership style make it impossible to anticipate where the individual is coming from. A supervisor who continually uses multiple leadership styles often confounds the personnel more than he or she helps them.

**Err on
the human side**

From time to time the supervisor will use an inappropriate style. A 9,1 approach will have worked well the last time, but this time a 1,9 would have been best. When unsure of what to do, it is best to err on the human side. A moderate Theory Y approach is usually superior to a moderate Theory X approach. A supervisor who is extremely humanistic can add a work-related dimension if it is needed and usually increase efficiency. However, a supervisor who is extremely work-related will not get the same results by adding a humanistic dimension. The personnel will see these efforts as manipulative attempts to con them. This is particularly true in white-collar jobs, where a human relations orientation is extremely important. Of course, a humanistic approach will sometimes prove to be too soft. However, over the long run the effective supervisor errs on the side of humanism rather than on that of authoritarianism.

UP AND DOWN: STARTING CASE REVISITED

Having read the chapter, you now realize that Susan was initially successful because she used an authoritarian style in a crisis situation. Her preferred style was the ideal one for straightening things out. However, the crisis has now passed and the workers are looking for a more relaxed environment. Susan has cracked the whip for too long.

Can she change her style? Probably not. So the best thing that can be done is to give her additional training or transfer her. Remember from the chapter: Change the situation, not the personality. Also remember the importance of contingency leadership. The style that works best in one situation will not necessarily work best in another situation.

INTERPRETATION OF SELF-ASSESSMENT QUIZ 9-1: WHAT IS YOUR SUPERVISORY LEADERSHIP STYLE?

After you have added up all five columns of numbers, check your mathematical accuracy by totaling the columns. Did you get 75? If not, add across each row and see if you get a total of 15 every time. You should have a 1, 2, 3, 4, and 5 in each row. Having corrected any mathematical mistakes, you are now ready to analyze your answers.

Enter your totals below beginning with the lowest number, which identifies your favorite leadership style. Then compute the mathematical differences between the totals.

Column totals	*Mathematical difference between totals*
_____	_____
_____	_____
_____	_____
_____	_____
_____	

Column I in the quiz indicates your preference for the 5,5 leadership style. Columns II through V represent the 1,1 style, the 9,1 style, the 9,9 style, and the

1,9 style, respectively. Which was your favorite? Most people choose the 9,9 while giving the 1,1 the lowest preference. The gap between the numbers indicates the degree of preference. The lowest total you could nave had was 5; the highest was 25. The closer your lowest number comes to 5, the greater your preference for that style; the closer your highest number comes to 25, the greater your dislike for that style. If there is a gap of 5 or more between one leadership style and the next popular one, this indicates that you would stay with the first style for an indefinite period of time. If the gap between one style and another is less than 5, you would be willing to switch from the first to the second if you felt that the former was not working well. In getting an idea of your supervisory leadership style, remember that this is your perception of your style. It is how you see yourself. It may not be the way your subordinates see you.

SUMMARY OF KEY POINTS

1. Leadership is the process of influencing people to direct their effort toward the achievement of some particular goal(s). There is no ideal profile of the successful leader, but some of the characteristics for success include: superior mental ability, emotional maturity, need-achievement drive, problem-solving skills, empathy, and the ability to represent workers to the next level of management.

2. Many supervisors have assumptions about worker behavior. Some subscribe to Theory X tenets, which see the worker as lazy, having little ambition, wanting security, and responding best to close control and coercion. Others subscribe to Theory Y tenets, which see the worker as not basically lazy, as committed to objectives that have desired rewards, and as self-directed, self-controlled, and creative.

3. Power is the ability to influence, persuade, or move another to one's point of view. There are five basic types of power: legitimate, coercive, referent, reward, and expert. Research indicates that informal power tends to be more important than formal power.

4. There are a number of basic supervisory leadership styles. One is the authoritarian leader who is heavily work-centered. A second is the paternalistic leader who is heavily work-centered but also has a concern for the personnel. A third is the participative leader who has a high concern for both the people and the work. A fourth is the laissez-faire leader who has a lack of concern for the people and the work.

5. A close analysis of supervisory styles reveals that there are two basic dimensions to leadership: concern for work and concern for people. These two dimensions are well reflected in the managerial grid and the path-goal approach. The managerial grid is a two-dimensional leadership model that helps supervisors identify, measure, and evaluate their current styles of leadership. The path-goal approach helps supervisors determine how much concern to evidence for both the people and the work.

6. There are a number of useful leadership tips for supervisors. Six of these are: know your people; match the people to the work; change situations, not personalities; act appropriately; be flexible; and err on the human side.

BUILD YOUR SUPERVISORY WORD POWER

These key leadership terms are presented in their order of appearance in the chapter. Effective supervisors have a working knowledge of them.

Leadership. The process of influencing people to direct their efforts toward the achievement of some particular goal(s).

Empathy. The ability to identify with others emotionally.

Theory X. A set of assumptions that managers have about their subordinates, including: (1) People dislike work and will avoid it when possible; (2) workers have little ambition and like to be directed; (3) they want security above all else; and (4) to get them to work, close control and coercion are necessary.

Theory Y. A set of assumptions that managers have about their subordinates, including: (1) Work is a natural phenomenon; (2) commitment to objectives is based on rewards; (3) the average worker will not only accept responsibility, but seek it; and (4) most workers have greater creativity and ingenuity than their jobs demand.

Power. The ability to influence, persuade, or move another to one's point of view.

Legitimate power. Power that is vested in the supervisor's position.

Coercive power. Power that is held by supervisors who can bring sanctions against those who do not comply with orders.

Referent power. Power based on the subordinates' identification with the supervisor.

Reward power. Power held by supervisors who can give rewards to those who do things well.

Expert power. Power held by supervisors who are seen by their people as having useful job-related knowledge and expertise.

Authoritarian leaders. Leaders who are heavily work-centered, with major emphasis given to task accomplishment and little to the human element.

Paternalistic leaders. Leaders who are heavily work-centered but who also have consideration for their people, treating them the way a parent would a child.

Participative leaders. Leaders who have a high concern for both their people and the work.

Laissez-faire leaders. Leaders who have a lack of concern for the people and the work.

Managerial grid. A leadership framework that uses a concern for production and a concern for people to explain and evaluate leadership behavior.

9,1 managerial style. A managerial style in which the manager has a high concern for production and a low concern for people. This manager is often referred to as a production pusher.

9,9 managerial style. A managerial style in which the manager has a high concern for production and a high concern for people. This manager is often referred to as a team manager.

1,9 managerial style. A managerial style in which the manager has a low concern for production and a high concern for people. This individual is often referred to as a country club manager.

1,1 managerial style. A managerial style in which the manager has a low concern for production and a low concern for people. This individual is often referred to as a do-nothing manager.

5,5 managerial style. A managerial style in which the manager has a moderate concern for production and a moderate concern for people. This individual is often referred to as an organizational manager.

Path-goal approach. A supervisory leadership approach which holds that on unstructured tasks the supervisor should provide assistance to subordinates by clearing a path to the goal and on structured tasks should provide praise, encouragement, and low directedness.

REVIEW YOUR UNDERSTANDING

1. In your own words, what is *leadership?*
2. What are some of the characteristics of successful leaders? Identify and describe three.
3. How does a Theory X manager view subordinates? How does a Theory Y manager view subordinates? Compare and contrast the two theories.
4. What is meant by the term *power?*
5. There are five basic types of power. What does this statement mean? In your answer be sure to identify and describe each type of power.
6. Some experts believe that informal power tends to be more important to the supervisor than formal power. What is the logic behind this? Explain your answer.
7. How does an authoritarian supervisor behave? How does this individual differ from a paternalistic supervisor?-
8. How does a participative supervisor differ from a laissez faire leader? Compare and contrast the two.
9. Describe how each of the following supervisors goes about leading his or her people: 1,1 manager; 1,9 manager; 9,1 manager; 5,5 manager; 9,9 manager. In your answer be sure to describe each manager's approach.
10. Of what value is the managerial grid to the study of effective supervision? Explain.
11. How can a supervisor use the path-goal approach in increasing his or her effectiveness as a manager? Give an example in your answer.

SUPPLEMENT YOUR KNOWLEDGE

In addition to the references listed at the end of this chapter, the following provide important, practical information that is of use to supervisors in leading their people:

Austin, Terence W.: "What Can Managers Learn from Leadership Theories?" *Supervisory Management*, July 1981, pp. 22–31.

Lester, Richard I.: "Leadership: Some Principles and Concepts," *Personnel Journal*, November 1981, pp. 868–870.

Polczynski, James J.: "Building a Foundation of Power," *Supervisory Management*, October 1982, pp. 36–39.

Thompson, Ken, and Robert E. Pitts: "The Supervisor's Survival Guide: Being Group Leader," *Supervisory Management*, March 1979, pp. 24–31.

Watson, Craig M.: "Leadership, Management, and the Seven Keys," *Business Horizons*, March–April 1983, pp. 8–13.

Weisbord, Marvin, and James C. Maselko: "Learning How to Influence Others," *Supervisory Management*, May 1981, pp. 2–10.

Weiss, Alan: "Leadership Styles: Which Are Best When?" *Supervisory Management*, January 1976, pp. 2–8.

YOU BE THE SUPERVISOR: AVERAGE AND EXCELLENT

Most workers in Clarence Hoover's department have a fixed opinion of him. Some refer to Clarence as hard-working; most admit that he rewards those who do a good job and makes life difficult for those who do a poor job. However, there are no major complaints about him. A recent attitude survey conducted at the workers' level reveals that Clarence has an image as a "reward and punishment" leader. The latest productivity report shows that Clarence's work group is average. His people have a greater amount of absenteeism and tardiness than most units; however, much of this is accounted for by 20 percent of the personnel, and these are the lowest producers. Approximately 25 percent of his people have above-average productivity performance, and these workers are seldom absent or late.

Teresa Menendez is another supervisor in the same work area. Teresa's people are very vocal in their praise of her. Most use the words *experienced, qualified,* or *effective* in describing her. The recent attitude survey reveals that Teresa has one of the highest-producing groups. Almost none of her people are ever absent and the tardiness rate is virtually nonexistent. Only three workers have missed a day's work during the last 6 months. The workers report that they enjoy working for Teresa because she is very job knowledgeable and can help them out if they get into trouble. Many of the workers also admit that they identify with her. "She is a manager who really cares about us," one of them wrote on the essay part of the attitude survey. "We all identify with her."

1. If you were a supervisor in the same work area as Clarence and Teresa, how would you seek to increase your power? What types of power would you pursue? Explain.
2. What type of leadership style would you employ with the workers in this case? Use the managerial grid in answering this question.
3. How would you use the path-goal approach in supervising these workers? Cite at least two examples in your answer.

YOU BE THE SUPERVISOR: HIGH EFFICIENCY, HIGH TURNOVER

When Lilli Forsythe came to work in Fred Atkin's department, she was totally unfamiliar with the way things were done. She had never worked in a retail catalog sales office and many of the procedures seemed strange. Fred understood this, and from the first day he went out of his way to help her. At first Lilli had difficulty filling out the order forms. There were so many pieces of information that had to be entered, from the buyer's name and address to the order number, quantity, and amount of purchase. Fred admitted that the form had not been well designed, but within a couple of days he had Lilli to the point where she could fill out an order form in less than 5 minutes. It took another week for Lilli, with the help of Fred, to master the rest of the job. By the end of the month she was one of the fastest people in the department. She had changed a lot. However, Fred had not.

Every day he would come by in the morning and again in the afternoon to check her work progress. He would look through all of the order forms, make sure that there were no mistakes, and then put the pile of forms back in the out box. By the end of the second week, Fred was unable to find one incorrect order form. Nevertheless, he kept coming by to check her work and talk to her about job-related matters.

Gradually, Lilli began to resent Fred's visits. It seemed as if he did not trust her to do the job right. Lilli mentioned this to a couple of other people in the department and they felt the same way she did. "The problem with Fred," one of them said, "is that he doesn't know when to let up. According to a friend of mine in the home office, his overall efficiency rating is one of the highest in the company. However, he has been unable to keep anyone for more than 6 months. He's got the highest turnover rate in the firm. This is why he hasn't gotten promoted in 5 years."

Over the next month, Lilli began to think more and more about transferring to another department. She talked to a friend who worked in shipping and learned that there was an opening there. Last week Lilli told Fred that she had decided to transfer to shipping. He was not happy with the news but accepted it with good grace. "I thought we worked well together. However, I think you should do what is in your own best interest. If you feel that shipping is better for you, that's where you should go. I'll sign off on the paperwork later today."

Lilli dropped in to say goodbye to Fred before she left. As she entered his office, he was talking to her replacement. "This job may be a little difficult to master, but I'll be working with you every step of the way. You can rely on me," he was telling the young man. The new employee seemed quite happy with the news.

1. What kind of leader is Fred: authoritarian, paternalistic, participative, or laissez-faire? What type would you be if you were in charge of this department? Explain your answer.

2. Using the managerial grid, how would you describe Fred's leadership style? If you were the supervisor of this department, what style would you use? Be complete in your answer.

3. How would you use the path-goal approach to manage this department? Explain.

NOTES

1. J. Clifton Williams, *Human Behavior in Organizations*, Cincinnati: South-Western, 1982, pp. 413–414.

2. Jay Hall, "To Achieve or Not: The Manager's Choice," *California Management Review*, Summer 1976, pp. 5–18.

3. Douglas McGregor, *The Human Side of Enterprise*, New York: McGraw-Hill, 1960.

4. McGregor, pp. 33–34.

5. McGregor, pp. 47–48.

6. John R. P. French, Jr., and Bertram Raven, "The Bases of Social Power," in D. Cartwright (ed.), *Studies in Social Power*, Ann Arbor, Mich.: Institute for Social Research, 1959, pp. 150–167.

7. Jerald G. Bachman, David G. Bowers, and Philip M. Marcus, "Bases of Supervisory Power: A Comparative Study in Five Organizational Settings," in Arnold S. Tannenbaum (ed.), *Control in Organization*, New York: McGraw-Hill, 1968, p. 236.

8. R. R. Blake and J. S. Mouton, *The Managerial Grid*, Houston, Tex.: Gulf Publishing, 1964.

9. Based on research conducted by the author.

10. Robert J. House, "A Path-Goal Theory of Leader Effectiveness," *Administrative Science Quarterly*, September 1971, pp. 321–338.

CHAPTER 10

APPRAISING AND REWARDING PERFORMANCE

**GOALS OF
THE CHAPTER**

At some point in time the supervisor must review the performance of the workers. There are three reasons for this. The first is to determine the strengths and weaknesses of the personnel for the purpose of providing additional training, development, and coaching. The second is to determine how well the people have done, thus providing a basis for rewarding performance. The third is to set objectives for the next evaluation period.

Performance appraisals are usually carried out once or twice a year depending on the nature of the work and the philosophy of the company. If the industry is very competitive and high output and quality are requirements for survival, appraisals will be more frequent because the firm will want to monitor worker performance continually and correct problems before they become too serious. On the other hand, many white-collar firms review their people annually because the costs of a second appraisal do not justify the benefits.

Appraisals are important to the reward system. However, since most supervisors have minimum authority over rewards, there is not too much they can do except recommend the best workers for higher raises than the other personnel. Nevertheless, there are things that the supervisor can do to help ensure that the firm's wage rates are both competitive and equitable.

When you have finished reading all the material in this chapter, you will be able to:

1. Describe how the performance appraisal process works.
2. Identify and discuss four of the most commonly used appraisal forms.
3. Discuss some of the most common problems that confront supervisors in their efforts to evaluate their personnel.
4. Compare and contrast validity and reliability and explain the importance of each to the performance evaluation process.
5. Discuss the steps the supervisor should follow in the appraisal interview.
6. Discuss the role that the supervisor should play in rewarding performance.

A STARTING CASE: ROUGH AND TOUGH RANDY

Randy Whitcomb is a new supervisor at Miller's, a regional retail chain. Randy was hired 2 months ago. Although he has had no experience in managing retail employees, he has been a supervisor for 3 years at a local bank. Randy left the bank because promotions were too slow. Most of the top people at the bank were young, and it would have been years before Randy would have been able to make it into the top-management ranks.

Although Randy has been at Miller's only a short time, there is a 6-month performance evaluation review for all personnel, and Randy's boss asked him to conduct the review with his own people. Based on his bank experience, Randy felt comfortable complying with the request.

Last week he held interviews with the six people in his work group. In each case Randy tried to be as specific and detailed as possible in pointing out both their strengths and weaknesses. He then provided each with a detailed list of things that he would like to see them work on. One person, for example, was told to be more alert to customers waiting for service. On a number of occasions Randy had found the woman talking to a fellow employee or arranging merchandise while the customer stood quietly waiting for assistance. Another worker was told to start coming back on time from his coffee breaks. Randy found him in the coffee shop 3 times last week when he should have been back on the floor.

Along with the interview, Randy filled out a performance appraisal form on each person. Four of the six workers were given average ratings, while the other two received below-average ones. In each case Randy told them that he knew they could do better and that he looked forward to seeing them prove it.

Yesterday Randy was called into his boss's office. "I wanted you to drop by," she told him, "because four of the people in your department have come in to ask for a transfer. It seems that they feel your performance evaluation was not fair. Do you want to tell me about the matter?"

Randy was taken aback by her comments but quickly regained his composure. "Well, I think I've got a very good group of workers, but they aren't measuring up to their potential. If they think my evaluation was too hard, they should have worked in the bank with me. Over there no one was ever given a superior rating. There seemed to be only two types of evaluations: average and poor. It was a tough system, but it weeded out the deadwood and encouraged the rest of us to work even harder. I think the people in my unit are upset over nothing. I told them that I was sure they would improve. Why are they angry?"

The boss then explained to Randy that most employees at Miller's get either superior or good ratings. Of all the supervisors in the store, Randy had the lowest evaluations. She closed by saying: "I think perhaps I failed to acquaint you with the way we evaluate people here. Let me put you in touch with two other supervisors. I'd like you to talk with them and get a feel for how we do things. Then the next time you'll have a better idea. Meanwhile, we'll let these current ratings stay as they are. You may be right. Maybe these people aren't measuring up to their full potential. We'll be able to tell after your next evaluation of them." With that the meeting ended and Randy left the office.

Where did Randy go wrong? Why did he make this mistake? Overall, what type of a rater is he in comparison to the other supervisors at Miller's? What is Randy likely to learn from his meeting with the other supervisors? How will this information be of value to him? Write down your preliminary answers to these questions. We will return to them at the end of the chapter.

HOW THE PERFORMANCE APPRAISAL WORKS

Performance appraisal is the process of evaluating how well an employee has done and then setting objectives for the individual for the next evaluation period.[1] (See Figure 10-1.) Sometimes this process is formally carried out; other times it is handled in a very informal manner. Sometimes the supervisor sets the objectives for the worker; other times it is a joint process. In either case, the four steps in Figure 10-1 are followed in sequential order.

Establishment of performance standards

The process begins with the establishment of performance standards. These standards are typically based on the job description.[2] (Table 10-1 provides an example of a job description.) If the job description is well written, the standards are easily identified. If not, the supervisor has to spell out to the worker what is expected. In an effort to provide uniformity of standards, some organizations have their supervisors meet and jointly identify what these standards should be for jobs in their area. In this way, all first-line managers know what is expected of their people and new supervisors can quickly learn these standards. In other cases, supervisors and workers jointly determine the standards. (Supervision in Action: Writing the Standards indicates how this can be done.)

Figure 10-1. Performance appraisal in action.

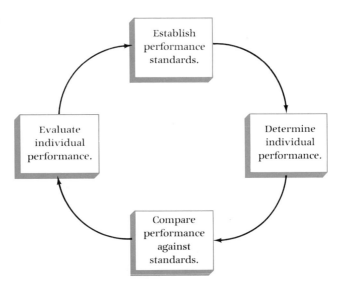

Table 10-1. Example
of a job description:
a stenographer-clerk

JOB TITLE

Stenographer-Clerk

Description of duties

Under direct supervision, takes and transcribes moderately difficult dictation from one or
more individuals, performs a variety of clerical duties, and usually carries out a regularly
assigned specific clerical task related to the functions of the unit. Performs miscellaneous
typing and related duties as assigned.

Typical examples of work

Takes dictation of moderate difficulty using shorthand or stenotype machine.
Transcribes notes by typing.

Performs rough draft or copy typing.

Performs a variety of clerical duties, which may involve the following related duties:

maintaining office files, including making additions, deletions, and revisions; looking up
materials from the files such as correspondence, reports, and requisitions;

composing and typing simple memoranda and correspondence;

maintaining reports and letters, recording data on predesigned forms, and, as requested,
summarizing data in weekly and monthly reports;

maintaining follow-up records on reports and correspondence;

distributing mail;

answering the telephone;

requisitioning office supplies.

Minimum qualifications

Education
Graduation from high school or its equivalent, with sufficient mental development to
perform clerical and stenographic duties. Requires training in stenography, typing, and
routine business procedures.
Experience
At least 3 months' experience in the company to become familiar with company and
departmental organization, policies, procedures, terminology, and general office
procedures. Requires 120 hours of on-the-job training to learn the details of departmental
assignments.
Knowledge
Knowledge of clerical methods and office procedures.
Ability and Skill
Ability to take general dictation using shorthand or stenotype machine, to record
statistics and arithmetical data on standard records and reports, and to compose and
type routine correspondence. Must be skilled in the use of the typewriter.
Personal Characteristics
Accuracy; dependability; mental alertness; thorough, pleasing personality; and good
memory for details.
Physical Requirements
Must pass company physical examination.

SUPERVISION IN ACTION: WRITING THE STANDARDS

The process of writing performance standards is initiated when the supervisor and the employee take time to discuss the job. The first step involves a listing of the employee's actual duties and responsibilities. The employee also considers his understanding of what primary expectations the supervisor might have. The operational phases of the job and the subordinate's work-related targets are also listed.

A review of the performance standard will show duplications and the need for editing and integration. This boiling-down process actively involves both the supervisor and employee in questioning, reacting, and seeking clarification of the standard. Every job is made up of segments for which specific standards can be written.

After completing the process of listing, editing, and integration, an approved performance standard can be written which will be quantifiable, measurable, and achievable. Each standard will measure a phase of the job but will be different for each employee. The differences between standards will lie in the specific quantity of output expected that will represent satisfactory performance.

Some record must be kept of the work performance so results can be systematically determined at regular intervals and compared with goals. When progress toward goals is not in accordance with plans, the problems must be identified and corrective action should be taken by the supervisor and the subordinate. Nothing is accomplished by writing performance standards unless a regular review of progress toward results is established. The review helps determine where and when progress is below expectations.

Supervisors must learn how to help employees prepare performance standards which will make them stretch but are not beyond their capabilities. Supervisors also must learn to effectively measure performance. They must learn to anticipate problems which threaten the achievement of goals and then take steps to cope with the problems.

Performance standards are normally related to unit management objectives. Goals should be balanced for the long haul, rather than reacting to immediate, pressing problems. Ideally, performance standards will help employees control their own jobs. Performance standards are desirable in each of the following areas:

Regular work. Refers to activities that make up the major part of the employee's responsibilities and will relate to improving the quality of product or service, operating more efficiently, and expanding the total amount produced.

Problem solving. Refers to definitions of major problems encountered or foreseen. The goal is to eliminate each defined problem.

Innovation. Refers to new ways of dealing with work and may relate to the acceptance of new ideas from employees. Also refers to the employee's continued growth in both technical areas and in working with others effectively.

Each employee is a collection of hereditary, educational, and environmental factors which influence his or her ability to perform at a given level. It is reasonable to expect more from some performers and to reward the extra performance. Likewise, it is necessary to identify areas in which less productive performers can improve their performance and earn extra rewards. Thus, all employees are rewarded for better performance and are encouraged to be more productive.

Source: Thomas C. Alewine, "Performance Appraisals and Performance Standards," © March 1982. Reprinted by permission of *Personnel Journal,* Costa Mesa, Calif.; all rights reserved.

Determining individual performance

The determination of individual performance is often the most difficult part of the process. Unless the supervisor has some basis for identifying how much work (quantity) someone has done, or how well (quality) the individual has done it, the performance appraisal can prove to be nothing more than an educated guess. To the extent that records are kept regarding work output, scrap or rejection rates, tardiness, absenteeism, job-related accidents, rule violations, etc., it becomes easier to determine how well each person in the unit has performed.

Comparing performance against standards

This step is not a difficult one if the previous two have been properly completed. It is really nothing more than a matter of placing actual work performance alongside desired work performance and comparing the two.

Evaluating individual performance

This step can take numerous forms. It usually begins with the superior deciding how well the subordinate has done. This information is placed on a formal performance evaluation form. Then there is typically an interview in which the supervisor discusses the review, points out the worker's strengths and weaknesses, and gives the latter a chance to ask questions, lodge disagreements, and/or seek assistance. Performance standards are then set for the next appraisal period and the process begins again.

COMMON APPRAISAL FORMS

A number of different types of appraisal forms are used by supervisors in evaluating worker performance. In general, these forms tend to be fairly simple and easy to complete, although in recent years some firms have begun adopting more complex, detailed ones. They have found that simple evaluation forms are often too general in content and do not adequately identify strong and weak areas of performance or offer sufficient information for improving future performance.[3] The following are four of the most common appraisal forms.

Graphic rating scales

Graphic rating scales are the most widely used of all performance appraisal tools. Figure 10-2 provides an example. A brief look at the figure shows that the instrument is easy to read and understand. In completing the form, the supervisor merely circles the factor degree that most accurately reflects the worker's performance. Not all graphic rating scales are as detailed as this one, which describes both the factors and the degrees of each as well as identifying the points per degree. These points are deliberately switched around so that the supervisor has to read each scale carefully before making a choice.

The biggest problem with using graphic rating scales is that the supervisors may not be fully aware of what the factors are designed to measure or what the dividing line is between one of the factor degrees and another. These interpretation problems are best resolved through supervisory meetings in which the first-line managers are taught how to fill out the forms and how to decide which degree of each to give to a worker.

Paired comparison method

The *paired comparison method* requires the supervisor to compare every individual in the work unit against every other individual in determining who is best on each of the factors being evaluated. An example is provided in Figure 10-3. Notice that in this figure two factors are being rated. In an actual setting it would not be uncommon for the supervisor to rate people on five to seven factors similar to those presented in the figure.

This evaluation is more time-consuming than graphic rating scales are. However, it also tends to be more accurate because it forces the supervisor to identify those who do the best work and those who are not as good. There can be only one person who ranks first on work quantity, work quality, etc. When the supervisor has finished ranking the workers on individual factors, an overall ranking can also be obtained. The easiest way is by giving a point value to each factor. For example, the person who is the highest on work quantity is given 5 points, on down to a 1 for the individual with the poorest performance. The supervisor can then add up all of the points and arrive at an overall ranking. If there is a tie, it can be broken by simply determining which factor is the most important of all. If it is deemed to be work quality, then the individual with the highest score here is placed ahead of the other person.

Perhaps the biggest drawback to the paired comparison is the amount of time required to fill out the various forms. Additionally, in the case of subjective factors like attitude or initiative, it can be difficult to determine who is better than whom. The supervisor may remember a particular instance when a worker volunteered to stay late and help out on a big job, but that does not mean that this worker has greater initiative than everyone else in the unit. On the other hand, it may be the only specific instance of initiative that the supervisor can recall. To the degree that the first-line manager lacks formal documentation, the paired comparison can be inac-

Figure 10-2. Illustration of a graphic rating scale.

<u>Instructions</u>: Before filling out this evaluation, carefully read each job factor and the degrees that follow it. Then, using your best judgment, circle the point value that most accurately reflects the worker's performance on that factor. If any of these factors does not apply, leave that row blank and write N/A in the "Total" box at the far right. When you have finished, add up all of the numbers in the "Total" box and place both the overall total points and the average overall points per factor at the bottom of the page. Then sign and date the form.

Employee's name _____

Department _____

Factor	Range of performance					Total
Work quantity Amount of satisfactory work output	Seldom meets work requirements output 7	Usually meets 14	Always meets 21	Generally exceeds 28	Always exceeds 35	
Work quality Degree of success in meeting quality work standards	Exceeds all quality work standards 35	Exceeds most 28	Meets all 21	Sometimes fails to meet all 14	Is unable to meet minimum 7	
Job knowledge Understanding of all phases of the work	Inadequate knowledge of the job	Knows the minimum for getting the job done	Knows the job well enough to do it properly	Has an expert knowledge of most phases of the work	Has an expert knowledge of all phases of the work	
Adaptability Ability to meet changing conditions	Very flexible and adaptive 10	Fairly flexible and adaptive 8	Can adjust to most conditions 6	Has trouble adjusting to changing conditions 4	Is unable to adjust to changing conditions 2	
Dependability Reliability and conscientiousness in performance of assigned work	Highly undependable 3	Often undependable 6	Somewhat dependable 9	Often dependable 12	Always dependable 15	

Factor					
Initiative Willingness to assume responsibility and use personal judgment	Always exercises high initiative 15	Often exercises high initiative 12	Usually exercises high initiative 9	Seldom exercises high initiative 6	Never exercises high initiative 3
Attitude Cooperativeness and willingness to carry out assignments	Highly negative attitude 2	Somewhat negative attitude 4	Fairly positive attitude 6	Positive attitude 8	Highly positive attitude 10
Attendance Amount of on-time job presence	Is never absent or tardy 10	Is seldom absent or tardy 8	Has average attendance 6	Is absent or late more than average 4	Is often absent or late 2
Team spirit Willingness to be an active member of the work team	Has extremely poor team spirit 3	Has poor team spirit 6	Has average team spirit 9	Has above-average team spirit 12	Has extremely high team spirit 15
Safety and housekeeping Compliance with rules related to worker safety and equipment maintenance	Always follows safety rules; workplace is well-kept 15	Always follows safety rules, but workplace is not always well-kept 12	Usually follows safety rules; workplace is always well-kept 9	Seldom complies with safety rules; workplace is usually well-kept 6	Does not comply with safety rules; workplace is not usually well-kept 3

Overall total points _____

Average points per factor _____

Supervisor _____

Date _____

Figure 10-3. Paired comparison method for rating employees on work quantity and work quality.

On the basis of work quantity				
Personnel being rated				
Acker	Burke	Charles	Donaldson	Edwards
As compared to:				
Acker	+	−	+	−
Burke	−		−	−	−
Charles	+	+		+	−
Donaldson	−	+	−		−
Edwards	+	+	+	+	

Burke has the highest ranking for work quantity

On the basis of work quality				
Personnel being rated				
Acker	Burke	Charles	Donaldson	Edwards
As compared to:				
Acker		−	+	+	+
Burke	+		+	+	+
Charles	−	−		+	−
Donaldson	−	−	−		−
Edwards	−	−	+	+	

Donaldson has the highest ranking for work quality

curate. One way of overcoming this is through the use of critical incident methods.

Critical-incident methods

The *critical-incident approach* calls for the supervisor to evaluate performance on the basis of specific job behaviors. In particular, it focuses on identifying things that the worker did that resulted in very good or very bad outcomes. There are three types of critical-incident methods: (1) employee performance records, (2) critical-incident techniques, and (3) behaviorally anchored rating scales.

Employee performance records. When employee performance records are kept, the supervisor has a basis for identifying all significant effective and ineffective incidents that a worker has performed. For example, in manufacturing firms it is common to keep track of both work quantity and the number of units that have been rejected because of quality problems. From this information, the supervisor can determine significant individual work quantity and work quality. In many lower-level white-collar jobs the firm keeps similar records, again making it easy for the supervisor to use the critical-incident approach.

On the other hand, many jobs do not lend themselves to such record keeping. In these cases, usually because of the expense associated with maintaining employee performance records, many companies do not collect such data. If a critical-incident approach is used, it is one of the remaining two methods.

Critical-incident techniques. The *critical-incident technique* involves a set of procedures for collecting direct observations of on-the-job behavior. The approach is somewhat time-consuming but can result in extremely effective performance appraisal. Typically it begins with a statement of the general purpose of the job. For example, if it is file clerks who are being evaluated, there will be a statement setting forth the objectives that these people should be pursuing. Then interviews are held with the supervisors and file clerks in order to obtain as many examples as possible of critical incidents. These incidents relate to areas such as work output, accuracy, neatness, and initiative. The supervisors and workers provide examples of very effective and very ineffective behavior in these areas. Based on these examples, a checklist of effective and ineffective behaviors is developed. In evaluating the personnel, the supervisor uses these checklists to rate the employees. Every time the supervisor sees a worker do something well or poorly, the supervisor places a check mark alongside the incident in the checklist.

The greatest advantage of the checklist approach is that it is job-related. The supervisor is recording something the worker actually did. Rather than waiting for performance evaluation time and then saying, "Let's see, what did George do well or poorly over the last 6 months?" the supervisor has specific, written feedback that has been collected during this time period. On the negative side, the approach is time-consuming. Additionally, there is no guarantee that the supervisor will see every highly effective or highly ineffective behavior performed by a worker. To this extent, the approach is incomplete as a means of performance appraisal.

Behaviorally anchored rating scales. *Behaviorally anchored rating scales (BARS)* consist of a series of critical incidents that have been ranked on scales from highly effective to highly ineffective and are used for evaluating the personnel. Figure 10-4 provides an illustration of one scale used by a state agency in evaluating the effective use of resources by an employment interviewer. In conducting the evaluation, the supervisor would use several scales in series (perhaps three to seven scales), each measuring behaviors such as adaptability to conditions, fulfillment of responsibilities, effective

<u>Effective uses of resources</u>: Plans effective use of own time and equipment.

Interviewers and claims deputies must plan their work far enough ahead and in sufficient detail that important aspects are not overlooked. Some plan their work effectively and seem to think ahead about what needs to be done; they can coordinate a great variety of tasks, such as interviews, evaluations, referrals, solicitations, and eligibility determinations. Others seem to need help in getting organized and in structuring their work efficiently. When making this rating, evaluate the person only on the basis of his planning effective work organization.

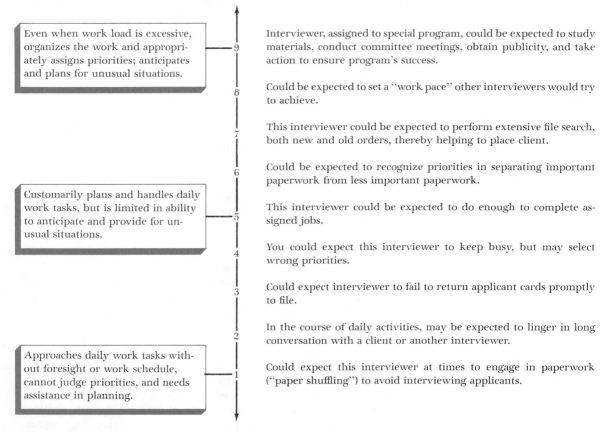

Even when work load is excessive, organizes the work and appropriately assigns priorities; anticipates and plans for unusual situations.

Customarily plans and handles daily work tasks, but is limited in ability to anticipate and provide for unusual situations.

Approaches daily work tasks without foresight or work schedule, cannot judge priorities, and needs assistance in planning.

Interviewer, assigned to special program, could be expected to study materials, conduct committee meetings, obtain publicity, and take action to ensure program's success.

Could be expected to set a "work pace" other interviewers would try to achieve.

This interviewer could be expected to perform extensive file search, both new and old orders, thereby helping to place client.

Could be expected to recognize priorities in separating important paperwork from less important paperwork.

This interviewer could be expected to do enough to complete assigned jobs.

You could expect this interviewer to keep busy, but may select wrong priorities.

Could expect interviewer to fail to return applicant cards promptly to file.

In the course of daily activities, may be expected to linger in long conversation with a client or another interviewer.

Could expect this interviewer at times to engage in paperwork ("paper shuffling") to avoid interviewing applicants.

Figure 10-4. A behaviorally anchored rating scale. (From Cheedle W. Millard, "The Development and Evaluation of Behavioral Criteria for Measuring the Performance of Non-Operational Employees," Ph.D. Dissertation, University of Nebraska, 1974, p. 182.)

interpersonal relationships, or the ability to learn new policies and procedures.

A brief look at Figure 10-4 shows that the scale is detailed and somewhat difficult to understand. This is a result of its comprehensiveness and attention to detail. A great deal of time and effort is expended in constructing these scales. The first step is to have people with a knowledge of the job(s) develop specific effective and ineffective behaviors. These critical incidents are then divided into categories (such as work quality, work quantity, and job attendance) and a 7- to 9-point scale ranking is developed for each category, or rating scale (such as that illustrated in Figure 10-4). Once each rating scale (category) has thus been developed, the result is a series of behaviorally anchored rating scales.

On the positive side, BARS is an excellent performance evaluation instrument because it is job-related.[4] The behaviors that are being measured are clear and relate to specific job performance. The supervisor who is evaluating the subordinate's effective use of resources has seven to nine descriptions of different types of such behaviors and can choose the one most descriptive of the worker. On the negative side, BARS is costly to develop and takes a lot of time to complete. For this reason, it is not as popular as the other appraisal methods discussed above.

Management by objectives

Management by objectives (MBO) was discussed in Chapter 2. At that time it was noted that MBO is a very effective planning approach. It is also commonly used for performance appraisal because of the focus it places on the feedback for control purposes. Of all the appraisal approaches discussed in this section, it continues to remain one of the most popular.

APPRAISAL PROBLEMS

Regardless of what appraisal form is used, there can be problems.

Sometimes the problems are caused by the appraisal instrument. For example, the company may be using graphic rating scales, and under the category of work quantity the supervisor has been asked to rate the amount of work an individual does. The range of choices extends from "a great deal" to "not very much." Unless the manager understands what these choices mean, there are likely to be problems. What one supervisor considers to be a great deal of work may be ranked as average by another.

Other problems are caused by supervisors themselves. For example, no matter how hard they try to be objective, many supervisors give a slightly better rating to those they like than to those they do not like even though the work performance of both groups is the same. Human nature can create prolems.

The following examines other common appraisal problems.

Central tendency

Central tendency is brought about by the reluctance of the supervisor to give either very good or very bad ratings. As a result, most workers end up being clustered in the middle, receiving an average score. In the case of 10 employees who range in performance from superior to extremely poor, the difference between accurate distribution and central tendency distribution would be something like this:

Person	Evaluation under an accurate distribution	Evaluation under central tendency
A	Excellent	Good
B	Excellent	Good
C	Good	Average
D	Good	Average
E	Average	Average
F	Average	Average
G	Average	Average
H	Average	Average
I	Poor	Poor
J	Unacceptable	Poor

Central tendency errors penalize the best workers and reward the poorest. They also make it difficult to determine who is promotable or worthy of the largest raises and who should be held back or let go.

Leniency and severity

Leniency is the tendency to give employees very good performance evaluations regardless of their actual job performance. *Severity* is the tendency to give employees low performance evaluations regardless of their actual job performance. Leniency occurs when supervisors give workers better evaluations on average than they have earned. Severity occurs when supervisors give workers poorer evaluations on average than they have earned. In contrast to central tendency, whereby the supervisor bunches most evaluations in the middle, leniency puts most people on the top end of the scale, and severity pushes them down toward the bottom.

Leniency discriminates against the best workers because it fails to differentiate between their superior performance and the lesser performance of coworkers also put on the top end of the scale. Severity discriminates against the best workers by failing to give them the evaluation they have earned, pushing them down the line toward the poorer performers. Both leniency and severity punish the best workers.

Halo effect

The *halo effect* occurs when a rater allows his or her rating on *one* factor to influence the evaluation of that person on *all* the factors being rated. For example, nurse A is excellent in dealing with patients but is very poor at keeping her records in order. The supervisor likes nurse A's interpersonal patient skills and allows this halo effect to spill over to the other dimensions of her job. She receives an outstanding evaluation every time. Nurse B is average in dealing with patients but is excellent at keeping her records in order; she receives an average performance evaluation score. Nurse C is poor in dealing with patients but excellent at record keeping; she receives a poor performance evaluation score. When the halo effect exists, the supervisor uses one dimension of the job to cover all dimensions of the work.

Seniority

Seniority, the length of time an individual has been on the job, can influence a person's rating. Some studies, for example, have found that the longer an individual has been on the job, the lower the person's ratings. Two reasons help explain this. First, if the individual were very good, he or she would have been promoted long ago. Second, since the individual is unlikely to be promoted, the supervisor is more likely to give a higher rating to someone for whom the evaluation will have more benefit.[5]

Acquaintanceship

Acquaintanceship, how well the supervisor and the workers know each other, can also influence an evaluation. However, this is not always a bad thing. As the supervisor gets to know how well a worker does the job and what the individual's strong and weak points are, the supervisor also gains insights into the performance evaluation that the individual deserves.

VALIDITY AND RELIABILITY

Most performance problems can be traced to a lack of validity and/or of reliability. Some evaluations are not valid; others are unreliable.

Measuring the right things

When a performance appraisal is *valid,* it measures what the supervisor wants it to measure. There are many reasons why performance evaluations are not valid.

One of the most common is the failure to measure performance-related behaviors. Many things can enter into an evaluation that do not belong there. For example, consider an assembly-line worker who installs stabilizer bars. What are the performance-related behaviors that a supervisor should be looking for? Some of the most important include: speed in getting the job done; accuracy, as measured by the number of cars that pass stabilizer-bar inspection; attendance, as measured by the number of times the individual shows up on time and is ready to start work when the shift begins; and safety, as measured by the lack of work-rule violations. Notice that all of these behaviors are related directly to the job; consequently, if the individual does well here, he or she should get a good evaluation. On the other hand, when the supervisor allows the worker's hair length, style of clothing, or personal political beliefs to influence the evaluation, the result is not valid. The performance evaluation is not measuring what it is supposed to measure.

A second common problem is the failure to develop performance measures appropriate to the particular hierarchical level. At the lower levels of the structure, managers should be evaluating their people in terms of measurable criteria, such as productivity, output, and costs. As the evaluation begins to take into account such criteria as morale, personality, ability to communicate effectively, and potential for promotion, it becomes less valid. The supervisor has a more difficult time measuring these latter criteria than in measuring things like productivity and costs. Additionally, most supervisors are not sufficiently skilled in evaluating subjective criteria, such as morale and personality.

Doing so consistently

When a performance evaluation is *reliable*, it provides a consistent measure of work performance. If a worker's job performance remains the same for 2 years, a reliable evaluation would give the same rating each time.

Reliability is easier to achieve than validity. Some performance evaluations do not measure what they should (validity), but the outcomes are consistent (reliability). One of the best examples is provided by the supervisor who believes that all of his people should be able to trade jobs even though this is not required by their work assignments. Failure to master all of the jobs in the area results in lower performance evaluations. Since the performance appraisal is not supposed to measure one's ability to master other jobs, it is not a valid evaluation. On the other hand, since everyone is evaluated on this basis, the rating is reliable, or consistent.

Two basic types of reliability problems face supervisors. One is called the *constant error*, which occurs whenever all evaluations are in error to the same degree and in the same direction. A supervisor who gives all of her people an evaluation that is one scale point higher than their true rating is making a constant error. A supervisor who gives all of his people an evaluation that is one scale point lower than their true rating is also committing a constant error.

The other is the *random error*, which occurs whenever an evaluation is unpredictably higher or lower than the rating the individual should receive. Random errors vary in both degree (one scale point, two scale points, etc.) and direction (higher or lower) and are often a result of confusion or lack of concern on the part of the supervisor.

When dealing with reliability errors, one can do a number of things. At the supervisory level, the most generally recommended approach is multiple observations. This means that if one of the criteria being evaluated is job speed, there should be two or more questions on the rating instrument that relate to job speed. In this way it is possible to check for reliability. If questions 3, 6, and 9 all relate to job speed, then these three answers should all be similar in content. If one of them shows that the worker is very slow and the other two say that the worker is very fast, there is an inconsistency in the answers. Multiple observations help supervisors refine their thinking and correct erroneous evaluation responses.

THE APPRAISAL INTERVIEW

After the supervisor has made the evaluation of the worker, the results have to be written up. Basically this is a five-step process (see Supervision in Action: Writing Up the Performance Appraisal). Once the results have been written up, it is time for the two to sit down and discuss them. This *appraisal interview*, or review discussion as it sometimes is called, should be conducted in a private area where both can talk without outside interruption. Depending on how many workers the supervisor has, the time for the review will vary; typically, it requires 15 to 30 minutes. During this meeting the supervisor should focus on job-related behavior, pointing out what the individual has done well, where the person needs improvement, and how this improvement can be brought about. In doing these things, there are five steps the supervisor should follow.

SUPERVISION IN ACTION:
WRITING UP THE PERFORMANCE APPRAISAL

The steps

Step #1—start smart. Ask yourself: How much time do I need to write these appraisals? How much time am I willing to spend? What are my time constraints? When do I really need to get started? When is the best time for me to write? Where's the best place for me to write? Is there anyone I can ask to look over my work or give me encouragement? What are the company's expectations and guidelines on what is to be written? Are there any exemplary samples of past appraisals that I can use as guides?

Know the answers to these questions before you begin. Make yourself a writing plan and stick to it.

Step #2—job notes. Record your thoughts anywhere—on napkins, scratch paper, or a tape recorder if you think of yourself as a talker rather than a writer. Carry a small pad around with you. Relying on your memory just won't do. Make it a habit to *record* those ideas that pop into your head when you least expect them.

Don't analyze or critique, *just write.* Keep a critical-incident file. Critical incidents are those events that make an employee stand out, either positively or negatively. What you need are specific examples of why you feel the way you do–what was or was not done, chronologically, to the minutest detail.

You can draw from your notes and critical-incident file the information you need to make your writing task easier. It's much easier this way than sitting down and staring at a blank piece of paper.

Step #3—organize. Gather together your notes, your company's performance appraisal form, your documentation, your critical-incident file, and your company's performance standards. Consolidate your notes according to what is to be written on the form. If your form has space for paragraph descriptions of employee performance, organize your notes first according to the performance factors being appraised. If further division of the material is necessary, divide it by simply looking for a logical beginning, middle, and end.

Find the method that works best for you. Don't worry that no one else uses your method of organization.

Step #4—write. If you've completed the first three steps, the writing step should really be quite easy. Work from the organization that you created in step three. Don't ponder each word, just spill it out. Promise yourself that no one will see this first draft but you. When you write, be sure that you are as specific as possible in describing the performance.

To give you an idea of what "specificity" really means, here are a few phrases, taken from an actual appraisal, that are *not specific.*

> . . . maintains good cost records . . . shows excellent results . . . demonstrates professional results . . . established an effective schedule.

What are "good cost records"? Are they organized? Neat? Systematic? What are "excellent results"? Are they accurate? Logical? What are "professional results"? How do they differ from excellent results? What is "an effective schedule"? Is it flexible, creative, consistent? See the problem?

It's remediable by using specific words and examples when you write a performance appraisal. To illustrate the point, think of one of your employees. Look at the words listed below and select one word that describes that employee's performance on the job. (Note that the words are both positive and negative.)

> ambiguous, apathetic, capable, clear thinking, careless, disorderly, efficient, helpful, hostile, inventive, organized, precise, thorough.

Now that you've selected one word that describes this employee's performance, build a sentence around the word. For example, for the key word *precise:*

> Sondra is precise in 90 percent of her secretarial work. She proofreads her work thoroughly and can be counted on to get the work out on schedule on a week-to-week basis.

Notice that the use of exact numbers helped the above example and made it more specific. Many supervisors try to avoid using exact numbers because they fear committing themselves on paper; they want to take a safe middle ground. This does nothing to maximize the potential effect a specific and exact performance appraisal can have.

Here are some other examples:

Instead of	*Why not use?*
Caused a significant loss	Caused a 53 percent loss
Has a good attendance record	Has a 96 percent attendance record
Sold a contract for a substantial amount	Sold a contract for $34 million

The more specific and exact the appraisal document is, the more helpful it will be to employees in formulating performance improvement plans. Being specific also protects you in the eyes of the law.

> **Step #5—edit.** After you've written the performance appraisal, put it away for an hour or two, if you're pressed for time, or better yet for 24 hours. Give yourself a break. When you go back to the performance appraisal, your editing needs will be clearer to you. Just cross out any unnecessary words, cut the jargon, and make sure that everything you have written is logical, specific, and easily understandable to anyone else who might read it. The test is to ask yourself: If another manager read this, would he or she be able to describe this employee's performance accurately?
>
> Source: Shelly Krantz, "Five Steps to Making Performance Appraisal Writing Easier," *Supervisory Management,* December 1983, pp. 8–10. © 1983 by AMACOM Periodicals Division, American Management Associations, New York. Reprinted by permission of the publisher; all rights reserved.

Be prepared

After the supervisor has completed the employee evaluation, he or she should have documentation to back up any points to be made. Where possible, objective data should be used. For example, if the supervisor says that the subordinate shows up late more than the average worker, there should be data showing that the individual comes late an average of once a week while the typical employee shows up late only once a month. These data help to defuse even the most belligerent employee.

Set the right atmosphere

The subordinate is often anxious or nervous about the interview. Will the supervisor say that he or she has not done a good job and suddenly present detailed information to back up this claim? Will the supervisor say that the worker does not get along with fellow employees and present documentation to this effect? These are the types of questions that may run through the subordinate's mind, even though the supervisor has no intention of saying or doing anything like this. Many workers believe that during the appraisal interview they should be prepared for the worst.

One way of allaying such fears is to put the employee at ease by providing a quiet, relaxed environment in which both can discuss the performance evaluation. The best place to hold the interview will vary from worker to worker. The supervisor's office is a good locale, but if this makes the individual nervous or tense, any quiet place in the building will do. The important thing is to get the worker to feel relaxed and prepared to discuss and accept feedback related to work performance.

Focus on total performance

Most people have some things that they have done well and some that they have done poorly. The supervisor needs to focus on total performance: Overall, how well has the worker performed? One of the most effective ways of doing this is first to discuss the strengths of the worker: Where has the individual done well? By recognizing good performance and employing an attitude of "Keep up the good work," the supervisor lets the worker know that the meeting is going to be a constructive one. Then problem areas can be identified. Quite often these are referred to as areas of opportunity and growth.

In discussing areas in which improvement is needed, the supervisor should talk in specific terms and work around personalities. Instead of saying, "You really do a terrible job when it comes to meeting quality standards," the supervisor should say, "Quality standards are an important part of your job and one in which you need to reduce the number of quality rejects." Notice that in the second statement the manager tries to explain why the area of quality standards is important, and in doing so focuses on objective performance.

Encourage feedback

Having given his or her opinion, the supervisor should now step back and let the subordinate talk. Perhaps there is something of which the supervisor has been unaware. For example, the worker may have been suffering a physical problem that has only been corrected in the past week. Or the individual may feel that the work standards that had been agreed upon previously could not be accomplished in the assigned time. Or the individual may argue that the support help being provided by the organization has been inadequate and that any shortcomings are more a reflection of company support than of personal ability. Some of these comments may be accurate; others may be merely defensive, self-serving statements designed to protect the worker's ego. In any event, the supervisor should write down what the individual says and make it a point to follow up and find out how much accuracy there is in each.

Formulate development plans

Having spelled out where improvement is needed and listened to the worker's explanations regarding why performance was not always up to par, the supervisor should now direct consideration to future improvement: What can be done to make things better? What specific shortcomings need to be overcome and how should this be done? What specific strengths does the worker have and how can the individual capitalize on these in the future?

For example, if the worker is too slow in preparing and submitting cost control reports, the individual may need to work with someone who knows how to fill out these reports quickly and accurately. It may be a matter of additional training and guidance. On the other hand, if the worker is extremely fast and accurate at identifying and correcting production mistakes before the unit is shipped down the line, the supervisor may want to give the individual more work in this area and turn the cost control report over to someone else.

The supervisor will address many kinds of problems throughout these performance interviews. For each kind, what the supervisor must do is focus on the cause of the problem and then try to formulate a solution for dealing with it. Table 10-2 provides some examples.

Table 10-2. Causes of and possible solutions to poor performance

Cause of problem	Possible solutions
1. Subordinate doesn't know what is expected.	Establish standards, expectations, and/or objectives.
2. Subordinate doesn't get feedback about the level and the quality of actual performance.	Establish some means of giving timely feedback. This could be periodic discussions with you or a self-monitoring system, such as a simple PERT chart.
3. Expected performance is difficult, "punishing," or in some way less desirable for the subordinate.	Remove or reduce the inhibiting factors to correct performance. Try to make performance matter.
4. Subordinate knows how to do what is expected but is "out of practice."	Provide practice.
5. Subordinate doesn't know how to do what is expected.	Arrange for training. Look into the availability of reference materials and other aids.
6. Something in the work environment interferes with performance.	Look at priorities, time expectations, mix of duties, physical environment, or availability of resources to determine the source of interference.
7. Performing below expectations is easier, "rewarding," or in some way more desirable for the subordinate.	Be sure expectations are known and the consequences for not performing up to expectations are also known (effect on future performance appraisals, your displeasure, interference with others' work). See if performing as expected can be made less difficult or more rewarding.

Source: Michael Smith and Jan Wing, "Five Steps to Improving Employee Performance," *Supervisory Management*, April 1983, pp. 40–41.

Summarize the session

When the interview is over, the supervisor should summarize what was said and what was agreed upon. In this way the worker is again made aware of personal accomplishments and shortcomings and knows what is to be expected in the future. At the same time, the supervisor should write down specific future assignments and/or objectives. For example, if it has been agreed that the worker will increase the number of units inspected from seven per hour to nine, this should be noted. If the worker has promised to complete an in-house productivity training program, this should be noted.

In some cases the objectives will be general, such as to improve one's attitude. Where possible, these objectives should be made more specific by turning them into quantifiable goals. Why does the supervisor want the worker's attitude to improve? If it is because the individual fails to coordinate her efforts with others in the work unit and is thus unable to produce 20 pieces per hour, the supervisor should also write down an objective of 20 pieces per hour. In this way the attitude improvement can be measured directly through the work output. It is not always possible to quantify objectives, but to the extent that they can be reduced to numbers, they should be. At the next review session the supervisor can produce these numbers and discuss job-related behavior in more objective terms than if the supervisor says, "OK, now let's take a look at your attitude and see if it has improved." The more difficult it is to measure a job-related behavior, the more hesitant the supervisor should be about agreeing to it as an objective. Especially at the worker level, objective and measurable behaviors should be given priority over all other forms of goals.

After the meeting is concluded, the supervisor should have the objectives typed up. One copy should be delivered to the worker and one kept by the manager. In some organizations, it is common to find a place on the page for both the worker and the supervisor to sign their names. In this way there is a formal document that shows what both have agreed the worker will do. When getting prepared for the next performance appraisal interview with the worker, the supervisor can begin by looking over the piece of paper and making notes regarding how well the individual has done in each of the agreed-upon areas. The worker can do the same. This procedure provides a basis for the futur review and helps ensure that the overall evaluation will be job-related in content.

REWARDING PERFORMANCE

Supervisors have limited authority when it comes to rewarding perform-ance. If there is a union, the contract typically dictates how much will be paid for each job and what the annual salary increase will be. The union negotiates labor's position while the personnel department looks after management's interests. If there is not a union, or it is a weak one, manage-ment will take a more decisive role in deciding wage rates. In these cases, the supervisor plays an important role in ensuring that competitive wages are paid.

External wage alignments

Every company needs to have its wages in line with those paid by the competition. If the firm pays too much, it unnecessarily gives away profit. If it pays too little, the best workers will leave and go to work for higher-paying competitors. One way in which the supervisor can help keep wages in line with the competition is by getting the necessary wage-rate information from the personnel department or from whoever is collecting this data for the firm.[6] If no one is doing this, the supervisor can use local newspaper ads and interviews with new recruits to help identify the going rates for jobs in the unit.

Internal wage alignments

Internal wage alignments take place when jobs are paid in relation to what they are worth relative to each other. For example, a very simple, menial job may pay $4.75/hour. A complex, challenging one may pay $8.75/hour. How much should a moderately difficult job pay? It should be more than $4.75/hour but less than $8.75/hour. In pricing jobs, many firms use *job evaluation*, which is a process for determining the overall value of a particular job. The process begins by identifying all the tasks required by the job. These tasks are then broken down into compensable factors, such as skill, effort, responsibility, and working conditions. This is what the firm is paying for. Finally, all of the jobs in the unit are compared against all others on the basis of these factors in determining which should get the highest wage and which should receive the lowest.[7]

The specific methods of evaluating jobs are beyond the scope of this book. However, whatever particular method is introduced, the supervisor should remain alert for problems once it has been introduced. Workers soon realize when one job is being paid more than another though it should not. By helping pinpoint these problems, the manager can assist the organization in correcting pay rates and ensuring that all wages are fair.

Wage increases   One of the direct ways in which the supervisor can reward performance is through the recommendation of a wage increase. Many nonunionized organizations have two parts to their wage-increase package: guaranteed and merit. The guaranteed part is given to everyone. The merit part is decided upon by the supervisor. For example, an organization might give a guaranteed 2 percent wage increase coupled with an average of 4 percent of merit money. The only limit on the supervisor's authority is that any raise of more than a particular amount, such as a total of 10 percent, must be reviewed and OK'd by a central compensation committee.

Perhaps the biggest challenge for the supervisor is that of differentiating between the best and the poorest performers. Many first-line managers prefer to give everyone approximately the same raise in order to prevent interpersonal problems with them. These forms of compensation are of three basic types: hourly wages, straight salary, and incentive pay.

Hourly wages. Under this arrangement, pay is based solely on how many hours the individual works. At $5.25/hour, a person working a 35-hour week will gross $183.75. Hourly pay systems are very common among blue-collar workers.

Straight salary. Under this payment arrangement, workers are paid a flat weekly or monthly sum. Office and clerical personnel, and white-collar employees in general, are typically paid a straight salary that is divided up by the number of pay periods. For example, a person who is paid $15,600 annually will receive a gross salary amounting to $300/week, $600 biweekly, or $1300/month depending on how often the company pays its people.

Incentive pay. There are many variations of incentive pay. The simplest is that used with salespeople in which a flat percentage rate is paid. For example, under a 10 percent arrangement, an individual would receive an annual salary of $25,000 for sales of $250,000. More commonly, incentive pay plans provide a guarantee as well as an incentive. In the above case the salesperson might receive a guaranteed salary of $12,500 and a 5 percent commission on all sales. The individual would still earn $25,000 annually but would not have to worry about being sick for a month and not earning any money at all.

Nonsales jobs also have incentive pay plans. For example, in production work it is common to find a bonus being paid for all output over and above a stated amount, such as $6.50/hour plus $1/unit for all weekly units in excess of 35. A person turning out 40 units in a 35-hour week would receive a total salary of $232.50 ($6.50 $\times$ 35 + $5).

Supervisors do not have a great deal of control over how much money people are paid. This is usually decided by the firm. However, to the extent that they remain alert to discrepancies or problems in the compensation package, they can help ensure fair and equitable wages and salaries.

ROUGH AND TOUGH RANDY: STARTING CASE REVISITED

Having read the chapter, you should now have a pretty good idea of what Randy did wrong and what he needs to do differently in the future. Basically, his mistake was that he did not understand that at Miller's it was standard fare to give good ratings. The store is not as demanding as the bank where he worked previously.

In terms of the type of rater he is, Randy is tough. If he makes any error, it is that of severity. He also seems to be guilty of letting the halo effect influence his judgment. Remember how he recalled specific, isolated things that the workers did wrong. He is letting this influence his overall evaluation.

His meeting with the other supervisors will help him understand how they evaluate their people. In this way his ratings will fall more into line with theirs. The biggest problem Randy had was that no one explained to him how things were done at Miller's. Undoubtedly his idea of "average" was quite different from theirs. Those who received average ratings from him would probably have gotten excellent evaluations from the other supervisors.

Overall, this starting case is designed to show how evaluations between supervisors can vary, thus causing problems among the personnel. This lack of uniformity can best be overcome by having the managers meet and discuss how the evaluations should be made. Only in this way can individual differences be resolved and everyone learn what is meant by excellent, good, average, and poor performance. Without this uniformity, evaluations have limited value because a person with an average evaluation in one department may be a much better employee than one in another department with an excellent evaluation.

SUMMARY OF KEY POINTS

1. Performance appraisal consists of four steps: (1) establishment of performance standards, (2) determination of individual performance, (3) a comparison of performance against standards, and (4) an evaluation of individual performance. These steps are carried out in sequential order.
2. There are a number of common appraisal forms. The most popular is the graphic rating scale. Others include paired comparison, critical-incident methods, and

management by objectives. Each has advantages and disadvantages. The simpler forms tend to be more popular, but the more complex ones tend to be more valid and reliable.

3. There are many different types of appraisal problems. Some of the most common include central tendency, leniency, severity, the halo effect, seniority, and acquaintanceship. Each of these was described in the chapter.

4. Most performance problems can be traced directly to validity and/or reliability problems. A performance appraisal is valid when it measures what the supervisor wants it to measure. It is reliable when it provides a consistent measure of work performance.

5. The appraisal interview is the final phase of the evaluation process. It provides the supervisor the opportunity to discuss the results of the evaluation, to encourage questions and comments from the worker, and to set performance goals for the next review period. This interview process requires the supervisor to do six things: be prepared, set the right atmosphere, focus on total performance, encourage feedback, formulate development plans, and summarize the session.

6. Supervisors have limited authority when it comes to rewarding performance. However, they can be extremely helpful in ensuring both external and internal wage alignments. Additionally, they should be prepared to recommend the largest raises for those who do the best work.

BUILD YOUR SUPERVISORY WORD POWER

These key appraisal and performance reward terms are presented in their order of appearance in the chapter. Effective supervisors have a working knowledge of them.

Performance appraisal. The process of evaluating how well an employee has done and then setting objectives for the individual for the next evaluation period.

Graphic rating scales. A form of appraisal instrument that provides the supervisor with factors, and sometimes with degrees of these factors, that describe the worker's behavior. The manager's job is to indicate how well the individual has performed in each of these areas.

Paired comparison method. A form of appraisal instrument that requires the supervisor to compare every individual in the work unit against every other individual in determining who is best on each of the factors being evaluated.

Critical-incident approach. A form of performance appraisal, it calls for the supervisor to evaluate worker performance on the basi of specific job behaviors.

Critical-incident technique. A form of performance appraisal, it involves a set of procedures for collecting direct observations of on-the-job behavior, which are then used as a checklist in evaluating the personnel.

Behaviorally anchored rating scales. A form of performance appraisal, BARS consists of a series of critical incidents that have been ranked on a scale from highly effective to highly ineffective and are used for evaluating the personnel.

Central tendency. A common performance appraisal problem, it is brought about by the reluctance of the supervisor to give either very good or very bad ratings.

Leniency. A common performance appraisal problem, it occurs when the manager gives very good performance evaluations to the employees regardless of their actual job performance.

Severity. A common performance appraisal problem, it occurs when the supervisor gives employees low performance evaluations regardless of their actual job performance.

Halo effect. A common performance appraisal problem, it occurs when the supervisor allows his or her rating on one factor to influence the evaluation of the worker on all of the other factors being rated.

Seniority. The length of time an individual has been on the job.

Acquaintanceship. A common performance appraisal problem, it exists whenever a supervisor allows his or her relationship with the worker to influence the evaluation.

Valid. One of the prerequisites for effective performance evaluation, the term means that the appraisal is measuring what it is intended to measure.

Reliability. One of the prerequisites for effective performance evaluation, the term refers to the consistency with which work performance is measured.

Constant error. A performance evaluation error, it exists whenever a supervisor's evaluations are in error to the same degree and in the same direction.

Random error. A performance evaluation error, it exists whenever an evaluation is unpredictably higher or lower than it should be. Random errors vary in both degree and direction.

Appraisal interview. A discussion during which the supervisor and the worker review the latter's performance, discuss strengths and weaknesses, and formulate objectives to be pursued during the next evaluation period.

Job evaluation. A process of determining the overall value of a particular job.

Hourly wages. A pay arrangement under which employees are compensated based directly on the number of hours they work.

Straight salary. A pay arrangement under which workers are paid a flat weekly or monthly sum.

Incentive pay. A pay arrangement under which workers are compensated in direct relation to the work they do. Sometimes this arrangement is totally incentive in nature, while other times it is used in conjunction with an hourly wage or straight salary.

REVIEW YOUR UNDERSTANDING

1. How does the performance appraisal process work? Put it in your own words, being sure to describe each of the four steps in the process.
2. What does a supervisor need to know about writing job standards? Offer practical advice in your answer.
3. How does a graphic rating scale work? Explain, and then discuss why it is such a popular form of performance appraisal.
4. How does the paired comparison method of performance evaluation work? Give an example, using a work unit with four subordinates.
5. Critical incidents can be used in three ways. What is meant by this statement? In your answer be sure to identify and describe each of these three ways.
6. Many experts of performance evaluation believe that BARS is an excellent appraisal instrument. On the other hand, many supervisors do not care for it. Why are the experts so positive about BARS? Why are the supervisors not as excited about the approach? Explain.

7. Some of the most common appraisal problems include: central tendency, leniency, severity, the halo effect, seniority, and acquaintanceship. In what way are these appraisal problems? In your answer be sure to define what each term means.

8. What is meant by the term *validity?* What is meant by the term *reliability?* Which is the most difficult to achieve? Why are both important to effective performance evaluations? Be complete in your answer.

9. What are the steps the supervisor should carry out in the appraisal interview? Identify and describe each.

10. How can the supervisor help ensure that the organization is paying fair and equitable rates? Cite two examples of things the individual can do.

11. There are three basic forms of compensation. What are they? Identify and describe each.

SUPPLEMENT YOUR KNOWLEDGE

In addition to the references listed at the end of this chapter, the following provide important, practical information that is of use to supervisors in appraising their people and developing effective approaches to rewarding performance:

Baker, H. Kent, and Stevan R. Holmberg: "Stepping Up to Supervision: Conducting Performance Reviews," *Supervisory Management*, April 1982, pp. 20–27.

Birch, William J.: "Performance Appraisal: One Company's Experience," *Personnel Journal*, June 1981, pp. 456–460.

Caruth, Don, Bill Middlebrook, and Frank Rachel: "Performance Appraisals: Much More Than a Once-a-Year Task," *Supervisory Management*, September 1982, pp. 28–36.

Collins, Samuel R.: "Incentive Programs: Pros and Cons," *Personnel Journal*, July 1981, pp. 571–575.

Curston, Louis C.: "Take the Fat Out of Job Evaluation," *Supervisory Management*, April 1976, pp. 11–17.

Dwortzman, Bernard: "The ABCs of Incentive Programs," *Personnel Journal*, June 1982, pp. 436–442.

Jaques, Elliott: "Taking Time Seriously in Evaluating Jobs," *Harvard Business Review*, September–October 1979, pp. 124–132.

Levine, Edward L.: "Let's Talk: Discussing Job Performance," *Supervisory Management*, October 1980, pp. 25–34.

Nix, Donald: "Getting Ready for the Appraisal Interview," *Supervisory Management*, July 1980, pp. 2–8.

Norton, Steven D.: "Performance Appraisal Advice for the New Supervisor," *Supervisory Management*, June 1982, pp. 31–34.

Olney, Peter B., Jr.: "Performance Review: Pitfalls and Possibilities," *Supervisory Management*, July 1976, pp. 2–16.

Pitts, Robert E., and Ken Thompson: "The Supervisor's Survival Guide: Using Job Behavior to Measure Employee Performance," *Supervisory Management*, January 1979, pp. 23–30.

Schuler, Randall S.: "Taking the Pain Out of Performance Appraisal Interviews," *Supervisory Management*, August 1981, pp. 8–12.

When he first joined the organization as a driver, Greg Kleminski had a short meeting with his supervisor, Mary Cardner. Mary explained to Greg that she ran a very tight ship. The company delivers packages across town. Typically, a call will come from a firm that needs to have some materials shipped to another company 50 blocks north. The firm will dispatch or reroute one of its trucks to pick up the package and deliver it to the other firm. Speed and accuracy are of greatest importance in this work. Mary's company guarantees that it will pick up the package within 1 hour of the time the call is received and will have it to the final destination within 90 minutes of this time. If the pickup or delivery is not within these time limits, the shipment is free.

Mary is in charge of the 30-truck fleet. Working closely with two dispatch operators, she keeps close control over how quickly the drivers do their job. Because a knowledge of the city is important, the firm tends to hire ex-cab drivers. However, even they make mistakes. Last week a driver drove to the wrong end of town and missed an important pickup by 15 minutes. The company lost $85 because of the mistake. Earlier this week another driver dropped a package off at the wrong firm and did not wait to have someone sign for it. It was not until later that day that the firm found out that the package was sitting in the wrong company's office. These types of mistakes are costly and the company works hard to prevent them.

Greg is an ex-cabbie with 7 years of experience. Mary explained to Greg that the most important thing was to get the job done right the first time. "If you have to reroute yourself because you are going to the wrong section of town, this costs us money. You also run the risk of a late pickup or delivery. Know where you're going before you start. If you have any questions, call the dispatcher and have him give you directions."

During the first month Greg found it a little difficult to keep up with the hectic pace. However, he soon fell into step and by the end of the second month was making more on-time pickups and deliveries than anyone else in the group. He found that one of the best habits was not to engage anyone in conversation. When he picked up or dropped off a package, he would simply sign the necessary forms and ask the other party to do the same. By cutting down on the small talk, he found that he could save himself between 10 and 15 minutes per package.

Last week marked the end of Greg's third month with the firm and, as required by company rules, he was given a written performance evaluation. He scored extremely high on work quantity. However, there were other factors on the form, such as attitude and interpersonal relations with customers. On these he was given low ratings. In particular, Mary had written on the form that a number of customers had remarked that Greg was too cold and hurried with them. One person had called him impersonal.

Greg was surprised to learn of these remarks. However, he was more surprised to find out that the firm actually contacted the customers to find out how he conducted himself. This had never been explained to him. Nor had it been made clear that attitude and interpersonal relations were important. He had been told that the only two things that counted were speed and accuracy. After reading the evaluation, he asked Mary if he could have a meeting with her regarding the matter. This will be held later this week.

1. What mistake did Mary make in setting forth the job standards? What did she fail to tell Greg?

2. Based on your understanding of validity and reliability, is the performance evaluation valid? Is it reliable? Defend your answer.
3. If you were the supervisor in this case, what type of performance appraisal instrument would you use? What would you include in the instrument? How would you avoid making the mistakes that Mary made? Be complete in your answer.

YOU BE THE SUPERVISOR: DESIGNING AN APPRAISAL FROM THE GROUND UP

The health care field has undergone major changes over the last decade. In particular, many large hospitals are finding that they are overbuilt and are unable to fill all of their beds. There is a scramble for patients.

General Hospital is a privately owned, 250-bed, general care facility located in a large northern city. The hospital caters to those who need minor surgery or are hospitalized for routine tests. It does not offer many of the services found at the nearby county hospital or the other five large hospitals in the area. General Hospital focuses on non-critical care patients who are seeking a pleasant environment where they can recuperate or have tests run while being assured privacy and comfort.

Most of General's patients are business executives, high-level government officials, professional artists and musicians, and/or wealthy people. General realizes that there are many hospitals in the nearby area and that in order to carve out a niche for itself, it must cater to a particular clientele not addressed by the competition.

General hires only nurses with previous training. It prefers those who have been private nurses, have worked with the elderly or infirm, and/or whose recommendations indicate that they have strong interpersonal skills. General believes that nurse-patient relations are the most important factor for success in the job. Technical training is important, but General feels that all nurses know this end of their business. The hospital must offer more than just good medical care. The administrator has often referred to General as "Disneyland North." By this he means that General must build a reputation of being a good place to go when one has to be hospitalized.

Over the last 5 years General has gotten a reputation as having the best environment of any hospital in the area. As a result, it has decided to expand by 100 beds and to open a special wing to cater exclusively to children. At the same time, the administrator has decided that more attention must be paid to the quality of the work force. "If we are going to expand," he said to his staff, "we are going to have to put more attention on supervising our personnel. It's during an expansion that things start to go haywire. I'd like to see us introduce a formal performance evaluation at the nurses' level. All supervisors should be required to evaluate their personnel on a semiannual basis." The nursing supervisors agree with the administrator, and later this week there is going to be a meeting regarding how these evaluations should be made and what form they should take.

1. Assume that you are one of the nursing supervisors. What type of appraisal instrument would you suggest be used in a nursing evaluation? What factors would you recommend be included on this appraisal instrument? Be complete in your answer.
2. What steps should be followed by the supervisor in carrying out this evaluation? How would you go about setting objectives for each person? How would you measure performance in each of the areas on the performance appraisal

instrument? How would you recommend that supervisors avoid falling into such traps as central tendency, leniency, severity, and the halo effect? What can they do?

3. Would you tie performance appraisal to rewards? How? What authority would you recommend for supervisors in terms of giving monetary rewards? Be complete in your answer.

NOTES

1. Virginia Bianco, "In Praise of Performance," *Personnel Journal,* June 1984, pp. 40–50.
2. Thomas C. Alewine, "Performance Appraisals and Performance Standards," *Personnel Journal,* March 1982, pp. 210–213.
3. Ed Yager, "A Critique of Performance Appraisal Systems," *Personnel Journal,* February 1981, pp. 129–133.
4. Cheedle W. Millard, *The Development and Evaluation of Behavioral Criteria for Measuring the Performance of Non-Operational Employees,* Ph.D. dissertation, University of Nebraska, 1974.
5. For more on this topic, see: Steven Altman, Enzo R. Valenzi, and Richard M. Hodgetts, *Organizational Behavior: Theory and Practice,* Orlando: Academic Press, 1985, chap. 14.
6. J. Spencer Ferebee, Jr., "What the Supervisor Should Know About Wage and Salary Administration," *Supervisory Management,* October 1976, pp. 26–35.
7. George L. Heller, "Demystifying Job Evaluation," *Supervisory Management,* January 1982, pp. 20–25.

CHAPTER 11

SUPERVISING PROTECTED GROUPS

GOALS OF THE CHAPTER

Every worker is entitled to an equal opportunity commensurate with his or her skills, training, experience, and knowledge. However, there are some groups that the supervisor has to pay extra attention to because they fall under the heading of "protected groups." Included here are minorities and the handicapped. On the one hand, the supervisor is not required to hire or promote these people merely because they are minorities. On the other hand, the manager is required to ensure that they are treated fairly, and because of their status, many of them need this extra attention. The overriding goal of this chapter is to examine who these people are and how the supervisor should manage each group. Particular attention is given to the laws and regulations that monitor the treatment of minorities. When you have finished reading all the material in this chapter, you will be able to:

1. Discuss some of the things supervisors should and should not do in supervising minorities.
2. Understand the importance of culture and language in supervising minorities.
3. Explain what is meant by sexual harassment and how to deal with this problem.
4. Discuss compensation issues and pregnancy policies and how they effect the supervision of women at work.
5. Discuss the role the supervisor should assume in organizational efforts to hire and retain handicapped workers.
6. Describe the challenges associated with supervising older workers.
7. Identify the major considerations involved in supervising Vietnam veterans and employees with different religious views.
8. Discuss what reverse discrimination is all about and how supervisors should deal with the issue.

A STARTING CASE: THE WORKER'S COMPLAINT

There are 26 people in Charles Warring's department. Fourteen of them are women, and all have been hired in the last 5 years. Three were brought on board last month, when the company announced that it had landed a large government contract and would be hiring another 145 people.

Because the department is fairly large, Charles does not have time to supervise every single person directly. He has four assistants who help him, and he spends more of his time working with these people than he does dealing with any of the other subordinates.

Two weeks ago one of the newly hired women came by to see Charles. She told him that one of the assistants was harassing her. She complained that the man made it a point to stand extremely close to her when showing her how to do something, put his hands on her shoulder as he talked to her, and in general made a nuisance of himself. "I don't like people getting that close to me or touching me," she told Charles. "It isn't necessary and I want it stopped or I'm going to file a sexual harassment grievance with the personnel department." Charles let her finish and then talked to her about her complaint. It appeared that she was serious about her allegation, although Charles felt that she was exaggerating things and was perhaps just upset with the assistant.

Later that day Charles called the assistant in and talked to him. He did not mention the worker's comments about sexual harassment, but he did tell the assistant that he had heard that the man was being "forward" with one of the women. "I think you know it's against the law to harass anyone in what could be considered a sexual manner. And what you consider totally innocent can be construed by the other person as sexual harassment. I want you to be extremely careful about your conduct around the women in your group. Do you understand me?" The assistant said that he did, but at the same time he indicated that he was shocked over someone making such a charge. He asked Charles where he had heard it, but Charles refused to tell him.

Yesterday Charles received a call from the personnel department. The woman who was in to see him the week before had filed a formal complaint of sexual harassment against the assistant. In her charge she noted that she had been to see Charles and had reported the incident to him. She also submitted to the personnel department director the handwritten notes she had made when her meeting with Charles was over. The director asked Charles to get the assistant and come upstairs immediately. When the two men were seated in the director's office, the latter told them: "We could have a real problem on our hands. Before we go see the company attorney, I want each of you to tell me your end of the story. I only hope that we can minimize the damage that has been done." Charles interrupted the man at this point and asked: "What damage? We haven't done anything. The burden of proof is on her. What are you talking about?" The personnel manager's face showed concern. "Look, Charles, I've got enough problems without you being a wise guy. You're in this up to your neck along with your assistant here. You two guys apparently think sexual harassment is a joke. You both better tell me what's been going on and not leave out any details." With that, the assistant began to give his version of what happened.

Is Charles in any trouble? Is his assistant? Why? What is sexual harassment all about and what has each of the men done wrong? Write down your answers and then put them aside. We will return to them at the end of the chapter.

NATURE OF THE CHALLENGE

Some personnel are known as protected employees because they are given special protection under the law. This protection is a result of legislation, such as: the Civil Rights Act and its accompanying equal employment opportunity regulations; the Equal Pay Act; the Age Discrimination in Employment Act; the Rehabilitation Act; and a host of presidential orders and court decisions. The objective of these decisions is to ensure equality in the workplace for minorities, women, the elderly, the handicapped, and Vietnam veterans, to name but five. Some of these legislative acts were briefly described in Chapter 6 under Recruiting and Selecting: The Legal Aspects. However, their impact does not stop after the recruiting and selection process is over. They also influence the way that supervisors manage protected employees on a daily basis. Table 11-1 sets forth some of the most common antidiscrimination laws, what they prohibit, and who is responsible for their enforcement.

The importance of common sense

Most protected groups are minorities, and in effectively supervising them, the supervisor should rely on common sense. Regardless of who the individual is, for example, there are some things the supervisor should avoid doing. These include:

1. Be careful not to allow stereotypes to affect expectations. Assuming that women work only because they want to earn spending money and really are not interested in a career will eventually result in a sex equity lawsuit. Believing that all racial minorities are lazy and will never do well in management positions simply invites a lawsuit. Supervisors have to look at each person on his or her own merits, realizing that each is unique regardless of his or her similarities to a particular minority group.
2. Do not treat minorities as different by according them special treatment or letting them break established work rules. This treatment will be viewed negatively by nonminorities and will result in the minorities wondering what the supervisor is really up to. The eventual outcome will be detrimental to unit efficiency.
3. Do not try to develop a relationship with protected group members too quickly. This leads them to regard the supervisor with suspicion.
4. Do not use the cliché "some of my best friends are. . . ." as part of an effort to win them over. Most minorities view such supervisors with skepticism.
5. Do not show off minority employees. Like everyone else, they dislike being put on display, especially when they feel that it is being done to enhance the image of the supervisor or the organization.
6. Do not share negative feelings about minorities with other employees. This only makes things worse. The supervisor who tells a worker, "You know, I think that new black worker is lazy," is creating gossip and sowing the seeds for problems later on. The greater the number of

Table 11-1. Some of the major antidiscrimination laws

Law	Discrimination prohibited	Employers covered
First and Fifth amendments to the Constitution	Deprivation of employment rights without due process of law	Federal government
Fourteenth Amendment to the Constitution	Deprivation of employment rights without due process of law	State government
Equal Pay Act of 1963	Sex differences in pay for substantially equal work	Private employers
Title VI, Civil Rights Act of 1964	Discrimination based on race, color, religion, sex, or national origin	Employers receiving federal financial assistance
Title VII, Civil Rights Act of 1964 (as amended in 1972 by the Equal Employment Act of 1972)	Discrimination or segregation based on race, color, religion, sex, or national origin	Private employers with 15 or more employees; federal, state, and local governments; employment agencies; unions and apprenticeship committees
Executive order 11141 (1964)	Age discrimination	Federal contractors and subcontractors
Age Discrimination in Employment Act (as amended in 1975)	Age discrimination against those between 40 and 70 years of age	Private employers with 20 or more people; unions with 25 or more members; employment agencies; apprenticeship and training programs
Title I (1968) Civil Rights Act	Interference with a person's rights in regard to race, religion, color, or national origin	People in general
Rehabilitation Act of 1973; Executive Order 11914 (1974)	Discrimination based on physical or mental handicap	Federal contractors; federal government
Vietnam Era Veterans Readjustment Act of 1974	Discrimination against disabled veterans and Vietnam era veterans	Federal contractors; federal government
State laws; fair employment practice laws	Similar to Title VII and the Equal Employment Act of 1972	Varies by state; has been passed by approximately 90 percent of all states

people who know about a problem, the more difficult it can be to resolve. The supervisor not only has to confront the worker but has to deal with the grapevine that is now carrying the manager's remarks throughout the organization.

7. Do not overreact to charges of discrimination or mistreatment. Instead, carefully review the situation, check the facts, talk to the individual who is making the charge, discuss the matter with those who are being

Harasser	Victim	Recommendation	Outcome
Supervisor	Employee	1. Victim notifies employer as soon as possible. 2. Supervisor is disciplined.	By advising supervisors that harassment may result in severe disciplinary action, employer attempts to eliminate supervisory harassment completely.
Coworker	Employee	1. Victim notifies supervisor as soon as possible. 2. Harasser is disciplined.	Hope for complete elimination of harassment, but when harassment occurs, taking immediate corrective action may satisfy the EEOC guidelines.
Nonemployee	Employee	1. Victim notifies supervisor as soon as possible. 2. Supervisor steps in to correct immediately; if the harasser is a customer, supervisor should also try to maintain good customer relations.	Difficult for supervisors to eliminate harassment from outsiders entirely. Taking immediate corrective action may satisfy the EEOC guidelines. If handled delicately, the employer may be able to keep customers while minimizing his or her liability.

Figure 11-1. National origin harassment: how to deal with it. (From Paul S. Greenlaw and John P. Kohl, "National Origin Discrimination and the New EEOC Guidelines," *Personnel Journal*, August 1981, p. 636. Reprinted by permission of *Personnel Journal*, Costa Mesa, Calif.; all rights reserved.)

accused of the practice, and weigh the evidence carefully. The supervisor should also keep his or her boss apprised of what is going on. If the situation warrants it, the boss will contact the personnel department or company counsel for advice on how to proceed.

8. Do not overlook or ignore discrimination, such as harassment based on national origin. These problems should be faced head on and dealt with on their merits. Figure 11-1 offers some advice on how to handle this type of harassment, although every type of harassment is a potential problem for the organization and should be treated seriously and expeditiously.

The above eight guidelines offer advice regarding what not to do. On the other hand, there are a number of things that the supervisor should do. These are explained in Supervision in Action: Managing Minorities Effectively.

SUPERVISION IN ACTION: MANAGING MINORITIES EFFECTIVELY

Some "dos" to practice
So far we have identified some of the practices supervisors should avoid. Now let's look at those strategies to be followed to maximize effectiveness.

Do analyze your own behavior and expectations. Supervisors don't have to change their personality or basic style of management, but they should review them and determine beforehand if there are factors under their control that might make working conditions more difficult for the minority employee. Let's use ethnic jokes as an example. Many people like to tell them, but few consider the feelings of those who would prefer not to hear them. To be on the safe side, the workplace should be free of ethnic and sexist jokes.

What seems funny to the supervisor may be offensive to the employee.

Do provide departmental personnel with advance notice that a minority employee will be employed. Making the announcement provides a supervisor with an opportunity to set the tone, communicate expectations, and reduce any apprehensions that departmental employees may feel. In addition, the supervisor can discuss the company's overall commitment to equal opportunity and the supervisor's personal goal of having all his or her employees succeed.

Do provide for open communication. All employees must be included in the organization's communication channel. It's particularly important that minority employees feel involved and free to discuss job-related matters with their boss.

Do monitor employee progress. An essential component of the supervisor-employee relationship is timely performance evaluations. All employees need feedback on their performance; the minority employee is no exception. New employees are especially interested in performance evaluations and anxiously await information that will indicate whether their performance is acceptable to their supervisor.

Needless to say, if the performance is unacceptable, it is even more critical that they be so advised as soon as deficiencies are noted, for unless the employee is aware of the need for improvement, it is very unlikely change will occur. Some inexperienced supervisors are reluctant to discuss performance problems with minority employees, but not doing so will only create further problems. In discussing job performance, supervisors should focus on what the employee is not doing and develop specific methods and subsequent goals that the individual can strive for. The employee deserves a fair chance to succeed, and a supervisor should work with the employee to ensure he or she gets it.

There are other examples we could discuss, but they lead us to the same conclusion: Employees, regardless of their sex, age, or race, have the same basic needs and should be treated fairly. The ideas presented are applicable to all people and represent a "common sense" approach to management. We do not have all the answers, but we believe a manager's effectiveness will be enhanced by utilizing these common-sense ideas.

Source: John Hodge, "Common-Sensical Approach to Supervising Minorities," *Supervisory Management,* September 1983, pp. 26–27.

**Culture and
language**

Minorities have their own subcultures, with values, beliefs, and attitudes that are sometimes different from those of nonminorities. An Anglo supervisor may have problems understanding or dealing with a Black male or Latin female because the manager does not fully understand "where they are coming from." For example, a woman who refuses a promotion because it requires her to go on the road and she wants to be able to go home to her husband and children every evening is making a decision that is in line with her values. However, the supervisor may be unable to understand the logic of the decision. Many times, male supervisors will look back on such a woman's decision and say: "I never did understand why Joan didn't take that job opening in industrial sales. It would have put her on a faster promotion track." What the male supervisor fails to realize is that his values are different from those of the woman. Additionally, if the supervisor does have children, he may be able to be away 2 or 3 days a week because his wife is taking care of them. However, if his wife decided to take a job that required her to travel, would he be willing to come home every evening, fix dinner, and take care of the children? To the extent that the supervisor's personal values influence the way he or she believes that minorities should act, there will be problems in managing them. The supervisor must try to understand the cultural values of protected employees and respect their right to these values. This often requires the first-line manager to work with minorities in getting an understanding of them and how to interact effectively with them in achieving unit objectives.

Language is another problem that supervisors have to confront. Many minorities that immigrate to this country do not speak English extremely well. They come to the United States with virtually no understanding of the language, and while the adults do attend night school, they often live in the same neighborhood as those who speak their native language. As a result, they do not become fluent in English, and on the job the supervisor may find it somewhat difficult to communicate with them. There are a number of ways of dealing with this problem. One is for the employer to continue to emphasize the importance of learning English. Some employers even offer on-site intensive English courses for minority employees. Another is to sensitize supervisors and managers in better understanding minority language patterns. For example, some large firms offer 1-day training programs to their managerial personnel to familiarize them with the culture and language of those minority groups who work in the organization.

What the supervisor needs to remember is that cultural and language barriers cannot be eliminated. Management must learn to work within these boundaries, and sometimes these cultural values are beneficial to the firm. For example, bilingual people can be very important to firms that are selling in a community where a significant percentage of the population is non-English-speaking. Spanish is particularly useful to supervisors in the San Antonio, Texas, and Miami, Florida, areas as well as in towns near the Mexican border.

SUPERVISING WOMEN

In 1980 over 40 percent of the labor force was female. By the end of the 1980s approximately 45 percent will be female and by 1995 over 70 percent of all women between the ages of 16 and 54 will be in the job market. These statistics illustrate the growing numbers of women in the workplace. Unfortunately, many of them have faced discrimination of various types, and supervisors need to be aware of the problems and issues involved in supervising women. One of the most serious is that some firms have not hired or promoted qualified women if there were men who could be given the job. In an effort to deal with discrimination in hiring, many firms and newspapers now subscribe to sexless, or unisex, ads. Figure 11-2 provides an illustration. Unless the job requires a man or woman, as in the case of a rest-room attendant, no designation of sex is used. This practice helps reduce discrimination in recruiting, although there are many other challenges that confront the supervisor on a day-to-day basis. One of the major ones is sexual harassment.

Sexual harassment

Sexual harassment is prohibited by Section 703 of Title VII of the Civil Rights Act as amended. While there is no uniform definition of the term, the following give a clear picture of what it means:

> [Sexual harassment includes any] repeated or unwarranted verbal or physical sexual advances (or) sexually explicit discriminatory remarks made by someone in the workplace which are offensive or objectionable to the recipient or which

Figure 11-2. Sexless job titles. (From Harvey L. Maslin, "How to Avoid Discrimination," *Supervisory Management,* February 1976, p. 4.)

Former Title	New Title
Cranemen	Crane operators
Forgemen and hammermen	Forge and hammer operators
Clergymen	Clergy
Public relations men	Public relations specialists
Credit men	Credit and collection managers
Newsboys	Newspaper carriers and vendors
Office boys	Office helpers
Foremen	Blue-collar supervisors
Pressmen	Printing press operators
Dressmakers and seamstresses	Dressmakers
Boatmen and canalmen	Boat operators
Fishermen and oystermen	Fishers, hunters, and trappers
Longshoremen	Longshore workers
Chambermaids and maids (except private households)	Lodging quarters cleaners
Busboys	Waiters' assistants
Firemen	Fire fighters
Policemen	Police
Laundresses (private household)	Launderers
Maids (private household)	Private household cleaners

cause the recipient discomfort or humiliation or which interfere with the recipient's job performance. (*Continental Can Co. v. Minnesota,* 22 FEP cases 1808 [Minnesota, 1980].)

Sexual harassment includes . . . continual or repeated verbal abuse of a sexual nature including, but not limited to, graphic commentaries on the victim's body, sexually suggestive objects or pictures in the workplace, sexually degrading words used to describe the victim, or propositions of a sexual nature. Sexual harassment also includes the threat or insinuation that lack of sexual submission will adversely affect the victim's employment, wages, advancement, assigned duties or shifts, academic standing, or other conditions that affect the victim's "livelihood." (Michigan Task Force on Sexual Harassment in the Workplace.)[1]

A number of things can be done to cope with sexual harassment effectively. One is to have a formal policy statement that is written by top management and communicated to all of the personnel. Of course, the supervisor plays virtually no role in writing such a policy; however, the individual should know if one exists and make the unit personnel aware of it.

Second, the supervisor should be aware of the legal problems associated with sexual harassment. At the present time, there has been no uniformity of decision. In some cases the courts have held that an employer is not liable for acts that go undiscovered by the supervisors and other management personnel. These decisions emphasize that the minute a supervisor knows something is happening, he or she must immediately investigate the matter. In a recent case, however, the court has held that the employer is liable under Title VII for acts committed by a supervisor even though the company argued that the manager's behavior was in clear violation of policy.[2] While this latter ruling does seem extreme, it helps emphasize the importance of not letting such behavior go unpunished.[3]

Third, the supervisor should have a plan of action for dealing with the situation. Supervision in Action: Coping with Sexual Harassment sets forth some very useful steps. More specifically, however, the supervisor should work closely with his or her superior in determining what to do. Even if there is no formal policy, the managers should keep a written record of all complaints regarding such harassment and spell out sanctions that will be used against those who are guilty. This strategy has a number of important benefits, including: (1) It shows that the organization will not tolerate sexual harassment, (2) it encourages those who are harassed to come forward and lodge their complaints, (3) it ensures that those guilty of harassment practices are punished, and (4) it protects the firm from legal action by employees who allege that such discrimination was allowed to continue.

Compensation

As noted earlier, the Equal Pay Act provides for equal pay for substantially equal work. For example, a male supervisor and a female supervisor working in the same department, doing similar work, and having the same

SUPERVISION IN ACTION: COPING WITH SEXUAL HARASSMENT

Annie, a project coordinator, is new to the company. She is an ambitious, eager, and hardworking person. Her unmarried boss, Dave, has started staring at her figure, massaging her neck, and making subtle, suggestive remarks. Annie likes Dave but is not interested in dating him. She doesn't know how to stop him from bothering her. An incident between Dave and Annie in an empty conference room causes a distraught Annie to seek out June, Dave's supervisor.

Janet, the only female machinist on her shift, is having problems being accepted by two of her coworkers. For the last few weeks, Allen and Phil have been commenting on her clothes in a sexual way, calling her "sweetie" and "girl," and telling obscene jokes in front of her. Janet has tried to ignore their antics. However, yesterday she found several crude sexual drawings in her locker. Tired of the harassment, she finally turns to Ron, her supervisor, for advice.

Employees are learning that they don't have to tolerate sexual harassment.

Coping with sexual harassment has become a new responsibility for supervisors. Your employees will probably begin coming to you for help in coping with sexual issues at work. If you're not receptive, the employee will not feel comfortable and may turn to the Equal Employment Opportunities Commission, the labor union, or an attorney for help.

A supervisor can mishandle a sexual harassment complaint by reacting hostilely, emotionally, or noncommittally. The issue may never be resolved. If harassment continues or worsens, employees may feel they have no choice but to take the case to court.

Employers are legally responsible for the actions of their employees with regard to sexual harassment when the employers knew or should have known about the conduct. The only exception is when the employers take corrective action immediately.

An employer is even legally responsible for the acts of nonemployees (like vendors, customers, or the public) with respect to sexual harassment when the employer knew or should have known about the offensive conduct and failed to take immediate corrective action.

Most sexual harassment incidents can be handled at the supervisory level and don't need to go any further. The newspapers just don't report on the supervisors coping successfully with harassment.

Here are basic steps to follow for coping with sexual harassment at work:

1. Find out if your organization has a policy on sexual harassment.
2. Determine your role in implementing the policy.
3. Inform your staff of the policy.
4. Act immediately and appropriately when a sexual harassment incident occurs.
5. Investigate all incidents objectively and empathetically.

6. Determine a course of action with the involved parties.
7. Follow up on all courses of action.

Source: Diane Saint James, "Coping with Sexual Harassment," *Supervisory Management,* October 1983, pp. 2, 4.

seniority and performance levels must be paid equally. Unfortunately, in few cases are the similarities so close. Quite often one of the individuals will have a larger department than the other or more seniority and the other will have a higher performance level. Now the question is, What is a fair salary for each?

At the lower levels of the hierarchy where everyone is doing the same basic job, equity disparities can be easily identified. For example, over the last decade many of the nation's largest firms have had lawsuits brought by women who claimed that they were being discriminated against. In many of these cases, the women either won in court or received an out-of-court settlement from the firm.

For the supervisor, compensation is an issue that requires familiarity with the law but does affect the individual's decision-making authority since few supervisors decide how much to pay their people. When they do, however, the supervisor needs to remember that those doing the same job, under the same conditions and with the same work experience, are entitled to the same pay.[4]

Pregnancy policies   A number of years ago it was not uncommon for pregnant women to quit working when their pregnant state became obvious. Today women are allowed to work as long as they and their physician agree that it is appropriate. This is a result of the Pregnancy Discrimination Act of 1978, which requires that pregnancy be treated no differently from illnesses or health disabilities if the employer has a disability plan. These company policies also grant the employee a leave of absence until she can return to work, usually 4 months after the birth of the baby.

Many employees who take pregnancy leave are assured of a job upon their return to work, but they are not guaranteed the same job or rate of pay. A *Fortune* survey of 1500 large firms found that 38 percent guaranteed women their same job back after a disability leave for childbirth, 43 percent provided a comparable job, 6 percent gave "some job," and 13 percent made no promise at all.[5] Additionally, if the firm has no disability policy, it does not have to rehire the woman because these same rights are not accorded to men. This is particularly common among nonunionized and/or small companies.

In recent years some firms have been sued by women under the provision of the respective state law that did provide for a return of their original job. In one major recent decision by a California Federal District Court, the judge declared that the state's legislation entitling every pregnant woman up to 4 months' unpaid leave without losing her job was unconstitutional.[6] This issue will eventually be decided in the United States Supreme Court.

For supervisors, the important thing is that they know the company's policy regarding the rights of returning women and that they plan accordingly. If a woman has the right to reclaim her previous job and salary, during her absence the supervisor must assign her tasks to other members of the unit or to a temporary replacement. If the woman has the right to a job but not necessarily her old one, the supervisor must find out if she is to be returning to the unit and, if so, what arrangements are to be made. Quite often the organization will have a policy regarding what is to be done. Based on this guideline, the supervisor can make the necessary decisions. If the woman is not going to be rehired, the manager must decide how to fill her position.

SUPERVISING HANDICAPPED WORKERS

There was a time when employers met their moral obligation to hire the handicapped by subcontracting certain routine jobs to them. For example, production, assembling, and packaging tasks would be given to sheltered workshops. The Rehabilitation Act of 1973 was a major turning point for handicapped employment. Under Section 503 of this act, companies with federal contracts or subcontracts valued at $2500 or more must hire and advance qualified handicapped individuals; Section 402 of the Vietnam Era Veterans Readjustment Act of 1974 mandates similar action. Under Section 504 of the Rehabilitation Act of 1973, many government agencies enforce similar requirements for companies receiving federal financial assistance, such as grants or other subsidies, that are outside of the normal procurement process. Employers not involved in federal government financial activities are not subject to these regulations; however, most states and many local governments have passed laws that closely mirror the federal statutes. As a result, employers should be well versed regarding their basic responsibilities in this area. One of the first questions a supervisor should be able to answer is; Who warrants special consideration because of this legislation?

The federal government holds that a qualified handicapped person is someone with a physical or mental impairment that substantially limits one or more major life activities and who can still perform the job. Also included are individuals who have a record of such impairment. This includes people with conditions such as: alcoholism, blindness, cerebral palsy, deafness, diabetes, drug addiction, mental retardation, and muscular dystrophy. In order to ensure that these people are recruited and hired, many firms have a formal *affirmative action program* (AAP) policy statement. A good example is provided by the Tennessee Valley Authority (TVA), a quasi-federal corporation that employs over 47,000 people, of whom approximately 8 percent are handicapped. Figure 11-3 sets forth their policy statement. When man-

Figure 11-3. TVA's handicapped affirmative action program policy statement. (From Gopal C. Pati and Edward F. Hilton, Jr., "A Comprehensive Model for a Handicapped Affirmative Action Program," © February 1980. Reprinted by permission of *Personnel Journal*, Costa Mesa, Calif.; all rights reserved.)

> **TVA's handicapped affirmative action program policy statement.**
>
> TVA conducts a program for the hiring, placement, and advancement of handicapped employees, former employees, applicants, and disabled veterans. Activities to promote, expand, and enhance employment opportunities are encouraged with special emphasis on returning injured employees to their original or alternate positions. Work environments are modified where possible to provide employment opportunities for handicapped persons. Handicapped employees are encouraged to increase their knowledge, skills, and abilities to facilitate their placement and upward mobility opportunities. Recruitment efforts to attract handicapped persons are enhanced by collaborative efforts with educational institutions, state Veterans Administration, and other vocational rehabilitation programs.

agement puts out the word to the supervisors that handicapped employment is a corporate goal, the policy gets implemented.

The supervisor's role

The supervisor can help ensure handicapped hiring in a number of ways. One is by setting forth the job requirements in such a way that it is obvious which jobs can be filled by handicapped workers. For example, if there is a warehouse position requiring the frequent operation of a motorized industrial truck, the manager should spell out to the personnel department exactly what qualifications a handicapped person must have to hold down this job. If the firm is making a concerted effort to hire the handicapped, the supervisor should also be prepared to visit with representatives of handicapped referral organizations, take them on a tour of the company's facilities, and work with them in refining the selection process. The supervisor can also help by ensuring that job testing focuses on job-related skills that are critical to the work, thereby ensuring that qualified handicapped applicants are hired.

Once a handicapped person has been brought on board, the supervisor should consider those changes which will make the job easier to perform. The following cites many examples: "Imaginative supervisors have eliminated the rotating shift responsibilities of an epileptic worker who needed a regular work schedule; provided air-conditioned work space for a worker with a respiratory ailment; secured a parking spot near the entrance for a worker in leg braces; provided cassette recorders for blind workers; allocated additional desk and shelf space for a blind worker's braille dictionary;

and requisitioned a special typewriter for a one-armed secretary who was then capable of typing the necessary 55 words per minute."[7] Another thing the manager must be careful about is his or her attitude toward the person. Handicapped people do not want to be treated with pity. They do not want the supervisor to feel sorry for them or to express amazement at their courage.[8] They merely want the chance to do their best.

The supervisor is a key person in every company's effort to hire the handicapped. This is seen in Figure 11-4, where the TVA's AAP is illustrated. Notice that the last step in working with the operating department involves placement activities and follow-up. This is where the supervisor comes into the picture. If things are well handled here, the program can be successful. If things are not well handled, the entire effort can prove to be a waste of time, money, and effort.

SUPERVISING OLDER WORKERS

The Age Discrimination in Employment Act of 1967 has been revised a number of times as well as influenced by court decisions. In essence, the act forbids discrimination against people in the 40- to 70-year-old category on the basis of age. For example, if two people apply for the same job and one is 32 and the other is 52, the employer cannot lawfully turn down the latter on the basis of age. The decision must be made on the basis of some other factor(s). However, this does not mean that the supervisor cannot choose one person over another on the basis of age. If the manager can prove that people over a particular age limit, such as 60 years, are not physically or mentally able to do the job, the individual can be excluded from consideration. The real problem for the supervisor is not that of excluding older people from the work group but that of managing them effectively.

Supervisors face a number of problems as they try to manage older-workers. The four most common are in the areas of physical, technological, societal, and motivational changes.

Physical changes

Physical changes relate to the worker's strength, endurance, and agility. As people get older, their ability to handle physically strenuous jobs tends to decline. Many also begin to forget details. The supervisor needs to take these things into consideration in managing the unit. The older worker may do 90 percent of the job as well as anyone else; it is the other 10 percent that the manager has to be aware of. If for some reason there is heavy equipment to be moved or there are detailed instructions to be followed, the supervisor is often wise not to assign this work to older employees unless past experience reveals that they will have no trouble carrying it out. Working around them is often no great chore, and many older workers make too great a contribution to the unit for this accommodation to be a stumbling block to their continued employment.

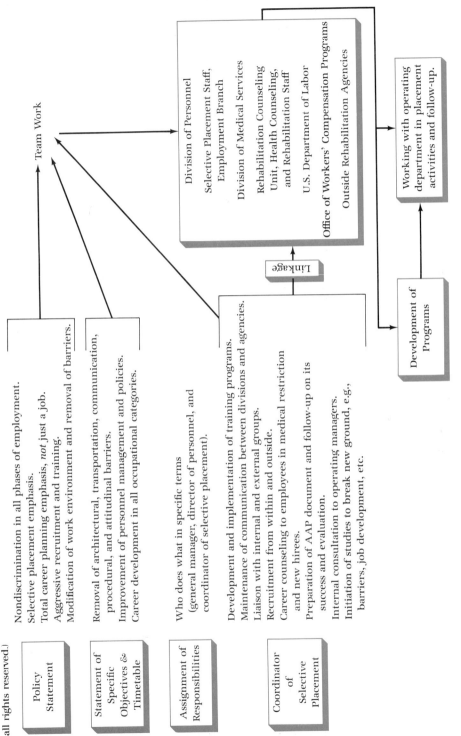

Figure 11-4. TVA's AAP for the handicapped: major program components. (From Gopal C. Pati and Edward F. Hilton, Jr., "A Comprehensive Model for a Handicapped Affirmative Action Program," © February 1980. Reprinted by permission of *Personnel Journal*, Costa Mesa, Calif.; all rights reserved.)

Policy Statement

Nondiscrimination in all phases of employment.
Selective placement emphasis.
Total career planning emphasis, *not* just a job.
Aggressive recruitment and training.
Modification of work environment and removal of barriers.

Statement of Specific Objectives & Timetable

Removal of architectural, transportation, communication, procedural, and attitudinal barriers.
Improvement of personnel management and policies.
Career development in all occupational categories.

Assignment of Responsibilities

Who does what in specific terms (general manager, director of personnel, and coordinator of selective placement).

Coordinator of Selective Placement

Development and implementation of training programs.
Maintenance of communication between divisions and agencies.
Liaison with internal and external groups.
Recruitment from within and outside.
Career counseling to employees in medical restriction and new hirees.
Preparation of AAP document and follow-up on its success and evaluation.
Internal consultation to operating managers.
Initiation of studies to break new ground, e.g., barriers, job development, etc.

Team Work

Division of Personnel
Selective Placement Staff,
Employment Branch
Division of Medical Services
Rehabilitation Counseling
Unit, Health Counseling,
and Rehabilitation Staff
U.S. Department of Labor
Office of Workers' Compensation Programs
Outside Rehabilitation Agencies

Linkage

Development of Programs

Working with operating department in placement activities and follow-up.

Technological changes

Technological changes are inevitable in many jobs. When they occur, it is often necessary to retrain individuals in the use of new equipment, processes, and/or knowledge. Many times older workers are reluctant to "retool." There are two major reasons for this. One is that many of them find it difficult to learn new ways. Their ability to adapt and adjust is not what it once was. A second is that many of them feel that they are within 5 to 10 years of retirement and wonder whether it is worth the time and effort to be retrained. "Besides," some of them argue, "if I learn this, it'll be outmoded within a few years and I'll have to start again." The supervisor must realize that these reasons represent genuine concerns on the part of the older worker. Yet the manager must try to overcome them by pointing out the need to maintain productivity at its highest levels and the responsibility that everyone in the work unit has toward this objective. The last thing the supervisor should do is threaten to fire anyone who does not want to be retrained. However, the supervisor can point out that the old job is going to be closed out, that the individual must therefore be prepared to switch to a new one, and that this can be accomplished through the retraining program. This can be a difficult challenge for the supervisor, but it is one that every manager who has older employees faces on a continual basis.

Societal changes

Societal changes are inevitable. Each generation's values are fashioned by its environment. Those who grew up during the great depression have values different from those who were raised in the post-World War II era, and both of these groups have different values from those raised in the Vietnam years. A close look at these groups indicates that the first are today's older workers, the second are the supervisors, and the third are the young workers. The supervisor must manage people from different generations and value systems. For example, many older workers have stronger work values; they believe that everyone should work long and hard. At the same time, many of them cannot understand why the supervisor is so lenient with younger workers. "How come these guys wear their hair so long and dress so shabbily?" some of them will ask. "We ought to fire them." Others wonder why the supervisor keeps everyone informed about what is going on. "These young guys want to be told everything that's happening," they will complain. "In my day we learned to take orders and keep quiet." Still others will question management's wisdom in assuming an active role in hiring women, the handicapped, and other minorities.

The supervisor must learn to listen to these people without agreeing with them. Older workers often have a great deal of valuable experience and the supervisor needs to draw on this expertise. Getting into discussions about differences in values does no good. The manager simply must remember that many things have changed since these older workers were born. Company attitudes toward the personnel and the relationship between management and unions have undergone significant changes. These are facts of life. Just as long as the biases and opinions of older workers do not affect work output or the rights of others, the supervisor must learn to get along with these people and tolerate their opinions.

Motivational changes

Motivational changes also take place among older workers and the supervisor must be aware of them. Most older workers know that there is little chance that they will be promoted up the ranks. They have risen as far as they are going to in the organization. For many of them, money is not as important a motivator as it was previously. Their house is paid for, their children are raised and have moved away from home, and their financial burdens are lighter than they were a decade ago. However, this does not mean that older workers cannot be motivated. Psychological rewards such as recognition for accomplishment, consultation by the supervisor regarding major unit decisions, and respect from fellow workers are all important. To the extent that the supervisor can promote and encourage this type of environment, older workers are motivated. In fact, many supervisors do get these people involved in projects where experience is important, such as reviewing the unit's plan for the next year and offering suggestions as to how it can be improved. Older workers are also useful resources in problem solving. Many of them have seen similar situations and remember how they were effectively dealt with the last time. Their knowledge of what works and does not work is very important.

Termination considerations

Unfortunately, not all older workers are as effective as they once were. Sometimes it is necessary to terminate them. In order to ensure that their rights are not violated under the Age Discrimination Act, the supervisor should be prepared to document their work performance and show why it is not acceptable. This is particularly important should a lawsuit arise. In most firms, an older person who is doing unacceptable work is told about it and often provided additional instruction or training. If the individual still fails to measure up, then he or she is terminated. However, many firms do not like to fire older workers. They keep the person on until retirement, feeling that they owe the individual something for all the years he or she has worked for the firm. Yet this is not always the case, and when termination is considered to be in order, it is important that the supervisor have adequately documented the case so as to support the action.

OTHER CONSIDERATIONS

Two other protected groups are Vietnam veterans and employees of different religious views. Each merits the supervisor's careful attention.

Vietnam veterans

As thousands of soldiers began returning from Vietnam, the government determined that their reentry into the civilian labor force would be facilitated if they were treated as a protected group. The Vietnam Era Veterans Readjustment Act of 1974 is designed to ensure that these individuals are accorded affirmative action. Many states and local governments provide the same protection, in many cases giving preferential employment treatment to these individuals. However, except in the case of those with physical or mental problems, once these people have adjusted to the work, they are supervised just like any other member of the unit. The supervisor's major responsibility is ensuring that these veterans are accorded the same opportunities available to other workers.

Different religious views

In recent years there have been court cases related to the non-discriminatory treatment of employees who hold different religious views. These decisions are not all consistent, but one fact has emerged clearly. The organization should make every reasonable effort to accommodate workers with different religious beliefs. This is particularly true in handling work and holiday schedules. For some people Saturday is a day of religious observance, while for others it is Sunday. For some, Hanukkah and Yom Kippur are religious holidays, while for others it is Christmas and Easter. Supervisors do not make the rules regarding workdays. However, they should strive to accommodate the personnel by developing work schedules that take religious practices into consideration.

REVERSE DISCRIMINATION

The supervisor has to realize that there are many laws designed to provide protection to special groups. At the same time, the supervisor should be aware that charges of *reverse discrimination* will occasionally arise. These charges are often brought by workers who feel that they are highly qualified for job opportunities or promotions but do not get them because they are not members of a protected group. In some cases these bypassed workers have brought lawsuits. Over the last decade, some of these reverse discrimination suits have made their way to the United States Supreme Court.

Legal rulings

One of the most famous reverse discrimination suits was brought by Alan Bakke, who was rejected for admission by the medical school at the University of California at Davis. Minority group members with lower test scores and grade point averages than he had been admitted. However, because the school had set a quota that guaranteed a certain number of minority enrollments, Bakke ended up being rejected. He brought a lawsuit under the Civil Rights Act, claiming reverse discrimination. The case eventually went to the United States Supreme Court, which held that Bakke could not be rejected for admission simply because he was not a member of a protected group. In writing for the majority, Justice Lewis Powell held that the purpose of helping certain groups whom the faculty of the medical school perceived as victims of societal discrimination does not justify a classification that imposes disadvantages upon people like Bakke, who bear no responsibility for the harm that these protected groups are thought to have suffered.[9] The Supreme Court apparently has decided that quotas for admission to universities are illegal. On the other hand, it did give some consideration to race in the admission process.

Another landmark case has been that of *Weber et al. v. Kaiser Aluminum & Chemical Corporation and United Steelworkers of America.* Brian Weber, a lab analyst for 10 years at the Kaiser Aluminum and Chemical Company in Gramercy, Louisiana, wanted to get a skilled-craft job because it promised higher pay, greater job security, and a chance to escape the grind of night work. He applied for a crafts-retraining program but was rejected. The program called for at least 50 percent black and female trainees and Mr. Weber was an Anglo. He filed a lawsuit in which he claimed reverse discrimination. He won in the lower courts, but the case was eventually appealed to the Supreme Court and it ruled against him. The company successfully argued that a ruling in favor of Weber would effectively destroy its voluntary affirmative action program. The court agreed.[10]

In more recent years, other decisions have supported the Weber case in their efforts to encourage affirmative action programs. In establishing voluntary AAPs, the courts feel that the programs should be designed to help members of protected groups just as long as their purpose is limited in duration, minimal in harm to innocent parties, restricted in their reverse discrimination impact, and flexible in implementation.[11]

Supervisor's role   The supervisor's role is that of knowing the organization's affirmative action program and what or she should do to help implement it. If there are any questions about how to do this or if a matter arises that could result in legal problems, the supervisor should immediately contact the superior and fill in the latter on what has happened. The supervisor should also refrain from making comments about hiring and promoting members of protected groups. These matters should be handled by the supervisor and the boss, who is in contact with higher-level management. A first-line manager who openly states, "The next five positions are all going to women regardless of their ability and the company has decided to promote as many minorities as possible," is only asking for trouble. The issue of reverse discrimination in any form is a sensitive one. As a member of the management team, the supervisor is expected to be more discreet with his or her comments.

THE WORKER'S COMPLAINT: STARTING CASE REVISITED

Charles and his assistant are indeed in a bind. There are two reasons for this. First, the woman related the incident to Charles, so she has evidence that she called the matter to her manager's attention. Charles cannot argue that he knew nothing about the situation. Second, while Charles did talk to his assistant, the latter apparently did not listen carefully. The two men are going to have to explain to the personnel director why they are not guilty of the charge. Charles is in the best position. He can prove that he talked to his assistant and told the individual to follow company policy. However, he should have taken written notes on the meeting and followed up by telling his own boss about the matter. In this way, he would have someone to support his claim that the minute he learned something was wrong, he took positive action.

The assistant is in more of a bind depending on the specific charges the woman files. Unless he has someone who can prove to the satisfaction of the personnel department or the legal people that he is being unjustly accused, he may well be terminated. The firm is going to take a very conservative position on a matter like this. The last thing they want is to go to court and lose. Unless the woman has made accusations like this before and they have been proven unfounded, the assistant is in trouble. The company will undoubtedly hold a hearing, do its best to straighten out the situation, and urge all supervisors in the future to take sexual harassment claims more seriously than Charles did. Meanwhile, pending some new information to support his counter claim, the assistant is likely to be transferred to another job or dismissed, depending on how accurate the woman's charges prove to be.

SUMMARY OF KEY POINTS

1. Some personnel in organizations are known as protected employees because they are provided special protection under the law. These include such individuals as minorities, women, the elderly, the handicapped, and Vietnam veterans. In supervising them, there are a number of things that supervisors should and should not do. These were spelled out in the beginning of the chapter.

2. Supervisors have to remember that in managing minorities there are often both cultural and language problems to be overcome. These barriers cannot be eliminated; the manager must learn to work within them.

3. The number of women in the work force is increasing every year. Every effective supervisor must know how to manage women in the workplace. Three of the most important areas of consideration are: sexual harassment, compensation, and pregnancy policies. Supervisors must be aware of what sexual harassment is and how to deal with it. Most compensation issues are tied directly to equal pay for equal work. Pregnancy policies dictate the rights of women who leave their jobs for childbirth; supervisors need to know the rights that these women have so that they can make the necessary personnel decisions for running the unit.

4. The Rehabilitation Act of 1973 and local and state regulations are designed to ensure equality in the workplace for handicapped people. Many firms also have policies whereby they give special hiring consideration to these people. The supervisor's role should be one of being familiar with the law and with company policy. The individual should also be prepared to spell out the specific requirements that must be filled by handicapped workers being hired for positions in the unit, ensure that screening tests are valid, look for ways of redesigning the workplace so that the job can be adequately performed by the individual, and try to treat the person as a regular worker rather than as someone who merits pity or extra special consideration.

5. Older workers are protected from discrimination by the Age Discrimination Act of 1967. At the same time, however, they can be dismissed if they are incompetent in their work, and they certainly do present special problems for the supervisor.

Four of the most common problems relate to physical changes, technological changes, societal changes, and motivational changes.

6. Two other protected groups are Vietnam veterans and employees of different religious views. The former merit special consideration when being hired but, once they have been integrated into the job, are treated just like everyone else. The latter present various types of work-scheduling problems, and the supervisor should do his or her best to accommodate the religious practices of these people.

7. In recent years reverse discrimination cases have been filed by members of nonprotected groups who felt that were denied equal opportunity under the law. The two most famous have been the Bakke and the Weber cases. The supervisor's job is that of knowing the organization's affirmative action program and doing the best possible job to implement it.

BUILD YOUR SUPERVISORY WORD POWER

These key terms are presented in their order of appearance in the chapter. They are terms for which supervisors have a working knowledge.

Sexual harassment. Any repeated or unwarranted verbal or physical sexual advance or sexually explicit discriminatory remarks that are offensive or objectionable to the recipient.

Affirmative action program. A program designed to ensure the hiring and retention of minorities and the handicapped.

Reverse discrimination. The hiring or promoting of individuals who are members of a protected group when employees who are not a member of this group are more qualified.

REVIEW YOUR UNDERSTANDING

1. In supervising minorities, what are some things that supervisors should not do? What are some things they should do? Offer at least three guidelines in each case.

2. In what ways do culture and language affect the way in which supervisors manage minorities? Explain.

3. What is meant by the term *sexual harassment?* How should supervisors handle such charges made by their people? Offer some recommendations for supervisory action.

4. In what way is compensation an issue in supervising female employees? In your answer be sure to discuss the concept of comparable worth.

5. Do women who have taken pregnancy leave have any employment rights with the company? Explain.

6. When a firm makes a concerted effort to hire the handicapped, whom are they hiring? Give some examples.

7. What is the supervisor's role in managing handicapped people? What does the supervisor need to know? What should the supervisor be prepared to do? Explain.

8. Who is protected by the Age Discrimination in Employment Act? Are these people guaranteed their jobs? What exactly are they guaranteed?

9. In managing older workers, the supervisor faces four common problems. What are these four? Identify and describe each, being sure to note how the supervisor should handle each one.

10. What do supervisors need to know about managing Vietnam veterans and individuals with different religious views? Be complete in your answer.
11. What is meant by the term *reverse discrimination?* Put it in your own words.
12. In what way have the Bakke and Weber decisions affected the area of reverse discrimination? Explain the impact of each.
13. What does the supervisor need to know about reverse discrimination? Explain.

SUPPLEMENT YOUR KNOWLEDGE

In addition to the references listed at the end of this chapter, the following provide important, practical information that is of use to supervisors in managing protected groups:

Driscoll, Jeanne Bosson: "Sexual Attraction and Harassment: Management's New Problems," *Personnel Journal*, January 1981, pp. 33–36.

Greenlaw, Paul S., and John P. Kohl: "Age Discrimination in Employment Guidelines," *Personnel Journal*, March 1982, pp. 224–228.

Hagen, Robert P.: "Older Workers: How to Utilize This Valuable Resource," *Supervisory Management*, November 1983, pp. 2–9.

Hodge, John: "Common-Sensical Approach to Supervising Minorities," *Supervisory Management*, September 1983, pp. 24–27.

Hoyman, Michele, and Ronda Robinson: "Interpreting the New Sexual Harassment Guidelines," *Personnel Journal*, December 1980, pp. 996–1000.

Kronenberger, George K., and David L. Bourke: "Effective Training and the Elimination of Sexual Harassment," *Personnel Journal*, November 1981, pp. 879–883.

Maslin, Harvey L.: "How to Avoid Discrimination," *Supervisory Management*, February 1976, pp. 2–5.

Niehouse, Oliver L., and Joanne Ross Doades: "Sexual Harassment: An Old Issue—A New Problem," *Supervisory Management*, April 1980, pp. 10–14.

Pati, Gopal C., and Edward F. Hilton, Jr.: "A Comprehensive Model for a Handicapped Affirmative Action Program," *Personnel Journal*, February 1980, pp. 99–108.

Renick, James C.: "Sexual Harassment at Work Why It Happens, What to Do About It," *Personnel Journal*, August 1980, pp. 658–662.

Rowe, Mary P.: "Dealing with Sexual Harassment," *Harvard Business Review*, May–June 1981, pp. 42–52.

Saint James, Diane: "Coping with Sexual Harassment," *Supervisory Management*, October 1983, pp. 3–9.

YOU BE THE SUPERVISOR: HIRING THE HANDICAPPED

Every year the mayor in Judson Corners undertakes a campaign to reduce unemployment in the area. Last year he got 190 firms to give summer jobs to 5 high school students each. This year his emphasis is on getting local firms to hire the handicapped. Part of his effort consists of a personal visit to the firm to ask for its support. When the mayor called on the president of the Manning Company he did not think he would get much support for his request. Nevertheless, he decided to give it his best pitch. "We've got 15 handicapped Vietnam vets in the area who are looking for work," he told the president, "and we are trying to get employers to make a special effort to hire them. They've made their contribution to this country. I think it's time we made ours. I'd like you to hire two of them." To the mayor's surprise, the president of the firm agreed. "Give us a week to get things worked out and we'll begin interviewing them. I promise you, we'll hire two of them. I know that we need some people in our production area, but I'm not sure how we can use them."

After the mayor had left, the president called in the vice president in charge of manufacturing and told him what he had promised the mayor. "I want you to look over your operations and see where we can use handicapped people," the president said. "I know there are some jobs where this isn't possible. However, there must be plenty of work down there that just about anybody can do." The vice president told him that he would take care of it at once.

Later that afternoon there was a meeting of all production supervisors. The vice president spelled out to them exactly what the president had told the mayor. The vice president also told them about his conversation with the president. "We're going to hire two handicapped veterans," the vice president said. "I don't know for sure who these people are, and until we do know, it's going to be a little difficult saying exactly what type of work we're going to give them. The mayor is going to find out how many of them would be interested in working in our type of business. From that group we're going to hire two. If it looks like we can hire more, I know the president is going to want us to do so. In any event, I want all of you to look over your own operations and let me know if there is any chance that you would be able to use a handicapped person. I'm sure the president would be willing to spend money to make any changes in the workplace that may be necessary to help the individual get around or perform the work more easily or safely. However, I have to get an idea of what type of work the individual could do if he or she were hired in your department. I also want to know how you would go about integrating the person into the work unit. What will you do in the way of easing the person into the job? Think about it and get back to me by tomorrow." All of the supervisors promised that they would.

1. If you were a supervisor in the plant and felt that your unit could hire a handicapped person, what suggestions would you make to the vice president regarding the types of testing the individual should be given during the screening process? Give an example.
2. What kinds of responsibilities would the supervisor have to assume if a handicapped person were assigned to his or her unit? Explain.
3. What types of things would the supervisor have to be careful not to do? Cite and describe at least four.

YOU BE THE SUPERVISOR: PAULA'S PLIGHT

Paula McCarthy has been a secretary in the typing pool in her firm for over 5 years. Paula's performance evaluations have always been excellent and her pay is 80 percent that of the lead secretary in the department, a woman who has been with the firm for over 15 years. Basically, Paula does the same job that this woman does. However, because the woman has been with the firm so much longer and typists are usually given across-the-board raises, Paula has never been able to close the gap between her salary and this woman's.

Three years ago Paula married. Her husband had just graduated from college and the two wanted to wait a couple of years before starting a family. Last week the doctor told Paula that she was pregnant. Paula intends to work until a month before the baby is due, assuming that there are no complications and that the doctor approves. Paula also intends to return to work as soon after the delivery as possible. Her mother, who lives nearby, will keep the child during the day, thus enabling Paula to continue her work career.

When Paula learned that she was pregnant, she talked to her supervisor. The latter informed her that the company does not have disability coverage and so she will not be able to take time off without losing pay. Additionally, it is the company's policy to rehire on an as-needed basis, and if Paula takes a pregnancy leave, the firm does not have to rehire her. However, the supervisor feels that Paula does such an exceptional job that, in his words: "If you want to return, I'll have something for you even if it's not your old job. You can bank on that."

Paula was distressed to learn that after the baby's birth the firm would not promise to give her back her old job. She feels that this is unfair and has talked to her husband, Jeff, about it. Jeff is not a lawyer, but he does have a B.S. degree in business. He believes that his wife is being discriminated against in two ways. The first is that she should be paid as much money as the lead secretary. "It's a blatant case of discrimination," he told her. "If you compare the skills you need to do your job effectively with those of that other woman, it's obvious that you are entitled to as much money as she is." He is even angrier over the pregnancy policy of the firm. "You are entitled to your job back," he continued. "It's the law. Women who take pregnancy leave can get their same job back at their same rate of pay, unless they stay out more than 4 months. It's right here in my company policy manual, and if my company has that guarantee, it must be because of the law. I think you should talk to your supervisor, and if you don't have any success, we should consult an attorney."

Paula has given a great deal of thought to her husband's comments. She thinks he may well be right, although she is somewhat confused as to why the supervisor would tell her she was not guaranteed her job. She is also a little concerned about bringing up the matter of equal pay for equal work. She wonders if the company really is discriminating against her on the basis of salary. In any event, she has decided to talk to her supervisor tomorrow morning as soon as she arrives at work.

1. If you were the supervisor, what would you tell Paula if she raised the issue of equal pay for equal work and compared her salary to that of the lead secretary? How would you defend the company's current wage scale? Is Paula being discriminated against? Explain.
2. Does Paula have a right to her old job back at the current salary? Why or why not? What would you tell her? Be as factual as you can in your answer.
3. Does the supervisor have to rehire her, or can the company simply terminate her employment if she takes pregnancy leave? Explain.

NOTES

1. Patricia Linenberger and Timothy J. Keaveny, "Sexual Harassment: The Employer's Legal Obligations," *Personnel*, November–December 1981, pp. 61–62.
2. Linenberger and Keaveny, pp. 64–65.
3. Terry L. Leap and Edmund R. Gray, "Corporate Responsibility in Cases of Sexual Harassment," *Business Horizons*, October 1980, pp. 58–65.
4. Randall S. Schuler, *Personnel and Human Resource Management*, 2d ed., St. Paul, Minn.: West, 1984, chap. 9.
5. Tamar Levin, "Maternity Leave: Is It Leave, Indeed?" *New York Times*, July 22, 1984, sec. F, pp. 1, 23.

6. Levin, pp. 1, 23.
7. A. B. Zimmer, "Smoothing the Way for the Handicapped Worker," *Supervisory Management*, April 1981, p. 7.
8. Robert B. Nathanson and Jeffrey Lambert, "Integrating Disabled Employees into the Workplace," *Personnel Journal*, February 1981, pp. 109–113.
9. "Excerpts of Four Justices' Opinions in the Bakke Case," *Chicago Tribune*, June 29, 1978, sec. 1, p. 6.
10. Fred Luthans, Richard M. Hodgetts, and Kenneth R. Thompson, *Social Issues in Business*, 4th ed., New York: Macmillan, 1984, p. 127.
11. Schuler, pp. 133–135.

PART THREE

THE WORK ENVIRONMENT

The purpose of this part of the book is to study how first-line managers supervise their work environments. This environment extends from on-the-job safety to dealing with unions, managing productivity, and controlling costs.

Chapter 12 examines how supervisors ensure employee safety and health. Included in this coverage are accident prevention, the effects of smoking, supervision of alcoholic workers, and employee assistance programs.

Chapter 13 deals with unions, grievances, and discipline. After discussing the growth of unions in America and the major objectives of unions, it considers the major laws that affect labor-management relations and discusses how the collective bargaining process works. It then discusses the supervisor's role in dealing with unions and spells out the ways in which discipline should be administered.

Chapter 14 addresses the areas of productivity and cost control. It describes the nature of the productivity challenge, spells out purchasing and inventory control techniques, and presents basic work-flow layouts. The latter part of the chapter discusses quality control, alternative work styles, and the necessary linkage between effective productivity plans and monetary incentives.

When you have finished studying all the material in these three chapters, you will know some of the major problems confronting the supervisor in his or her efforts to manage the work environment. You will also be aware of the current status of some of the most recent developments in safety, health, union negotiations, and productivity improvement efforts.

CHAPTER 12

ENSURING EMPLOYEE SAFETY
AND HEALTH

**GOALS OF
THE CHAPTER**

Every organization must provide its employees with safe and healthful working conditions. The supervisor's job is to ensure that these conditions remain in existence. Any change in the physical environment or the behavior of individuals that threatens the health and safety of the workers must be addressed. The overriding purpose of this chapter is to examine the specific areas of safety and health with which the supervisor must be familiar. When you have finished reading all the material in this chapter, you will be able to:

1. Describe the nature, purpose, and requirements of the Occupational Safety and Health Act.
2. Explain the importance of worker compensation programs.
3. Identify some of the most common accident prevention rules and discuss the supervisor's responsibility for enforcing them.
4. Discuss the impact of smoking on employee health and performance.
5. Discuss how supervisors should manage alcoholic employees.
6. Describe the nature and importance of employee assistance programs.

A STARTING CASE: THE TROUBLED SALESPERSON

Terry Anderson was the number one salesperson in Pete Seacrest's department. Over the last 5 years Terry's annual sales rose from $1.2 to $3.4 million. However, about eight months ago Pete noticed that Terry's performance was beginning to taper off. Terry lost two of his biggest accounts and began checking into the office late on Monday and leaving early on Friday.

Once, about four months ago, Pete joined him for lunch with one of the firm's biggest accounts. They met at 11:30 A.M. in a nearby restaurant. As Pete approached the front door, he saw the client coming from the opposite direction. He waited, shook hands with the man, and then held the door for him. As they entered the restaurant and started to check their coats, Terry called to them. He was sitting at the bar having a drink. They joined him while he ordered a round for everyone. A few minutes later the maître d' came and told them their table was ready. As they were leaving the bar, Terry said to the bartender, "Do it again, will you, and have the drinks brought to the table."

Once they were seated, they began small talk and then ordered lunch. Terry had the waiter bring out a bottle of the house's best wine. During lunch the client discussed some of his company's specific needs and Terry took notes. He then told the client that the company could deliver on everything that was wanted. The client was delighted. "That's what I like about doing business with your firm. Terry is the best salesperson I've come across in years."

After lunch, Terry and Pete walked back to the office together. As they chatted it became obvious to Pete that Terry was under a great deal of stress. Terry explained that his youngest son had been diagnosed as having a serious heart condition and might not live more than another year. Pete expressed his concern and asked if there was anything he could do. "No," said Terry, "it's a personal problem. However, I have to stay closer to home, and that's what's cutting into my sales performance." Pete said he understood.

Over the next 4 months Terry's sales took a nosedive. Pete, aware of Terry's problem at home, said nothing. Then last week he received a call from the company attorney, who asked Pete to come to her office as soon as possible. When Pete arrived, the attorney explained that Terry would have to be fired by the firm. It seems that he was arrested the previous evening for drunk driving and that this was the second arrest in 8 months. "He faces a minimum of 6 months in jail," she explained. "The last time, his license was suspended for a year, so he shouldn't even have been behind the wheel of a car. Did you know anything about this?" Pete said that he did not, although he admitted that Terry's work performance had dropped off dramatically.

Once back in his office, Pete put in a call to Terry's wife. He expressed his concern and sorrow over the matter, told her of his conversation with the attorney, and asked if this development would have any effect on the family's ability to provide the needed medical care for their young son. Terry's wife expressed surprise. "Why, there's nothing wrong with Tommy. Where did you get the idea he had a heart problem? Everyone's health is just fine." Pete beat a hasty retreat, saying that he must have gotten his facts turned around. He then asked her to feel free to call on him if she needed some assistance and hung up. Sitting back in his chair, Pete began to ponder what had happened.

Exactly what did happen to Terry? Why did Pete not see it coming? Should he have known something was wrong? What lessons can Pete learn from this that will make him a more effective supervisor?

SAFETY AND THE LAW

Every organization is required to provide its people with safe and healthful working conditions. There are many things an organization can do in meeting this objective. Two of the major ones are: complying with the Occupational Safety and Health Act of 1970 and providing protection in the form of workers' compensation. Before reading on, take Self-Assessment Quiz 12-1.

SELF-ASSESSMENT QUIZ 12-1:
HOW MUCH DO YOU KNOW ABOUT WORKER SAFETY AND HEALTH?

Read each of the following statements and enter an X in the appropriate column. Then check your answers at the end of the chapter to see how much you currently know about worker safety and health.

	True	*False*
1. At least once every 2 years the government makes a safety inspection of every organization that employs 25 or more people.	____	____
2. If an employee is killed in a work-related accident, a formal report must be filed with the Occupational Safety and Health Administration (OSHA).	____	____
3. OSHA has the authority to make businesses provide a work environment that is free from employee exposure to all hazards.	____	____
4. All states require employers to have workers' compensation plans.	____	____
5. On a national basis, the total cost of accidents on the job exceeds $10 billion annually.	____	____
6. The supervisor's responsibility for job safety begins with an understanding of the company's rules.	____	____
7. There is a higher absenteeism rate among nonsmokers than among smokers in the work force.	____	____
8. Smoking can contribute to a person taking a disability retirement.	____	____
9. Productivity among smokers tends to be higher than that among nonsmokers.	____	____
10. The current annual cost of allowing people in the workplace to smoke is in excess of $5000/person.	____	____
11. Effective supervisors encourage smoking in the workplace.	____	____
12. Alcoholism is a major cause of absenteeism.	____	____
13. Workers who have one or two drinks at lunch are more productive than those who do not.	____	____
14. If a supervisor finds that a worker is an alcoholic, he or she should immediately begin counseling the individual.	____	____
15. Employee assistance programs, popular in the 1970s, have faded because of their inability to promote worker safety and health.	____	____

The *Occupational Safety and Health Act of 1970* is a comprehensive piece of legislation that calls for safety and health hazard inspections of organizations and investigations of all accidents and allegations of hazards. The act is well-intentioned but soon came under serious attack by critics, who claimed that it focuses on minor problems and overlooks major ones. Many businesses also contended that those enforcing the law were overburdening them with compliance demands and were antibusiness in their attitude. During the Reagan administration, the Labor Department, which is charged with enforcing this act, began to lessen this adversarial relationship to the point where critics now claim that the act does not go far enough in protecting the health and safety of the workers. In any event, there are three specific areas of the act that the supervisor should know about. These relate to inspection, record keeping, and the establishment of standards.

Inspection. The Occupational Safety and Health Administration (OSHA) has been responsible for setting up and enforcing occupational safety and health standards and for inspecting and issuing citations to organizations that violate these standards. Of course, given the fact that there are only a small number of OSHA inspectors and millions of businesses in the country, there is not a very high likelihood that any particular organization will be inspected during a given year. In fact, the inspectors can get to less than 2 percent of all organizations in a year. For this reason, the focus tends to be on the most flagrant and frequent violations of OSHA rules.

Most recently the agency has been moving toward changing its inspection procedures so that: (1) Companies with a low injury rate, such as less than six lost-workday cases per 100 workers, will be exempt from inspection; (2) less immediate inspections are made in response to worker complaints unless there is an imminent danger, and then only if the problem is not corrected after written OSHA notification to the firm; and (3) there is exemption from inspection for firms with in-house worker-management committees that respond to worker complaints, conduct monthly inspections, and ensure that hazards are eliminated.

Record keeping. Whether or not an OSHA inspection is made of the facilities, organizations are required to keep safety and health records so that accurate statistics on work injuries and illnesses can be reported. The OSHA guide to determining what must be recorded is illustrated in Figure 12-1. A number of different types of safety and health rates must be recorded. Two of the most common types of compiled statistics are those relating to the incidence rate and the frequency rate. OSHA requires these statistics for use in comparing the performance of one company against that of similar firms. Many organizations also keep these records for the purpose of developing more effective safety and health programs. The *incidence-rate formula* is used for combining job-related illnesses and injuries. The formula is computed this way:

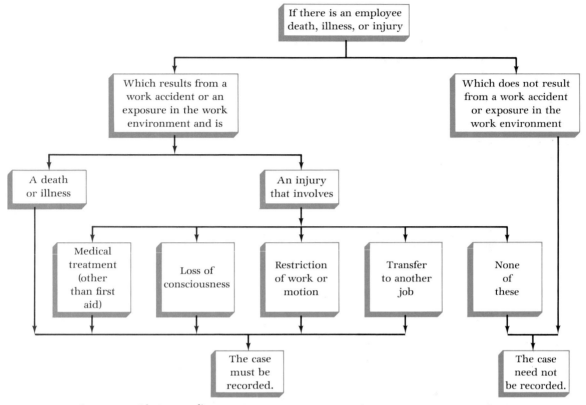

Figure 12-1. The OSHA guide to recording cases.

$$\text{Incidence rate} = \frac{\text{number of recordable injuries and illnesses} \times \text{1 million}}{\text{number of employee exposure hours}}$$

Using the above formula, if an organization had 20 recordable injuries and illnesses and 1000 employees, it would determine the number of exposure hours by multiplying the number of employees by 40 hours and 50 weeks: $1000 \times 40 \times 50 = 2,000,000$. It would then divide the numerator (20,000,000) by the denominator (2,000,000) to arrive at an incidence rate of 10. In recent years, this rate would be a little higher than average.

The *frequency-rate formula* is similar to the incidence-rate formula except that it reflects the number of injuries and illnesses per million hours worked rather than per year. The formula is:

$$\text{Frequency rate} = \frac{\text{number of disabling injuries} \times \text{1 million}}{\text{number of employee hours worked}}$$

In addition to maintaining statistics on occupational safety and health, organizations must either show or give to the employees, to their designated representatives, and to OSHA their on-the-job medical records as well as records showing the amount of exposure the individual has had to toxic substances. This permits both the employee and OSHA to know about any health hazards faced by the workers on the job. Some states have gone further, requiring firms to label chemicals and to identify their potential health threats. Of these many chemicals, Table 12-1 describes 10.

Establishing standards. In recent years, the way that OSHA establishes standards has changed. Previously it set what are called no-risk standards. This meant that the agency could tell businesses that they had to make the work environment free from any risk of employee exposure. Because of

Table 12-1. Ten suspected hazards in the workplace

Potential dangers	Diseases that may result	Workers exposed
Arsenic	Lung cancer, lymphona	Smelter, chemical, oil-refinery workers; insecticide makers and sprayers—estimated 660,000 exposed
Asbestos	White-lung disease (asbestosis); cancer of lungs and lining of lungs; cancer of other organs	Miners; millers; textile, insulation, and shipyard workers—estimated 1.6 million exposed.
Benzene	Leukemia; aplastic anemia	Petrochemical and oil-refinery workers; dye users; distillers; painters; shoemakers—estimated 600,000 exposed
Bischloromethylether (BCME)	Lung cancer	Industrial chemical workers
Coal dust	Black-lung disease	Coal miners—estimated 208,000 exposed
Coke-oven emissions	Cancer of lungs, kidneys	Coke-oven workers—estimated 30,000 exposed
Cotton dust	Brown-lung disease (byssinosis); chronic bronchitis; emphysema	Textile workers—estimated 600,000 exposed
Lead	Kidney disease; anemia; central-nervous-system damage; sterility; birth defects	Metal grinders; lead-smelter workers; lead storage-battery workers—estimated 835,000 exposed
Radiation	Cancer of thyroid, lungs and bone; leukemia; reproductive effects (spontaneous abortion, genetic damage)	Medical technicians; uranium miners; nuclear-power and atomic workers
Vinyl chloride	Cancer of liver, brain	Plastic-industry workers—estimated 10,000 directly exposed

Source: *U.S. News & World Report*, February 5, 1979, p. 42. © 1979 by U.S. News & World Report, Inc.

court decisions and budgetary cutbacks, however, OSHA now focuses on eliminating significant risks. If these efforts are unsuccessful, the agency can then force the firm to adhere to the more stringent no-risk standards; and if significant risks are found to exist, OSHA can demand compliance regardless of the costs involved.

OSHA was created to provide employees with protection against accidents and diseases on the job. Workers' compensation programs are designed to provide financial aid for those who are unable to work because of accidents and diseases.

Workers' compensation programs

Supervisors also have to be aware that there are *workers' compensation programs,* which provide financial awards to those who are unable to work because of physical injury or illness. In recent years, the courts have also been awarding compensation in job-related cases of anxiety, depression, and mental disorders. For example, the Texas Supreme Court held that an employee who became terrified and highly anxious and unable to work because of a job-related accident had a compensable claim even though he had no physical injury (*Bailey v. American General Insurance Company,* 1955). In a more recent case (*James v. State Accident Insurance Fund,* 1980) an Oregon court ruled in favor of a worker's claim for compensation for inability to work due to job stress resulting from conflicting work assignments.

All states today require employers to have workers' compensation plans for their employees. While state laws differ, in general all plans provide workers who are injured on the job with payments for a specified time. The purpose of this compensation is to offset the wages lost because of injury or inability to work. Usually the payment is a percentage of the worker's salary. Additionally, payments are typically made to cover medical expenses, and if the individual is killed on the job, there is a survivor's benefit paid to the deceased's spouse, parents, or next of kin. The cost of these plans varies based on the employer's previous safety record. Those with good records pay less than those with poor ones. This cost factor has encouraged many organizations to implement safety improvement programs. One of the prime areas of attention has been accidents.

ACCIDENT PREVENTION

The National Safety Council estimates that on a national basis the cost of accidents exceeds $14 billion annually, which averages out to more than $150/worker. There are many reasons for job accidents. One is chance occurrences, such as the brakes on a forklift truck suddenly going out, causing the vehicle to crash into a load of boxes that is being transported across the plant floor, injuring the driver and causing damage to the equipment and inventory. Despite management's best efforts, there will always be chance occurrences that cannot be predicted or totally controlled. However, research shows that less than 2 percent of all work-related accidents are due to chance. The rest are avoidable if the firm takes the proper safety steps.

Rules and procedures

Many firms attempt to reduce the accident rate by identifying and correcting hazards in the workplace. They inspect the facilities for the purpose of identifying such things as defective machinery, the hazardous arrangement of equipment, dangerous storage of inventory, improper ventilation, and inadequate lighting. They also focus attention on areas that are most susceptible to accidents. For example, the Aetna Insurance Company has noted that particular consideration should be given to:[1]

- Situations in which heavy, awkward material is handled using trucks, cranes, and hoists.
- Situations requiring the use of machinery that can injure the user, such as metal- and wood-working machines, machines with exposed gears, belts, or chains, and paper cutters.
- Climbing up ladders or using scaffolding where people can slip and fall.
- Blocked aisles and stairways and unsafe passageways.
- Lack of access to fire extinguishers and fire alarms.

It is also common to find the company developing safety inspection checklists that can be used to ensure that all safety steps are being taken. Sometimes these checklists are given to the supervisor, who uses them to monitor work behavior. More commonly, they are also given to the workers. An example of a set of general plant safety rules is provided in Table 12-2. These rules are not meant to be degrading or to imply that the worker is stupid; rather, they are designed to spell out things which the average employee should know and which are often not obvious to the person.

The supervisor's responsibility

The supervisor's responsibility for job safety begins with an understanding of the company's rules. If the first-line manager knows how the workers are supposed to be acting and why, attention can then be focused on worker safety. In carrying out this responsibility, there are six things the supervisor must do:

1. ***Understand the causes.*** Accidents occur for a number of reasons. Some of the most common are:
   a. Safety instructions are inadequate.
   b. Safety rules are not enforced.
   c. Safety has not been built in as part of the job.
   d. Work hazards have not been corrected.
   e. Safety devices have not been provided.
   f. There has been infrequent contact with the employees regarding safety rules and procedures and the importance of following them. When accidents are examined, one or more of these six reasons often explain why they occurred.

Table 12-2. Examples of general plant safety rules

1. Unless there is an emergency, running on plant property is forbidden.
2. Smoking is permitted in designated areas only.
3. Know the location of all fire and safety exits.
4. All emergency equipment—such as fire extinguishers, fire alarms, and exit doors—must be kept clear of obstacles.
5. Safe shoes must be worn at all times; sandals or canvas-type shoes are not permitted on the plant floor.
6. Safety glasses must be worn in all specified areas of the plant; these areas are marked with warning signs.
7. The wearing of jewelry such as watches, rings, or necklaces, or of long ties while working around or operating movement equipment is prohibited.
8. Do not attempt to use defective machinery.
9. Tampering with or the unauthorized use of machinery is forbidden.
10. The removal of any "Danger, Do Not Operate" tags or locks on machinery is prohibited.
11. All tools are to be maintained in a good state of repair.
12. If machinery must be cleaned or requires adjusting while in motion, special permission must first be obtained from the supervisor.
13. If climbing is required, a ladder is to be used; do not stand on machines or tables.
14. Forklift trucks are built to accommodate only one person, and only the driver is to ride on the truck.
15. Keep your work area clean at all times.
16. When going on or coming off duty, carefully examine all apparatus and equipment under your responsibility to ensure that it is in good working order. If any repairs or other attention is needed, call your shift supervisor at once.
17. Horseplay and practical jokes are forbidden.
18. No one is permitted on the premises who is in possession of firearms, ammunition, or articles of a similar nature unless that person has the written permission of the plant manager.
19. Each person is responsible for his or her own safety as well as for that of fellow workers.
20. Report all injuries to your supervisor immediately.

2. ***Be aware of the mental condition of the employees.*** No matter how hard the supervisor tries to create an accident-free environment, if the workers do not join in this effort there will be accidents. There are many reasons why workers do not approach accident prevention with the same enthusiasm as the first-line manager. Some of these include: a lack of safety awareness on their part; inattention; lack of emotional stability; improper attitude; temperament; and nervousness. These causes contribute to accidents on the job.

3. ***Be aware of the physical condition of the employees.*** Sometimes the workers want to obey the company's safety rules but are prevented from doing so for physical reasons. These include: extreme fatigue, poor eyesight, poor hearing, and generally poor health. Taken together with items 1 and 2 above, these constitute what are called the contributing causes to accidents.

4. ***Realize the immediate causes of accidents.*** These fall into two categories: unsafe conditions and unsafe acts. Unsafe conditions include such things as ineffective safety devices, improper illumination

and/or ventilation, improper clothing or dress for the job, defective equipment or tools, and hazardous working conditions. Unsafe acts include: horseplay; hazardous running around, jumping, or climbing over things; improper handling of equipment or materials; and a failure to abide by safety rules and regulations.

5. ***Be aware of the costs of accidents.*** This includes minor injuries, major injuries, production delays, spoilage, and time lost. All of these affect the bottom line of the company's income statement.

6. ***Realize that with proper supervision, accidents can be prevented.*** In carrying out this step, there are many things the supervisor can do. One is to ensure that all the people in the work unit have had safety training. By making them aware of what they should do and why, the supervisor increases the likelihood that accidents will decline. A second important step is to keep one's eye on those who have the greatest number of accidents. For whatever reason, they are more likely to have recurring problems. Some people refer to these individuals as "accident prone." Whether or not this is true, these workers merit more attention than the others. Other important steps are presented in Supervision in Action: Some Important Things to Do.

SUPERVISION IN ACTION: SOME IMPORTANT THINGS TO DO

How well supervisors meet their responsibility in the area of safety is a major factor in the development of safety attitudes throughout an organization. Because managers play such an important safety role, the following guidelines are offered. They are admittedly only ground rules, but your own imagination and creativity should add the appropriate substance, tailoring these rules to the particular needs of your organization and your work group.

- *Set a good example.* Your attitude and the example that you set in the area of safety are significant factors in the formation of your subordinates' safety attitudes. By showing your subordinates that you are sincerely committed to safety, you will be encouraging them to develop a positive safety attitude. So, take a close look at your own safety attitude, and ask yourself if this attitude will motivate positive attitudes in your subordinates.

- *Build safety habits from the first day.* New employees are subject to more than their share of changes. Therefore, even before the first day that they are on the job, remind them to keep safety in mind when they are in the process of moving away from their old homes and jobs. Employees during the job transition period are most vulnerable to accidents.

    As part of a new employee's first-day orientation, make sure that you review the company's and your personal commitment to safety and discuss briefly the company's safety program. This initial safety orientation is very important, since the employee will be able to use the information received to develop work habits that should include a safety awareness.

- *Reinforce positive safety performance.* Be sure to take the time to recognize employees who have safe records or participate in safety activities. If an employee consistently attends safety meetings, has no accidents, and takes the time to maintain a safe work area, be sure to let him or her know that you approve.

- *Communicate your concern for safety.* Effective communications can help formulate safety attitudes. Supplement written communications with discussions on safety at your group meetings. See to it that each employee feels free to offer suggestions and ideas on safety matters. Make sure that you use every possible communication medium, and that the message carried in each medium is consistent and reflects your positive safety attitude.

- *Encourage participation in safety programs.* Such participation helps to personalize safety attitudes. Employees are generally more interested in safety matters when they participate than when they merely see and hear safety discussed. By participating, the employee will also be more likely to identify directly with the safety program.

  The value of participative management is that employees tend to support what they help develop. This is just as true in safety matters as it is in other areas. And don't limit participation to your subordinates; take part, too, in the activities. This helps to set a good example for other employees to follow.

- *Set safety objectives.* One of the most effective ways to show your commitment to safety is to include safety objectives in your management-by-objectives program. This is evidence to your subordinates that, along with quality, productivity, and the like, you view safety as an important part of getting the job done. In addition, the normal process of reviewing objectives throughout the year will enable you periodically to review and discuss with your subordinates their safety attitudes.

  These guidelines barely touch the surface in terms of how attitudes are formed, but they should give you a feel for how important you are in the formation of these attitudes. You owe it to your subordinates and to yourself to ensure that accidents are avoided. By fostering positive safety attitudes, you can help yourself, your subordinates, and your organization manage change *safely*.

Source: Edward F. Konczai, "The Supervisor's Role in Accident Prevention," *Supervisory Management,* July 1979, pp. 32–34.

**SMOKING:
DEALING WITH A
HEALTH HAZARD**

In 1964 the Surgeon General issued a report demonstrating the adverse effects of smoking on health. In 1979 a second report was issued, and this one was even more emphatic in its conclusions about the dangers of smoking. What many business firms are only now beginning to realize is that smoking in the workplace is also detrimental to organizational efficiency. It can cause illness, lost on-the-job time, increased insurance costs, and higher property damage and maintenance.

Statistics and costs

Among U.S. adult males, over 35 percent are smokers, while among U.S. adult females it is over 30 percent.[2] Government statistics show that smokers have a 50 percent greater incidence of absenteeism than do nonsmokers.[3] In fact, smoking takes such a toll on the work force that by their mid-40s, many absence-prone smokers leave the work force altogether.[4] This has led some organizations to hire only nonsmokers. For example, the fire chief of the Alexandria, Virginia, Fire Department found that over a 5-year period, 73 percent of those taking early retirement were smokers. This is a significant statistic, given the fact that only 33 percent of the adult population takes early retirement.[5] It also helps explain why the fire chief no longer hires smokers. It is too costly to the taxpayer to employ people who will be taking disability retirement before they are 60 years old. Smoking translates into extremely high operating costs.

One is the cost of disability insurance. As more and more workers take early disability retirement, these expenditures are eventually passed back to the business in the form of higher insurance premiums. If the company has a large number of claims, it will be adjudged a poorer risk than most other firms and will have to pay a higher rate for disability coverage.

A second cost is the on-the-job time and accompanying productivity that are lost due to the smoking ritual. Estimates of job time lost to cigarette smoking (lighting the cigarette, puffing it, putting it out, taking informal breaks while smoking, etc.) range from 8 to 30 minutes per day[6] and up to 55 minutes per day for pipe smokers.[7]

A third is the cost of property damage caused by damage to furniture, carpeting, draperies, etc., that are burned or pick up tobacco odors that must be removed. Other costs include the cleaning of interior glass surfaces (windows, showcases) and the repainting of interior walls, which require more maintenance if smoking on the premises is permitted. Some estimates of these costs range from $500 to $1000 per worker per year!

A fourth cost is that of training people to replace those who have left due to disability or have died prematurely because of smoking. The overall mortality rate for smokers is 70 percent greater than that for nonsmokers. Even more distressing is the fact that many of these people are struck down during their prime working years. Men between the ages of 35 and 44 who smoke 40 or more cigarettes per day are almost 3 times as likely to have a fatal heart attack as are their nonsmoking counterparts.

A fifth cost is the impact of smoking on nonsmokers. These people are

Table 12-3. Annual cost of employing smokers and allowing smoking in the workplace

Absenteeism	$ 310
Medical care	230
Morbidity and early mortality	765
Insurance (excluding health)	90
On-the-job time lost	1,820
Property damage and depreciation	500
Maintenance	500
Involuntary smoking	522
Total cost per smoker per year	$4,737

Source: Wayne F. Cascio, *Costing Human Resources: The Financial Impact of Behavior in Organizations*, Boston: Kent, 1982, p. 74.

subjected to the same types of problems as are smokers, although at a lower rate. Researchers estimate that the damage from involuntary or passive smoking is equal to that suffered by light smokers (1 to 10 cigarettes per day), which is about 20 percent of the damage to normal smokers.[8] Do all of these costs really add up to much money? The answer is yes. One researcher, after making an investigation of the actual costs, estimated the annual expenses to be over $4700 per person in 1981 dollars (see Table 12-3). Allowing an average increase of 5 percent per year for inflation brings today's total to well over $6000.

The supervisor's role

Supervisors do not make the rules regarding smoking. However, if they have any effect on this decision, they are wise to advocate a ban, or heavy restriction, on smoking in the workplace. If they themselves smoke, every effort should be made to stop. The statistics are too one-sided to justify the habit.

If the firm does have a ban on smoking, it should be strictly enforced. Some people argue that such a rule is a violation of "smokers' rights." However, Johns-Manville has prohibited smoking in all of its asbestos mines and plants in the United States and Canada. Other firms have followed suit, feeling that it is unfair for individuals to practice a habit that causes absenteeism, disability, early mortality, and substandard productivity and is a major hazard for coworkers.

If there is no ban, the supervisor should encourage the personnel not to smoke. The manager should also urge the personnel department to compare the absenteeism and productivity records of smokers in the unit with that of nonsmokers. A cost comparison over 3 to 5 years is likely to show the dangers of smoking, although if the number of personnel is quite small or the group is young (age 20 to 29), the statistics may not show much difference between smokers and nonsmokers. It may be necessary to look at these statistics for the company at large.

Finally, the supervisor should keep in mind that firms that have instituted a smoking ban have had very favorable results. Some of the specific reported outcomes include:[9]

1. A decline in personnel costs because the same workload is able to be done by fewer people.
2. A decline in maintenance costs.
3. A slowdown in the actual physical depreciation of furniture and equipment.
4. A decline in insurance rates brought about by a decrease in health, accident, and disability claims.
5. An improvement in employee morale.

SUPERVISING THE ALCOHOLIC

Alcoholism is a major problem in American industry. It is estimated that 5 percent of the labor force suffers from alcoholism, and this percentage is constant everywhere on the organizational ladder: lower, middle, and upper.[10] The major reason why alcoholism is a supervisory problem is that it affects productivity.

Cost of alcoholism

Alcoholism affects productivity in a number of ways. Some of these include: (1) overtime costs caused by absenteeism, (2) increased life and health insurance costs, (3) reduced work quantity, and (4) diminished work quality. Alcoholic employees are not as productive as other employees. In fact, the National Council on Alcoholism reports that alcoholic employees are absent 3 times as often as the average employee, are involved in 2 to 4 times as many on-the-job accidents, and make sickness and accident benefit claims that are 3 times greater than those of the average employee.[11] Overall, the losses caused by alcoholism are equal to approximately 3 percent of a company's total payroll, in addition to increased health insurance premiums, higher workers' compensation payments, and greater turnover and lower morale among the employees.

Understanding employer liability

In addition to the above losses, the organization runs a legal risk because it is responsible for the acts that employees commit while engaged in company business.

For example, Joe and other members of the work unit have broken early in order to have a small Christmas party in the supervisor's office. After a few hours of social drinking, everyone is ready to go home for the holidays. However, there is one job that still has to be done. A crate of boxes must be moved from one end of the plant to the other. Joe agrees to load the boxes on the forklift truck and drive it to the other end of the plant. While doing so he turns a corner and accidentally runs down two workers from another unit. Is the company responsible for Joe's mistake? Yes, because the supervisor should have known that Joe was drunk and unable to perform the job safely. The supervisor did not use reasonable care in assigning the work.

One way to reduce company liability is to have a rule that prohibits intoxication on the job. In this way, if someone does operate machinery while under the influence and is responsible for an accident, the company can limit its liability by noting that the worker was operating outside the scope of his or her authority. To do this, recommends one lawyer, the company should follow these steps:[12]

1. Publicize the rule.
2. Hire people who will follow it.
3. Assign work with it in mind.
4. Stay informed as to violations.
5. Communicate to the employees that the rule is important and will be enforced.
6. Offer assistance to potential violators.
7. Enforce the rule quickly and uniformly.
8. If a violation occurs, do the following:
   a. *Immediately,* on the spot, suspend the "employee" status of the violator.
   b. *Order* the violator off the premises or to report to the medical department.
   c. *Later,* when he or she is no longer intoxicated, the temporary suspension can be removed and whatever steps deemed necessary can be taken.

Signs of alcoholism

An employee who reports for work in an alcoholic state for the first time in her 15-year career or the worker who has too much to drink at the annual Christmas party are minor problems for the supervisor. These people are intoxicated, but they are not habitual drinkers. The supervisor's biggest challenge is dealing with employees who are alcoholics. These people cannot get through the day without having a drink. Sometimes this is a result of problems at home. Other times it arises as part of the job, as in the case of a salesperson who entertains clients at lunch every day. In the latter case, the employee may slowly become more and more dependent on alcohol. Without realizing it, the individual has a few drinks with lunch and even more with dinner even on those days when clients are not being entertained.

Some supervisors do not realize that some of their people are alcoholics because they do not know what to look for. For example, when they go to lunch with the salesperson and alcohol is ordered, the manager sees this as a sign of a good socializer. "He certainly knows how to treat a customer," the supervisor will conclude. "We ought to get a real big order this time." In the case of those workers who do not entertain on the job, the supervisor will be unaware that they have a bottle on the premises or take long lunch hours during which they have a couple of drinks. It never occurs to the manager to check the individual's work performance after lunch to see how much is being done. The alcoholic often works hard in the morning in order to clear up much of the day's work and ensure that the afternoon is free from important matters. In this way, he or she is less likely to be identified as having a drinking problem. When the supervisor checks the total work output, this person is found to be doing as much as anyone else.

If the supervisor does think there is a drinking problem among some of the personnel, he or she often looks for the wrong signs. The individual concludes such things as: Men are more likely to be alcoholics than women, so I'll keep my eye on them; blue-collar types tend to be bigger drinkers than white-collar types, so they'll get the bulk of my attention; less educated people tend to be bigger drinkers than better-educated people, so I'll monitor them more closely. These conclusions may be true for the supervisor's own work group, but in the main they are not accurate descriptions of problem alcoholics. Some of the characteristics of these people include:[13]

- 50 percent of alcoholics are women.
- 25 percent are white-collar workers, such as secretaries, bookkeepers, and other office workers.
- 30 percent are blue-collar workers, normally in the more skilled crafts, such as machinists and electricians.
- 45 percent are professional or managerial personnel.
- 13 percent have completed less than a grammar school education.
- 37 percent are high school graduates and 50 percent have completed or attended college.

It is dangerous to generalize about who in the work unit is drinking too much. For this reason, the supervisor should best focus on observable behavior patterns. Table 12-4 provides a description of some of these. Notice that alcoholics go through a series of stages during which absenteeism, general behavior, and job performance all change. As things get worse, the supervisor needs to be alert to these changes and be prepared to take corrective action. The first area on which the manager needs to focus his or her attention is absenteeism. Quite often alcoholics begin coming to work late on Monday or missing altogether. A weekend of hard drinking has taken its toll. Soon thereafter, work-related problems begin to manifest themselves. As the worker moves from the early to the terminal stage of alcoholism, these telltale signs become progressively worse and easier to spot. The effective supervisor picks them up early and begins to do something about the situation. In doing so, however, the individual must be aware of the role that he or she should play in this process. Most supervisors are not guidance counselors or psychologists, so their function is limited. Nevertheless, the supervisor's role is an important one.

The supervisor's role

In the case of alcoholic employees, the primary responsibility of the supervisor is to work effectively with the individual. In doing so, there are a number of things that supervisors should do, including pointing out the importance of getting professional help. Five of the major steps the manager should follow include:

Table 12-4. Observable behavior patterns among alcoholic employees

Stage	Absenteeism	General behavior	Job performance
	Alcohol addiction time		
I. Early	Tardiness Quits early Absence from work situations ("I drink to relieve tension")	Complaints from fellow employees for not doing his or her share Overreaction Complaints of not "feeling well" Makes untrue statements	Misses deadlines Commits errors (frequently) Lower job efficiency Criticism from the boss
II. Middle	Frequent days off for vague or implausible reasons ("I feel guilty about sneaking drinks"; "I have tremors")	Marked changes Undependable statements Avoids fellow employees Borrows money from fellow employees Exaggerates work accomplishments Frequent hospitalization Minor injuries on the job (repeatedly)	General deterioration Cannot concentrate Occasional lapse of memory Warning from boss
III. Late middle	Frequent days off; several days at a time Does not return from lunch ("I don't feel like eating"; "I don't want to talk about it"; "I like to drink alone")	Aggressive and belligerent behavior Domestic problems interfere with work Financial difficulties (garnishments, etc.) More frequent hospitalization Resignation: does not want to discuss problems Problems with the laws in the community	Far below expectation Punitive disciplinary action
IV. Approaching terminal stage	Prolonged unpredictable absences ("My job interferes with my drinking")	Drinking on the job (probably) Completely undependable Repeated hospitalization Serious financial problems Serious family problems: divorce	Uneven Generally incompetent Faces termination or hospitalization

Source: Gopal C. Pati and John I. Adkins, Jr., "The Employer's Role in Alcoholism Assistance," © July 1983. Reprinted by permission of *Personnel Journal*, Costa Mesa, Calif.; all rights reserved.

1. Make it clear that if job performance does not improve, the worker may be terminated.
2. Point out that programs are available to people who want to resolve personal problems. (If there is internal assistance, be sure to tell the worker about this.)
3. Make it clear that the employee is the one who must decide whether or not to accept the assistance.
4. Emphasize the positive aspects of the program.

5. Remember that alcoholism is a progressive disease that never gets better without treatment. Professional help is needed.

(The above alluded to the fact that sometimes the organization will have an in-house program or use an outside referral group in counseling alcoholic employees. When this is done, it is commonly handled through an employee assistance program.) Other useful steps are presented in Supervision in Action: Useful Supervisory Guidelines.

SUPERVISION IN ACTION: USEFUL SUPERVISORY GUIDELINES

How should the alcoholic be supervised? While there are many things the supervisor should do, the following nine guidelines have been found to be particularly helpful:

1. Be alert to changes in work performance and unusual behavior of all employees under your supervision.
2. Document all specific instances in which an employee's work performance or compliance with the rules falls below standard.
3. Before taking corrective action, conduct an interview with the employee. The primary purpose of the interview should be to gather factual data.
4. Question the employee about deteriorating job performance and/or rule violations, reviewing all your documentation of the case with him. The interview may be an opportunity to show the employee how much he has lost in wages because of his problem. You may also decide that this is a good time to tell the employee about the organization's substance-abuse or employee assistance program. Notify the employee that his job performance must improve immediately and that the required level of performance must be maintained.
5. Continue documenting job performance and rule violations if the deficient performance continues. Do not let poor performance or violations snowball. Additional interviews should be conducted and disciplinary action taken when management can prove guilt unless there are mitigating circumstances. Whether the action taken involves formal disciplinary penalties or informal coaching and counseling, you should remind the employee of the organization's employee assistance procedure and offer to make it available to the employee on a strictly confidential basis. Legal experts believe that it is wise, even in discharge cases, to offer assistance programs to substance abusers so as to protect the organization from possible legal liability in the future.
6. If the employee has been admitted to the program but continues to be intoxicated or to "trip out" at work, normal organizational procedures should be followed. The employee should not be excused, nor should the infraction be soft-pedaled, because "Jim is on the program." Disciplinary action, however, should be corrective—not punitive—insofar as your intent is concerned.

7. If the substance abuser is showing noticeable improvement as a result of your coaching, counseling, and cautioning, or perhaps as the result of some other factor that you are (or are not) aware of, every effort should be made to take note of the improvement, to recognize it, and to encourage the employee. But be careful. This can be overdone. Use positive reinforcement with care and judgment. The key is to be supportive, not punitive or harsh, toward an employee who is obviously trying to improve his performance.

8. There are times when you may become privy to confidential information about an employee, which should never be revealed to anyone. When pressed for confidential information by higher supervision, it should be enough to report that the employee was counseled; the date, time, and place of the interview; and pertinent information about job performance. Do not reveal the fact that the employee may have confided in you about personal, marital, financial, legal, sexual, or personality problems. To do so creates a serious situation for you when the information "leaks," as it often does. Also, a breach of confidence may make a professional liable for legal action involving invasion of privacy, defamation, and related tort actions. If the court regards you as a professional, you would be in the same position as a counselor, doctor, social worker, or lawyer who has breached a confidence.

9. Many organizations have supervisors who dispense aspirins, bandages, cough medicines, and so forth to employees. If you are authorized to do so, you may want to review the departmental medicine chest to make sure none of its wares contains chemicals that could trigger a dormant substance-abuse habit. A few drops of certain cough medicines and sleeping potions have been known to cause recovering alcoholics with many years of sobriety to go on a binge, and in some instances the binge has lasted for the remainder of the alcoholic's shortened life. One alcoholic described himself as a person who didn't need a drink until he had one. Recovering substance abusers also report that their recovery is jeopardized by tranquilizers such as Valium, Librium, and Thorazine, as well as by such painkillers as codeine. The supervisor who dispenses medication without being authorized is reminded of the aphorism: "Fools rush in where angels fear to tread." Giving medicine containing a few drops of alcohol to an alcoholic may trigger violent physical trauma or even death if he is using Antabuse as a part of the recovery process.

Source: Joseph J. Walker, "Supervising the Alcoholic," *Supervisory Management,* November 1978, pp. 30–31.

At the same time, the supervisor must be aware of some things that should not be done. These include:[14]

1. Do not be misled by sympathy-evoking tactics; alcoholics are experts at doing this.

2. Do not discuss the worker's problem with anyone except the personnel assigned to the program or those in direct line of authority above you.
3. Do not try to diagnose the problem; stick to observing the behavior.
4. Do not discuss drinking unless it occurs on the job or the employee reports to work intoxicated.
5. Do not moralize; restrict all comments to job performance or attendance.

EMPLOYEE ASSISTANCE PROGRAMS

Employee assistance programs (EAPs) are designed to help employees deal with alcohol and other substance-abuse problems, such as drugs. Recent research reveals that the cost of personal problems in terms of absenteeism, poor workmanship, lost productivity, and related factors is now running over $10 billion annually.

Today there are over 2000 EAPs nationwide. The pattern used in setting up these plans is typically the following:[15]

1. The company issues a policy statement indicating that it is supportive of the program. The statement also points out that employees sometimes need this type of personal assistance because of factors beyond their control and that the assistance is available to them.
2. If there is a union in the organization, the group's support is secured and it is afforded representation on the committee that is overseeing the establishment of the EAP.
3. Qualified counselors and other skilled personnel are brought in to help in diagnosing and referring people for professional assistance.
4. A comprehensive insurance benefit package covering this assistance is provided to all of the employees.
5. A comprehensive approach to evaluating the effectiveness and impact of the EAP is developed.

EAP benefits

Many firms have reported success with their EAPs. For example, at Gates Rubber absenteeism during the first year of the program was dramatically reduced from 11,174 hours to 4106 hours resulting in a cost savings of $56,000. At the same time, medical visits to the company clinic fell by 43 percent. The company estimated that it saved $3 for every $1 spent on the EAP. Over the first 6 years of the program, Gates reduced absenteeism by 300 percent, medical visits to the company clinic by over 200 percent, and employee terminations by 1000 percent.[16]

At Kennecott Copper, after 13 months the firm found that its attendance rate had improved by 5.2 percent and that its hospital, medical, and surgical costs had gone down by 55.4 percent.[17] At Control Data a researcher predicted that the program would save the firm $3.5 million annually.[18] Many other well-known firms have also reported success with EAPs, including Hughes Aircraft, Employers Insurance Company of Wausau, and Illinois Bell Telephone, to name but three.[19]

The supervisor's role

The supervisor's role is one of identifying the alcoholic employee and then getting the individual to accept treatment. Once there are signs that the employee is having alcohol problems, the supervisor should talk to the person. The basis for the discussion should always be work performance. If a salesperson has a drink while entertaining a client at lunch and still manages to turn in superior performance, the supervisor has no job-related basis on which to speak to the individual. The first-line manager may feel that drinking at lunch is not a good habit, but there is no bottom-line reason for insisting that the individual stop. The supervisor should get involved only when employee performance declines.

When this happens, the supervisor should call in the employee for a talk, discuss the deteriorating job performance, and get the individual to confront the problem. If the worker says, "You're right, I'm drinking too much and it's beginning to affect my work, and I've got to do something about this," then the supervisor can suggest that the employee take advantage of the company's employee assistance program (see Figure 12-2). If the employee does not recognize the problem, the supervisor should let things continue. Job performance is bound to deteriorate further, and when it does, the supervisor can then call in the individual again and this time give a warning as well as suggest professional help. The supervisor must remember that because he or she is not a skilled counselor, no advice or suggestions should be given regarding how to combat this drinking problem. This is not the supervisor's job. However, the supervisor should document the discussions that take place with the employee, should it be necessary to terminate the worker, and this should be done if performance does not turn around in the near future.

On the other hand, if the employee does feel that he or she needs assistance, the supervisor should refer the individual to the in-house person who coordinates the program. Sometimes supervisors have this person sit in on the initial meeting so that if the worker admits that drinking might be a problem, the coordinator can explain to the individual the benefits of the EAP. Once this happens, the supervisor leaves the room and allows the two to talk privately.

If an individual does join an EAP and work performance goes up, the problem is resolved and the company does not put a record of this in the individual's personnel file. It is a closed chapter as far as the organization is concerned. This policy is extremely important in getting people to face up to drinking problems. Many workers are afraid of admitting a problem for fear the organization will never forget it. In 10 years they will be in line for a promotion and someone will open their file, read it, and say: "This person had a drinking problem 10 years ago. I wonder if this is still a problem? In

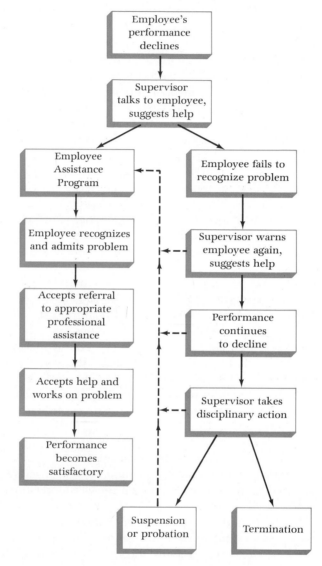

any event, why take a chance? Let's move on to the next candidate and get someone whose past record indicates a more stable personality." Successful EAPs are designed to help the employee, not to be punitive in nature. The supervisor must use them in the spirit in which they have been created.

THE TROUBLED SALESPERSON: STARTING CASE REVISITED

Terry quite obviously has a drinking problem. Pete failed to pick it up because he believed that Terry's work performance decline was a result of his son's heart condition. Obviously, Terry told him that story in order to cover up the fact that he was drinking too much and his sales performance was taking a nosedive. The first lesson for Pete is that alcoholics always have a story to cover up what they are doing. They either seek sympathy or make up a story that wins over the other person. How could Pete call Terry into the office and tell him his sales were dropping dramatically when the man had such a burden to carry at home?

The second lesson for Pete is not to get involved in the personal matters of the employees. If people have personal problems that are affecting their work, they need to seek professional counseling.

The third lesson is that if work performance begins to decline, the supervisor should objectively check the facts. Pete should have looked at Terry's observable behavior patterns and then checked with clients to find out why Terry was not getting their repeat business. There might be some reason to explain the turndown other than Terry's personal problem. However, if one or two of the clients had said that Terry missed meetings with them, made them promises he could not deliver, or embarrassed them by coming to the meeting drunk or drinking too much during the meeting, Pete would have begun to get conflicting signals and could have checked into the matter more closely.

Pete cannot save this one, but in the future he can use these lessons to guide him in dealing with alcoholic employees.

INTERPRETATION OF SELF-ASSESSMENT QUIZ 12-1: HOW MUCH DO YOU KNOW ABOUT WORKER SAFETY AND HEALTH?

1. False. There are not enough government inspectors to check every one of these businesses. Instead, the focus of attention is placed on the most flagrant and frequent violators.
2. True. This is required by OSHA guidelines.
3. False. This was the original goal of OSHA, but it has had to settle for the elimination of "significant" risks.
4. True.
5. True. In fact, it runs over $14 billion annually.
6. True.
7. False. It is just the opposite. Smokers have a higher absenteeism rate.
8. True. In fact, many of them do.
9. False. Nonsmokers have higher productivity because they waste less time in the smoking ritual.
10. True. It is close to $6500 today.

11. False. They discourage it because of the expenses associated with smoking.

12. True. Alcoholics have more absentee days than the average worker.

13. False. There is no empirical data to support this. In fact, it is likely that they do less work.

14. False. The supervisor is not a trained counselor. He or she should send the worker to someone who is professionally able to do this.

15. False. It is just the opposite. EAPs are growing in popularity because of their effectiveness in promoting worker safety and health.

SUMMARY OF KEY POINTS

1. Every organization is required to provide its people with safe and healthful working conditions. One of the ways this is done is through the Occupational Safety and Health Act, a comprehensive piece of legislation that calls for safety and health hazard inspections of organizations. A second is through workers' compensation programs. All states require employers to have these programs.

2. Accident prevention is one of the supervisor's main responsibilities. Many firms attempt to reduce accidents by formulating and distributing lists of rules and procedures that should be followed in the workplace. The supervisor's job is to see that these rules are followed. This involves being aware of why accidents occur, how much they cost the organization, and how proper supervision can minimize or eliminate them.

3. Smoking is a costly habit. It leads to increased absenteeism, medical care, early mortality, higher health insurance premiums, lost on-the-job time, and higher maintenance costs. If there is a no-smoking rule, the supervisor should strictly enforce it; if there is no such rule, the individual should encourage the people in the unit not to smoke and should try to follow this same advice.

4. Alcoholism is a major problem in many organizations. It affects people at all levels of the hierarchy and increases operating costs through absenteeism, higher life and health insurance rates, reduced work quantity, and diminished work quality. The supervisor should be aware of the observable behavior patterns that accompany alcoholism and take action as soon as it is obvious that such a problem exists. In particular, the supervisor should remember that the organization is responsible for the acts of employees who are intoxicated while on company business.

5. Employee assistance programs (EAPs) are designed to help employees deal with alcohol and other substance-abuse problems such as drugs. If the supervisor finds that one of the employees is becoming addicted to alcohol and this is affecting the individual's work performance, the supervisor should talk to the individual about getting help. This is where EAPs come in. They are proving to be extremely effective in helping businesses deal with such problems and overcome the accompanying absenteeism, poor workmanship, lost productivity, and other telltale signs of alcoholism.

BUILD YOUR SUPERVISORY WORD POWER

These key employee safety and health terms are presented in their order of appearance in the chapter. Effective supervisors have a working knowledge of them.

Occupational Safety and Health Act. A comprehensive piece of legislation that calls for safety and health hazard inspections of organizations and investigations of all serious accidents and allegations of hazards.

Incidence-rate formula. A formula used for determining job-related illnesses and injuries.

Frequency-rate formula. A formula used for determining the number of injuries and illnesses per million hours worked.

Workers' compensation programs. Programs that provide financial awards to those unable to work because of physical injury or mental anxiety, depression, or disorder.

Employee assistance programs. Programs designed to help employees deal with alcohol and other substance-abuse problems such as drugs.

REVIEW YOUR UNDERSTANDING

1. What do supervisors need to know regarding OSHA requirements related to inspection, record keeping, and the establishment of standards? Explain.
2. In examining job-related illnesses and injuries, how are the incidence rate and frequency rate computed? What does each of these statistics mean?
3. Of what value are workers' compensation programs to the area of employee safety and health? Explain.
4. What are some of the most common general safety rules? Identify five.
5. What is the supervisor's responsibility for job safety? Identify and describe all six things the individual should do.
6. How does smoking increase the cost of doing business? Cite at least three examples.
7. What is the supervisor's role in dealing with smoking in the workplace? Be complete in your answer.
8. In what way does alcohol affect productivity? Explain.
9. Do organizations have any responsibility for injuries caused by the personnel if the latter are under the influence of alcohol? Defend your answer.
10. How can a supervisor know if one of the workers in the unit is having a drinking problem? In your answer, cite some examples.
11. How should the supervisor deal with employees who have drinking problems? Set forth your recommendations, inluding what the manager should not do.
12. Of what value are employee assistance programs to an organization? What should the supervisor know about them? Explain.

SUPPLEMENT YOUR KNOWLEDGE

In addition to the references listed at the end of this chapter, the following provide important, practical information that is of use to supervisors in ensuring the safety and health of their personnel

Milbourne, Gene, Jr.: "Alcohol and Drugs: Poor Remedies for Stress," *Supervisory Management*, March 1981, pp. 35–42.

Phillips, Donald A., and Harry J. Older: "Alcoholic Employees Beget Troubled Supervisors," *Supervisory Management*, September 1981, pp. 2–9.

Walker, Joseph J.: "Supervising the Alcoholic," *Supervisory Management*, November 1978, pp. 26–32.

Weis, William L.: "Profits Up in Smoke," *Personnel Journal*, March 1981, pp. 162–163.

Zepke, Brent E.: "Employer Liability for Intoxicated Employees," *Supervisory Management*, July 1977, pp. 32–39.

YOU BE THE SUPERVISOR: THE SAFETY INSPECTION

There was an inspection of the Grandling Manufacturing firm last week by an OSHA inspector. The inspector spent over 3 hours walking around, looking at the facilities, talking to the employees, and reading the accident reports that had been filed by the company. When it was over, the inspector asked to talk to the senior foreman. Before this meeting could be held, however, the president of the firm learned that the inspector was on site and came down to meet him. "Hi, I'm Roger Grandling," he told the inspector. "I can't say that I'm delighted to see you, but I know that the job you do is important, and if there's anything that's wrong with the facilities, you can bet that we're going to get them fixed up." The inspector did not reply directly to this statement, preferring to wait until the senior foreman showed up.

The two men then began a tour of the facilities. The president tagged along because he wanted to hear what the inspector had to say. Within 15 minutes, the president was glad he had done so. The inspector had found a great number of problems in the plant. One of the first things he pointed out was that two of the five fire exits were blocked with boxes containing steel castings. "There is supposed to be easy access to all fire exits. Those boxes not only block the exits but they cannot be shoved aside by one or two people because they are too heavy. If there were a fire in this area, anyone caught in this section would be injured or killed."

Another problem the inspector found was that materials were stored in racks above the machinery and, even as he pointed this out, some of the workers were climbing on top of the machines to bring down material. "These machines are not built to be stood on. Their surfaces are polished, and it would be quite easy for someone to slip off them and injure himself. You should either store the materials in a more accessible place or put in ladders so that the workers can safely reach the materials. Also, look at the shoes that everyone is wearing. They are not safety shoes; they are everyday walking shoes. It's extremely dangerous to climb anywhere with them."

As they continued walking around, their conversation was interrupted by one of the workers who was shouting to another. The first person was standing on a platform about 25 feet above the ground floor. "Hey, Chuck, catch this," he yelled. With that, the worker dropped a wrench to his friend below. Chuck kept his eye on it and as it neared him, he stepped to the side and made a backward sweeping catch. The inspector walked over to Chuck and asked him why his friend had thrown down a wrench. "Oh, I need it to make an adjustment on this machine, and if he throws it down it'll save time. We do this all the time. The worst that can happen is that I miss it and it hits the floor, but it usually doesn't damage the wrench. These things are plenty strong." The inspector did not say anything. He just looked at the foreman and the president and then continued walking around the plant talking to them.

Later, when the three men were back in the foreman's office, the inspector repeated all of the safety and health violations he had found. "I'm going to write these up and you have 30 days in which to correct them. Then I'll be back to see that they've been taken care of." Both men assured him that all of the violations would be handled. After he left, the president said: "I can't believe all of the things we've been doing wrong. Look, I want you to hire a new supervisor who knows a lot about worker safety. Have the individual take over group 5, to replace Andy, who is retiring this week, and at the same time give us recommendations regarding how we can prevent problems in the future." The foreman agreed that this was a good idea.

1. If you were the new foreman, what is the first thing you would do? Explain your answer.
2. If you put together a list of safety rules, what would these entail? Identify and describe five of the rules you would have on that list.
3. What are some of the things you would attempt to teach the other supervisors so that they, too, could become more safety conscious? Be complete in your answer.

YOU BE THE SUPERVISOR: THE COSTS OF SMOKING

Until a few years ago, a large west-coast-based insurance company had rented its facilities. However, the chairman of the board felt that a company of this stature should have its own building and made such a proposal to the board. In defending the action, the president brought up many arguments, including: "We'll be able to reduce our rent and maintenance costs. The person who owns the building passes the expenses along to the renters. By building our own, we'll be able to sidestep some of these expenses." The board listened carefully and agreed. The building was completed 8 months ago.

During the last monthly meeting one of the members of the board noticed that there was an expenditure of $27,500 for maintenance. "This seems pretty high," he noted. "What is this for?" The president did not know, so he put the question to the vice president of finance. The latter also professed a lack of information but said that he would have an answer within 2 days and send a memo on it to every member of the board.

After checking with the maintenance department, the vice president sent the following memo to the president and other board members:

> The $27,500 expenditure for maintenance was a result of three different costs: (1) $7600 to repaint major parts of the building that are now beginning to fade or turn gray; (2) $13,800 for new furnishings, including area carpeting, that have been damaged by cigarette burns (these areas are those often used by clients and it was felt that they should be kept in top shape at all times); and (3) $6100 for general maintenance above the normal contract price (in particular, all of the interior windows throughout the building are having to be cleaned twice as often as had been planned for in the budget).

After the president read the memo, he called in the vice president and asked why these expenditures were suddenly showing up. "We didn't have them in the last building, did we?" he asked. The vice president explained that the company did have them but that they were absorbed by the firm that owned the building. "That's one reason why we decided to leave that building. The rental company had put so much money into maintenance that it wanted to raise our rent 14 percent above the going rate. Now we have to pay those costs out of our own pocket. Most of them are a result of people smoking on the job. However, we've allowed them to smoke for years and I think it would be a little difficult to stop it now."

The president pondered what the vice president had said. "Will our smoking-related expenses continue at this level?" he asked.

"Worse than that," said the vice president, "they'll gradually go up because it'll cost more and more money to maintain the building as it gets older. However, I'm afraid that that's just a cost of doing business that we're going to have to absorb."

The president was not pleased to hear this. "I think we should ban smoking throughout the building," he said. "I don't care how angry it makes the personnel. This is ridiculous. I want you to form a group of supervisors to study the impact of smoking in their work areas and then report back to me with their findings. I want to know exactly how much this habit is costing us. Heaven knows, we give reduced insurance rates to nonsmokers. Why do we let our own people smoke?" The vice president said that he would start putting together the group of supervisors within a week.

1. Assume that you are a supervisor who has been chosen to be in this group. In addition to property damage, what other costs would you find associated with smoking? Explain.
2. How would you get data to prove your answers to the above question? How could the personnel department be helpful to you? Explain.
3. Is the president's argument against smoking a good one from a dollar-and-cents standpoint? Defend your answer.

NOTES

1. "A Safety Committee Man's Guide," Aetna Life and Casualty Insurance Company, Catalog 872684.
2. Wayne F. Cascio, *Costing Human Resources: The Financial Impact of Behavior in Organizations*, Boston: Kent, 1982, p. 67.
3. Cascio, p. 68.
4. Cascio, p. 69.
5. Cascio, p. 69.
6. Cascio, p. 70.
7. *Wall Street Journal*, May 8, 1979, p. 1.
8. Cascio, p. 73.
9. William L. Weis, "Can You Afford to Hire Smokers?" *Personnel Administrator*, May 1981, p. 77.
10. Richard J. Tersine and James Hazeldine, "Alcoholism: A Productivity Hangover," *Business Horizons*, November–December 1982, p. 68.
11. Tersine and Hazeldine, p. 69.
12. Brent E. Zepke, "Employer Liability for Intoxicated Employees," pt. 2, *Supervisory Management*, November 1977, p. 40.
13. Gopal C. Pati and John I. Adkins, Jr., "The Employer's Role in Alcoholism Assistance," *Personnel Journal*, July 1983, p. 568.
14. Pati and Adkins, p. 572.
15. Thomas N. McGaffey, "New Horizons in Organizational Stress Prevention Approaches," *Personnel Administrator*, November 1978, p. 28.
16. Edwin J. Busch, Jr., "Developing an Employee Assistance Program," *Personnel Journal*, September 1981, pp. 710–711.
17. Julian L. Carr and Robert T. Hellan, "Improving Corporate Performance Through Employee-Assistance Programs," *Business Horizons*, April 1980, p. 59.
18. David J. Reed, "One Approach to Employee Assistance," *Personnel Journal*, August 1983, p. 652.
19. Carr and Hellan, p. 58.

CHAPTER 13

DEALING WITH UNIONS, GRIEVANCES, AND DISCIPLINE

GOALS OF THE CHAPTER

Many organizations are unionized, and the labor-management agreement spells out the rights of both the workers and the managers. Today's supervisor must be aware of the impact of unions on organizations and how this affects the way things are done. The primary goal of this chapter is to examine and study how supervisors should conduct themselves in a unionized environment. This requires an understanding of the objectives of unions, a knowledge of the major labor laws affecting union-management relations, an understanding of how labor contracts are hammered out through the collective bargaining process, and a knowledge of the supervisor's role in dealing with the union. The second major goal is to review the discipline process and to set forth recommendations for effectively handling this challenge. When you have finished reading all the material in this chapter, you will be able to:

1. Discuss the growth of unions in the United States, including the reason for current membership trends.
2. Identify the major objectives of unions.
3. Describe the major laws that affect labor-management relations, including: the Railway Labor Act of 1926, the Norris-LaGuardia Act of 1932, the National Labor Relations Act of 1932, the Labor-Management Relations Act of 1947, the Labor-Management Reporting and Disclosure Act of 1959, and the Civil Service Reform Act of 1978.
4. Explain how collective bargaining works.
5. Discuss the supervisor's role in dealing with unions.
6. Compare and contrast mediation and arbitration.
7. Explain when discipline is required and what initial steps the supervisor should take.
8. Discuss the value of progressive discipline in ensuring employee conformity to organizational rules.

A STARTING CASE: THE AGGRESSIVE SUPERVISOR

The Eattle Corporation, an office supply firm, was founded in 1954. By purchasing in large quantities so as to obtain big purchase discounts, and selling at prices that allowed but razor-thin margins, Eattle began to dominate the competition. By the mid-1980s the firm had three major warehouses that supplied its nine-state sales region, and there were plans to expand into three more states during the next year.

Because of its large market share, Eattle had been the target of union activity since the late 1970s. Each year there had been an eelection, and each year the union effort had failed. Last year was the closest vote ever. Encouraged by the results, the union began to step up its latest effort. In turn, management began holding meetings with its own people in an effort to defeat the union movement. In particular, the company wanted to remind its managers that the best way to defeat union efforts was by showing that the firm was being fair, open, and honest in its dealings.

Jane Burke, a new supervisor at Eattle, listened carefully to the management spokesperson. The more she heard, the angrier she became over the union effort. "Why," she asked herself, "don't the workers realize that management has their best interests at heart? The union can't do anything for the workers that management isn't doing already."

Later that day Jane was talking to some of the workers in her unit. They were discussing the pros and cons of unionizing. It was obvious from the conversation that while some of the workers were in favor of unionizing, most were undecided. Jane decided to try to sway them toward management's position. She talked for about five minutes. Part of her talk went as follows:

> You know, management has been going out of its way to provide the best salaries and benefits in the industry. If you look at how much the company's profit was last year, you know that its return on investment is lower than most of the competition. If the union gets in, it's likely that the union will demand higher wages. This will mean that the company will have to cut back on the number of people and get everyone to do more work. It only makes sense. So the union may be able to get higher salaries, but only at the expense of jobs.

One of the workers chimed in and said that the union would not allow management to cut back the work force. However, Jane countered by noting that all of this would have to be worked out in the labor-management agreement and that the company would not give in to higher wages unless there was an accompanying cut in employment.

Later that day Jane had a call from her boss. "What are you talking to the workers about?" he asked. "Are you trying to talk them into voting against unionizing? Who authorized you to do this? Do you want us to wind up with an unfair labor practice lawsuit?" With that he hung up.

What did Jane do wrong? What does she need to know about the role of the supervisor during a union drive? Write down your answers and then put them aside. We will return to them later.

UNIONS IN THE UNITED STATES

Unions in the United States can be traced back hundreds of years. In 1778 journeyman printers in New York City banded together to demand a wage increase. In 1786 Philadelphia printers struck for a $6/week minimum wage. Many of these early unions, however, disbanded after attaining their demands.

National growth

In 1869 the Knights of Labor was founded. This was the beginning of permanent national unions. The Knights were very successful for a while and by 1886 the membership was over 700,000. However, internal difficulties led to the union's demise. In its place came the American Federation of Labor (AFL). Led by Samuel Gompers, it was a craft union made up of skilled workers such as carpenters, plumbers, and printers. By 1920 three-fourths of all organized workers were members of this union. In 1935 a union was formed within the AFL for industrial workers, who were ineligible for membership in a craft union. In 1938 the group, which had now called itself the Congress of Industrial Organizations (CIO), was expelled from the AFL because the latter felt the affiliation with an industrial union would threaten its status and security. In 1955, however, the two merged into today's AFL-CIO. Most large unions are affiliated with the AFL-CIO, although the Teamsters, with a membership close to 2 million, remains independent. Before continuing on, take Self-Assessment Quiz 13-1 and see how much you currently know about unions.

SELF-ASSESSMENT QUIZ 13-1:
WHAT DO YOU KNOW ABOUT UNIONS?

Carefully read each of the following and enter an *X* in the appropriate column—true or false. Answers are provided at the end of the chapter.

	True	*False*
1. Union membership over the last 20 years has declined by about 15 percent.	X	✓
2. In a union shop, all employees must be union members in order to be hired.		ı
3. Unions favor a spread-the-work policy.	✓	ı
4. Yellow-dog contracts, which are pledges not to join a union or attempt to form one, are outlawed by federal legislation.	ı	
5. It is illegal for management to take any action against an employee as a means of encouraging or discouraging union membership.	ı	
6. It is illegal for management to refuse to bargain collectively with those representatives chosen by the employees to represent them in drawing up a labor-management contract.	ı	

7. Certification elections, whereby the membership votes for union representation, cannot be held more than once a year. _____ _____

8. Once a union gets into an organization, there is no way for the members to vote it out. _____ _____

9. If the workers want to get rid of the union, they are allowed to form a joint committee with the management to work up a strategy to achieve their aims. _____ _____

10. While some unions are considered to be corrupt, the federal government has maintained that it has no authority to interfere in the internal workings of these unions and has refused to pass legislation to this effect. _____ _____

11. Shop stewards are members of the regular work force who are chosen by coworkers to serve as their on-site union representative. _____ _____

12. Workers who feel that they have been unfairly treated by the company, which has in their view violated the labor-management agreement, can file a grievance to this effect. _____ _____

13. Mediators can make recommendations that are binding on both the union and the management. _____ _____

14. Arbitration is often used to help solve union-management impasses. _____ _____

15. In fact, there is no difference between mediation and arbitration. _____ _____

Membership trends

Over the last 20 years union membership has grown more slowly than the work force. In 1970 the percentage of unionized nonagricultural workers was 22.3; in 1980 this percentage had declined to 20.8. On the other hand, union membership continued to increase from approximately 21 million in 1970 to 23 million in 1980. Much of this growth has been accounted for by union success among white-collar workers such as teachers and office personnel.

Two major reasons explain the slow growth of unions during the last decade. One is the decline in employment in industries that typically have been heavily unionized. A second is the failure of the unions to make headway in growth industries like computers and high technology. In fact, over the last two decades, union attempts to organize workers have been losing ground steadily. Table 13-1 illustrates this downward slide.

Objectives

While unions have many objectives, most of them are directed toward guaranteeing their members better economic conditions. The following are pursued by most unions:[1]

Table 13-1. The decline in union victories

Year	Number of persons eligible to vote	Number of persons becoming represented	Percentage of union victories
1960	483,964	286,048	58.6
1964	551,751	295,230	57.1
1968	566,164	292,053	57.2
1972	586,155	297,127	53.7
1976	475,404	173,385	48.2
1980	521,600	195,515	45.7

Source: Randall S. Schuler, *Personnel and Human Resource Management*, 2d ed., St. Paul, Minn.: West, 1984, p. 531.

Higher wages and shorter hours. These two objectives are intertwined. If the union can secure a 5 percent raise for the workers, the latter will make more money. If the union is unable to negotiate a salary increase but can get a reduction in the work week (for example, from 37 to 35 hours and management still needs everyone to work 37 hours), this will also benefit the employees economically since, in most cases, overtime is 1½ times the regular hourly rate of pay. Of course, if the union can negotiate a salary raise *and* a reduction in the regular work week, so much the better.

Guaranteed seniority rights. Most union contracts, especially in blue-collar organizations, guarantee seniority rights so that those who have held their jobs for the longest period of time are given certain privileges. For example, if there is a cutback, it is often done on a last-hired–first-laid-off basis; likewise, rehiring is done on a last-laid-off–first-rehired basis. In some contracts a worker who is laid off from one job is allowed to "bump" a person with less seniority on another job, provided that the first worker has had experience in doing the other person's job. For example, an expediter who used to be a quality control inspector can bump the latter to prevent being laid off. In turn, the control inspector may be able to bump someone else. The last-hired–first-laid-off approach guarantees that senior people get to keep their jobs.

Union security. Unions would like all workers to be members. However, not everyone wants to join. To counter this resistance, various types of shop agreements have been formulated and won through favorable legislation and collective bargaining. The specific type of union security will vary by state and company. The following examines some of the most common:

- The *union shop* is one in which all current employees must join as soon as the union is certified as the legitimate bargaining unit. All new workers have to join after a probationary period, usually 30 days. Union shops exist in many states, although they are outlawed in those which have *right-to-work* laws, which give employees the right to work with or without union membership.

- The *modified union shop* is one in which some employees can elect not to join that union. People who have been employed before a given date, part-time employees, and students participating in work-study programs are examples. However, all workers who are already members of the union at the time the modified-union-shop agreement goes into effect must remain as members or lose their jobs, but nonmembers can refuse to join.

- The *maintenance-of-membership shop* requires that all employees who voluntarily join a union must remain as members during the life of the labor agreement with the employer. However, sometimes there is an escape period during which those who wish to do so can drop their membership.

- In an *agency-shop* arrangement, employees who are not members of the union still have to pay union dues. The union argues that this is only fair since all of the workers are covered by the labor contract and benefit from the union's efforts. The agency shop has been held to be legal by the courts.

- The *open shop* is one in which membership is voluntary for all existing and new employees. Anyone who decides not to join the union is not required to pay union dues.

- The *closed shop* is one in which all employees must be members. When bringing in new employees, only union members are hired. The union shop is illegal, but it continues to exist, especially in the skilled-craft areas. If a construction company is hiring carpenters, a nonunion carpenter may apply for the job, but one with a union card will be hired. It may be illegal, but it is reality.

Job retention. Another major objective is job retention. The union wants to keep jobs so that it loses none of its members. One way is through the seniority system discussed above. A second is through the use of a *spread-the-work* policy. Under this agreement, the union gets the firm to agree that if things start to go badly for the firm, it will cut back the number of weekly work hours before laying anyone off. So instead of reducing the number of employees by 25 percent, the company will reduce the number of work hours by 25 percent.

In understanding how unions work, the supervisor needs a fundamental knowledge of these union objectives, including the various types of union security. The manager also needs to know the major laws that have shaped the growth and development of unions in this country.

MAJOR LABOR LEGISLATION

A number of laws have significantly influenced what unions can and cannot do. The following are some of the most important:

Railway Labor Act of 1926

While this act applied only to the railroad industry, portions of it were used to frame other labor legislation in the years after its passage. Three of the main things this act did were: (1) It required employers to bargain collectively with the employees, (2) established procedures for settling labor-management disputes, and (3) outlawed the *yellow-dog contract*, which was a written pledge not to join a union or attempt to form one.

Norris-LaGuardia Act of 1932

This act outlawed the use of yellow-dog contracts in all industries. It also prohibited employers, except in specific instances, from using court injunctions to prevent work stoppages. Many people believe that this law guaranteed the survival of unions.

National Labor Relations Act of 1935

This act, often known as the *Wagner Act*, was designed to help workers organize into unions that were free from employer domination. It also required companies to recognize those unions which were duly chosen by the members as their representatives. In achieving these goals, the act listed five unfair labor practices in which employers were forbidden to engage:

1. Interfering with or restraining employees involved either in self-organizing activities or collective bargaining with the firm.
2. Dominating or interfering in the formation or administration of any labor organization or contributing financially to its support.
3. Taking any action against employees as a means of encouraging or discouraging union membership.
4. Firing or taking action against employees because they filed or gave testimony under the act.
5. Refusing to bargain collectively with those representatives chosen by the employees.

The act also set up a National Labor Relations Board (NLRB) consisting of three members (later expanded to five) affiliated with neither industry nor labor. The purposes of the board are (1) to decide unfair-labor-practice suits and render decisions that are consistent with the act and (2) to conduct elections among employees to determine if they will unionize and who will be their representative at the collective bargaining table.

Labor-Management Relations Act of 1947

Many people felt that the National Labor Relations Act went too far in its support of labor. In an effort to swing the pendulum back toward the center and give management many of the same rights that labor was accorded, the Labor-Management Relations Act of 1947 was passed. Often called the *Taft-Hartley Act*, this legislation was an amendment to the Wagner Act, and except as amended or repealed by Taft-Hartley, the Wagner Act remains in effect. Some of the specific provisions of Taft-Hartley include:

1. Employees are allowed to refrain from union activity as well as to engage in it (as long as this is in accord with the labor-management contract).
2. The closed shop is outlawed.
3. There must be written authorization from employees before union dues can be deducted from their paychecks.
4. Unions composed of supervisors do not need to be recognized.
5. Employers have the right to file charges against unfair labor practices such as coercing workers to join unions, refusing to bargain in good faith, engaging in featherbedding activities, and coercing employers to discriminate against those who will not join the union.
6. Unions cannot charge excessive or discriminatory fees to their members.
7. Certification elections, whereby the membership votes for union representation, cannot be held more than once a year.
8. Employees have the right to initiate decertification elections, whereby they can get rid of the union.

Labor-Management Reporting and Disclosure Act of 1959

In 1959 the Labor-Management Reporting and Disclosure Act, often known as the Landrum-Griffin Act, was enacted. The purpose of the act is to regulate internal union affairs. In particular, it provides for equality of rights for union members in nominating and voting in elections; controls increases in union dues; controls the suspension and fining of union members; requires that there be elections every 3 years for local offices and every 5 years for national or international offices; defines the type of person who can hold union office; and requires the filing of annual reports with the Secretary of Labor. The act is designed to protect employees from corrupt or discriminatory labor unions.

Federal employee regulations

The above laws were enacted to govern labor relations in the private sector. For example, the Wagner Act specifically excluded the U.S. government, government corporations, states, and municipal corporations in its definition of the word *employer*. For a long time government employees lacked the legislative protection that was afforded private-sector workers. Rather, federal employee labor relations were controlled by presidential executive orders. More recently, however, a civil service reform act has been passed.

Executive orders. The first set of regulations for federal employee labor relations was introduced by President John F. Kennedy in 1962. This order prohibited federal agencies from interfering with employee organizing and provided for recognition of employee organizations, but the act was limited in the amount of authority it gave to the employees. For example, employee organizations were denied the right to strike; and economic issues were not part of the bargaining process, because these were fixed by the civil service classification system. Agency heads were made the ultimate authority on grievances, and managers were excluded from the bargaining units. This order did not give the employees a great deal when compared with their counterparts in the private sector. However, it was a beginning. In 1970, 1971, and 1975 additional executive orders were issued. From these the Federal Labor Relations Council was created. It is authorized to hear appeals from the decisions of agency heads. The Federal Service Impasses Panel was also established; it is responsible for acting on negotiation impasses.

Civil Service Reform Act. In 1978 the Federal Service Labor-Management Relations Statute was passed as Title VII of the Civil Service Reform Act. This act has been called the most significant change in federal personnel administration since the passage of the Civil Service Act of 1883. Some of the most significant changes brought about by this act include:

1. A Federal Labor Relations Authority (FLRA), modeled after the NLRB, was created as an independent, neutral, full-time, bipartisan agency to remedy unfair labor practices within the government.
2. Anyone who feels that he or she has been the target of an unfair labor practice can seek judicial review by the FLRA.
3. Negotiated grievance procedures, which must be included in all agreements, have to provide for arbitration as the final step.

State and local regulations

State and local employee regulations vary. Collective bargaining is permitted in most states and covers wages, hours, and other terms and conditions of employment. However, the rights and privileges of these public-sector labor organizations are not as extensive as those in the private sector; for example, management still exercises a great deal of authority over employees such as police, fire fighters, and teachers. Nevertheless, even in these areas the supervisor must be familiar with the rights of the employees. Two of the most important things the supervisor must know are how collective bargaining works and how grievances are resolved, as discussed in the following sections.

HOW COLLECTIVE BARGAINING WORKS

Collective bargaining is the process in which the union and management come together and negotiate a labor contract. When the contract runs out, the two then work out the terms for a new one. In the process, each side attempts to win its way with the other.

The bargaining process

In the bargaining process, each side typically has three identifiable positions.[2] For the union, the first position is called the *initial demand point*, which represents more than what it believes it will get. The second is the *target point*, which is its realistic assessment of what it can get. The third is the *resistance point*, which is the least it will accept. In the case of hourly salaries for clerical help, for example, the union's initial demand point may be $6.00, its target point may be $5.75, and its resistance point may be $5.50.

Management also has three identifiable positions. One is its *initial offer*, which is the amount that it first offers. The second is its *target point*, which is where it would like to reach an agreement. The third is its *resistance point*, above which it will not go. For management, assume that these three points are $5.35, $5.55, and $5.80, respectively.

The three points for each side can be brought together as in Figure 13-1. Notice that the two resistance points create what is called a settlement range. The union will not go below this point, and management will not go above it. The settlement range is between $5.50 and $5.80, respectively, and it is likely that the two parties will agree on a salary rate within this 30-cent spread.

Issues for negotiation

This above approach is a typical one in negotiating wages. However, in large firms there is more to the process than simply haggling over rates for various jobs. Often there are negotiating committees and predetermined strategies that are thought out well in advance of the formal negotiations. Each side goes to the bargaining table with a basic idea of how it stands on issues such as pensions, paid vacation, paid holidays, sick leave, health and life insurance, dismissal or severance pay, supplemental unemployment

Figure 13-1. Negotiating a salary rate.

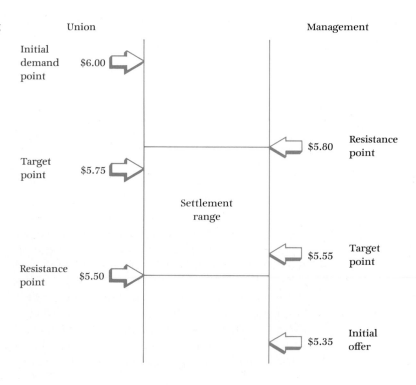

benefits, job security, seniority, safety and health, discharge and discipline, production standards, and grievance procedures. In small firms the process is often a much simpler one since there is less to negotiate. However, the process itself is similar. When all is said and done, a labor contract is hammered out.

THE SUPERVISOR AND THE UNION

The supervisor needs to understand the laws that affect the labor contract. The individual also needs to know how a contract is arrived at in the first place and what the company has agreed to do and not do. However, the essence of the supervisor's job is to work with management in ensuring that the letter and spirit of the contract are carried out. Some supervisors believe that this means discouraging union activity, trying to talk employees into voting against unionization, or using coercion and close control to monitor the activities of those associated with the union. All of this is nonsense. Effective supervisors work within the law. Supervision in Action: Supervisors and Union Organizing sets forth some of the things that first-line managers cannot do and can do.

SUPERVISION IN ACTION: SUPERVISORS AND UNION ORGANIZING

Supervisors need to understand what they can and cannot do about union organizing. There are types of conduct that are totally improper; there are actions that are completely within the law. The following looks at both.

Improper conduct
The following are examples of improper conduct whether expressed directly or implied:

Threats. Supervisors must not threaten employees with discharge or disciplinary action if they engage in union activities during nonworking time or if they should choose a union. Likewise, employees must not be threatened with loss of wages or benefits, changes in site practices, reduced operations or plant shutdown, or other penalties for participating in union activity or electing to be represented by a union.

Interrogation. Supervisors may not probe employees about their union activities, what they think about unions, whether or not they have signed an authorization card or attended a union meeting, or how they intend to vote. (However, supervisors may listen to and discuss any information about union activities that employees freely volunteer.)

Promises. Supervisors must not promise better wages, benefits, working conditions, promotions, or other rewards for rejecting a union or supporting no-union activities.

Surveillance. Watching employees participating in off-site union activities (such as union meetings or other gatherings) or giving the impression that union activities are being watched is prohibited.

Coercion. Supervisors may not call employees into their offices to talk about unions as this may be considered coercive or intimidating. Discussions should be held at the employees' work station or in the cafeteria or some other neutral area. (However, supervisors may answer questions and discuss unions if the subject is raised by employees during office meetings.)

Discrimination. Any discipline or other unfavorable treatment of employees because of their legal union activities, or any reward or other favorable treatment of employees because of their no-union activities, is prohibited.

A convenient method for avoiding violations of employees' Section 7 NLRA rights is to remember the catchword "TIPS," which stands for:

> Threats
> Interrogation
> Promises
> Surveillance

By stopping to consider if his or her statements or actions are any of these TIPS, a supervisor can avoid a possible charge of an unfair labor practice while still communicating management's position on the union organizing campaign.

What management can do

As mentioned earlier, the Taft-Hartley Act amended the NLRA and states that

> The expression of any view, argument, or opinion, or the dissemination thereof, whether in written, printed, graphic, or visual form, shall not constitute or be evidence of an unfair labor practice under any of the provisions of this Act, if such expression contains no threat of reprisal or force or promise of benefit.

As a result, management and management representatives can express their opinions and answer employees' questions using facts. Examples of permissible actions and statements by supervisors during a union campaign are:

- Continue to function as usual. Supervisors should not change standards, work practices, or methods of discipline just because of union activity.
- Affirm the company policy regarding no-union status.
- Remind employees that they are free *not* to participate in union activities or join a union.
- Inform employees of the disadvantages of belonging to a union such as the possibility of strikes, serving on picket lines, union dues, and initiation fees.
- Emphasize that a union can promise anything to employees but can guarantee nothing because no company is required to agree to any union demands it feels are too costly or otherwise unreasonable.
- Point out to employees that with a union they may lose the right to

speak and act for themselves and that their problems may have to go through the shop steward instead of directly to the supervisor.

- Correct untrue or misleading statements made by union organizers.
- Remind employees of the benefits they now enjoy and reaffirm that they got these without a union, and that they do not need a union to keep them or to improve them.
- Inform employees that even though they signed a union card, this does not obligate them to vote for the union.
- Explain employee rights and election procedures.

A supervisor using statements such as these would not be committing an unfair labor practice because the statements deal only with facts and contain no indication of reprisal or benefit.

Source: Christopher F. Carney, "What Supervisors Can Do About Union Organizing," *Supervisory Management,* January 1981, pp. 13–15.

Supervisors have a limited role in negotiating the labor agreement. This role is typically limited to their boss asking them about specific inputs to the contract. For example: "Are there any working conditions that your employees lead you to believe need to be corrected? Are there any demands that you believe the union will make and, if so, what are they? Is there anything you personally believe we should be aware of in getting ready to negotiate the contract?" At this point, the supervisors step aside and let management negotiate the contract. When this process has been completed, the supervisor then assumes a major role: enforcing the labor agreement.

Enforcing the labor agreement

The labor agreement will cover many areas, including wages, working conditions, hours of work, overtime, holidays, and paid vacations. These will be spelled out to some degree, but there is always room for interpretation. It is the supervisor's job to ensure that management's rights are not lost in this interpretation.

Quite often this means talking to the boss to find out exactly what management's position is regarding various parts of the contract. For example, the agreement may allow workers to trade jobs if the work is boring; however, this does not mean that people can trade with individuals who are not trained to do the other job. The supervisor can prevent job trading among those who lack such experience. When it comes to the part of the contract that deals with management's right to discipline or discharge for "just or proper cause," management may not be willing to allow the supervisor to determine this without consultation with the boss. In this way the company reduces the likelihood that the union will file an unfair-labor-practice suit claiming that a worker was terminated for a minor infraction.

In enforcing the contract, the supervisor also spends a great deal of time interfacing with the shop steward.

The supervisor and the shop steward

The supervisor's primary link with the union is the *shop steward*, who is elected by the coworkers to be their on-site union representative. The steward is both a worker and a union representative and tends to be very well informed regarding the nature and scope of the labor agreement.

The supervisor and the shop steward have a lot in common. Both are the first line of defense for their respective groups. If a worker does something that is a direct violation of the contract, the supervisor is management's representative on site while the shop steward is the union's (worker's). Since the two work together on a daily basis, it is common to find them keeping each other informed about decisions made by their respective groups and sharing information about sources of trouble. One of the most common problems for both is the worker grievance.

Grievances. A worker *grievance* is a formal charge made by a worker when he or she is dissatisfied with a supervisor's disposition of a work-related complaint. Grievances always allege that there has been a violation of the labor contract. Quite often the situation begins as a gripe by the worker, but when the problem is not handled to the worker's satisfaction, a grievance is filed. (Managers can also file grievances, although this is outside the scope of the current discussion.) Some of the most common types of grievances deal with the following:

Discipline and discharge—absenteeism; insubordination; misconduct; poor work
Seniority—calculating seniority; layoffs; bumping; rehiring
Leave of absence—paid sick leave; personal leave; union business
Promotion—basis for promotion; measurement of ability; transfer
Vacation—eligibility; scheduling; pay
Holidays—eligibility for pay; pay for holiday work
Wages and hours—incentive pay plans; overtime; premium pay

When there is a grievance, the first thing a supervisor should do is find out what the grievance is all about.[3] What happened? To whom? When? Where? Why? How? Many firms have their supervisors make a formal written report on what they learned in their grievance investigation. In this way, if the grievance is not solved at the lower levels, top management can read the report and be better prepared to deal with the situation.

The grievance procedure. While grievances can be handled in a number of ways, the formal procedure is often spelled out in the labor-management agreement. Figure 13-2 illustrates the most common approaches used in small firms and large firms.

Once a grievance has been filed, the first thing that usually occurs is a

Figure 13-2. Typical grievance procedures.

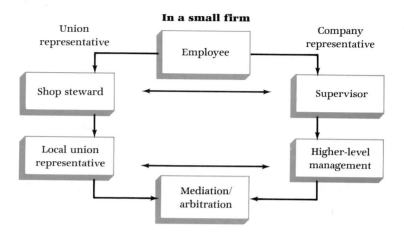

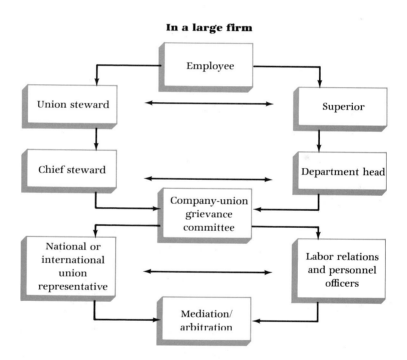

meeting between the supervisor, the shop steward, and the employee who has filed the grievance. If the steward has handled things properly to this point, he or she will have investigated the employee's grievance, found out what it was all about, and determined whether the company has addressed it in a fair and proper manner as called for in the labor-management agreement.[4] Now the employee and the steward will ask the supervisor to correct the situation. For example, the company may have a rule saying that anyone who endangers the health and safety of a fellow worker is to be dismissed immediately. The worker may have been charged with smoking in a no-smoking area. The supervisor, having reviewed the facts in the situation, will present management's side of the picture. If the manager personally saw the individual smoking, the worker's grievance is much weaker than if the supervisor learned about it secondhand and fired the individual on the basis of this information. In any event, the supervisor will listen to what the worker and the steward have to say and then give his or her side of the story. It may turn out that the worker was smoking in the area but was unaware of the fact that only in the previous 24 hours had management designated it as a no-smoking area. Or the individual who claimed that the worker was smoking may be the only one who says this; none of the other workers may have seen the person smoking. Depending on the relationship that exists between the union and the management, the supervisor may agree to reinstate the individual (perhaps with a penalty, such as 3 days off with no pay) or may stick to the original decision. If the matter is not solved at this level, it then moves up the line.

In small firms, someone in higher-level management will review the supervisor's decision while the shop steward will consult with a local union representative to see what should now be done. In large firms, the supervisor's boss and the shop steward will meet on the matter. (See Figure 13-2.) Again an effort will be made to resolve the matter. At this point it is unlikely that the worker and the steward will be charging that the incident never happened. Higher-level management would not allow it to get to this point unless the supervisor's facts were in order. On the other hand, the union representative may argue that the penalty is too harsh and will be asking for some milder form of punishment. This gives both sides a chance to win their points. The supervisor's decision can be upheld but also modified.

If the grievance is not resolved at this point, many contracts call for the use of mediation or arbitration. In small firms, this is the next step. In large firms, however, there is first a company-union grievance committee to which the matter is referred; if the matter still cannot be resolved by the two parties, then they turn to a third party for mediation or arbitration. While similar in nature, there are important differences between the two approaches to grievance resolution.

Mediation

Mediation is a procedure in which a third party helps the union and management negotiators reach a voluntary agreement regarding how to settle a grievance. The mediator is a facilitator. He or she works to bring both sides together. In this role, the individual often makes suggestions or recommendations and tries to reduce the emotions and tensions that are causing the two parties to remain at an impasse. In order to be successful, the mediator must have the trust and respect of both parties and have sufficient expertise and experience to convince both the company and the union that he or she will be fair and equitable. The U.S. government operates the Federal Mediation and Conciliation Service to make experienced mediators available both to companies and to unions, and many of these individuals have had great success in helping resolve labor-management disputes.

The important thing to remember is that the individual's recommendations are not binding upon the parties. For example, in the case of the worker who was fired for smoking in a no-smoking area, the mediator might recommend that the individual be reinstated but not be given any back pay for all of the work days that have been lost while the matter was under review. The penalty is all of the lost days from the time the individual was fired by the supervisor until the present day. The company does not have to go along with this, but it often will, reasoning that the worker has suffered enough and that management has made its point about enforcing the "no smoking in restricted areas" rule.

Arbitration

Arbitration is a procedure in which a neutral third party studies the grievance, listens to the argument of both sides, and then makes recommendations that are binding on both. There are two common types of arbitration.

The most common type is the extension of bargaining. This involves the arbitrator attempting to reach an equitable decision that is acceptable to both parties. To some extent, the individual's role in this process is similiar to that of the mediator.

The other approach is known as final-offer arbitration. This involves the arbitrator choosing between the final offer of the two sides. For example, if the union insists that the worker be reinstated and paid for all days that have been lost and the company insists that the worker's termination remain effective as of the day of the firing, the arbitrator must decide which position to back. Since it is an all-or-nothing approach, the pressure is on both sides to be as fair as possible because this is the basis on which the arbitrator will choose.

When a grievance is going to arbitration, both sides are usually involved in choosing the arbitrator. Sometimes the two already have agreed on a permanent arbitrator and this person is asked to hear the grievance. More likely, however, they contact the American Arbitration Association, or some similar group at the state level, and ask for a list of arbitrators. If neither side is familiar with any of the people, each will check up on the arbitrators by asking around about the individual's integrity, fairness, etc. Then the two groups will sit down with the list and take turns "striking out" names. For example, if there are five people on the list, the union may begin by saying, "We don't want number three." The management will then counter by saying, "We don't want number five." Continuing this process, the two will end up with one person. Neither side may get its first choice, but it will avoid having to take its two least favorite choices.

In conducting the arbitration process, it is common for the arbitrator to call witnesses, have testimony recorded, and in general conduct the proceedings in a manner similar to that of a court of law. At the end of the hearing, the individual then renders a decision.[5] For example, the arbitrator may reinstate the worker with full back pay because management has not satisfactorily proven that the individual was smoking in the area. Or the arbitrator may hold that the worker should be reinstated with no back pay. Whatever the decision, it is binding on both parties.

Fortunately, not every attempt of the supervisor to admonish the subordinate or enforce the rules ends up in a grievance. In most cases the supervisor will tell the worker what to do, or not do, and that is the end of the matter. If the individual fails to comply, the supervisor will discipline the worker and the matter will never get to mediation or arbitration. This is particularly true for minor problems or for matters that are not negotiable, such as management's right to enforce safety regulations.

EFFECTIVE DISCIPLINING

Discipline is the process of educating subordinates to practice self-control and of dispensing appropriate punishment for wrongdoing. Many supervisors use negative discipline, i.e., reprimanding or punishing subordinates for breaking rules or not carrying out job responsibilities. However, discipline should begin on a positive note, i.e., showing the individual where he or she went wrong and how to correct the situation.

When discipline is needed

There are a number of times when discipline is required. Some of the most common are:

- Excessive tardiness
- Excessive absenteeism
- Defective workmanship
- Inadequate work performance
- Poor attitudes that affect the morale of others
- Insubordination

When these things happen, the supervisor must take action. To allow them to continue without comment is akin to sanctioning them. What the first-line manager must decide is the specific type of discipline needed: positive or negative. The first step should be an analysis of the situation. This should be followed, if possible, by the use of positive discipline.

Initial steps

First, before doing anything else, the supervisor should investigate what happened and why it happened. Seven sets of questions should be answered in this investigation:

1. What really happened? Is there direct evidence to support this, or is it circumstantial evidence or just suspicion?

2. How serious is the offense? Was it major or minor? Were others involved?
3. Did the individual know of the rule or standard? Did the person have a reasonable excuse? Were there extenuating circumstances?
4. What is the individual's past disciplinary record? Has he or she had problems previously, or is this the first one?
5. Should this person receive the same treatment as others who have committed this offense? Or is there a reason for treatiing this person differently?
6. Is the offense properly documented should the need for an outside review arise?
7. What steps can be taken to prevent this problem from occurring in the future?

Second, the supervisor should not take any action until he or she is sure of being objective. Becoming angry, yelling at the employee, or placing one's hand on the individual should be avoided at all costs. Loss of self-control or displays of anger result in the supervisor compromising his or her objectivity and fairness.

Third, all disciplining should be done in private.[6] Public reprimands humiliate the employee in front of the coworkers and weaken the overall morale of the group. Of course, if someone openly refuses to obey an order or violates a rule in front of the supervisor (such as lighting a cigarettte in a no-smoking area), the first-line manager should consider on-the-spot action. In this way the supervisor lets everyone know who is in charge. However, the supervisor must be careful not to go overboard. Telling the employee, "You're fired," may be too harsh and the boss may later have to back down under pressure from the union because the penalty does not fit the offense. A better way is to say, "I want to see you in my office immediately." In this way the supervisor can handle the problem on his or her own turf and not that of the employee.

Fourth, where possible, *positive discipline* should be used. This means the promotion of understanding and self-control.[7] The first aim of discipline should be to correct a problem situation. One of the most direct ways of doing this is by making the rules clear and getting people to understand why they should be followed. By explaining why safety glasses must be worn in the metal-cutting area or why special earphones that block out all noise must be worn while working around the printing presses, the supervisor helps the worker understand that the rule is designed for employee safety. Management is interested in the welfare of the worker. Once this is clear, the worker can take over the function of self-control by assuming personal responsibility for complying with the rule. The supervisor should not have to be around in order to ensure that the rule is obeyed.

Progressive discipline

If it becomes obvious that disciplinary steps must be taken, the manager should employ a number of principles. Some of these are spelled out in

Supervision in Action: How to Discipline. Equally important is the idea of *progressive discipline.*[8] The supervisor should start with a general warning and then use increased degrees of negative discipline.

SUPERVISION IN ACTION: HOW TO DISCIPLINE

A neophyte supervisor may inwardly tremble the first time he or she has to reprimand an employee. This supervisor may wonder whether the employee will accept the reprimand, get angry, or need further disciplining. Even the experienced supervisor may still have these feelings. However, inexperienced or experienced, supervisors need to keep several points in mind to successfully administer discipline.

First, a supervisor must know and understand the organization's rules and regulations and be sure that his or her copy of them is the most current one. If the rules seem unclear, the supervisor should ask his or her boss, someone in personnel, or perhaps another supervisor to explain them. Caution is advisable in talking to other supervisors, for they may not be fully knowledgeable either. Since a supervisor is supposedly an expert in the eyes of his or her subordinates, to take disciplinary action and then be wrong does not help the individual's credibility. It is even worse when the subordinate is the one who corrects the supervisor! So there is no excuse for not knowing the company's rules and regulations.

Another important point is learning how to confront subordinates when administering discipline. Part of being an effective first-line supervisor is to be aware of a subordinate's behavior and to notice little problems before they become huge ones. This means learning how to approach the employee, knowing what to say, and how to say it. The supervisor will need to become adept at treating employees differently with regard to confrontation. One employee may be very embarrassed that the supervisor found it necessary to reprimand him or her; therefore, the supervisor should be very tactful with this subordinate. Another employee might require the supervisor to be very abrasive just to get his or her attention.

The supervisor should also learn to confront the individual and not the group unless it is a group problem. For example, a supervisor who brings things up at group meetings takes the approach that the guilty party will hear the comments and improve his or her behavior. Of course, this never happens. All the employees know who the guilty party is and become very resentful that the supervisor does not talk to the employee in question. A supervisor must develop the fortitude to confront subordinates and deal with disciplinary matters; a supervisor is not paid to avoid problems.

Some supervisors will confront their employees but never quite tell them exactly what the problems are and where they stand. Sometimes supervisors only hint at problems and assume that employees know what they are doing wrong. But employees are no more capable of mind reading than supervisors. The supervisor should be crystal clear: Instead of telling subordinates they need to improve the quality of their work, if, for example, neatness in correcting typing errors is the problem, the supervisor should say so.

Another important principle in administering discipline is to be consistent. If one employee is reprimanded for sloppy work, any employee with this problem should be reprimanded. Special mitigating circumstances come into play in deciding what punishment to administer, not whether or not to discipline. Inconsistency is one reason why a supervisor's actions are overturned by higher management or arbitrators. Inconsistency can also lead to charges by subordinates of supervisory favoritism.

First-line supervisors should be objective. They should not make decisions based on emotions but should investigate work problems and come to a decision based on verifiable facts. For example, a supervisor should not automatically assume that an employee is lying simply because the individual may have lied in the past. Objectivity adds to supervisors' credibility and increases employees' respect for them.

It is also important for supervisors to be firm. They should make decisions regarding disciplinary action, after investigating the facts, and stick with them. Employees know what to expect from a firm supervisor and act accordingly.

At the same time supervisors should be prepared for various reactions from subordinates when they are reprimanded, suspended, or terminated. An employee may become quiet or belligerent, cry, swear, shout, or simply walk away. A supervisor experiencing any of these reactions for the first time may become upset and inadvertently aggravate the situation. The supervisor needs to remain cool and remember that the subordinate is not necessarily reacting to the *supervisor* but to being reprimanded or disciplined. Most people will undergo some embarrassment, so a supervisor should give some thought to how not to react. It may be necessary to hold two meetings with an employee—one simply to relate the decision and another to discuss it after the individual has calmed down.

Source: Marcia Ann Pulich, "What Supervisors Should Know About Discipline," *Supervisory Management*, October 1983, pp. 22–23.

The first step in progressive discipline is an oral warning. At this stage the supervisor tells the worker what the latter has been doing wrong. For example, the manager may say: "Joe, you've been taking extended lunches. As you know, we have only a 30-minute lunch break. Since you leave at 12:30 P.M., you are supposed to be back by 1:00 P.M. I expect you to abide by this rule from now on or I'll have to take action."

If the individual conttinues to come back late, the supervisor should document this. One way is by keeping a written record of those days the individual was not back on time. Another way, often used to supplement

TO: Leslie Forrester
DATE: 1/29/82
FROM: Tammy Hausner
RE: Written Warning

Earlier, we discussed the matter of your frequently extended lunch periods. I have discussed your lengthy lunch periods with you three times in the past two months. Yet, during the past two weeks, you overstayed your lunch period on five occasions, without working additional time. On each of these occasions you exceeded your lunch period by 10 to 15 minutes.

You indicated that you enjoy jogging during the noon hour. I responded that jogging must not interfere with your work hours or job performance. Company rules establish 30 minutes for lunch unless additional time is made up each day.

You indicated that you would either quit jogging or take an hour lunch and work 30 minutes longer each day on a consistent basis. I trust you to keep your word as I consider you to be a good employee, with the exception of your lunch-time tardiness.

In this matter, you must show improvement during the next three weeks. Otherwise, you will be subject to disciplinary action, including suspension. At the end of three weeks, on February 19, we will privately review your problem.

this personal record, is by sending the individual a written warning.[9] Figure 13-3 provides an illustration.

If the individual still does not comply, the next step is usually a suspension from the job without pay. The worker is sent home for a week. It is hoped that this loss of pay will be enough to convince the individual that the company is serious about its 30-minute-lunch-break rule. At this point, many employees will quit. They are unwilling to tolerate this form of discipline.

If the individual does return to the job, he or she is usually informed that the next infraction of the rule will lead to dismissal. In this case, the problem is resolved. The worker either shapes up or is shipped out.

The above represents the most typical approach to progressive discipline. However, the supervisor does not always follow it. If the infraction is serious, the worker may be dismissed on the spot; examples include: gross insubordination, drunkenness on the job, willful destruction of property, and theft or dishonesty. In regard to dishonesty, for example, if an individual lies on the job application about previous work experience, regardless of how effective the person is in the work place, the company usually dismisses him or her upon learning of the lie. The firm reasons that if the employee lied about something like job experience, the person probably lied about other things, and it does not have the time or inclination to determine where the individual has and has not been truthful.

THE AGGRESSIVE SUPERVISOR: STARTING CASE REVISITED

Jane meant well, but she violated the law by attempting to influence the workers' decision regarding unionizing. Remember from the chapter's discussion of the National Labor Relations Act (Wagner Act) and from Supervision in Action: Supervisors and Union Organizing that the supervisor is prohibited from doing certain things. These include threatening the workers, promising them better wages in order to influence them, using coercion or arm-twisting techniques, and employing surveillance to monitor unionizing efforts. Jane tried to influence her work group by using coercion in the form of fear, i.e., if you vote for the union, some of you are going to lose your jobs. Jane needs to learn what supervisors legally can and cannot do. She needs a basic review of the material in the first part of this chapter.

INTERPRETATION OF SELF-ASSESSMENT QUIZ 13-1: WHAT DO YOU KNOW ABOUT UNIONS?

1. False. Union membership is still going up, although at a very slow rate.
2. False. In a union shop new employees must join within a predetermined time period, such as 30 days.
3. True. This is one way they help their members stay employed.
4. True. This was done by the Norris-LaGuardia Act.
5. True. This was done by the Norris-LaGuardia Act.
6. True. This is outlawed by the Taft-Hartley Act.
7. True. This is also a provision of Taft-Hartley.
8. False. The union can be voted out.
9. False. Management cannot get involved; this is a violation of the Wagner Act.
10. False. The Labor-Management Reporting and Disclosure Act does just this.
11. True. This is an accurate description of the shop steward.
12. True. Workers can file grievances if they feel this way.
13. False. Mediators make suggestions, but these are not binding on the parties.
14. True. Arbitrators are often used for this purpose.
15. False. The arbitrator has a lot more power than does a mediator.

SUMMARY OF KEY POINTS

1. Unions have existed in the United States for over 200 years. However, it was not until the late nineteenth century that they began their dramatic growth. Today over 23 million workers are unionized, although over the last two decades this growth rate has begun to slow.
2. Unions have many objectives. Some of the most common are: higher wages, shorter hours, guaranteed seniority rights, union security, and job retention.
3. A number of laws have significantly influenced what unions can and cannot do. Some of the most important pieces of legislation have been: the Railway Labor Act

of 1926, the Norris-LaGuardia Act of 1932, the National Labor Relations Act (Wagner Act) of 1935, the Labor-Management Relations Act (Taft-Hartley Act) of 1947, and the Labor-Management Reporting and Disclosure Act of 1959. In recent years federal employees have also been able to benefit from legislation in the form of executive orders, the Civil Service Reform Act, and state and local regulations.

4. Collective bargaining is the process in which the union and management come together and negotiate a labor contract. This process typically involves a give and take on both sides, and there are many issues covered, from wages and salaries to job security, grievance procedures, and pension benefits.

5. The supervisor does not negotiate the labor-management agreement, but it is the supervisor's job to help enforce it. In this capacity, the supervisor interacts daily with the shop steward, who is selected by the coworkers to be their on-site union representative. If a grievance is filed, the steward will stand by the employee throughout the proceedings.

6. Some grievances are solved very quickly. Others end up going to mediation or arbitration. Mediation is a procedure in which a third party helps the union and management negotiators reach a voluntary agreement regarding how to settle the grievance. Arbitration is a procedure in which a neutral third party studies the grievance, listens to the argument of both sides, and then makes recommendations that are binding on both.

7. Discipline is the process of educating subordinates to practice self-control and of dispensing appropriate punishment for wrongdoing. When discipline is needed, the supervisor should always opt for positive over negative discipline. Whenever possible, the supervisor should also use a progressive approach, giving the employee every opportunity to straighten out before finally letting the individual go.

BUILD YOUR SUPERVISORY WORD POWER

These key labor-management and discipline terms are presented in their order of appearance in the chapter. Effective supervisors have a working knowledge of them.

Union shop. A union security arrangement in which all current workers must join the union and new ones have to join after a probationary period.

Right-to-work law. A law that gives employees the right to work, with or without union membership.

Modified union shop. A union security arrangement whereby those who are union members when the labor agreement goes into effect must remain in the union but nonmembers can refuse to join.

Maintenance-of-membership shop. A union security arrangement that requires all employees who voluntarily join the union to remain as members during the life of the labor contract, although there is sometimes an escape period for those who want to drop their membership.

Agency shop. A union security arrangement under which employees who are not members of the union must still pay union dues.

Open shop. A union security arrangement under which membership is voluntary for all existing and new employees.

Closed shop. An organization in which all employees must be union members.

Spread-the-work policy. A policy of cutting work hours rather than personnel in an effort to minimize the economic impact of a cutback.

Yellow-dog contract. A written pledge not to join a union or attempt to form one.

Wagner Act. A law designed to aid unions, it sets forth unfair labor practices in which employers are forbidden to engage.

Taft-Hartley Act. A law designed to aid management, it sets forth unfair labor practices in which unions are forbidden to engage.

Collective bargaining. The process in which the union and management come together to negotiate a labor contract.

Shop steward. The primary, on-site union representative who interfaces directly with the supervisor and is charged with seeing that the workers are treated properly.

Grievance. A formal charge related to an alleged violation of the labor-management contract.

Mediation. A procedure in which a third party helps the union and management negotiators reach a voluntary agreement regarding how to settle a grievance.

Arbitration. A procedure in which a third party studies a grievance, listens to the arguments of both sides, and then makes recommendations that are binding on both parties.

Discipline. The process of educating subordinates to practice self-control and of dispensing appropriate punishment for wrongdoing.

Positive discipline. Discipline that promotes understanding and self-control.

Progressive Discipline. Discipline that starts with a general warning and then uses increased degrees of negative discipline.

REVIEW YOUR UNDERSTANDING

1. Why is union membership growth slowing up? Explain.
2. What objectives do unions try to attain for their members? Identify and describe three.
3. Describe how the following union security arrangements work: union shop, maintenance-of-membership shop, agency shop, open shop, closed shop. Are any of these illegal? Explain.
4. List and explain what supervisors need to know about the following acts: Norris-LaGuardia Act, National Labor Relations Act, Labor-Management Relations Act, Labor-Management Reporting and Disclosure Act, Civil Service Reform Act. Be as complete as possible in your answers.
5. Explain how the union uses the following in the bargaining process: initial demand point, target point, resistance point. Explain how management uses the following: initial offer, target point, resistance point. In your answeer, use a specific example and then explain how the resistance points create a settlement range.
6. What role does the supervisor play in the creation of the labor-management contract? Give an example.
7. In what way do the supervisor and the shop steward perform similar duties? Compare and contrast their jobs.
8. How are grievances handled? In your answer be sure to discuss the role of mediators and arbitrators.
9. What is meant by the term *discipline?* When is discipline required? Cite some examples.
10. What are the initial steps a supervisor should take in using discipline? Explain.
11. How does progressive discipline work? Why is it so effective? Explain.

SUPPLEMENT YOUR KNOWLEDGE

In addition to the references listed at the end of this chapter, the following provide important, practical information that is of use to supervisors in dealing with union and discipline matters:

Cabot, Stephen, and Jerald R. Cureton: "Labor Disputes and Strikes: Be Prepared," *Personnel Journal*, February 1981, pp. 121–123, 136.

Harrison, Edward L.: "Legal Restrictions on the Employer's Authority to Discipline," *Personnel Journal*, February 1982, pp. 136–141.

Kaufman, Lois, and John Wolf: "Cutting Down on Complaints," *Supervisory Management*, March 1981, pp. 14–17.

Larson, Charles C., and Sheila D. Melville: "How Far Can a Rule Bend?" *Supervisory Management*, December 1980, pp. 11–14.

Miller, Ronald L.: "Handling Employee Complaints," *Supervisory Management*, February 1978, pp. 38–42.

Picard, Hans, and Lyra Picard: "Team Discipline: The Supervisor as Coach," *Supervisory Management*, November 1980, pp. 37–39.

Pulich, Marcia Ann: "Train First-Line Supervisors to Handle Discipline," *Personnel Journal*, December 1983, pp. 980–986.

Sullivan, Frederick L.: "Union Organizing in the 1980s: Prelude to a Union Campaign," *Supervisory Management*, June 1982, pp. 20–23.

Tidwell, Gary L.: "The Supervisor's Role in a Union Election," *Personnel Journal*, August 1983, pp. 640–647.

Weiss, Bernard: "Constructing Your Criticism," *Supervisory Management*, May 1981, pp. 12–18.

YOU BE THE SUPERVISOR: JOE'S GRIEVANCE

Four weeks ago the Fairfield Company announced that it was going to start cutting back its work force. Over the last 12 months the firm has sustained losses in excess of $1.2 million and is being forced to downsize operations. As part of the labor-management agreement, the company announced its intention to reduce the quality control department by 25 percent. Following the philosophy of "last hired, first laid off," the company told Joe Keel that he would be laid off from quality control effective the end of the month.

Before coming to work in quality control 3 years ago, Joe had spent 2 years as a lathe operator. Since the union contract allows for interdepartmental bumping, Joe went to see the supervisor in the lathe department. The latter has 20 people in his department and has been ordered to lay off 5. This will be done on a seniority basis. The five who are scheduled to be laid off all have less than 1 year's experience. Two others, who will be kept on, have only 1½ years of experience. Joe told the supervisor that he had 2 years of experience and that, on the basis of interdepartmental bumping, he wanted to return to this department after he was laid off by quality control.

The next day the supervisor called Joe and told him that he could not honor his request. "You were a member of this department before we installed these new, sophisticated machines. You have no experience operating them and so, for all practical purposes, you would come into the department as a trainee. The labor contract allows for bumping on the basis of work experience, but in this case you bring no work experience with you." Joe was upset when he heard the news and immediately sought out his shop steward. As calmly as possible, he explained to the steward what had happened. The stewaard then visited with the supervisor. When he came back, he told Joe: "I've had no success talking to that guy. However, I've looked over the labor contract very carefully, and while he's technically right, you are still entitled to move into his department."

The steward then helped Joe write up a grievance and submit it through channels. Joe is not the only one in the company who has filed such a grievance. There are 19 people in all who claim that the company is misinterpreting the bumping rule in the contract and that they are entitled to jobs in other departments.

The initial grievance meeting between Joe and the steward on the one hand, and the supervisor and a company representative on the other, is scheduled for tomorrow afternoon. If the situation is not amicably resolved at that point, Joe intends to appeal to the union-management grievance committee and then demand arbitration. "If I lose my appeal," he told the steward, "I'm out of the work force forever. I'm 59 years old. Who is going to hire me?" The steward urged him to relax and wait for the hearing. "It may all work out a lot better than you think," he told Joe.

1. If you were the supervisor in the lathe machine department, what steps would you take in getting ready for the meeting with Joe and the shop steward? Describe these steps.
2. Will higher-level management play any role in helping you prepare for this meeting? Explain your answer.
3. If the grievance eventually goes to arbitration and the arbitrator says that Joe must be taken into your department, are you required to go along with this ruling or is this merely a strong recommendation? Defend your answer.

YOU BE THE SUPERVISOR: SARA'S DECISION

Sara Guillen considers herself a rather mild-mannered supervisor. She seldom raises her voice and always tries to reason with her people. However, last week she became extremely angry. While walking through the workplace she noticed that one of the people in her unit was not wearing his protective headgear. Sara's people work in a very noisy environment with machines all around them. The special headgear is designed to protect them should something fall off one of the two-story machines and strike them. The headgear also has special earphones through which music is piped. These earphones screen out all of the harsh, unpleasant noise and, in the process, reduce the likelihood of hearing damage.

Last month one of the employees won a lawsuit against the firm. The individual had been working here for over 25 years and for all of this time had never worn protective ear covering of any type. The noise eventually resulted in his going partially deaf. He sued for disability retirement and won. Additionally, the courts awarded him $125,000 for pain and suffering. Immediately after losing the lawsuit, the company had a team of experts into the plant to design something that would eliminate the noise and reduce the likelihood of future legal actions.

Last month the management revealed the results of the experts' efforts: the protective headgear with the accompanying earphones. When the gear was given out to the workers, they were told that it was mandatory that they wear this equipment at all times. Management has been assured by its attorneys that if they enforce this rule, the chances of future disability cases are very small. However, if they do not enforce the rule, even though they have distributed the headgear, they are still liable for any physical injury to the workers.

When Sara saw the man not wearing his headgear, she went over to him and told him to report to her office immediately. Once in the office, she informed him that because he had not been wearing his headgear, she was firing him effective immediately. The man protested that he had taken the gear off only a few minutes before. "The helmet and earphones are very confining. I took them off for a minute to give myself a chance to relax. I intended to put them right back on when you came by and caught me not wearing them." Sara listened to his counterclaim but felt that it was not true. In any event, she knew what the company's rule was and she stuck by her guns.

About an hour later the shop steward came by to see her. He asked if she would consider a less harsh penalty. "Send him home for the day," the steward suggested. "Or make it 2 days." The word will get around that you're serious about the rule, and no one will ever do this again." Sara would not budge.

Early the next morning, Sara learned that the worker had filed a grievance. She also received a phone call from her boss asking her to drop by in an hour to discuss the matter. "Let's see if we can settle this before it moves up the line and gets out of our hands," he said to Sara. During her meeting with the boss, however, it was evident to Sara that he wanted her to drop her punishment in favor of something milder. She was reluctant to do this but did not see what else she could do.

Finally, Sara agreed to give the man 2 days off without pay. This made both the supervisor and the steward very happy. However, Sara felt that she had made a mistake. "I should have stuck to my guns," she told herself.

In this morning's paper there was a story about a worker who was suspended for two days, without pay, for not wearing safety glasses in a work area where this was mandatory. It seems that the worker appealed the ruling to an arbitrator and was given 1 day off without pay and reinstated. After reading the article, Sara began to think that maybe her boss was right all along in getting her to reduce her discipline penalty.

1. As far as discipline goes, if you were the supervisor, would you have done the same thing Sara did, i.e., fire the person on the spot? Why or why not? Explain.

2. Would you have brought any supporting materials with you when you went to visit your boss? What would they have been? How would they have helped you? Explain.

3. If you were giving Sara advice regarding how to handle similar situations in the future, what would you recommend? Outline your suggestions and then briefly elaborate on each one.

NOTES

1. Richard M. Hodgetts, *Introduction to Business,* 3d ed., Reading, Mass.: Addison-Wesley, 1984, pp. 226–229.

2. Randall S. Schuler, *Personnel and Human Resource Management*, 2d ed., St. Paul, Minn.: West, 1984, pp. 556–559.

3. Charles W. Eisemann and Stuart L. Lourie, "Grievance Handling: How to Carry the Ball," *Supervisory Management*, November 1983, pp. 35–38.

4. Lanning S. Mosher, "Grievance Procedures," *Supervisory Management*, August 1976, pp. 20–26.

5. John E. Tobin, "How Arbitrators Decide to Reject or Uphold an Employee Discharge, Part 1: General Guidelines," *Supervisory Management*, June 1976, pp. 20–23.

6. Robert W. Braid, "Seven Rules for Disciplining Problem Employees," *Supervisory Management,* May 1983, p. 7.

7. Richard G. Martin, "Five Principles of Corrective Disciplinary Action," *Supervisory Management,* January 1978, pp. 24–28.

8. George L. Heller, "Laying Down the Law—Progressively," *Supervisory Management,* August 1981, pp. 14–16.

9. Ira G. Asherman and Sandra Lee Vance, "Documentation: A Tool for Effective Management," *Personnel Journal,* August 1981, pp. 641–643.

CHAPTER 14

IMPROVING PRODUCTIVITY
AND COST CONTROL

Productivity has become a major concern for many businesses. Over the last two decades, U.S. firms have steadily lost ground to international companies because of their inability to produce goods as efficiently as their overseas competitors. The overriding goal of this chapter is to examine current productivity and cost control concerns and discuss the supervisor's role in meeting these challenges. In particular, concern is focused on some of the approaches that are most likely to produce the greatest benefits with the least expenditure of resources. When you have finished reading all the material in this chapter, you will be able to:

1. Define the term *productivity.*
2. Set forth the six steps that must be undertaken if an organization is to increase its productivity.
3. Discuss purchasing and inventory control practices that can reduce costs.
4. Discuss how effective work-flow layout can help control costs and increase productivity.
5. Define the term *quality control* and discuss how quality control circles work and what their value is in increasing employee productivity.
6. Identify some of the most popular alternate workstyles and discuss the advantages and disadvantages associated with flextime.
7. Explain why monetary incentives are so important to the success of productivity efforts.

A STARTING CASE: JOE'S PRODUCTIVITY PLAN

When last year's fourth-quarter results were published, Joe Stafford knew there would be a change in top management. This was the seventh successive losing quarter for the firm. Prior to this, the company had not lost money since 1933.

The new management team that came in 6 months ago immediately introduced a host of changes. One of them was the productivity bonus. The idea was quite simple. If a division, department, or unit had an increase in productivity, the managers in the area all got to share in the cost savings. In Joe's case, management estimated that it should cost about $37,000/month to run the unit. This estimate included salaries, supplies, utility costs, maintenance, etc.

The new management also sponsored a series of seminars for both managers and workers. The purpose of the seminars was to acquaint the personnel with ways in which productivity could be increased. Some of the specific ideas included flextime, quality circles, inventory control, and work layout. Joe attended all five seminars. Many of the ideas that were presented had direct application to Joe's department and he was determined to use them.

Joe estimated that a 20 percent increase in productivity could be achieved through better work layout and performance. Under the new productivity plan, if Joe could save 20 percent of the monthly cost of operating the unit, this $7400 would go into a special fund. At the end of the year, the total value of the fund would be divided between the company and Joe on a 3:1 basis. Joe estimated that he could save the company at least $60,000/year.

He began by focusing attention on work layout. By rearranging the work flow and physically changing the location of some desks and machines, Joe hoped to reduce the work time and increase the output. He also held a meeting of his people and set up a productivity improvement committee. The purpose of the committee was to make recommendations for changes that would reduce the costs or increase the work output.

All of this occurred 2 months ago. Since then Joe's monthly cost for running the unit has risen from $37,000 to $39,250. The productivity committee has offered but seven ideas. Three of these Joe rejected straightaway, two others were implemented but actually led to an increase in costs, and the last two were introduced a week ago, so it is still too early to judge their value.

At yesterday's management meeting, all of the supervisors reported the effects of their productivity efforts. Ten of them had monthly cost savings of between $100, and $250; the rest reported either no change or increases in costs. No one had as large an increase as Joe, although no one had introduced as many changes either. On the way out of the room, one of Joe's friends said, "If you put in any more productivity-related ideas, you'll double the monthly cost of running your unit." Everyone laughed, including Joe. However, back at his desk he began to ponder what had been going wrong. No one had been trying as hard as he had, yet he was having the poorest results of all.

What is wrong? Why is Joe having such poor results? What should be done? Write down your answers and put them aside. We will return to them later.

THE PRODUCTIVITY CHALLENGE

Productivity is measured by the equation: output/input. If a company produces 20 widgets with an input of $20, the cost per widget is $1. If through laborsaving tools and techniques the firm can reduce this input to $18 and still turn out 10 widgets, it has increased productivity. Another way of improving productivity is by leaving inputs the same but increasing the output, such as by turning out 21 widgets with $20 of input. A third way is by increasing output faster than input. Before continuing on, take Self-Assessment Quiz 14-1 and see how much you currently know about productivity.

SELF-ASSESSMENT QUIZ 14-1:
WHAT DO YOU KNOW ABOUT PRODUCTIVITY?

Carefully read each of the following statements and indicate whether it is true (T) or false (F). Answers are provided at the end of the chapter.

	True	*False*
1. Productivity is talked about a lot, but it is not possible to measure it quantitatively.	____	____
2. Since World War II, U.S. productivity growth has slowed down.	____	____
3. The major reason for low productivity is obsolete plant and equipment.	____	____
4. One major area in which cost savings often can be attained is that of purchasing.	____	____
5. More and more firms today are turning to hand-to-mouth inventory practices even though these may lead to occasional stockouts.	____	____
6. Work-flow layout often affects productivity.	____	____
7. One of the biggest differences between U.S. and Japanese approaches to product quality is that the Americans believe that low costs per unit can be achieved with small production runs, while the Japanese believe that low costs per unit can be achieved only with large production runs.	____	____
8. Quality circle members are assigned to the circle by the supervisor.	____	____
9. Effective quality circle leaders tend to have a 9,9 leadership style.	____	____
10. Productivity plans that offer psychological rewards tend to be more effective than those which offer monetary rewards.	____	____

Over the last 40 years, U.S. productivity growth has been slowing down dramatically. From 1948 to 1965 the annual rate was 3.2 percent. During the 1970s it fell to an annual rate of less than 2 percent, and from 1978 to 1982 it was virtually zero. Since then it has been rising slowly. Yet for the first time in decades, it is a major concern for many firms. The supervisor's role in this process is an important one.

Many firms have long argued that their inefficiency is a result of such things as excessive government taxes, the decline of the work ethic, problems with government regulations, obsolete plant and inequipment, insufficient research and development (R&D), and poor labor relations. The truth of the matter is that these things have little to do with U.S. industry's faltering productivity.[1] Most firms have productivity problems because their own efforts have been misdirected and uncoordinated.

One of the major problems is that the scope of productivity improvements in most companies is too narrow. They focus almost exclusively on cost savings in one or another part of the firm, and this piecemeal approach provides short-run benefits only. A second major problem is that many companies concentrate their efforts on symptoms of productivity rather than on productivity causes. They do not find out why productivity is low in the first place. A third major problem is that the top management often is not very involved in these productivity efforts. At best, they offer lukewarm support. What, then, needs to be done? The answer is that management must create the right environment so that the supervisor's efforts are not in vain. This calls for six steps:[2]

1. Top management must support productivity efforts. Unless the supervisors and the employees are convinced that a productivity improvement program has top management's support, they are unlikely to take the program seriously.
2. The organizational structure must be designed to support productivity improvement objectives. Many firms have set up productivity steering committees that share the responsibility for educating and assisting supervisors and work groups in both measuring and improving productivity.
3. The company climate must be conducive to a productivity effort. This requires four things:
   a. Employees have to be made aware of management productivity objectives as well as of the tools and techniques available in attaining these goals.
   b. Management must be sure that the employees understand these objectives.
   c. There must be direct employee involvement in the productivity efforts.
   d. The company must recognize the contributions of the personnel through appropriatte reward systems, such as bonuses, citations, and employee- or supervisor-of-the-month awards.
4. Realistic productivity goals must be set, and methods of measuring progress must be determined. Some of the most common measures include: units per work hour, sales per payroll dollar, sales per employee, sales per asset dollar, and costs per unit.
5. The firm must be continually on the lookout for new techniques for productivity improvement. Some of the most common approaches

include: work simplification, automation, employee suggestion systems, time and motion studies, quality circles, and job enrichment.

6. There must be a schedule for implementing the productivity program and committing the resources. Productivity improvement has to be planned and systematically pursued.

PURCHASING AND INVENTORY CONTROL

Two main areas in which significant cost savings and productivity increases can be attained are purchasing and inventory control. The two are interrelated in that many firms will usually purchase and store materials and parts until they are used. Not wanting to have too much on hand at any one time, however, they will seek to balance the risk associated with stockouts against the costs of storing excess amounts.

Purchasing practices and productivity

Just about every firm purchases some things from outside suppliers. As a result, it is important to have well-defined purchasing practices and an organizational structure that efficiently handles purchase decisions. The supervisor can help by continually reviewing these practices to see where inefficiencies can be eliminated. Some of the most common approaches include the following:

1. A centralized purchasing department buys all of the major items that are supplied by outside vendors.
2. Minor or one-of-a-kind purchases are bought directly by the departments that need them.
3. Buyers are required to have a sound understanding of the engineering specifications and requirements of all items being purchased from outside.
4. All purchases in excess of $10,000 are handled on the basis of low bid, commensurate with the reputation of the supplier.
5. No special rebates or favors are accepted from any suppliers regardless of the conditions under which these are offered.

Guidelines of this nature are designed to ensure that the company is able to obtain the best quality merchandise at the fairest possible prices. In many cases these guidelines apply directly to the purchasing department since it will be the department responsible for the purchase of expensive components and parts as well as for all large orders, regardless of the individual cost per item in the order. On the other hand, to the extent that the individual supervisor is involved in purchasing, the focus should be on cutting purchasing costs without suffering shortages or stockouts.

Inventory control practices

Supervisors can also help control costs by monitoring inventory levels. In many firms this is done through the use of material requirements planning and/or of just-in-time production methods.

Material requirements planning. *Material requirements planning* (*MRP*) is a systematic, comprehensive planning and controlling technique used to increase the efficiency of both material handling and inventory control. The formulation of an MRP begins with an annual sales forecast, which is used to get an initial idea of the demand for the company's products. Each of these products is then "exploded" to determine the materials and parts that will be needed to produce each. The amount of inventory on hand is then subtracted from the total needed in order to determine the amount to be ordered. Then the time between when an order is placed and when delivery can be expected is calculated, along with the lead time necessary to ensure that the materials and parts are received in time for production. The forecasts and the materials requirement plan often have to be revised based on actual sales so that demand and supply can be kept in balance. However, when the system works properly, the firm can avoid costly ripple effects either from a sharp, unexpected drop in sales or from delivery problems created by suppliers. By carefully monitoring the MRP the supervisor can ensure that everything does happen according to schedule.

JIT production. Another recent development, related to inventory control, is just-in-time (JIT) inventory production. *JIT production* is the purchase and/or production of small quantities of materials and parts just in time for use. This hand-to-mouth approach leads to smaller inventories and reduces the need for storage space, inventory-related equipment (such as forklifts and racks), and material support personnel. Most important, because of the absence of extra inventories, the organization should be able to run an error-free operation.

In some ways, JIT production is not new. Organizations have always sought to minimize inventories while maintaining full-scale production. For example, many large firms producing standard products have been able to reduce their inventory to 1 or 2 days without interrupting the work flow. Through the use of continuous delivery and/or production of the needed materials, the company has been able to operate at full capacity. Yet JIT production is not restricted to large firms; it can also be employed by small ones.

The biggest problem in using JIT production is that the firm may run out of inventory from time to time, resulting in work stoppages. The cost of such occasional problems, however, is more than offset by the savings associated with carrying less inventory. Companies are now beginning to realize that by removing inventories from the shop floor, moving machines closer together, and permanently reallocating floor space that once held inventory, productivity can be increased and costs controlled.

The supervisor's job in this process is to be aware of the benefits of JIT production and to work closely with higher-level management to implement this approach. The supervisor needs to be particularly alert to problems that arise from the approach. For example, there may be a late delivery by a supplier, or the quality of the inventory may not be right. By identifying these problems, the supervisor helps the firm correct them; for instance, a new and more reliable supplier may be needed, or the firm may find that it is better to buy from someone located closer to its facilities. In his or her role as problem identifier, the supervisor helps higher-level management formulate strategies for dealing with the problem.

WORK-FLOW LAYOUT

Another critical area for increasing productivity is *work-flow layout*, the process of determining the physical arrangement of the productive system. If personnel and machines are scattered in a haphazard arrangement, productivity will suffer. If these machines can be arranged in an orderly, logical, cost-effective manner, productivity can be increased. In a well-designed work-layout arrangement, some of the major benefits include: (1) minimization of investment, (2) more effective use of existing space, (3) reduction in material-handling costs and overall production time, (4) maintenance of operational flexibility, and (5) assurance of employee safety and convenience.

Supervisors need to understand the basic layout formats and the advantages and disadvantages of each. The three basic layout formats are: product, process, and fixed position. All other layouts are simply variations of these three.

Product layout

In a *product layout*, machines, equipment, and personnel are arranged according to the progressive steps used in building the product. A good example is the auto assembly plant. As the basic frame of the car moves down the line, parts are put onto it until a finished auto emerges at the end of the line (see Figure 14-1a). In assembling large numbers of manufactured products, it is common to find machines and personnel placed at fixed workstations along the line, with each making a contribution to the product as it moves past.

This type of layout has both advantages and disadvantages. On the positive side, the workers do not have to be very skilled. Most assembly lines are staffed with semiskilled personnel. Additionally, one supervisor can usually oversee the work of many people. Therefore, direct management costs tend to be low.

On the negative side, the firm is locked into one type of layout. Changing to another major form is extremely costly. Second, the assembly line is no stronger than its weakest link. If a person cannot keep up or a machine goes down, it may be necessary to stop the line; if the firm runs out of parts, it is impossible to continue assembly. Finally, in recent years more and more workers have begun to rebel against the monotony, boredom, and specialization of the line. They want more authority and control of their work environment.

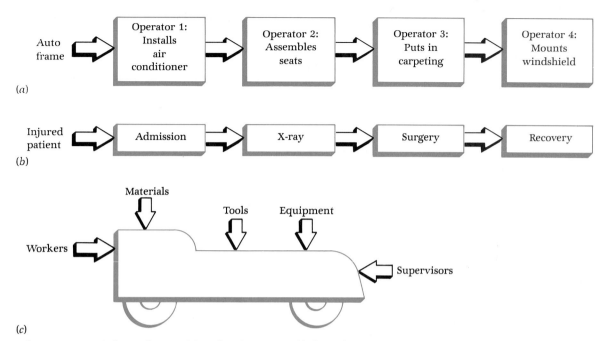

Figure 14-1. Basic layout formats. (a) Product (auto assembly line); (b) process (hospital); (c) fixed-position (locomotive).

Process layout

A *process layout* is one in which all components are grouped on the basis of the functions they perform. All lathe machines are placed in one area; all welding machines are placed in another. In job shops where the product can be moved from one area to another, process layout works well. Yet the layout is not restricted to manufacturing. Hospitals (Figure 14-1b) also employ this layout form. The patient literally is moved to some of these departments (x-ray, surgery), while others (dietetics, pharmacy) come to him or her.

The process layout has both advantages and disadvantages. On the positive side, these arrangements are more flexible than product layouts. They are also more suitable for the custom processing of diverse outputs because they can address themselves to the specific needs of the latter. On the negative side, it is necessary to schedule work carefully; otherwise some departments will be overscheduled while others sit idle.

Fixed-position layout

A *fixed-position layout* is one in which the workers come to the work (Figure 14-1c). Aircraft, diesel locomotives, and oil tankers are examples. The process is too large and/or heavy to be moved, so the workers and the equipment come to the product.

On the positive side, the resources are more efficiently used because it is too costly to build the product any other way. Additionally, workers like this form of layout because it allows them to move about during their workday.

On the negative side, this work design is expensive because it requires the firm to duplicate resources. For example, if there are three locomotives being built simultaneously, the company will have to draw 3 times as many crews and 3 times as much equipment, materials, etc.

QUALITY CONTROL

Quality control is the process of ensuring that goods and services meet predetermined specifications. Quality control has two important parts: philosophy and practice. The philosophy of quality control relates to the ways that management and the personnel view their responsibilities for turning out a quality product or service. The practice of quality control relates to the ways in which the organization ensures that its goods and services are meeting predetermined specifications, such as through the use of quality control circles. The following examines both of these.

Philosophy

Many organizations are beginning to realize that their approach to quality control is ineffective. Perhaps the main reason is because they are attempting to correct mistakes as soon as they are identified rather than trying to prevent them in the first place. The Japanese are an excellent example of this latter approach. Their philosophy is based on two major beliefs: (1) things should be done right the first time, and (2) everyone has a responsibility for quality control, not just the people in the quality control department.[3] They also believe that it is possible to turn out a small number of units at the same cost and with the same quality as achieved by American firms in large production runs. Some of these contrasts are presented in Table 14-1.

A second important facet of a quality control philosophy is the acceptance of the use of computers. The Japanese use robots much more than the Americans and this is reflected in the low defect rate of their manufactured goods. The supervisor's role here is to work to overcome employee fear and anxiety regarding replacement by computers. In truth, most firms do not replace their people with computers. They use the machines to help the workers do their jobs more efficiently. When someone is replaced, the

Table 14-1. Philosophy of quality: U.S. firms versus Japanese firms

United States	Japan
Quality is the responsibility of the quality control department personnel.	Everyone is responsible for quality control.
With large production runs, low costs per unit can be achieved.	With small production runs, low costs per unit can be achieved.
There is a tradeoff between cost, quality, and delivery.	There need never be a tradeoff between cost, quality, and delivery.
Poor quality should be kept to a minimum.	Poor quality should be totally eliminated.
High quality will bring about higher costs and lower productivity.	Higher quality will bring about lower costs and higher productivity.
Quality checks should be performed by inspectors.	Quality checks should be performed by each worker.

individual is typically assigned work elsewhere in the organization. Far from causing unemployment, computers have actually created job opportunities in industry.

Quality circles

Quality circles are small groups, usually 8 to 12 people, who meet to identify and solve work-related problems. These groups typically get together once a week on company time to discuss progress and to plan future actions. Membership in the group is almost always voluntary; if an employee does not want to participate, he or she does not.

Every circle has a leader. Quite often this is the regular supervisor. The leader's job is to direct the efforts of the group in solving job-related problems. The leader is charged with helping the circle identify those problems it wants to solve, analyze the information, and then present it to management at a formal meeting.

Firms that have many quality circles often have formal weekly meetings that everyone is invited to attend. At these meetings, two or three circles will report what they have done, their recommendations for action, and the cost savings that will accrue as a result of these recommendations. For example, one quality circle in a large manufacturing firm recently found that it had to wait an average of 30 minutes per day for a cart on which to ship its finished products to the quality control area. The cost of an additional cart was $99.50. The circle recommended buying one and showed through its calculations that the firm would recover the investment in less than 10 working days. In another case, an auto-assembly-line circle showed how redesigning the size of a stabilizer bar so that it was ¼ inch shorter would make it easier and faster to install. The original design looked good on paper, but it was too long. The redesigned bar is now installed in 40 seconds, compared with the 70 seconds needed for the old bar. In a third case, a group of workers showed how a rerouting of paperwork would result in a 10 percent increase in the daily amount of work completed. These weekly meetings allow the members of other circles to learn what approaches are being taken by workers in other departments and how successful they have been. If nothing else, the get-togethers give the personnel a chance to exchange information regarding the success of their respective circles.

The first step in developing a quality circle program is to choose a leader who can help the members identify and solve job-related problems. Quite often this is the supervisor. A facilitator is also chosen. This individual's job is to provide assistance to the circle. For example, if the group needs to get information about an engineering-related problem, the facilitator will seek out the appropriate person in the organization and see that this engineer is at the next circle meeting. The facilitator usually reports to a steering committee, which is made up of all the facilitators and representatives from the various areas of the organization. The committee, in turn, coordinates the activities of the circles and publicizes their progress and success. (See Figure 14-2.)

Figure 14-2. Quality circles program structure.

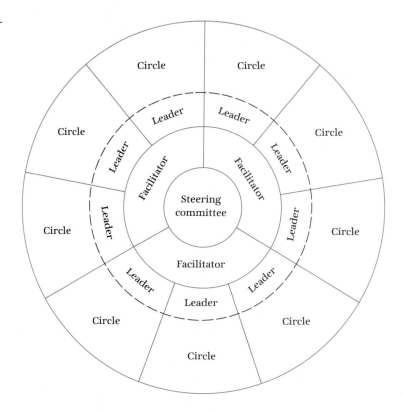

The supervisor plays three distinct roles in a quality circle. First, the individual is a teacher who helps the members learn how to identify, analyze, and solve job-related problems. Second, the individual is a trainer who acquaints the members with the various tools and techniques that can be used in carrying out problem identification, analysis, and solution. Third, the individual is a leader who runs the quality circle and ensures that the morale and productivity of the group remain high. (See Supervision in Action: Running an Effective Quality Circle.) Recent research shows that leadership style is a major variable in the success of circles; in managerial grid terms, the 9,9 style seems to be the most effective (see Table 14-2).

Table 14-2. Comparison of leadership styles of first-level managers in a quality circle (*n* = 58)

	Leadership style				
	9,9	**9,1**	**1,9**	**5,5**	**1,1**
Extremely effective quality circle	15	11	2	4	0
Average effective quality circle	6	6	0	2	0
Low effective quality circle	0	4	3	4	0

Source: Merle O'Donnell and Robert J. O'Donnell, "Quality Circles—The Latest Fad or a Real Winner?" *Business Horizons*, May–June 1984, p. 51.

SUPERVISION IN ACTION:
RUNNING AN EFFECTIVE QUALITY CIRCLE (QC)

Becoming an effective QC leader

Leadership is a skill that one develops over a period of time. The experience of many supervisors, however, shows that the following points are useful in improving one's ability to lead a quality circle group.

Master the quality circle technique. The supervisor is more than a leader to a quality circle group. He or she is, first of all, a teacher who presents to them the principles and techniques involved, guiding them through the different phases of problem identification and solving. It is essential therefore that the supervisor himself or herself understand QC techniques thoroughly. This learning process begins during the leadership training program, but it shouldn't stop there. As the circle deals with more sophisticated problems, many organizations provide advanced training in statistical analysis and group dynamics to the QC leaders and their groups. The leader should make good use of this opportunity to update himself or herself and acquire new skills.

Be thorough in training members. There is evidence to suggest that the more thorough the training members receive in quality circles, the better the group performance. Furthermore, good training reduces the workload that the supervisor has to carry in the future. To be sure, more thorough training implies more than superficial coverage of the material; it requires that the leader fully acquaint members with what each technique entails.

Effective running of quality circle meetings. The weekly meeting of a quality circle is an extraordinary gathering, providing as it does an opportunity for the employees to work on issues of interest to them and to the company. From the company's viewpoint, it is a chance to utilize employees' special skills and creativity in a meaningful way. To take full advantage of these sessions the leader should:

- *Plan the meeting well.* The supervisor should review the minutes of the last meeting and follow up with individuals in the organization to get data and relevant information for the group if needed. Also, the leader should have a clear idea of the issues to be covered in the next meeting.
- *Keep attendance records up to date.* This is important for two reasons. First, employees are usually compensated for attending the meetings. Hence, good record keeping is a must. Second, members who stop attending the weekly meetings may be doing so to express their discontent with the circle process. Poor attendance therefore may be a warning signal of loss of interest. If that's the case, the supervisor should contact the individuals and discuss their feelings regarding the circle. Care must be exercised here, though, since membership in the circle is voluntary.

- *At the beginning of the meeting, summarize the work done by the group on the issue at hand.* Feedback is crucial to continued interest. Furthermore, a status report helps keep the circle's activities focused on the problem.
- *Refrain from telling members what to do.* Essential to a circle's success is a guarantee of free participation and self-expression. The leader needs to remember that he or she is only *one* member of the group. The challenge awaiting the leader is to encourage members to come up with ideas and put them to practical use.
- *Emphasize a democratic, participatory style.* Indeed, the most critical test of quality circle leadership is the existence of group participation, including willingness to involve members in decision making.
- It should be noted that a more participatory leadership style is not an easy thing to develop. American organizations tend to use technical competence as the major criterion in identifying employees for promotion to supervisor. As a result, some supervisors lack the ability to lead people effectively and develop an autocratic orientation in defense. It takes time and skill for a participatory supervisory style to develop. The process can be speeded up, however, if the supervisor emphasizes this style outside the quality circle meetings—that is, in the workplace. It is through practice and doing that this style is achieved.
- *Maintain circle focus.* Over a period of months, special interest subgroups may emerge within the circle and vie for the leader's attention. If this happens, the leader should resist the temptation to accommodate these subgroups' demands. The opinion of the majority should prevail. The leader, however, should not ignore "minority" concerns, adding the problems identified by these interest groups to the list of issues likely to be considered. The members can then vote in accordance with the democratic principles of quality circles to determine whether these issues should be discussed.
- *Keep them informed of the results.* An effective leader will keep QC members, the program coordinator, and immediate managers informed of the progress made by the group. The leader should realize that some middle managers are suspicious of circles. This is because, unfortunately, many organizations have implemented quality circles without involving middle managers. The astute supervisor should try to make up for this for two obvious and practical reasons. First, middle managers are in the position to circumvent circle activities by withholding data if they do not appreciate the merits of the program. Second, middle managers usually appraise the performance of the supervisors and make decisions regarding retention, promotion, and the like.

There are three effective ways to involve middle managers. The first is to meet with the managers frequently for informal updates of quality circle work. The leader should solicit the manager's input. A simple question such as, "What do you think of what the group decided to do?" often paves the way to a fruitful discussion.

> The second way to keep middle managers informed is to provide brief progress reports that, formally, summarize circle accomplishments and point out areas that may be of interest to the managers. The third method is to invite the managers, from time to time, to join the weekly meetings. A manager may be asked to be an observer or invited as an expert on a specific issue. A circle in a manufacturing firm had a problem collecting data on a breakdown of a piece of machinery. After several frustrating weeks, the leader of the circle contacted the chief industrial engineer who, unbeknownst to the group, was independently working on the same issue. The engineer was invited to attend the next circle meeting to share his observations with the group. A fruitful discussion of possible ways of improving cooperation between the circle and industrial engineering developed— and an important link to middle management was made.
>
> Source: Shaker A. Zahra, "How to Be an Effective QC Leader," *Supervisory Management,* September 1983, pp. 21–23.

In the final analysis, the bottom line dictates the value of the quality circle. Often an organization will spend quite a bit of time and money on each circle. In addition to the meetings, which are held during working hours, there is the cost of training the circle leaders and members. Circle leaders often receive training in small-group leadership, adult learning techniques, motivation, and communication. Members typically receive instruction in the use of measurement techniques, histograms, cause-and-effect diagrams, quality strategies, and various types of check sheets.[4] Many firms are finding that these circles are well worth the expenses involved in setting them up. Additionally, as a circle begins to pay off, the morale of the group goes up because financial bottom-line results have an impact on the attitudes of the members, culminating in a desire to undertake still other projects. Research shows that supervisors also benefit from participation in quality circles (see Table 14-3).

ALTERNATE WORKSTYLES

Another approach to productivity is the use of alternate workstyles. Many firms are finding that if they provide their people a flexible work schedule, output will increase and/or costs will go down. A number of different workstyles are currently in use.

Commonly used forms

Alternate workstyles take many different forms. One of the most common is *full flextime*, which allows employees to decide each day, without informing the supervisor, when they will arrive at and leave work. When employees show up, they then proceed to work for the required 7 or 8 hours.

A second approach is *modified flextime*, in which the employee chooses when to begin working. The earlier in the day the person gets started, the earlier the person can leave. For example, for an 8-hour working day, an

Table 14-3. Summary of responses by supervisors (leaders and nonleaders)

Statements[a]	Frequency of responses (%)[b]				
	SA	A	N	D	SD
Since we started quality circles in this organization . . .					
Effect on the organization					
1. Management and workers (employees) have become closer.	25.0	62.5	10.1	0.0	3.1
2. Working conditions have improved.	20.3	60.9	6.7	6.3	6.6
3. Quality of work has improved.	14.1	46.9	17.2	14.1	1.6
4. Productivity in my department has improved.	14.9	35.9	28.1	14.1	7.7
5. Employee performance has improved.	21.3	27.3	16.3	14.1	21.0
6. Employee tardiness has declined.	17.4	23.7	11.4	17.6	29.9
7. Employee attendance has increased.	18.3	24.5	15.5	16.3	25.4
8. Communication in the company has improved.	22.1	26.7	13.2	18.4	19.6
9. Employee attitudes have improved.	19.3	34.3	20.8	16.6	10.0
Effect on the leader					
10. I feel closer to my subordinates.	21.3	32.3	30.8	8.3	7.3
11. My job has become more interesting.	14.7	36.3	35.0	12.2	1.8
12. I use more skills on my job.	21.3	34.5	30.4	10.1	3.7
13. I communicate *better* with my subordinates.	31.2	26.1	29.4	7.1	6.2
14. I communicate *more* with my subordinates.	23.7	27.1	31.1	9.9	8.2
15. My job satisfaction has increased.	10.8	29.6	39.4	16.3	3.9
16. I am more committed to my work.	12.7	40.1	24.8	10.2	12.2
17. I am more committed to my company.	8.7	42.5	14.4	21.1	13.3
18. My interpersonal skills have improved.	8.6	36.7	35.2	11.1	8.4
19. I have become a better leader.	13.6	54.7	21.4	8.3	2.0
20. I manage my time better.	2.6	12.5	44.9	23.6	16.4
21. I feel more anxiety on the job.	8.9	24.0	20.1	35.4	11.6
22. I have lost some of my authority.	4.7	6.3	4.6	64.1	20.1
23. It has become more difficult for me to make decisions.	16.3	34.3	15.6	18.6	15.2
24. I have lost some of my enthusiasm for my job.	9.3	11.8	26.3	43.1	10.5
General					
25. Being a quality circle leader helps one's career.	12.4	56.3	20.3	4.7	6.3

[a] These statements were "scrambled" in the original questionnaire and were rearranged here for clarity of presentation.

[b] SA = strongly agree; A = agree; N = neutral; D = disagree; and SD = strongly disagree.

Source: Shaker A. Zahra, "What Supervisors Think About QCs," *Supervisory Management*, August 1984, pp. 30–31.

individual arriving at 7 A.M. can leave at 3 P.M.; a person coming in at 10 A.M. goes home at 6 P.M. Once an employee sets his or her schedule, the individual must stay with it until a new arrangement is negotiated with the management. Also, in many organizations there are *core hours* when everyone must be present, such as 11 A.M. to 2 P.M. Flexible schedules are built around these core times.

A third approach is the *compressed workweek*, in which people do their work in less than the usual 5 days. An example is the 4-day, 40-hour week.

A fourth is *flexplace*. Under this arrangement, people work at home or at some place other than the regular business setting.

There are other forms of alternate workstyles, including work sharing, permanent part-time work, seasonal work, and project work. However, they are not as popular as the first four. In fact, the term *alternate workstyle* is most often used in referring to versions of flextime and the compressed workweek.

At the present time over 20 million nonfarm workers operate under some version of flextime. It is estimated that by 1990 over 50 million will be.[5]

Advantages and disadvantages

Flextime arrangements have a number of benefits. Some of the most important are the following:[6]

1. *Reduced tardiness and absenteeism.* Since employees set their own working hours, they can choose the times that best fit with their lifestyle and personal responsibilities.
2. *Increased morale.* Under a flextime arrangement, employees have more freedom, responsibility, and participation in decision making. These functions tend to lead to higher morale.
3. *Increased productivity.* Many employees on flexible work schedules are better prepared, both physiologically and psychologically, to meet the challenges of their job. They also learn to do other jobs while covering for fellow employees, thus increasing their overall capabilities.
4. *Reduced turnover.* Flextime arrangements often lead to increased employee satisfaction. The result is lower turnover.
5. *Increased customer service.* Many service organizations, such as insurance companies and banks, are able to extend their hours of operations with flextime arrangements. This allows them to provide increased customer service.
6. *Improved planning and communication.* The supervisor will not always be on hand during the workday because some employees will be arriving before the manager or leaving after. This results in the supervisor developing more effective planning and communication techniques for dealing with this lack of face-to-face contact.

Flextime also has drawbacks. Six of the most commonly cited ones are the following:

1. *Additional operating costs.* When people are coming in earlier or staying later than usual, operating costs go up. In particular, lighting, heating, and air-conditioning expenses rise.
2. *Limited use.* Flextime does not lend itself to everyone or every situation. Some people do not like flexible work arrangements; they do best on a 9 to 5 schedule. Some jobs, such as auto assembly (where there is a high degree of interdependency between the workers), do not allow the use of flextime.
3. *Increased employee responsibility.* Under a flextime arrangement, some workers will not be on hand the first thing in the morning, while others will be gone by the close of business. This arrangement means

that employees will sometimes have to fill in for others during noncore hours. An attitude of "that's not my job" will cause productivity problems. Everyone must be willing to pitch in and assume increased responsibility.

4. *Reduced overtime.* The increases in productivity brought about by flextime often result in a loss of overtime pay for some workers. The organization is able to meet all of its work demands without paying a premium for additional work hours.

5. *Loss of supervisory control.* Many supervisors feel that since they are not on hand at all times, they are unable to control operations the way they could before flextime was introduced. Additionally, some of them feel that under a flextime arrangement, the employees try to exploit the situation and do as little work as possible.

6. *Need for supervisory planning.* Since the supervisor will not be around during all working hours, the individual must do more planning. This calls for delegating work activities and establishing formal communication channels among the personnel to ensure cooperation throughout the workday.

Overall, many organizations are finding that the advantages of flextime outweigh the disadvantages. In particular, this workstyle gives people more control over their workday, allowing them to choose those hours which best meet their personal and job-related responsibilities. For example, people who are basically "morning people" because they do their best work before lunch can come in early in the morning and be more productive than they were when operating on a 9 to 5 schedule. Conversely, those who are basically "afternoon people" can arrive in the late morning and get more done than they did under the old 9 to 5 arrangement. However, as seen in Supervision in Action: Meeting the Challenge, the supervisor's role in making the arrangement work is an important one.

SUPERVISION IN ACTION: MEETING THE CHALLENGE

Regardless of the type of alternative workstyle that a company adopts, and it may be a combination of two or three, you as the supervisor will be responsible for resolving potential problems in the areas of scheduling, coordination, communication, discipline, performance, and training. These new workstyles represent a challenge to a manager's ingenuity. To assist you, consider these key steps:

- *Screen candidates carefully.* An alternative workstyle is not right for every employee. An individual's temperament, professional goals, and employment history will give you clues as to whether he or she will adapt well to the new work system.

  When interviewing potential flextime workers, for example, you might look for self-starters who require less supervision than nine to fivers. Job sharers should be compatible with each other and capable of setting joint goals and articulating points of disagreement. People who want to work a compressed workweek schedule should have the motivation and stamina to be productive for a longer workday. Office temporaries should be prescreened by the service before they come to your office to see that their skills, attitudes, and personalities match the company's requirements.

- *Establish a viable work plan.* More alternative workstyles fail because of inadequate preparation on the part of management than because of a flaw in the system itself. Whether you use part-timers, free-lancers, flextime workers, or temporaries, it is important to determine in advance the scope of the tasks employees will be required to perform, where they will work (part-timers may share an office, for example, and attention must be given to where work in progress will be stored), and who will supervise the employees in your absence.

  A staggered schedule of lunch hours and break times should also be established so that office equipment never remains idle.

- *Set appropriate performance goals.* During the transition period from a traditional to an alternative work situation, you must see to it that productivity remains high and ultimately increases. To accomplish this, set a production schedule, share your goals with your workers, and enlist their support in achieving them. Always monitor production to ensure that the goals set can be realistically met. Remember to adjust your expectations for part-time workers; they should not be expected to complete a full-time workload in fewer hours.

- *Develop a flexible training program.* At the very least, all workers must be familiar with office procedures and protocol. To hold training sessions when employees work on varying schedules, careful planning and coordination is needed.

  If workers must acquire new skills, as is the case when a transition is made to an automated office, some employees may have to temporarily adjust their schedules to be available when a professional is in the office to teach the group. In such a situation, a company might even prefer to use the services of a skilled staff member from a temporary service to train employees. An advantage to this procedure is that the staffer would be available to conduct training sessions on second shifts, during weekends, or whenever the need existed. At the same time, temporaries could be hired to run the automated equipment at capacity level, maintaining production during the training period.

- *Provide ongoing managerial support.* One reason for resistance to alternative workstyles is the fear that employees who work on different schedules may not fulfill their commitments because there is not always someone on hand to oversee their work. Generally this fear is unfounded, for employees on alternative work schedules are usually well-motivated and apt to produce at consistently high levels. However, many companies still prefer continuity of managerial support and occasionally rotate supervisors' schedules, ensuring that all workers have access to a manager to help resolve immediate problems.

The presence of a manager is also important in helping employees feel their contributions are recognized and appreciated.

Disciplinary action should be taken quickly if abuses in the system are discovered. For example, an employee who is chronically late, whose output is low, or who takes extended breaks or lunch periods must be dealt with swiftly so that coworkers are not led to believe that such conduct is acceptable.

- *Maintain open communication at all levels.* A pitfall inherent in most alternative workstyles is lack of communication between employee and supervisor because of the different work schedules. To mitigate this problem, you should try to meet regularly with employees, even if this means that you must change your own hours. Perhaps you could hold two or three meetings during the course of a week to share information with the staffers and handle any problems that have arisen. On occasion, you might delegate the leadership of such meetings to a capable subordinate.

During employee-supervisor sessions, workers on alternative schedules should be encouraged to express their feelings about the system; to discuss any expectations on the part of management that they feel are unrealistic; and, when feasible, to offer input into policies that will facilitate the company's smooth operation.

Maintaining open lines of communication is also crucial in helping part-timers and office temporaries feel a part of the work environment. These employees should receive all directives and written communications related to the work. Knowing that the supervisor cares about their job satisfaction and the quality of their performance contributes to a sense of "belonging" that can boost morale and productivity.

- *Remain flexible.* In most cases, much planning and commitment of resources go into the decision to implement an alternative workstyle, and it deserves a fair trial. If it becomes apparent after start up that the system is not functioning to management's satisfaction, you should be prepared to make some modifications. The solution may be as simple as requiring someone to come in an hour earlier to ensure supervision between shifts or to leave an hour later in order to participate in key meetings. If problems are more complex, the entire program might have to be reevaluated.

Source: William Olsten, "Effectively Managing Alternative Work Options," *Supervisory Management*, April 1984, pp. 12–14.

PRODUCTIVITY AND INCENTIVES

While increased productivity is a challenge, the solutions do not have to be either sophisticated or expensive. If management can introduce cost-saving techniques and motivate the personnel to work harder and reward them for doing so, productivity will increase. One popular approach is goal setting.

Goal setting

The basic premise behind goal setting is that people will work harder when the goals are clear and challenging and when they are provided feedback on performance and rewards for accomplishment. An example is provided in Figure 14-3. When individuals are assigned work with no specific standards or work measurement, they usually perform at 40 to 60 percent of the normal rate. When goal setting is used, this amount often increases to the 60 to 90 percent range. If incentive pay is tied into the arrangement, performance can rise to the 115 to 135 percent range.

Four basic requirements are vital to the success of a goal-setting approach:

1. The goals must be clear. Rather than urging people to do more work, the supervisor should set a specific goal, such as "Turn out 10 more units per day."
2. If possible, the work should allow for self-control. In this way the employee can tell how well he or she is doing and make any necessary changes. If the work does not allow for self-control, the supervisor should provide frequent feedback, thereby letting the worker know the status of his or her performance.

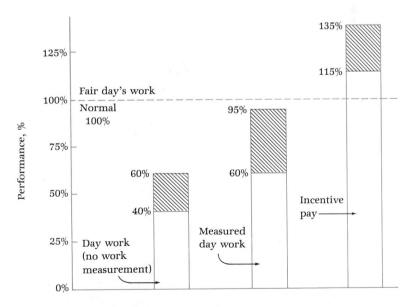

Figure 14-3. Productivity from different forms of motivation. (From Robert C. Kyser, Jr., and James Meade, "Work Measurement: America's Answer to the Productivity Challenge," *Supervisory Management*, October 1981, p. 32.)

3. The goals should be challenging, yet attainable. They should "stretch" the person, encouraging the individual to do more and better work than before.
4. There should be some form of incentive plan for rewarding those who do well.

Reward systems

When an organization implements a new purchasing or inventory control system, redesigns its plant layout, introduces flextime, or creates a quality control circle, productivity often increases. However, the overall success of the effort is heavily influenced by the reward system that accompanies the change. Supervisors need to be aware of two basic facts:

1. Productivity programs that offer job satisfaction as the prime reward for involvement will be supported by only a small portion of the work force and will tap but a fraction of the potential for improvement.
2. Productivity programs that offer financial rewards by sharing productivity improvement through formal productivity-sharing plans will create high levels of support, produce results very quickly, and raise productivity to much higher levels than those achieved by nonfinancial reward programs.

These findings point out the value of developing productivity-sharing plans. At the present time a number of such plans are being used. According to the General Accounting Office, the most popular is the *Scanlon plan*. Under this plan, the total payroll dollars are divided by the total dollar sales value of production in determining productivity gains. These are then shared with the workers on a 3:1 basis. For example, consider a firm that has found from past experience that for $1 million in payroll it is able to produce goods worth $2 million in sales revenue. Under the Scanlon Plan, if $2 million worth of goods can be produced for less than $1 million in payroll, or if more than $2 million worth of goods can be produced for $1 million in payroll, this is regarded as a productivity gain. This gain is shared between the workers and the management on a 3:1 basis.

Another popular productivity-sharing arrangement is the *Rucker plan*, which is similar to the Scanlon plan but more sophisticated in design. Under the Rucker plan, using past performance, the company establishes the relationship between the total earnings of the hourly rated employees and the production value created by the company. Productivity gains are then shared with the workers. One compensation expert has explained the specifics of the plan this way:

Assume that the company puts $0.55 worth of materials, supplies, and power into production to obtain a product worth $1.00. Value added or production value is thus $0.45 for each $1.00 of sales value. Assume also that analysis shows that 40 percent of production value is attributable to labor. The productivity ratio becomes 2.5, and for a payroll (plus benefits) of $100,000, standard production value is $250,000. If actual production for the month is

$300,000, a gain of $50,000 is available for bonus and is distributed 40 percent to labor and 60 percent to the company. Labor's bonus share for the month is $20,000.[7]

There are many other group productivity plans, but they all have one thing in common: Using some predetermined formula, they reward employees for productivity increases. In some cases these gains have proved to be dramatic.

The supervisor must realize that in productivity-sharing plans there are two major considerations. First, financial rewards must be given to the employees. Second, management must secure worker support. Without these two elements, productivity efforts will be less than ideal. Job redesign coupled with improved work layout and technology is incomplete. There must be monetary rewards as well, for money is a major motivator in productivity efforts.

JOE'S PRODUCTIVITY PLAN: STARTING CASE REVISITED

The problem with Joe's approach is that it is all one-sided. If the unit saves money, Joe and the management divide it up between themselves. There is no reward for the workers, and yet it is they who are generating the productivity savings. Sure, Joe thinks up the productivity approaches, but the personnel have to implement them. The case does not directly state that the workers are being uncooperative, but it does say that Joe has more productivity plans in operation than anyone else and that his unit has had the poorest results. Also notice that no unit has saved more than $200, so the overall payoff has at best been marginal. As noted at the end of the chapter, if management does not give rewards for productivity efforts, the results will not be as good as they can be. Joe needs to talk to his boss about sharing productivity rewards with the personnel.

INTERPRETATION OF SELF-ASSESSMENT QUIZ 14-1: WHAT DO YOU KNOW ABOUT PRODUCTIVITY?

1. False. It most certainly can be measured if input and output data are available.
2. True. It is starting to pick up but is still quite low.
3. False. While a commonly cited reason, this is not a major cause.
4. True. It is one primary source of cost savings.
5. True. JIT inventory is becoming very popular.
6. True. This is explained in the chapter.
7. False. It is just the opposite.
8. False. Membership is voluntary.
9. True. This is explained in the chapter.
10. False. It is just the opposite; monetary rewards are very effective.

SUMMARY OF KEY POINTS

1. Productivity is measured by the equation: output/input. Today productivity is a major concern for many American firms. Two of the major reasons why organizations have productivity problems are: (a) Their scope of productivity improvement has been too narrow, and (b) they focus their attention on productivity symptoms rather than on productivity causes.

2. In order for productivity to increase, there must be top-management support for the effort. Additionally, the organizational structure and climate must support the effort, realistic goals must be set, and there must be a plan for achieving these objectives.

3. One way of reducing costs and increasing productivity is through effective purchasing and inventory control practices. Carefully designed purchasing policies are very important. So are inventory control practices, such as material requirements planning and JIT production.

4. Another way of increasing productivity is through effective work-flow layout. Supervisors should know when to use product, process, and fixed-position layout arrangements.

5. Quality control is the process of ensuring that goods and services meet predetermined specifications. Part of the success of every quality control effort is management's philosophy regarding how to address the problem. A second part is the use of control techniques, such as quality circles. The latter were described in detail in the chapter.

6. Another approach to productivity is alternate workstyles, such as flextime. There are many different types of flextime, and management must compare the advantages and disadvantages of each.

7. No matter how well conceived a productivity effort is, there must be some consideration of employee motivation. Research reveals that productivity efforts that are tied to monetary rewards are more effective than those which are nonfinancial in nature.

BUILD YOUR SUPERVISORY WORD POWER

These key terms are presented in their order of appearance in the chapter. They are terms for which supervisors have a working knowledge.

Productivity. Output/input.

Material requirements planning. A systematic, comprehensive planning and controlling technique used to increase the efficiency of both material handling and inventory control.

JIT production. The purchase and/or production of small quantities of materials and parts just in time for use.

Workflow layout. The process of determining the physical arrangement of the productive system.

Product layout. The arrangement of machines, equipment, and personnel according to the progressive steps used in building the product.

Process layout. A work-flow layout in which all components are grouped on the basis of the functions they perform.

Fixed-position layout. A work-flow layout in which the workers come to the work. Examples include aircraft, locomotives, and ships.

Quality control. The process of ensuring that goods and services meet the predetermined specifications.

Quality circles. Small groups that meet to identify and solve work-related problems.

Full flextime. An alternate workstyle in which employees decide, without informing the supervisor, when they will arrive at and leave work.

Modified flextime. An alternate workstyle in which employees set their work hours and remain with this arrangement until a new one is negotiated with management.

Core hours. Hours when everyone in a flexible work arrangement must be on the job.

Compressed work week. An alternate workstyle in which people do their work in less time than the usual 5 days.

Flexplace. An alternate workstyle in which people work at home or at some place other than the regular business setting.

Scanlon plan. A productivity-sharing plan in which workers and managers divide productivity gains on a 3:1 basis.

Rucker plan. A productivity-sharing plan in which the workers and management share productivity gains based on their contribution to the plan.

REVIEW YOUR UNDERSTANDING

1. What is meant by the term *productivity?* Define it in your own words.
2. How can management create the right environment for productivity? Identify and describe five steps in this process.
3. How can more effective purchasing guidelines help increase productivity? What role can the supervisor plan in this process?
4. What kinds of inventory control practices can firms use in controlling their costs? Identify and describe two.
5. What is meant by the term *work-flow layout?* How many basic types of work-flow layout are there? Identify and describe each.
6. How can a company's philosophy of quality control make an impact on the quality of its goods and services? Give an example using U.S. and Japanese philosophies.
7. How does a quality control circle work? Put it in your own words.
8. Of what value are quality control circles to productivity efforts? Explain.
9. Of what value is goal setting in increasing productivity? Explain.
10. In what way are reward systems of importance to productivity efforts? Defend your answer.
11. How do the Scanlon and Rucker productivity plans work? Which is the better one? Why?

SUPPLEMENT YOUR KNOWLEDGE

In addition to the references listed at the end of this chapter, the following provide important, practical information that is of use to supervisors in increasing productivity:

Blair, John D., and Carlton J. Whitehead: "Can Quality Circles Survive in the United States?" *Business Horizons*, September–October 1984, pp. 17–23.

Graber, Jim M.: "Let's Get a Handle on QWL," *Supervisory Management*, June 1983, pp. 26–34.

Jenkins, Kenneth M., and Justin Shimada: "Quality Circles in the Service Sector," *Supervisory Management*, August 1981, pp. 2–7.

O'Donnell, Merle, and Robert J. O'Donnell: "Quality Circles—The Latest Fad or a Real Winner?" *Business Horizons*, May–June 1984, pp. 48–52.

Olsten, William: "Effectively Managing Alternative Work Options," *Supervisory Management*, April 1984, pp. 10–15.

Santavicca, Gary, and Sandra F. Jewell: "Goal Setting: How to Work Smarter," *Supervisory Management*, September 1984, pp. 12–14.

Zahra, Shaker A.: "What Supervisors Think About QCs," *Supervisory Management*, August 1984, pp. 27–33.

YOU BE THE SUPERVISOR: COPYING THE COMPETITION

The Chandell Corporation is a medium-size manufacturing firm that has been quite successful in the subcontracting business. The company typically bids on those jobs which the government mandates must be subcontracted to medium-size and small firms.

Chandell has found that by pumping 5 percent of its total revenue back into new machinery and equipment, it is able to keep its production facilities in top shape. There are no competitors who have better tools for doing the work. Nevertheless, this technological edge is not so important as it used to be. Over the past 12 months the company has lost 60 percent of the contracts on which it bid. Last year it lost 50 percent of them, and the year before it bid unsuccessfully 35 percent of the time.

A close analysis of the situation reveals that the competition is underbidding Chandell. Two years ago the firm lost seven big contracts by an average of 5.5 percent on the bid price. Last year its bid on 11 big contracts was 9.3 percent higher than the competition's. This year it has already lost eight major contracts because, on average, its bid was 16.1 percent higher than that of the winning firm.

The engineering people have looked the plant facilities over from top to bottom. They can find no problems with either the layout or the machinery. "I don't know how those guys are managing to underbid us," the chief engineer told the company president, "but it can't be on the basis of machine efficiency. No one can produce materials and parts any cheaper than we can. The only thing I can figure out is that they're either paying less money to their people or they're taking less profit on the bottom line." The president thought about the engineer's comments but could not get himself to accept them. "Everyone in the industry pays about the same rates," he reasoned, "and no one would be dumb enough to cut his profits any lower than ours. Every subcontracting job is awarded on its own merits. It makes no sense to take less than a fair return. There has to be something we're overlooking." Unable to figure out what it was, Chandell decided to hire a supervisor away from one of its major competitors.

The new manager came on board last week. Once the supervisor was acquainted with the situation, the individual explained how the competition was beating out Chandell. "Productive equipment isn't enough," he explained. "You also need productive people who can figure out nonmechanical ways of cutting costs and increasing productivity. We've been doing it through the use of quality circles. We've found that these circles help us identify problem areas and get the personnel involved in solving them. About 18 months ago we introduced the idea, and within 6 months we were able to generate enough savings to cut our bid price by 8 percent. Each 6 months following, things have gotten even better. If we introduce quality circles in this firm, I know we can cut bid prices by 10 to 15 percent the first year and more after that." The president agrees and has ordered the creation of quality circles.

1. Assuming that you are the new supervisor, how would you explain quality circles to the other supervisors? Be complete in your answer.
2. What are the benefits of quality circles? Explain.
3. Will these circles help improve productivity? Explain.

YOU BE THE SUPERVISOR: CHANGING THE WORK SCHEDULES

Private University is located in a large metropolitan area. Founded over 50 years ago, the university has built a national reputation for its nighttime programs. Many working people are enrolled at the institution, and its graduate programs in business and the liberal arts are the largest in the area.

Most local universities open at approximately 7:30 A.M. and close at 5 P.M. Those offering night programs have a small administrative staff that remains to around 7 P.M. to handle student problems, etc.; the secretarial staff and other direct support personnel, however, leave by 5 P.M. Private University has found that it must have a full contingent of administrative and secretarial staff on hand during the evening as well as the daytime hours since 65 percent of all its courses are taught at night. Quite often the professors, many of whom are moonlighting here while working full-time in the business district or for state or local organizations, will turn in exams for typing or will need assistance in other work-related matters, such as photocopying of handouts for the students or proctoring exams for large sections. The students are usually unable to get to the university except during the evening, so there-must be support help for the professors during these hours.

Over the last 20 years the university has doubled the number of support and administrative personnel. The institution now has two shifts of people. The first works from 7:30 A.M. to 3:30 P.M. and the second shift from 3:30 P.M. to 10:30 P.M. The busiest hours for these people are 2 to 3 P.M. and 6 to 7 P.M. The daytime faculty and students usually place the heaviest burden on the support and administrative personnel during the early afternoon; the nighttime faculty and students usually require the greatest amount of assistance during the early evening to midevening hours. During these periods, the personnel find that they often cannot keep up with all of the demands on their time.

Private University recently conducted a study which showed that it has too many support and administrative personnel. Part of the report read as follows:

From 7:30 A.M. until noon there are too many personnel on hand. Most of these people are sitting around doing nothing. On the other hand, between 2 and 3 P.M. they are swamped with work. The same is true for the night group. They come in at 3:30 P.M., right after the midafternoon rush, and do not really do much work until 6 P.M. However, by 7:30 P.M. they have taken care of most problems and then take it easy until 10:30 P.M., when they go home. The university needs to rearrange work schedules so that there are fewer people on hand at opening and closing times and more people on hand during the busy hours.

The university president has read the report very carefully and thinks the consultants are on the right track. Since the organization is not unionized, there is no reason why there cannot be either a cutback in employment or a rearrangement of work schedules. However, the president is not sure how this should all be done. One of the deans has recommended the use of alternate workstyles. "There are a lot of things that we can do to improve the situation," he told the president. "Just talk to some of the supervisors in the various departments. They'll know how to improve things. They've been around a long time and know how many people they need every hour of the day and which ones can be either assigned different jobs or let go." The president has decided to do just this.

1. If you were a supervisor working at the university, what type of alternate workstyles would you recommend to the president? Identify and describe three.
2. How would flextime be of value to the university? Explain by citing some of its advantages.
3. If the university did decide to go to flextime for the groups mentioned in the case, how would the idea be put into practice? Outline a plan that could be used to balance the number of people on hand with the demand from the faculty and students.

NOTES

1. Arnold S. Judson, "The Awkward Truth About Productivity," *Harvard Business Review*, September–October 1982, p. 93.
2. Y. K. Shetty, "Key Elements of Productivity Improvement Programs," *Business Horizons*, March–April 1982, pp. 15–22.
3. William A. Mahon and Richard E. Dyck, "Japanese Quality Systems from a Marketing Viewpoint," *Industrial Management*, September–October 1982, p. 10.
4. James F. Harmon, "The Supervisor and Quality Control Circles—Studying a Problem Area," *Supervisory Management*, March 1984, pp. 38–43.
5. Susan G. Schroeer, "Alternate Workstyles: A Solution to Productivity Problems," *Supervisory Management*, July 1983, p. 28.
6. The material in this section can be found in: Sally A. Coltrin and Barbara D. Barendse, "Is Your Organization a Good Candidate for Flexitime?" *Personnel Journal*, September 1981, pp. 712–715.
7. David W. Belcher, *Wage and Salary Administration*, 2d ed. (Englewood Cliffs, N.J.: Prentice-Hall, Inc., 1962), pp. 444–445.

PART FOUR

SUPERVISING YOURSELF

The purpose of this part of the book is to present important areas of personal interest that are of value to the modern supervisor. The three major ones covered in this part are: time management, stress management, and the development of a career plan.

Chapter 15 addresses time management and stress management. The first part of the chapter examines the nature of time management and sets forth useful time management guidelines that can help the supervisor work smarter rather than harder. The second part of the chapter looks at stress management, what it is, and how it can affect the supervisor. The chapter closes by offering guidelines for dealing with stress.

Chapter 16 examines the steps to be taken in developing a supervisory career plan. The first part of the chapter looks at how a candid self-appraisal should be carried out. Then attention is devoted to how a specific career plan of action can be implemented. Consideration is also given to practical steps for managing one's career. The last part of the chapter offers useful career guidelines for the supervisor who has decided to leave the firm.

When you have finished studying all the material in this part of the book, you will know how to manage time and stress more effectively. You will also be aware of specific steps you need to take in developing a career plan that will take you up the line from first-line supervisor to as far as your abilities and talents will carry you.

CHAPTER 15

MANAGING TIME AND STRESS

GOALS OF THE CHAPTER

Most supervisors work a full day and, in many cases, also take work home with them. Many report that they are constantly on the go. How can they get all of their work done and manage their hectic pace at the same time? The answer is, With effective time and stress management techniques. The overriding goal of this chapter is to examine what supervisors need to know about time management and stress management. When you have finished studying all the material in this chapter, you will be able to:

1. Compare and contrast the three basic types of time.
2. Explain how supervisors can identify what they do with their time.
3. Describe a dozen of the leading time wasters.
4. Set forth useful time management guidelines for improving work efficiency.
5. Define the term *stress* and describe factors that cause stress.
6. Explain how type A people approach work and why these individuals often suffer burnout.
7. Set forth recommendations that supervisors can use in helping their subordinates deal with stress and in dealing with stress themselves.

A STARTING CASE: WORKING SMARTER, NOT HARDER

It seems to Janice Whitney that the workday is never long enough. Not once in the last 4 months has she been able to finish everything in her in-box. By closing time there is usually at least 4 hours of work there, although on some days there is twice that amount. Janice typically takes the first couple of reports or memos that are on top, puts them in her attaché case, and finishes them at home after she has had supper.

Last month Janice's boss talked to her about two reports that she had submitted late. Janice admitted that she had been unable to get to them because of all the other things she had to do. "I'm swamped with work from morning till night," she explained. "From the time I get into the office until the time I go home, I never stop going." Her boss found this hard to believe. "None of my other supervisors has this problem," he explained. "Are you sure it's the amount of work you have to do and not the way you're doing it?" Janice was confused as to what he meant. "I mean, do you have too much work or are you having trouble managing your time properly?" Janice admitted she did not know the answer to the question. "I suppose it could be a combination of the two, but I'm not sure."

Her boss decided to check into the situation and find out exactly what the problem was. "For the next 2 weeks I want you to keep a time log on what you do. Every hour I want you to write down what you have done during the previous 60 minutes. Then you and I are going to sit down and see how you are spending your time. If it turns out that you need additional assistance, I'll get it for you. On the other hand, if it turns out that you need to manage your time better, then we'll focus on helping you work smarter rather than harder." The idea sounded fine to Janice. Beginning the next day, she started writing down exactly how she was spending all of her time. At the end of 2 weeks, Janice reported that she still had more work than ever. Her in-box was crammed with material, and she estimated that during this 2-week period her backlog of work had increased from 4 to 7 hours.

"That's all well and good," her boss told her. "However, I'd first like to see how you've been spending your time. Let me see your time log for the last 10 working days." Her boss carefully looked over the entries. Many of them were similar in nature. A typical day was the following:

8:30	Arrived at work
8:35–9:00	Worked on cost control report that is due next week.
9:00–10:15	Nancy Jakes came by to ask questions about some new work orders she received. Nancy is unclear regarding how to implement these orders.
10:15–11:00	Called away to a meeting with the United Fund group, of which I am a member. They wanted to review the strategy that we will be using in this year's campaign.
11:00–12:00	Weekly supervisory meeting
12:00–12:45	Lunch
12:45–1:15	Continued work on the cost control report.
1:15–2:00	Visit from Andy Daley regarding assistance on some productivity data that he is gathering and analyzing. He seems unclear as how to proceed with the assignment. He and I agree to each work up some of the information.
2:00–3:00	Completed working on the material for Andy's report.
3:00–3:20	Continued work on the cost control report.
3:20–4:00	Meeting with the boss regarding performance evaluations that must be submitted next week.
4:00–4:30	Called away to a meeting regarding new work procedures that will go into effect next month.
4:30–4:45	Continued work on the cost control report.
4:45–5:00	Cleared the desk and put materials into the attaché case to take home, including the cost control report.

After her boss looked over the time log, he smiled. "I know how I can help you out," he said. "You don't need more people. You need better time management practices."

What did the boss mean by his comment? How can Janice improve her management of time? What are some of the things that she is doing wrong? How much time can she save through better practices? Write down your answers and put them aside. We will return to them later.

NATURE OF TIME MANAGEMENT

Throughout the last 14 chapters, many of the challenges and responsibilities facing the supervisor have been discussed. The first-line manager is a very busy person. This is why time management is so important to the individual. The first thing the supervisor must realize is that there are some types of time demands that can be managed.

Types of time

There are three types of time: boss-imposed, subordinate-imposed, and personal. *Boss-imposed time* is taken up with assignments delegated by the supervisor's boss. These time requirements must usually be handled personally by the supervisor. This is why the boss delegates them directly to the first-line manager, who is best equipped to handle them.

Subordinate-imposed time is taken up helping subordinates with their work. Typical examples include explaining new work rules, assisting people in understanding how to fill out reports, and answering questions regarding how to handle work-related problems. In contrast to boss-imposed time, subordinate-imposed time can be reduced if the supervisor knows how to do it. One of the most effective rules is: Never allow a subordinate to delegate any work to you unless you do the same. When the supervisor agrees to help one of the workers write up a report, the manager should also delegate something else to the individual to do while he or she is working on the report. In this way the supervisor does not become a dumping ground for the subordinates' work. Many first-line managers, unfortunately, go out of their way to help their people and, in turn, find themselves working 10 to 12 hours daily while some of the workers are able to cut down their own work from 8 to 7 or 6 hours daily.

Personal time is that time which the manager has for getting his or her own work done. Personal time is equal to the number of hours the individual works minus the amount of time given over to boss-imposed and subordinate-imposed time. In effectively managing personal time, the supervisor needs to do two things: (1) keep subordinate-imposed time to a minimum, and (2) use time management tools and techniques in getting the most out of personal time. The first step in doing these things is for the supervisor to find out how he or she is spending an average day, i.e., where is the individual's time going?

**Identifying
time use**

There are many ways of identifying time use. One of the most helpful is for the supervisor to write down what he or she does every hour of the working day. However, this can be a time-consuming chore. An easier way is through the use of personal and business-related time charts. The first of these is illustrated in Table 15-1. This chart focuses on how the supervisor spent the previous week and includes both working and nonworking time. The reason for incorporating all 168 hours of the week is that it forces the supervisor to think about time in general and how he or she uses it. The first part of Table 15-1 has the supervisor divide each day into hours of sleeping and hours awake. Then the latter is broken into various categories. When supervisors fill out this form they are often surprised at the large number of hours they spend on work-related activities. For example, many of them list 8 hours of work at the office and 1 hour at home each night. Some also spend an hour commuting to work, during which time they dictate memos into a tape recorder. Since they are working and traveling at the same time, some of their commuting time must be transferred to their total of work at home. Likewise, if they eat breakfast or lunch and read reports at the same time, they must take some of their eating time and assign it to their work total. As they begin doing this, the total number of work hours rises.

After determining the number of working hours, the supervisor now concentrates on identifying what was done during each of these hours and determining if any of them could have been saved by delegating the work to others. In so doing, the supervisor needs to keep in mind the 80/20 theory of time management: 80 percent of the results a supervisor achieves are accomplished with 20 percent of the individual's time. This means that

Table 15-1. Supervisory time log: identifying personal and work-time activities*

	M	T	W	Th	F	Sa	Su	Total
I. Hours sleeping								
II. Hours awake								
A. Work at office and home								
B. Commuting/travel								
C. Eating								
D. Dressing/personal hygiene								
E. Family/personal work								
F. Education/self-development								
G. Community and professional activities								
H. Leisure								

Instructions: Determine the amount of time you sleep each night and enter the totals in row I above. Put the remaining number of daily hours in row II. Then divide up the latter hours based on how long you spend on each of the listed activities. Remember that the total of A through H must be equal to the total number of hours awake.

Figure 15-1. The 80/20 theory of time management.

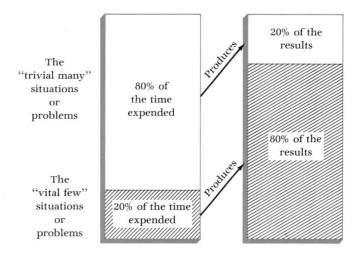

there are many hours of the week when the individual is not getting a great deal done. Much of this work is minor and can be delegated to others with no drop-off in efficiency. (See Figure 15-1.) Table 15-2 is designed to help the supervisor examine work-related time and identify those segments which can be delegated to others. Many supervisors find that when they examine their current time management habits, they are able to cut 10 to 20 percent of their time simply by delegating work that does not require their personal attention.

Identifying time wasters

Once the supervisor has determined what he or she must do personally, time management techniques can be applied to these tasks. In a manner of speaking, these techniques help the manager work smarter, not harder. One of the first things the individual should realize is that certain time wasters are common among many managers. A dozen of the most important are the following:

1. Telephone interruptions that disrupt the supervisor's work progress.
2. Visitors who drop by without appointments and proceed to take up time.
3. Meetings, especially unscheduled ones.
4. Crisis situations for which there has been no contingency planning.
5. A failure to set objectives, deadlines, and priorities.
6. Personal disorganization that prevents the supervisor from finding materials and reports and getting things organized in proper order.
7. Too much involvement in routines and details that should be left to others.
8. Trying to do too much at once and underestimating the amount of time that it will take.
9. A failure to set up clear lines of authority and responsibility.

Table 15-2. Supervisory time long: managing work time effectively*

I. Work activity	II. Time for this activity	III. Must be personally handled	IV. Can be delegated
	Total		

Instructions: Take the total of row A in Table 15-1 (the amount of time spent working at the office and home) and enter it at the bottom of column II above. Then fill in columns I and II, indicating the work activities associated with these times: e.g., meetings—7 hours; report writing—5 hours; telephone conversations—3 hours; etc. If there are any activities that take less than 1 hour per week, group them under miscellaneous. Then examine each work activity and determine what needs to be done personally and what can be delegated to others. If you are unable to delegate all of the time you are currently spending on an activity, determine whether you can delegate a part of it, and then divide the total time between columns III and IV. Your totals of columns III and IV should equal that of column II.

10. An inability to say no to others.
11. Lack of progress reports that enable the supervisor to keep track of work developments.
12. Physical fatigue.

Whether they realize it or not, most supervisors fall prey to at least half of these. The most effective way of sidestepping them is first to make an evaluation of personal time habits. This can be done by undertaking a survey of current habits. Self-Assessment Quiz 15-1 provides an answer. Before continuing on, take this quiz and then read the evaluation provided at the end of the chapter.

SELF-ASSESSMENT QUIZ 15-1:
WHAT ARE YOUR CURRENT TIME MANAGEMENT HABITS?

Instructions: Read each of the following statements and check whether or not you do them. If the statement does not apply (because as in the first one, for example, you do not have a secretary), simply pass it by and go on.

	Yes	No
1. In the case of incoming phone calls, your secretary screens them in advance.	—	—
2. When you return calls, you first group them and then set aside a specific time for making them.	—	—
3. You plan your phone calls in advance, listing all of the important points that are to be discussed.	—	—
4. When you get on the phone, you are able to get to the point without spending a lot of time socializing.	—	—
5. If the other party begins to get long-winded, you have the ability to terminate the call quickly.	—	—
6. You set aside time each day for drop-in visitors or unscheduled events.	—	—
7. When you are busy, you tell visitors, "I have very little time, so let's get right to the point."	—	—
8. You predetermine how long visitors can spend talking to you rather than just allowing things to take their own course.	—	—
9. You encourage people to set appointments with you rather than simply drop by unannounced.	—	—
10. Your secretary screens all visitors before allowing them to get to you.	—	—
11. When appropriate, you personally make decisions rather than referring them to committee.	—	—
12. You always use agendas for meetings and you follow the agendas closely.	—	—
13. Well in advance of the meeting, you make sure that everyone who is to attend has an agenda.	—	—
14. You set a time limit for meetings and quit at the established time.	—	—
15. You discourage too many meetings and use them only when they are needed and can prove profitable.	—	—
16. You draw up a daily list of things you have to do and arrange them in order of priority so that you put the focus of attention on the most important ones.	—	—

17. You are able to determine the times during the day when you do the best work, and you undertake the most important projects during these times. ___ __

18. You set aside "quiet" time for yourself every day, and during this time you reflect on what has happened over the last couple of days and plan what must be done during the next couple of days. ___ __

19. You continually think about ways of improving your job results. ___ __

20. You take time to get things right the first time rather than having to redo them later on because they were done in haste. ___ __

21. You make sure that the workload among your people is properly balanced and that they all do their fair share. ___ __

22. You take work breaks to relieve boredom, tension, and stress. ___ __

23. You keep a time log as a means of improving your time use. ___ __

24. You delegate work, avoiding the tendency to do everything yourself. ___ __

25. You continually look for new ways of getting control of your time. ___ __

An interpretation of your answers is provided at the end of the chapter.

Having identified time use and time management problems, the supervisor's next step is to develop guidelines for dealing with them. Some of the most important of these are discussed in the following section.

TIME MANAGEMENT GUIDELINES

There are many useful time management guidelines. The following examines eight of the most helpful.

Use a daybook

A daybook helps the supervisor plan his or her workday. Figure 15-2 provides an illustration. By laying out the workday in advance, the supervisor is able to keep track of what has to be done and has time to plan an effective approach. Meetings, conferences, major deadlines, etc., can all be blocked out in advance.

Effective supervisors also know the importance of having some quiet time during the day when they can get away from the hustle-bustle of the workplace and sit back and think about how to handle job-related problems. This gives them time to reflect on major issues that require concentration and thought. For this reason, seldom are all of the work hours in their daybooks filled in.

Establish priorities

There are two reasons why supervisors need to establish priorities. First, priorities provide a basis for delegating work. Low-priority tasks do not warrant the personnel consideration of the supervisor and should be given to subordinates. Second, priorities help the supervisor decide what to do

Figure 15-2. An example of a day book.

Schedule of planned activities

	Monday	Tuesday	Wednesday	Thursday	Friday
8:00–9:00					
9:00–10:00					
10:00–11:00					
11:00–12:00					
12:00–1:00					
1:00–2:00					
2:00–3:00					
3:00–4:00					
4:00–5:00					
5:00–6:00					
Evening					

today and what to put off for tomorrow. Unless personal work is prioritized, one will end up doing things that could wait while more important assignments go uncompleted. Priorities help the supervisor be both effective and efficient. *Effectiveness* means doing the right things. *Efficiency* means doing things well. The supervisor should focus first on being effective and then on being efficient. Prioritizing helps one identify the right things to do.

Delegate work to subordinates

It is not enough simply to delegate tasks to subordinates; the supervisor must be sure that the right tasks are being delegated. By matching the abilities of the workers with the demands of the assignment, the supervisor ensures that the work will be done right. Otherwise, the personnel will end up coming back to the manager for assistance and advice, taking up the supervisor's time in the process.

Know your best times

Some supervisors are morning people. When they have a major project or a challenging assignment, they make their greatest progress in the morning. Other supervisors are afternoon people. It takes them longer to warm to the task. After lunch they are at their best.

By determining when they do their best work, supervisors can match the work project with the time of day. If they are morning people, they can get started on the project within an hour of the time they arrive at the office. If anyone needs to see them or there is to be an unscheduled committee meeting, they can try to delay it until after lunch. Conversely, if they are afternoon people, they can take care of minor problems and unscheduled meetings during the morning and clear their calendar for after lunch.

Use a work-reward approach

No one can work for extended periods of time without becoming fatigued. This is particularly true if the work is mentally exhausting. Inevitably, however, most supervisors have a full day of work facing them. To finish their work easily and efficiently, they need to employ a work-reward approach. After they have worked on a difficult task for 60 to 90 minutes or have completed a demanding chore, such as having to tell someone that she has not been given a promotion, they need to reward themselves by doing something that is easy or that they like. For example, after an hour of working on the monthly cost control report, the supervisor will turn to the morning mail and spend 30 minutes reading memos and other correspondence. Or the individual will relax by returning the half-dozen calls that have piled up over the last hour. Each supervisor must choose those tasks which are personally most enjoyable. The important thing is to mix business and pleasure so that rewards accompany the completion of hard work.

Learn to say no

Too many supervisors are reluctant to say no to their people. No matter what type of assistance is requested, they go out of their way either to provide it perssonally or to see that someone else does. As a result, their workers call on them every time they need help and subordinate-imposed time takes up more and more of the supervisor's day.

One of the most common examples is someone dropping by the manager's office and asking, "Do you have a minute?" These visits seldom take less than 15 minutes and often involve minor matters. If the manager cannot say, "No, I don't have any time now but I will fit you in later when I do have free time in my schedule," he or she should say, "Sure, but not more than 5 minutes." When this time is up, the manager should terminate the discussion. It is difficult for most supervisors to act this way, but unless they are willing to take a firm stand they will be unable to manage their time effectively.

Be efficient

The best way to explain this guideline is with the cliché Do it right the first time. Too often supervisors find that they have to do the same thing 2 and 3 times. A good example is verbal communications. The supervisor will tell the subordinate what to do and then find the individual coming back to ask questions. If the manager were efficient, he or she would first have outlined the information to be communicated, conveyed it to the other party, invited questions, and then asked some questions to ensure that the person did indeed understand the message.

Handling written correspondence is another area in which time is often wasted. Many supervisors need over an hour a day to read all of their incoming messages and to dictate responses. One way of cutting down on this time is to stand up when reading. People tend to read faster and more accurately when they are in an uncomfortable position. Another helpful rule is to read everything only once. This means that if the supervisor starts reading a memo and realizes that it requires a detailed response, the memo should be put aside until it can be answered. The supervisor who reads the entire memo now is going to have to reread it again later, being unlikely to remember all of its major points by then. A third useful rule is to learn to read with one's eyes and get away from the habit of subvocalizing (reading to oneself), because this limits the speed with which one can cover the material.

Stay in charge

Time management is a personal challenge. If the supervisor wants to manage his or her time, it can be done. If the individual is indifferent, it will not happen. Success depends on two things: desire and a plan of action. Of course, there will be some days when the supervisor will find unscheduled meetings and boss-imposed time demands taking up a lot of time; the individual will come to the end of the day and realize that very little personal work has been accomplished. However, these days will be more the exception than the rule if the supervisor is determined to control work time and follows the guidelines that have been set forth in this part of the chapter. In making this point clearer, look closely at the two lists below and see if you can determine the major differences between the reasons cited for not completing all of the assigned work by the end of the day.

List A	*List B*
I did not get complete information from my people.	I tried to do too much at once.
My employees took up too much of my time.	I procrastinated.
I was called away to three unscheduled meetings.	I found myself unable to say no to requests from some of my people for assistance.
I had too many telephone calls to return.	I failed to communicate clearly with my people.
I am responsible for too many outside activities.	I refused to let others do some of the work.
My boss made too many demands on me.	I was unorganized.

The major difference between the list on the left and the one on the right is that the first rationalizes why the supervisor was unable to get things done, while the second puts the blame at the supervisor's door. The first list is a series of external reasons, i.e., I could not get everything accomplished because other people and outside events prevented me from doing so. The second list is a series of internal reasons, i.e., I did not manage things well; I made mistakes. The successful supervisor realizes that most of the reasons for failure to manage time well are similar to those in the second list. Moreover, even when they are not, the supervisor assumes personal responsibility for straightening things out. The individual works to stay in charge of events rather than being controlled by them. Still other useful guidelines are provided in Supervision in Action: Using Time Efficiently.

SUPERVISION IN ACTION: USING TIME EFFICIENTLY

In addition to the suggestions presented earlier, here are other useful guidelines followed by supervisors in using time efficiently.

Get organized. First, clean up your desk and files, to reduce the amount of time needed to search for items. File papers away neatly after using them, to save time later on. Avoid having an IN basket; it just gets in the way. Throw out all unnecessary papers. Ask yourself, "What would be the worst thing to happen if this paper or file were thrown out?"

Clarify objectives. Know what is expected of you in order to avoid duplication and wasted effort. This involves good goal-setting and communication practices, key aspects of time management. Don't attempt too much at once; this often leads to disorganiztion.

Shuffle your paperwork. Avoid cluttering your desk with correspondence. If possible, examine a single piece of paper only once, then act on it (if at all possible), forward it, or file it in a dated file that ensures you will act on it on a given date in the future.

Combine tasks. Group similar tasks together whenever possible. For example, respond to all correspondences between 3 P.M. and 4 P.M.; answer all phone calls between 1 P.M. and 2 P.M.

Break up tasks. If you're having trouble getting started—for example, if you are procrastinating—break each task up into smaller tasks. Don't write a book; write chapters or sections.

Use tidbits of time. Make efficient use of tidbits of time—for example, waiting in offices, etc. One time management consultant suggests that you always carry three kinds of folders—one manila, containing current response items such as letters; one pink, for materials on discretionary projects under way; and one blue, for future activities or new ideas. When in peak form, go through the ideas in the blue folder and decide which ones should be transferred to the pink folder. If the tidbit is brief, just go through the items in the manila folder.

Reduce interruptions and time leaks. Establish a quiet period in the office (preferably during your most productive hours) during which time you will not schedule meetings, accept phone calls, etc. In addition, rearrange your desk so your back is facing the door, in order to avoid interruptions. Cut down on time wasters—for example, lengthy coffee breaks and lunches, chit chat, etc. Recognize that if you're earning $40,000 per year, and if you waste a total of just one-half hour per day, it will cost your company more than $2500 over the course of the year.

Avoid perfectionism. Become results-oriented, but recognize the trade-off between efficiency and perfection. As suggested by Sir Simon Marks, former chairman of the Marks and Spencer retailing chain, "the price of perfectionism is prohibitive."

Source: Warren Keith Schilit, "A Manager's Guide to Efficient Time Management," *Personnel Journal,* September 1983, p. 740.

NATURE OF STRESS MANAGEMENT

Over the last 20 years increased attention has been focused on the area of stress. Management is coming to realize that excess stress is bad and can result in both physical and psychological personnel problems. Stress is particularly evident at the supervisory level, management's primary link with the work force. The following examines the nature of stress and what supervisors need to know about it.

Stress and stressors

Stress is a feeling of anxiety, tension, or pressure. Many things can cause stress, from job-related happenings to everyday occurrences. Table 15-3 shows some of these and their potential impact on a person. According to the researchers who put together this table, the higher the total of life-change units, the greater the stress the individual is suffering. Of course, not every person is going to feel the effect in the exact same way, so these life-change units have to be adjusted on a person-by-person basis. Also, the scale was constructed 20 years ago, so any references to financial values have to be greatly increased. Overall, however, the table is important because it illustrates that the stress under which supervisors and their personnel find themselves is a result of more than just organizational factors. People encounter stress in their daily lives as well, and often bring this to the workplace with them.

Stress is brought about by *stressors*, which are environmental factors that cause anxiety, tension, or pressure. There are many types of stressors, including:

The physical environment—light; noise; temperature
Individual-level stressors—too much work; responsibility for others; unclear job assignments
Group-level stressors—lack of group cohesiveness; conflict in the work group; conflict with other work groups
Organizational-level stressors—too much red tape; lack of top-management support; no general direction in the organization
Extraorganizational-level stressors—illness in the family; financial concerns; a move to another geographic location

The supervisor's primary concern is with those which are directly work-related, but non-work-related factors will also cause stress and the first-line supervisor must realize that the two cannot always be separated.

Stress and work behavior

Most people perform best under moderate degrees of stress. If there is too little, the individual is *underloaded* (see Figure 15-3) and often will be bored, irritable, or absent from work. If there is too much, the individual is *overloaded* and is likely to suffer such symptoms as lack of memory, indecision, and poor judgment. When individuals function between these two extremes, they tend to perform to the best of their ability. They are motivated, mentally alert, energetic, and productive.

When people are underloaded, the supervisor's task is to give them more work. Sometimes this can be done in terms of work quantity, such as

Table 15-3. The Holmes-Raye social readjustment scale

Event	Life-change units
Death of a spouse	100
Divorce	73
Marital separation from mate	65
Detention in jail or other institution	63
Death of a close family member	63
Major personal injury or illness	53
Marriage	50
Being fired at work	47
Marital reconciliation with mate	45
Retirement from work	45
Major change in the health or behavior of a family member	44
Pregnancy	40
Sexual difficulties	39
Gaining a new family member	39
Major business adjustment	39
Major change in financial state	38
Death of a close friend	37
Changing to a different line of work	36
Major change in the number of arguments with spouse	35
Taking on a mortgage greater than $10,000	31
Foreclosure on a mortgage or loan	30
Major change in responsibilities at work	29
Son or daughter leaving home	29
In-law troubles	29
Outstanding personal achievement	28
Wife beginning or ceasing work outside the home	26
Beginning or ceasing formal schooling	26
Major change in living conditions	25
Revisions of personal habits	24
Troubles with the boss	23
Major change in working hours or conditions	20
Change in residence	20
Changing to a new school	20
Major change in usual type and/or amount of recreation	19
Major change in church activities	19
Major change in social activities	18
Taking on a mortgage or loan less than $10,000	17
Major change in sleeping habits	16
Major change in number of family get-togethers	15
Major change in eating habits	15
Vacation	13
Christmas	12
Minor violations of the law	11

Source: T. H. Holmes and R. H. Raye, "The Social Readjustment Rating Scale," *Journal of Psychosomatic Medicine*, vol. 11, 1967, pp. 213–218.

additional assignments. Other times it should be done in terms of work quality, such as more interesting, challenging, meaningful jobs. By carefully monitoring the personnel, the supervisor should be able to identify those who are underloaded. However, the reverse is not always true. When work-

Figure 15-3. Stress and productivity.

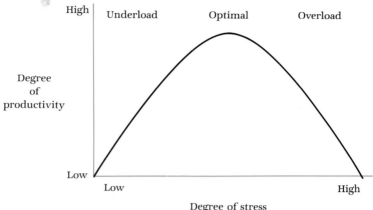

Underload	Optimal	Overload
Overqualified	Highly motivated	Absent
Absent	Mentally alert	Accident-prone
Negative attitude	Energetic	Indecisive
Irritable	Exhilarated	Withdrawn
Lethargic	Calm under pressure	Poor judgment

ers are overloaded, the supervisor may not see it. Why not? Because many times the symptoms show up very slowly and it is not until the situation is quite far along that the manager realizes there is a problem. The same is true for the supervisor, personally. He or she may feel, "Oh, I'm not really working that hard," and the next day the individual has a heart attack. One of the most effective ways of dealing with the problem of overload is to understand the relationship between stress and personality.

Stress and personality

Figure 15-3 describes some of the effects of underload and overload. Those who are underloaded might, quite naturally, want more work. However, why would people allow themselves to be overloaded with work? The answer is that some people actually enjoy this. They are *workaholics,* who enjoy working all of the time. Many of these people have *type A* personalities; they enjoy trying to get more and more done in less and less time. This is in contrast to their *type B* counterparts, who pace themselves and are content to work hard without bringing themselves to the point of mental and physical exhaustion. Before continuing, take Self-Assessment Quiz 15-2 and measure your own personality type.

SELF-ASSESSMENT QUIZ 15-2:
ARE YOU A TYPE A OR A TYPE B PERSON?

This exercise is designed to help you determine whether you exhibit type A or type B behaviors. For each item, there are two alternatives. Indicate in the margin which of the two is most descriptive of you by using the following scale:

If statement A is totally descriptive of you and B is not descriptive of you at all, give yourself 5 points.

If statement A is much more descriptive of you and B is only somewhat descriptive, give yourself 4 points.

If statement A is slightly more descriptive of you than is statement B, give yourself 3 points.

If statement B is slightly more descriptive of you than is statement B, give yourself 2 points.

If statement B is much more descriptive of you and A is only somewhat descriptive, give yourself 1 point.

If statement B is totally descriptive of you and A is not descriptive at all, give yourself 0 points.

1. A. During an average day, you usually work at a hectic pace.
   B. During an average day, you usually work at a relaxed pace.
2. A. You hate days off because you do not get to do any job-related work during them.
   B. You enjoy days off because they allow you to get away from work and to relax.
3. A. You enjoy fighting deadlines.
   B. You prefer to pace yourself so that you do not fight deadlines.
4. A. Your primary satisfaction comes from work.
   B. Your work is satisfying, but you also enjoy sports, social gatherings, etc.
5. A. You talk very fast.
   B. You talk at a moderate rate of speed.
6. A. You set high standards for yourself and get upset if you don't meet them.
   B. You set reasonable standards for yourself and do not get upset if you fall short.
7. A. When you play games, you play to win.
   B. You enjoy games but do not always have to win.
8. A. When you listen to slow or rambling speakers, you want to finish the conversations for them.
   B. When you listen to slow or rambling speakers, you focus on what they are saying rather than on how they are saying it.
9. A. When you eat, you eat very fast.
   B. When you eat, you eat at a leisurely pace.

10. A. You are always in a hurry even when you do not have to be.
    B. You seldom rush anywhere.
11. A. You often try to do two things at the same time.
    B. You concentrate on doing one thing at a time.
12. A. You are often angry and upset at the way people behave.
    B. You seldom get angry about the way people behave.
13. A. Waiting makes you nervous.
    B. When you have to wait, you try to take the time to relax.
14. A. You always measure progress in terms of time and performance.
    B. You like achieving things but do not always try to measure them in terms of time and performance.
15. A. You want people to respect you for what you do.
    B. You want people to respect you for who are you.
16. A. You often wear yourself out by doing too much work.
    B. You seldom wear yourself out by doing too much work.

Take your answers from the margins and enter them below. An interpretation is provided at the end of the chapter.

1.	3	5.	0	9.	5	13.	2
2.	4	6.	3	10.	3	14.	1
3.	1	7.	2	11.	3	15.	4
4.	3	8.	3	12.	2	16.	3

_____ + _____ + _____ + _____ = _____
                                                    Total

Type A personalities are most prone to *burnout,* which is a response to chronic stress that results in emotional and/or physical exhaustion. Burnout is a result of continuously high stress. Some of the signs include: chronic exhaustion, hypertension, mental depression, unwillingness to talk to others, and mental detachment from the job.[1] Once these signs begin to show up, the individual needs to get help. A complete physical, a change of work assignments, and psychological or psychiatric counseling are often in order. When a person suffers burnout, the situation is beyond the supervisor's direct control. However, the individual can help by addressing the problem before it becomes serious.

DEALING WITH STRESS

Supervisors can do a number of things to help their subordinates and themselves deal with stress. The following examines some of these.

Recognize individual differences

The supervisor must realize that some people can tolerate a great deal of stress, while others can take very little. One of the causes is physical health. People in poor health do not stand up to stress as well as those in good health. A second is experience. Those who know their jobs well suffer lower stress than do their less experienced counterparts. A third is control. Most people who have control over the pace of their work have less stress than those who must closely conform to predetermined rules and procedures. A fourth is the specific occupation. Some jobs are very stressful and people carrying them out are likely to suffer tension, anxiety, and pressure, while other jobs are very low in stress. Examples include:

High Stress	*Low Stress*
Air traffic controllers	Farm laborers
Secretaries	Maids
Waiters	Stock handlers
Assembly-line foremen	College professors[2]

Cope effectively

Stress is self-induced, and so the supervisor's ability to help subordinates deal with stress is limited. However, the individual personally can cope effectively with stress if he or she follows the suggestions that are set forth here.

First, diet is important. Many experts in the area believe that "you are what you eat," and most people, according to doctors, consume too much salt, sugar, red meat, eggs, and butter. Many supervisors also drink too much coffee. More attention should be paid to a balanced diet, with greater consumption of fruit, vegetables, fish, fowl, whole-grain breads, and decaffeinated beverages. Also, many supervisors skip breakfast or have only a small amount to eat; they prefer to have their large meal in the evening. This is the wrong time for a heavy meal because there is no chance to burn off the calories and, for many of them, weight becomes a problem. A hearty breakfast and a light dinner are better for the average person.

Second, physical fitness is important in dealing with stress. Today, many organizations offer their personnel some form of physical-fitness program. These programs help supervisors keep their weight under control while working off tension. Unfortunately, most managers do very little physical exercise. One national study found that only 40 percent of organizational personnel did anything more strenuous than exercise walking and most of the rest hardly ever walked for exercise.[3]

Third, mental relaxation can help one slow down. There are a number of ways of doing this. One of the most popular is to breathe deeply and slowly, holding it in for about 5 seconds, and then exhaling slowly. This procedure helps one slow down and relax and is particularly useful when under pressure. A second is to work on becoming aware of when stress is building up and then mentally get hold of the situation and talk oneself back to a more relaxed state.

These three approaches are very popular in dealing with stress.[4] Supervision in Action: Getting Rid of Stressors presents others that have proven useful.

SUPERVISION IN ACTION: GETTING RID OF STRESSORS

Studies on work and leisure have shown that the most effective way to deal with a heavy workload is to work in hour blocks. Spend 50 minutes in concentration followed by 10 to 15 minutes of rest. Mental health professionals have long adopted this pattern, and it would be wise for managers to schedule their work accordingly. Here are other remedies for stress:

Leave it. Following the fight-or-flee philosophy, it is often advantageous, when stress becomes too great, for a manager to walk away from the source of stress for a short period of time. A walk around the block or an interlude of shopping can provide the time necessary to release feelings of tension.

Talking it out. Often a person under stress will feel better just by having someone listen to concerns. The best listeners are individuals who understand the nature of the work but who are not directly associated with it. One might also consider talking to a trusted mentor or friend. Talking to a superior can be detrimental because information relayed may be used against the manager instead of to help him or her.

Short naps. For many people, short naps can provide the tension release they need. Naps of from 15 to 20 minutes (more than 30 minutes and you might feel worse) can be refreshing. Thomas Edison's work schedule included short naps followed by long work periods. This enabled him to work almost around the clock.

Action. Procrastination can be a major stressor. Often just getting started on a postponed project can be enough to energize, instead of demobilize, an individual.

Expressing anger. Stress can be caused by unexpressed anger and hostility. Jogging, punching a bag, throwing plates, banging cupboard doors have all been successful in helping individuals let off steam. One manager regularly writes "memos" to her boss about problems that concern her. Instead of sending the memo, she waits until her temper has subsided and then goes in to talk to her boss in person (angry comments recorded on paper can be perpetually haunting).

One U.S. firm has come up with an innovative means to express anger. Claiming it is cheaper than seeing a therapist, the firm rents individuals a sledge hammer. For up to an hour a session, the individual is free to slam away at wrecked automobiles.

Professional counseling. Conditioned to believe that a person ought to be able to handle his or her own stress-related problems, many individuals are reluctant to obtain professional counseling. However, when fear of reprisals or loss of self-esteem are at issue, professional counseling may be a viable alternative. In the safe confines of the counselor's office, an individual is free to express fears, anxieties, and concerns.

Source: Vandra L. Huber, "Managing Stress for Increased Productivity," *Supervisory Management,* December 1981, pp. 1–12.

WORKING SMARTER, NOT HARDER: STARTING CASE REVISITED

If you have carefully looked over Janice's time log, you realize that she is using three types of time. Some of it is for boss-imposed work. The weekly supervisory meeting is an example; the United Fund meeting may also be. Some of it is for personal time, the best example being the cost control report. A large portion of the rest is being spent helping her subordinates.

In particular, Andy Daley has taken up 1¾ hours of Janice's time. Notice that Janice agreed to help him out but did not give him any of her work. What is Andy doing while Janice is working on his report? Probably not much. Could Janice get all her work done if she saved 1¾ hours a day? Also look at how much time Nancy Jakes took up—1¼ hours. Is all of this time necessary? Could it have been handled more expeditiously? Janice's biggest problem is that she is letting her subordinates take time away from her own work. She needs to follow some of the guidelines in this chapter, including saying no, delegating work, and freeing up time for high-priority items.

INTERPRETATION OF SELF-ASSESSMENT QUIZ 15-1:
WHAT ARE YOUR CURRENT TIME MANAGEMENT HABITS?

This quiz did not survey all of the areas of time management, but it did focus on five major areas (as listed below). If you checked no to more than two statements in any area, you need to pay closer attention to that area. Additionally, all of your no responses should be examined because each indicates a poor time management practice. The breakdown of the quiz by area is as follows:

Questions *Area*

1–5	How you manage telephone-related matters
6–10	How you handle drop-in visitors
11–15	How you use committees
16–20	How much time management planning you do
21–25	How you go about delegating, making decisions, and controlling your time

INTERPRETATION OF SELF-ASSESSMENT QUIZ 15-2:
ARE YOU A TYPE A OR A TYPE B PERSON?

Your total number of points tells whether you perceive yourself as a type A or type B person. The higher the number of points, the more you see yourself as a type A person; the lower the number of points, the more you see yourself as a type B person. More specifically, the following provides a sharper picture of your personality:

Points	Interpretation
0–16	You have a strong type B personality.
17–32	You have a moderate type B personality.
33–48	You have a mixture of type A and type B personalities; you do not exhibit any clear pattern.
49–64	You have a moderate type A personality.
65–80	You have a strong type A personality.

SUMMARY OF KEY POINTS

1. There are three basic types of time: boss-imposed, subordinate-imposed, and personal. The supervisor usually cannot sidestep the first of these. However, the second can often be minimized by learning how to help subordinates without doing the work for them. The third warrants the use of effective time management practices.

2. One way of managing time effectively is by determining how it is being used and where it is being wasted. Guidelines for doing this were provided in the chapter. The supervisor can also profit from the use of time management guidelines, including: use a daybook, establish priorities, delegate work to subordinates, know your best times, use a work-reward approach, learn to say no, be efficient, and stay in charge.

3. Stress is a feeling of anxiety, tension, or pressure. It is brought about by stressors, most of which were identified in the chapter. When people have too little to do or it is boring, they are underloaded. When they have too much to do and it is physically and/or psychologically overburdening, they are overloaded. The latter is of particular concern to the supervisor.

4. Some people enjoy being overloaded. They are workaholics, typified by type A personalities. These individuals are most prone to burnout. In dealing with these types of subordinates, as well as with personal stress, the supervisor must realize a number of things. One is to be alert to the signs of burnout among subordinates and take steps to help the individual deal with the situation. Another is personally to look after oneself through good diet, physical fitness, and mental relaxation.

BUILD YOUR SUPERVISORY WORD POWER

These key terms are presented in their order of appearance in the chapter. They are terms for which supervisors have a working knowledge.

Boss-imposed time. Time that is taken up with assignments delegated by one's boss.

Subordinate-imposed time. Supervisory time that is taken up helping subordinates with their work.

Personal time. Time that an individual has for getting his or her work done.

Effectiveness. Doing the right things.

Efficiency. Doing things well.

Stress. A feeling of anxiety, tension, or pressure.

Stressors. Environmental factors that cause anxiety, tension, or pressure.

Underloaded. A situation that exists when people have too little to do and, as a result, are bored, irritable, or absent from work.

Overloaded. A situation that exists when people have too much to do and, as a result, suffer from lack of memory, indecisiveness, and poor judgment.

Workaholics. People who enjoy working all of the time.

Type A. A personality type that is characterized by individuals who enjoy trying to get more and more done in less and less time.

Type B. A personality type that is characterized by individuals who pace themselves and are content to work hard without bringing themselves to the point of mental and physical exhaustion.

Burnout. A response to chronic stress that results in emotional and/or physical exhaustion.

REVIEW YOUR UNDERSTANDING

1. Of the three types of time, which is the most difficult for the supervisor to control? Which is the easiest? Explain your answers.
2. How can a supervisor determine how and where his or her time is spent? Use Tables 15-1 and 15-2 in your answer.
3. What are some of the most common time wasters? Identify and describe five.
4. What is the 80/20 theory of time management? What value does it have for effective supervision?
5. Of all of the time management guidelines offered in this chapter, which five are the most valuable? Identify and describe each. Then defend your choices.
6. How does underload lead to stress? How does overload lead to stress? Explain your answers.
7. There are many types of stressors, including the physical environment, individual-level stressors, group-level stressors, organizational-level stressors, and extraorganizational-level stressors. What is meant by this statement? In your answer be sure to identify two stressors from each of the above-mentioned categories.
8. How does a type A personality differ from a type B personality? Compare and contrast the two in your own words.
9. What is meant by the term *burnout?* Why is an understanding of this term useful to the supervisor? Explain.
10. How can supervisors help their people deal with stress? Offer at least three guidelines.
11. How can supervisors personally deal with stress? Offer at least three recommendations.

SUPPLEMENT YOUR KNOWLEDGE

In addition to the references listed at the end of this chapter, the following provide important, practical information that is of use to supervisors in managing time and stress:

Alexander, Larry D.: "Effective Time Management Techniques," *Personnel Journal*, August 1981, pp. 637–640.

Ashkenas, Ronald N., and Robert H. Schaffer: "Managers Can Avoid Wasting Time," *Harvard Business Review*, May–June 1982, pp. 98–104.

Baker, H. Kent, and Stevan Holmberg: "Stepping Up to Supervision: Managing Time and Job Pressures," *Supervisory Management*, December 1981, pp. 25–32.

Behling, Orlando, and F. Douglas Holcombe: "Dealing with Employee Stress," *MSU Business Topics*, Spring 1981, pp. 53–61.

Gmelch, Walter H.: "A Regimen for Stress Reduction," *Supervisory Management*, December 1982, pp. 16–24.

Helliwell, Tanis: "Are You a Potential Burnout?" *Training and Development Journal*, October 1981, pp. 25–29.

Jackson, Susan E., and Randall S. Schuler: "Preventing Employee Burnout," *Personnel*, March–April 1983, pp. 58–68.

Kreitner, Robert: "Personal Wellness: It's Just Good Business," *Business Horizons*, May–June 1982, pp. 28–35.

Niehouse, Oliver L.: "Measuring Your Burnout Potential," *Supervisory Management*, July 1984, pp. 27–33.

Sailer, Heather R., John Schlacter, and Mark R. Edwards: "Stress: Causes, Consequences, and Coping Strategies," *Personnel*, July–August 1982, pp. 35–48.

YOU BE THE SUPERVISOR: GETTING THINGS DONE ON TIME

The Golding Corporation evaluates its people every 90 days. This approach is not very common, for most companies evaluate every 6 months or annually. However, Golding has found that it is able to identify its best people and to spot problem areas much faster if it uses more frequent evaluations. Unfortunately, this puts quite a bit of pressure on the supervisors, who have to fill out a detailed questionnaire on each person in their units every 3 months. One of the supervisors recently expressed her feelings about the evelution by noting, "The worst thing about completing these performance evaluations is knowing that I'm going to have to do them again in 13 weeks."

The evaluations are reviewed by management and serve as the basis for quarterly and semiannual salary raises. For this reason, they must be completed on time.

Last week, for the third quarter in a row, Jenny Lafferly's evaluations were late and her boss, Jim Crowley, was called on the carpet. When the meeting with his boss was over, Jim called Jenny in for a conference.

I've just had a meeting with the boss. He's on my back over the fact that you're late with your performance evaluations again. This is the third straight time. You told me that it wouldn't happen again and I took you at your word. Exactly what is your problem? Why aren't you getting your supervisory work done? I've asked you, if you're going to be late on something like an evaluation, to get in touch with me and ask for assistance. What seems to be the problem?

Part of Jenny's explanation related to the fact that she felt that performance evaluations were required too often. However, another part of her explanation was the following:

Many of the people who work for me depend on me. I spend over 80 percent of my time out of the office, helping them get things done. You'd be surprised how many bottlenecks there are in this operation that require a supervisor's time. I really don't have time to get all of my office work done. There's too much to be done elsewhere.

Jim was not sure how many of these comments were accurate. However, since he needed the performance evaluations finished immediately, he told Jenny to work exclusively on them and that he would send someone over to help her handle employee requests for assistance. The person he sent was Carol King, a floating supervisor whose job is to help out with trouble spots. Jim asked Carol to keep her eye out for why Jenny was unable to get her work done. "Find out what she's doing with all of her time and get back to me," he told her.

Earlier today, Carol and Jim had a meeting at which she gave her explanation of why Jenny was late with her work. The heart of her explanation was the following:

Jenny spends most of her time outside the office because she likes getting involved in the personnel's work. She hates paperwork detail. During the 4 days that I helped her out, she had me take care of these matters while she interfaced with her people. Basically, she gets involved in minor matters while important ones are put on hold. On the positive side, she works very hard. On the negative side, she spends a lot of time doing trivial work while the supervisory stuff gets low priority.

1. If you were a supervisor sent in to help Jenny overcome the problems identified in the case, where would you begin? Explain.
2. What specific things is Jenny doing wrong? Identify and describe at least three of them.
3. What time management guidelines would you recommend that she follow? Offer at least four, and explain each.

YOU BE THE SUPERVISOR: THE BEDRIDDEN ASSISTANT

When the telephone rang, Bert Schorr rolled over on his side and answered it.

"Mr. Schorr," the voice said, "this is University Hospital calling. We admitted a Mr. Henry Thomssen 4 hours ago. He asked that we call and tell you."

It took Bert a couple of seconds to clear his head. "Uh, what's wrong with him?"

"Mr. Thomssen suffered a heart attack earlier this evening. He is currently in intensive care. He's been sedated and the doctors are with him. You'll be able to see him tomorrow in all likelihood, but please call before you come in."

Bert said that he would. He then looked at the clock. It was 4:10 A.M. For the rest of the night Bert did not sleep very much. The impact of the news began to take its effect.

Henry Thomssen is Bert's administrative assistant. Henry came to work for the company about five years ago, and within a few months it was obvious that he was one of the hardest working people in the department. It seemed that no task was too difficult for Henry. He took responsibility for just about everything that came his way.

Two years ago Bert was involved in a major reorganization of the department. The undertaking took 3 months of intensive effort. Without Henry's help, it would have taken a lot longer. When the project was completed, Bert's boss congratulated him. "Your reorganization was the best one of all the departments," his boss said. "In our meeting yesterday, the senior vice president went out of his way to say that he had read all of the reorganization plans in detail and that yours was a model for the rest." Based on these comments and on his own evaluation, Bert promoted Henry to assistant supervisor of the department.

After this, Bert began to depend more and more on Henry. When there were unscheduled meetings, unexpected problems, or detailed work that he did not want to undertake, Bert delegated it to Henry. In the beginning, Henry seemed to have trouble getting a handle on things; however, within a few months he was able to do all that was asked of him. In fact, Henry continually asked Bert if there was anything more he could do, and there was hardly an evening that Henry did not take work home with him.

About four months ago Bert and Henry went for their annual company physicals.

Both were told that they were in good health, although the doctor cautioned Henry about working too hard. "You seem to be somewhat overworked. I want you to slow down a bit. If possible, try not to work on weeknights or weekends." Henry promised. However, within a few days he was back to his regular routine and Bert was happy to see it. There was so much work to be done before the end of the fiscal year in 2 weeks that Henry, too, found himself having to take work home.

Bert now wondered how he would ever get everything done by the end of the year. He also wondered how Henry could have passed his physical and then suffered a heart attack within a month. Most important, he was concerned with how Henry could have gotten into his current predicament. "He certainly didn't look overworked to me," Bert mused. "He's always been in a hurry, working all of the time. How come now he suddenly develops a problem?"

Looking at his clock, Bert realized it was time to get ready for work. As he showered, he began thinking of everything he would have to get done at the office. The first thing would be delegating Henry's work to other personnel, he decided. Once that was taken care of, Bert thought, he should get over to the hospital, visit with Henry, assure him that everything was going to be all right, and then talk to the doctor regarding when Henry might be able to come back to work.

1. If you were giving advice to Bert, what would you tell him that he did wrong in his work relationship with Henry? Explain.
2. Why did Bert not see the problem developing? Since he works with Henry every day, how could he have missed it?
3. What mistake is Bert making in his approach to the problem created by Henry's illness? How does this mistake mirror the stress management problem that has existed all along? Defend your answer.

NOTES

1. Steven Altman, Enzo R. Valenzi, and Richard M. Hodgetts, *Organizational Behavior: Theory and Practice*, Orlando, Fla.: Academic Press, 1985, p. 428.
2. Altman, Valenzi, and Hodgetts, p. 443.
3. Robert Kreitner, Steven D. Wood, and Glenn M. Friedman, "Just How Fit Are Your Employees?" *Business Horizons*, August 1979, p. 44.
4. For more on this, see: Richard M. Hodgetts, *Management*, Orlando, Fla.: Academic Press, 1985, pp. 615–617.

CHAPTER 16

DEVELOPING A CAREER PLAN

GOALS OF THE CHAPTER

The basic focus of this book has been on practical, applicable, efficiency-oriented ideas that can be of value to the modern supervisor. In this last chapter, the focus of attention is on an area that has until now been neglected: a career plan for helping the supervisor rise in the organization. At the same time, the formal approach that has been used will be dropped in favor of a more informal approach. The discussion will now be about you, rather than some impersonal supervisor or first-line manager.

The first goal of this chapter is to discuss how you can carry out a candid self-appraisal. This appraisal will address both work performance and personal interests. The second goal is to set forth practical steps that you can use in developing a specific career plan. The third goal is to describe some of the most useful approaches for guiding your career. The last goal is to provide information that is beneficial in writing a résumé and handling a job interview. When you have finished reading all the material in this chapter, you will be able to:

1. Identify the types of work performance and personal interest areas that you should examine when making a candid self-appraisal.
2. Describe how career goals should be written.
3. Fill out a career path plan that states your goals, describes the risks and the commitment of personal resources, and specifies how progress toward these career goals can be monitored.
4. Identify and describe a half-dozen practical guidelines for managing your career.
5. Write a detailed and attention-getting résumé.
6. Effectively handle a supervisory or middle-management job interview.

A STARTING CASE: CLIFF'S CAREER PROGRESS

When Cliff Packard joined the Amthall Corporation 4 years ago, he set two career objectives for himself: supervisor in 4 years, and office manager 5 years later.

Within a month of the time he started, Cliff realized that the most important thing was to distinguish himself in some way from the rest of the people. Aware that it would take some time to figure out exactly how to do this, Cliff decided to start with the most obvious approach. Every morning he arrived 15 minutes before everyone else and every evening he stayed 15 minutes late. The results of this strategy began to pay off. Within 6 months Cliff was doing 15 percent more work than anyone else in the unit and his boss soon became aware of it.

Gradually the boss began giving Cliff special assignments. At first it was busywork, but eventually Cliff got more challenging jobs. On one occasion he was made responsible for compiling statistics and writing a report related to the effects of a new productivity program that was introduced into the department a year earlier. Cliff had to compare absenteeism, tardiness, turnover, cost, and productivity data from the previous year to that of the present one in order to show how effective the productivity program had been. His boss estimated that it would take 3 days or so to gather and analyze all of the data and another 2 days to write the report. Cliff did all of it in 1 day and spent the second day working up slides and charts that could be used when the boss presented the findings at the supervisors' meeting. His boss was very impressed with the job, and when the presentation proved to be the best of those given at the meeting, Cliff was chosen as that month's outstanding employee in the department.

Two years after Cliff started at Amthall, his boss was promoted. Nine people in the department had been there longer than Cliff, and two of them were considered to be the major contenders for the supervisory position. However, at Amthall it is an unwritten rule that supervisors name their own replacement. Cliff was given the job.

The promotion put him 2 years ahead of his game plan. It also meant that he would again be reporting directly to his old boss. If he could do the same job as before, Cliff felt that within 5 years he would be office manager. However, things did not work out this way. Somehow Cliff could not establish the same relationship as before. Many of the other supervisors were just as hard-working as he was and often managed to upstage him with the boss. For example, on one occasion Cliff put together a recommended productivity improvement plan that would have increased output by 15 percent; however, one of the other supervisors formulated a more detailed plan that would result in a 17.5 percent increase in output. On another occasion the office manager announced that there were four openings for a supervisory development seminar that would be held the following week. Cliff's workload was so great that he was forced to pass it up; he later learned that this seminar was considered vital for supervisory promotion. On a third occasion Cliff found that while he was able to complete in 3 months a 6-month supervisory self-study program that was offered by the firm on an in-house basis, four of the other supervisors had finished the entire program in less than 2 months.

Last month marked the third anniversary of Cliff's promotion to supervisor. It also heralded the promotion of the office manager to general manager. The supervisor chosen for the promotion to office manager had been in her job 6 months less than Cliff had. In terms of job tenure, Cliff had the second-longest time as supervisor, while the woman who was promoted was eighth out of 10. Cliff believes that the next office manager promotion will probably not be for at least 3 more years, meaning that he will not be able to attain his objective of becoming office manager within 5 years. Thinking back on the last 3 years, Cliff still cannot figure out how he lost his momentum.

What happened? Why was Cliff initially so successful but unable to maintain his progress? What did he do right when he was a worker but not do right when he became supervisor? Write down your answers and put them to the side. We will return to them later.

CANDID SELF-APPRAISAL

The first place to begin developing a supervisory career plan is with a candid self-appraisal. You need to answer questions such as: What do you do well? What do you do poorly? What do you like to do? What do you not like to do?

Appraisal of work performance

A good place to start is with an appraisal of your work performance. This can be done in a number of ways. One of the most effective is with an instrument such as that in Self-Assessment Quiz 16-1, which focuses on some of the major questions that should be asked in determining how well you are doing your job. These questions cover a wide range of supervisory activities and are meant only to be representative of the many that should be asked. A complementary work-related evaluation is provided in Self-Assessment Quiz 16-2, which focuses on your ability to carry out specific tasks and duties. It is skills-oriented.

Before filling out these two self-appraisals, keep in mind that there can be a problem of bias. Few people see themselves as others see them. To increase the value of the self-appraisals, it is useful to get outside input. For example, you should ask both your superior and your subordinates to fill out the instruments. In this way, your perception can be compared with those of personnel with whom you interact on a daily basis. Before continuing on, fill out the two self-assessment quizzes.

SELF-ASSESSMENT QUIZ 16-1: HOW WELL DO YOU DO YOUR JOB?

Read each of the following questions and, unless you are instructed to do otherwise, check the answer that best describes you.

1. How well do your subordinates understand their roles and responsibilities?
    _____ a. Very well.
    _____ b. Well.
    _____ c. Somewhat.
    _____ d. Not well at all.

2. How willing are you to pitch in and help your people complete their work?

    _____ a. Very willing.

    _____ b. Somewhat willing.

    _____ c. Not very willing.

    _____ d. Not willing.

3. How active are you in ensuring that your people have safe and healthful working conditions?

    _____ a. Very Active.

    _____ b. Active.

    _____ c. Not very active.

    _____ d. Not active at all.

4. How often do you discuss with your employees your appraisal of their performance and how they can improve it?

    _____ a. Daily.

    _____ b. At least quarterly.

    _____ c. At least semiannually.

    _____ d. At least annually.

5. Are you acquainted with your fellow supervisors and able to call on them for assistance and advice?

    _____ a. Yes.

    _____ b. I think so.

    _____ c. I'm not sure.

    _____ d. No.

6. How valuable are you to your boss?

    _____ a. Very valuable.

    _____ b. Valuable.

    _____ c. Somewhat valuable.

    _____ d. He or she does not really count on me for much.

7. Do you continually look for ways to improve your unit's efficiency and effectiveness?

    _____ a. All the time.

    _____ b. Quite often.

    _____ c. From time to time.

    _____ d. Never.

8. In how many professional or technical societies, such as the American Management Association or the National Association of Purchasing Agents, are you active?

    _____ a. 1–2.

    _____ b. 3–4.

    _____ c. 5–6.

    _____ d. 7+.

9. How many different technical or professional magazines or journals do you read on a monthly basis in order to learn more about successful supervision?

_____ a. 1.

_____ b. 2–4.

_____ c. 5–10.

_____ d. 11 +

10. How have you tried to improve your own basic supervisory education? (Check all that apply.)

    _____ a. Night courses, correspondence courses, and/or formal programs of self-education.

    _____ b. Reading of professional and technical magazines and journals.

    _____ c. Informal discussions with other supervisors.

    _____ d. Conscientious efforts to improve job-related knowledge while at work.

11. Do you use an open-door policy with your subordinates?

    _____ a. Yes; they can come and see me any time.

    _____ b. Yes, but it is in effect only during certain hours of the day.

    _____ c. No, but I make it clear to my people that I am available if they need me.

    _____ d. No; they have to wait for me to come to see them.

12. How would you describe your leadership style?

    _____ a. Autocratic.

    _____ b. Paternalistic.

    _____ c. Democratic.

    _____ d. Laissez-faire.

An interpretation of your answers can be found at the end of the chapter.

SELF-ASSESSMENT QUIZ 16-2:
HOW EFFECTIVE ARE YOU AS A SUPERVISOR?

Read each of the following statements and evaluate your performance accordingly.

	Excellent	Good	Fair	Needs improvement
Ability to set specific, measurable objectives for your people.	_____	_____	_____	_____
Ability to organize operations efficiently.	_____	_____	_____	_____
Ability to distinguish between problems and causes.	_____	_____	_____	_____
Ability to apply sound reasoning and logic in problem solving.	_____	_____	_____	_____
Ability to generate creative solutions.	_____	_____	_____	_____
Ability to make a decision and stick to it.	_____	_____	_____	_____

Ability to go to bat for your people.	_____	____	____	_____
Ability to cope with stressful conditions.	_____	____	____	_____
Ability to express yourself clearly in writing.	_____	____	____	_____
Ability to express yourself verbally.	_____	____	____	_____
Ability to listen to others.	_____	____	____	_____
Ability to adjust to changing conditions.	_____	____	____	_____
Ability to motivate your personnel.	_____	____	____	_____
Ability to manage your time effectively.	_____	____	____	_____
Ability to influence your subordinates.	_____	____	____	_____

Go back and note how many check marks you placed in each column. Enter the number below and compute the total. An interpretation of your score can be found at the end of the chapter.

	Number of check marks		*Points per check mark*	*Overall points*
Excellent	_____	×	10	_____
Good	_____	×	8	_____
Fair	_____	×	6	_____
Needs improvement	_____	×	3	_____
			Total	_____

Appraisal of personal interests

Personal interests are another important part of every career plan. People tend to excel at those things they like. If you enjoy interacting with others, helping people solve problems, and assuming responsibility for work projects, you are undoubtedly doing well as a supervisor. As you move up the hierarchy, you will find these interests complementing the skills you will be needing in managing others.

Another aspect of personal interests is social and family life. If you are unmarried, you will likely take a somewhat different career path than will a first line-manager who is married. You may be willing to accept promotions that provide additional upward mobility or career promise, while the married supervisor may be reluctant to accept any job that takes him or her away from the family for more than 1 day at a time.

Work is an important part of life. However, personal interests and concerns must also be addressed. In addition to appraising your work performance, it is important to examine your nonwork interests and goals. Quite often some sacrifices will have to be made. However, neither area, work or personal, can be totally overlooked. After completing this preliminary candid self-assessment, you should be ready to focus on a specific program of action.[1]

DEVELOPING A SPECIFIC CAREER PLAN

An evaluation of your work performance and personal interests should give you a pretty good idea of your strong and weak points. Now you need to focus on a career plan that can do two things: help you capitalize on your strong points and assist you in avoiding or minimizing your weak points. There are a number of ways of doing this.

The most effective way is to identify those goals which you would like to attain over the next 5 years. If you are 25 to 45 years of age, this career plan will have to be reviewed (and in all likelihood revised) a number of times before retirement. This is one of the benefits of putting together such a plan early in your career. It helps you evaluate how well you are doing and serves as a reference point in revising long-range goals. For example, if you set a personal goal of getting promoted within 5 years and at the end of this time are still a supervisor, you must either reset the goal or admit that it was too ambitious. It may even be time to admit that this is the wrong firm and that it is time to move on to another. Conversely, if you are promoted within 3 years, you need to start setting more ambitious career goals. You are moving along at a much faster-than-anticipated clip.

Career goals

There are many different types of goals that you can set. When possible, these should be quantifiable. They should state what is to be attained and by when. The following provides a handful of examples:

Be promoted to senior supervisor within 36 months.

Average 8.5 percent annually in raises over the next 3 years.

Be assigned as a project supervisor for new product development within 18 months.

Be given responsibility for a work group of at least 35 people by December 31 of next year.

Join at least two professional societies and be promoted to elective office in at least one within 24 months.

Complete the six-part in-house supervisory development course by December 15 of this year.

Receive the highest semiannual performance evaluation of any supervisor in this department at least twice over the next 3 years.

Be promoted to general manager within 5 years.

These objectives are typical of those set by supervisors. Two of the most important characteristics of effective objectives are: (1) They are attainable; and (2) they involve a stretching or reaching upward, i.e., they force you to excel.

Some supervisors fail because they set unrealistic objectives for themselves. They want to move along as quickly as possible but do not allow themselves the time needed to learn their jobs fully. This is particularly true of first-line managers who take a promotion to move to another firm. After 6 to 12 months in a supervisory position, they are contacted and offered a middle-management position in another company (or see an ad in the newspaper and apply for the job) and feel that they have sufficient knowledge to handle the challenge.

Others make the opposite mistake. They stay in a supervisory position so long that when they finally do decide to move up, their application is regarded with skepticism. "How come he's been a supervisor for 15 years and only now is deciding that he'd like to be in middle management?" someone will ask. "Maybe he's a slow learner. Maybe he lacks motivation. Maybe he really doesn't know what he wants but has decided to apply before it's too late." Questions of this nature are likely to be raised, and the supervisor will often find that younger, more ambitious people are chosen instead.

The best way of dealing with these two problems is to weigh the risks and opportunities associated with different career decisions. In this way you can mesh your career objectives with the risks and opportunities that you are likely to confront over the next 2 to 5 years. The process by which this is done is known as career path planning.

Career path planning

While many supervisors write down the objectives they intend to pursue, some formulate the plan of attack only in their head. A better way is to bring together *both* the goals and the formal plan in *written* form. This is called *career path planning* and forces the manager to consider the steps, risks, and commitments associated with each. Attention can also be focused on how progress toward the objectives will be measured. Figure 16-1 provides an example.

Notice that the first thing you have to do is to identify your career objectives specifically. It is best to focus on no more than a handful. If you can attain these, you should be successful. Next, determine the steps that must be taken in order to reach these objectives. For example, if you want to complete an in-house supervisory development course, the steps would entail such things as registering for the course, getting the books and assignments, attending the meetings, and turning in all required work. There may not be much of a risk associated with this objective, but a commitment of personal resources has to be made in the form of time in order both to attend the sessions and to complete the assignments. Progress can be measured in terms of the number of sessions attended. If it is a self-study program, progress can be measured in terms of the number of lessons completed.

Each objective on the career-planning worksheet follows the same procedure. As you describe how each objective will be pursued and monitored, a detailed plan of action begins to emerge. When the entire plan is complete, you then need to look it over in its entirety. Quite often you will find

Figure 16-1. Career planning worksheet (partial form, continued on next page).

Name _____   Date _____

Present position duties: _____

_____

_____

Career path planning period: _____ years

In the designated areas below, write down the career objectives you would like to attain during the career path planning period. List your objectives in their order of priority. Then complete the planning material that follows each objective.

I. Career objective 1

_____

_____

A. What steps must be taken in order to maintain this objective? Identify and describe them below; be sure to list them in chronological order, beginning with the one that must come first.

   1. _____

   2. _____

   3. _____

   4. _____

   5. _____

B. What risks or commitments of personal resources will be necessary to attain this objective? Identify and describe each below, beginning with the most important.

   1. _____

   2. _____

   3. _____

   4. _____

   5. _____

C. How will you monitor your progress toward this objective? Be as specific as possible in terms of both quantitative results and time frames.

   1. _____

   2. _____

   3. _____

   4. _____

   5. _____

that you are pursuing too many objectives. There is not enough time in the day to get everything done. The plan is too ambitious. This can only be determined, however, by placing each of the objectives and its accompanying support plan alongside the others. By looking back and forth across the write-ups, risks, commitments, and monitoring, you can compare all of the

II. Career objective 2

_____

_____

A. What steps must be taken in order to attain this objective? Identify and describe them below; be sure to list them in chronological order, beginning with the one that must come first.

1. _____

2. _____

3. _____

4. _____

5. _____

B. What risks or commitments of personal resources will be necessary to attain this objective? Identify and describe each below, beginning with the most important.

1. _____

2. _____

3. _____

4. _____

5. _____

C. How will you monitor your progress toward this objective? Be as specific as possible in terms of both quantitative results and time frames.

1. _____

2. _____

3. _____

4. _____

5. _____

activities. If you feel that something should be cut, the choice is a simple one: Since the objectives are written down in order of importance, the last one should be dropped, and this should continue to the point at which you are convinced that the remaining ones are manageable and will result in the desired career progress.[2]

MANAGING YOUR CAREER

An effective career plan requires two things: (1) knowing where you want to go and (2) determining how you will get there. Many supervisors are unable to attain their career objectives because they do not manage their progress properly.

A first-line manager who sets an objective of being promoted into middle management within 5 years or seeking a job somewhere else knows where he or she wants to go. However, this does not mean that the individual has a complete game plan. What will the supervisor do if no promotion is forth-coming? Is there a fallback position? Even more important, why did the individual not get promoted? Has the person done something wrong? Is the individual on the wrong career track? Has he or she teamed up with, or become associated with, individuals who are regarded as being over the hill or no longer members of the "in" group in the organization?

Thus, besides setting up a specific program with goals and strategies, you need a game plan for managing your career. The following set forth some of the most useful recommendations for doing this.

Be a high-level performer

Nothing succeeds like success. A supervisor who does well is more likely to be promoted than is one who is a mediocre or poor performer. If nothing else, your success will make the boss look good, and people are most likely to reward those who help them. As your job performance gets better and better, the boss's star in the organization will rise even higher. At the middle and upper levels of the organization, human and conceptual skills are important, but for most supervisors it is technical skill and measurable work output that count. Additionally, in many organizations supervisory per-formance is carefully monitored so as to minimize any charges of discrimi-nation in promotion. By being able to point to the supervisor and say, "His work unit had higher productivity than any other for each of the last 18 months and that's why we promoted him," the boss is also saying that the promotion was based solely on merit. It would be pretty difficult to chal-lenge this promotion on the basis of "He only got promoted because he's the boss's favorite supervisor. Around here all that counts is friendship." The work record shows that performance was the reason behind the pro-motion, and nothing more.

Know the formal evaluation criteria

Most organizations formally evaluate their people on a semiannual or annual basis. These evaluations are very important. If you get a poor evalua-tion, you may find your career in jeopardy. This is particularly true if most superiors give their supervisors good-to-excellent evaluations. A poor eval-uation means that you have lost a step on all of the others. When promo-tions are considered, you will not have the same performance ratings to show. For this reason, regardless of your boss's reputation, you should find out what the formal evaluation criteria are. If you are to be judged on the basis of work quality, work quantity, effort, and attendance, these are the four things you should focus on. Now you should find out how these are measured. How does the boss determine whether one's work quality is excellent, good, fair, or poor? What measurable criteria are used? The same questions should be asked regarding the informal evaluation criteria.

Know the informal evaluation criteria

Many bosses rate their people on informal as well as on formal criteria. One informal criterion is loyalty, which is measured by answers to questions such as: Are you a team player? Can you be relied on to pitch in and support the department? However, this is not the only way that loyalty is evaluated. Another is work effort. How hard do you work? Those who come in early, leave late, and are busy throughout the entire day are rated as more loyal than those who do not. A third form of loyalty is protection of the department. Do you cover for the boss and support the individual in conversations with outside members? If so, you are seen as highly loyal. A fourth form of loyalty is obedience. If you do as you are told, do not ask a lot of questions, and treat the boss with respect, you are seen as highly loyal. For you, the primary question is, How can I prove my loyalty? Only by determining what this word means to the boss will you be able to meet this informal evaluation criterion. The same is true for all other informal criteria used by the boss.

Help your boss succeed

Your superior is the most critical link in your career plan. If this individual decides to help you move along, he or she can pull the right strings. If the boss decides that you are not middle-management timber, just the reverse can occur. Effective supervisors try to become crucial subordinates, of which there are two types.

One is the *complementary crucial subordinate*. This individual helps the boss overcome his or her weaknesses. If the superior hates giving public talks, the supervisor fills in at the local Chamber of Commerce luncheon. If the boss dislikes filling out the monthly cost control report, the supervisor gathers the necessary data and completes the report in time for the superior to sign off and submit it. If the boss is uncomfortable writing memos, the supervisor works them up and gives them to the boss to look over and make minor changes or suggestions for rewriting, and sees that they are then prepared in final form.

The other type of crucial subordinate is the *supplementary subordinate*, who helps the boss in areas in which the individual is capable but wants to expand his or her expertise. For example, the boss believes that public speaking is an important skill to develop and welcomes every opportunity to talk at luncheons and dinners. The subordinate helps free up the boss for these assignments by taking on additional chores that would prevent the boss from getting away to talk. The boss may also feel that writing skills are important and wants to develop these skills. Thus, every time the boss writes a report or a memo, the subordinate reads it over and tries to find problems with the wording or flow of the material. In this way, the boss gets feedback on how others will interpret the material and begins to hone his or her writing skills.

Some supervisors find they have the temperament to be effective complementary crucial subordinates but not supplementary subordinates. Some are just the opposite. Others can function well in both categories. In deciding which (or both) to be, you must assess the boss and his or her own personal approach to doing things. Then work on complementing this approach. In this way there can be a blending of styles. Supervision in Action: Assessing the Boss explains this idea in more depth.

SUPERVISION IN ACTION: ASSESSING THE BOSS

We all have a natural tendency to think in categories. Assessing a boss employs this process. There are many labels for executives: game players, egocentrics, abrasive personalities. However, there are four categories developed by Peter Drucker that may be more useful than others in learning about your boss. These distinctions suggest style and approach rather than specific traits, and to that extent they may have more universal application.

Readers. Bosses who are readers want to digest all reports and other data before discussion and decisions are made. They want to be briefed first and brainstorm second. They may feel uncomfortable about being confronted in a meeting with new information or unexpected circumstances. So if you want to reduce conflict with such a boss and improve his or her acceptance of your ideas or proposals, you should first submit a written memo or report.

On the other extreme end of this continuum are those bosses who would reject an employee suggestion just because the subordinate walked into the boss's office, sat down, and threw out the idea. The same concept might have been received more favorably had the employee sent a memo, waited a day or two, then approached the boss.

Listeners. These bosses like the process of discussion. It allows them to verbalize their thoughts. This is how they clarify their ideas as well as the views of others. They read as little as possible. Reports are for reference; they want written material outlined or summarized and won't bother reading it otherwise. Employees who don't get this message are often discouraged to discover that the boss hasn't read a report that the employee believes is crucial to a proper decision. They may wrongly assume that the boss is disinterested in the problem or, worse, in themselves.

To be effective with a boss who is a listener, you need to learn to discuss your ideas, let the ideas be modified in these discussions, sometimes let the ideas rest with the boss awhile, then follow up the discussion with written documentation.

Systematic. Bosses who are systematic value their analytical ability and want employees, either verbally or in writing, to outline premises, options, and scenarios. They want rational arguments along with timetables and other data. They love numbers. If you make a proposal or disagree with a systematic boss on an issue, you had better be prepared to defend your stand using the approach the boss respects. That means having the facts and being prepared to present them in an organized fashion.

Intuitive. These bosses are hunch players. They trust their emotions and gut reactions. They must feel right about a decision or all the data in the world won't convince them. An intuitive boss is likely to be impressed by subtleties and insights, not by ratios and cost-benefit analyses. This kind of boss may be just as analytical as the systematic thinker and may reach similar conclusions, but the means are very different from the systems-oriented thinker.

Of course, most bosses are not entirely listeners or readers. Nor are they 100 percent systematic or intuitive. It is a matter of degree, and assessment involves detecting predominant patterns. In most instances, the same individual may be a listener at certain times or with specific individuals and be a reader in other circumstances. An aware subordinate will take the time to evaluate the situational changes in a boss's style and make adjustments in approach accordingly.

No one executive style or pattern is superior to another. Successful executives may be listeners, readers, systematic, or intuitive.

Perhaps the most important issue related to your adaptability to your boss's style is your own style. If you are a reader, you'll have to make a significant adjustment if your boss is a listener. If you're systematic, you may become very frustrated with and even underestimate the competence of an intuitive boss. The burden of assessment and adjustment falls more on you than on your boss. In any confrontation, after all, it is you who have more to lose by misjudgment than your boss.

There may come a point in your relationship with your boss when you may decide that your style is so different from his or hers that a smooth and effective pairing is not possible. In such a situation, you may have no choice but to accept the situation while you look for a job elsewhere.

Source: Donald Sanzotta and Lois Drapin, "Getting Along with the Boss," *Supervisory Management,* July 1984, pp. 14–16. © 1984 by AMACOM, a division of American Management Associations, New York. Reprinted by permission of the publisher; all rights reserved.

Document your accomplishments

You hope your boss will keep a record of your accomplishments and you will be rewarded for them. However, not everything you do is likely to be in your file. So when your boss is deciding whom to recommend for a promotion or to give a special assignment that will be helpful later in one's career, he or she may be in a quandary. Quite often the boss will say: "Tell me why I should recommend you for this new job. I've gone through your file and you have a very good record. However, so do Tom and Mary." The boss is looking for something "extra," and if you have kept a record of your accomplishments, you may be able to provide it. Perhaps the boss forgot about the special project team that you helped put together 6 months ago, or the boss may not realize that the president personally congratulated you on the work you did in helping with the latest union-management relations.

Another way of documenting your accomplishments is through empire building. When promotions are made, two factors tend to weigh most heavily: performance and current responsibilities. The person with the best performance often ranks at the top of the list. However, if two or three people have excellent performance, management often chooses the individual who currently carries the greatest responsibility. This is why supervisors with large units tend to be promoted faster than do those with small units. Management will reason, "A person effectively managing 20 people should be better able to handle a promotion to the next level, where there is more responsibility but fewer people to supervise, than would a person effectively managing only 10 people." Size often equates with power, and power helps bring about promotion.

Train your replacement

Few organizations promote a supervisor without having someone to fill that position. Sometimes this is done from the outside, but most organizations prefer to promote internally. If there is an unexpected opening at the next-highest level and you are tapped for the job, one of the first things your boss will ask is, "Do you have someone who can take over your unit?" If you say no, you have something of a problem. On the one hand, you must find out what your new responsibilities will be and move into that job as quickly as possible (often 10 days or less); on the other hand, you must scurry to train someone to handle your current responsibilities. If you have been following some of the ideas set forth in the previous chapter, you have been delegating work to your people and should be doing only supervisory tasks. Now you must train someone to handle these. One way of avoiding this problem is to identify the person best equipped to fill your shoes and to start giving that individual more and more supervisory-related responsibility so that when you are tapped for a promotion you can assume the job within a week's time.

Also remember that by training people to move up, you are helping them with their own careers, and this, too, is part of your job. Nor is upward movement the only way they can go. In some cases, they may be better off with a horizontal or lateral move, and since this, too, is a career change, you should be aware of how to help your people with their own careers. Supervision in Action: Helping Subordinates with Their Own Careers provides an example.

SUPERVISION IN ACTION: HELPING SUBORDINATES WITH THEIR OWN CAREERS

Option 1: Moving up

Most individuals are interested in moving up—probably because they are unaware of the opportunities offered by the other options. Also, for many, upward mobility is considered the only acceptable and rewarding way to develop a career. Upward mobility provides additional status, responsibility, compensation, and weight of title to a professional reputation. For many, movement "up" equals success; all other movement either does not count or counts against. And most literature on career development (both scientific and popular) continues to tout the idea that "up" is the best and only direction in which anyone should desire to move.

You can assist your employees by discussing positions at the next higher level or by organizing resource material to help them make plans. Resource materials might include job listings by salary grade or title, reports showing job families and subfamilies, job descriptions showing entry requirements, and specially designed job content profiles. If such information cannot be provided directly, you might show employees where they can obtain this information on their own. For example, you could identify key contact people within the organization who might act as information resources. You can also encourage employees to use data available in the system, such as job posting bulletins, so that they can determine what the job requirements are for positions in other parts of the organization.

Option 2: Moving across

Horizontal or lateral moves clearly demonstrate the concept of the transferability of skills, abilities, and job knowledge. An employee who has strong product knowledge from a background in production, and who has also demonstrated successful sales skills by "selling" production proposals to top management, may, indeed, be qualified to make a lateral move into a position in marketing by virtue of transferable skills and knowledge.

Moving across involves a change in function and/or title without necessarily undergoing a change in status or salary. Although such moves were once considered a way of dealing with "deadwood" employees, they are fast becoming a way of demonstrating adaptive abilities and broadening skills, learning about other areas of the organization, and developing new talents. Lateral movement is one way that organizations with limited advancement opportunities can continue to challenge their highly motivated employees. Further, providing individuals with this kind of exposure is becoming a grooming mechanism for positions in higher management since it broadens an individual's base of knowledge and is an opportunity to demonstrate management skills.

Before presenting horizontal movement as a viable option to your employees, you should be aware of the cultural norms concerning such a move within your organization. By *norms* we mean biases for or against such movement.

In many companies horizontal moves occur frequently and are considered part of routine training and development. Job rotation programs are also common, ongoing processes in certain companies. Such programs are designed to prevent overspecialization and to encourage understanding of the unique demands faced by each function within the organization. In such organizations, a lateral move would not cause any problems.

Where horizontal movement is infrequent and/or seen as a sign of probable failure, the manager may be able, with the assistance of human resource professionals in the company, to determine whether and how such mobility can be legitimized. It may be as simple as pointing out that the frequency of such moves is actually greater than it is perceived to be by most employees. Based on this information, the company newsletter, for example, may be encouraged to present miniwork histories of several successful people who have benefited from making lateral moves.

> More formally, managers might suggest that a job posting or transfer system be instituted, or, if already in effect, that it be publicized as providing an opportunity both as a means of transferring skills to new work areas and learning more about other parts of the organization. Internal job rotation programs designed to rotate people on a temporary basis can also be implemented, thus encouraging employees to experiment with transferring their present skills to similar level jobs in other departments.
>
> There are a variety of ways that an organization can show that it is open to horizontal mobility, and it is the manager's job to convey this message to his or her subordinates.
>
> Source: Beverly L. Kaye, "Up Is Not the Only Way," *Supervisory Management*, February 1980, pp. 3–5. Reprinted by permission.

Be prepared to take action

Quite often, career success depends on your willingness to take action to improve your situation. If you find that your career path is blocked because you are in the wrong area (supervisors in production are rapidly promoted and you are in sales, where promotions are very slow) or in the wrong type of job (line managers are promoted very quickly, but you hold a staff position), consider moving to a firm where your expertise does result in upward promotion. Find an organization where your skills would be of primary importance to its success. Likewise, if your career path is blocked because those ahead of you are younger and have no intention of leaving the firm, start looking around for another position. You will not move up if you stay, so leave.

Finally, if you find that you do not like working for your present firm, start looking for something else. Sometimes a job is initially very challenging and rewarding and then becomes boring and mundane. Or you get a new boss with whom you have a poor relationship and this limits your career opportunities. The sooner you realize that things are not going well, the better off you will be. Like it or not, a work change is in order. Before examining what you should do when you make up your mind to leave, remember that you should always leave at your convenience and on good terms.

Having made up your mind that it is time to go, decide how you will explain the decision to recruiters or prospective employers. Some supervisors will say: "I'm leaving because that firm is a terrible place to work. Only a fool would stay there." Others will say: "My boss is totally ineffective. He doesn't know what he's doing, and he spent all of his time criticizing me and the other supervisors. I can't work for a guy like that. I have to leave." These comments are too critical. Prospective employers wonder whether these supervisors are not relating more about themselves than about their company or their boss. A better way to handle the situation is to say: "I believe I'm ready for increased responsibility and more challenging work. My current firm provided me excellent training, but I think there's more that I can do in terms of exercising my abilities. I'm looking for a company that is operating in a more challenging environment and where the chances for promotion are likely to be faster. That's what attracted me to apply for a job at your firm." Notice that this last statement puts the focus on issues rather than on personalities. Sure, some of it may be total hogwash, and the recruiter or manager who is conducting the interview may realize this. At the same time, however, the individual will see that you are not backbiting or being vindictive. This will count in your favor as the person evaluates you.[3] Before getting to this point, however, it is important to understand the steps to take after you decide to leave your current employer.

IF YOU DECIDE TO LEAVE

Regardless of the reason, if you decide to leave there are two things you should know. One is how to prepare a proper résumé. The other is how to go about interviewing for another job.

The résumé

A *résumé* is a short biographical sketch of oneself. There are many forms a résumé can take. Figure 16-2 provides a development guide in preparing one. The format suggested in this guide is only one of many that can be used, but it does cover all of the important information that should be in a résumé.

In preparing the résumé, you should keep eight things in mind:

1. The résumé should be neatly typed and up to date. If you are going to be sending more than half a dozen copies out in response to newspaper ads or taking them along to interviews, it pays to type the résumé and make good-quality copies.
2. The information should not be crowded onto the pages. It should be spaced out so that it looks both orderly and neat.
3. It is important to stay away from gimmicks, such as fancy typefaces or slick paper that are designed to catch the reader's attention. You will be hired on the basis of your past accomplishments and future potential, not because the recruiter is influenced by an eye-appealing résumé.
4. If the résumé is going to have a picture with it, the photo should be a conservative-looking one and be placed in the upper left-hand corner.
5. Past experience and performance are what the recruiter is looking for, and the résumé should be written so as to focus on this.
6. The résumé should be no more than two pages long, unless, for some special reason, it is important to expand or elaborate on some area that carries the sketch beyond this recommended limit. Remember that most long résumés have unnecessary information. If the résumé does its job, you will get an interview and then can explain or elaborate on those things which it does not fully cover.

Figure 16-2. Résumé development guide. (Courtesy of Placement Office, Florida International University, Miami, Fla.)

The following guide is an important instrument when seeking a professional position. It represents you and your image when you are not there. As a result, it should be grammatically correct, clear, concise, and professional-looking. It should also present you in the best possible light, so if you feel that the categories below should be changed so as to better emphasize your assets—do so.

NAME:

ADDRESS: (include ZIP code)

TELEPHONE: (include area code, and both home and business numbers if applicable)

CAREER OBJECTIVE/GOAL

Briefly describe the position for which you wish to be considered. Example: An office supervisor with an organization providing upward mobility. (You may also include the date you are available to start.)

PERSONAL DATA (OPTIONAL)

Date of birth: Marital status:
Height and weight: Citizenship:
Place of birth: Health:
Number of dependents: Languages:

EDUCATION

Dates attended, name and city of college/university, degree received, major field(s). List in chronological order, beginning with the most recent. Do not use personal pronouns.

EXPERIENCE

Dates of work, name of firm, address of firm, position held, and brief description of DUTIES. If applicable, describe your accomplishments, supervisory responsibilities, and administrative responsibilities. Do not use personal pronouns in your description. *List most recent position first.*

MILITARY EXPERIENCE

(If you do not have any activities to list, omit this section.)

If you have had military experience, list branch of service, active-duty data, rank or rating at time of discharge, and current status. Briefly describe your duties in the service.

PROFESSIONAL EXPERIENCE

(If you do not have any activities to list, omit this section.)

Describe professional organizations to which you belong, offices held, and awards given.

ADDITIONAL INFORMATION

Describe other ASSETS, those skills or experiences significant to your career objectives which are not easily organized or included under another heading, such as special projects you have managed or business-community activities in which you played an important role.

REFERENCES

Indicate that your references will be "available on request." Be sure that you have at least three references who can attest to your ability as a supervisor.

7. In writing the résumé, choose your action words and self-descriptive words carefully. Table 16-1 provides some of the most helpful of both.
8. It is usually best not to list references. Simply note that they are available on request.[4]

Handling the interview

Getting another job can sometimes be a difficult process. What you need to do is to get someone to read your résumé or hear about you from a friend or acquaintance and then invite you for an interview. Most supervisors who decide to leave their present jobs learn about new openings from friends or acquaintances. Another source is employment ads in the local newspaper. These are not the only ways of getting in contact with prospective employers, but they are the two most common. If you have written your résumé following the guidelines set forth in the above section, you will be invited for interviews. It is at this point that you must put your best food forward. There are a number or guidelines that you should follow in preparing for

Table 16-1. Key words for résumé preparation

Action words			
actively	eliminated	motivated	responsible
accelerated	established	organize	responsibilities
adapted	evaluate	originate	revise
administer	expanded	participated	review
analyze	expedite	perform	schedule
approve	founded	plan	significantly
coordinate	generate	pinpointed	simplicity
conceived	increased	program	set up
conduct	influence	proposed	solve
completed	implemented	proved	strategy
control	interpret	provide	structure
created	improve	proficient	streamline
delegate	launched	recommend	successfully
develop	lead	reduced	supervise
demonstrate	lecture	reinforced	support
direct	maintain	reorganized	teach
effect	manage	revamped	

Self-descriptive words			
active	determined	independent	realistic
adaptable	diplomatic	logical	reliable
aggressive	disciplined	loyal	resourceful
alert	discreet	mature	respective
ambitious	economical	methodical	self-reliant
analytical	efficient	objective	sense of humor
attentive	energetic	optimistic	sincere
broad-minded	enterprising	perceptive	sophisticated
conscientious	enthusiastic	personable	systematic
consistent	extroverted	pleasant	tactful
constructive	fair	positive	talented
creative	forceful	practical	will travel
dependable	imaginative	productive	will relocate

this interview and conducting yourself during it. The following are nine of the most useful:

1. Gather background information on the firm so that you have a working knowledge of their product lines, their services, their customers, etc. This allows you the more adequately to fit yourself into their scheme of things.

2. Make a list of at least a dozen questions that you are likely to be asked and mentally rehearse them. If possible, discuss them with a knowledgeable friend and talk about your answers.

3. Make sure you are well groomed. Wear something that is appropriate for a supervisor in that organization.

4. Arrive a little bit ahead of schedule, i.e., 10 or 15 minutes early. By all means, do not be late; first impressions play an important role in many interviews.

5. Let the interviewer lead the discussion. This individual knows where he or she wants to go. Just sit back and let this person run things for a while. When you are asked a question, be as clear and concise as you can. Do not feel obligated to expand on your answers. If the interviewer wants to know more, you will be asked follow-on questions.

6. When you see the chance to do so, indicate your work experiences or accomplishments. Let the interviewer know that you have learned a lot about how to be an effective supervisor. Do not go overboard, but remember that humility seldom wins you points when you are trying to convince someone to hire you as a manager.

7. Before the interview is over, you should have been given a number of opportunities to ask questions. If you have not, then before the meeting is over, simply say, "Before we wrap this up, there are a few questions I'd like to ask you." Two of the things you should focus on are job responsibilities and career opportunities, but do not get into the matter of salary during the first interview. There may be a number of people who are being interviewed for the job and the interviewer may not be prepared to discuss salary at this point. If you are invited back for a second interview or are called up and offered the job, then you can talk money. If you are asked during the first interview how much you would like, give a range based on industry standards for a person with your qualifications.

8. Do not leave without knowing when you will be contacted regarding a follow-up interview or the final decision. Remember that you do not want to sound anxious for the job, but neither do you want to appear uninterested. Additionally, you may go on four interviews and find that the first firm wants you to make a decision within 3 weeks. If you know when the others will be getting back to you, you may be able to stall the first until you are able to compare that job against other offers.

9. If you are made an offer on the spot and asked when you can start, do not say, "Right away." Indicate that you have to give your employer advance notice. This reveals a basic loyalty to one's company and illustrates that should you ever leave this new firm, you will again give notice. Some firms will not make an offer but will ask, "When could you start if we got together on terms?" Those who say, "Immediately," sometimes find that one of the other finalists gets the job.

CLIFF'S CAREER PROGRESS: STARTING CASE REVISITED

The most direct way of answering the questions posed at the end of the case is by referring to the career management guidelines presented in the chapter. Notice that when Cliff was a worker, he did a number of things very well. In particular, he maintained his basic career competencies, he knew the formal and informal evaluation criteria, he was a top-notch performer, he stood out from the pack, and he was crucial to his boss. When he became a supervisor, it became more difficult for him to do these things. The major reason was that there were a number of supervisors who were as aware as he was of the importance of these guidelines, and in many cases they simply beat him out. Cliff was good but was unable to keep up with them. When he did something well, they did it better. When he was unable or unwilling to do something, they did do it.

Knowing how to manage one's career is important, but being able to act on this information is even more important. If Cliff hopes to be promoted in the future, he is going to have to focus on standing out from the crowd. Right now he is simply a hard-working, reliable supervisor. There is no reason to believe that he will be fired or demoted, but unless he can get in gear the way he did earlier in his career, there is little chance that he will be promoted in the future. Someone will always come by and beat him out of it. Cliff has to figure out what he is doing wrong and overcome it. The competition for promotion is fiercer now than it was earlier—and Cliff has to respond to this challenge or face the fact that he is unlikely to be promoted again.

INTERPRETATION OF SELF-ASSESSMENT QUIZ 16-1: HOW WELL DO YOU DO YOUR JOB?

The following is the scoring key for this quiz. Circle the number of points you receive for each answer.

1. 10 points   b. 7 points   c. 2 points   d. 0 points
2. Answer *a* is a time management trap. Answer *b* is more preferable.
   a. 5 points   b. 10 points   c. 5 points   d. 0 points
3. a. 5 points   b. 4 points   c. 1 point   d. 0 points
4. Answer *a* indicates excessively close control. You need to back off.
   a. 0 points   b. 15 points   c. 10 points   d. 5 points

5. a. 10 points   b. 7 points   c. 4 points   d. 0 points
6. a. 15 points   b. 12 points   c. 8 points   d. 0 points
7. a. 15 points   b. 12 points   c. 6 points   d. 0 points
8. You should belong to at least one, but three or more are too many for active involvement.

    a. 10 points   b. 5 points   c. 2 points   d. 1 point
9. There are so many good monthly journals that a magazine or two every week is not that demanding. However, after 10 the payoff begins to go down.

    a. 3 points   b. 7 points   c. 15 points   d. 10 points
10. Here you can get up to a total of 20 points. Notice that formal study and on-the-job learning are worth more than magazine and journal reading because the former have greater practical value and payoff for the supervisor.

    a. 8 points   b. 2 points   c. 6 points   d. 4 points
11. A restricted or limited open-door policy is the most effective.

    a. 2 points   b. 10 points   c. 6 points   d. 0 points
12. The point assignment here is based on what is best under most conditions. If you feel that the assignment warrants changing, do so.

    a. 5 points   b. 7 points   c. 15 points   d. 0 points

Now take your points, enter them below, and total them.

1. _____   5. _____   9. _____
2. _____   6. _____   10. _____
3. _____   7. _____   11. _____
4. _____   8. _____   12. _____

_____ + _____ + _____ = _____

                                                       Total

Overall evaluation

Points   **Interpretation**

121–150   You see yourself as doing a very good job.
 91–120   You see yourself as doing a better-than-average or average job.
 61–90   You see yourself as doing an average or below-average job.
  0–60   You see yourself as doing a poor job.

INTERPRETATION OF SELF-ASSESSEMENT QUIZ 16-2: HOW EFFECTIVE ARE YOU AS A SUPERVISOR?

This assessment can be heavily biased, depending on your perception. For this reason, it is a good idea to compare your evaluation with that of others with whom you work. An interpretation of your scores is the following:

Points	*Interpretation*
135–150	You see yourself as extremely effective.
105–134	You see yourself as fairly effective.
75–104	You see yourself as being of average effectiveness.
Less than 75	You see yourself as needing more development of your skills and abilities.

SUMMARY OF KEY POINTS

1. The first place to begin developing a supervisory career plan is with a candid self-appraisal. This involves consideration of both work performance and personal interests.

2. After the self-appraisal, you should determine your objectives. These goals should be, whenever possible, quantitative. They should state what is to be attained and by when. Then you should spell out the steps, risks, and opportunities associated with each goal. This can be done with the use of a career planning worksheet. An example is provided in Figure 16-1.

3. An effective career plan requires two things: knowing where you want to go and determining how to get there. The latter requires the effective management of your career progress. In doing this, you should follow a number of important guidelines. Some of the major ones are: be a high-level performer, know the formal evaluation criteria, know the informal evaluation criteria, help your boss succeed, document your accomplishments, train your replacement, and be prepared to take action.

4. If you decide to leave your present job, the first thing to do is to put together a résumé. This is a short biographical sketch that sets forth personal data, career objectives, education, experience, and any other information that you feel will help you get a job. Figure 16-2 provided a résumé development guide that can be helpful in doing this.

5. If you have written an effective résumé and have the requisite experience and training, you will be contacted by prospective employers and asked to come in for an interview. This is when you must sell yourself. Some of the most effective guidelines in doing so were presented in the chapter.

BUILD YOUR SUPERVISORY WORD POWER

These key terms are presented in their order of appearance in the chapter. They are terms for which supervisors have a working knowledge.

Career path planning. A plan that sets forth career objectives, steps that must be taken to attain these objectives, the risks and the commitment of personal resources necessary in attaining these objectives, and an identification of the way(s) in which progress will be monitored.

Complementary crucial subordinate. A subordinate who helps the boss overcome his or her weaknesses.

Supplementary subordinate. A subordinate who helps the boss in areas in which the latter is capable but wants to expand his or her expertise.

Résumé. A short biographical sketch.

REVIEW YOUR UNDERSTANDING

1. How can you go about making a candid self-appraisal of your work perform-ance? What are some of the questions you should be able to answer? Cite at least four.

2. How can you go about making a candid self-appraisal of your personal interests? What are some of the questions you should be able to answer? Cite at least four.

3. In developing a career plan, what are some typical objectives that you would pursue? Write down four of them. What are the two characteristics these objectives should have? Explain.

4. What is meant by the term *career path planning?* How can a career-planning worksheet help in this process? Explain, being sure to incorporate Figure 16-1 into your answer.

5. What specific steps should you use in managing your career? Identify and describe five.

6. What is a résumé? What format should it take? In your answer, be sure to include a discussion of Figure 16-2.

7. In preparing a résumé, there are a number of useful guides. What are some of them? Identify and describe five.

8. In a résumé, of what value is the information contained in Table 16-1? Explain.

9. A friend of yours is going for an interview. What guidelines would you urge the individual to follow? Cite and describe six.

10. At the end of your initial interview, you are offered a job. The interviewer then asks you, "How much money are you looking for?" and "When can you begin?" How should you handle these two questions? Explain.

SUPPLEMENT YOUR KNOWLEDGE

In addition to the references listed at the end of this chapter, the following provide important, practical information that is of use to supervisors in career planning:

Bell, Robert R., and J. Bernard Keys: "Preparing for a Move to Middle Management," *Supervisory Management*, July 1980, pp. 10–16.

Green, Connie: "From Roadblocks to Rapport: Understanding Your Boss," *Black Enterprise*, June 1984, p. 245.

Gutteridge, Thomas G., and Fred L. Otte: "Organizational Career Development: What's Going On Out There?" *Training and Development Journal*, February 1983, pp. 22–26.

Hillis, Donald J.: "An Operational View of Career Planning," *Personnel Journal*, July 1983, pp. 574–579.

Kaye, Beverly: "Up Is Not the Only Way," *Supervisory Management*, February 1980, pp. 2–9.

Leach, John J.: "The Career Planning Process," *Personnel Journal*, April 1981, pp. 283–287.

McArthur, Shirley: "The Fine Art of Finding the Right Job," *Black Enterprise*, Febru-ary 1985, pp. 101–103.

McEwan, Bruce E.: "The Risk Management Approach to Career Planning," *Super-visory Management*, January 1984, pp. 12–18.

Near, Janet P.: "The Career Plateau: Causes and Effects," *Business Horizons*, October 1980, pp. 53–57.

YOU BE THE SUPERVISOR: JOSÉS AMBITIONS

The Alterne Company is a large manufacturing firm located in the midwest. Alterne hires between 200 and 250 people every year. Over the last 5 years its sales have increased at an annual rate of 20.2 percent, and the company intends to start building another plant within the next 18 months.

The turnover at Alterne is quite low, but because of its sales growth, there have been a number of supervisory openings over the last year. The most recent promotions from the worker to the supervisory level occurred last week. One of the individuals who was promoted was José Rodriguez. José has been with the company for over 2 years and has been consistently ranked as the outstanding worker in his department. His boss recommended him for a promotion based on this performance, and when it came through, José was delighted.

His first couple of weeks on the job were spent learning the ropes. José came out of the quality control department and is now working in the parts department, and it took him a while to get a handle on the job. Nevertheless, he believes he now knows how the department operates and can settle back and begin focusing on his job as a supervisor. At the same time, he would like to begin sketching out a career plan. When José first joined the company, he set an objective of promotion to the supervisory level within 2 years. Now that he has attained that objective, he realizes that he has to set additional goals and work out a plan of action for attaining them.

While he has not spent a great deal of time actually writing down his objectives, some of the goals he wants to reach include the following: Have the highest productivity of any department in the division; get an average annual salary raise of 8 percent over each of the next 3 years; complete all of the in-house supervisory training programs within 24 months; be promoted to the next level of the hierarchy within 4 years.

For the moment, José realizes that these are just ideas floating around in his head. He has not worked out exactly how he should go about reaching each of them. However, he does have a supervisory friend in another department with whom he has lunch every day. This friend has talked to José on a number of occasions about his own goals and aspirations at Alterne, and it seems to José that his friend has a pretty clear idea of what he wants to achieve and how he should go about doing it. José would like to develop a similar plan of attack. Where he needs help is in writing out his career objectives and figuring out all of the steps that have to be taken in reaching his goal. He also needs to bounce his ideas off someone so that his final plan is realistic and takes into account the problems and pitfalls he is likely to confront.

1. Assume that you are José's friend. How would you help him write his objectives so that they are clearly stated and serve as career targets? Do so by rewriting the ones he set forth.
2. How could a career path worksheet help José? Be complete in your answer.
3. In addition to the worksheet, what other advice would you give him regarding things to do (or not do) in managing his career? Be specific in your answer.

YOU BE THE SUPERVISOR: SALLY'S PREDICAMENT

One of the things that attracted Sally Penn to the Garbell Company was its dramatic growth. Over the previous 5 years Garbell's sales had increased an average of 42.9 percent annually. At the same time, the firm was building three more computer component manufacturing plants. The company had received firm orders for over

$125 million of computer equipment and estimated that over the next 5 years it would have an average annual sales growth of between 37 and 41 percent.

When Sally was hired 6 months ago, the recruiter painted her a very rosy picture. "We now have 119 supervisors," he said, "and will be needing at least that many more to meet future demands. Once we start staffing our three new facilities, we are going to be promoting people from inside into these positions. We are also going to be needing senior supervisors and department managers. If you are looking for upward mobility, you've come to the right company." Sally had just been graduated from State University and this was her first job. She was scheduled to start as a supervisor in one of the main departments in plant 2. Other firms had offered her middle-management positions, but Sally felt certain that within a year or two at Garbell she would be promoted to senior supervisor and a few years after that could make department manager. As long as the firm continued to grow, she would be able to move up much faster than if she went with one of the other firms that had given her job offers. Unfortunately, these plans are not going to materialize.

Three months ago Garbell was informed that two of its major customers had decided to start producing many of their components themselves. These customers reasoned that it was cheaper over the long run to manufacture than to contract out the work. These decisions have had a dramatic effect on Garbell's future projections. Next year's sales forecast was in the range of $160 to $175 million but has now been reduced to the $70 to $80 million range. At the same time, the firm has announced that it is going to cut back its work force and is looking for buyers for the three plants it had under construction. It appears very likely that the two major customers who decided to go in-house with their production will be willing to buy the new plants.

Sally's immediate reaction to the new sales forecast was to find out the impact it would have on her. Her boss indicated that every unit is going to be affected but that because of her college degree and her outstanding work performance, she will not be laid off unless things get worse. "We're going to have a big layoff next week," he told her. "I think that will take care of all our problems. However, if there is a second layoff after that, you may end up going. For the moment, sit tight and let's see what develops."

Sally knows that her boss was trying to put her at ease. However, she feels that her time at Garbell is limited. This may be a good point at which to start looking around for another job. Quite obviously her career objectives cannot be attained if she stays. Her biggest problem is that she does not know much about how to get another job. A number of other supervisors are in the same predicament, and Sally has been thinking about asking them what they are going to do.

1. Assume that you are a fellow supervisor and that Sally has come to see you. What would you tell her about how to get another job? What is the first thing she should do? Explain.
2. What would you tell her about getting her résumé into shape? What types of suggestions would you make? Be as complete in your answer as possible.
3. What pointers would you give her regarding job interviews? Be as practical as possible in your suggestions.

NOTES

1. For more on making a candid self-appraisal, see: Richard M. Hodgetts, *Introduction to Business*, 3d ed., Reading, Mass.: Addison-Wesley, 1984, pp. 630–634.

2. For another approach to this topic, see: Bruce E. McGowan, "The Risk Management Approach to Career Planning," *Supervisory Management*, January 1984, pp. 12–18.

3. Other useful ideas can be found in: Brian H. Kleiner, "Managing Your Career," *Supervisory Management*, March 1982, pp. 17–21.

4. Also see: "Résumés that Open Doors," *Black Enterprise*, February 1985, p. 102.

NAME INDEX

SUBJECT INDEX

Get Video
of Passion for Ex.